THE COMPLETE INVESTOR: INSTRUMENTS, MARKETS AND METHODS

THE COMPLETE INVESTOR: INSTRUMENTS, MARKETS AND METHODS

Geoffrey A. Hirt

Chairman, Department of Finance
DePaul University

Stanley B. Block

Texas American Bank/Fort Worth Chair of Finance
Texas Christian University

DOW JONES-IRWIN
Homewood, Illinois 60430

A classroom edition of this book is available through Richard D. Irwin, Inc., under the title
Fundamentals of Investment Management, Second Edition

© RICHARD D. IRWIN, INC., 1983, 1986, and 1987

This publication is designed to provide accurate and
authoritative information in regard to the subject matter
covered. It is sold with the understanding that neither the
author nor the publisher is engaged in rendering legal, accounting,
or other professional service. If legal advice or other expert
assistance is required, the services of a competent
professional person should be sought.

*From a Declaration of Principles jointly adopted by a Committee
of the American Bar Association and a Committee of Publishers.*

ISBN 0-87094-939-X

Library of Congess Catalog Card No. 86–50778

Printed in the United States of America
1 2 3 4 5 6 7 8 9 0 DO 4 3 2 1 0 9 8 7

Dedicated to our fathers: Arnold Hirt and Abe Block

PREFACE

A visit to any well-stocked bookstore will convince the reader of the breadth and depth of the investment field. Books about stocks, bonds, options, futures, real estate, mutuals funds, and the many other topics that this interesting discipline comprises line the shelves. Some of these books are intended for the novice, others are addressed to the advanced investor.

In *The Complete Investor* we have attempted to provide the reader with a thorough coverage of all important investment subjects, beginning with the basics, and building to a theoretical level that is both challenging and useful. Every effort has been made to make the discussion clear, and to avoid esoteric subjects or models having little or no application in the real world.

We believe that the book will provide a sound foundation of understanding for those beginning their studies of investing, and that advanced readers will be challenged to expand the boundaries of their knowledge.

We wish to thank those who contributed directly to the preparation of the book.

For their valuable reviews and helpful comments we are grateful to Keith E. Boles (University of Colorado, Colorado Springs), Jerry D. Boswell (College of Financial Planning), Paul Grier (SUNY-Binghamton), John D. Markese (DePaul University), John W. Peavy III (Southern Methodist University), Tom S. Sale (Louisiana Tech University), Ira Smolowitz (Siena College), Frank N. Tiernan (Drake University), Bismarck Williams (Roosevelt University), Sheri Kole (Copeland Companies), Art Schwartz (University of South Florida), Jane H. Finley (University of South Alabama), Don Taylor (University of Wisconsin, Platteville), Carol J. Billingham (Central Michigan University), and Gerald A. Blum (University of Nevada, Reno).

Finally, we are especially grateful to our families for their patience and tolerance throughout the project.

Geoffrey A. Hirt
Stanley B. Block

CONTENTS

THE COMPLETE INVESTOR:
INSTRUMENTS, MARKETS AND METHODS

Part One

INTRODUCTION TO INVESTMENTS

In Part One of the text, we establish the groundwork that is essential to the development of investment stragey and the management of financial resources.

The place to begin is with the setting of investment objectives. Not only is this the first step in any well-managed investment program, but it is often the most important ingredient. Among the factors the investor considers are willingness to take risks, desire for current income, need for liquidity, and tax considerations. The reader also considers the concepts of risk and return and examines historical rates of return on different types of investments.

A discussion of security markets follows in Chapter 2. An important distinction is made between primary markets (for new issues) and secondary markets (for existing issues). We discuss the major organized exchanges, such as the New York Stock Exchange, the American Stock Exchange, and the Chicago Board Options Exchange, as well as the over-the-counter market. We also take a look at future developments in the securities industry relating to computerized security trading.

In Chapter 3 the actual steps necessary to participate in the market are considered, with a description of the types of accounts that can be opened, the forms of orders that can be executed, and the commission costs involved. Tax considerations are also covered, with an emphasis on the proper timing of investment decisions to minimize taxes.

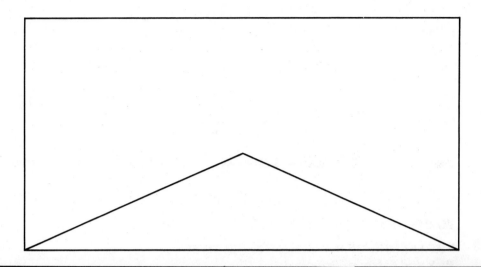

As part of the goal of establishing the groundwork for investment management in Part One, sources of investment information are covered in Chapter 4. The reader is presented with an overview of aggregate economic data sources generated by the government and industry/company data developed by investment advisory services, such as Value Line and Standard & Poor's. The uses of periodical indexes, journals, and computer data bases are also highlighted.

Chapter 1
THE INVESTMENT SETTING

Chapter 2
SECURITY MARKETS—PRESENT AND FUTURE

Chapter 3
PARTICIPATING IN THE MARKET

Chapter 4
SOURCES OF INVESTMENT INFORMATION

Chapter 1

The Investment Setting

FORMS OF INVESTMENT

THE SETTING OF INVESTMENT OBJECTIVES
Risk and Safety of Principal
Current Income versus Capital Appreciation
Liquidity Considerations
Short-Term versus Long-Term Orientation
Tax Factors
Ease of Management

PROFILE ANALYSIS

MEASURES OF RISK AND RETURN
Risk

ACTUAL CONSIDERATION OF REQUIRED RETURNS
Real Rate of Return
Anticipated Inflation Factor
Risk Premium
Determining the Risk Premium
Systematic and Unsystematic Risk
Summary of Return Considerations

In the last decade, we saw an unusual series of economic events. Oil went from $2 to over $30 a barrel. Gold went from $35 an ounce to $875 and then fell by over 60 percent. Silver increased from $4 an ounce to over $50 an ounce and then declined by 80 percent. Interest rates moved between 8 percent and 20+ percent, and inflation was at double-digit levels, moderating only at later points in time. This was in sharp contrast to the stable economic environment of the 1950s and 1960s.

How does one develop an investment strategy in such an environment? Suggestions come to the investor from all directions. He or she is told how to benefit from the coming monetary disaster as well as how to grow rich in a new era of prosperity. The intent of this text is to help the investor sort out the various investments that are available and to develop analytical skills that suggest what alternates might be most appropriate for a given portfolio.

We shall define an investment as the commitment of current funds in anticipation of receiving a larger future flow of funds. The investor hopes to be compensated by forgoing immediate consumption, for inflation, and for taking a risk.

The process of investing may be both exciting and challenging. The first-time investor who pours over the financial statements of a firm and then makes a dollar commitment to purchase a few shares of stock often has a feeling of euphoria as he or she charges out in the morning to secure the daily newspaper and read the market quotes. Even the professional analyst may take pleasure in leaving his Wall Street office to evaluate an emerging high technology firm in Austin or Palo Alto. Likewise, the buyer of a rare painting or late 18th-century U.S. coin may find a sense of excitement in attempting to outsmart the market. Even the purchaser of a bond or money market instrument must do proper analysis to assure that anticipated objectives are being met.

However, the seasoned investor often learns that there are failures that go with successes. The professional money manager is under tremendous pressure to outperform the popular market averages, and failure to do so may mean loss of a valuable account or perhaps a job. The individual investor may also feel a sense of frustration as he or she observes a "sure thing" go sour. The primary task is to establish your investment objectives so that both successes and temporary setbacks can be reasonably anticipated and accepted as part of the process.

FORMS OF INVESTMENT

In the text, we break down investment alternatives between financial and real assets. A financial asset represents a financial claim on an asset that is usually documented by some form of legal representation. An example would be a share of stock or a bond. A real asset represents an actual tangible asset that may be seen, felt, held, or collected. An example would be real estate or gold.

In Table 1–1, we list the various forms of financial and real assets.

As indicated in part A of Table 1–1, financial assets may be broken down into five categories. *Direct equity claims* represent ownership interests and

TABLE 1–1   Overview of Investment Alternatives

A. Financial assets
   1. Equity claims—direct:
      Common stock.
      Warrants.
      Options.
   2. Equity claims—indirect:
      Investment company shares.
   3. Creditor claims:
      Savings accounts.
      Money market funds.
      Commercial paper.
      Treasury bills.
      Bonds (straight and convertible to common stock).
   4. Preferred stock (straight and convertible to common stock).
   5. Commodity futures.
B. Real assets
   1. Real estate—office buildings, apartments, shopping centers, personal residences.
   2. Precious metals—gold, silver.
   3. Precious gems—diamonds, rubies, sapphires.
   4. Collectibles:
      Art.
      Antiques.
      Stamps.
      Coins.
      Rare books.
   5. Other:
      Cattle.
      Oil.
      Common metals.

include common stock as well as other instruments that can be used to purchase common stock, such as warrants and options. Warrants and options allow the holder to buy a stipulated number of shares in the future at a given price. Warrants usually convert to one share and are long-term in nature, whereas options are generally based on 100 share units and are short-term in nature.

Indirect equity can be acquired through placing funds in investment companies (such as a mutual fund). The investment company pools the resources of many investors and reinvests them in common stock (or other investments). The individual enjoys the advantages of diversification and professional management (though not necessarily higher returns).

Financial assets may also take the form of *creditor claims* as represented by debt instruments offered by financial institutions, industrial corporations, or the government. The rate of return is often initially fixed, though the effective yield may vary with changing market conditions. Other forms of financial assets are *preferred stock*, which is a hybrid form of security combining some of the elements of equity ownership and creditor claims, and *commodity futures,* which represent a contract to buy or sell a commodity in the future at a given price. Commodities may include wheat, corn, copper, or even such financial instruments as Treasury bonds or foreign exchange.

As shown in part B of Table 1–1, there are also numerous categories of real assets. The most widely recognized investment in this category is *real estate,* either commercial property or one's own residence. For greater risk, *precious metals* or *precious gems* can be considered, and for those seeking psychic pleasure as well as monetary gain, *collectibles* are an investment outlet. Finally, the *other (all-inclusive)* category includes cattle, oil, and other items that stretch as far as the imagination will go.

Throughout the text, each form of financial and real asset is considered. What assets the investor ultimately selects will depend on his or her investment objectives as well as the economic outlook for the future. For example, if the investor believes that inflation will be relatively strong in the future, there may be a preference for real assets that have a replacement value reflecting increasing prices. In a more moderate inflationary environment, stocks and bonds may be preferred.

THE SETTING OF INVESTMENT OBJECTIVES

The setting of investment objectives may be as important as the selection of the investment. In actuality, they tend to go together. A number of key areas should be considered.

Risk and Safety of Principal

The first factor that the investor must consider is the amount of risk that he or she is prepared to assume. In a relatively efficient and informed capital market environment, risk tends to be closely correlated with return. Most of the literature of finance would suggest that those who consistently demonstrate high returns of perhaps 20 percent or more are greater-than-normal risk takers. While there may be some clever investors who are able to prosper on their wits alone, most high returns may be perceived as compensation for risk.

And there is not only the risk of losing invested capital directly (a dry hole perhaps), but also the danger of a loss in purchasing power. At 8 percent inflation (compounded annually) a stock that is held for four years without a gain in value would represent a 36 percent loss in purchasing power.

The investor who wishes to assume low risks will probably confine a large portion of his or her portfolio to short-term debt instruments in which the party responsible for payment is the government or a major bank or corporation. Some conservative investors may choose to invest in a money market fund, in which the funds of numerous investors are pooled together and reinvested in high-yielding, short-term instruments. More aggressive investors may look toward longer-term debt instruments and common stock. Real assets, such as gold, silver, or valued art, might also be included in an aggressive portfolio.

It is not only the inherent risk in an asset that must be considered, but also the extent to which that risk is being diversified away in a portfolio. Though an investment in gold might be considered risky, such might not be fully the case if it is combined into a portfolio of common stocks. Gold thrives on bad news, while common stocks generally do well in a positive economic environment. An oil embargo or foreign war may drive down the value of stocks while gold is advancing, and vice versa.

The age and economic circumstances of an investor are important variables in determining an appropriate level of risk. Young, upwardly mobile people are generally in a better position to absorb risk than are elderly couples on a fixed income. Nevertheless, each of us, regardless of our plight in life, has different risk-taking desires. A surgeon earning $200,000 a year may be more averse to accepting a $2 per share loss on a stock than an aging taxicab driver.

One cruel lesson of the last decade is that those who thought they were buying conservative investments often found quite the opposite to be true. For example, an 8 percent U.S. government bond maturing in 1998 was trading at 75 percent of its stated value in the mid-1980s.

Current Income versus Capital Appreciation

A second consideration in the setting of investment objectives is a decision on the desire for current income versus capital appreciation. Though this decision is closely tied to an evaluation of risk, it is a separate matter.

In purchasing stocks, the investor with a need for current income may opt for high-yielding, mature firms in such industries as public utilities, machine tools, or apparel. Those searching for capital gains may look toward smaller, emerging firms in high technology, energy, or electronics. The latter firms may pay no cash dividend at all, but the investor hopes for an increase in value to provide the desired return.

Liquidity Considerations

Liquidity is measured by the ability of the investor to convert an investment into cash within a relatively short period of time with a minimum capital loss on the transaction. Most financial assets provide a high degree of liquidity. Stocks and bonds can generally be sold within a matter of minutes at a price reasonably close to the last traded value. Such may not be the case for real estate. Almost everyone has seen a house or piece of commercial real estate sit on the market for weeks or months.

Liquidity can also be measured indirectly by the transaction costs or commissions involved in the transfer of ownership. Financial assets generally trade on a relatively low commission basis (perhaps 1 or 2 percent), whereas many real assets have transaction costs that run from 5 percent to 25 percent or more.

In many cases the lack of immediate liquidity can be justified if there are unusual opportunities for gain. An investment in real estate or precious gems may provide sufficient return to more than compensate for the added transaction costs. Of course, a bad investment will be all the more difficult to unload.

The investor must carefully assess his or her own situation to determine the need for liquidity. If you are investing funds to be used for the next house payment or the coming semester's tuition, then immediate liquidity will be essential, and financial assets will be preferred. If funds can be tied up for long periods of time, bargain-buying opportunities of an unusual nature can also be evaluated.

Short-Term versus Long-Term Orientation

In setting investment objectives, you must decide whether you will assume a short-term or long-term orientation in managing the funds and evaluating performance. You do not always have a choice. Those who manage funds for others may be put under tremendous pressure to show a given level of performance in the short run. The appliers of pressure may be a concerned relative or a large pension fund that has placed funds with a bank trust department. Even though you are convinced your latest stock purchase will double in the next three years, the fact that it is currently down by 15 percent may provide some discomfort to those around you.

Market strategies may also be short-term or long-term in scope. Those who attempt to engage in short-term market tactics are termed *traders*. They may buy a stock at 15 and hope to liquidate if it goes to 20. To help reach decisions, short-term traders often make use of technical analysis, which is based on evaluating market indicator series and charting. Those who take a longer-term perspective try to identify fundamentally sound companies for a buy-and-hold approach. A long-term investor does not necessarily anticipate being able to buy right at the bottom or sell at the exact peak.

Tax Factors

Investors in high tax brackets will have different investment objectives than those in lower brackets, or tax-exempt charities, foundations, or similar organizations. An investor in a high tax bracket may prefer municipal bonds (interest is not taxable), real estate (with its depreciation and interest write-off), or investments that provide tax credits or tax shelters, such as those in oil and gas or railroad cars.

In recent times many investment advisers have cautioned investors not to be blinded by the beneficial tax aspects of an investment but to look at the economic factors as well.

Ease of Management

A final item of consideration in setting up an investment program is ease of management. The investor must determine the amount of time and effort that can be devoted to an investment portfolio and act accordingly. In the stock market, this may determine whether you want to be a daily trader or to assume a longer-term perspective. In real estate, it may mean the difference between personally owning and managing a handful of rental houses or going in with 10 other investors to form a limited partnership in which a general partner takes full management responsibility and the limited partners merely put up the capital.

Of course, there is a minimum amount of time that must be committed to any investment program. Even when investment advisers or general partners are in charge, their activities must be monitored and evaluated.

PROFILE ANALYSIS

The editors of *Consumer Guide* have developed an interesting survey to see what types of investments are appropriate for investors, based on their age and economic circumstances. The questionnaire is presented in Appendix 1–A. After you have read this chapter you may want to try it. You can apply the questions to your own or your family's economic conditions.

MEASURES OF RISK AND RETURN

Now that you have some basic familiarity with the different forms of investments and the setting of investment goals, we are ready to look at concepts of measuring the return from an investment and the associated risk. The return that you receive from any investment (stocks, bonds, real estate) has two primary components: capital gains (or increase in value) and current income. The rate of return from an investment can be measured as:

$$\text{Rate of return} = \frac{(\text{Ending value} - \text{Beginning value}) + \text{Income}}{\text{Beginning value}} \qquad (1\text{--}1)$$

Thus if a share of stock goes from $20 to $22 during 1986 and also pays a dollar in dividends during the year the total return is 15 percent. Using Formula (1–1):

$$\frac{(\$22 - \$20) + \$1}{\$20} = \frac{\$2 + \$1}{\$20} = \frac{\$3}{\$20} = 15\%$$

Where the formula is being specifically applied to stocks, it is written as:

$$\text{Rate of return} = \frac{(P_1 - P_0) + D_1}{P_0} \qquad (1\text{--}2)$$

Where:

P_1 = Price at the end of the period.
P_0 = Price at the beginning of the period.
D_1 = Dividend income.

Risk

The risk for an investment is related to the uncertainty associated with the outcomes from the investment. For example, an investment that has an absolutely certain return of 10 percent is said to be riskless. Whereas, another investment that has a likely or expected return of 12 percent, but also the possibility of minus 10 percent in hard economic times and plus 30 percent under optimum circumstances, is said to be risky. An example of three investments with progressively greater risk is presented in Figure 1–1. Based on our definition of risk, investment C is clearly the riskiest because of the large uncertainty (wide dispersion) of possible outcomes.

In the study of investments, you will soon observe that the desired or required rate of return for a given investment is generally related to the risk associated with that investment. Because most investors do not like risk, they will require a higher rate of return for a more risky investment. That is not to

FIGURE 1–1   Examples of Risk

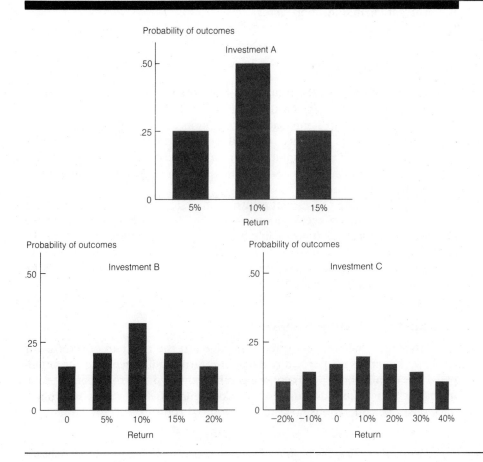

say that investors are unwilling to take risks—they simply wish to be compensated for taking the risk. For this reason, an investment in common stocks (which inevitably carries some amount of risk) may require an anticipated return 4 or 5 percent higher than a certificate of deposit in a commercial bank. This 4 or 5 percent represents a risk premium. You never know for sure whether you will get the returns you anticipate, but at least your initial requirements will be higher to justify the risk you are taking.

ACTUAL CONSIDERATION OF REQUIRED RETURNS

Let's consider how return requirements are determined in the financial markets. Although the following discussion starts out on a theoretical "what if" basis, you will eventually see empirical evidence that different types of investments do provide different types of returns.

There are basically three components that make up the required return from an investment:

A. The real rate of return.
B. The anticipated inflation factor.
C. The risk premium.

Real Rate of Return

The real rate of return is the return that investors require for allowing others to use their money for a given time period. This is the return that investors demand for passing up immediate consumption and allowing others to use their savings until the funds are returned. Because the term *real* is employed, this means it is a value determined before inflation is included in the calculation. The real rate of return is also determined before considering any specific risk for the investment.

Historically, the real rate of return in the U.S. economy has been of the magnitude of 2 to 3 percent. However, in the 1980s it has been somewhat higher (4 to 6 percent). It is possible that the greater volatility in the financial markets (in terms of interest rates and stock prices) has led to this higher real-rate-of-return requirement. Over the long-term, perhaps 3 percent may still be the most reasonable estimate.

Anticipated Inflation Factor

The anticipated inflation factor must be added to the real rate of return. For example, if there is a 3 percent real-rate-of-return requirement and the anticipated rate of inflation is 5 percent, we combine the two to arrive at an approximate 8 percent required return factor.[1] Combining the real rate of return and inflationary considerations gives us the required return on an investment be-

---

[1] We use the word *approximate* to denote that mathematical procedures actually produce an answer slightly over 8 percent.

fore explicitly considering risk. For this reason, it is called the risk-free required rate of return or, simply, *risk-free rate (R_F)*.

We can define the risk-free rate as:

$$\text{Risk-free rate} = (1 + \text{Real rate})(1 + \text{Expected rate of inflation}) - 1 \qquad (1-3)$$

Plugging in numerical values, we would show:

$$(1.03)(1.05) - 1 = 1.0815 - 1 = .0815, \text{ or } 8.15\%$$

The answer is approximately 8 percent. You can simply add the real rate
of return (3 percent) to the anticipated inflation rate (5 percent) to get an 8
percent answer or go through the more theoretically correct process of Formula 1–3 to arrive at 8.15 percent. Either approach is frequently used.

The risk-free rate (R_F) of approximately 8 percent applies to any investment as the minimum required rate of return to provide a 3 percent *real
return* after inflation. Of course, if the investor actually receives a lower return,
his real rate of return may be quite low or negative. If the investor receives a 4
percent return in a 5 percent inflationary environment, there is a negative real
return of 1 percent. The investor will have 1 percent less purchasing power
than before he started. He would have been better off to spend the money *now*
rather than save at a 4 percent rate in a 5 percent inflationary economy. In
effect, he is *paying* the borrower to use his money. Of course, real rates of
return and inflationary expectations change from time to time, so the risk-free
required rate (R_F) also changes.

We have now examined the two components that make up the minimum
risk-free rate of return that apply to any investment (stock, bonds, real estate,
etc.). We now consider the third component, the risk premium. The relationship is depicted in Figure 1–2.

FIGURE 1–2   The Components of Required Rate of Return

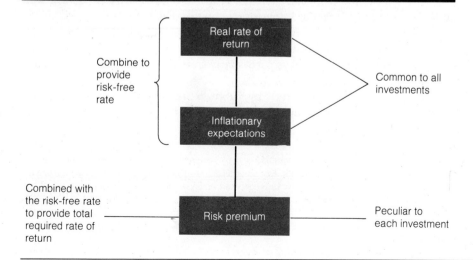

Risk Premium

The risk premium will be different for each investment. For example, for a federally insured certificate of deposit at a bank or for a U.S. government Treasury bill, the risk premium approaches zero. All the return to the investor will be at the risk-free rate of return (the real rate of return plus inflationary expectations). For common stock, the investor's required return may carry a 4 or 5 percent risk premium in addition to the risk-free rate of return. If the risk-free rate were 8 percent, the investor might have an overall required return of 12 to 13 percent on common stock.

+ Real rate	3%
+ Anticipated inflation	5%
= Risk-free rate	8%
+ Risk premium	4% to 5%
= Required rate of return	12% to 13%

Corporate bonds fall somewhere between short-term government obligations (virtually no risk) and common stock in terms of risk. Thus, the risk premium may be 2 to 4 percent. Like the real rate of return and the inflation rate, the risk premium is not a constant, but may change from time to time. If investors are very fearful about the economic outlook, the risk premium may be 8 to 10 percent for a high-risk investment.

The normal relationship between selected investments and their rates of return is depicted in Figure 1–3.

There have been a number of empirical studies that tend to support the risk–return relationships shown in Figure 1–3 over a long period of time. Perhaps the most widely cited is the Ibbotson and Sinquefield study presented in Table 1–2, which covers data from 1926–83. Note the high-to-low return scale is in line with expectations based on risk.[2] Of particular interest is the first column, labeled geometric mean. Nonstatisticians will be pleased to know that this is simply the compound annual rate of return. The arithmetic mean in column 2 is an average of yearly rates of return and has less meaning. We will study the concept of standard deviation (column 3) later in the text.

Because the study covered over half a century (including a decade of depression), the rates of return are somewhat lower than those currently available in the economy. This is particularly true for the bonds and Treasury bills shown in the table.

In Table 1–3, you see a study by Salomon Brothers, an investment banking firm, that covers 14 different investment categories and the CPI (consumer price index).

---

[2] Similar long-term studies of financial assets by Fisher and Lorie produced the same type of risk–return relations. Examples include Lawrence Fisher and James H. Lorie, *A Half Century of Returns on Stocks and Bonds* (Chicago: University of Chicago Graduate School of Business, 1977); James H. Lorie and Lawrence Fisher, "Rates of Return on Investment in Common Stock," *Journal of Business*, January 1964, pp. 1–17; and Lawrence Fisher and James H. Lorie, "Rates of Return on Investment in Common Stock: The Year-by-Year Record 1926–1965," *Journal of Business*, July 1968, pp. 219–316.

FIGURE 1–3   Risk-Return Characteristics

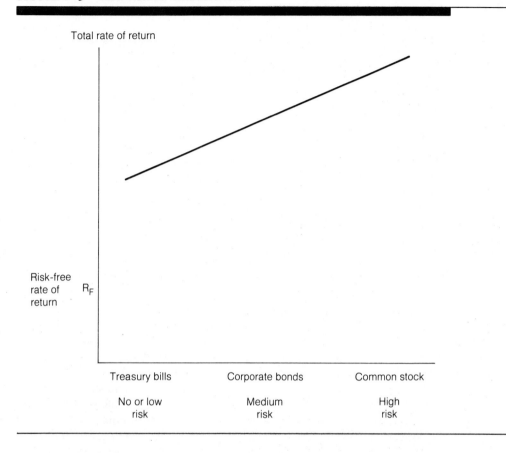

TABLE 1–2   Annual Returns of Financial Assets (1926–1983)

Series	(1) Geometric mean	(2) Arithmetic mean	(3) Standard deviation
Common stocks	9.6%	11.8%	21.4%
Small stocks	12.8	18.7	36.5
Long-term corporate bonds	4.2	4.4	7.6
Long-term government bonds	3.5	3.7	7.4
U.S. Treasury bills	3.1	3.2	3.2
Inflation	3.0	3.1	5.0

Source: *Stocks, Bonds, Bills and Inflation, 1984 Yearbook* (Chicago: R. G. Ibbotson and Associates, Inc., 1984),
p. 5.

TABLE 1–3   Compounded Annual Rates of Return*

	15 years (ranking)		10 years (ranking)		5 years (ranking)		1 year (ranking)	
Oil	20.4%	(1)	10.1%	(4)	14.8%	(2)	0.0%	(8)
Coins	17.3	(2)	21.4	(1)	11.3	(5)	7.4	(3)
Gold.	16.3	(3)	9.5	(6)	7.4	(8)	−4.0	(12)
U.S. stamps	16.1	(4)	17.1	(2)	9.8	(6)	−4.0	(13)
Chinese ceramics	13.7	(5)	5.9	(14)	15.7	(1)	3.0	(6)
Silver	11.7	(6)	7.2	(12)	2.4	(13)	−25.2	(15)
Diamonds.	10.4	(7)	9.8	(5)	6.1	(9)	0.0	(7)
Farmland	9.6	(8)	9.4	(7)	3.3	(12)	−0.7	(9)
Treasury bills	9.0	(9)	10.1	(3)	12.7	(4)	9.4	(2)
Old masters	8.5	(10)	9.1	(8)	1.5	(14)	14.3	(1)
Housing	8.5	(11)	8.6	(10)	5.8	(10)	5.5	(4)
Consumer price index . .	7.2	(12)	7.9	(11)	7.9	(7)	4.6	(5)
Bonds.	5.7	(13)	6.3	(13)	4.6	(11)	−7.2	(14)
Stocks.	5.3	(14)	9.0	(9)	13.5	(3)	−1.2	(10)
Foreign exchange.	3.0	(15)	0.9	(15)	−4.9	(15)	−3.0	(11)

* Values computed through June 1, 1984.
Source: Salomon Brothers Inc.

The study is different from Table 1–2 in that it covers real assets as well as financial assets. The information runs through June 1, 1984.

For the 15-year and 10-year periods, real assets tend to dominate the return rankings. This is primarily due to the high rate of inflation that was present during the 1970s and early 1980s. Real assets, because of increasing replacement value and scarity, tend to perform best during periods of high inflation. However, in the 5-year column, you will observe that many real assets, such as silver, diamonds, farmland, and gold performed poorly as inflationary expectations diminished in the 1983–84 time frame. Stocks, which were poor performers over the 15- and 10-year periods, showed a strong performance during the five-year time frame. The one-year rankings are almost meaningless because of short-term influences.

Because much of the material in the Salomon Brothers study was gathered during one of the most inflationary time periods in U.S. history (aided by major oil price increases), you should not overly generalize from the results. Over longer periods of time, common stock tends to perform at approximately the same level as such real assets as real estate, coins, stamps, etc.,[3] with each

---

[3] Examples of longer-term studies on comparative returns between real and financial assets are: Roger G. Ibbotson and Carol F. Fall, "The United States Wealth Portfolio," *The Journal of Portfolio Management,* Fall 1982, pp. 82–92. Roger G. Ibbotson and Lawrence B. Siegel, "The World Market Wealth Portfolio," *The Journal of Portfolio Management,* Winter 1983, pp. 5–17. (While Ibbotson and Siegel showed superior returns for metals between 1960 and 1980, metals have greatly underperformed other assets in the 1980s). Alexander A. Robichek, Richard A. Cohn, and John J. Pringle, "Returns on Alternative Media and Implications for Portfolio Construction," *Journal of Business,* July 1972, pp. 427–43.

tending to show a different type of performance in a differing economic environment. More will be said about the impact of inflation and disinflation on investments in later parts of the text.

Determining the Risk Premium

We have attempted to demonstrate the importance of risk in determining the required rate of return for an investment. As previously discussed, it is the third key component that is added to the risk-free rate (composed of the real rate of return and the inflation premium) to determine the total required rate of return. How does one *actually* go about determining the risk that is to be rewarded from a given instrument?

Systematic and Unsystematic Risk

You will recall that earlier we defined risk as related to the uncertainty of outcomes for a given investment. But it is not just the risk for an individual security that must be considered. Financial theory also requires that we consider the relationship between two or more investments to determine the combined risk level. Part of the risk of one investment may be diversified away with a second investment. For example, an investment in an oil company may be somewhat risky in nature because oil prices may drop, but if you have a second investment in a petrochemical company that will benefit from lower oil prices, then you have diversified away part of the risk. Similarly, investments in foreign stocks often move in the opposite direction of investments in U.S. stocks. If you combine stocks from two or more countries, part of the risk is diversified away. Because diversification can *eliminate* part of the risk in an investment, not all risk is thought to be compensated for by proportionally higher returns.

Financial theory can be used to break down risk which is systematic and unsystematic in nature. We'll talk about the latter item first. Unsystematic risk is risk that can be diversified away in a well-constructed portfolio and thus is not assumed to be rewarded with higher returns in the financial markets. It represents the type of risk described in the preceding paragraph. Systematic risk, on the other hand, is inherent in the investment and cannot be diversified away, and is assumed to be rewarded in the marketplace. The relationship is indicated below.

Total Risk in a Stock

Systematic (cannot be eliminated)   Unsystematic (can be diversified away)

Systematic risk is measured by the related movement of a stock to the market. Even in a totally diversified portfolio, each stock will be vulnerable to changes in the *overall* market even if individual characteristics of the stocks have been largely diversified away. Based on systematic risk, if the market goes up or down by 10 percent, our stock may go up or down by 10 percent. The joint movement between a security and the market in general is defined as the beta coefficient. If a stock has equal volatility to the market (if the market changes by 10 percent, the stock changes by 10 percent) the beta coefficient is 1. If the stock is 50 percent more volatile than the market, the beta coefficient is 1.5 and so on. Systematic risk, as measured by the beta coefficient, is assumed to be compensated for by higher potential returns. That is, stocks that have high systematic risk or betas are assumed to provide higher returns to compensate for the additional risk. This same type of risk analysis can be applied to other types of investments as well.

In Chapter 19, we will give a more thorough mathematical definition of how you separate out systematic and unsystematic risk. It is enough for now that you understand that the differences exist, and that the two forms of risk are not equally compensated. In the prior discussion of unsystematic risk, we mentioned the importance of diversifying away nonmarket-related risks. We discussed oil versus petrochemicals as representing potential for diversifying oil price risks. Also foreign stocks versus U.S. stocks were given as an example. Undoubtedly you can think of others. The auto part replacement market may move in the opposite direction of new auto sales; the same can be said for the market for defense systems and public works projects. In order to establish an efficiently diversified portfolio, the investor must consider how projects correlate with each other. Generally, highly correlated projects provide little diversification benefits, while projects that have low correlations or are negatively correlated provide maximum diversification benefits.

Summary of Return Considerations

Based on our analysis to this point, we can say that each investment requires a total return that comprises a real rate of return, compensation for inflationary expectations, and a risk premium. The risk premium should be related to systematic risk (as opposed to unsystematic risk).[4]

When you get to Chapter 6, "Valuation of the Individual Firm," you will see how the required rate of return influences the valuation of an investment. You should also be aware that just because an investor has a required return expectation does not mean that the expectation will be met. For example, an investor may purchase a bond with an expected return of 10 percent. But if the inflation expectations go up, the new required return on such a bond may now be 13 percent. The only way for the old bond to offer the going market rate, based on its low 10 percent interest payments, will be for the bond to go down in value. This lower value will offer the *new* bondholders the return they desire but will mean *old* bondholders are suffering market value losses in the

---

[4] Some analysts prefer to view risk in terms of internal corporate considerations such as business or financial risk. Our emphasis for now is on systematic risk.

meantime. They started out hoping to receive 10 percent, but now their annual rate of return will be less because of the drop in the bond value.[5] The same thing can happen to common stock investors.

_____

[5] Of course, if inflation expectations go down, the required return would be less and the bond price would go up. Now investors would receive a return higher than the 10 percent they initially expected.

Chapter 2

SECURITY MARKETS— PRESENT AND FUTURE

MARKET FUNCTIONS
Market Efficiency and Liquidity
Competition and Allocation of Capital
Secondary Markets
Primary Markets

ORGANIZATION OF THE PRIMARY MARKETS—THE INVESTMENT BANKER
Underwriting Function
Distribution

ORGANIZATION OF THE SECONDARY MARKETS
Organized Exchanges
Consolidated Tape
Listing Requirements for Firms
Membership for Market Participants

OTHER ORGANIZED EXCHANGES
The American Stock Exchange
The Chicago Board Options Exchange
Futures Markets

OVER-THE-COUNTER MARKETS
NASDAQ
Debt Securities Traded Over-the-Counter
The Third and Fourth Markets—Part of Over-the-Counter Trading

THE TRANSFORMATION AND FUTURE OF THE CAPITAL MARKETS
Competition in Financial Services
The National Market System

REGULATION OF THE SECURITY MARKETS
Securities Act of 1933
Securities Exchange Act of 1934
The Securities Acts Amendments of 1975
Other Legislation
Insider Trading

Change in the securities markets that began in the 1970s has greatly accelerated in the 1980s. Deregulation of financial institutions created new competitors for retail brokerage houses and allowed banks and savings and loans to offer discount brokerage services and money market deposit accounts. Mergers continued to increase the consolidation of financial resources into well-capitalized financial-service-oriented companies, such as Merrill Lynch, Sears, Bank of America, and Shearson Lehman/American Express. One result is that investors probably have more alternative investments (securities) currently available to them than at any other time.

The market for stock options and financial futures has recently expanded to include options on futures and options on stock indexes. The popularity of individual retirement accounts (IRAs) has added to the demand for mutual funds, and these funds have increased the emphasis on traditional products as well as short-term money market funds, real estate investment trusts, and funds investing in international securities.

Even the traditional markets for common stocks have changed as the over-the-counter market through its NASDAQ automated quotation system has successfully increased its share of equity trades at the expense of the New York and American Stock Exchanges. Computer and communications technology is affecting the way securities are traded not only in the international market systems but also by the individual and institutional investors. As debt has become more widespread, markets for federal government securities, municipal bonds, and corporate debt have all expanded. The combined effects of all these events are still creating structural changes in the markets.

The impact of these changes as well as a complete discussion of securities available for investment will be presented in various chapters throughout the book. In this chapter we examine how the market system operates, with an eye toward efficiency, liquidity, and allocation of capital. We then look at the role of the secondary or resale market for stocks, bonds, and other securities. Finally, we examine some key protective legislation for the investor.

MARKET FUNCTIONS

Many times people will call their stockbroker and ask, How's the market? What they are referring to is usually the market for common stocks as measured by the Dow Jones Industrial Average, the New York Stock Exchange Index, or some other measure of common stock performance. The stock market is not the only market. There are markets for each different kind of investment that can be made.

A market is simply a way of exchanging assets, usually cash for something of value. It could be a used car, a government bond, gold, or diamonds. There doesn't have to be a central place where this transaction is consummated. As long as there can be communication between buyers and sellers, the exchange can occur. The offering party does not have to own what he sells. He can be an agent acting for the owner in the transaction. For example, in the sale of real estate, the owner usually employs a real estate broker/agent who advertises and sells the property for a percentage commission. Not all markets have the same procedures, but certain trading characteristics are desirable for most markets.

Market Efficiency and Liquidity

In general, markets are efficient when prices respond quickly to new information, when each successive trade is made at a price close to the preceding price, and when the market can absorb large amounts of securities or assets without changing the price significantly. The more efficient the market, the faster prices react to new information, the closer in price is each successive trade, and the greater the amount of securities that can be sold without changing the price.

In order for markets to be efficient in this context, they must be liquid. Liquidity is a measure of the speed with which an asset can be converted into cash at its fair market value. Liquid markets exist when continuous trading occurs, and as the number of participants in the market becomes larger, price continuity increases along with liquidity. Transaction costs also affect liquidity. The lower the cost of buying and selling, the more likely it is that people will be able to enter the market.

Competition and Allocation of Capital

An investor must realize that all markets compete for funds; stocks against bonds, mutual funds against real estate, government securities against corporate securities, and so on. The competitive comparisons are almost endless. Because markets set prices on assets, investors are able to compare the prices against their perceived risk and expected return and thereby choose assets that enable them to achieve their desired risk-return trade-offs. If the markets are efficient, prices adjust rapidly to new information, and this adjustment changes the expected rate of return and allows the investor to alter his/her investment strategy. Without efficient and liquid markets, the investor would be unable to do this. This allocation of capital takes place on both secondary and primary markets.

Secondary Markets

Secondary markets are markets for existing assets which are currently traded between investors. It is these markets that create the prices and allow for liquidity. If secondary markets did not exist, investors would have no place to sell their assets. Without liquidity, many people would not invest at all. Would you like to own $10,000 of Eastman Kodak common stock but be unable to convert it into cash if needed? If there were no secondary markets, investors would expect a higher return to compensate for the increased risk of illiquidity and the inability to adjust their portfolios to new information.

Primary Markets

Primary markets are distinguished by the flow of funds between the market participants. Instead of trading between investors as in the secondary markets, participants in the primary market buy their assets directly from the source of the asset. A common example would be a new issue of corporate bonds sold by AT&T. You would buy the bonds through a brokerage firm acting as an agent for an investment banking firm or for AT&T. Your dollars would flow to AT&T rather than to another investor. The same would be true of buying a piece of art directly from the artist rather than from an art gallery. Primary markets allow corporations, government units, and others to raise needed funds for expansion of their capital base. Once the assets or securities are sold in the primary market, they begin trading in the secondary market. Price competition in the secondary markets between different risk-return classes enables the primary markets to price new issues at fair prices to reflect existing risk-return relationships. So far, our discussion of markets has been quite general but applicable to most free markets. In the following section, we will deal with the organization and structure of specific markets.

ORGANIZATION OF THE PRIMARY MARKETS—THE INVESTMENT BANKER

The most active participant in the primary market is the investment banker. Since corporations, states, and local governments do not sell new securities daily, monthly, or even annually, they rely on the expertise of the investment banker when selling securities.

Underwriting Function

The investment banker acts as a middleman in the process of raising funds, and in most cases, he takes a risk by *underwriting* an issue of securities. Underwriting refers to the guarantee the investment banking firm gives the selling firm to purchase its securities at a fixed price, thereby eliminating the risk of not selling the whole issue of securities and having less cash than desired. The investment banker may also sell the issue on a "best efforts" basis where the issuing firm assumes the risk and simply takes back any securities not sold after a fixed period of time.

We can see by inspecting Table 2–1 that on average the best-efforts offerings in recent years only equal about 20 percent of the total securities sold through public distribution, and the overwhelming majority of these issues were common stock. The more risk the investment banker takes, the higher the selling fee to the corporation. Some stock issues are so risky that the investment banker may charge too much of a fee for underwriting risk and distribution so the firm chooses the best-efforts method as a cheaper alternative. With underwriting, once the security is sold, the investment banker will usually make a market in the security, which means active buying and selling

TABLE 2–1 Corporate Issues by Method of Distribution and by Type of Security: 1981–1984 (Primary Issues Registered under the Security Act of 1933; in millions)

Year	Underwritten				Agency best-efforts				Direct by issuer			
	Total	Debt	Preferred	Common	Total	Debt	Preferred	Common	Total	Debt	Preferred	Common
1983	$40,826	$16,049	$4,918	$19,859	$ 8,454	$ 152	$16	$8,286	$2,543	$ 339	$28	$2,176
1982	36,674	21,570	4,558	10,546	9,935	1,305	10	8,620	4,138	2,589	6	1,542
1981	46,678	32,499	1,678	12,451	10,139	1,206	4	8,929	6,689	3,091	10	3,589

Source: Annual Report of the U.S. Securities and Exchange Commission, 1984.

to ensure a continuously liquid market and wider distribution. In the case of best efforts and for direct offerings, which are even smaller than best efforts, the firm assumes the risk of not raising enough capital and faces no guarantees that a continuous market will be made in the company's securities. Table 2–1 shows that most long-term capital raising efforts by corporations are through investment bankers and not directly by corporations.

Corporations may also choose to raise capital through private placements rather than through a public offering. With a private placement the company may sell its own securities to a financial institution such as an insurance company, pension fund, mutual fund, etc. or it can engage an investment banker to find an institution willing to buy a large block of stock or bonds. Most private placements involve bonds (debt issues) instead of common stock but, in general, as Table 2–2 demonstrates, private offerings of bonds have become less popular in recent years.

TABLE 2–2   Gross Proceeds of Corporate Bonds Publicly Offered and Privately Placed

Year	Publicly offered (in millions)	Privately placed (in millions)
1983	n.a.	n.a.
1982	$43,428	$ 7,748
1981	37,653	6,989
1980	41,587	11,619
1979	25,814	14,394
1978	19,815	17,057
1977	24,072	17,943
1976	26,453	15,927
1975	32,583	10,172
1970	25,384	4,931
1965	5,570	8,150
1960	4,806	3,275
1955	4,119	3,301
1950	2,360	2,560

n.a. = Not available.
Source: Selected issues of the *Federal Reserve Bulletin.*

Distribution

In a public offering, the distribution process is extremely important and on large issues an investment banker does not undertake this alone. More often, other investment banking firms will share the risk and the burden of distribution by forming a group called a syndicate. The larger the offering in dollar terms, the more participants there generally are in the syndicate. For example, the tombstone advertisement for Texaco Capital's issue of 13 percent notes due in 1991 shows 19 participating investment bankers (Figure 2–1). Texaco

FIGURE 2–1 Advertisement of Distribution

This announcement is neither an offer to sell nor a solicitation of an offer to buy these securities.
The offer is made only by the Prospectus Supplement and the related Prospectus.

New Issue / August 6, 1984

$500,000,000

Texaco Capital Inc.

13% Notes Due 1991

Unconditionally Guaranteed by

Texaco Inc.

Price 99.54% and accrued interest from August 1, 1984

Copies of the Prospectus Supplement and the related Prospectus may be obtained
in any State in which this announcement is circulated only from such of the
undersigned as may legally offer these securities in such State.

Merrill Lynch Capital Markets   **Salomon Brothers Inc**

PaineWebber   **Atlantic Capital**   **Becker Paribas**   **Daiwa Securities America Inc.**   **Dillon, Read & Co. Inc.**
Incorporated   Corporation   Incorporated
Donaldson, Lufkin & Jenrette   **E. F. Hutton & Company Inc.**   **Kidder, Peabody & Co.**   **The Nikko Securities Co.**
Securities Corporation   Incorporated   International, Inc.
Nomura Securities International, Inc.   **Prudential-Bache**   **Swiss Bank Corporation International**
                                                      Securities   Securities Inc.
Wertheim & Co., Inc.   **Dean Witter Reynolds Inc.**   **Yamaichi International (America), Inc.**

Thomson McKinnon Securities Inc.   **Wood Gundy Corp.**

Source: *The Wall Street Journal,* © Dow Jones & Company, Inc. (August 7, 1984).

Capital is a subsidiary of Texaco and the debt is fully guaranteed by the parent company. Merrill Lynch Capital Markets and Salomon Brothers Inc. are the managing underwriters, with the other 17 firms participating in the syndicate. The firms are usually listed in the tombstone advertisement based on their clout in the investment banking community. The firms at the top of the advertisement usually have taken the biggest dollar position and the firms at the bottom, e.g., Thomson McKinnon Securities Inc., a relatively small position.

Each banker is responsible for selling the agreed-upon number of bonds or stock.

For most original offerings, the investment banker is extremely important as a link between the original issuer and the security markets. By taking much of the risk, the investment banker enables corporations and others to find needed capital and thus allows investors an opportunity to participate in the ownership of securities through purchase in the secondary markets. Notice that the bonds are priced at 99.54 percent of par value which means that the bonds are selling for $995.40 per $1,000 bond. In the case of the Texaco offering, the investment banker took some risk that interest rates would not rise during the offering period. Since rates did later rise, the price fell below par of $1,000 and the syndicate's profit was less than expected.

Investment bankers are in business to make a profit by selling new issues as quickly as possible so that they can use their capital for more offerings. The advantage of having a large number of investment bankers is that more potential public and institutional buyers are available to improve the liquidity and geographic distribution of the issue. Another advantage is that risk is reduced by spreading the selling effort between many investment bankers. The sale of bonds is primarily to large institutional investors in large blocks and so a large broker network is not as necessary as with common stock.

TABLE 2–3   Leading Underwriters for U.S. Issuers, 1985

Manager	Total amount managed ($ billions)	IN U.S. ($ billions)		Outside U.S.† ($ billions)	Fees ($ millions)
		Debt	Equity*		
Salomon Bros.	$34.2	$23.9	$4.9	$5.4	$402
First Boston	25.7	17.2	3.3	5.7	272
Goldman Sachs	19.9	10.9	5.0	4.1	348
Merrill Lynch	17.6	9.3	5.5	2.8	333
Drexel Burnham Lambert	13.3	9.9	3.3	.1	402
Morgan Stanley	12.7	6.6	3.0	3.0	196
Shearson Lehman	10.3	5.1	4.4	.8	212
Kidder Peabody	3.9	1.7	1.8	.3	95
Union Bank of Switzerland	3.0	—	—	3.0	59
PaineWebber	2.9	1.9	1.0	—	65

*Includes equity and equity-related offerings.
†Includes nondollar issues.
Source: IDD Information Services. Reprinted by permission of *The Wall Street Journal,* © Dow Jones & Company, Inc. (January 2, 1986). All rights reserved.

A significant change that is taking place in the investment banking area can also be noted in previously discussed Figure 2–1. An offering of $500 million in the 1970s would have included at least twice as many investment bankers in the syndicate. As firms have merged, the financial strength of the investment bankers has increased to the point where they are able to assume more risk and thus larger dollar positions in new offerings.

Table 2–3 shows the top 10 underwriters for 1985. The top few firms clearly consolidated their dominant position in this market. The rankings are used as a tool to convince clients that the investment banker can raise capital. The rise of shelf-registration under SEC Rule 415 (discussed in Chapter 9) increased the dominance of the large investment bankers specializing in bonds. A shelf registration allows firms to register their securities (mostly bonds and notes) with the Securities and Exchange Commission and then sell them at will as funds are needed. This allows investment bankers to buy portions of the shelf issue and immediately resell the securities to institutional clients without forming the normal syndicates or tying up capital for several weeks.

Some initial offerings, such as Treasury bills or other federal government securities, do not use investment bankers. They rely on Federal Reserve banks to auction the securities to government securities dealers who make markets by buying and selling to large financial institutions. Individuals desiring to buy initial offerings from the Treasury can place orders directly with the nearest Federal Reserve branch bank.

ORGANIZATION OF THE SECONDARY MARKETS

Once the investment banker or the Federal Reserve (for U.S. government securities) has sold a new issue of securities, it begins trading in secondary markets that provide liquidity, efficiency, continuity, and competition. The *organized exchanges* fulfill this need in a central location where trading takes place between buyers and sellers. The *over-the-counter markets* also provide markets for exchange but not in a central location. We will first examine the organized exchanges and then the over-the-counter markets.

Organized Exchanges

Organized exchanges are either national or regional, but both classifications are organized in a similar fashion. Exchanges have a central trading location where securities are bought and sold in an auction market by brokers acting as agents for the buyer and seller. Stocks usually trade at various trading posts on the floor of the exchange. Brokers are registered members of the exchanges, and their number is fixed by each exchange. The national exchanges are the New York Stock Exchange (NYSE) located at the corner of Broad and Wall Street in New York City and the American Stock Exchange (AMEX) located at the corner of Hanover and Wall Street, also in New York City. Both these exchanges are governed by a board of directors consisting of one half exchange members and one half public members.

The regional exchanges began their existence trading securities of local firms. As the firms grew, they became listed on the national exchanges, but they also continued to trade on the regionals. Many cities, such as Chicago, Cincinnati, Baltimore, Detroit, Boston, and others, have regional exchanges. Today most of the trading on these exchanges is done in nationally known companies. Trading in the same companies is common between the NYSE and such regionals as the Midwest Exchange in Chicago, the Pacific Coast Exchange in San Francisco and Los Angeles, and the smaller regionals. In fact, about 90 percent of the companies traded on the Midwest and Pacific Coast Exchanges are also listed on the NYSE.

August 3, 1984, was the busiest day in the history of the New York Stock Exchange, and Table 2–4 shows that over 275 million shares of NYSE-listed stock was traded. Since some of these shares are dually listed on other exchanges and even traded over-the-counter, not all volume was transacted in

TABLE 2–4   Data on Trading Volume

NYSE-Composite Transactions

Friday, August 3, 1984

Quotations include trades on the Midwest, Pacific, Philadelphia, Boston and Cincinnati stock exchanges and reported by the National Association of Securities Dealers and Instinet

Friday's Volume
275,309,660 Shares; 649,000 Warrants

TRADING BY MARKETS

	Shares	Warrants
New York Exchange	236,570,000	648,000
Midwest Exchange	17,967,700	....
Pacific Exchange	7,331,100	....
Nat'l Assoc. of Securities Dealers	6,401,760	1,000
Philadelphia Exchange	4,607,700	....
Boston Exchange	1,917,700	....
Cincinnati Exchange	416,600	....
Instinet System	97,100	....

NYSE – Composite

Volume since Jan. 1:	1984	1983	1982
Total shares	16,202,304,430	15,172,333,820	9,131,951,746
Total warrants	56,607,800	98,163,900	22,587,150

New York Stock Exchange

Volume since Jan. 1:	1984	1983	1982
Total shares	13,664,668,450	13,018,334,165	7,851,651,596
Total warrants	54,697,800	97,683,100	22,558,800

New York. For example, the Midwest Exchange in Chicago accounted for almost 18 million shares of stock listed on the NYSE, while the NYSE traded 236 million shares in its own listed stocks.

Consolidated Tape

Although dual listing and trading has existed for some time, it was not until June 16, 1975, that a consolidated ticker tape was instituted. This allows brokers on the floor of one exchange to see prices of transactions on other exchanges in the dually listed stocks. Any time a transaction is made on a regional exchange or over-the-counter in a security listed on the NYSE, this transaction and any made on the floor of the NYSE are displayed on the composite tape. The composite price data keeps markets more efficient and prices more competitive between exchanges at all times.

The NYSE and AMEX are both national exchanges and for years did not allow dual listing of companies traded on their exchanges. As of August 1976, securities were able to be dually listed between these exchanges. There doesn't seem to be any advantage to this since both are located in New York City, and traditionally, shares traded on one exchange are not traded on the other.

Table 2–5 displays the number of trades (not number of shares) on all markets participating in the Consolidated Tape. We can see that trading volume has risen dramatically since 1976. However, the New York Stock Exchange is getting a smaller piece of the total number of trades in its own listed stock. Its percentage of trades in 1983 slipped to 77.68 percent, its lowest level since the inception of the Consolidated Tape.

During this same time the percentage of *shares* traded on the NYSE peaked in 1978 at 88.43 percent and declined to almost 82 percent by the end of 1983. Volume statistics on participating markets in NYSE listed stocks are shown in Table 2–6.[1] In general, the New York Stock Exchange is meeting tough competition from other exchanges and the over-the-counter NASDAQ system, but it is faced with a possible loss of prestige and profits during the rest of the 1980s as competition becomes even more intense.

Listing Requirements for Firms

Securities can only be traded on an exchange if they have met the listing requirements of the exchange and have been approved by the board of governors. All exchanges have minimum requirements that must be met before trading can take place in a company's common stock. Since the NYSE is the biggest exchange and generates the most dollar volume in large, well-known companies, it is not surprising that its listing requirements are the most restrictive.

---

[1] The NYSE has a larger percentage of the share volume (Table 2–6) than the trade volume (Table 2–5) because its average trade involves more shares than other exchanges.

TABLE 2-5   Number of Trades Shown on the Consolidated Tape

Consolidated tape trades by market, 1983

Year	NYSE	AMEX	PSE	MSE	PHLX	BSE	CSE	NASD	INST	Total
1983	15,050,791	43	1,661,907	1,318,868	751,002	241,520	94,171	248,820	7,250	19,374,372
1982	12,609,104	13	1,326,460	944,862	628,217	159,865	134,106	231,036	6,304	16,039,967
1981	11,701,098	673	910,634	644,176	547,219	129,593	123,911	136,519	3,329	14,197,152
1980	13,074,382	1,021	817,957	548,416	530,659	118,000	108,169	112,923	3,019	15,314,546
1979	10,442,237	244	665,073	402,196	333,805	78,087	63,689	71,858	4,123	12,061,312
1978	10,087,834	725	653,769	366,654	255,359	75,471	54,065	96,165	1,911	11,591,953
1977	8,264,036	1,982	548,507	328,653	150,234	74,263	155,804	178,020	2,062	9,703,561
1976	9,646,200	1,535	545,685	399,266	168,119	95,096	86,735	268,324	1,560	11,217,536

Distribution of consolidated tape trades, 1976–1983

Year	NYSE	AMEX	PSE	MSE	PHLX	BSE	CSE	NASD	INST	Total
1983	77.68%	0.00%	8.58%	6.81%	3.88%	1.25%	0.49%	1.28%	0.04%	100.00%
1982	78.61	0.00	8.27	5.89	3.92	1.00	0.84	1.44	0.04	100.00
1981	82.42	0.00	6.41	4.54	3.85	0.91	0.87	0.96	0.02	100.00
1980	85.37	0.01	5.34	3.58	3.47	0.77	0.71	0.74	0.02	100.00
1979	86.58	0.00	5.51	3.33	2.77	0.65	0.53	0.60	0.03	100.00
1978	87.02	0.01	5.64	3.16	2.20	0.65	0.47	0.83	0.02	100.00
1977	85.16	0.02	5.65	3.39	1.55	0.77	1.61	1.83	0.02	100.00
1976	85.99	0.01	4.86	3.56	1.50	0.85	0.77	2.39	0.01	100.00

Participating markets: NYSE, New York; AMEX American; PSE, Pacific; MSE, Midwest; PHLX, Philadelphia; BSE, Boston; CSE, Cincinnati; NASD, National Association of Securities Dealers; INST, Instinet.
Source: *New York Stock Exchange Fact Book* (New York: New York Stock Exchange, 1984).

TABLE 2–6   Share Volume Shown on the Consolidated Tape

Consolidated tape volume by market, 1983 (thousands of shares)

Year	NYSE	AMEX	PSE	MSE	PHLX	BSE	CSE	NASD	INST	Total
1983	21,589,577	188	802,012	1,634,760	416,206	182,812	51,325	649,261	36,320	25,362,458
1982	16,458,037	1	664,089	1,091,081	307,357	104,085	59,328	486,028	33,593	19,203,590
1981	11,853,740	194	451,591	700,830	215,000	74,406	47,226	319,081	17,125	13,679,194
1980	11,352,294	584	385,970	577,710	212,296	70,747	53,236	268,097	14,679	12,935,607
1979	8,155,914	76	297,379	359,615	160,550	54,711	34,148	180,297	11,357	9,254,044
1978	7,205,055	238	236,417	326,727	118,156	49,381	20,089	184,983	6,530	8,147,569
1977	5,273,767	771	201,841	267,189	80,208	40,054	49,126	234,413	5,803	6,153,173
1976	5,360,116	786	213,041	256,032	85,275	46,558	30,844	281,118	5,771	6,281,008

Distribution of consolidated tape volume, 1976–1983

Year	NYSE	AMEX	PSE	MSE	PHLX	BSE	CSE	NASD	INST	Total
1983	82.12%	0.00%	3.16%	6.45%	1.64%	0.72%	0.20%	2.56%	0.14%	100.00%
1982	85.70	0.00	3.46	5.68	1.60	0.54	0.31	2.53	0.17	100.00
1981	86.66	0.00	3.30	5.12	1.57	0.54	0.35	2.33	0.13	100.00
1980	87.76	0.00	2.98	4.47	1.64	0.55	0.41	2.07	0.11	100.00
1979	88.13	0.00	3.21	3.89	1.73	0.59	0.37	1.95	0.12	100.00
1978	88.43	0.00	2.90	4.01	1.45	0.61	0.25	2.27	0.08	100.00
1977	85.71	0.01	3.28	4.34	1.30	0.65	0.80	3.81	0.09	100.00
1976	85.34	0.01	3.39	4.08	1.36	0.74	0.49	4.48	0.09	100.00

Participating markets: NYSE, New York; AMEX American; PSE, Pacific; MSE, Midwest; PHLX, Philadelphia; BSE, Boston; CSE, Cincinnati; NASD, National Association of Securities Dealers; INST, Instinet.
Source: *New York Stock Exchange Fact Book* (New York: New York Stock Exchange, 1984).

Initial listing.   Although each case is decided on its own merits, according to the *NYSE Fact Book,* the minimum requirements for a company to be listed on the New York Stock Exchange for the first time are as follows:

1.   Demonstrated earning power under competitive conditions of: *either* $2.5 million before Federal income taxes for the most recent year and $2 million pre-tax for each of the preceding two years, *or* an aggregate for last three fiscal years of $6.5 million *together with* a minimum in the most recent fiscal year of $4.5 million. (All three years must be profitable.)
2.   Net tangible assets of $16 million, but greater emphasis is placed on the aggregate market value of the common stock.
3.   Market value of publicly held shares, subject to adjustment depending on market conditions, within the following limits.

Maximum	$18,000,000
Minimum	$ 9,000,000
Present (2/13/84)	$18,000,000

(The market value requirement is subject to adjustment, based on the NYSE Index of Common Stock Prices. The base in effect as of February 13, 1984, is the Index on July 15, 1971 (55.06). The Index as of January 15 and July 15 of each year (if lower than the base) is divided by the base, and the resulting percentage is multiplied by $18 million to produce the adjusted market value standard. The adjustment formula is used only when the current Index is below the base).
4.   A total of 1,100,000 common shares publicly held.
5.   *Either* 2,000 holders of 100 shares or more, *or* 2,200 total stockholders *together with* average monthly trading volume (for the most recent six months) of 100,000 shares.

The other exchanges have requirements covering the same areas, but the amounts are smaller.

Corporations desiring to be listed on exchanges have made the decision that public availability of the stock on an exchange will benefit their shareholders. The benefits will occur either by providing liquidity to owners or by allowing the company a more viable means for raising external capital for growth and expansion. The company must pay annual listing fees to the exchange and some fees based on the number of shares traded each year.

Delisting.   The New York Stock Exchange also has the authority to remove (delist) or suspend a security from trading when the security fails to meet certain criteria. There is much latitude in these decisions but generally a company's security may be considered for delisting if there are fewer than 1,200 round-lot (100 share owners), 600,000 shares or fewer in public hands and market value of the security is less than $5,000,000. A company that easily exceeded these standards on first being listed may fall below them during hard times.

Membership for Market Participants

We've talked about listing requirements for corporations on the exchange, but what about the investment houses or traders that service the listed firms; or trade for their own account on the exchanges? These privileges are reserved for a select number of people. The NYSE has 1,366 members who own "seats" which may be leased or sold with the approval of the NYSE. While the price of a seat was $425,000 in the mid-1980s, it could have been bought for a recent low of $35,000 in 1977. These 1,366 members can be divided into five distinct categories, each with a specific job.

Commission brokers.   Commission brokers represent commission houses, such as Merrill Lynch or E. F. Hutton, that execute orders on the floor of the exchange for customers of that firm. Many of the larger retail brokerage houses have more than one commission broker on the floor of the exchange. If I call my account executive (stockbroker) and place an order to buy 100 shares of Exxon, he will teletype my order to the NYSE where it will be transmitted to one of the firm's commission brokers who will go to the appropriate trading post and execute the order.

Floor brokers.   You can imagine that a commission broker could get very busy running from post to post on a heavy volume day. In times like these, he will rely on some help from a floor broker, who is registered to trade on the exchange but is not an employee of a member firm. Instead, the floor broker owns his own seat and charges a small fee for his services (usually around $4 per 100 shares).

Registered traders.   Registered traders own their own seat and are not associated with a member firm (such as Merrill Lynch). They are registered to trade for their own accounts and, of course, do so with the objective of earning a profit. Because they are members, they don't have to pay commissions on these trades; but in so trading, they help to generate a continuous market and liquidity for the market in general. There is always the possibility that these traders could manipulate the market if they acted in mass, and for that reason, the exchanges have rules governing their behavior and limiting the number of registered traders at one specific trading post.

Odd-lot dealers.   Odd lots (less than 100 shares) are not traded on the main floor of the exchange, so if a customer wants to buy or sell 20 shares of AT&T, the order will end up being processed by an odd-lot dealer. The dealer owns his own inventory of the particular security and buys and sells for his own account. If he accumulates 100 shares, he can sell them in the market, or if he needs 20 shares, he can buy 100 in the market and hold the other 80 shares in his inventory. A few very large brokerage firms, such as Merrill Lynch, have begun making their own odd-lot market in actively traded securities, and it is expected that this trend will become common practice at the other large commission houses. Odd-lot trading on other exchanges is usually handled by the specialist in the particular stock.

Specialists.   Specialists are a very important segment of the exchange and make up about one fourth of total membership. Each stock traded has a specialist assigned to it, and most specialists are responsible for more than one stock. The specialist has two basic duties with regard to the stocks he supervises. First, he must handle any special orders that commission brokers or floor brokers might give him. For example, a special order could limit the price someone is willing to pay for General Telephone (GTE) stock at $40 per share for 100 shares. If the commission broker reaches the General Telephone trading post and GTE is selling at $41 per share, the broker will leave the order with the specialist to execute if and when the stock of GTE falls to $40 or less. The specialist puts these special limit orders in his "book" with the date and time entered so he can execute orders at the same price by the earliest time of receipt. A portion of the broker's commission is then paid to the specialist.

The second major function of specialists is to maintain continuous, liquid, and orderly markets in their assigned stocks. This is not a difficult function in the actively traded securities, such as General Motors, Du Pont, and American Telephone, but it becomes more difficult in those stocks where there are no large, active markets. For example, suppose you placed an order to buy 100 shares of Ametek at the market price. If the commission broker reaches the Ametek trading post and no seller is present, he can't wait for one to appear since he has other orders to execute. Fortunately, he can buy the shares from the specialist who acts as a dealer—in this case buying for and selling from his own inventory. To ensure his ability to maintain continuous markets, the exchange requires a specialist to have $500,000 or enough capital to own 5,000 shares of his assigned stock, whichever is greater. At times, specialists are placed under tremendous pressure to make a market for securities. A classic case occurred when President Eisenhower had a heart attack in the 1950s and specialists stabilized the market by absorbing wave after wave of "sell" orders.

The New York Stock Exchange actually keeps statistics on specialist performance and their ability to maintain price continuity, quotation spreads, market depth, and price stabilization. These data are given in Table 2–7. Price continuity is measured by the size of the price variation in successive trades. Column 1 is the percentage of transactions with no change in price or a minimum change of ⅛ of a dollar. Column 2 presents the percentage of the quotes where the bid and asked price was equal to or less than ¼ of a point. Market depth (column 3) is displayed as a percentage of the time that 1,000 shares of volume failed to move the price of the stock more than ⅛ of a point. Finally the NYSE expects the specialist to stabilize the market by buying and selling from his own account against the prevailing trend. This is measured in column 4 as the percentage of shares purchased below the last different price and the percentage of shares sold above the last different price. While these

TABLE 2-7   Market Quality and Specialists' Stabilization

	(1) Price continuity	(2) Quotation spreads	(3) Market depth	(4) Stabilization rate
1983	88.7%	60.7%	86.2%	90.0%
1982	89.5	65.1	85.2	88.9
1981	87.2	60.4	81.6	90.2
1980	86.4	60.6	80.4	90.9
1979	90.6	71.1	84.9	90.0
1978	90.8	72.9	84.4	90.0
1977	92.5	75.9	86.0	90.8
1976	90.3	71.0	—	92.5
1975	88.1	59.9	—	91.4
1974	84.3	44.9	—	91.1

Source: *New York Stock Exchange Fact Book* (New York Stock Exchange, 1984).

statistics are not 100 percent, it would be quite unreasonable for us to expect specialists to maintain that kind of a record in all types of markets. However, some critics of the specialist system on the NYSE think that these performance measures could be improved by having more than one specialist for each stock. Many market watchers feel that competing dealers on the over-the-counter market provide more price stability and fluid markets than the NYSE specialist system.

OTHER ORGANIZED EXCHANGES

The American Stock Exchange

The American Stock Exchange trades in smaller companies than the NYSE and, except for one dually listed company on the NYSE in 1983, the stocks traded on the AMEX are completely different from those on any other exchange. Because the small companies on the AMEX do not meet the liquidity needs of large institutional investors, the AMEX has been primarily a market for individual investors.

In an attempt to differentiate itself from the NYSE, the AMEX traded warrants in companies for many years before the NYSE allowed them. Even now, the AMEX has warrants listed for stocks trading on the NYSE, while the NYSE has very few warrants listed at all. The AMEX also trades put and call options in over 100 stocks, with most of the underlying common stocks being listed on the NYSE. This market has been a stabilizing force for the AMEX. The AMEX (as well as the NYSE) has also recently entered into commodity futures trading through interest rate futures. Although the AMEX also trades about 200 corporate bonds, this is not the major market for corporate bonds.

The Chicago Board Options Exchange

Trading in call options started on the Chicago Board Options Exchange (CBOE) in April of 1973 and proved very successful. The number of call options listed grew from 16 in 1973 to approximately 400 by 1985. A call option gives the owner the right to buy 100 shares of the underlying common stock at a set price for a certain period of time. The establishment of the CBOE standardized call options into three-month, six-month, and nine-month expiration periods on a rotating monthly series. For example, one series is January, April, July, October. A second series is December, March, June, September, and the last series is November, February, May, August. When the CBOE began, only the first series was traded, but the growth in the market dictated the need for other dates. The CBOE and the AMEX currently have many options that are dually listed, and the competition between them is fierce. The two exchanges also trade put options (options to sell). A number of smaller regional exchanges also provide for option trading, and the New York Stock Exchange began trading options in 1985.

A new wrinkle in the options game has been options on stock market indexes or industry groupings (called subindexes). The CBOE offers puts and calls on the Standard & Poor's 100 and 500 stock indexes; the NYSE has options on the NYSE Index; the AMEX has options on the AMEX Market Value Index and several options available on industry indexes such as the Computer Technology Index, the Oil and Gas Index, and the Transportation Index. Even the regional Philadelphia Exchange has options on a Gaming and Hotel Index and a Gold and Silver Index. More about these markets will be presented in Chapter 16.

Futures Markets

Futures markets have traditionally been associated with commodities but, more recently, also with financial instruments. Purchasers of commodity futures own the right to buy a certain amount of the commodity at a set price for a specified period of time. When the time runs out (expires), the futures contract will be delivered unless sold before expiration. One major futures markets is the Chicago Board of Trade, which trades corn, oats, soybeans, wheat, silver, plywood, Ginnie Mae futures, and Treasury bond futures. There are also other important futures markets in Chicago, Kansas City, Minneapolis, New York, and other cities. These markets are very important as hedging markets and help set commodity prices. They are also known for their wide price swings and volatile speculative nature.

In recent years trading volume has increased in foreign exchange futures such as the West German mark, Japanese yen and British pound as well as in Treasury bill and Treasury bond futures. One new product having a direct effect in the stock market is the development of futures contracts on stock market indexes. The Chicago Merchantile Exchange, Chicago Board of Trade, New York Futures Exchanges (a division of the NYSE) and the Kansas City Board of Trade have all developed contracts in separate market indexes such as the Standard & Poor's 500 and the Value Line Index. Market indexes will be presented in the following chapter and we will spend more time discussing futures markets in Chapters 15 and 16.

OVER-THE-COUNTER MARKETS

Unlike the organized exchanges, the over-the-counter markets (OTC) have no central location where securities are traded. Being traded over-the-counter implies that the trade takes place by telephone or electronic device and that dealers stand ready to buy or sell specific securities for their own accounts. These dealers will buy at a bid price and sell at an asked price that reflects the competitive market conditions. The National Association of Securities Dealers (NASD), a self-policing organization of dealers, requires at least two market makers (dealers) for each security, but often there are 5 or 10 or even 20 for government securities. As previously mentioned, the multiple dealer function in the over-the-counter market is an attractive feature for many companies, in comparison to the single specialist arrangement on the NYSE and other organized exchanges.

OTC markets exist for stocks, corporate bonds, mutual funds, federal government securities, state and local bonds, commercial paper, negotiable certificates of deposits, and various other securities. Altogether these securities make the OTC the largest of all markets in the United States in dollar terms.

In the OTC market, the difference between the bid and asked price is the spread; it represents the profit the dealer earns by making a market. For example, if XYZ common stock is bid 10 and asked 10½, this simply means the dealer will buy at least 100 shares at $10 per share or will sell 100 shares at $10.50 per share. If his prices are too low, more buyers than sellers will appear, and he will run out of inventory unless he raises prices to attract more sellers and balances the supply and demand. If his price is at equilibrium, he will match an equal number of shares bought and sold, and for his market-making activities, he will earn 50 cents per share traded. Although in the future, many OTC stocks will no longer be reported on the basis of bid and ask prices, but simply a closing price, the concept of dealer spreads will remain.

There are actually several segments of the over-the-counter stock market, and the National Association of Securities Dealers divides the 5,000+ companies into the National Market System, the national list, and regional and local companies. Stocks in the National Market System receive the quickest and best reporting of their trading activity.

On the National Market System, stocks of companies such as Apple Computer, Coors Brewing, Intel and MCI Communications can be found. These companies all have a diversified geographical shareholder base,[2] while the national list and regional or local companies are usually smaller or closely held by management or the founding family. The small local stocks may not appear

---

[2] The standards for inclusion on the National Market System were reduced by the NASD in 1984 (with permission of the SEC). By early 1986, 2,500 OTC firms will be on the National Market System.

in *The Wall Street Journal*, but will be found on the financial pages of large city newspapers in Dallas, Cleveland, Chicago, Minneapolis, Los Angeles, and other major cities under the heading "Local Over-The-Counter Markets." OTC markets have always been very popular for bank stocks and insurance stocks because these stocks do not generate enough trading volume or have enough stockholders to merit their listing on the organized exchanges. Another reason is that many are small and have only local interest.

NASDAQ

NASDAQ stands for the National Association of Securities Dealers Automated Quotations System. This system is linked together by a computer network and provides up-to-the-minute quotations on over 4,000 of the OTC stocks traded on the NASDAQ system.

Table 2-8 presents the qualification standards for initial and continued listing on various OTC markets. The big difference between the OTC standards and the NYSE listing requirements are that the OTC requires fewer shareholders of record, smaller assets and less net income. While these qualifications allow many small companies to be included in the trading system, they do not preclude many large companies such as Apple Computer or Intel from trading. In fact the National Association of Securities Dealers estimates that over 600 companies on the National Market System would be eligible for listing on the New York Stock Exchange and many more would be eligible for the American Stock Exchange.

The OTC market used to be thought of as only an equity market for low-priced common stocks, but that is all changing with the advent of the National Market System. Table 2-9 depicts the OTC market and the most active stocks in dollar volume on August 3, 1984. On this day when the NYSE set a new trading high of 237 million shares, the OTC's volume was 122 million shares. Notice that some of the names of the most active stocks may be familiar to you. The prices range between $7.75 and $62.50 per share and the dollar volume is quite large. On August 3, 1984 the total number of issues traded was 4,157, which is more than the NYSE and AMEX combined.

During the mid-1980s many articles appeared comparing the New York Stock Exchange and the American Stock Exchange to the over-the-counter market and, in particular, to the inroads that the National Association of Securities Dealers had made in retaining companies on their automated quotation system. Traditionally companies that would reach listing qualifications would jump to the AMEX and then eventually to the NYSE. This cannot be assumed to happen any more. During the first half of 1984, NASDAQ's over-the-counter share volume amounted to about 65 percent of the volume on the NYSE and almost 10 times the volume on the AMEX. The AMEX seems to be suffering most of all in this battle, as the number of listings has fallen by about one third since 1974. The multiple dealer system as well as the enhanced reporting capability can be listed as reasons for the increased competitive nature of the OTC markets.

TABLE 2–8 NASDAQ, National List and NASDAQ NMS Qualification Standards

Standard	For initial NASDAQ inclusion (domestic common stocks)*	For continued NASDAQ inclusion (domestic common stocks)*	For newspaper national list inclusion — Alternative 1	Alternative 2	SEC criteria for mandatory NMS† inclusion‡	SEC criteria for voluntary NMS† inclusion‡
Registration under Section 12(g) of the Securities Exchange Act of 1934 or equivalent	Yes	Yes	Yes	Yes	Yes	Yes
Total assets	$2 million	$750,000	$2 million	$2 million	—	—
Tangible assets	—	—	—	—	$2 million	$2 million
Capital and surplus	$1 million	$375,000	$1 million	$8 million	$1 million	$1 million
Net income	—	—	$300,000 in latest or 2 of 3 last fiscal years	—	—	—
Operating history	—	—	—	4 years	—	—
Public float (shares)	100,000	100,000	350,000	800,000	500,000	250,000
Market value of float	—	—	$2 million	$8 million	$5 million	$3 million
Minimum bid	—	—	$3	—	$10 on 5 business days	$5 on 5 business days
Trading volume	—	—	—	—	Average 600,000 shares/month for 6 months	Average 100,000 shares/month for 6 months
Shareholders of record	300	300	300	300	300	300
Number of market makers	2	1	2	2	4 on 5 business days	4 on 5 business days

* Qualification standards for other types of securities are available upon request from the NASDAQ Operations Department in Washington, D.C.
† NMS—National Market System.
‡ A number of their standards were further reduced in 1984 to expand participation in the National Market System.
Source: *NASDAQ Fact Book* (Washington, D.C.: National Association of Securities Dealers, Inc., 1983).

Debt Securities Traded Over-the-Counter

Debt securities also trade over-the-counter. Actually, government securities of the U.S. Treasury provide the largest dollar volume of transactions on the OTC and account for billions of dollars in trades each week. These securities are traded by government securities dealers who are often associated with a

TABLE 2–9

Over-the-Counter Markets
Quotations From the Nasdaq System
4:00 p.m. Eastern Time Prices
Friday, August 3, 1984

Friday's Volume
All Issues, 122,230,800 Shares

SINCE JANUARY 1

	1984	1983	1982
Total sales	8,838,208,441	9,687,409,358	4,023,347,879

MARKET DIARY

	Fri	Thur	Wed	Tues	Mon
Issues traded	4,157	4,155	4,152	4,154	4,153
Advances	1,665	1,401	1,139	728	615
Declines	300	350	441	689	727
Unchanged	2,192	2,404	2,572	2,737	2,811
xNew highs	138	84	61	33	24
xNew lows	39	64	71	154	132

x-Based on 4 p.m. Eastern time bid quote.

ACTIVE STOCKS

	Dollar Volume	Close	Chg.
Apple Computer	71,386,000	27⅜	+ 3¼
Intel Cp	43,973,000	35¼	+ 2¼
MCI Commun	30,234,000	7¾	+ ¼
Digital Switch	27,255,000	27⅜	+ ⅛
American Intl Grp	24,127,000	62½	+ 2½
Tandem Computers	21,688,000	16⅝	+ 1⅜
Intergraph	20,878,000	53¼	+ 3¾
Tandon Cp	19,621,000	9⅝	+ ⅝
Apollo Computer	18,747,000	27½	+ 3
Convergent Tech	17,182,000	14⅛	+ ¼

division of a large financial institution, such as a New York, Chicago, or West Coast money market bank or a large brokerage house like Merrill Lynch. These dealers make markets in government securities, such as Treasury bills, Treasury bonds, or federal agency securities like Federal National Mortgage Association issues.

Municipal bonds of state and local governments are traded by specialized municipal bond dealers who, in most cases, work for large commercial banks. Commercial paper, representing unsecured, short-term corporate debt, is traded directly by finance companies, but a large portion of commercial paper sold by industrial companies is handled by OTC dealers specializing in this market. Every security has its own set of dealers and its own distribution system. On markets where large dollar trades occur, the spread between bid and ask could be as little as $1/16$ or $1/32$ of $1 per $1,000 of securities.

The Third and Fourth Markets—Part of Over-the-Counter Trading

Prior to the mid-1970s, commissions on the NYSE were fixed. This meant that the same commission schedule applied to all transactions of a given size, and one broker could not undercut the other on the New York Stock Exchange. Several OTC dealers, most notably Weeden & Co., decided to make a market in about 200 of the most actively traded NYSE issues and to do this at a much smaller cost than the NYSE commission structure would allow. This trading in NYSE-listed securities in over-the-counter markets became known as the third market.

The third market diminished in importance for awhile as the NYSE became more price competitive. However, in the mid-80s this market made a comeback as OTC dealers accounted for 2.5 percent of the dollar volume in listed stocks for 1983. One advantage of the OTC market is that more than one specialist trades a security and there is greater flexibility in trading. During July of 1984, ITT Corporation reported a significant dividend cut and lower earnings after the NYSE was closed, but Jefferies Corporation, an over-the-counter trading firm, traded over 3 million shares by the time the NYSE opened the next morning. Another example occurred when the Justice department announced the breakup of AT&T on a Friday. MCI, a competitor in communications, traded OTC while AT&T traded on the NYSE. AT&T trading was halted until Monday because the specialist was unable to stabilize the market, whereas the 29 market makers in MCI stock transacted over $75 million dollars of securities before AT&T opened on Monday morning. It is the multimarket maker system that many people think makes the OTC market more competitive. At the time of this writing, much discussion is being held at the New York Stock Exchange about expanding trading hours, revising rules, and generally competing more effectively with the third market and the OTC.

The fourth market is that market in which institutions trade between themselves, bypassing the middleman broker altogether (replacing him with a computer). Much of the trading in this market is done through Instinet, Institutional Networks Inc. Instinet provides a low-cost automated stock trading system, with transactions available on over 3,500 securities, both listed and over-the-counter. The system allows banks, insurance companies, mutual and pension funds, etc. to enter an order over a computer terminal for up to 1,000 shares. The computer searches a nationwide trading network until it finds the trader with the best price, then the computer holds the order 30 seconds so that another trader may offer a better price. While Instinet is only a small trading system, Merrill Lynch bought 8 percent of the company and has plans to tie the trading system into the quote-terminal desktop computer that it is developing with IBM.

THE TRANSFORMATION AND FUTURE OF THE CAPITAL MARKETS

Financial institutions, such as banks, pension funds, insurance companies, and investment companies (mutual funds), have always invested and traded in securities. However, the growth of these institutions and their participation in the capital markets has increased dramatically in recent years. Part of the increased share activity can be found in the accelerated growth of pension plans during this period. Also, the rapid rise in stock prices during the post–World War II period attracted a lot of individual investors into mutual funds.

Table 2–10 on institutional activity shows that significant changes have taken place over the last two decades as institutional trading has accounted for a relatively larger percentage of total trading on the New York Stock Exchange. A block trade is a transaction of 10,000 shares or more and is almost always carried out by institutions rather than individuals. In 1965 block trades accounted for only 3.1 percent of the reported volume on the NYSE but by 1983 block trades increased to over 45 percent, an amount more than 14 times greater than that of two decades ago. This increased institutional activity is also evident by an examination of the second column of Table 2–10 which shows that between 1965 and 1983 the average number of block trades per day increased from 9 to 1,436.

TABLE 2–10   Institutional Activity on the New York Stock Exchange

Year	*(1)* *Block trades as a percent of reported NYSE volume*	*(2)* *Average Number of block transactions per day*	*(3)* *Average Number of shares per trade*
1965	3.1	9	224
1967	6.7	27	257
1969	14.1	61	356
1971	17.8	106	428
1973	17.8	116	449
1975	16.6	136	495
1977	22.4	215	641
1979	26.5	385	787
1981	31.8	575	1,013
1982	41.0	1,007	1,305
1983	45.6	1,436	1,434

Source: *New York Stock Exchange Fact Book* (New York: New York Stock Exchange, 1984).

Proof of the decreased importance of small investors and the increased importance of the institutional trader is seen in the average number of shares per trade, which soared more than 540 percent—from 224 shares in 1965 to 1,434 shares by 1983. These statistics do not necessarily mean that individual investors are not getting a "piece of the action" in the stock market, but that many are investing indirectly in stocks through mutual funds, IRAs, and private pension plans at work.

In the early 1960s and before, the NYSE had been a market primarily for the individual investor. As this shift toward the institutions occurred, the market structure also changed. Because of fixed commissions on the NYSE, the third market and fourth market developed. The increased activity in these markets, and federal legislation, eventually forced the NYSE to eliminate its fixed commissions. When fixed commissions were replaced by negotiated rates, many smaller, research-oriented investment firms were unable to compete with the larger, retail brokerage houses. These firms eventually merged with other firms, went out of business, moved into portfolio management, or changed their emphasis toward a small market niche.

Competition in Financial Services

After negotiated commissions were in place, brokerage houses started charging individuals for research reports that previously had been distributed free of charge. This forced the individual to either buy research or simply take his or her account executive's advice. Under these conditions the individual investor started looking for services on a competitive fee basis and many ended up using brokers that only charged for making trades but gave no research advice. Because these brokers charged lower prices than the large retail brokerage firms, they became known as "discount brokers." This segment of the market is growing rapidly as many banks and savings and loans are now indirectly offering discount brokerage service to their customers. For example, many banks have simply linked up with the large discount brokers and are providing this investment service through trading desks located in their own buildings. This is an attempt to retain bank clients and their funds.

As previously mentioned, the rise of financial service companies has become commonplace. Starting in 1981, financial service firms purchased brokerage houses in order to diversify their consumer base. Prudential Insurance bought Bache Halsey Stuart Shields; Sears acquired Dean Witter; American Express bought Shearson and, later, Lehman Brothers; and Equitable Life purchased Donaldson, Lufkin and Jenrette. Most of these firms were adding brokerage houses to other financially-oriented companies. Sears, with its Allstate Insurance, Coldwell Banker real estate brokers, Sears Savings Bank, and Dean Witter brokerage services, now has financial service centers in many of its retail stores and is trying to take advantage of its relationship with 25 million Sears credit-card holders.

Shearson Lehman/American Express is a better example of a financial service company. Known world-wide for its card and travelers checks, it bought Fireman's Fund Insurance in 1968, a large casualty insurance company. In 1981 it acquired Shearson, the second largest retail brokerage firm; in 1983 it bought IDS, a Minneapolis-based life insurance company and one of the biggest mutual fund management companies; and in 1984 it purchased

Lehman Bros. Kuhn Loeb Inc., a prestigious investment banking house specializing in bonds. American Express International Banking Corporation bought the Swiss-based Trade Development Bank in 1984 and is now trying to combine its international banking firms. Shearson Lehman/American Express is currently attempting to integrate its operations to take advantage of the many services it offers. Shearson, perhaps more than any other company except Sears, has a huge client base that includes almost 18 million American Express cards. By crossing client lists from Shearson, IDS, and Fireman's Fund, the company hopes to develop a faithful group of customers taking advantage of all its many services, not to mention the new products it hopes to develop. The market has not seen the last of the changes brought about by deregulation and increased competition, but many observers feel that more firms like Shearson Lehman/American Express and Sears will be around by the end of the 1980s.

The National Market System

A national market system was mandated by Congress in the Securities Amendments Act of 1975. This is envisioned as a coordinated national system of security trading with no barriers between the various exchanges or the OTC market. There is sometimes confusion between the concept of a national market system and the National Market System listing segment of the OTC market. It is the former system that is the subject of the present discussion: The latter has already been discussed.

While there has been some delay in the implementation of a national market system due to industry foot-dragging and political changes in Washington, it is still a goal for the future. The implementation of the system is strongly supported by the SEC. No one knows exactly what form this national market might take, but there are several things that will be required. Some are easily achieved, while others are not. The first is already in place, and that is the composite tape that reflects trades on all exchanges for listed NYSE companies. There will also have to be competition between specialists and market makers. This is already occurring between the regional exchanges and the NYSE in dually listed securities. The prices seem to be more stable and the spreads between the bid and ask prices are closer for securities with competing market makers. A third occurrence is that the NYSE will most likely have to abolish Rule 390, which prohibits members of the NYSE from trading off the exchange in NYSE-listed securities.

Possibly the biggest dilemma in creating a national market system is fully developing a computerized system to execute limit orders. Currently, NYSE specialists execute most limit orders, which specify that a security must be bought or sold at a limited price or better. The national market system will need a computerized system to handle limit orders from all markets. Progress along these lines was being required by the SEC, and by the mid-1980s the NYSE had created several computer systems to aid in trading. The designated order turnaround system (Super DOT) allows members to transmit orders of up to 599 shares directly to the correct trading post on the floor of the exchange. After the transaction, the execution report is returned back to the order origination point, and the NYSE states that 95 percent of the market orders are confirmed in two minutes. This electronic system transmits market and limit orders. In 1984 the AMEX announced that it had installed Autoper, an electronic order execution system that processes specialists' trades in a few seconds. This system uses a touch-screen that virtually eliminates clerical errors and allows market price trades of 300 shares or limit orders of up to 500 shares.

The national market system mandated by Congress could take the form of NASDAQ where several competing dealers make markets electronically. Clearly the National Association of Securities Dealers hopes that the national market system will follow its trading practices rather than the auction markets of the exchanges. The exchanges have complained to the SEC that the NASD's use of the term *National Market System* for its largest OTC companies should not be allowed because it gives the appearance that the OTC is *the* national market. Certainly the NYSE will not capitulate easily to an over-the-counter system of trading. The traditional exchange auction markets have been able to absorb block trades without difficulty and serve the needs of institutional customers and individuals. The NYSE does not want to give up its dominant market position, but it had better stop to look at who is catching up to it.

It is clear that any truly national market system will rely on computers more than ever and the trend seems to show no sign of ceasing. There are even systems in existence today that allow individual investors to use their personal computers to place stock market orders.

Expanded hours for trading is another issue. Charles Schwab, the largest discount broker and a subsidiary of Bank of America, takes orders 24 hours a day and orders received after the markets close are executed the next morning. Some envision an eventual 24-hour market. As the international markets link up to provide continuous trading in commodities such as gold, silver, and currencies, it has also been thought that continuous trading could exist in the common stock of multinational companies such as IBM, Sony, Royal Dutch Petroleum, Nestlé, and others. Speculating on the future of the markets may be foolish but we know they do not look like they did 10 years ago and we expect them to keep changing.

REGULATION OF THE SECURITY MARKETS

Organized securities markets are regulated by the Securities and Exchange Commission (SEC) and by the self-regulation of the exchanges. The OTC market is controlled by the National Association of Securities Dealers. There are three major laws governing the sale and subsequent trading of securities. The Securities Act of 1933 pertains to new issues of securities, while the Securities Exchange Act of 1934 deals with trading in the securities markets. The Securities Acts amendments of 1975 are the latest legislation, and their main emphasis is on a national securities market. The primary purpose of these laws was to protect unwary investors from fraud and manipulation and to make the markets more competitive and efficient.

Securities Act of 1933

The Securities Act of 1933 was enacted after congressional investigations of the abuses present in the securities markets during the 1929 crash and again in 1931. The act's primary purpose was to provide full disclosure of all pertinent investment information whenever a corporation sold a new issue of securities. For this reason it is sometimes referred to as the "truth in securities" act. The Securities Act has several important features:

1. All offerings except government bonds and bank stocks that are to be sold in more than one state must be registered with the SEC.[3]
2. The registration statement must be filed 20 days in advance of the date of sale and include detailed corporate information. If the SEC finds the information misleading, incomplete, or inaccurate, they will delay the offering until the registration statement is corrected. The SEC in no way certifies that the security is fairly priced but only that the information seems to be factual and accurate. Under certain circumstances, the previously mentioned shelf registration is being used to modify the 20-day waiting period concept.
3. All new issues of securities must be accompanied by a *prospectus,* a detailed summary of the registration statement. Included in the prospectus is usually a list of directors and officers; their salaries, stock options, and shareholdings; financial reports certified by a CPA; a list of the underwriters; the purpose and use for the funds to be provided from the sale of securities; and any other reasonable information that investors may need to know before they can wisely invest their money. A preliminary prospectus may be distributed to potential buyers before the offering date, but it will not contain the offering price or underwriting fees. It is called a "red herring" because stamped on the front in red letters are the words "Preliminary Prospectus."
4. Officers of the company and other experts preparing the prospectus or registration statement can be sued for penalties and recovery of realized losses if any information presented was fraudulent, or factually wrong, or if relevant information was omitted.

Securities Exchange Act of 1934

This act created the Securities and Exchange Commission to enforce the securities laws. It was empowered to regulate the securities markets and those

[3] Actually the SEC did not come into existence until 1934. The Federal Trade Commission had many of these responsibilities prior to the formation of the SEC.

companies listed on the exchanges. Specifically, the major points of the 1934 Act are as follows:

1. Guidelines for inside trading were established. Insiders must hold securities for at least six months before they can sell them. This is to prevent them from taking quick advantage of information which could result in a short-term profit. All short-term profits were payable to the corporation. Insiders were generally thought to be officers, directors, major stockholders, employees, or relatives. In the late 1960s the SEC widened its interpretation to include anyone having information that was not public knowledge. This could include security analysts, loan officers, large institutional holders, and many others who had business dealings with the firm.
2. The Federal Reserve Board of Governors became responsible for setting margin requirements to determine how much credit one had available to buy securities.
3. Manipulation of securities by conspiracies between investors was prohibited.
4. The SEC was given control over the proxy procedures of corporations (a proxy is an absent stockholder vote).
5. In its regulation of companies traded on the markets, it required certain reports to be filed periodically. Corporations must file quarterly financial statements with the SEC, send annual reports to stockholders, and file 10-K Reports with the SEC annually. The 10-K Report has more financial data than the annual report and can be very useful to an investor or loan officer. Most companies will now send 10-K Reports to stockholders on request.
6. The act required all securities exchanges to register with the SEC. In this capacity, the SEC supervises and regulates many pertinent organizational aspects of exchanges, such as listing and trading mechanics.

The Securities Acts Amendments of 1975

The major focus of the Securities Acts amendments of 1975 was to direct the SEC to supervise the development of a national securities market. No exact structure was put forth, but the law did assume that any national market would make extensive use of computers and electronic communication devices. Additionally, the law prohibited fixed commissions on public transactions and also prohibited banks, insurance companies, and other financial institutions from buying stock exchange memberships to save commission costs for their own institutional transactions. This act is a worthwhile addition to the securities laws since it fosters greater competition and more efficient prices.

Other Legislation

In addition to these three major pieces of legislation, a number of other acts deal directly with investor protection. For example, The Investment Advisor Act of 1940 is set up to protect the public from unethical investment advisers.

Any adviser with over 15 public clients (excluding tax accountants and lawyers) must register with the SEC and file semiannual reports. The Investment Company Act of 1940 provides similar oversight for mutual funds and investment companies dealing with small investors. The act was amended in 1970 and currently gives the NASD authority to supervise and limit commissions and investment advisory fees on certain types of mutual funds.

Another piece of legislation dealing directly with investor protection is the Securities Investor Protection Act of 1970. The Securities Investor Protection Corporation (SIPC) was established to oversee liquidation of brokerage firms and to insure investors' accounts to a maximum value of $500,000 in case of bankruptcy of a brokerage firm. It functions much the same as the Federal Deposit Insurance Corporation (for banks) and the Federal Savings and Loan Insurance Corporation. SIPC resulted from the problems encountered on Wall Street during the period from 1967 to 1970. Share volume surged to then all-time highs, and many firms were unable to process orders fast enough. A back-office paper crunch caused Wall Street to shorten the hours the exchanges were formally open for new business but even this didn't help. Investors lost large sums, and for many months, they were unable to use or get possession of securities held in their names. Even though SIPC insures these accounts, it still does not cover market value losses suffered while waiting to get securities from a bankrupt brokerage firm.

Insider Trading

The Securities Exchange Act of 1934 established the initial restrictions on insider trading. However, over the years these restrictions have often proved to be inadequate. As previously indicated the definition of *insider* may go beyond officers, directors, and major stockholders to include anyone with special insider knowledge. Both the Congress and the Securities and Exchange Commission are attempting to grapple with the issue of making punitive measures severe enough to discourage the illegal use of nonpublic information for short-term profits.[4] Current and future legislation is likely to go beyond civil penalties to criminal prosecution. Also the penalties for improper action will expand beyond simple recovery of profits to a penalty three or more times the profits involved.

Regulators are also concerned about security analysts and financial writers who attempt to trade on the basis of their own analysis shortly before it is published. A classic case was the use of "Heard on the Street" material from *The Wall Street Journal* to achieve short-term profits. In this case, it was not so much the authors of the material, but friends of the authors who benefited. Federal regulators initiated quick and strong action to penalize the abuse.

On balance, all the legislation we have discussed has tended to increase the confidence of the investing public. In an industry where public trust is so critical, some form of supervision, whether public or private, is necessary and generally accepted.

---

[4] Insiders, of course, may make proper long-term investments in a corporation.

Chapter 3

PARTICIPATING IN THE MARKET

MEASURES OF PRICE PERFORMANCE—MARKET INDEXES

STOCK MARKET INDEXES AND AVERAGES
Dow Jones Indexes
Standard & Poor's Indexes
Value Line Average
Other Market Indexes

BUYING AND SELLING IN THE MARKET
Cash or Margin Account
Long or Short?—That Is the Question

TYPES OF ORDERS

COST OF TRADING

TAXES
Short-Term versus Long-Term Gains and Losses
Timing of Gains and Losses

There are many different kinds of investors participating in the market, from the individual to the professional, and each participant needs to know about the structure and mechanics of the market in which he or she might invest. In this chapter, we examine the use of indexes to gauge market performance, the rules and mechanics of opening and trading in an account, and basic tax considerations for the investor.

MEASURES OF PRICE PERFORMANCE— MARKET INDEXES

We first look at tracking market performance for stocks and bonds. Each market has several market indexes published by Moody's, Standard & Poor's, Dow Jones, and other financial services. These indexes allow investors to measure their portfolio's performance against an index which approximates their portfolio composition; thus different investors prefer different indexes. While a professional pension fund manager might use the Standard & Poor's 500 Stock Index, a mutual fund specializing in small, over-the-counter stocks might prefer the NASDAQ (National Association of Securities Dealers Automated Quotations) index, and a small investor might use the Value Line average as the best approximation of his or her portfolio.

STOCK MARKET INDEXES AND AVERAGES

Dow Jones Indexes

Since there are many stock market indexes, we will cover the most widely used ones. Dow Jones, the publisher of *The Wall Street Journal* and *Barron's,* publishes several indexes, of which the Dow Jones Industrial Average (DJIA) is the most popular. This average consists of 30 large industrial companies, and is considered a "blue chip" index (stocks of very high quality). Many people criticize the DJIA for being too selective and representing too few stocks. Nevertheless, the Dow Industrials do follow the general trend in the market, and these 30 common stocks comprise over 25 percent of the market value of the 1,550 firms listed on the New York Stock Exchange. Dow Jones also publishes an index of 20 transportation stocks, 15 utility stocks, and a 65-stock composite average. The companies that make up these Dow Jones averages are shown in Table 3–1, while the listing of indexes that appear in *The Wall Street Journal* are shown in Table 3–2.

The Dow Jones Industrial Average used to be a simple average of 30 stocks, but when a company splits its stock price, the average had to be adjusted in some manner. For the Dow Jones Industrials, the divisor in the formula has been adjusted downward from the original 30 to slightly more than 1. Each time a company splits its shares of stock (or pays a stock dividend), the divisor is reduced to maintain the average at the same level prior to the stock split. If this were not done, the lower-priced stock after the split

TABLE 3–1   Companies in the Dow Jones Averages

```
COMPONENTS
DOW JONES 65 STOCKS AVERAGES
  The Dow Jones Stock Averages are compiled daily by
using the New York Stock Exchange only closing prices and
adjusting by the then current appropriate average divisor. The
divisors appear in the second column of the Market Labora-
tory page under the data for the yearly Dow Jones Stock
Average. A list of the stocks on which these averages are
based follows:
                    INDUSTRIALS
Allied Corp.      General Electric     Owens-Illinois
Aluminum Co.      General Foods        Procter & Gamb
Amer Brands       General Motors       Sears Roebuck
Amer Can          Goodyear             Std Oil of Calif
Amer Express      Inco                 Texaco
AT&T              IBM                  Union Carbide
Bethlehem Steel   Inter Harvester      United Technologies
Du Pont           Inter Paper          US Steel
Eastman Kodak     Merck                Westinghouse El
Exxon             Minnesota M&M        Woolworth

                  TRANSPORTATION
AMR Corp.         Eastern Air Lines    Santa Fe So Pac
Burlington North  Federal Express      Transway Int'l
CSX Corp          Norfolk Southern     TWA
Canadian Pacific  Northwest Air        UAL Inc
Carolina Freight  Overnite Trans       Union Pac Corp
Consolid Freight  Pan Am World Air     USAir Group
Delta Air Lines   Rio Grande Indus

                    UTILITIES
Am Elec Power     Consol Nat Gas       Panhandle E Cp
Cleveland E Ill   Detroit Edison       Peoples Energy
Colum-Gas Sys     Houston Indust       Phila Elec
Comwlth Edison    Niag Mohawk P        Pub Serv E&G
Consol Edison     Pacific Gas & El     Sou Cal Edison
```

would lower the average, giving the appearance that investors are worse off. Figure 3–1 depicts the daily graph that appears in *The Wall Street Journal* covering the Dow Jones Averages.

The Dow Jones Industrial Average is a *price-weighted average,* which means that each stock in the average is weighted by its price. To simplify the meaning of price-weighted: if you had three stocks in a price-weighted *index* that had values of 10, 40, and 100, you would add the prices and divide by three.[1] In this case you would get an average of 50 (150 divided by 3). A price-weighted index is similar to what you normally use in computing averages. Price-weighted *averages* tend to give a higher weighting bias to high-price stocks than to low-price stocks. For example, in the above analysis, if the $100 stock goes up by 10 percent, with all else the same, the average will go up over three points from 50 to 53.3. However, if the $10 stock goes up by 10 percent, with all else the same, the average will only go from 50 to 50.3. It is not necessary that you go back and do these computations, only that you understand the basic principle.

----

[1] This assumes there have been no prior stock splits affecting the denominator.

TABLE 3–2   Indexes and Averages Found in *The Wall Street Journal*

STOCK MARKET DATA BANK   January 3, 1985

Major Indexes

HIGH	LOW	(12 MOS)	CLOSE	NET CH	% CH	12 MO CH	%	FROM 12/31	%
DOW JONES AVERAGES									
1286.64	1086.57	30 Industrials	1189.82	− 9.95	− 0.76	− 92.42	− 7.21	−21.75	− 1.80
612.63	444.03	20 Transportations	555.58	+ 1.88	+ 0.34	− 53.89	− 8.84	− 2.55	− 0.46
149.93	122.25	15 Utilities	147.26	− 0.51	− 0.35	+ 13.06	+ 9.73	− 2.26	− 1.51
514.02	421.36	65 Composite	483.02	− 1.94	− 0.40	− 29.10	− 5.68	− 6.84	− 1.40
NEW YORK STOCK EXCHANGE									
98.12	85.13	Composite	95.05	− 0.38	− 0.40	− 2.29	− 2.35	− 1.33	− 1.38
114.40	99.73	Industrials	108.87	− 0.52	− 0.48	− 4.75	− 4.18	− 1.71	− 1.55
51.65	42.94	Utilities	51.17	− 0.04	− 0.08	+ 3.39	+ 7.10	− 0.40	− 0.78
100.46	73.11	Transportation	89.43	− 0.15	− 0.17	− 10.11	− 10.16	− 1.18	− 1.30
97.87	76.74	Finance	96.57	− 0.37	− 0.38	− 0.82	− 0.84	− 1.06	− 1.09
STANDARD & POOR'S AVERAGES									
169.28	147.82	500 Index	164.57	− 0.80	− 0.48	− 4.24	− 2.51	− 2.67	− 1.60
191.48	168.88	400 Industrials	183.14	− 0.96	− 0.52	− 7.01	− 3.69	− 3.22	− 1.73
161.64	117.21	20 Transportations	142.01	− 0.14	− 0.10	− 18.63	− 11.60	− 1.90	− 1.32
76.47	62.90	40 Utilities	75.21	− 0.25	− 0.33	+ 6.14	+ 8.89	− 0.68	− 0.90
18.88	14.09	40 Financials	18.56	− 0.09	− 0.48	− 0.22	− 1.17	− 0.24	− 1.28
NASDAQ									
287.90	225.30	OTC Composite	246.41	+ 0.50	+ 0.20	− 38.04	− 13.37	− 0.94	− 0.38
336.16	250.18	Industrials	259.40	+ 0.55	+ 0.21	− 72.01	− 21.73	− 1.33	− 0.51
283.91	226.87	Insurance	281.76	− 0.51	− 0.18	+ 19.67	+ 7.51	− 1.35	− 0.48
230.77	192.51	Banks	230.77	+ 0.54	+ 0.24	+ 25.94	+ 12.66	+ 1.00	+ 0.44
NASDAQ NATIONAL MARKET									
103.95	93.94	Composite	104.25	+ 0.30	+ 0.29			− 0.47	− 0.45
109.51	92.55	Industrials	97.47	+ 0.28	+ 0.29			− 0.56	− 0.57
OTHERS									
227.73	187.16	Amex	203.19	− 0.82	− 0.40	− 23.68	− 10.4	− 1.07	− 0.52
200.32	162.46	Value-Line	176.97	− 0.17	− 0.10	− 22.36	− 11.2	− 1.01	− 0.57
1766.132	1508.829	Wilshire 5000	1680.128	− 5.604	− 0.33	− 81.176	− 4.61	−21.87	− 1.29

Source: Reprinted by permission of *The Wall Street Journal,* © Dow Jones & Company, Inc. (January 4, 1985). All rights reserved.

In early-1985, Eastman Kodak was trading at 55, while International Harvester was trading at 6¾. Clearly an up or down 10 percent price movement in Eastman Kodak would have a greater impact on the Dow Jones Industrial Average than a 10 percent movement in International Harvester. Thus, we see the bias toward high-price stocks in the Dow Jones Industrial Average.

Barron's, which is also a publication of Dow Jones, publishes Barron's 50 Stock Average and an index of low-priced securities which meets the needs of many small investors. *Barron's* also publishes a weekly average called Barron's Group Stock Averages, covering 32 industry groups. These averages are especially useful to the analyst following the performance of a specific industry relative to the general market, and they are shown in Table 3–3.

FIGURE 3–1   Dow Jones Averages

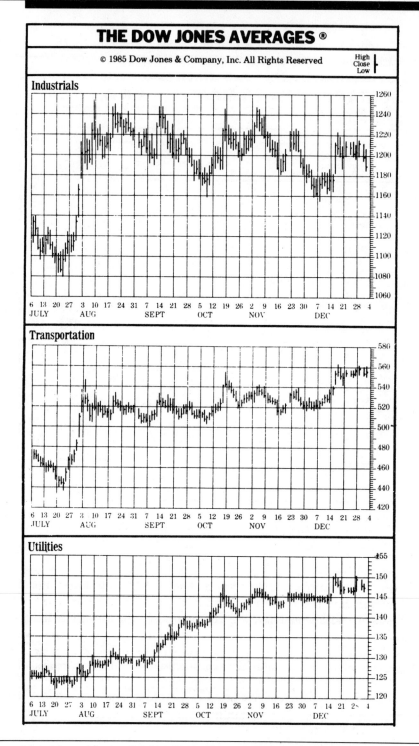

TABLE 3–3   Barron's Group Stock Averages

BARRON'S GROUP STOCK AVERAGES

1984 High-a	Low-a			May 31	May 24	% change
816.34	631.98	Aircraft manufacturing		667.56	657.01	+ 1.61
247.91	181.45	Air transport		191.85	186.66	+ 2.78
128.26	98.61	Automobiles		99.63	99.54	+ .09
324.19	244.16	Automobile equipment	L	243.79	244.16	− .15
342.01	258.04	Banks	L	245.56	258.04	− 4.84
255.92	224.92	Bldg material, equipment		230.13	231.51	− .60
475.85	393.25	Chemicals		414.85	412.08	+ .67
49.18	38.75	Closed-end invest	L	38.48	39.12	− 1.63
2,438.91	2,214.12	Drugs	L	2,210.00	2,234.38	− .09
929.75	756.74	Electrical equipment	L	743.26	756.74	− 1.
542.21	389.62	Farm equipment		394.00	389.62	+ 1.12
584.61	520.41	Foods and beverages		575.11	576.48	− .24
933.24	723.77	Gold mining		816.67	794.62	+ 2.77
475.31	404.73	Grocery chains	L	395.45	404.73	− 2.29
410.12	310.47	Installment financing	L	303.49	318.43	− 4.69
1,308.21	1,102.36	Insurance	L	1,071.20	1,102.36	− 2.83
1,351.50	1,160.51	Liquor		1,173.87	1,188.26	− 1.21
262.19	202.13	Machine tools		204.70	205.80	− .54
194.75	150.49	Machinery (heavy)	L	144.89	150.49	− 3.72
896.06	726.90	Motion pictures		813.96	832.68	− 2.25
238.37	194.73	Non-ferrous metals	L	180.56	194.73	− 7.28
4,391.61	3,766.42	Office equipment		3,802.15	3,766.42	+ .95
760.76	621.26	Oil		716.02	724.47	− 1.17
594.39	442.21	Packing	L	435.63	452.88	− 3.81
428.72	352.93	Paper	L	347.19	352.93	− 1.63
341.04	216.42	Railroad equipment		217.59	225.11	− 3.34
1,344.96	1,004.56	Retail merchandise		1,062.23	1,084.37	− 2.04
442.22	337.69	Rubber	L	333.94	337.69	− 1.11
215.75	158.93	Steel and iron	L	157.82	158.93	− .70
389.47	270.77	Television	L	261.06	270.77	− 3.59
351.64	281.21	Textiles	L	280.96	281.36	− .14
407.65	351.77	Tobacco	L	349.78	351.77	− .56
1,286.64	1,103.43	Dow-Jones Industrials		1,104.85	1,103.43	+ .13
612.63	461.32	Dow-Jones Transportation		467.08	461.32	+ 1.25
134.83	123.55	Dow-Jones Utilities	L	122.69	123.55	− .70
514.02	429.08	Dow-Jones Composite		430.32	429.08	+ 1.29

a-1984 highs and lows through preceding week ended Thursday. In this table daily closings for trading week ended last Friday used in the range for the Dow Jones Averages. L-New low.

Change in Components: Chemicals: Allied Corp; 3-for-2 split, new multiplier is 12. Electrical Equipment: Westinghouse; 2-for-1 split, new multiplier is 32. Paper: Kimberly Clark; 2-for-1 split, new multiplier is 16.

Standard & Poor's Indexes

Standard & Poor's Corporation publishes several indexes, but two of the most important are the S&P 400 Industrials and the S&P 500 Stock Index. These indexes are followed by professional investors and others as measures of broad stock market activity. The S&P 400 consists of industrial common stocks and make up over 50 percent of the market value of NYSE-listed companies. The S&P 500 Stock Index includes the 400 industrials plus 20 transportation firms, 40 utilities, and 40 financial firms. The stocks in the Standard & Poor's 500 Stock Index are equivalent to 75 percent of the total value of the 1,550 firms listed on the New York Stock Exchange.[2]

These indexes are true indexes in that they are linked to some base value, in this case stock prices in the period from 1941 to 1943. The base period price in 1941 to 1943 was 10, so the S&P 500 Stock Index of 164.57 in early 1985 indicates that the index has increased by 1,545.7 percent over this period.

These indexes are *value-weighted,* which means that each company is weighted in the index by its own total market value as a percentage of the total market value for all firms. For example, in a value-weighted index comprising the following three firms, the weighting would be:

Stock	Shares	Price	Total market value	Weighting
A	150	$10	$ 1,500	12.0%
B	200	20	4,000	32.0
C	500	14	7,000	56.0
			$12,500	100.0%

In each case the weighting is determined by dividing the total market value of the stock by the total market value for all firms. In the case of stock A, that would be $1,500 divided by $12,500, or 12 percent. The same procedure is followed for stocks B and C.

Even though stock C has only the second highest price, it makes up 56 percent of the average because of its high total market value based on 500 shares outstanding. This same basic effect carries through in the Standard & Poor's Indexes, with large companies such as IBM, AT&T, and Exxon having a greater impact on the index than do small companies. For example, IBM makes up approximately 3.9 percent of the 500 company index, while Jonathan Logan Inc. makes up .01 percent. Value-weighted indexes do not require special adjustments for stock splits because the increase in the number of shares automatically compensates for the decline in the stock value caused by the split.

The Standard & Poor's 400 and 500 Stock Indexes provide a good measure of the direction of the market for large firms. Often the S&P 400 and S&P

---

[2] Actually there are also some large, over-the-counter firms in the S&P Indexes, though the indexes are predominantly made up of New York Stock Exchange firms.

500 are used as a proxy for market return when calculating the risk measures (betas) of individual stocks and portfolios.

Standard & Poor's also compiles value-weighted indexes for 90 different industries, and they are reported in the *Outlook,* a weekly Standard & Poor's publication.

Value Line Average

The Value Line Average represents 1,700 companies from the New York and American Stock Exchanges and the over-the-counter market. Some individual investors use the Value Line Average because it more closely corresponds to the variety of stocks the small investor may have in his or her portfolio.

Unlike the previously discussed price-weighted average (the Dow Jones Industrial Average) and value-weighted indexes (S&P 400 and 500), the Value Line Average is *equal-weighted.* This means that each of the 1,700 stocks, regardless of market price or total market value, is weighted equally. It is as if there were $100 to be invested in each and every stock. In this case IBM or Exxon is weighted no more heavily than Wendy's International or Mattel Inc. The equal-weighting characteristic also more closely conforms to the portfolio of individual investors.

Other Market Indexes

Indexes are also computed and published by the New York Stock Exchange, American Stock Exchange, and the National Association of Securities Dealers. Each index is intended to represent the performance of stocks traded in a particular exchange or market. As was seen in Table 3–2, the NYSE publishes a composite index as well as an industrial, utility, transportation, and financial index. Each index represents the stocks of a broad group or type of company. The American Exchange Market Value Index (AMEX) is composed of all stocks trading on the American Stock Exchange.

The National Association of Securities Dealers, which is the self-governing body of the over-the-counter markets, also constructs several indexes to represent the companies in their market. They publish the NASDAQ OTC composite, industrial, insurance, and banking indexes (which are also listed in Table 3–2). The NASDAQ also publishes subindexes for stocks listed in the National Market System.

The indexes of the New York Stock Exchange, American Stock Exchange, and NASDAQ are all *value-weighted* indexes.[3]

A relatively new index is the Wilshire 5000 Equity Index. It represents the *total dollar value* of 5,000 stocks, including all New York Stock Exchange and American Stock Exchange issues and the most active over-the-counter issues. By the very fact of including total dollar value, it is *value-weighted.* In

---

[3] Up until October 1973 the American Stock Exchange Index was price-weighted.

1984 the Wilshire Index had a range of $1,508 billion to $1,766 billion. The index literally tells you of the value of virtually all important equities daily. A typical daily change might be plus or minus $10 billion.

The direction of the indexes are all closely related, but they do not necessarily move together all the time. If a pension fund manager is trying to "outperform the market," then the choice of index may be crucial as to whether the fund manager maintains his or her accounts. The important thing for you, as well as a professional, when measuring success or failure of performance is to use an index that represents the risk characteristics of the portfolio being compared to the index. If you only want a general idea as to whether the market is going up or down over time, the choice of the average or index is not that critical since they all move fairly closely together.

Bond market averages.   Performance in the bond market is not widely followed by way of an index or average but usually is gauged by interest rate movements. Since rising interest rates mean falling bond prices and falling rates signal rising prices, investors can usually judge the bond market performance by yield curve changes or interest rate graphs. *Barron's* does publish an

TABLE 3–4   Lipper Mutual Fund Investment Performance Averages, Thursday, May 31, 1984

LIPPER MUTUAL FUND INVESTMENT PERFORMANCE AVERAGES
Thursday, May 31, 1984

LIPPER FUND INDICES

	Close	Percentage Change Year to Date	Weekly
Growth Funds	191.49	– 13.01	– 0.20
Growth Income	301.57	– 8.55	– 0.32
Balanced Funds	245.54	– 9.14	– 0.86

OTHER MARKET INDICATORS

	Close	Percentage Change Year to Date	Weekly
D. J. Industrial	1,104.84	– 12.22	+ 0.13
S. & P. 500	150.55	– 8.72	– 0.45
S. & P. 400	171.14	– 8.11	– 0.31
N.Y.S.E. Comp.	86.71	– 8.90	– 0.28
Amex Index	198.63	– 10.93	+ 0.34

AVERAGE FUND PERFORMANCES

No.	Type of Fund	Percentage Change Year to Date	Weekly
88	Capital Appreciation	– 14.28	– 0.13
173	Growth Funds	– 12.34	– 0.17
23	Small Co. Growth Fds	– 14.11	– 0.70
91	Growth & Income	– 7.84	– 0.26
33	Equity Income	– 5.31	– 0.68
408	Average Performance	– 11.28	– 0.25
24	Balanced Funds	– 6.71	– 0.42
25	Income Funds	– 4.69	– 0.83
8	Natural Resources	– 2.47	– 0.84
16	Specialty Funds	– 9.50	– 0.95
17	Global Funds	– 7.80	– 1.12
10	International	– 6.55	– 2.41
11	Gold Oriented	+ 5.75	+ 4.17
5	Option Growth	– 10.88	– 0.06
10	Option Income	– 4.63	– 0.18
142	Fixed Income	– 3.20	– 0.69
676	Average Performance	– 8.55	– 0.37
676	Median Performance	– 7.33	– 0.43

Data supplied by Lipper Analytical Securities Corp. Year to date and weekly percentage changes on Thursday for mutual funds include reinvestment of income dividends and capital gains distributions, other market indicators do not. Only funds in existence for the entire period covered are included. Total number of funds, by objective, may include funds with net asset values unavailable at compilation time.
Source: Lipper Analytical Securities Corp.

index of 20 bonds (10 utility bonds and 10 industrial bonds), and other bond indexes are published by Salomon Brothers, and Lehman Brothers Kuhn Loeb (a part of Shearson Lehman/American Express).

Mutual fund averages. Lipper Analytical Services publishes the Lipper Mutual and Investment Performance Averages shown in Table 3–4, taken from *Barron's.* Lipper publishes three basic fund indexes for growth funds, growth-with-income funds, and balanced funds. Additionally, the average performances on a year-to-date and weekly basis are provided for many other categories of funds in the right-hand portion of the table.

BUYING AND SELLING IN THE MARKET

Once you are generally familiar with the market and perhaps decide to invest directly in common stocks or other assets, you will need to set up an account with a retail brokerage house. Some of the largest and better-known retail brokers are Merrill Lynch; Shearson Lehman/American Express; Bache; and E. F. Hutton, but there are many other good houses, both regional and national. When you set up your account, the account executive (often called stockbroker) will ask you to fill out a card listing your investment objectives, such as: conservative, preservation of capital, income oriented, growth plus income, or growth. The account executive will also ask for your social security number for tax reporting, the level of your income, net worth, employer, and other basic information. Basically he or she needs to know the client's desire and ability to take risk in order to give good advice and proper management of the investor's assets.

Cash or Margin Account

The account executive will need to know if you want a cash account or margin account. Either account allows you five business days to pay for any purchase. A cash account requires full payment, while a margin account allows the investor to borrow a percentage of the purchase price from the brokerage firm. The percentage of the total cost the investor must pay is called the margin and is set by the Federal Reserve Board. During the great crash in the 1920s, margin on stock was only 10 percent, but it was as high as 80 percent in 1968. It has been at 50 percent since January 1974. The margin percentage is used to control speculation. When the Board of Governors of the Federal Reserve System thinks that the markets are being pushed too high by speculative fervor, they raise the margin requirement, which means that more cash must be put up.

Margin accounts are used mostly by traders and speculators or by investors who think their long-run return will be greater than the cost of borrowing. Most brokerage houses require a $2,000 minimum in an account before loaning out money, although many brokerage houses have higher limits. Here is how a margin account works. Assume you purchased 100 shares of GE (General Electric) at $60 per share on margin and that margin is 50 percent.

Purchase: 100 shares of GE at $60 per share	$6,000
Borrow: Cost (1 − margin percentage)	−3,000
Equity contributed, cash or securities	$3,000

You can borrow $3,000 or the total cost times (1 − margin percentage). The percentage cost of borrowing is generally 1 to 2 percent above the prime rate, depending upon the size of the account. Rather than putting up $3,000 in cash, a customer could put $3,000 of other approved financial assets into the account to satisfy the margin. Not all stocks may be used for margin purchases. The Securities and Exchange Commission publishes a list of approved securities which may be borrowed against.

One of the reasons people buy on margin is to leverage their returns. Assume that GE rises to $80 per share. The account would now have $8,000 in stock and an increase in equity from $3,000 to $5,000.

100 shares of GE at $80	$8,000
Loan	−3,000
Equity	$5,000

This $2,000 increase in equity creates a 67 percent return on the initial $3,000 of equity. The 67 percent return was accomplished on the basis of only a 33 percent increase in the price of the stock ($60 to $80). With the increased equity in the account, the customer could now purchase additional securities on margin.

Margin is a two-edged sword however, and what works out to your advantage in up markets works to your disadvantage in down markets. If GE had gone to $40, your equity would decrease to $1,000.

100 shares of GM at $40	$4,000
Borrowed	−3,000
Equity	$1,000

There are minimum requirements for equity in a margin account called *minimum maintenance standards* (usually 25 percent). Your equity would now be at minimum maintenance standards where the equity of $1,000 equals 25 percent of the current market value of $4,000. A fall below $1,000 would bring a margin call for more cash or equity. Many brokerage firms have maintenance requirements above 25 percent, and when margin calls are made, the equity often needs to be increased to 35 percent or more of the portfolio value. Normally you must maintain a $2,000 minimum in your account, so you would have been called for more equity when the stock was at $50 even though the minimum maintenance requirement had not yet been reached.

An important feature of a margin account is that securities may not be delivered to the customer. In this case, the GE stock would be kept registered in the street name of your retail brokerage house (e.g., Shearson Lehman/

American Express), and your account would show a claim on 100 shares which are held as collateral for the loan. It is much like an automobile loan; you don't hold title to the car until you have made the last payment. In the use of margin, however, there is no due date on the loan. The use of margin increases risk and is not recommended for anyone who cannot afford large losses or who has no substantial experience in the market.

Long or Short?—That Is the Question

Once you have opened the account of your choice, you are ready to buy or sell. When investors establish a position in a security, they are said to be "long" if they purchase the security for their account. It is assumed that the reason they purchased the security was to profit on an increase in price over time and/or to receive dividend income. An investor who is long may take delivery of the securities (keep them in physical possession) if he or she has a cash account. An investor with a cash account may also choose to keep them on deposit in his/her brokerage account to facilitate bookkeeping, dividends, safe-keeping, and ease of sale. A margin account user has no choice but to keep them with the broker in "street name."

Sometimes investors anticipate that the price of a security may drop in value. If they are long in the stock, some may sell out their position. Those who have no position at all may wish to take a "short" position in order to profit from the expected decline. When you short a security, you are borrowing the security from your broker and selling it with the obligation to replace the security at a future time. How you can sell something you don't own is an obvious question. Your broker will simply loan you the security from the brokerage house inventory. If your brokerage house doesn't have an inventory of the particular stock you want to short, the firm will borrow the stock from another broker.

Once you go short, you begin hoping and praying that the price of the security will go down so that you can buy it back and replace the security that you sold at a lower price. In a perverse way, bad news starts to become good news. When you read the morning paper, you look for signs of unemployment, high inflation, and high interest rates in hopes of a stock market decline.

A short sale can only be made on a trade where the price of the stock advances (an uptick), or if there is no change in price, the prior trade must have been positive. These rules are intended to stop a snowballing decline in stock values caused by short sellers.

There is a margin requirement associated with short selling, and it is currently equal to 50 percent of the securities sold short. Thus if you were to sell 100 shares of Wrigley short at $70 per share, you would be required to put up $3,500 in margin (50 percent of $7,000). In a short sale, the margin is considered to be good-faith money and obviously is not a down payment toward purchase. The margin protects the brokerage house in case you start losing money on your account.

The way that you would lose money on a short sales position is if the stock that you sold short starts going up. Assume that Wrigley goes from $70 to $80. Since you initially sold 100 shares short at $70 per share, you have suffered a $1,000 paper loss. Your initial margin or equity position has been reduced from $3,500 to $2,500.

Initial margin (equity)	$3,500
Loss	−1,000
Current margin (equity)	$2,500

We previously specified that there is a minimum 25 percent margin maintenance requirement in buying stock. There is a similar type requirement in selling short. The equity position must equal at least 30 percent of the *current* value of the stock that has been sold short. In the present example, the equity position is equal to $2,500, and the current market value of Wrigley is $8,000 ($80 × 100). Your margin maintenance percentage is 31.25 percent ($2,500 ÷ $8,000) or slightly above the minimum requirement. However, if the stock goes up another point or two and your losses increase, you will be asked to put up more margin to increase your equity position.

Of course, if the value of Wrigley stock goes down from its initial base of $70, you would be making profits off the bad news. A 20-point drop in Wrigley would mean a $2,000 profit on your 100 shares. Most market observers agree that it requires a "special breed of cat" to be an effective short seller. You often need nerves of steel and a contrariant outlook that can not be easily shaken by good news.

Aside from risk takers, some investors sell short to establish beneficial tax positions. For example, if you had bought Digital Equipment at $60 and five months later it was $100, you would have a $40 per share profit on paper. If you want to preserve the profit but wait until next year to pay the tax, you can "sell short against the box." This means you can short shares against those you already hold. Since you own the stock and also have a short position, you can neither gain nor lose by price movements in the stock. In the following tax year, you can deliver the shares you hold to cover your short position. At that point, you will incur the tax obligations associated with the transactions. The total net profit will still be $40.

TYPES OF ORDERS

When an investor places an order to establish a position, he or she has many different kinds of orders from which to choose. When the order is placed with the account executive on a NYSE-listed stock, it is teletyped to the exchange where it is executed by the company's floor broker in an auction market. Each stock is traded at a specific trading post on the floor of the exchange, so the floor broker knows exactly where to go to find other brokers buying and selling the same company's shares.

Most orders placed will be straightforward market orders to buy or sell. The market order will be carried by the floor broker to the correct trading post and will usually trade close to the last price or within ¼ of a point. For example, if you wanted to sell 100 shares of AT&T at market, you would probably have no trouble finding a ready buyer, since AT&T may be trading 300,000 to 500,000 shares per day. On the other hand, if you wanted to sell 100 shares of Bemis, there might be as little as only 1,000 shares traded in a day, and no other broker would be waiting at the Bemis post to make a transaction with the floor broker. If the broker finds no one else wishing to buy the shares he is selling, he will transact the sale with the specialist who is always at the post ready to buy and sell 100-share "round lots." If the broker wants to sell, the specialist will either buy the shares for his own account at ⅛ to ¼ less than the last trade or will buy out of his book in which special orders are kept.

There are two basic special orders, the "limit order" and the "stop order." A limit order limits the price at which you are willing to buy or sell and assures you that you will pay no more than the limit price on a buy or receive no less than the limit price on a sell. Assume you are trying to buy a thinly traded stock that fluctuates in value and you are afraid that with a market order you might risk paying more than you want. So, you would place a limit order to buy 100 shares of Bell Industries, as an example, at 16½ or a better price. The order will go to the floor broker who goes to the post to check the price. The broker finds Bell Industries trading at its high for the day of 16⅞, and so he leaves the limit order with the specialist who records it in his book. The entry will record the price, date, time, and brokerage firm. There may be other orders in front of yours at 16½, but once these are cleared and assuming the stock stays in this range, your order will be executed at 16½ or less. Limit orders are used by investors to buy or sell thinly traded stocks or to buy securities at prices thought to be at the low end of a price range and to sell securities at the high end of the price range. Investors who calculate fundamental values have a basic idea of what they think a stock is worth and will often set a limit to take advantage of what they view to be discrepancies in values.

Many traders are certain that they want their order to be executed if a certain price is reached. A limit order does not guarantee execution if orders are ahead of you on the specialist's book. In cases where you want a guaranteed "fill" of the order, a stop order is placed. A stop order is a two-part mechanism. It is placed at a specific price like a limit order, but when the price is reached, the stop turns into a market order which will be executed at close to the stop price but not necessarily at the exact price specified. Often there will be a common price that many short-term traders will view with optimism for a certain trading strategy. When the stock hits the price, it may pop up on an abundance of buy orders or decline sharply on a large volume of sell orders, and your "fill" could be several dollars away from the stop price. Assume that AXE Corporation stock has been trading between $25 and $40 per share over the last six months, reaching both these prices three times. A trader may follow several strategies. One strategy would be to buy at $25 and sell at $40 using a stop buy and a stop sell order. There may be some traders putting in a stop buy at $41 thinking that if the stock breaks through its peak trading range it will go on to new highs, and finally some may put in a stop sell at $23 to either eliminate a long position or establish a short position with the assumption that the stock has broken its support and will trend lower. When used to eliminate a long position, a stop order is often called a stop-loss order.

Limit orders and stop orders can be "day orders" that expire at the end of the day if not executed, or they can be GTC (good till cancelled) orders. GTC orders will remain on the specialist's books until taken off by the brokerage house or executed. If the order remains unfilled for several months, most brokerage houses will send reminders that the order is still pending so that the client does not get caught buying stock for which he is unable to pay. Orders have been known to stay on the specialist's books for years.

COST OF TRADING

Since May 1, 1975, commissions have been negotiated between the broker and customer, with larger orders getting smaller percentage charges. Before "May Day" commissions were fixed, and all brokers charged the same fee out of a published table for a given size order. Now there are individual variations, so check with several brokers. If commissions are of concern, you may want to do business with a "discount" broker who charges a discount of up to 70 percent from the old fixed-commission schedule.

Discount brokers sprung up as bare-bones operators providing only transactions and no research. They have found a niche with those investors who make up their own minds and do not need advice or personal service. Discount brokers do not have many regional offices located around the country (but may be represented in some of the largest cities, such as New York, Chicago, and Los Angeles). Instead, they rely on toll-free, long-distance "WATS" lines for their customers. Many discount brokers advertise in *The Wall Street Journal* and other newspapers.

Regular brokerage houses still offer more personal service and more variety of services and are often part of a financial corporation involved in underwriting and investment banking, managing mutual funds, pension funds, economic advising, government bond dealings, and more. Unfortunately, you pay extra when dealing with a full-service broker. Table 3–5 sets forth the fees for one national brokerage house.

TABLE 3–5   Example of Round-Lot Commissions

Trades	Commissions
Under → $800	2.500% + $11
801–2,500	1.875 + 16
2,500–5,000	1.395 + 28
5,000–20,000	1.255 + 35
20,000–30,000	0.910 + 104
Over 30,000	0.560 + 209

Most full-service brokers still use a formula for computing commissions, but they also negotiate rates on large transactions, and are willing to give actively trading customers discounts from the formula if their business over the year makes them a large trader in volume.

The fees in Table 3–5 are not necessarily an industry standard, and you may find variations of these fees from broker to broker. However, most firms will have a similar structure, charging a commission based on the dollar value of the transactions and the number of shares purchased. Don't be embarrassed to ask your broker what the commission will be before you make any trades.

TAXES

In the previous sections, we discussed trading strategies and different types of orders that can be used to transact purchases and sales. In the brief example about selling short against the box, it was indicated that for tax reasons an investor would choose to defer taxes. As we go through this section, the basics of taxation on investment income will be considered.

Short-Term versus Long-Term Gains and Losses

There are different effective tax rates on short-term and long-term holdings. The Internal Revenue Service defines long-term as being over six months for stocks, bonds, and other assets. Up until June 22, 1984, the holding period for long-term capital gains was one year. However, the Deficit Reduction Act of 1984 reduced the time frame to six months.

Short-term gains are taxed as ordinary income, which is at the effective marginal tax rate of the investor. The marginal tax rate of the investor is the tax to be applied to each succeeding dollar of income. For example, a single investor who had $25,000 in salary would be in an approximate 30 percent marginal tax rate bracket. New income would be taxed at the marginal tax rate (though income between 0 and $25,000 had been taxed at a lower rate). A single individual with $85,000 of income would be in the 50 percent marginal tax bracket. For married couples filing joint returns, the marginal tax rate goes up at a slower pace.

Our initial comment was that short-term gains would be taxed at the marginal tax rate of the investor. What about short-term losses? Short-term losses may be used to offset short- or long-term gains. Any remaining short-term loss after the above deductions may be deducted from ordinary income—up to $3,000 per year. For example, if an investor had $10,000 in short-term losses beyond that written off against other gains, he could deduct $3,000 from salary and other income in 1985 and carry forward the $7,000 difference into 1986 to again be used to offset gains. Net short-term losses can be carried forward indefinitely until used up.

Long-term gains receive preferential tax treatment. The IRS allows 60 percent of long-term gains to be excluded from taxation so that the maximum tax an investor will pay is his or her marginal tax rate times $(1 - .6)$. If you are in the 40 percent marginal bracket your maximum tax would be $40\% \times (1 - $

.6), or 16 percent. This reduced rate maker long-term gains very advantageous and is one good reason to prefer long-term gains to short-term gains. Table 3–6 sets forth the tax liability of different gains, demonstrating the advantages of long-term gains.

TABLE 3–6   Short-Term versus Long-Term Gains

Short-term gain	$10,000	Long-term gain	$10,000
No exclusion	–0–	60% excluded	6,000
Taxable gain	$10,000	Taxable gain	$ 4,000
Marginal tax rate	40%	Marginal tax rate	40%
Tax	$ 4,000	Tax	$ 1,600
Effective tax rate	40%	Effective tax rate	16%

Note in Table 3–6 there would be a 40 percent marginal tax rate applied to short-term capital gains, but the effective tax on long-term capital gains is only 16 percent. This is because $6,000 of the $10,000 of gain was excluded from taxable income before the 40 percent tax was applied. The $1,600 in tax represents only 16 percent of $10,000. Once again, the effective tax rate to be applied to long-term capital gains is always the marginal tax rate times $(1 - .6)$. For an investor in a 50 percent tax bracket, the effective tax rate on long-term capital gains is 20 percent:

$$50\% \times (1 - .6) =$$
$$50\% \times .4 = 20\%$$

The investor is never required to pay more than 20 percent on long-term capital gains on stock transactions. Many years ago, the maximum long-term capital gains tax rate was 35 percent.

Long-term capital losses must first be written off against long-term gains and then short-term gains in a given year.[4] This is done on a dollar-for-dollar basis. Any remaining losses may be deducted from ordinary income to provide a write-off of $3,000 per year. However, long-term losses can only be written off against ordinary income at the rate of 50 cents on the dollar. Thus, $6,000 of long-term capital losses are necessary to provide a $3,000 deduction against ordinary income. You will recall that, in contrast, short-term losses can be deducted against ordinary income on a one-to-one basis. However, the maxi-

---

[4] As indicated above, any loss, such as a long-term loss, must be first written off against long-term gains and then against short-term gains. The same applies to short-term losses. They must first be written off against short-term gains and then long-term gains. Any unused losses are then written off against ordinary income to the extent allowable by law. Any loss that is carried forward to future years retains its original character. A short-term loss that is carried forward will be considered short-term in the next year, and a long-term loss will be considered long-term.

TABLE 3–7   Treatment of Capital Gains

	Short-Term
Gains	*Loss*
Taxed at marginal tax rate	After deductions against any short-term or long-term capital gains on a dollar-for-dollar basis, $3,000 may be written off against other ordinary income in a given year, also on a one-to-one basis. Additional losses may be carried forward.
Long-Term (over 6 months)	
Taxed at marginal tax rate times $(1 - .6)$	After deductions against any long-term or short-term capital gains on a dollar-for-dollar basis, a $3,000 deduction against ordinary income may be taken. However, long-term capital gains can only be deducted against ordinary income at the rate of 50 cents on the dollar, so $6,000 of long-term losses would be necessary to take the maximum $3,000 deduction against other ordinary income in a given year. Additional losses may be carried forward.

mum annual write-off is still only $3,000. In Table 3–7, we summarize the points related to short-term and long-term capital gains.

Timing of Gains and Losses

Because of the tax laws, the best kind of gain is long-term, which minimizes the tax, and the best kind of loss is short-term, because it maximizes your deductions. The worst tax combination would be to take long-term gains and short-term losses in the same year because they are netted out before the long-term gains receive any exclusion.

Investors should try to separate or combine short-term and long-term transactions in the appropriate year or year(s) for tax purposes. While this may not always be feasible because investments may move in unanticipated directions, it is still a worthwhile goal for which to strive. Examples of tax planning implications over two years are presented in Table 3–8.

In alternative A of Table 3–8, a $3,000 short-term capital loss is taken in the first year. This can be written off against ordinary income such as salary. Since the investor is in a 40 percent tax bracket, he or she will save $1,200 in other taxes on ordinary income. In the second year of alternative A, a $3,000 long-term capital gain is taken. Given the 60 percent exclusion on long-term capital gains, the tax is only $480. ($3,000 \times (1 - .6) \times 40\%$).

TABLE 3–8   Short-Term Loss and Long-Term Gain—Implications for Tax Planning

Alternative A

Year 1

Short-term loss	($3,000)
Marginal tax rate, 40%	
Tax saving on ordinary income	$1,200

Year 2

Long-term gain	$3,000
Exclusion 60%	1,800
Taxable income	1,200
Marginal tax rate, 40%	
Tax	($ 480)
Net tax savings over 2 years ($1,200 − $480)	$ 720

Alternative B

Year 1 only

Short-term loss	($3,000)
Long-term gain	3,000
Net taxable gain or loss	0

Thus over the two-year time period in alternative A, there is a $1,200 tax savings and a $480 tax obligation. The net difference is $720 in tax savings.

Under alternative B, both the short-term loss and long-term gain are taken in the same year. All the benefits of the short-term loss are used up against the normally low-tax long-term capital gains. The net tax is 0. This figure represents $720 less than the tax savings in alternative A. The investor following alternative A has properly timed his transactions, while the investor in alternative B has not been so fortunate.

There are many other combinations that could be covered. In each instance, tax planners consider ways to match up various types of gains and losses and evaluate the impact. There are many other tax consequences an individual should be aware of, such as tax shelters, estate planning, and gift taxes. These will be covered more fully in later chapters. Also, there has been a strong tendency for tax laws to change rapidly in the 1980s. The basic rules presented in this section are valid as we go to press in late 1985. However, future changes are always possible. Nevertheless, the *basic principles* presented in this section will serve you well even if there are some future modifications to the capital gains tax laws.

Chapter 4

SOURCES OF INVESTMENT INFORMATION

AGGREGATE ECONOMIC DATA
Federal Reserve Bulletin
Federal Reserve Banks
Federal Reserve Bank of St. Louis
Survey of Current Business
Business Conditions Digest
Other Sources of Economic Data

INVESTMENT ADVISORY SERVICES
Moody's
Standard & Poor's
Value Line
Other Investment Services

INDEXES, SEC FILINGS, PERIODICALS, AND JOURNALS
Indexes
Securities and Exchange Commission Filings
Periodicals and Newspapers
Journals

COMPUTER DATA BASES
The Use of Mainframe Computers
The Use of Personal Computers

INFORMATION ON NONTRADITIONAL MARKETS
Commodity Yearbook
Scott Publishing Company

We are continually exposed to much information in this world of expanding and rapid communications. As the scope of investments has grown to include more than stocks and bonds, investment information has expanded to cover items such as gold and silver, diamonds, original art, antiques, stamps and coins, real estate, farm land, oil and gas, tax shelters, commodities, mutual funds, and other specialized assets. The problem investors are faced with is not only which investments to choose from the many available, but also where to find relevant information on specific investments.

First of all, the investor needs a basic knowledge of the economic environment. After determining the economic climate, the investor will proceed to a more detailed analysis of industries and unique variables affecting a specific investment. It is often said that the sign of an educated person is whether he or she knows where to find information to make an intelligent decision. The rest of this chapter will attempt to provide a list and description of the basic information sources for some of the more common forms of investments as well as sources for general economic data.

You may want to refer back to this chapter as you go through the chapters that follow. This chapter is not intended to be a guide for analysis—only an overview of what information is available. You may have heard the old phrase "a picture is worth a thousand words." You will find that is certainly true of the tables and figures in this chapter. It is virtually impossible to discuss each and every variable found in the figures and tables. To acquaint yourself more fully with information sources we suggest that you visit your college and local library and spend time browsing through their collection of economic and financial services. Appendix 4–A at the end of the chapter contains the addresses of a number of the sources mentioned in this chapter.

AGGREGATE ECONOMIC DATA

Economic data are necessary for analyzing the past and predicting future trends of the economy. The economic environment that exists today and the one expected in the future will bear heavily on the types of investments selected when creating or managing an investment portfolio. Information on inflation, wages, disposable income, economic growth rates, interest rates, money supply, demographic trends, and so on are important economic data that will influence investor decisions. This information is available in many publications from the government, commercial banks, and periodicals. What follows is a brief description of some of the major sources of economic data.

Federal Reserve Bulletin

The *Federal Reserve Bulletin* is published monthly by the Board of Governors of the Federal Reserve System, Washington D.C. It contains an abundance of monetary data, such as money supply figures, interest rates, bank reserves, and various statistics on commercial banks. Fiscal variables, such as U.S. budget receipts and outlays and federal debt figures are also found in the *Bulletin.*

This publication also contains data on international exchange rates and U.S. dealings with foreigners and overseas banks.

Since a complete description of the *Federal Reserve Bulletin* is outside the scope of this chapter, a partial listing of the table of contents should suffice to provide a better idea of what information it contains. Each heading may be divided into more detailed sections that provide information for the previous month, the current year on a monthly basis, and several years of historical annual data.

> Domestic Financial Statistics
> Federal Reserve Banks
> Monetary and Credit Aggregates
> Commercial Banks
> Financial Markets
> Federal Finance
> Securities Markets and Corporate Finance
> Real Estate
> Consumer Installment Credit
> Domestic Non Financial Statistics
> International Statistics
> Securities Holdings and Transactions
> Interest and Exchange Rates

The Federal Reserve Board also publishes a *Federal Reserve Quarterly Chart Book* and an annual *Historical Chart Book* depicting the data in the *Bulletin* in graphic form.

Federal Reserve Banks

There are 12 Federal Reserve Banks in the Federal Reserve System, representing different geographical areas (districts) of the United States. Each bank publishes its own monthly letter or review which includes economic data about its region and sometimes commentary on national issues or monetary policy. The 12 banks by district are as follows: Boston (1), New York (2), Philadelphia (3), Cleveland (4), Richmond (5), Atlanta (6), Chicago (7), St. Louis (8), Minneapolis (9), Kansas City (10), Dallas (11), and San Francisco (12).

Federal Reserve Bank of St. Louis

One district bank, the Federal Reserve Bank of St. Louis, publishes some of the most comprehensive economic statistics on a weekly and monthly basis. *U.S. Financial Data* is published weekly and includes data on the monetary base, bank reserves, money supply, a breakdown of time deposits and demand deposits, borrowing from the Federal Reserve Banks, and business loans from the large commercial banks. The publication also includes yields and interest rates

FIGURE 4–1

SELECTED INTEREST RATES
AVERAGES OF DAILY RATES ENDED FRIDAY

LATEST DATA PLOTTED ARE AVERAGES OF RATES AVAILABLE FOR THE WEEK ENDING: JULY 20, 1984

1984	FEDERAL FUNDS ▪	3-MONTH TREASURY BILL	6-MONTH TREASURY BILL ▪▪	1-YEAR TREASURY BILL	5-YEAR TREASURY SECURITIES	LONG-TERM TREASURY SECURITIES
MAY 4	10.70	9.73	9.88	10.18	12.65	12.85
11	10.46	9.97	10.27	10.46	12.99	13.16
18	10.52	9.88	10.40	10.59	13.24	13.42
25	9.75	9.79	10.38	10.73	13.35	13.49
JUNE 1	10.30	9.76	10.62	10.94	13.69	13.71
8	10.72	9.81	10.57	10.80	13.34	13.38
15	10.85	9.95	10.66	10.87	13.36	13.35
22	11.49	9.91	10.49	10.97	13.49	13.41
29	11.27	9.81	10.49	11.09	13.72	13.62
JULY 6	10.91	9.92	10.54	11.01	13.67	13.65
13	11.25	10.04	10.52	10.94	13.39	13.31
20 ▪	11.21	10.10	10.60	10.92	13.27	13.21
27						

▪ AVERAGES OF RATES AVAILABLE.
▪▪ SEVEN-DAY AVERAGES FOR WEEK ENDING WEDNESDAY TWO DAYS EARLIER THAN DATE SHOWN.
    CURRENT DATA APPEAR IN THE BOARD OF GOVERNORS' H.15 RELEASE.
▪▪▪ NEW ISSUE RATE
RATES ON LONG-TERM TREASURY SECURITIES ARE COMPUTED BY THE FEDERAL RESERVE BANK OF ST. LOUIS.
TREASURY BILL YIELDS ON DISCOUNT BASIS.

PREPARED BY FEDERAL RESERVE BANK OF ST. LOUIS

on a weekly basis on selected short-term and long-term securities. An example of these published interest rates appears in Figures 4–1 and 4–2.

Monetary Trends is published monthly by the St. Louis Fed and includes charts and tables of monthly data. The information is similar to that found in *U.S. Financial Data* but covers a longer time period. The tables provide compound annual rates of change, while the graphs include the raw data with trend changes over time. Additional data are available on federal government debt and its composition by type of holder and on the receipts and expenditures of the government for both the National Income Account Budget and the High Employment Budget.

FIGURE 4–2

YIELDS ON SELECTED SECURITIES
AVERAGES OF DAILY RATES ENDED FRIDAY

LATEST DATA PLOTTED ARE AVERAGES OF RATES AVAILABLE FOR THE WEEK ENDING: JULY 20, 1984

1984	90 DAY CD'S	30-DAY COMMERCIAL PAPER	90-DAY BANKERS' ACCEPTANCES	CORPORATE Aaa BONDS	CORPORATE Baa BONDS	MUNICIPAL BONDS ▓
MAY 4	10.60	10.28	10.42	13.00	14.46	9.99
11	11.17	10.52	10.98	13.15	14.61	10.19
18	11.32	10.54	11.07	13.33	14.75	10.36
25	11.14	10.19	10.93	13.42	14.91	10.83
JUNE 1	11.31	10.32	10.92	13.56	15.04	11.07
8	11.09	10.56	10.81	13.46	14.95	10.78
15	11.13	10.75	10.85	13.48	15.01	10.59
22	11.46	10.98	11.27	13.55	15.06	10.56
29	11.67	11.07	11.46	13.71	15.20	10.76
JULY 6	11.75	11.11	11.44	13.69	15.29	10.69
13	11.60	11.13	11.41	13.53	15.16	10.44
20 ▓	11.56	11.04	11.36	13.35	15.15	N.A.
27						

▓ AVERAGES OF RATES AVAILABLE.
▓▓ BOND BUYER'S AVERAGE INDEX OF 20 MUNICIPAL BONDS, THURSDAY DATA.
N.A. - NOT AVAILABLE

PREPARED BY FEDERAL RESERVE BANK OF ST. LOUIS

National Economic Trends is also published by the St. Louis Federal Reserve Bank and presents monthly economic data on employment, unemployment rates, consumer and producer prices, industrial production, personal income, retail sales, productivity, compensation and labor costs, gross national product, the implicit price deflator for the GNP, personal consumption expenditures, gross private domestic investment, government purchases of goods and services, disposable personal income, corporate profit after taxes, and inventories. This information is presented in graph form and in tables showing the compounded annual rate of change on a monthly basis. If raw data is needed, other economic publications are required.

Survey of Current Business

The *Survey of Current Business* is published monthly by the Bureau of Economic Analysis of the U.S. Department of Commerce. It contains monthly and quarterly raw data rather than compound annual growth rates as found in the St. Louis Federal Reserve's publications. The *Survey of Current Business* contains a monthly update and evaluation of the business situation, analyzing such data as GNP, business inventories, personal consumption, fixed investment, exports, labor market statistics, financial data, and much more. For example, if personal consumption expenditures are broken down into subcategories, one would find expenditures on durable goods, such as motor vehicles and parts, and furniture and equipment; nondurables, such as food, energy, clothing, and shoes; and services.

The *Survey* can be extremely helpful for industry analysis as it breaks down data into basic industries. For example, data on inventory, new plant and equipment, production, and more can be found on such specific industries as coal, tobacco, chemicals, leather products, furniture, paper, and many others. Even within industries, such as lumber, production statistics can be found on hardwoods and softwoods right down to Douglas fir trees, southern pine, and western pine. The Commerce Department publishes a weekly update to the *Survey* called *Weekly Business Statistics.* This publication updates the major series found in the *Survey of Current Business* and includes 27 weekly series and charts of selected series. To provide a more comprehensive view of what is available in the *Survey of Current Business* and *Weekly Business Statistics,* a list of the major series updates follows:

GNP	Housing Starts and Permits
National Income	Retail Trade
Personal Income	Labor Force, Employment and
Industrial Production	Earnings
Manufacturers Shipments, Inventories and Orders	Banking
Consumer Price Index	Consumer Installment Credit
Producer Price Index	Stock Prices
Construction Put in Place	Value of Exports and Imports
	Motor Vehicles

Business Conditions Digest

The *Business Conditions Digest* is published monthly by the Bureau of Economic Analysis of the U.S. Department of Commerce. The information differs from the other publications previously discussed in that its primary emphasis is on cyclical indicators of economic activity. The National Bureau of Economic Research (NBER) analyzes and selects the time series data, based on each series' ability to be identified as a leading, coincident, or lagging indicator over several decades of aggregate economic activity.

Over the years, the NBER has identified the approximate dates when aggregate economic activity reached its cyclical high or low point. Each time

FIGURE 4–3

NOTE: Numbers entered on the chart indicate length of leads (–) and lags (+) in months from reference turning dates.
Current data for these series are shown on page 60.

Source: *Business Conditions Digest* (U.S. Department of Commerce, Bureau of Economic Analysis, April 1985).

series is related to the business cycle. Leading indicators are those that move prior to the business cycle, coincident indicators move with the business cycle, and lagging indicators follow directional changes in the business cycle. Figure 4–3 represents the composite index of 12 leading, 4 coincident, and 6 lagging indicators that have consistently performed well relative to the general swings in the economy. The 22 indicators were selected out of several hundred found in the *Business Conditions Digest* and time-tested by the NBER. This publication can be very helpful in understanding past economic behavior and in forecasting future economic activity with a higher degree of success.

Other Sources of Economic Data

So far, we have presented the basic sources of economic data. Much other data is available or duplicated in other publications. What is available to each investor may vary from library to library, so here are some brief notes on other sources of data.

Many universities have bureaus of business research that provide statistical data on a statewide or regional basis. Major banks, such as Citicorp, Morgan Guaranty Trust, Harris Trust, and Bank of America, publish monthly or weekly letters or economic reviews, including raw data and analysis. Several other government sources are available, such as *Economic Indicators* prepared by the Council of Economic Advisors and the *Annual Economic Report of the President.* Additionally, many periodicals, such as *Business Week, Fortune,* and *Barron's,* contain raw data as well as economic commentary. Moody's and Standard & Poor's Investment Services (introduced on the following pages) both publish economic data along with much other market-related information.

INVESTMENT ADVISORY SERVICES

Investment information and advice is available from many sources—from large corporate financial services to individuals writing investment letters. A look through such financial magazines as *Barron's, Forbes,* and *Financial World* will turn up hundreds of investment services charging fees large and small for the information they sell. Most public libraries and universities subscribe from several of the major publishers, such as Moody's, Standard & Poor's, or Value Line.

Moody's

Moody's is owned by Dun & Bradstreet and publishes several data bases for bonds and stocks. *Moody's Manuals* are widely used and present not only historical financial data on the companies listed but also on their officers and the companies' general corporate condition. The *Manuals* are divided into several categories (Banks and Finance, Industrial, Municipals and Government, OTC Industrial, Public Utility, and Transportation). Each manual has a biweekly news supplement that updates quarterly earnings, dividend announcements, mergers, and other news of interest. *Moody's Manuals* are comprehensive, with each category taking up one or two volumes and over several thousand pages.

Moody's Bond Record contains data on corporates, convertibles, governments, municipals, and ratings on commercial paper and preferred stock. Corporate bond information includes the interest coupon, payment dates, call price, Moody's rating, and yield to maturity. The current price as well as the yearly and historical high-low price are presented. The total amount of the bond issue outstanding is given with a designation for a sinking fund and the original issue date. Data on convertible bonds also include the conversion price, conversion value, and conversion period. Information on industrial revenue and municipal bonds is usually limited to the Moody's rating. *Moody's Bond Record* also contains historical yield graphs for various types of bonds over at least 30 years. This is a monthly publication.

Moody's also publishes a weekly *Bond Survey* that reviews the week's activity in the bond market, rating changes, new issues, and bonds called for redemption. *Moody's Dividend Record* presents quarterly dividends and the date of declaration, date of record, date payable, and ex-dividend dates. This is an annual publication. *Moody's Handbook of Common Stock* is a quarterly reference guide that summarizes a company's 10-year historical financial data along with a discussion of corporate background, recent developments, and prospects. Approximately 1,000 companies are listed in the *Handbook*. *Moody's Stock Survey* is a weekly publication that discusses the weekly investment climate and market performance. This publication also presents some selected stocks for purchase. Only a brief description has been given for each Moody's publication, but enough has been presented for you to know whether a particular one may be worth looking at further.

Standard & Poor's

A second major source of information is the Standard & Poor's Corporation, a subsidiary of McGraw-Hill. Standard & Poor's has very comprehensive coverage of financial data. The following items will not all be discussed, but they provide a good look at what Standard & Poor's makes available to the investor.

Analysts Handbook   *Industry Survey*
Bond Guide   *International Stock Reports*
Called Bond Record   *Investment Advisory Survey*
Convertible Bond Reports   *Municipal Bond Selector*
Corporation Records   *Opportunities in Convertible*
Daily Stock Price Records   *Bonds*
Dividend Record   *The Outlook*
Earnings Forecaster   *Poor's Register of Corporations,*
Fixed Income Investor   *Directors and Executives*

Registered Bond Interest Record
The Review of Securities Regulation
Security Dealers Directory
Stock Guide
Stock Reports (A.S.E., N.Y.S.E., O-T-C and Regional Exchanges)

Stock Summary
Standard & Poor's Statistical Service
Transportation Service
Trendline Charts

Standard & Poor's Corporate Records are similar to *Moody's Manuals* except that they are organized alphabetically rather than by trade categories. The *Corporate Records* are published monthly, and the six volumes are updated by daily supplements. Information found in the volumes includes historical company background, financial statements, news announcements, earnings updates, and other news of general interest. Companies found in the *Corporate Records* are listed, and their subsidiary companies are cross-listed.

Something that may be overlooked when examining the *Corporate Records* is the statistical section found in the T–Z volume. The statistical section includes a mutual fund summary, an address list of many no-load mutual funds, and foreign bond statistics. Special tables contained in the T–Z volume list new stock and bond offerings on a monthly basis. This volume also presents a classified index of industrial companies listed by Standard Industrial Classification code numbers (SIC). For example, if you want to find out about cereal breakfast food companies, you would first find the corresponding SIC number for cereal breakfast foods which is listed in alphabetical order. The number, 2043, then leads you to the cross-listing of companies in the *Standard & Poor's Corporate Records.* These are the companies one would find listed under *2043 Cereal Breakfast Foods:*

Carnation Co.
The Clorox Company
General Foods Corp.
General Mills, Inc.
Gerber Products Co.
Iroquois Brands, Ltd.
Kellogg Company

Liggett Group Inc.
Nabisco, Inc.
Nestlé S.A.
The Quaker Oats Co.
Ralston Purina Co.
George Weston Limited

All of these companies make up an industry classification and may be found in the *Corporate Records.* This industry listing can certainly be helpful when trying to put together a list of companies for an industry analysis.

Several other Standard & Poor's publications are quite useful and present concise, thumbnail sketches of companies, common stock variables, and corporate bonds. Figure 4–4 depicts two pages from the *Stock Guide.* This is a monthly publication that enables investors to take a preliminary look at the common and preferred stock of several thousand companies and almost 200 mutual funds. The introduction to the *Stock Guide* presents recommendations

FIGURE 4–4 Sample pages, Standard & Poor's Stock Guide

214 Ten-Tho

Standard & Poor's Corporation

Index	Ticker Symbol	Name of Issue (Call Price of Pfd. Stocks)	Market	Com. Rank. & Pfd. Rating	Par Val.	Inst.Hold Cos	Inst.Hold Shs. (000)	Principal Business	Price Range 1971-83 High	Low	1984 High	Low	1985 High	Low	Mar. Sales in 100s	March, 1985 Last Sale Or Bid High	Low	Last	%Div. Yield	P-E Ratio
1	TNY	Tenney Engineering	AS	B+	10¢	7	467	Environmental test eq	6⅛	⅜	4⅞	3⅛	5⅜	3⅛	625	6⅛	5⅛	5¾	...	15
2	TEN	Tensor Corp	AS	C	10¢		3	Hi-intensity lamps	14⅞	⅜	10⅜	5⅛	6⅜	4	129	5⅜	4⅛	4⅞	...	d
3	TRRA	TERA Corp	OTC	NR	No	13	1219	Computer sys/pkgd software	39½	5¼	9¼	4	6¾	4¼	950	5¾	4⅜	4¾B	...	d
4	TRA	Teradyne Inc	NY	B	12½¢	184	15942	Electr ind automatic test eq	39⅞	1¼	39⅜	21⅛	32⅜	21⅛	32423	28⅜	21⅜	21⅜	...	13
5	TERM	Terminal Data	OTC	B		9	942	Document microfilming sys	16½		13		9¼	6¼	1934	8¾	6⅜	7⅝B	...	13
6	TMEXF	Terra Mines Ltd	OTC,Vc	NR	50¢	6	231	Int'l silver producer	8⅝	1	4⅜	1⅜	1⅞	1¼	3076	1⅞	1½	1⅞B	s.	d
7	TDSC	Tesdata Systems	AS	C	1¢	3	148	Computer perf measure sys	25½	1	9⅜	2⅝	1⅞	1½	515	1½	1½	1⅜B	...	d
8	TSO	Tesoro Petroleum	NY,B,M,P,Ph	BB-	16¾¢	27	3759	Integrated oil company	32¼	6⅜	20⅞	9¼	15	9¾	16396	15	10¼	12¾	3.2	50
9	Pr	$2.16 cm Cv Pfd(25)vtg	NY,M	BB		4		Trinidad, Indonesia, U.S.	55½	18¾	36¾	20⅜	27½	20⅜	605	27¼	22⅜	25¼	8.6	2
10	TEVIY	Teva Pharm Indus ADR	OTC	NR	‥	4	5	Pharmac'ls,veterinary prod	10⅜	2⅜	4½	2⅞	2⅜	1½	475	2½	2½	2½B	1.2	2
11	TXC	Texaco Canada	AS,Ph,Mo,To	A-	No	61	1352	Large factor in Canadian oil	38	5¾	33	25¼	27¾	25¼	331	25¼	22½	25¼	4.8	7
12	TX	Texaco Inc	NY,B,C,M,P,Ph,To	B+	6¼	587	76153	Major international oil co	54¾	20	48¾	31½	36⅛	31½	135447	36⅛	34¾	36⅛	8.3	35
13	TEX	Texas Air	AS,M	C	4	48	3253	Hldg: regional airlines	16⅜	8¾	9⅜	6½	11⅛	6½	11726	11	10⅛	10⅛	...	8
14	TXA	Texas Amer'n Bancsh	NY,M	B	5	48	3061	Multiple bank hldg:Ft Worth	45¾	8¾	42	33¾	37⅛	33¾	2709	36⅜	32⅜	33¾	4.5	8
15	TAE	Texas Amer'n Energy	AS	B-		9	542	Hldg:oil&gas prod'n:refinery	17		10⅛	4	7½	4¾	2859	7	6	7	s.	50
16	Pr	$2.575cm Cv''Exch Pfd(**22.3175)		B+	No	4	127	Multiple bank hldg:Houston	46¾	6¾	22¼	16¼	20	16¼	432	20	19¼	19¾	13.0	6
17	TCB	Texas Commerce Bkshr	NY,M,P	A+	198		16508	Gas: sys:petrol mkt/distr	46⅞	6¾	45	36¼	44	32¾	46838	43¾	32⅜	33⅜	4.7	8
18	TGB	Texas Oil & Gas Corp	AS,C,M,P	A+	3½	250	24172	Oil & gas sys:gathering	64⅝	13¾	46½	36¾	44¼	36¾	30542	43¾	30⅛	34⅛	6.4	9
19	Pr	Texas Pac Ld Tr Ctfs		A+	1		512	Holds surface rights/royalties	62⅝	13¾	56½	42¾	57¼	42¾		56½	54¼	56½	1.1	10
20	TXI	Texas Indus	NY,B,M,Ph	B+	1	46	1796	Concrete prod: constr: r. e.	44¾	2⅞	38⅜	25	34¼	25	2361	31	25¾	27¾	s29	13
21	TXN	Texas Instruments	NY,B,C,M,P,Ph	A-		349	18051	Semiconductors:el'tronic eqp	176	39¾	149½	111¾	131¾	105¼	17585	114	105¼	111¼	1.8	9
22	TEI	Texas Int'l	NY,M,P,Ph,To	C	10¢	35	3280	Oil & natural gas	46⅞	1¹¹⁄₁₆	5⅜	3⅛	3⅝	1¾	9207	2⅜	1⅞	1⅞	...	d
23	TPL	Texas Oil & Gas	NY,B,C,M,Ph	B+	50¢	460	115229	Gas gathering:oil & gas	26¼	¾	27⅜	16½	21⅜	16¼	171027	19¾	16¼	17⅛	1.1	10
24	TXU	Texas Utilities	NY,B,C,M,Ph	A+	No	436	82741	Electric utility holding co.	36	14¼	28¼	24½	28¾	25⅜	89804	28⅜	26¼	28	9.0	7
26	TXF	Texfi Indus	NY,M	C	20¢	5	490	Fabrics for apparel indus	67½	1	8¼	2	3½	1¾	922	3½	3⅛	3½	2.0	9
27	TXON	Texon Energy	OTC	NR	20¢	5	1342	Oil & gas royalty interests	12⅜	⅛	6¾	2	1⅜	1¼	2433	1⅛	1½	1⅜B	...	d
28	TXS	Texscan Corp	AS	B	20¢	23	1667	CATV eq:radio freq:test'g eq	27½	⅞	20	6¼	7¾	3¾	7440	5⅞	3¾	3⅜	...	56
29	TXTN	Textone Inc	OTC	AS	20¢	3	44	Wall paneling board:doors	29¾	1	19¼	6¾	18¾	14¾	5667	18⅜	14¾	16⅛	1.5	11
30	TXT	Textron, Inc.	NY,B,C,M,Ph	A	25¢	140	11378	Aerosp:electr:consumer prod	38½	11¾	43½	25%	45¾	32¾	49995	45¾	39¼	45¾	4.0	15
31	Pr A	$2.08 cm Cv A Pfd(50)vtg	NY,B	BBB	No	14	233	outdoor,ind'l prod,machine	46½	19	47¼	28¾	49½	36	128	49½	43½	49½B	4.2	d
32	Pr B	$1.40 cm Cv B Pfd(45)vtg	NY,M	B	No	3	235	Deols:engineered fasteners	25¼	14	38⅜	23¾	40⅜	23¾	1366	40⅛	36¼	40⅛	3.5	
33	THK	Thackeray Corp	NY	CCC	10¢	3	114	hardware:RE	27	4½	6⅝	2⅞	6¾	2¾	366	6½	2⅜	26⅛B	15.6	d
34	Pr	$4.15 cm Pfd(*27.90:SF25)	OTC	NR	1¢	12	323	Mfrs custom window units	13¼		15	7½	14¼	12½	3033	14¼	12½	12⅜B		21
35	THPR	Thermal Profiles	OTC																	
36	THMD	Thermedics Inc	OTC	NR	1	29	50	Mfrs biomedical prod & sys	8⅜	6⅜	10¼	6¾	17½	8	2923	17¼	13	15½B	...	d
37	TMO	Thermo Electron	NY,M	B	39		1659	Eng'd ind'l pr: environ instr	26¼	2¾	10¼	6⅛	26	18	5638	26	21	25⅛	...	23
38	TDYN	Thermodynetics	OTC	NR	25¢			Mfr twisted metal tubing	2¾	1	1%		9¾	6¾	2382	10¾	9½	9⅜B	...	37
39	THFR	Thetford Corp	OTC	B+	10	11	403	Toilet sys:recreat veh,boat	26⅜	2⅜	15	6¾	10⅜	7½		10½	9¾	9¾B	3.5	d
40	TDAT	Third Nat'l	NY,B,M	A+		40	3721	Multi-bank hldg:Tennessee	26⅜	6¼	33½	21¼	37¼	33	1171	37¼	36¼	36½B	...	8
41	TCBY	This Can't Be Yogurt	OTC	NR	No	128	9833	Franchises frozen yogurt strs	38¼	8¾	8¾	2¾	27¼	18	7967	19¼	19¾	19¾	...	40
42	TNB	Thomas & Betts	NY,M,P	A	50¢	226	2286	Elec connectors, accessories	19½	2¼	38	28¾	43¼	34¼	6524	41½	36¼	36⅛	3.4	15
43	TII	Thomas Indus	NY,M	A-		16	984	Lighting fix:decor hm:tools	14¾	¾	18	13	18	15	1362	18	15	16⅜	2.4	9
44	TNEL	Thomas Nelson	OTC	B+	10¢	23	816	Book publ:prod'r,mktr-Bible	26	3¼	26¼	13¼	18¾	13¼	4883	18⅜	13¾	14¼	2.8	79
45	THM.A	Thomson Newspaper A	To,Mo	A+	No	63	1931	Large newspaper publisher	39	6¾	52¼	37	60	48	2048	58¾	54¼	58¾	2.1	19

Uniform Footnote Explanations—See Page 1. Other: ¹P:Cycle 1. ²P:Cycle 2. ³AS:Cycle 1. ⁴AS. ⁵CBOE:Cycle 1. ⁶P:Cycle 3. ⁷Ph:Cycle 1. ⁸CBOE:Cycle 1.
¹Pro forma,excl shrs held by co. ²⁸$0.98,'84. ³Incl reorg liab & new financing. ⁴$0.45,'83. ⁵$0.14,'81. ⁶$0.01,'84. ⁷$1.20,'84. ⁸$0.45,'83. ⁹Co opt fr 5-1-86exch for $20 amt 12%Cv2014. ¹⁰To 4-30-85,scale to $20 in '94.
¹¹Com price equals 140%Cv price-20 trad'g days. ¹²Subsid Pfd in M/S. ¹³$4.00,'84. ¹⁴Thru 5-31-85:min 7½%,max 15.1/2%. ¹⁵Thru 11-30-92,then $50. ¹⁶Stk dstr of Regal Int'l. ¹⁷$0.05,'80.
¹⁸$0.19,'82. ¹⁹Nortek Inc plan acq 1.09 shrs. ²⁰$1.87,'80. ²¹$0.14,'81. ²²$0.28,'82. ²³$0.07,'84. ²⁴To 8-15-85,scale to $25 in '94. ²⁵$0.50,'81.

FIGURE 4-4 *(concluded)*

Common and Preferred Stocks

Ten-Tho 215

Splits ◆ / Dividends

Index	Cash Divs. Ea. Yr. Since	Per$	Date	Ex. Div.	So Far 1985	Ind. Rate	Paid 1984
1◆	....	None Paid			....	Nil	....
2	....	None Paid			....	Nil	....
3	....	None Since Public			....	Nil	....
4◆	....	None Paid			....	Nil	....
5◆	....	....			....	Nil	....
6◆	....	5% Stk	1-28-85	1-8	5% Stk	Stk	5% Stk
7	....	None Since Public			....	Nil	....
8	1980	Q0.10	2-25-85	2-5	0.10	0.40	0.40
9	1976	Q0.54	3-15-85	2-25	0.54	2.16	2.16
10◆	1984	0.01½	1-29-85	1-7	0.01½	0.03	0.035
11◆	1944	gQ0.30	3-1-85	2-5	g0.30	1.20	g1.20
12	1903	Q0.75	3-8-85	1-30	0.75	3.00	3.00
13	....	0.04	7-31-83	7-6	....	Nil	....
14◆	1934	Q0.38	4-2-85	3-11	0.76	1.52	1.52
15◆	....	5% Stk	8-1-84	7-10	....	Stk	5% Stk
16	1984	Q0.64⅜	2-1-85	1-15	0.64⅜	2.57½	0.987
17◆	1920	Q0.39	4-1-85	3-4	0.78	1.56	1.42
18◆	1950	Q0.55	3-1-85	2-5	0.55	2.20	2.16¼
19	1983	1.506	3-1-85	2-5	1.506	5.82½	6.37½
20◆	1962	Q0.20	2-28-85	1-28	0.20	0.80	s0.784
21	1962	Q0.50	4-29-85	3-26	1.00	2.00	2.00
22◆	....	h**	5-28-82	6-1	....	Nil	....
23◆	1965	Q0.04½	4-12-85	3-27	0.09	0.18	0.17
24◆	1956	A0.40	3-12-85	2-26	0.40	0.40	0.40
25	1917	Q0.63	4-1-85	3-13	1.22	2.52	2.32
26	....	None Paid			....	Nil	....
27	....	None Since Public			....	Nil	....
28◆	....	None Since Public			....	Nil	....
29	1983	0.25	1-16-85	12-24	0.25	0.25	0.25
30	1942	Q0.45	4-1-85	3-11	0.90	1.80	1.80
31	1968	Q0.52	4-1-85	3-11	1.04	2.08	2.08
32	1968	Q0.35	4-1-85	3-11	0.70	1.40	1.40
33	....	0.30	6-5-74	5-6	....	Nil	....
34	1983	Q1.03¾	2-15-85	1-28	1.03¾	4.15	4.15
35	....	None Since Public			....	Nil	....
36◆	....	None Since Public			....	Nil	....
37◆	....	None Paid			....	Nil	....
38	....	None Since Public			....	Nil	....
39	....	None Since Public			....	Nil	....
40◆	1929	Q0.32	4-1-85	3-7	0.59	1.28	1.046
41◆	....	None Since Public			....	Nil	....
42◆	1934	Q0.31	4-1-85	3-4	0.62	1.24	1.17
43◆	1955	Q0.17	4-1-85	3-4	0.324	0.68	0.604
44◆	1975	Q0.05	4-19-85	3-29	0.10	0.20	0.17
45◆	1962	Q0.10	4-15-85	3-25	0.20	0.40	0.40
46	1966	gQ0.30½	3-15-85	2-25	g0.30½	1.22	g1.17½

Financial Position / Capitalization

Index	Cash& Equiv.	Curr. Assets	Curr. Liab.	Balance Sheet Date	Lg Trm Debt Mil-$	Pfd.	Com.
1	3.46	11.4	3.13	9-30-84	4.98	...	3484
2	0.03	2.05	4.69	9-30-84	2.58	...	546
3	6.19	31.4	14.0	12-31-84	...	...	7507
4	0.78	186.	46.7	9-29-84	58.7	...	22232
5	1.21	26.4	13.4	12-31-84	7.38	...	4471
6	....	3.57	5.59	9-30-84	0.92	...	9967
7	0.26	5.34	1.80	9-30-84	0.01	...	1295
8	10.5	368.	328.	12-31-84	147.	4199	13731
9	Cv into 1.7241 shr com=$14.50				...1323		
10	398.	5903	4519	j3-31-84	438.	54186848	
11	423.	1828	663.	j12-31-84	94.0	900	120768
12	1576	7501	6405	12-31-84	★11766	12627	237380
13	203.	448.	266.	9-30-84	56 1113	4955	13015
14	Book Value=$31.68			12-31-84	128.	...	10604
15	3.26	39.6	23.3	9-30-84	75.0	700	6719
16	Cv into 2.1 com shrs				...	700	...
17	Book Value=$35.15			12-31-84	180.	...	32459
18	180.	1341	2029	9-30-84	53 1316	323	52686
19	Callable at $51.50 fr 12-1-87★⁵				★926±1835		1
20	21.4	126.	50.1	11-30-84	137.	19	7517
21	274.	1858	1412	12-31-84	388.	...	24616
22	12.2	55.0	54.5	9-30-84	346.	...	27458
23	8.40	404.	373.	11-30-84	678.	...	210174
24	3.13			9-30-84	...	...	±4035
25	n/a	658.	832.	12-31-84	3340	55 2763	★133586
26	n/a	20.8	15.5	2-1-85	26.4	...	3480
27	0.40	1.52	2.51	10-31-84	12.5	413	★7625
28	0.11	90.5	26.4	1-31-85	48.6	...	6721
29	5.67	13.7	1.43	9-30-84	2.53	...	p1169
30	42.9	1515	645.	12-29-84	200.	1994	33791
31	Conv into 1.1 shrs common				...1453		...
32	Conv into 0.9 shrs common				...541		...
33	1.71	35.7	10.1	9-30-84	34.3	730	5107
34					...730		...
35	1.45	10.1	4.83	12-31-84	7.16	...	2743
36	4.52	5.60	0.42	9-29-84	...	...	6126
37	9.52	95.3	46.2	9-29-84	47.1	...	6020
38	0.57	2.58	0.52	12-31-84	0.04	...	8113
39	0.80	10.4	3.56	12-31-84	2.21	...	1803
40	Book Value $28.53			9-30-84	58.2	...	8661
41	1.06	2.26	1.79	8-31-84	0.86	...	★2907
42	53.0	190.	60.1	12-31-84	7.22	...	15534
43	14.0	119.	32.2	12-31-84	43.1	...	8487
44	3.31	51.6	20.8	12-31-84	24.5	...	5126
45	21.8	83.3	24.5	8-31-84	...	...	9560
46	68.7	171.	90.7	j12-31-83	97.8	155	±49236

Earnings $ Per Shr.

Index	End	1980	1981	1982	1983	1984	Last 12 Mos.
1	Dc	0.21	0.24	0.19	0.22	P⁵¹0.03	0.39
2	Dc	*0.04	*0.21	d0.86	2.84	...	d3.73
3	Je	0.38	0.51	0.71	0.30	d0.48	d0.31
4	Dc	0.68	0.25	0.24	52 1.08	P1.87	1.87
5	Sp	d0.18	0.39	0.55	0.44	0.68	0.56
6	Dc	*0.19	d0.22	*0.08	d0.30	Pd1.17	jd1.17
7	Dc	*0.53	d0.18	d0.92	▲d1.00	...	d2.49
8	Sp	7.15	■4.84	2.90	▲3.05	0.59	0.25
9	Sp	b5.11	b7.63	b6.24	b3.23	b1.56	...
10	Mr	0.89	0.71	0.56	55 1.00	...	1.00
11	Dc	2.92	2.45	2.15	2.74	3.41	j3.41
12	Dc	*8.31	8.75	■4.92	4.80	P■1.03	1.03
13	Dc	0.55	d8.11	d7.27	d14.58	P*⁵71.24	1.24
14	Dc	■3.65	■4.52	■4.82	■3.66	▲4.06	4.06
15	Dc	0.67	d0.08	d0.33	D■0.84	P0.14	0.14
16	Dc						Call restr to 5-1-86⁶¹
17	Dc	■3.48	■4.49	5.35	5.50	■5.64	5.64
18	Dc	4.36	4.35	...	2.97P▲■34.04	4.04	
19	Dc			b2.12	b2.22	b2.80	...
20	My	5.16	3.76	2.28	2.34	1.54	2.06
21	Dc	9.22	4.62	6.10	■d6.09	▲13.05	13.05
22	Dc	△⁷⁰0.76	D0.54	D■0.37	D■3.26 P▲d0.85	d0.85	
23	Au	0.67	0.91	1.17	1.40	1.65	1.67
24	Dc	2.12	1.40	1.69	2.00	P1.77	1.77
25	Dc	3.18	3.51	3.85	3.90	P4.21	4.21
26	Oc	■d6.24	■▲d0.09	▲d1.36	*0.51	d3.83	d3.82
27	Ap	d0.05	d0.05	*0.03	d0.21	d0.24	d0.29
28	Ap	0.26	0.46	0.68	0.89	0.70	0.06
29	Dc	0.28	0.71	1.03	2.11	P1.45	1.45
30	Dc	▭⁷⁴4.17	△⁷³3.92	△⁷⁵2.02	2.40	3.11	3.11
31	Dc	b4.55	b3.87	2.57	b3.11	b3.76	....
32	Dc	b4.55	b3.87	b2.57	b3.11	b3.76	....
33	Dc	△*0.52	d0.81	d0.31	*Nil	P*d0.17	d0.17
34	Dc				b0.98	...	...
35	Mr	*0.03	d0.05	*0.18	0.50	...	0.60
36	Dc			Nil	d0.01	Pd0.09	d0.09
37	Dc	1.20	1.35	0.40	0.01	P1.01	1.01
38	Mr	*0.02	*0.01	*0.01	*0.03	...	0.02
39	Dc	d0.56 *d1.17	*d1.30	*1.43	1.37		
40	Dc	■d2.54	■3.02	■3.22	3.82	P4.46	4.46
41	Nv			*0.13	0.09	P0.45	0.49
42	Dc	2.11	2.15	1.52	1.74	2.51	2.51
43	Dc	1.27	1.44	0.88	■1.09	1.87	1.87
44	Mr	0.41	0.49	0.57	0.68	...	0.10
45	Dc	1.00	1.03	1.16	1.65	P2.20	2.20
46	Dc	▭1.53	△1.96	■2.01	2.55	P3.11	3.11

Interim Earnings — $ Per Shr.

Index	Period	1983	1984
1	9 Mo Sep	d1.60	d2.49
2	6 Mo Dec	d0.16	0.01
3			
4	3 Mo Dec	0.13	0.01
5			
6	9 Mo Sep	▲d0.65	■d2.14
7	3 Mo Dec	0.40	0.06
8			
9			
10			
11	9 Mo Sep	3.80	3.39
12			
13			
14			
15			
16			
17			
18			
19	9 Mo Feb△	0.36	0.88
20			
21	3 Mo Nov	0.38	0.40
22			
23			
24			
25			
26	3 Mo Jan△	*0.06	*0.05
27	6 Mo Oct	d0.11	d0.16
28	3 Mo Jan△	0.48	d0.16
29			
30			
31			
32			
33	Mand Red 10% fr 8-15-89		
34	9 Mo Dec	0.36	0.46
35			
36			
37			
38	9 Mo Dec	*0.02	*0.01
39	3 Mo Dec	0.06	Nil
40			
41	3 Mo Feb△	0.02	0.06
42			
43	9 Mo Dec	0.52	d0.06
44			
45			
46			

◆ **Stock Splits & Divs By Line Reference Index** ¹4-for-3,'81. ¹'82:5-for-4,'80,'83,'84. ²2-for-1,'82,'83. ³3-for-1,'81:5-for-4,'83,'84:10%,'81,'85. ⁴10%,'80,'81(ex'80):Adj to 5%,'85. ⁵07-for-5,'82. ¹¹4-for-1,'80. ¹⁴10%,'80:5-for-4,'81. ¹⁵Adj to 5%,'84. ¹⁷2-for-1,'84. ²⁰Adj to 4%,'84. ²²2-for-1,'81. ²³10%,'80,'83:2-for-1,'81(wi'80)'84(wi'83). ²⁴3-for-1,'80. ²⁶6-for-5,'80:2-for-1,'81:5-for-4,'82. ³⁵5-for-4,'85. ³⁷3-for-2,'83. ⁴⁰6-for-5,'81,'82:3-for-2,'84. ⁴²3-for-2,'84,'85. ⁴³2-for-1,'84. ⁴⁵Adj for 5%,'83(ex'82):10%,'80,'81,'83,'84. ⁴⁴5-for-4,'80:2-for-1,'81:6-for-5,'82:3-for-2,'83. ⁴⁵5-for-4,'82:2-for-1,'83.

Source: *Standard & Poor's Stock Guide*, April 1985.

of common stock for price appreciation and income, and provides name changes, new exchange listings, common stock rating changes, and a graph of Standard & Poor's Stock Price Indexes.

The *Bond Guide* is of the same format as the *Stock Guide*. It is a monthly publication in booklet form that presents data on corporate and convertible bonds. Figure 4–5 shows one page on corporate bonds with a long list of Texas Electric Service bonds at the top. The Standard & Poor's rating is presented along with the bond form (either a coupon or registered bond), refunding dates, call prices, sinking funds, yields, prices, and other information. Figure 4– 6 is one page of convertible bonds from the *Bond Guide*. Looking at Allied Stores, we see three convertible bonds having different coupons, interest payment dates, and maturity. Again, the Standard & Poor's rating is given. All the conversion data is presented with bond prices and common stock prices. Can you find how many shares of common stock an investor will receive for each $1,000 bond of Allied Stores having a 9½ percent coupon and a maturity of 2007?[1]

One of the more popularly used Standard & Poor's publications is the *Corporate Reports*. These reports are often mailed out from brokerage houses to customers who want basic information on a company. In Figure 4–7, Texas Instruments provides a good example of what one would expect to find in such reports. This information can be compared to the entry in Figure 4–4, line 21, for Texas Instruments to see the difference in the depth of coverage between the *Corporate Reports* and the *Stock Guide*. The *Corporate Reports* are contained in three separate multiple-volume sets, the New York Stock Exchange Stocks, American Stock Exchange Stocks, and Over-the-Counter and Regional Stocks. Each company is updated quarterly with new earnings, dividends, and recent developments. About 1,020 NYSE stocks are selected and bound in an annual publication called the Standard & Poor's *Stock Market Encyclopedia*, which contains end-of-the-year *Corporate Reports*. To develop an appreciation for the other Standard & Poor's services, try perusing this material at your library.

Value Line

Value Line Investment Survey is a publication of Arnold Bernhard & Co. It is one of the most widely used investment services by individuals, stockbrokers, and small bank trust departments. The *Value Line Investment Survey* follows 1,700 companies, and each common stock is covered in a one-page summary (see the one for Texas Instruments in Figure 4–8). Value Line is noted for its comprehensive coverage, which can be seen by comparing Figure 4–8 to Figures 4–4 and 4–7. Raw financial data is available as well as trendline growth rates, price history patterns in graphic form, quarterly sales, earnings and dividends, and a breakdown of sales and profit margins by line of business.

---

[1] The answer is 25 shares.

FIGURE 4–5 Page from *Standard & Poor's Bond Guide* (corporate bonds)

CORPORATE BONDS

Title-Industry Code & Co. Finances (In Italics) Individual Issue Statistics Exchange Interest Dates	I n d	Chgs. 1982	S&P Quality Rating	Eligible Bond Form	-Legality- M a N	N Y	Cash &Eqv Current Assets Liabs Date Million $	Redemption Provisions Refund Earliest/ Other	Call For S.F.	Price-Reg ular	L.Term Debt (Mill $) Out-std'g (Mill$)	Underwriter Firm Year	Debt % Prop	Period 1972-83 High Low	Times Earn. 1983 1984	Price Range 1984 High Low	1985 High Low	Mo. End Price Sale(s) or Bid	Yield Curr to Yield Mat.
Texas El Sv 1st 7¼s 2001	Ao		A+	X R	√		.....	101.21	104.69		25.0	K1 '71		102⅜ 49⅜	68⅜ 57⅜	69 64¼	64¼ 64¼	11.63 12.75
1st 7⅞s 2002	Jj		A+	X R	√√√		.....	101.24 ±104.50			30.0	F2 '72		101⅞ 55⅜	65 54¼	65⅜ 61⅜	61⅜ 61⅜	11.61 12.76
1st 8⅜s 2004	Ao		A+	X R	√√√		.....	101.17 ±106.20			40.0	B9 '74		109⅝ 55⅞	74⅜ 62⅜	75¾ 70¾	70¾ 70¾	12.23 12.79
1st 9⅝s 2004	jD		A+	X R	√√√		.....	100 106.07			60.0	B9 '74		112 60⅜	80⅜ 63⅜	81¼ 76¾	76¾ 76¾	12.44 12.81
1st 8⅞s 2005	Jd		A+	X R	√√√		.....	2.00 ±105.78			50.0	B9 '75		112 56⅜	75⅜ 63⅜	76¼ 71¾	71¾ 71¾	12.39 12.84
1st 8⅞s 2006	Ms		A+	X R	√√√		.....	±101.20 ±107.04			75.0	F2 '76		112 59⅞	75⅜ 63⅜	76⅜ 71⅜	71⅜ 71⅜	12.43 12.84
1st 9⅝s 2009	Fa		A+	X R	√√√		.....	2.00 ±106.98			75.0	B9 '79		101⅜ 59⅜	79⅜ 66⅜	80⅜ 74¾	74¾ 74¾	12.69 12.91
1st 14⅜s 2010	Ms		A+	X R	√√√		1112.54	2.00 ±111.28			75.0	B10 '81		121⅜ 83⅜	114⅜ 95⅜	116⅜ 108⅜	108¼ 108¼	13.00 12.95
1st 15⅜s 2011	jD		A+	X R	√√√		2112.27	100 ±113.80			50.0	D2 '81		121⅞ 95⅜	118⅜ 95⅜	116⅜ 112⅜	112⅜ 112⅜	14.06 14.01
1st 16s 2012	Ao		A+	X R	√√√		2112.27	2.00 113¾			75.0	D2 '82		121⅜ 97⅜	117⅜ 104⅜	116⅜ 116¼	113⅜ 113⅜	14.14 14.10
1st 11⅜s 2012	jD		A+	X R	√√		3108¾	2.00 ±109.90			75.0	G2 '82		99⅜ 89⅜	95⅜ 80⅜	96⅜ 89¾	89¾ 89¾	12.95 12.99
SF Deb 6⅝s '93	Fa		A+	X CR	√√			100.47 ±102.20	537	9.84	7.65	K2 '68		99⅜ 53⅜	74 63⅜	74¾ 71	71 71	9.31 12.51
• Texas Gas Transmission⁴	73a	3.27	A+	3.46	Dc		11.8	649			233	30.0		9 Mo Sep	3.35 4.33				8.28 11.50
SF Deb 7⅜s '86	aO		A+	X R	√√√			•.00 100			30.0	D3 '76		102⅜ 77⅜	95⅜ 91⅜	95 94	90¾ 95¾	8.28 11.50
SF Deb 6⅜s '87	ao		A+	X R	√√√			•.00 100.72			10.5	D3 '67		89⅜ 62⅜	90⅜ 82⅜	91 90⅜	90⅜ 90⅜	7.19 11.66
SF Deb 9⅜s '90	⁶jd		A+	X R	√√√			•.00 101.92			15.9	D3 '70		91⅜ 69⅜	91⅜ 81⅜	92⅜ 91⅜	91 91	10.44 11.94
SF Deb 12⅜s '90	fA15		A+	X R	√√√		7101.57	•.00 104.71			18.0	D3 '80		103⅜ 78⅜	100⅜ 92⅜	100⅜ 98⅜	98⅜ 98⅜	12.26 12.41
SF Deb 9⅝s '90	jJ		A+	X R	√√√			8.00 ±102.43			18.0	D3 '70		103⅜ 70⅜	91⅜ 81⅜	93 93	90⅜ 90⅜	10.76 12.13
SF Deb 8⅛s '91	Jj		A+	X R	√√√			•.00 ±102.01			16.9	D3 '71		105⅜ 62	83⅜ 73⅜	84⅜ 82⅜	82⅜ 82⅜	9.83 12.30
SF Deb 13s '92	Mn		A+	X R	√√√		10100	10100 110			100	D3 '81		114⅜ 93⅜	110⅜ 101⅜	111⅜ 108⅜	109 109	13.76 13.01
• Texas Industries	13a	1.66	A+	2.13	1.77 Mj		21.4	126	50.1 11.84		137	64.0		6 Mo Nov	2.02 2.46				10.60 13.50
• Sub SF Deb 7⅞s '92	mN15	5.35	B+	Y R	7.46 Dc			100	14½ 12.84		12 15.0	D3 '72		76⅜ 50	76⅜ 64	75 72½	72½ 73¾	10.60 13.50
• Texas Instruments	24b		AA-	3.46				1858	1412		388	26.2		9 Mo Sep			No Sale		
SF Deb 4.80s '86	mN		AA-	X R	√√√			•.00 101			10.1	M8 '65		78 48⅜	68 48⅜	71 71	70 70	6.86 12.40
SF Deb 12.70s 2005	Fa		A+	X R	√√√		13102½	14.00 105¾			200	M8 '80		110 78⅜	101⅜ 78⅜	102⅜ 98	100 100	12.70 12.70
• Texas Intl Airlines¹⁵	4	0.08	D	d1.66	De		File bankruptcy Chapt 11				ⁱ⁶882		64.0	9 Mo Sep	d2.22 1.35				Flat
Sub SF Deb 10¾s '98	§Ao15	Z		d1.27	√		Default 10.15-83 int				17.6	S6 '78		100 35	57 38	71½ 54½	69%		Flat
• Texas International	49b	1.27	CCC	R	√		12.2	55.0	54.5 9.84		346	140		9 Mo Sep	d0.38 0.58		65 65	65 65	13.85 15.98
• Sr Sub Oil Ind N¹⁰ 9s '95	aO		CCC	√	22.		23100	24.00 100			50.0	D7 '83		103⅜ 100	70 70	65 61	62%	21.13 23.79
• Sr Sub Nts 13⅞s '93	jJ15		CCC	√			25100	24.00 100			100	D7 '83		95⅜ 85	90 70	58 46	§52¾ 52%	21.75 23.33
• SubSFDeb('77) 11⅝s '97	Ao		CCC	Y R	√√√		25100	25.00 102.30			12 30.0	D7 '77		107⅜ 60	76 46	58 46	s52¾	21.75 23.33
• SubSFDeb('78) 11⅛s '97	Ao		CCC	Y R	√√√			25.00 102.30			20.0	D7 '78		97⅜ 66	77⅜ 49	57⅜ 47½	52%	21.75 23.33
• Texas & Pacific RR	A6			Assumed by Southern Pacific Trans, see							39.3	F2 '46		70 35	57⅜	No Sale	69%	4.87 11.66
• 1st & Ref C 3⅜s '90	A4	1.98	BBB	X CR	V	√		104⅜	51.4 100¾		98.6	38.3		12 Mo Sep	2.28 2.36				
*Texas-New Mexico Pwr*³⁴	72a		A	X R	√	Dc		43.5	373⁷ 11.84			22.2					No Sale	69%	4.87 11.66
1st G²⁷ 4.70s '93	jJ		A	X CR	√√√			±100.74 ±101.70			10.4	S1 '63		69⅜ 40⅜	76⅜ 51⅜	62⅜ 61⅜	60 60	7.82 12.61
1st J²⁸ 4.95s '95	Ms		A	X CR	√√√			±100.43 ±101.92			4.13	S1 '65		70⅜ 43⅜	57⅜ 48⅜	56⅜ 56	56 56	8.80 12.65
1st J²⁹ 6.075s '96	Mn		A	X CR	√√√			±100.36 ±103.59			8.58	S1 '66		82⅜ 44⅜	63⅜ 53⅜	63¾ 61	61 61	9.94 12.70
1st J³⁰ 7.99s '99	aO		A	X R	√√√			±100.44 ±101.54			8.58	S1 '69		110⅜ 56⅜	78⅜ 66⅜	79 75¾	75¾ 75¾	11.94 12.77
1st K 8⅞s 2001	Mn		A	X R	√√√			±101.35 ±105.60			7.04	S1 '71		107⅜ 52⅜	73⅜ 70⅜	74¾ 70¾	70% 70%	11.99 12.81
1st M 8.70s 2006	mS		A	X R	√√√		30100	100 ±106.30			9.30	S1 '76		104⅜ 52⅜	71⅜ 60⅜	73⅜ 69%	69% 69%	12.50 12.91
1st N 15⅝s '91	mN		A	X R	√√√		31110.60	100 ±110.17			15.0	S1 '81		113⅜ 94⅜	102⅜ 97⅜	114⅜ 111½	105% 105%	12.88 12.81
1st O 13⅜s 2013	jD		A	X R	√√√		32115.40	100 ±111.66			14.9	S4 '83		104⅜ 97⅜	101⅜ 85⅜	104 100⅜	102% 101%	12.82 12.86
1st P 13s 2013	mS	4.12	A	6.26	√√	Au	32.00	373⁷ 11.84			100	'83		100 96	101 96	103 99%	101%	12.82 12.81
Texas Oil & Gas	73c		AA	R			8.40	404	373⁷ 11.84		678	22.2						
• 1st C 7⅛s '92	Fa		AA	X R	√√			100 ±101½			15.9	K2 '72		101 No Sale	76⅜ 73	81¾ 80	79¾ 79¾	9.43 11.97
• 1st D 7⅜s '92	mN15		NR	X R	√√			100 ±101½			1.54	K2 '72		58⅜ 58½		77¾ 71⅜	77%	9.63 11.99
• 1st E 8⅞s '94	Fa		AA	X R	√√			100 ±104.04			19.0	K2 '74		108⅜ 73⅜	86 78	No Sale	77%	10.43 12.17
• 1st F 10⅜s '95	Mn		AA	X R	√√		33104	100 ±104.60			32.1	K2 '75		108⅜		88½ 87¾	90%	11.33 11.89

Uniform Footnote Explanations—See Page 1. Other: ¹Red rest'n(15.907%)to 12-1-86. ²Red rest'n(16.109%)to 4-1-87. ³Red rest'n(11.701%)to 12-1-87. ⁴Subsid of Texas Gas Resources(CSX Corp).
⁵Due Jun 1. ⁶Due Apr 1. ⁷Red rest'n(12.324%)to 8-15-88. ⁸Fr 8-15-87. ⁹Due Oct 1. ¹⁰Red rest'n(12.34%)to 11-15. ¹¹Red rest'n(15.184%)to 5-1-89. ¹²Fr 5-1-90. ¹³Incl disc. ¹⁴Red rest'n(12.7%)to 2-1-90. ¹⁴Fr 2-1-91.
¹⁵Subsid of Continental Airlines Corp. ¹⁶Incl Chapt 11 liabs. ¹⁷Red rest'n(10 7/8%)to 4-15-88. ¹⁸Fr 4-15-88. ¹⁹Indexed Prin Amt(IPA)due 10-1-95,as defined.
²⁰Hldr's rept'n opt on es SF red date,as defined. ²¹Red for SF fr 10-1-86 at IPA,as defined. ²²Red if IPA equals/exceeds $2,000,as defined. ²³Red rest'n(6 1/4%)to 7-15-88. ²⁴Fr 7-15-89.
²⁵Red rest'n(11 1/2%)to 4-1-87. ²⁶Subsid of TNP Enterprises. ²⁷Int incr fr 4 1/2%,7/1/74. ²⁸Int incr fr 4 3/4%,8/1/74. ²⁹Int incr fr 5 7/8%,11/1/74. ³⁰Red rest'n(15.4%)to 11-1-88.
³¹Red rest'n(13 1/4%)to 12-1-87. ³²Red rest'n(13%)to 9-1-88. ³³Red rest'n(10.28%)to 5-1-85.

Source: *Standard & Poor's Bond Guide*, April 1985.

II

FIGURE 4–6 Page from *Standard & Poor's Bond Guide* (convertible bonds)

STANDARD & POOR'S CORPORATION

CONVERTIBLE BONDS — Issue, Rate, Interest Dates and Maturity	S&P Quality Rating	B F o o d m	Oustdg. Mil.$	Conv. Ex-pires	Shares per $1,000 Bond	Price per Share	Div. Income per Bond	1985 RANGE Hi	Lo	Curr Bid Sale(s) Ask(A)	Curr. Return	Yield to Mat	Stock Value of Bond	Conv. Parity	STOCK DATA Curr. Price	P/E Ratio	Yr. End	1983	1984	Last 12 Mos	1983 Dil-u't'n
[1]Acapulco Y LA Rest. 13⅞s Qjul 1996	NR	R	9.99	1996	108.70	9.20	‑	84	83	84	16.0	16.6	47¾	7%	4¾	15	Dc	✸□2.05	✸0.25	0.29	n/r
●AccuRay Indus[2] 5⅝s Jd 1991	B–	R	11.2	1991	27.87	35.88	5.57	75	72	72	7.64	12.0	55%	25%	19%	12	Dc	1.31	P1.64	1.64	n/r
●Action Indus 9s Ao 1998	NR	R	1.95	1998	101.32	9.87	‑	185	98¾	111¼	8.07	7.59	111¾	25%	◆19%	20	E	1.28	◆0.44	d0.54	n/r
●Advest Group 9s Mn15 2008	NR	R	27.5	2008	60.90	16.42	7.31	88⅛	70	80¾	8.12	11.4	111%	13%	◆.9¾	11	Sp	1.61	●0.10?d0.09		n/r
●Aeroflex Labs 9¾s Ms15 2005	B–	R	25.0	2005	66.67	15.00	‑	100	99	99	9.47	9.48	79%	14%	●11%	11	Je	0.91	0.96	1.04	n/r
Aeronca,Inc 8⅞s Fa 1993	NR	R	10.0	1993	170.21	5.875	‑	129½	112¾	127¾	9.79	7.73	127%	7%	●7%	13	Dc	✸▲0.63	P▲0.58	✸0.58	✸0.50
●AFG Indus 8⅞s Ao 2005	BBB–	R	40.0	2005	39.49	25.32	‑	100	100	100	8.38	8.38	84%	25%	21%	13	Dc	1.43	P1.82	1.82	‑1.93
●Alaska Airlines 9s mN15 2003	BBB	R	25.0	2003	55.17	18.125	7.72	119	101	s118¾	7.58	7.16	108%	21%	●19%	9	Dc	1.45	2.19	2.19	‑1.93
Alaska Airlines'B' 9s mN15 2003	BBB	R	10.0	2003	55.15	18.125	7.72	117¾	100¾	100%	8.31	8.13	108%	21%	●19%	9	Dc	1.45	2.19	2.19	‑1.93
●Alco Standard 9s mS30 2007	BBB+	R	50.0	2007	27.03	37.00	32.44	109¾	93	109	8.20	8.05	93%	40%	34%	12	Sp	2.70	2.85	2.95	2.77
Alco Standard 8¼s Ms31 2010	BBB+	R	60.0	2010	22.99	43.50	27.59	100¾	99¾	100%	8.48	8.47	79%	43%	●34%	12	Sp	2.70	2.85	2.95	2.77
●Alexander & Alex Sv 11s Ao15 2007	BBB+	R	74.4	2007	25.64	39.00	25.64	103	91¾	103	10.6	10.6	79%	40%	●31	12	Dc	●NiP	▲d1.92	d1.92	0.88
●Alexander's 5⅝s Jj 1996	B	R	16.4	1996	31.01	32.25	‑	83	74¾	s79%	6.90	8.39	69%	25%	●22%	19	Jl	1.03	◆0.89	1.19	0.88
●Allegheny Beverage 6⅞s tA 1988	B	R	1.44	1988	190.11	5.26	76.04	430¾	309	373%	1.68	…..	373%	19%	●19%	19	Ja	1.74	‑	1.03	1.67
Allied Stores 4¾s Ms15 1992	NR	R	0.76	1992	44.94	22.25	95.27	256	231½	257%	1.75	…..	257%	57%	●57%	9	Ja	6.15	P6.71	6.71	5.98
Allied Stores 5¾s mN 2007	A–	R	124	2007	40.00	53.00	38.82	146¾	125	143%	6.64	5.99	143%	57%	●57%	9	Ja	6.15	P6.71	6.71	5.98
Allied Stores 8¾s Jj15 2009	A–	R	125	2009	18.31	54.625	‑	116	104	s114%	7.64	7.44	104%	62%	●57%	9	Ja	6.15	P6.71	6.71	5.98
●Amer Adventure[4] 10s Ao 1998	CCC	R	12.3	1998	86.96	11.50	‑	113	95	95	10.5	10.7	90%	14%	10%	4	Sp	1.32	P2.31	2.41	1.62
Amer Brn Ins Gr(3"91) 9¾s jD 2004	BBB	R	635.0	2004	50.25	13.65	36.63	108	102¾	104	9.38	9.30	93%	14%	10%	9	Dc	●1.42	P▲1.49	1.49	n/r
[7]Amer Can Int'l[8] 4¾s Mn15 1988	NR	R	30.0	1988	717.76	56.30	51.50	No Sale		94%	5.01	6.59	94%	53%	●.53	11	Dc	✸4.08	P4.74	4.74	4.50
●Amer Cap Bd Fd('83x0)[10] 11.35s[11]Jj 1990	AAA	R	50.0	1995	52.08	19.20	114.58	102¾	100	97	11.7	12.2	143%	18%	●18%		Je	✸▲1.10	▲✸1.97	0.45	1.80
[13]Amer Century Corp[12] 7s Ao 1990	NR	R	61.67	1990	76.39	13.09	‑	100	65½	78	8.97	13.1	67%	10%	●8%	20	E	✸▲1.10	▲✸1.97	0.45	1.80
[13]Amer Century Tr 6¾s Jd15 1991	NR	R	68.41	1991	39.87	25.08	39.78	77	64¾	71	9.51	13.8	35%	17%	●8%	20	E	✸▲1.10	▲✸1.97	0.45	1.80
●Amer[14]Gen'l 5⅝s mS 1987	A+	R	1.90	1987	12.24	s181.70	39.78	88	88	s88	6.25	11.3	76%	71%	●62%	21	Dc	△3.00	△3.00	3.00	2.90
[7]Amer Gen'l 11s Fa8 2007	A+	R	128	2007	54.56	18.33	54.56	170¾	141½	158%	6.95	6.12	158%	29	●.29	10	Dc	△3.00	△3.00	3.00	2.90
●Amer Gen'l 11s mN4 2008	A+	R	176	2008	54.56	18.33	54.56	170¾	66½	s163	6.75	5.98	158%	29%	●.29	10	Dc	△3.00	△3.00	3.00	2.90
●Amer Hoist & Der 4¾s Jd 1992	NR	R	0.58	1992	63.86	15.66	18.00	66½	57¾	s65	7.14	11.8	65%	10%	●10%	d	Nv	d7.17	▲d3.57	d3.57	n/r
●Amer Hoist & Der 5⅞s Jd 1993	NR	R	6.21	1993	50.25	19.90	‑	65½	57¾	s65	8.46	12.4	51%	12%	●10%	d	Nv	d7.17	▲d3.57	d3.57	n/r
●Amer Int'l Group 4¾s jJ 1997	AAA	R	6.64	1997	36.63	27.30	16.12	285¾	238	268%	1.49	…..	268%	73%	●73%	17	Dc	●5.77	P4.27	4.27	7.03
●Amer Israeli Paper 11¾s AaN15 1997	NR	R	13.3	1997	58.58	17.07	‑	78¾	75	77	15.1	15.8	38%	13%	●6%	4	Mr	1.73	‑	1.73	n/r
●Amer Maize-Prod 11¾s fA 2000	BB+	R	25.0	2000	41.02	24.38	28.61	113	105	s115	11.0	10.9	86	19%	●.15%	8	Dc	0.73	P1.92	1.92	n/r
●Amer Medical Int'l 9½s mN15 2001	A–	R	125	2001	41.02	24.38	29.53	98½	81¾	s115	8.26	7.86	103%	28	●.25%	12	Au	2.05	1.64	2.04	n/r
●Amer Medical Int'l 8⅛s Ao 2008	NR	R	63.6	2008	43.00	40.00	18.00	82½	81¾	s86%	9.54	9.72	63%	34%	●.25%	12	Au	2.05	1.64	2.04	n/r
●American Motors 6s tA 1988	CCC	R	16.3	1988	133.69	7.48	‑	82½	78	s79	7.59	13.7	43%	5%	●.3%	d	Dc	d2.11	*Nil	▲Nil	n/r
[17]Amer Tobacco Int'l 5⅞s tA 1988	C	R	1.11	1988	s755.56	18.00	216.68	No Sale		385%	1.36	…..	385%	69%	●.69%	10	Dc	6.76	7.20	7.20	7.03
●Ames Dept Stores 8½s aO 2009	BB+	R	40.0	2009	29.74	33.625	5.95	120	102	s119%	7.11	6.84	105%	40%	●.35%	18	Ja	1.53	P2.00	2.00	n/r
●Amfac 5s Ms 1989	B+	R	11.6	1989	28.00	35.714	‑	77	72¾	73%	6.80	14.0	73%	26%	●.26%	d	Dc	d4.99	P0.93	d0.93	n/r
●Amfac 5⅝s Mn 1994	B+	R	24.3	1994	22.90	43.67	‑	82½	64	82%	6.36	7.99	60%	36	●.26%	d	Dc	d4.99	P0.93	d0.93	n/r
●Anacomp,Inc(Sr)[18] 10s jJ 1995	R		19.9	1995	250.00	4.00	‑	106¼	50	87%	…..	Flat	87%	3%	●.3%	d	Dc	19d0.38	▲d0.84	d7.07	n/r
●Anacomp,Inc.[20] 13⅞s Jj15 2002	CC	R	[23]23.2	2002	57.14	17.50	‑	72	54¼	s71	5.60	Flat	20	12%	●.3%	d	Sp	19d0.38	▲d0.84	d7.07	n/r
●Andal[21]Corp[22] 5⅞s mS15 1997	NR	R	2.27	1997	44.44	22.50	‑	47	44	46%	11.8	15.1	22%	10%	●.5	12	Dc	□1.35	P0.41	0.41	n/r
●Andersen Group 10¾s aO15 2002	NR	R	9.98	2002	61.84	16.17	‑	97	81¾	96	10.9	11.0	74%	15%	●.12		Dc	0.72	0.82	0.85	1.16
●Anixter Bros 8⅞s Jj 2003	BBB	R	42.0	2003	36.43	27.45	10.20	93¾	83¾	84%	9.79	10.1	56%	23%	●15%	18	Jl	▲1.72	P▲1.96	1.96	1.73
[24]Apache Corp 6s jJ 1990	B	R	2.40	1990	247.62	21.00	81.91	114¼	105¾	107%	5.60	4.46	107%	22%	●22%	6	Dc	2.45	P2.67	2.67	2.65

Uniform Footnote Explanations—See Page XVI. Other: [1]Now Acapulco Restaurants. [2]Was Ind'l Nucleonics. [3]Plan fiscal chge to Mar. [4]Was Great Outdoor Amer Adventure. [5]Hldr's rep't option on 12-1-91 at 110. [6]Incl disc. [7]Cv into & data of Amer Can. [8]Offered outside U.S. P&I pay in U.S.$. [9]Hldr's rep't option on 1-1-90. [10]Int thru 12-31-89,adj aft as defined. [11]Due 1-1-95. [12]Was Amer Century Mtg Inv. [13]Now Amer Century Corp;was Amer Century Mtg Inv. [14]Was Lincoln Amer. [15]Cv into $3.25 Cv Jr pfd. [16]Into Cl'A'. [17]Cv into & data of Amer Brands. [18]Co option to pay int in cash/com,as defined. [19]Fiscal Jun'83 & prior. [20]Int:1-15-84,pd 3-21-84;7-15-84,pd 8-15-84. [21]Was Nat'l Kinney. [22]Int 5 1/4% to 3-9-82. [23]Due Jan 31. [24]Cv into & data of Continental Telecom.

Source: *Standard & Poor's Bond Guide*, April 1985.

FIGURE 4–7   Sample pages, *Standard & Poor's Corporate Reports*

Texas Instruments   2208

NYSE Symbol TXN   Options on CBOE (Jan-Apr-Jul-Oct)

Price	Range	P-E Ratio	Dividend	Yield	S&P Ranking
Mar. 29'85	1985				
111¼	131¾- 105½	9	2.00	1.8%	A−

Summary

Texas Instruments is the leading producer of semiconductor products, and has important representation in other segments of the electronics industry, in geophysical exploration, and in specialty metal products. Following the strong gain in 1984, earnings for 1985 are expected to decline significantly, reflecting weakness in semiconductors in the first half of the year due to the recent industrywide slump. However, a pick-up in the semiconductor business is anticipated for the latter half of 1985.

Current Outlook

Earnings for 1985 are projected at $7.00 a share, down sharply from 1984's $13.05.

Dividends at $0.50 quarterly are the minimum expectation.

A modest sales decline is anticipated for 1985, reflecting a poor first half for semiconductors. That segment will continue to be affected by inventory adjustments by customers which has resulted in weak order levels. Profitability in semiconductors will be adversely affected by the lower sales volume and by declining prices. However, a much improved performance is seen for the second half. Digital products will be aided by new product introductions. Government electronics should benefit from a changing mix toward new weapons systems. Geophysical services are not expected to show much improvement, since that market has remained weak. Metallurgical materials should move with the economy. Long-term prospects appear favorable.

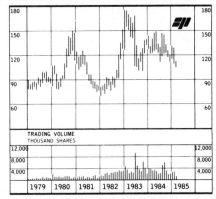

Net Sales (Million $)

Quarter:	1985	1984	1983	1982
Mar.	---	1,339	1,174	1,079
Jun.	---	1,464	1,100	1,093
Sep.	---	1,423	1,007	1,048
Dec.	---	1,516	1,299	1,107
	---	5,742	4,580	4,327

Sales for 1984 rose 25% from those of the preceding year, primarily reflecting strong gains in components. Results benefited from wider components margins and the absence of losses related to home computer operations. Net income equaled $316,000,000 ($13.05 a share), in contrast to a net loss of $145,400,000 ($6.09).

Common Share Earnings ($)

Quarter:	1985	1984	1983	1982
Mar.	E1.00	3.32	0.30	1.17
Jun.	E1.00	3.57	d5.00	1.56
Sep.	E2.25	3.54	d4.64	1.57
Dec.	E2.75	2.64	3.23	1.80
	E7.00	13.05	d6.09	6.10

Important Developments

Feb. '85—The company said that due to continued weakness in semiconductor markets worldwide, it would continue to reduced work schedules at its semiconductor plants through the first half of 1985. TXN added that the shortened work schedule would primarily affect overseas plants.

Next earnings report due in late April.

Per Share Data ($)

Yr. End Dec. 31[1]	1984	1983	1982	1981	1980	1979	1978	1977	1976	1975
Book Value	62.58	50.06	57.53	53.44	50.08	41.75	37.12	32.64	28.89	25.53
Earnings	13.05	d6.09	6.10	4.62	¹9.22	¹7.58	¹6.15	¹5.11	¹4.25	¹2.71
Dividends	2.00	2.00	2.00	2.00	2.00	2.00	1.76	1.41	1.08	1.00
Payout Ratio	16%	NM	33%	43%	22%	26%	29%	28%	25%	37%
Prices—High	149½	176	152½	126¼	150¾	101	92½	102¼	129¾	119⅜
Low	111¾	101	70½	75	78⅝	78	61⅜	68⅝	93⅛	61
P/E Ratio—	11–9	NM	25–12	27–16	16–9	13–10	15–10	20–13	31–22	44–23

Data as orig. reptd. 1. Ful. dil.: 9.04 in 1980, 7.52 in 1979, 6.12 in 1978, 5.10 in 1977, 4.23 in 1976, 2.70 in 1975. NM-Not Meaningful. d-Deficit. E-Estimated.

April 8, 1985   Standard & Poor's Corp.
25 Broadway, NY, NY 10004

FIGURE 4–7 *(concluded)*

2208

Texas Instruments Incorporated

Income Data (Million $)

Year Ended Dec. 31	Revs.	Oper. Inc.	% Oper. Inc. of Revs.	Cap. Exp.	Depr.	Int. Exp.	Net Bef. Taxes	Eff. Tax Rate	Net Inc.	% Net Inc. of Revs.
1984	5,742	948	16.5%	¹705	423	48.9	487	35.0%	316	5.5%
1983	4,580	63	1.4%	¹454	351	36.0	d323	NM	d145	NM
1982	4,327	574	13.3%	¹329	339	33.1	213	32.4%	144	3.3%
1981	4,206	586	13.9%	¹341	333	41.3	175	38.0%	109	2.6%
1980	4,075	676	16.6%	548	257	44.3	379	44.0%	212	5.2%
1979	3,224	507	15.7%	435	187	19.5	309	44.0%	173	5.4%
1978	2,550	385	15.1%	311	131	8.4	257	45.5%	140	5.5%
1977	2,046	319	15.6%	200	108	9.2	211	44.7%	117	5.7%
1976	1,659	250	15.1%	138	87	8.3	178	45.3%	97	5.9%
1975	1,368	207	15.1%	71	92	10.8	116	46.4%	62	4.5%

Balance Sheet Data (Million $)

Dec. 31	Cash	Current Assets	Current Liab.	Ratio	Total Assets	Ret. on Assets	Long Term Debt	Common Equity	Total Cap.	% LT Debt of Cap.	Ret. on Equity
1984	274	1,858	1,412	1.3	3,423	10.2%	381	1,541	1,921	19.8%	22.8%
1983	185	1,452	1,231	1.2	2,713	NM	225	1,203	1,428	15.8%	NM
1982	420	1,527	959	1.6	2,631	5.8%	214	1,361	1,575	13.6%	11.0%
1981	150	1,197	765	1.6	2,311	4.6%	212	1,260	1,472	14.4%	8.9%
1980	140	1,299	971	1.3	2,414	9.7%	212	1,165	1,376	15.4%	19.9%
1979	117	1,083	882	1.2	1,908	10.1%	18	953	970	1.8%	19.2%
1978	115	915	637	1.4	1,518	10.1%	19	845	864	2.2%	17.7%
1977	257	815	467	1.7	1,255	9.8%	30	745	774	3.8%	16.6%
1976	294	783	418	1.9	1,128	9.4%	38	660	698	5.5%	15.7%
1975	267	663	302	2.2	941	6.5%	48	585	633	7.5%	11.0%

Data as orig. reptd. 1. Net of curr. yr. retirement and disposals. NM-Not Meaningful. d–Deficit.

Business Summary

Texas Instruments produces a variety of electrical and electronics products for industrial, consumer and government markets. Contributions by industry segment in 1984:

	Sales	Profits
Components	46%	79%
Digital products	19%	Nil
Government electronics	24%	24%
Metallurgical materials	3%	2%
Services	8%	–5%

Operations outside the U.S. accounted for 29% of sales and 48% of operating profits in 1984.

Components include semiconductor integrated circuits (microprocessors, memories and digital and linear circuits), semiconductor discrete devices (transistors, and optoelectronic products), assembled modules (microprocessor and memory printed circuit boards), and electrical and electronic control devices.

Digital products include minicomputers, electronic data terminals and peripherals, geophysical and scientific equipment, electronic calculators, learning aids and other products. In October, 1983 the company withdrew from the consumer home computer business.

Government electronics products include radar, infrared surveillance systems and missile guidance and control systems.

Metallurgical materials primarily involve clad metals which are used in variety of applications.

Services mainly consist of the collection and electronic processing of seismic data in connection with petroleum exploration.

Dividend Data

Dividends have been paid since 1962.

Amt. of Divd. $	Date Decl.	Ex-divd. Date	Stock of Record	Payment Date
0.50	Jun. 15	Jun. 19	Jun. 25	Jul. 30'84
0.50	Sep. 28	Oct. 2	Oct. 9	Oct. 29'84
0.50	Dec. 20	Dec. 26	Jan. 2	Jan. 28'85
0.50	Mar. 22	Mar. 26	Apr. 1	Apr. 29'85

Next dividend meeting: mid-Jun. '85.

Capitalization

Long Term Debt: $380,700,000.

Common Stock: 24,670,380 shs. ($1 par).
Institutions hold about 74%.
Shareholders of record: 30,701.

Office— 13500 North Central Expressway, Dallas, Texas 75265. Tel—(214) 995-3773. Chrmn—M. Shepherd, Jr. Pres & CEO—J. F. Bucy. VP-Secy—R. J. Agnich. VP-Treas—W. A. Aylesworth. Investor Contact—M. Post. Dirs—H. W. Bell, J. F. Bucy, D. C. Garrett, Jr., S. T. Harris, D. C. Harvey, J. R. Junkins, E. R. Kane, P. F. Lorenz, P. W. McCracken, M. Shepherd, Jr., C. J. Thomsen, J. C. Toomay, J. M. Voss, W. P. Weber. Transfer Agents & Registrars—RepublicBank, Dallas; Morgan Guaranty Trust Co., NYC. Incorporated in Delaware in 1938.

FIGURE 4–8 *The Value Line Investment Survey*

Value Line contains 13 sections divided into several industries each. The first few pages beginning an industry classification are devoted to an overview of the industry, with the company summaries following. Each section is revised on a 13-week cycle.

Value Line has a unique evaluation system that is primarily dependent on historical relationships and regression analysis. From the valuation model, each company is rated 1 through 5, with 1 being the highest positive rating and 5 the lowest. Each company is rated on timeliness and safety. It should be noted that Value Line minimizes human judgment in making its evaluation, which is consistently mechanical from period to period.

The *Investment Survey* of Value Line also contains some information and advice on put and call options. This is updated weekly as are the stock rankings of the total sample. Data on options are presented in Figure 4–9. Value Line also publishes a separate *Options and Convertible Bond Survey*, which analyzes and recommends action on convertibles based on the underlying common stock, interest rate movements, and related market behavior. Other Value Line publications are *Special Situations, OTC Stocks*, and the *New Issue Service*.

Other Investment Services

Dun & Bradstreet publishes *Key Business Ratios* in bound form. This publication contains 14 significant ratios on 800 different lines of business listed by SIC (standard industrial classification) code. Examples of ratios included are current assets to current debt, net profits on net sales, and total debt to tangible net worth. This publication has replaced the old Dun & Bradstreet 11-page pamphlet on key business ratios for 125 lines of business. Another good source of ratios is Robert Morris Associates, which provides ratios on over 150 industry classifications.

Dun's Marketing Services division of Dun & Bradstreet also publishes the *Million Dollar Directory* and *Billion Dollar Directory*. Companies are listed in alphabetical order, by geographical location by city and state, and by product classification. The data provide names, addresses and phone numbers, and sales for each company. This could be helpful in identifying companies in the same industry or in writing to request such information as annual reports or product lists.

Another publication is the *Dow Jones–Irwin Business Almanac*. Almost everyone has looked through an almanac at some time and probably remembers being overwhelmed by all the facts and figures. This almanac is no exception. For our specific purposes, there is a section on finance and accounting which covers key business ratios, financial statement ratios by industry, and corporate profits and margins. A section on the stock market covers over 100 pages and includes market averages, mutual funds, dividends, common stock prices and yields, and much more. Information on commodities, banks, financial institutions, economic data, and a great deal more is contained in this 600-page business almanac.

FIGURE 4–9

OPTIONS—RELEVANT INFORMATION FOR BUYERS AND WRITERS

Ratings & Reports Page No.	Stock Name	Stock Ticker Symbol	Where Option Trades	Recent Stock Price	Timeliness (3-6 mos.)	Technical	Safety	Stability Index	Beta	P/E Ratio	Est'd Div'd Yield (next 12 mos)	Industry Group	Industry Rank
980	Colgate-Palmolive	CL	CBO	25	▲3	3	1	85	0.80	12.6	5.1	Household Products	89
1310	Colt Ind., Inc.	COT	PHL	57	2	3	3	50	0.95	8.4	4.6	Machinery	43
1311	Combustion Eng.	CSP	PAC	33	4	3	3	55	1.15	14.7	5.6	Machinery	43
2050	Comdisco, Inc.	CDO	PAC	15	2	3	4	5	1.45	8.6	1.3	Financial Services (Div)	1
1090	Commodore Int'l	CBU	PHL	10	5	5	4	5	1.55	10.5	NIL	Computer And Peripherals	64
708	Commonwealth Edison	CWE	CBO	30	3	2	3	95	0.65	6.7	10.7	Electric Util. (Central)	37
763	Communic. Satellite	CQ	PHL	32	▲2	2	3	50	1.05	9.2	3.9	Telecommunications	36
1278	Community Psych Ctrs.	CMY	PHL	34	1	2	3	30	1.45	23.8	0.7	Medical Services	3
2105	Computer Sciences	CSC	CBO	15	3	3	3	30	1.00	9.4	NIL	Computer Software & Svcs	48
1092	Computervision Corp	CVN	PHL	16	5	3	3	15	1.60	16.0	NIL	Computer And Peripherals	64
188	Consol. Edison	ED	ASE	33	▼4	1	1	100	0.65	7.9	7.5	Electric Utility (East)	42
764	Cont'l Telecom Inc.	CTC	ASE	23	4	2	2	95	0.75	8.1	7.8	Telecommunications	36
1093	Control Data	CDA	CBO	30	4	4	3	40	1.45	16.0	2.4	Computer And Peripherals	64
1313	Cooper Ind.	CBE	ASE	31	3	3	3	45	1.25	13.5	5.0	Machinery	43
224	Coopervision Inc.	EYE	ASE	22	—	—	3	NMF	NMF	14.7	1.8	Medical Supplies	50
1006	Corning Glass Works	GLW	CBO	38	3	3	2	80	1.05	14.3	3.4	Electrical Equipment	44
1095	Cray Research	CYR	PAC	73	▲1	3	3	15	1.45	17.9	NIL	Computer And Peripherals	64
933	Crown Zellerbach	ZB	ASE	42	—	3	3	50	1.20	13.0	2.4	Paper & Forest Products	57
2106	Cullinet Software	CUL	CBO	27	1	3	3	20	1.60	28.4	NIL	Computer Software & Svcs	48
1469	Dart & Kraft Inc.	DKI	ASE	93	3	2	1	100	0.75	9.5	4.9	Food Processing	35
1096	Data General Corp.	DGN	PAC	39	4	3	3	15	1.40	18.5	NIL	Computer And Peripherals	64
1097	Datapoint Corp.	DPT	CBO	14	4	5	4	5	1.45	NMF	NIL	Computer And Peripherals	64
1098	Dataproducts Corp.	DPC	PAC	12	5	4	3	15	1.70	9.6	1.3	Computer And Peripherals	64
1650	Dayton Hudson Corp.	DH	PAC	40	3	2	2	70	1.05	13.6	1.9	Retail Store	16
1433	Deere & Co.	DE	ASE	28	3	3	3	70	1.05	22.4	3.6	Agricultural Equip./Div.	55
257	Delta Air Lines	DAL	CBO	42	▼2	3	3	40	1.15	7.0	1.9	Air Transport	28
410	Diamond Shamrock	DIA	PAC	19	3	4	3	50	1.05	10.7	9.3	Petroleum (Integrated)	79
1125	Diebold, Inc.	DBD	CBO	40	3	3	3	55	1.00	8.5	2.6	Office Equipment&Supply	8
1099	Digital Equipment	DEC	ASE,CBO	103	3	3	2	50	1.25	14.3	NIL	Computer And Peripherals	64
1756	Disney (Walt) Prod.	DIS	ASE,CBO	79	2	3	3	60	0.90	16.6	1.5	Recreation	65
1221	Dome Mines	DM	PHL	9¼	5	4	4	10	1.35	33.2	2.2	Gold (No. American)	91
190	Dominion Resources	D	PHL	30	3	4	2	100	0.60	8.5	9.3	Electric Utility (East)	42
1242	Dow Chemical	DOW	CBO	30	3	4	2	80	1.20	12.6	6.0	Chemical (Basic)	76
1846	Dresser Ind.	DI	PHL	21	3	4	3	40	1.20	12.7	4.3	Oilfield Services	87
191	Duke Power	DUK	PHL	33	3	1	2	100	0.60	8.0	7.7	Electric Utility (East)	42
1791	Dun & Bradstreet	DNB	ASE	76	2	2	1	90	0.90	20.4	2.9	Publishing	6
1243	Du Pont	DD	ASE,CBO	58	▼4	3	2	80	1.15	11.6	5.3	Chemical (Basic)	76
154	EG & G, Inc.	EGG	PHL	38	3	3	3	40	1.30	17.8	1.3	Precision Instrument	25
557	E-Systems	ESY	PAC	30	2	3	3	40	1.20	14.7	1.9	Aerospace/Diversified	18
1877	Eastern Gas & Fuel	EFU	PHL	22	4	3	3	55	0.95	13.7	5.9	Coal & Uranium	80
155	Eastman Kodak	EK	CBO	67	3	3	1	95	0.85	11.3	5.6	Precision Instrument	25
785	Eckerd (Jack) Corp.	ECK	CBO	27	3	3	3	65	1.00	10.7	3.9	Drug Store	11
1183	Edwards (A.G.) Inc.	AGE	CBO	31	3	3	2	20	1.70	14.8	2.7	Securities Brokerage	30
1009	Emerson Electric	EMR	ASE	72	2	3	1	95	0.90	12.0	3.6	Electrical Equipment	44
259	Emery Air Freight	EAF	PHL	16	▼4	3	3	25	1.30	10.3	3.1	Air Transport	28
1894	Engelhard Corp.	EC	CBO	27	4	3	3	55	0.95	12.0	2.7	Chemical/Diversified	66
453	ENSERCH Corp.	ENS	PAC	26	3	3	3	55	1.10	15.8	6.2	Natural Gas(Diversified)	75
411	Exxon Corp.	XON	CBO	52	3	1	1	100	0.85	7.5	6.8	Petroleum (Integrated)	79
260	Federal Express	FDX	CBO	38	4	2	3	35	1.40	22.2	NIL	Air Transport	28
1156	Federal Nat'l Mtg.	FNM	PHL	16	3	3	4	20	1.45	NMF	1.0	Savings & Loan	10
1157	Fin'l Ccrp. Of America	FIN	PHL	6½	3	5	5	5	1.85	NMF	NIL	Savings & Loan	10
130	Firestone Tire	FIR	ASE	20	3	3	3	60	0.95	10.0	4.0	Tire & Rubber	58
1184	First Boston Inc.	FBC	CBO	68	2	2	3	30	1.35	8.7	3.4	Securities Brokerage	30
650	First Chicago Corp.	FNB	CBO	25	4	3	3	50	1.05	6.7	5.3	Bank (Midwest)	13
1896	First Mississippi	FRM	ASE	9⅛	▼3	3	5	20	1.35	8.5	3.0	Chemical/Diversified	66
1560	Fleetwood Enterprises	FLE	ASE	22	3	3	3	20	1.35	10.4	1.7	Manu Housing/Rec Veh	31
870	Fluor Corp.	FLR	CBO	19	▲3	3	3	35	1.35	NMF	2.1	Building	32
105	Ford Motor	F	CBO	43	3	3	3	45	1.15	3.0	5.8	Auto & Truck	9
1367	Foster Wheeler	FWC	PAC	14	▲3	3	4	35	1.20	13.9	3.1	Machinery(Const.&Mining)	53
1223	Freeport McMoRan	FTX	CBO	21	3	4	3	25	1.40	13.5	2.9	Metals & Mining(General)	62
1897	GAF Corp.	GAF	PHL	32	1	2	3	35	1.00	10.6	0.6	Chemical/Diversified	66
158	GCA Corp.	GCA	ASE	25	3	3	4	10	1.60	10.7	NIL	Precision Instrument	25
766	GTE Corp.	GTE	ASE	41	3	3	1	95	0.90	7.8	7.6	Telecommunications	36
561	Gen'l Dynamics	GD	CBO	70	▼2	3	3	40	1.30	7.1	1.6	Aerospace/Diversified	18
1015	Gen'l Electric	GE	CBO	61	3	3	1	95	1.00	11.2	3.8	Electrical Equipment	44
1475	Gen'l Foods	GF	CBO	64	4	1	1	95	0.80	10.4	4.1	Food Processing	35
1052	Gen'l Instrument	GRL	PHL	17	▼5	4	3	25	1.40	NMF	1.5	Electronics	84
107	Gen'l Motors	GM	CBO	70	3	3	2	80	1.10	6.0	7.1	Auto & Truck	9
1053	GenRad	GEN	PHL	17	5	4	4	10	1.45	17.0	0.6	Electronics	84
117	Genuine Parts Co.	GPC	PAC	33	3	3	1	80	0.90	14.0	3.3	Auto Parts (Rep)	82
1850	GEO Int'l	GX	ASE	4⅞	4	4	4	10	1.45	NMF	NIL	Oilfield Services	87
937	Georgia-Pacific	GP	PHL	23	3	3	3	50	1.40	8.9	3.5	Paper & Forest Products	57
1103	Gerber Scientific	GRB	PHL	18	▼2	3	4	5	1.85	11.3	0.7	Computer And Peripherals	64
818	Gillette	GS	ASE	62	3	2	1	90	0.80	11.5	4.2	Toiletries/Cosmetics	33
1851	Global Marine	GLM	ASE	4⅛	5	5	5	10	1.55	NMF	6.0	Oilfield Services	87
1774	Golden Nugget	GNG	ASE	12	2	3	4	10	1.50	16.7	NIL	Hotel/Gaming	41
1160	Golden West Fin'l	GDW	PHL	30	1	2	4	10	1.50	6.2	0.8	Savings & Loan	10
133	Goodyear Tire	GT	ASE	27	4	3	3	75	1.05	8.0	5.9	Tire & Rubber	58
1054	Gould Inc.	GLD	ASE	22	4	4	3	40	1.15	11.2	3.1	Electronics	84
1898	Grace (W. R.)	GRA	ASE	41	4	3	2	90	0.95	13.8	6.8	Chemical/Diversified	66
1161	G't Western Fin'l	GWF	CBO	27	2	3	3	20	1.50	8.0	3.3	Savings & Loan	10
1391	Greyhound Corp.	G	ASE	28	3	3	2	75	1.10	9.2	4.3	Multiform	38
438	Gulf Canada Ltd.	GOC	PHL	15	▲2	3	3	25	1.30	11.3	2.9	Canadian Energy	67
1392	Gulf & Western Ind.	GW	CBO	38	4	3	3	70	1.10	10.7	2.4	Multiform	38
2076	Hall (Frank B.) & Co.	FBH	ASE	26	3	3	3	55	0.90	14.7	3.8	Insurance (Diversified)	69
1852	Halliburton Co.	HAL	CBO	32	4	5	3	40	1.35	11.6	6.0	Oilfield Services	87
1055	Harris Corp.	HRS	ASE	25	▼4	4	3	55	1.10	10.8	3.5	Electronics	84
626	Hecla Mining	HL	ASE	17	4	4	4	10	1.30	NMF	NIL	Lead. Zinc & Mining	71
1245	Hercules Inc.	HPC	CBO	33	3	3	3	60	1.10	9.6	4.8	Chemical (Basic)	76
1104	Hewlett-Packard	HWP	CBO	34	3	3	2	55	1.30	13.9	0.7	Computer And Peripherals	64
1775	Hilton Hotels	HLT	PAC	68	—	2	3	75	1.00	16.0	2.6	Hotel/Gaming	41
1571	Hitachi Ltd. (ADR)	HIT	CBO	32	3	4	3	55	0.90	10.6	1.2	Foreign Stocks/Japanese	22
1776	Holiday Inns Inc.	HIA	CBO	54	▲1	3	3	55	1.20	13.5	1.9	Hotel/Gaming	41
1226	Homestake Mining	HM	CBO	25	3	3	3	25	1.20	46.3	0.8	Gold (No. American)	91
1105	Honeywell, Inc.	HON	CBO	57	3	3	2	65	1.20	8.7	3.6	Computer And Peripherals	64
1280	Hospital Corp Of Amer	HCA	PAC	42	2	3	3	55	1.25	10.9	1.4	Medical Services	3
2053	Household Int'l Inc.	HI	ASE	36	3	3	2	75	0.90	8.1	4.9	Financial Services (Div)	1

ASE—American Stock Exchange
CBO—Chicago Board Options Exchange
PAC—Pacific Stock Exchange
PHL—Philadelphia Stock Exchange

Weisenberger Services, Inc., publishes one of the best-known sources of information on mutual funds. The annual issue covers a 10-year statistical history (a sample page appears in Chapter 20) and is updated quarterly. Another publication which is like an investment service is the annual issue of The Individual Investor's Guide to No-Load Mutual Funds published by the American Association of Individual Investors.

Retail stockbrokers have long provided information to their clients. Of course, the more you can afford to pay and the bigger your account, the more research you may receive. Most large brokers, such as Merrill Lynch; Shearson Lehman/American Express; Bache; and E. F. Hutton, will provide investors information free and for a fee. You name what you want, and they have it—industry-company analysis, bond market analysis, futures and commodities, options advice, tax shelters in oil and gas and real estate, and so on. The brokerage industry provides much more sophisticated coverage of investments outside of stocks and bonds than they have in the past. This is partly because investors themselves have become more sophisticated in response to inflation and partly because of the increasing numbers and complexity of alternative investments.

INDEXES, SEC FILINGS, PERIODICALS, AND JOURNALS

Indexes

One way to find relevant articles in periodicals and journals is to use indexes. There are many that will lead an analyst to useful information. The *Business Periodicals Index* references subjects in approximately 170 periodicals in the fields of accounting, advertising, banking, communications, economics, finance, insurance, investments, labor management, marketing, taxation, and other specific topics. The *Funk and Scott Index of Corporations and Industries* indexes articles from over 750 publications in two volumes. Each article covered includes a brief description of the article's contents. The articles are taken from business, financial, and trade magazines, major newspapers, bank newsletters, and investment advisory services. One very popular index is *The Wall Street Journal Index,* which identifies the date, page, and column of articles appearing in *The Wall Street Journal.* The index is presented in two parts—corporate news and general news. Many libraries have several years of *The Wall Street Journal* on microfiche or microfilm. There are many other indexes, such as *Who's Who in Finance and Industry,* Dun & Bradstreet's *Reference Book of Corporate Management,* and Standard & Poor's *Register of Corporations, Directors and Executives.* These last three focus on people and can provide important qualitative information about management.

Securities and Exchange Commission Filings

As discussed in Chapter 2, the Securities and Exchange Commission (SEC) was established by the Securities Exchange Act of 1934 and has the power to regulate trading on the exchanges and to require corporate disclosure of information relevant to the stockholders of publically traded companies. The SEC even has the power to dictate accounting conventions such as the mandatory inflation-adjusted accounting statements required in corporate annual reports.

Information available through the SEC consists primarily of corporate income statements, balance sheets, detailed support of accounting information, and internal data not always found in a company's annual report. There are specific reports that companies are required to file with the SEC. The annual 10-K report is perhaps the most widely known and can usually be obtained free of charge directly from the company rather than paying the SEC a copying charge. This report should be read in combination with the firm's annual report as it contains the same type of information, but in greater detail. The 8-K report must be filed when the corporation undergoes some important event that stockholders would be interested in knowing about, such as: changes in control, bankruptcy, resignation of officers or directors, and other material events. 10-Q statements are filed quarterly no later than 45 days after the end of the quarter. This report includes quarterly financial statements, changes in stockholdings, legal procedings, and other matters.

There are many other SEC reports. The most common are proxy statements which disclose information relevant to stockholders' votes; a prospectus which must be issued whenever a new offering of securities is made to the public, and a registration trading statement which is required for new issues by firms trading on an organized exchange or over-the-counter. Figure 4–10 presents a detailed listing of information available from SEC filings, including reports required for tender offers and acquisitions. This table is taken from Disclosure Inc., a firm providing on-line computer access to SEC filings and other information sources to subscribers. These reports can be obtained from the Disclosure retrieval system at 37¢ a page with a one-business-day turnaround, or they can be ordered from the Securities and Exchange Commission at 10¢ per page with a seven-business-day turnaround.[2] They can also be read at the SEC regional office, where the corporation is headquartered, or in the SEC's regional New York, Chicago, or Los Angeles offices. A list of SEC addresses is given in Appendix 4–B at the end of this chapter.

Periodicals and Newspapers

After using the *Business Periodical Index,* an investor will most likely be referred to several of the most popular business periodicals, such as *Fortune, Business Week, Forbes, Dun's Business Month, Financial World,* and others. *Fortune* is published biweekly and is known for its coverage of industry problems and specific company analysis. *Fortune* has several regular features that make interesting reading. One, called "Business Roundup," usually deals with a major business concern, such as the federal budget, inflation, productivity, etc.

---

[2] The costs will obviously change over time.

FIGURE 4–10   Securities Exchange Commission Filings

REPORT CONTENTS	10-K	19-K 20-F	10-Q	8-K	10-C	6-K	Proxy Statement	Prospectus	Registration Statements '34 Act F-10 8-A 8-B	'33 Act "S" Type	ARS	Listing Application	N-1R	N-1Q
Auditor														
Name	A	A	■				■		A	A		A	A	
Opinion	A	A	■				■		A			A	A	
Changes				A			■							
Compensation Plans														
Equity	■		■				F	F	A	F		■	■	
Monetary	■						F	A	F			■	■	
Company Information														
Nature of Business	A	A				F	A	A	A		■			
History	F	A					A		A					
Organization and Change	F	F		A	■	F	F	A	A	F				
Debt Structure	A					F	A	A	A	A	A			
Depreciation & Other Schedules	A	A				F	A	A	A					
Dilution Factors	A	A		F		F	A	A	A	A				
Directors, Officers, Insiders														
Identification	F	A				F	A	A	A		A	F		
Background	■	A				F	F	A	■		A			
Holdings	■	A		■			A	A	A	A				
Compensation	■	A		■			A	A	A	A				
Earnings Per Share	A	A	A			F			A			A	A	
Financial Information														
Annual Audited	A	A							A		A		A	
Interim Audited		A					■			■				
Interim Unaudited	■		A			F	■	F		F	F			
Foreign Operations	A						■	A	A	A		F		
Labor Contracts									F	F				
Legal Agreements	F			■					F	F				
Legal Counsel								A	A			■		
Loan Agreements	F		F				■		F	F		■		
Plants and Properties	A	F		■			■	F	A	F				
Portfolio Operations														
Content (Listing of Securities)														A
Management												A		
Product-Line Breakout	A							A	A		■			
Securities Structure	A	A			■			A	A	A				
Subsidiaries	A	A						A	A	A				
Underwriting								A	A	A				
Unregistered Securities	■			■				F	F					
Block Movements	■			F			■		A			■		

TENDER OFFER/ACQUISITION REPORTS	13D	13 G	14D-1	14D-9	13E-3	13E-4
Name of Issuer (Subject Company)	A	A	A	A	A	A
Filing Person (or Company)	A	A	A	A	A	A
Amount of Shares Owned	A	A				
Percent of Class Outstanding	A	A				
Financial Statements of Bidders			F		F	F
Purpose of Tender Offer			A	A	A	A
Source and Amount of Funds	A		A		A	
Identity and Background Information			A	A	A	A
Persons Retained, Employed or to be Compensated			A	A	A	A
Exhibits	F		F	F	F	F

Legend

A-always included - included-if occured or significant   **F**-frequently included

■ special circumstances only

Source: "A Guide to SEC Corporate Filings," (Bethesda, Md.: Disclosure, Inc. April 1983), pp. 12–13.

Another feature, "Personal Investing," is always a thought-provoking article presenting ideas and analysis for the average investor.

Forbes is also a biweekly publication featuring several company-management interviews. This management-oriented approach points out various management styles and provides a look into the qualitative factors of security analysis. There are several regular columnists who discuss investment topics from a diversified perspective. *Business Week* is somewhat more general in nature than *Forbes.* It includes a weekly economic update on such economic variables as interest rates, electricity consumption, and market prices while also featuring articles on industries and companies. Many other periodicals, such as *The Harvard Business Review,* and *Money Magazine,* are helpful to the financial manager or personal investor. Unfortunately, space limits describing very many.

Most major city newspapers (Chicago, Dallas, and Cleveland, to name a few) have good financial sections. The *New York Times* has an exceptional financial page. However, the most widely circulated financial daily is *The Wall Street Journal,* published by Dow Jones. This is the paper that is read by millions of investors in order to keep up with the economy and business environment. Feature articles on labor, business, economics, personal investing, technology, and taxes appear weekly. Corporate announcements of all kinds are published. Figure 4–11, "Digest of Earnings Reports," is a daily feature that updates quarterly and annual earnings of firms.

New offerings of stocks and bonds are also advertised by investment bankers in the *Journal.* Prices of actively traded securities are presented by market. Common stock prices are organized by exchange and over-the-counter markets. Figure 4–12 is an example of common stock prices on the New York Stock Exchange. Along with the prices, notice that trading volume by markets is presented, and that the most active securities for the day are listed.

Many other prices are printed in *The Wall Street Journal.* An investor will find prices of mutual funds, government Treasury bills, notes and bonds, put and call prices from the option exchanges, government agency securities, foreign exchange prices, and commodities future prices. Figure 4–13 is an example of the future prices from the *Journal.* The prices are listed by category and exchange. Because of the comprehensive price coverage on a daily basis and other features, it is hard to believe that an up-to-date intelligent investor would be able to function without *The Wall Street Journal.* Each Fall *The Wall Street Journal* publishes an educational edition which explains how to read *The Wall Street Journal* and interpret some of the data presented.

Barron's National Business and Financial Weekly is also published by Dow Jones (every Monday). It contains regular features on dividends, put and call options, international stock markets, commodities, a review of the stock market, and many pages of prices and financial statistics. *Barron's* takes a weekly perspective and summarizes the previous week's market behavior. It also has regular analysis of several companies in its section called "Investment News and Views." The common stock section of *Barron's* not only

FIGURE 4–11

Digest of Earnings Reports

ADVANCED MICRO DEVICES (N)

13 wk June 24:	1984	1983
Sales	$234,266,000	$108,034,000
Net income	38,202,000	8,124,000
Avg shares	58,038,000	a57,048,000
Shr earns (com & com equiv):		
Net income	.66	a.14

a-Adjusted for a two-for-one stock split paid in August 1983.

AMERICAN ECOLOGY CORP. (O)

Quar June 30:	1984	1983
Sales	$10,656,000	$10,403,000
Net income	1,341,000	930,000
Shr earns:		
Net income	.46	.32
6 months:		
Sales	19,202,000	20,217,000
Net income	1,940,000	1,507,000
Shr earns:		
Net income	.67	.52

AMERICAN SECURITY CORP. (O)

Quar June 30:	1984	1983
Net income	$4,594,000	$7,405,000
Shr earns:		
Net income	.40	a.67
6 months:		
Net income	11,768,000	15,089,000
Shr earns:		
Net income	1.04	a1.36

a-Adjusted to reflect a three-for-two stock split paid in May 1984.

ASTROSYSTEMS INC. (O)

9 mo May 31:	1984	1983
Sales	$6,413,000	$6,831,000
Net income	2,063,000	2,241,000
Shr earns (primary):		
Net income	.39	.41
Shr earns (fully diluted):		
Net income	.39	.40

BANCO DE PONCE (O)

Quar June 30:	1984	1983
Income	$3,017,494	$2,747,338
Extrd cred	2,488,458	
Net income	5,505,953	2,747,338
Shr earns:		
Income	1.86	1.69
Net income	3.39	1.69
6 Months:		
Income	6,029,506	5,670,166
Extrd cred	2,488,458	
Net income	8,517,964	5,670,166
Shr earns:		
Income	3.72	3.49
Net income	5.25	3.49

BEECHAM GROUP PLC (O)

Year Mar 31:	1984	1983
Sales	$2,560,200,000	$2,242,100,000
Net inco	213,100,000	200,100,000

The above results have been computed at the pound's current rate.

BINKS MANUFACTURING CO. (A)

Quar May 31:	1984	1983
Sales	$41,012,000	$29,718,000
Net income	1,764,000	1,228,000
Shr earns:		
Net income	.57	.40
6 months:		
Sales	67,572,000	55,543,000
Net income	2,945,000	2,120,000
Shr earns:		
Net income	.96	.69

BLUESKY OIL & GAS LTD. (O)

Year Apr 30:	1984	a1983
Revenues	$23,735,936	$17,854,336
Net income	9,213,072	5,344,693
Shr earns:		
Net income	.34	.20

a-Restated.
Amounts in Canadian dollars.

CHEMFIX TECHNOLOGIES (O)

Quar May 31:	1984	1983
Sales	$253,832	$1,456,260
Net loss	518,620	b128,731
Shr earns:		
Net loss	...	c.03
9 months:		
Sales	3,059,890	4,332,485
Net loss	649,976	b316,965
Shr earns:		
Net loss	...	c.06

b-Income. c-Income; adjusted for a three-for-one stock split paid in July 1983.

COMPACT VIDEO INC. (O)

Year Apr 30:	1984	f1983
Revenues	$35,741,000	$29,024,000
Loss cnt op	a1,686,000	b720,000
Inco dis op	...	c677,000
Net loss	a1,686,000	b1,397,000
Shr earns:		
Loss cnt op	...	e.22
Net loss	...	e.43
Quarter:		
Revenues	10,852,000	7,937,000
Loss cnt op	a1,795,000	e188,000
Inco dis op	...	c196,000
Net loss	a1,795,000	e384,000
Shr earns:		
Loss cnt op	...	e.06
Net loss	...	e.12

a-Includes charge of $1,438,000 primarily from writedown of assets and certain assessments. b-Income; includes gain of $908,000 from sale and leaseback of real estate. c-From gain on disposal of discontinued operations. e-Income. f-Restated.

FEDERAL CO. (N)

Year June 2:	1984	1983
Revenues	$1,303,754,000	$1,122,844,000
Net income	41,367,000	25,707,000
Shr earns:		
Net income	5.03	3.13
Quarter:		
Revenues	377,011,000	295,568,000
Net income	13,304,000	3,467,000
Shr earns:		
Net income	1.62	.42

FLAGLER BANK CORP. (O)

Quar June 30:	1984	1983
Net income	$473,088	$318,077
Shr earns:		
Net income	.37	a.25
6 months:		
Net income	901,128	595,802
Shr earns:		
Net income	.71	a.47

a-Adjusted for a four-for one stock split paid in January 1984 and a 10% stock dividend paid in December 1983.

GENERAL MILLS INC. (N)

Year May 27:	1984	1983
Sales	$5,600,800,000	$5,550,800,000
Net income	233,400,000	245,100,000
Avg shrs	46,900,000	50,100,000
Shr earns:		
Net income	4.98	4.89
13 weeks:		
Sales	1,361,100,000	1,341,300,000
Net income	40,500,000	55,100,000
Avg shrs	45,700,000	49,200,000
Shr earns:		
Net income	.90	1.13

GENERAL MICROWAVE CORP. (O)

Quar June 2:	1984	1983
Sales	$3,173,694	$2,594,054
Net income	368,472	225,633
Avg shares	1,329,312	917,367
Shr earns:		
Net income	.28	.25

H & H OIL TOOL CO. (O)

Quar May 31:	1984	1983
Revenues	$4,207,000	$3,406,000
Net loss	34,000	318,000

HADRON INC. (O)

Year Mar 31:	1984	a1983
Revenues	$29,554,000	$28,263,000
Inco cnt op	156,000	1,232,000
Loss dis op	2,882,000	859,000
Loss	2,726,000	c373,000
Extrd cred	b23,000	b129,000
Net loss	2,703,000	c502,000
Shr earns:		
Inco cnt op	.01	.10
Loss	...	c.03
Net loss	...	c.04

a-Restated to reflect discontinued operations. b-Tax-loss carry-forward. c-Income.

HIGHWOOD RESOURCES (O)

Year Jan 31:	1984	1983
Revenues	$167,025	$275,967
Net loss	a561,333	80,431

a-Includes a $366,513 write-down of non-productive Canadian petroleum and natural gas properties. Amounts in Canadian dollars.

KOGER PROPERTIES INC. (N)

Year Mar 31:	1984	1983
Revenues	$41,760,000	$37,675,000
Net income	3,876,000	4,185,000
Shr earns (com & com equiv):		
Net income	.61	.68

NATIONAL ENVIRON CNTRLS (O)

Quar May 1:	1984	1983
Sales	$2,315,939	$1,996,271
Net loss	187,640	c81,748
Shr earns:		
Net loss	...	c.02
9 months:		
Sales	6,634,888	5,771,564
Net loss	142,734	c307,788
Shr earns:		
Net loss	...	c.09

c-Income.

SCHULMAN (A.) INC. (O)

Quar May 31:	1984	1983
Sales	$87,371,000	$72,409,000
Net income	3,148,000	2,764,000
Shr earns:		
Net income	.60	a.52
9 months:		
Sales	238,541,000	197,084,000
Net income	8,155,000	6,335,000
Shr earns:		
Net income	1.54	a1.20

a-Adjusted for a two-for-one stock split paid in November 1983.

TRECO INC. (O)

Year Mar 31:	1984	1983
Revenues	$29,044,139	$29,576,764
Income	2,766,564	2,044,141
Extrd cred	b1,889,000	a6,265,689
Net income	4,655,564	8,309,830
Shr earns (primary):		
Income	.56	.41
Net income	.95	1.67
Shr earns (fully diluted):		
Income	.35	.26
Net income	.60	.98
Quarter:		
Revenues	10,445,312	8,158,493
Income	414,147	2,713,966
Extrd cred	b639,000	b1,784,000
Net income	1,053,147	4,497,966
Shr earns (primary):		
Income	.05	.61
Net income	.17	1.01
Shr earns (fully diluted):		
Income	.05	.31
Net income	.15	.55

a-Consists of a $2,420,689 gain from early extinguishment of debt and a $3,845,000 tax-loss carry-forward. b-Tax-loss carry-forward.

VALLEY NATIONAL BANCORP (N)

Quar June 30:	1984	1983
Net income	$4,128,551	$3,554,434
Shr earns:		
Net income	1.74	1.50
6 months:		
Net income	8,173,522	7,012,922
Shr earns:		
Net income	3.45	2.96

VYQUEST INC. (O)

Quar May 31:	1984	a1983
Inco cnt op	$944,000	$13,000
Loss dis op	...	65,000
Net income	944,000	d52,000
Shr earns (primary):		
Inco cnt op	.25	...
Net income	.25	...
Shr earns (fully diluted):		
Net income	.24	...
6 months:		
Inco cnt op	1,346,000	326,000
Loss dis op	22,000	168,000
Net income	1,324,000	158,000
Shr earns (primary):		
Inco cnt op	.35	b.08
Net income	.34	b.04
Shr earns (fully diluted):		
Inco cnt op	.34	b.08
Net income	.33	b.04

a-Restated to reflect discontinued operations. b-Adjusted for a two-for-one stock split paid in January 1984. d-Loss.

FIGURE 4–12   Common Stock Prices

Thursday's Volume
100,777,200 Shares; 180,200 Warrants

TRADING BY MARKETS

	Shares	Warrants
New York Exchange	85,230,000	180,200
Midwest Exchange	6,171,800	
Pacific Exchange	3,317,900	
NASD Assoc. of Securities Dealers	3,434,940	
Philadelphia Exchange	1,438,100	
Boston Exchange	844,700	
Cincinnati Exchange	174,400	
Instinet System	165,400	

NYSE–Composite

	1984	1983	1982
Volume since Jan. 1:			
Total shares	14,778,612,529	14,069,232,820	8,484,830,046
Total warrants	52,416,500	91,796,400	21,308,850

New York Stock Exchange

	1984	1983	1982
Volume since Jan. 1:			
Total shares	12,454,764,269	12,076,685,005	7,296,119,596
Total warrants	50,521,100	90,845,300	21,282,500

ACTIVE STOCKS

	Open	High	Low	Close	Chg.	Volume
ITT Corp	22¼	24	22	23¾	+1¾	2,703,500
Amer T&T n	17¾	18	17¾	17⅞	+ ¼	1,855,500
Unocal	35¼	38¾	35¼	38	+2⅞	1,451,000
ContilICp	4⅜	4¾	3⅞	3½	− 1	1,388,400
Ramada Inn	6	6½	5¾	5¾	− ¾	983,700
StRegisCo	46½	47¾	43¼	44	−2¾	970,800
AMD s	29¼	29¾	26¾	26⅞	−2⅞	966,400
Phila Elec	11¼	11¼	9	10¾	− 1	912,000
IBM	107¾	107¾	106¼	107	− ⅝	895,900
Pfizer	30¾	30¾	29¾	29¾		889,500
Revlon	39	39⅛	38¼	39¼	+ ¼	887,700
FordMot s	38½	39¾	38¼	38¾	− ¼	872,300
ComdreInt	22¾	22⅜	19¾	20	−2¼	821,000
LTV Corp	10¼	10⅜	10	10¼	− ⅛	800,500
Colg Palm	23	23	22½	22¾	− ¼	792,700

[The remainder of the page consists of dense multi-column stock quotation tables (52 Weeks High/Low, Stock, Div., Yld. %, P-E Ratio, Sales 100s, High, Low, Close, Net Chg.) listed alphabetically from A through H, which are too small to transcribe reliably.]

FIGURE 4–13

Futures Prices

Thursday, July 19, 1984

Open Interest Reflects Previous Trading Day.

FIGURE 4–14 Market Transactions from *Barron's*

INDEX TO STATISTICS

WEEK'S MARKET TRANSACTIONS

NYSE COMPOSITE

Detailed stock quotation table with columns: 52-Weeks High Low; Name and Dividend; Sales 100s; Yield Pct.; P-E Ratio; Week's High Low Last Chg.; Net Chg.; Interim or Fiscal Year; Year ago; Latest divs; Record date; Payment date. (A–B–C–D–E sections)

Footnote legend (symbols a through xw and M, S, X, etc.):

a Also extra or extras
b Annual rate plus stock dividend
c Liquidating dividend
d New 52-week low
e Declared or paid in preceding 12 months
g Dividend or earnings in Canadian money. Stock trades in U.S. dollars. No yield or PE shown unless stated in U.S. money
i Declared or paid after stock dividend or split up

j Paid this year, dividend omitted, deferred or no action taken at last dividend meeting
k Declared or paid this year, an accumulative issue with dividend in arrears
m Months for which share results are given
n New issue in the past 52 weeks. The high-low range begins with the start of trading in the new issue and does not cover the entire 52-week period.

q Quarterly
r Declared or paid in preceding 12 months plus stock dividend
rt Rights
s Stock split or stock dividend amounting to 25 per cent or more in the past 52 weeks. The high-low range is adjusted from the old stock. Dividend begins with the date of split or stock dividend.
sa Semi-annual

u New 52-week high
un Units
v Trading halted on primary market
w Weeks for which share results are given
wd When distributed
wi When issued
wt Warrants
ww With warrants
x Ex-dividend or ex rights
x-dis Ex-distribution
xw Without warrants

y Ex-dividend and sales in full
z Sales in full
cld Called
vj In Bankruptcy or receivership or being reorganized under the Bankruptcy act, or securities assumed by such companies
D Deficit per share
Def Deficit
E Estimated
L Includes non-recurring loss

M Monthly
S Payments in stock
X Includes non-recurring profit
Y Latest dividend paid on date indicated
♦ Dividend declared
♦ Dividend omitted or deferred
➤ New earnings

provides weekly high-low-close prices and volume, but also informs investors as to the latest earnings per share, dividends declared, and the dividend record and payable dates. This can be seen in the middle portion of Figure 4–14.

One unique feature of *Barron's* is the "Market Laboratory" covering the last five pages of each issue. Weekly data on major stock indexes are presented with the week's market statistics. Special weekly tables also include: Pulse of Industry and Trade and Economic and Financial Indicators. Figures 4–15 and 4–16 show some of the tables from *Barron's* Market Laboratory. Careful reading of this publication will turn up useful data in a compact summary form not found in other publications.

Other major papers would be *The Wall Street Transcript* (weekly) and the *Commercial and Financial Chronicle* (weekly). *The Media General Financial Weekly* is an exceptional source of fundamental and technical indicators for the professional manager. Over 3,400 common stocks are divided into 60 industrial groups and analyzed based on relative strength (whether they are leading or lagging the market), trends, earnings, and other variables that may be useful to the analyst.

Journals

Most journals are academic and, because of this, are more theoretical than practical or trade oriented. However there are several that are industry oriented, such as the *Financial Analysts Journal,* which is a publication of the Financial Analysts Federation. This journal has both academic and practitioner articles that deal mainly with analytical tools, new laws and regulations, and financial analysis. *The Journal of Portfolio Management* and the *Institutional Investor* are also well read by the profession. The more scholarly, research-oriented academic journals would include the *Journal of Finance, Journal of Financial Economics, Financial Management,* and the *Journal of Financial and Quantitative Analysis.* These journals include information on the development and testing of theories, such as the random walk and efficient market hypothesis, capital asset pricing model, portfolio theories, and much empirical research on a variety of financial topics. Lastly, the *Journal of Financial Education* includes articles on classroom topics and computer applications.

COMPUTER DATA BASES

More computer-accessible data bases have become available in the last several years as home computer usage has increased and data-based storage management has improved. Currently, there are several major sources of data that are available for use in large mainframe computers on magnetic tapes, or that are accessible on an interactive, time-sharing basis. Many of these data bases are now accessible from a personal computer.

FIGURE 4–15

BARRON'S MARKET LABORATORY

Dow Jones Hourly Averages

30 Industrials

	May 6	7	8	9	10
Open	1246.91	1248.23	1248.67	1251.88	1268.99
11:00	1250.77	1252.21	1251.10	1254.09	1268.11
12:00	1249.45	1257.73	1250.33	1253.86	1272.75
1:00	1250.55	1256.29	1246.80	1253.64	1273.30
2:00	1249.56	1255.08	1247.35	1255.30	1275.84
3:00	1249.89	1251.88	1247.78	1259.05	1275.18
Close	1247.79	1252.76	1249.78	1260.27	1274.18
High	1256.40	1261.37	1258.94	1265.57	1282.46
Low	1241.39	1243.15	1239.51	1246.58	1261.59
Change	+0.55	+4.97	−2.98	+10.49	+13.91
Advances	16	21	10	22	26
Declines	9	6	18	5	0
Unchanged	5	3	2	3	4
Intra-day range:		High 1282.46		Low 1239.51	

20 Transportation Cos.

Open	585.25	586.47	588.80	595.22	610.27
11:00	587.58	586.80	588.24	597.43	610.94
12:00	586.47	588.68	589.90	597.21	612.05
1:00	587.36	587.91	590.35	598.10	614.04
2:00	588.35	587.80	591.78	598.65	617.91
3:00	588.13	586.47	591.78	602.30	617.21
Close	587.36	588.46	594.66	604.30	617.03
High	592.01	591.23	597.54	606.51	621.46
Low	582.04	584.15	584.48	592.34	607.06
Change	+2.88	+1.10	+6.20	+9.64	+12.73
Advances	12	10	12	17	18
Declines	7	4	6	1	1
Unchanged	1	6	2	2	1
Intra-day range:		High 621.46		Low 582.04	

15 Utilities

Open	154.75	155.42	157.57	157.98	159.31
11:00	154.90	156.34	158.03	158.39	159.26
12:00	155.06	156.39	157.78	158.65	159.47
1:00	155.42	156.24	157.57	158.75	159.42
2:00	155.21	156.19	157.88	158.34	159.98
3:00	154.90	156.29	158.03	158.85	159.83
Close	155.47	157.67	157.83	159.11	159.73
High	155.98	158.14	159.62	159.73	160.60
Low	153.93	154.75	156.24	157.06	158.19
Change	+0.52	+2.20	+0.16	+1.28	+0.62
Advances	7	10	7	10	12
Declines	3	1	6	2	3
Unchanged	5	4	2	3	0
Intra-day range:		High 160.60		Low 153.93	

65 Stocks Composite

Open	507.12	508.05	509.78	512.24	520.45
11:00	508.64	509.52	510.46	513.48	520.37
12:00	508.15	511.28	510.53	513.51	521.82
1:00	508.80	510.69	509.70	513.72	522.39
2:00	508.70	510.35	510.33	514.03	524.17
3:00	508.57	500.34	510.48	516.02	523.87
Close	508.18	510.71	511.54	516.90	523.45
High	511.54	513.61	515.27	518.97	526.86
Low	504.66	505.98	505.95	509.86	517.39
Change	+1.06	+2.53	+0.83	+5.36	+6.55
Advances	35	41	29	49	56
Declines	19	11	30	8	4
Unchanged	11	13	6	8	5
Intra-day range:		High 526.86		Low 504.66	

Shares Traded on N.Y. Exchange

	May 6	7	8	9	10
10–11	23,290	23,580	27,080	26,480	44,730
11–12	13,010	19,910	17,140	16,430	24,270
12– 1	12,530	15,690	15,640	13,390	20,680
1– 2	9,900	9,270	11,020	9,900	18,700
2– 3	10,370	13,900	10,820	16,700	15,350
3– 4	16,550	17,800	19,550	28,090	16,530
Total, ths	85,650	100,150	101,270	110,990	140,260
Dow Jones Stock Averages					
30 Ind	7,100.7	9,141.1	9,708.6	16,318.6	16,462.4
20 Tran	3,701.1	3,780.1	3,873.2	3,635.7	7,913.4
15 Util	2,928.6	3,362.8	3,102.0	2,067.0	2,635.7
65 Stock	13,730.4	16,284.0	16,683.8	22,021.3	27,011.5

Ratio of 10 Most Active Stocks (Composite) to total
trading: 13.57 11.52 10.25 13.09 9.89
Average closings (Composite) of 10 Most Active
Stocks: 43.36 32.22 43.12 46.74 38.35

Dow Jones Bond Averages

	May 6	7	8	9	10
20 Bonds	75.19	75.40	75.35	75.46	75.75
10 Util	72.12	72.62	72.55	72.45	72.90
10 Ind	78.26	78.18	78.15	78.45	78.61

NYSE Odd-Lot Trading

	May 3	6	7	8	9
Purch ths shs	188.7	183.6	195.5	186.9	180.9
Sales, ths shs	398.4	438.0	418.5	363.2	414.8
Short sales, sh	17,043	4,654	2,753	695	1,741

Dow Jones Weekly Averages

Dow Jones Stock Averages

	First	High	Low	Last	Chg.
Indus	1247.79	1274.18	1247.79	1247.18	+ 26.94
Trans	587.36	617.03	587.36	617.03	+ 32.55
Utils	155.47	159.73	155.47	159.73	+ 4.78
Comp	508.18	523.45	508.18	523.45	+ 16.33

Dow Jones Stock Diary

	Advances	Declines	Unchanged
Indus	24	5	1
Trans	9	8	0
Utils	13	0	2
Comp	57	5	3

Dow Jones Bond Averages

	First	High	Low	Last	Chg.
20 Bonds	75.19	75.75	75.19	75.75	+ 0.69
10 Util	72.12	72.90	72.12	72.90	+ 0.93
10 Ind	78.26	78.61	78.15	78.61	+ 0.45

Dow Jones Averages for 1985

Dow Jones Stock Averages

	First	High	Low	Last	Chg	%
Ind	1198.87	1299.36	1184.96	1274.18	+ 62.61	+ 5.17
Trp	553.70	635.30	553.03	617.03	+ 58.90	+ 10.55
Util	147.77	159.73	146.54	159.73	+ 10.21	+ 6.83
Cmp	484.96	528.78	480.93	523.45	+ 33.59	+ 6.86

Stock averages are compiled daily by using
the following divisors: Industrials, 1.132; Transports, 1.129; Utilities, 2.437; 65 Stks Comp., 4.830.

Dow Jones Bond Averages

	First	High	Low	Last	Chg	%
20 Bds	72.64	75.75	72.27	75.75	+ 3.30	+ 4.55
10 Util	68.75	72.90	68.62	72.90	+ 4.07	+ 5.91
10 Ind	76.53	78.61	75.61	78.61	+ 2.54	+ 3.34

Dow Jones Price-Earnings Ratio

	May 10	April 10	May 10	May 10
	1985	1985	1984	1983
Industrials	11.2	11.1	16.1	13.4
Trnsprt Cos	9.9	9.5	13.1	18.7
Utilities	7.6	7.4	6.6	7.0

Per share earnings for 12 months ended Dec. 31.

Standard & Poor's Price-Earnings Ratio

	Last Week	Prev. Week	Last Year
500 Composite	10.80	10.66	11.38
400 Industrials	11.14	11.04	12.28

Based on week ended Wednesday. Per share
earnings for 12 months ended Dec. 31.

NASDAQ OTC Indexes

Index	5/10/85	% Chg.
Industrial	299.58	+ 2.66
Composite	287.46	+ 2.55
Bank	270.61	+ 1.23
Insurance	345.00	+ 3.27
Other Finance	354.55	+ 2.22
Transportation	360.61	+ 3.33
Utilities	277.05	+ 2.44

(February 5, 1971, equals 100.00)

Other Market Indicators

	May 6	7	8	9	10
NYSE Comp.	104.18	104.59	104.56	105.31	106.64
Ind.	118.90	119.32	119.15	119.83	121.40
Util.	55.72	55.98	56.09	56.41	56.94
Tran.	95.68	96.10	96.62	97.97	99.58
Fin.	111.22	111.85	112.23	113.67	115.98
Amex Index	225.78	226.04	225.07	226.64	228.17
OTC-a Comp.	279.85	280.89	281.07	283.27	287.46
Ind.	290.82	291.91	291.65	294.38	299.58
Insur.	334.84	336.41	338.13	340.92	345.00
Banks	267.22	268.14	268.77	270.07	270.61
NMS-b Comp.	118.01	118.47	118.60	119.58	121.45
NMS-b Ind.	108.00	108.41	108.39	109.48	111.52
S&P500Comp.	179.99	180.76	180.62	181.92	184.28
S&P 400 Ind.	199.63	200.44	200.06	201.45	203.95
Value Line	191.10	191.74	191.96	193.29	195.60

a-NASDAQ. b-National Market System.

Week's Market Statistics

	Last week	Prev. week	Last year
Sales NYSE, th sh	538,475	504,642	439,565
Sales AMEX, th sh	36,640	34,100	27,840
Sales OTC, th sh-a	383,140	347,220	285,896
Sales Dow Indus, th sh	58,731	50,094	42,814
Sales Dow Transp, th sh	22,904	24,937	15,269
Sales Dow Utils, th sh	14,096	12,540	10,949
Sales Dow Comp, th sh	95,731	87,571	69,032
Bond offerings, th $-v	2,693,460	2,826,800	1,047,031
Stock offerings, th $-v	383,044	544,995	219,950
Low Price Stk. Index-v	245.12	241.31	247.75
Volume, th sh	674.6	1,077.8	1,450.7
%vol to DJI vol	1.32	2.14	3.09

20 Most Active Stocks:
Average price	43.22	47.20	42.49
% vol to total vol	14.34	20.77	15.61

NYSE volume report, Apr. 26:
Buy/sell, th sh-w	484,712	459,017	431,889
Total shorts, th sh	37,304.6	37,277.2	41,129.2
Public shorts, th sh	7,710.6	7,279.6	8,514.9

Member trading, Apr. 26:
Member shrt, th sh-x	29,594.0	29,997.6	32,614.3
Speclst shrt, th sh	14,180.8	15,316.9	13,648.9
Purchases, th sh	128,378.0	120,984.0	118,952.4
Sales,th sh-z	125,829.0	127,039.8	121,139.3
Net buy/sell, th sh	+2,549.0	−6,055.8	−2,186.9
% vol to NYSE vol	26.22	27.02	27.80

Odd-lot trading, Apr. 26:
Purchases, th sh	1,564	1,827	1,526
Purchases, th $	58,459	64,550	52,353
Sales, th sh-z	3,417	3,748	3,367
Sales, th $	134,557	136,786	124,187
Short sales, actual	33,447	43,813	12,409
Bond vol, NYSE, th $	182,380	144,627	163,318

Best Grade Bonds %-y	11.58	11.61	12.39
Intrm Grade Bonds %-y	12.42	12.54	13.85
Confidence Index-c	93.2	92.6	89.5
T-Bill/Eurodollar			
Futures Spread, %	+0.88	+0.94	+1.80
Saloman Govt./Corp.			
Yield Spread, %	−1.58	−1.59	N.A.
Stock/Bond Yield Gap-s	−6.77	−6.71	−7.61

Yield Returns on Dow-Jones Averages:
30 Industrials, %	4.81	4.90	4.78
20 Transports, %	2.38	2.50	2.71
15 Utilities, %	8.67	8.92	10.18
20 Bonds, %-y	12.04	12.14	13.51
10 Utils, %-y	12.46	12.58	14.64
10 Indus, %-y	11.61	11.71	12.38
Bond Buyers' 20 Muni			
Bond Index, %-y	9.11	9.37	10.19

a-NASDAQ. c-Ratio best grade to intermediate
grade bonds. r-Revised. s-Spread between dividend yield on DJI and yield to maturity on best
grade bonds. v-Ended Thursday. w-Shares
and warrants. x-Includes specialists short sales.
y-Yield to maturity week ended Thursday. z-In-
cludes short sales.

NYSE Most Active Stocks

	High	Low		Sales	High	Low	Last	Chg.
AtlRich	64¾	40%		11,348,600	64¼	61⅛	62½	− ⅜
AT&T	22½	15		7,570,000	22½	21	22¼	+ 1¼
Mobil	34¾	23¾		6,485,100	34¾	30¼	30½	− 2¾
BethStl	24	14¼		5,840,500	16⅝	15¾	16⅛	+ ¼
IBM	138¼	99		5,495,300	130⅝	124⅜	130¼	+ 5¼
HewlPk	44¼	31¼		4,118,000	34¾	32¼	34¼	+ ¼
USFG	36	17¾		4,012,800	34¾	32¾	34¼	+ 1¾
NtSemi	14¾	9½		3,946,500	11⅞	10¼	11⅜	+ 1
Exxon	51¾	38		3,774,100	52¾	49½	50	− ⅞
GMot	85	61		3,772,800	69¾	67¾	68¾	+ 2⅞
DowCh	32	25%		3,765,200	31½	30	31¼	+ ⅝
FordM	51¾	34		3,721,600	43¾	41	43	+ ¼
PanAm	6%	3		3,588,900	5⅜	4⅜	5¾	+ ½
Uniroyl	26⅝	14¾		3,576,400	20¾	19⅜	19¾	+ ¾
AmExp	46	25		3,552,800	46	42⅞	45⅜	+ 2⅜
PhilMr	95%	62½		3,536,400	86	81½	84¾	+ 1¾
WrnCm	30	17		3,504,800	30¾	28¼	28¾	− ½
Arkla	24%	16		3,253,200	24⅛	23	23	+ ¼
GenEl	63%	48¼		3,215,200	60¾	58¾	60¾	+ 2⅛
Boeing	66¾	37		3,169,400	62¾	57¾	62¼	+ 4¾

Weekly Composite Diary

Week ended May 10, 1985
	NYSE	AMEX	NASDAQ
Total	2,235	910	4,131
Advances	1,469	456	1,629
Declines	546	290	981
Unchanged	220	164	1,521
New Highs	341	76	
New Lows	58	36	

NYSE Common Stock Diary

	May 6	7	8	9	10
Total	1,492	1,486	1,500	1,495	1,497
Advances	603	722	565	843	995
Declines	525	419	581	335	262
Unchanged	364	345	354	317	240

NYSE Composite Diary

	May 6	7	8	9	10
Total	2,001	2,013	2,010	2,027	2,008
Advances	815	907	764	1,078	1,233
Declines	688	608	765	498	393
Unchanged	498	498	481	451	382
New Highs	81	81	91	114	196
New Lows	17	13	23	12	11
Sales ths shs	101,955	119,181	122,290	130,287	162,510

AMEX Composite Diary

	May 6	7	8	9	10
Total	747	765	768	785	809
Advances	264	266	255	317	399
Declines	275	247	274	213	203
Unchanged	208	252	239	255	207
New Highs	19	15	22	36	34
New Lows	11	7	11	14	7
Sales ths shs	7,486	8,162	7,765	7,729	10,867

NASDAQ OTC Market Diary

	May 6	7	8	9	10
Total	4,131	4,130	4,133	4,136	4,131
Advances	765	1,005	828	1,123	1,329
Declines	871	713	835	631	491
Unchanged	2,495	2,412	2,470	2,382	2,311
New Highs	122	158	145	181	233
New Lows	76	71	75	57	39
Sales ths shs	59,314	70,938	76,848	80,740	95,508

New York Exchange Bond Diary

	May 6	7	8	9	10
Total	885	965	944	957	1,013
Advances	393	508	378	467	670
Declines	286	263	358	275	181
Unchanged	206	194	208	215	162
New Highs	83	103	79	80	176
New Lows	2	3	8	4	7
Sales ths $	29,630	36,810	35,730	34,610	45,600

Sales ths $ May 2 corrected to 27,390.

AMEX Bond Diary

	May 6	7	8	9	10
Total	55	64	71	63	82
Advances	26	20	33	27	52
Declines	17	24	23	17	17
Unchanged	12	20	15	19	13
New Highs	3	5	6	6	12
New Lows	3	1	0	2	0
Sales ths $	1,670	3,550	3,300	2,270	2,510

Weekly Trading by Markets in NYSE Listed Stocks

	Last Week	Prev. Week	Last Year
NYSE	538,475	504,642	439,565
Midwest	41,329	37,036	38,810
Pacific	20,514	21,657	17,825
NASDAQ	18,129	19,753	15,238
Phila.	9,317	10,494	9,438
Boston	6,682	7,770	5,094
Cincinnati	1,131	1,052	917
Instinet	800	1,337	565
Total	636,377	603,741	527,452

STOCK EXCHANGE VOLUME TRENDS

(Volume, th shs)

		NYSE		(%)	AMEX		(%)	NASDAQ	
		Up	Down	QCHA	Up	Down	QCHA	Up	Down
May	6	39,558	34,385	+ .10	2,317	2,767	− .04	16,218	18,655
	7	60,098	25,649	+ .25	3,953	1,530	+ .19	20,440	15,384
	8	45,985	42,905	+ .07	2,482	2,580	− .12	20,825	23,076
	9	81,100	18,271	+ .61	3,900	1,009	+ .66	41,701	15,077
	10	114,047	17,473	+ .58	6,139	1,001	+ .52	50,000	9,007

Supplied by QUOTRON, th of shares. "QCHA" is the average percentage movement for all exchange
listed stocks each day on an unweighted basis.

FIGURE 4–16   From *Barron's* Market Laboratory—Trade and Foreign Data

PULSE OF INDUSTRY AND TRADE

	Latest date	Latest period	Preceding period	Year ago
Production—What They Make:				
Autos, U.S. domestic units	May 11	e178,652	r181,029	170,699
Electric power, mil kw hrs	May 4	43,927	44,467	43,008
Paper, th tons	May 4	651	r656	692
Paperboard, th tons	May 4	626.7	r611.9	681.9
Petroleum, daily runs, th bbls	May 3	11,604	11,692	11,631
Petroleum, rated capacity, %	May 3	75.9	76.7	73.0
Rotary rigs running (Hughes)	May 6	1,950	1,962	2,317
Steel production, th tons	Apr. 27	1,823	1,841	2,128
Steel, rated capacity, % (AISI)	Apr. 27	71.1	71.8	81.9
GNP (adjusted annual rate)	1st qtr.	+ 1.3	+ 4.3	+ 10.1
Factory operating rate, %	Feb.	80.7	81.4	80.1
Industrial Production (FRB)	Mar.	165.4	r164.9	160.8
Manufacturing a	Mar.	p167.1	r166.5	162.1
Durable Mfg a	Mar.	p158.5	r157.7	151.4
Non-durable Mfg a	Mar.	p179.5	r179.1	177.6
Mining a	Mar.	p123.5	r123.1	123.8
Utilities a	Mar.	p184.7	r184.8	180.0
Newsprint, U.S. & Can., th metric tons	Mar.	1,244	1,147	1,100
Distribution—What They Sell:				
Business sales, bil $	Feb.	419.21	r418.21	401.78
Autos, U.S. domestic units	Apr.	788,281	768,927	721,091
Autos, imports	Apr.	196,000	198,040	171,000
Retail store sales, bil $	Mar.	110.54	r112.74	103.87
Factory Shipments, bil $	Feb.	192.03	r192.71	185.00
Durable goods, bil $	Mar.	101.83	r101.72	96.99
Machine tools, mil $	Mar.	227.7	166.2	189.3
Inventories—What's Left on Hand:				
Business inventories, bil $	Feb.	576.89	r574.79	531.90
Domestic crude oil, th bbls	May 3	349,244	342,075	347,191
Gasoline, th bbls	May 3	214,961	214,339	249,216
Factory Inventories, bil $	Feb.	285.70	r284.79	246.07
Newsprint, U.S. & Can., th metric tons	Mar.	1,372	r1,373	1,146
New Orders Received:				
New Factory Orders, bil $	Mar.	191.61	193.44	196.48
Durable goods, bil $	Mar.	99.74	102.85	105.18
Non-durable goods, bil $	Mar.	91.87	90.59	91.29
Machine tools, mil $	Mar.	297.3	r237.5	208.5
Unfilled Orders:				
Factory orders backlog	Mar.	348.65	r350.05	348.71
Failures (D. & B.)				
Business Failures b	Apr. 26	107.0	109.4	96.5
Business Incorporations (D. & B.)				
New Incorporations	Nov.	53,490	r52,587	51,642
Purchasing Power:				
Whlesle Food Price Index (D&B) $	Apr. 30	16.39	16.38	17.25
Leading Indicators Composite Index a	Mar.	167.1	167.5	165.5
Consumer Price Index a	Mar.	318.8	317.4	307.3
Producer Price Index Finished Goods a	Apr.	293.1	292.4	291.6
Inventory-to-sales ratio	Feb.	1.38	1.37	1.32
Employment:				
Civil labor force, th	Apr.	115,370	r115,510	113,202
Employed, th	Apr.	106,950	r107,120	104,402
Unemployed, th	Apr.	8,430	r8,390	8,800
Unemployment Rate, %	Apr.	7.3	7.3	7.7
Construction:				
Advance Planning (ENR), mil $	May 9	3,153.4	3,444.1	3,636.5
Bldg contracts, (Dodge), mil $	Mar.	227.75	204.15	
Construction Spending, bil $	Mar.	324.2	r323.8	309.7
Private Spending, bil $	Mar.	265.6	r265.7	254.9
Public Spending, bil $	Mar.	58.6	r58.1	54.8
Lumber production, mil bd ft	Jan.	2,727	2,295	2,740
Lumber shipments, mil bd ft	Jan.	2,666	2,411	2,589
New housing starts, th units	Mar.	1,895	r1,631	1,645

a-1967 equals 100. b-5 week moving average. e-Estimate. p-Preliminary. r-Revised.

THE WILSHIRE 5000 EQUITY INDEX
(Published by Wilshire Associates, Santa Monica, California)

	Current (5/10/85)	Last Week (5/3/85)	Last Month (4/10/85)	Last Year (5/10/84)
Wilshire Index, Bil $	1,899.715	1,852.921	1,849.821	1,641.335
Net Change, Bil $		46.794	49.895	258.380
Percent Change		2.53	2.70	15.74

The Wilshire 5000 Equity Index is the total market value of all stocks listed on the New York Stock Exchange and American Stock Exchange as well as those actively traded over-the-counter.

FOREIGN

SOUTH AFRICAN ADR's

Closing prices of selected issues in U.S. currency.
May 10, 1985

Name of Stock	Week's Close		Week's Change
Bracken	1.80	+	.30
Consol. Modderfontein	7.40	+	.275
Deelkraal	3.125	+	.375
Doornfontein	18.75	+	1.75
Durban Deep	14.75	+	1.75
ERPM	8.00	+	.50
Elandsrand	8.75	+	.375
Elsburg	2.75	+	.35
ERGO	5.25	+	.125
Gen Mining	xd14.75	+	1.50
Grootvlei	8.625	+	1.00
Harmony	15.75	+	1.875
Hartesbeestfontein	5.625	+	.375
Impala Platinum	10.625	+	.25
Kinross	20.00	+	.50
Leslie	13.25	+	.25
Libanon	24.75	+	2.00
Loraine	4.875	+	.875
Lydenburg Platinum	7.50	+	1.00
Randfontein	10.90	+	.70
Rustenburg Platinum	8.375	+	.375
So. African Breweries	3.75	+	.25
So. A. Manganese Amcor	xd2.875	+	.125
Southvaal	47.00	+	3.00
Stilfontein	8.125	+	.875
Unisel	10.625	+	1.125
Venterspost	9.00	+	1.00
West Rand Cons	4.50	+	.25
Western Areas	4.25	+	.25
Winkelhaak	33.00	+	2.00
Zandpan	.95	+	.10

Source: S.G. Warburg, Rowe & Pitman, Akroyd, Inc.

STOCK INDEXES

	1984–'85— High	Low	May 7 Close	Week's Change
Australia	889.90	646.30	884.70	+ 18.50
Belgium	2.309.65	1,817.31	2,220.45	+ 14.75
Canada	2,657.78	2,175.58	N.A.	N.A.
France	211.36	165.49	211.36	+ 2.85
Hong Kong	1,621.45	746.02	1,613.36	+ 62.56
Italy	1,870.00	1,006.00	1,263.00	+ 53.00
Japan	12,683.26	9,897.15	12,536.31	+ 74.52
Netherlands	213.00	149.70	209.1	– 3.00
Singapore	1,071.01	764.38	798.14	+ 2.37
Sweden	484.80	362.50	399.40	+ 1.00
Switzerland	353.30	272.30	353.30	+ 5.90
U.K.	1,308.40	770.30	1,001.90	+ 12.00
W.Germany	1,244.50	922.60	1,244.50	+ 21.90

GOLD COINS

NAME OF COIN	Price	Premium Over the Value of the Gold Contained in Coin In $ Per Coin	As a % of Gold Value
Krugerrand	326.75	10.50	3.32
Maple Leaf	326.75	10.50	3.32
Mexican 1 oz	326.75	10.50	3.32
Mexico Peso	394.00	12.73	3.34
Austria crown	309.50	– .49	– .16
Sovereign	77.00	2.56	3.44

MOCATTA'S spot Gold price $316.25.
Wholesale dealer offering price on Friday.
Source: Mocatta Metals Corp.

GOLD AND SILVER PRICES

Handy & Harman's base for pricing gold content of shipments and for making refining settlements was $314.50 a troy ounce Friday. The company's silver price was $6.32 a troy ounce.

ECONOMIC AND FINANCIAL INDICATORS

	Latest period	Preceding period	Year ago
Fed Reserve Condition Report, Mil $, Apr. 24			
Loans, leases, securities, net	834,776	r-837,989	761,052
US Treasury agency securities, total	85,471	86,882	80,927
Other securities, total	48,785	48,792	49,774
Other loans and leases, gross	661,752	r-663,493	598,597
Commercial & industrial, total	253,744	254,780	237,045
Commercial & industrial, adjusted	251,088	251,727	233,907
Real estate	165,653	165,218	150,017
Depository, financial institutions	39,661	r39,396	40,289
Nonbank depository & others	23,723	23,968	24,439
Total Assets	1,053,277	1,067,064	990,626
Deposits, total	685,110	r698,086	633,683
Demand deposits, total	182,808	r193,048	181,288
Domestic depository institutions	20,893	r23,570	19,547
Transaction balances, total	37,676	r40,518	34,031
Nontransaction balances, total	464,626	r464,520	418,364
Liabilities for borrowed money	198,514	r200,800	191,054
Total Liabilities	979,450	r993,194	923,721
Federal Reserve Bank Changes, Mil $, May 8:			
Gov't. securities bought outright	168,164	167,089	154,534
Federal agency issues bought outright	8,371	8,372	8,556
Borrowings from Fed	634	1,272	1,098
Seasonal Borrowings	164	172	161
Extended credit	119	672	52
Float	743	r120	892
Total reserve bank credit	195,663	r195,059	175,410
Treasury gold stock-z	11,091	11,091	11,107
Currency in circulation	181,965	180,477	171,473
Treasury deposits with Fed banks	12,557	16,463	5,651
Total	203,766	r206,115	185,764
Fed Monetary & Reserve Aggregates			
Daily Average, Mil $; Two Weeks Ended May 8:			
Total Reserves (sa)	40,962	r41,352	36,230
Nonborrowed Reserves (sa)	40,009	r40,194	35,166
Required Reserves (sa)	40,155	r40,470	35,639
Excess Reserves	807	r882	591
Borrowings from Fed (nsa)-a	557	392	1,002
Free Reserves (nsa)	+ 250	r- +490	– 411
Monetary Base, Bil $	205,058	r203,842	190,581
Money Supply (M1) Bil $, sa Apr. 29:	575.2	r576.1	541.0
Federal Reserve Interest Rates, % May 3:			
Federal Funds	8.35	7.69	10.70
Treasury bill (90 day)	7.78	7.77	9.99
Commercial paper (dealer, 90 day)	8.19	8.08	10.33
Certfs of Deposit (resale, 90 day)	8.29	8.20	10.60
Eurodollar (90 days)	8.58	8.49	10.99
Money Market Funds, bil $, May 8:			
Total Assets	210.13	208.3	171.6
Treasury Statement, bil $, May 8:			
Total Public Debt Outstanding	1,744.6	1,744.0	1,489.3
Total Subject to Limit	1,745.2	1,744.7	1,490.0

a-Excluding extended credit. r-Revised. nsa-Not seasonally adjusted. sa-Seasonally adjusted. z-Actual. NA-Not available; Fed monetary and reserve aggregates released by Fed only every other week.

Monthly Economic And Financial Indicators

	Latest period	Preceding period	Year ago
Bank Debits, bil $, sa, Feb.:			
All Banks	143,281.5	140,678.6	126,749.9
New York City	63,157.0	64,474.7	55,776.7
Other Banks	80,124.5	76,203.9	70,973.1
Avg. Deposits Outstanding, bil $, sa, Feb.:			
All Banks	303.9	300.2	291.6
New York City	33.2	32.1	31.9
Other Banks	270.7	268.1	259.7
Velocity Rate of Deposit Turnover, Feb.:			
All Banks	471.4	468.6	434.7
New York City	1,902.2	2,008.6	1,747.7
Other Banks	295.9	284.2	273.3
Money Supply, bil $, sa, Mar.:			
Total (M1)	r572.0	569.3	537.3
Total (M2)	r2429.3	r2420.9	2229.1
Total (M3)	r3055.4	r3041.4	2765.4
Currency	r161.3	160.5	151.2
Travelers Checks	r5.4	5.3	5.0
Demand Deposits	251.9	251.7	245.5
Other Checkable Deposits	r153.4	151.7	135.6
Savings Deposits, total	288.9	r289.6	302.9
Small Time Deposits, total	r878.5	r877.2	802.3
Large Time Deposits, total	r423.5	419.7	349.7

sa-Seasonally adjusted.

The Use of Mainframe Computers

The following data bases are all made to be used on large mainframe computers. *Compustat* is published by Investors Management Science Company, a subsidiary of Standard & Poor's Corporation. The Compustat tapes are very comprehensive, containing 20 years of annual financial data for over 3,000 companies. Each year's data for the industrial companies include over 120 balance sheet, income statement, and market-related items. Compustat has an industrial file that includes company data from the New York and American Stock Exchanges and the over-the-counter market. There is also a file on utilities and banks. Besides the annual file, which is updated weekly, users can order tapes with quarterly data also updated weekly.

A second data base created by Compustat is called the Price-Dividend-Earnings tape (PDE) which contains monthly data on per-share performance. These tapes are leased to financial institutions for a fairly large sum or to nonprofit educational institutions at a significant discount. The tapes may be paid for in cash or in soft dollars (commissions funneled through an S&P brokerage subsidiary).

These tapes are useful for the analysis of large numbers of companies in a short time period. Ratios can be created, analyzed, and compared. Trends and regression analysis can be performed. Searches can be implemented for specific kinds of companies. For example, one could read through the tapes and sort out companies meeting certain parameters, such as:

1. Dividend yield greater than 6 percent.
2. Earnings growth greater than 15 percent per year.
3. Price–earnings ratio less than the Standard & Poor's 500 Index.
4. Market price less than book value.

It should be noted that Interactive Data Corporation also provides the same information as the Compustat tapes on a time-sharing basis.

The *CRSP Tapes* are maintained by the University of Chicago in the Center for Research in Security Prices. The information provided is oriented to earnings, dividends, stock prices, and dates of mergers, stock splits, stock dividends, etc. The tapes are extremely useful (data begin in 1926) for historical research on stock performance. They are widely used in academia for research on the efficient market hypothesis, the capital asset pricing model, and other portfolio questions.

Value Line also has made computer tapes of its 1,700 companies available. Again these would have market price data as well as financial statement items. The Federal Trade Commission has industry trade topics available on aggregate industry data and the Federal Reserve Bank of St. Louis has been known to make tapes of monetary data available for academic researchers.

The Use of Personal Computers

During the last few years there has been a proliferation of data bases for the personal computer. The owner of a personal computer with communications ability and a modem (phone hook-up), can now dial up a data base such as the Dow Jones News Retrieval System. This data base is oriented to the business user and includes financial data, current and historical information on stock quotes, commodity quotes, access to Disclosure's SEC reports mentioned previously and much more.[3] Other information outlets, such as The Source and CompuServe, also provide financial data, general information, government statistics, and electronic mail. Chase Econometrics and Nite-Line specialize in financial, business, and economic data, while Citishare Corporation offers U.S. economic statistics. Many old line financial companies such as Value Line (Value/Screen, and ValuePak) and Standard & Poor's (Stockpak II) are offering their financial data on micro-computer floppy disks with monthly updates. One good place to look for more complete information on these sources is in a computer magazine such as *Personal Computing* or *Byte*.

In addition to the data bases available for the personal computer, new software to access and analyze the data is being created at an extremely rapid pace. The raw data can either be "downloaded" (quickly transferred) onto a floppy disk or into your computer memory to save time and analyzed later, or it can be read directly into a software program which is designed to perform calculations on the raw data.

There are programs that analyze and create charts of the technical behavior of price movements, and others that evaluate the financial data from income statements and balance sheets. Using the Dow Jones Investment Evaluator, you can access the Dow Jones News Retrieval System to obtain information for stocks, bonds, warrants, options, mutual funds, or treasury issues. Information related to 10K statements, ratios, earnings growth rates, earnings per share forecasts, etc. are available on 2400 companies. The Dow Jones Market Analyzer, The Dow Jones Microscope, and the Dow Jones Investor Workshop all allow access to the Dow Jones information network. Once the correct data is entered into these software programs, they then create standardized analysis from preprogrammed instructions. Also, new programs are now able to transfer data from a news retrieval service straight into a spread sheet program such as Lotus 1-2-3 or SuperCalc. This saves time and money and allows the individual flexibility to create his or her own financial analysis. Not all these programs are available for every personal computer. Most programs are for the IBM personal computer and compatible systems, or for the Apple computer. Before buying one, check to make sure which software programs run on your computer.

INFORMATION ON NONTRADITIONAL MARKETS

For the purposes of this section, we define nontraditional as being out of the realm of stocks, bonds, and government securities. A major area that received increased attention during the last decade has been commodities and financial futures. A major source of information on commodities is the *Commodity Yearbook*.

Commodity Yearbook

This is a yearly publication which can be supplemented by the *Commodity Yearbook Statistical Abstract* three times per year. The *Commodity Yearbook*

---

[3] There is generally a monthly subscription fee associated with this and other such services.

runs several feature articles of educational interest, covering commodities or situations that are currently in the forefront of commodity trading. For 1984, the articles included such items as, "the Petroleum Futures Complex: Factors Affecting Supply/Demand and Prices," and "Understanding the Aluminum Futures Market."

In addition to the featured articles, the *Yearbook* covers each traded commodity from alcohol to zinc. For example, corn is covered in six pages. The first page is a description of the corn crop and occurrences for the 1983–84 year. The next five pages cover much data in tabular form for the last 13 years. The tables show world production of corn, acreage, and supply of corn in the United States, corn production estimates and disposition by value in the United States, corn supply and disappearance, distribution of corn in the United States, corn price support data, average price received by farmers for corn in the United States, and of course, weekly high-low-close of the nearest month's futures price. Each commodity has a similarly detailed evaluation and statistical summary.

There are other publications about commodities from main-line brokerage houses and specialty commodity brokers. In addition, the commodities exchanges publish educational booklets and newsletters. The International Monetary Market publishes the *I.M.M. Weekly Report,* which discusses the interest rate markets, the foreign exchange markets, and gold. It also presents weekly prices for all interest rate futures, foreign exchange markets, gold, and selected cash market information, such as the federal funds rate and the prime rate. The Chicago Board of Trade publishes the *Interest Rate Futures Newsletter.* As investors continue to become active in these markets, an investor (speculator) can be sure to find more available data.

Scott Publishing Company

The Scott Publishing Company has long been involved in the philatelic (stamp) market. They turn out annual catalogues with price data and pictures with descriptions. Recently, Scotts has added a *Stamp Market Update,* which is a quarterly report on current trends and prices. It features prices of major U.S. stamps and popular foreign stamps, information for specialized collectors, investment opportunities and strategies as stated by recognized experts, and special articles, statistical tables, and graphs.

Part Two

ANALYSIS AND VALUATION OF EQUITY SECURITIES

While we often praise the investor who is fortunate enough to receive a hot tip and capitalize on it, in the real world, events do not normally follow this course. In the second section of the text, we examine the in-depth analytical process that the typical security analyst must pursue.

Initially, we look at key variables influencing the economy. The security analyst must consider the role of fiscal and monetary policy, and their impact on economic conditions in the near term and over a long period of time. The security analyst also should examine business cycles, their length, and causation. An understanding of leading indicators and their ability to provide warnings about peaks and troughs in the economy is also important. We take a look at many of these items, although clearly we are drawing from a vast body of knowledge (exact and inexact) from which we can only consider the most relevant material.

As part of the consideration of economic movements, we also evaluate industry patterns. What industries peak with the economy, which go against the grain? Not only are industries influenced by the business cycle, but also by their own life cycle which is related to the ability to adjust to technological change.

The evaluation of the individual firm is the next logical step in the valuation process. We first examine valuation procedures based on the present value of future dividends and earnings of the firm. The widely used concept of the price–earnings ratio (earnings multiplier) is also a major item for consideration.

In assessing value, the security analyst also devotes much time and attention to the examination of the financial statements of the firm. Key ratios must

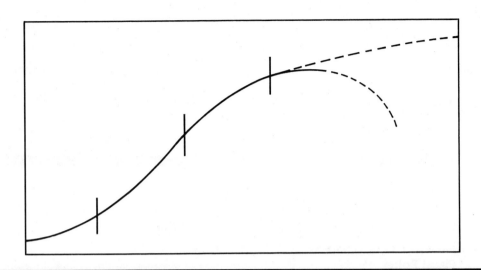

be computed and additional analysis done. Very little on the financial statements should be accepted at face value.

Finally, a key question for any security analyst is whether the security markets are assumed to be "efficient." In an efficient market environment, securities are assumed to be correctly priced at any point in time. All relevant information is thus presumed to be impounded into the value of the security at a given point in time. At the end of this section, we will consider the pros and cons of the arguments related to this efficient market hypothesis. We also present a discussion of technical analysis (the use of charting and key indicator series to predict stock prices) and its role in investment analysis.

Chapter 5
ECONOMIC AND INDUSTRY ANALYSIS

Chapter 6
VALUATION OF THE INDIVIDUAL FIRM

Chapter 7
FINANCIAL STATEMENT ANALYSIS

Chapter 8
A BASIC VIEW OF TECHNICAL ANALYSIS AND MARKET EFFICIENCY

Chapter 5

ECONOMIC AND INDUSTRY ANALYSIS

To determine the value of the firm, the process of fundamental analysis relies on long-run forecasts of the economy, the industry, and the company's financial prospects. Short-run changes in business conditions are also important in that they influence investors' required rates of return and expectations of corporate earnings and dividends. This chapter presents the basic information for analysis of the economy and industry, while the next chapter focuses specifically on the valuation of the individual firm. In Chapter 7, we extend our discussion to include financial statement and ratio analysis for the firm.

Figure 5–1 presents an overview of the valuation process as an inverted triangle. The process starts with a macro analysis of the economy and then moves into industry variables. Next, common stocks are individually screened out according to expected risk-return characteristics, and finally the surviving stocks are combined into portfolios of assets (portfolio management is discussed in Part Five). This figure is not inclusive of all variables considered by an analyst, but is intended to indicate representative areas applicable to most industries and companies.

ECONOMIC ACTIVITY AND THE BUSINESS CYCLE

An investor begins the valuation process with an economic analysis. The hope is that an accurate forecast and examination of economic activity will provide the basis for accurate stock market predictions and indicate which industries may prosper. The analyst needs information on present and expected interest rates, monetary and fiscal policy, government and consumer spending patterns, and other economic data. To be successful, investors must understand business cycles and be able to forecast accurately. Unfortunately, these are not easy tasks, but the rewards can be significant if the timing is right.

Whether or not an analyst uses statistical methods, such as regression analysis and probability theory, or simply seat-of-the-pants judgment, he or she is still basing the forecast on expectations related to past data and experiences. Past information usually is not extrapolated into the future without being adjusted to conform with the subjective beliefs of the decision maker. Even when highly sophisticated statistical methods are used, subjectivity enters into the decision in some fashion.

Most likely, past knowledge will be helpful, but modifications for the present effects of worldwide currency fluctuations, international debt obligations and other factors, which were not so important previously, need to be included in any forecast now. Since most companies are influenced to some degree by the general level of economic activity, a forecast will usually start with an analysis of the government's economic program.

FEDERAL GOVERNMENT ECONOMIC POLICY

Government economic policy is guided by the Employment Act of 1946 and subsequent position statements by the Federal Reserve Board, the President's Council of Economic Advisors, and other acts of Congress. The goals estab-

FIGURE 5–1   Overview of the Valuation Process

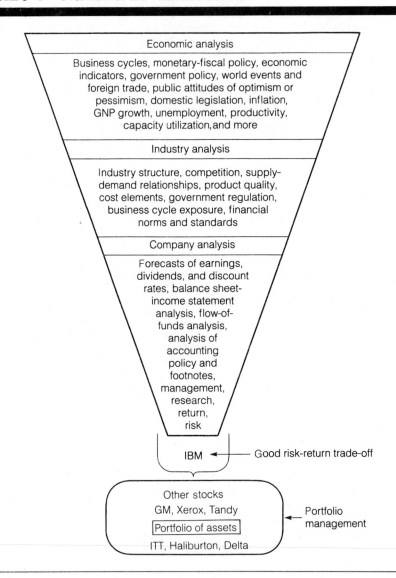

lished by the Employment Act still hold and cover four broad areas. These
goals are the focus of monetary and fiscal policy, and they are as follows:

1. Stable prices.
2. Business stability at high levels of production and employment.
3. Sustained economic growth.
4. A balance in international payments.

These goals are often conflicting in that they do not all respond favorably to the same economic stimulus. Therefore, goal priorities and economic policies change to reflect current economic conditions. In the 1950s and early 1960s, the United States did not have an international trade problem or spiraling inflation, so the focus of economic policy was on employment and economic growth. The economy grew rapidly between 1961 and 1969, and because of the Vietnam War, unemployment reached very low levels. The demand for goods and competition for funds was very high during the war, and eventually war expenditures, large budget deficits, full employment, and large increases in the money supply caused many problems. Inflation accelerated to high levels, interest rates reached record heights, and an imbalance of international payments finally resulted in two devaluations of the U.S. dollar in the early 1970s.

By the time Jimmy Carter took office in January 1977, it was recognized that the primary goals were once again to reduce unemployment, control inflation, and create a moderate level of economic growth that could be sustained without causing more inflation (a very difficult task indeed!). The achievement of these goals was thrown into the hands of the Federal Reserve Board. The Fed's tight money policy caused a rapid increase in interest rates in order to control inflation. These high rates depressed common stock prices as the required rate of return by investors reached record levels. Ronald Reagan inherited most of the same problems as Carter but tried new ways of reaching the goals. As the 1980s began, Reagan relied more on fiscal policy than previous administrations in his desire to control inflation and increase economic growth. He instituted a three-year tax cut to increase disposable income and stimulate consumption and thus economic growth, and at the same time he negotiated reductions in government spending. These policies were successful in sharply reducing inflation and creating strong growth in the gross national product (GNP), but they were accomplished with record government deficits and high interest rates. While the Reagan administration's economic policies have been the object of praise in some quarters, many others have expressed concern that continuation of these policies could cause renewed government stimulus of inflation.

Fiscal Policy

Fiscal policy can be described as the government's taxing and spending policies. These policies can have a great impact on economic activity. One must realize at the outset that fiscal policy is cumbersome. It has a long implementation lag and is often motivated by political rather than economic considerations since Congress must approve budgets and develop tax laws. Figure 5–2 presents a historical picture of government income and expenditures. When the government spends more than it receives, it runs a deficit which must be financed by the Treasury.

A forecaster must pay attention to the size of the deficit and how it is financed in order to measure its expected impact on the economy. If the deficit

FIGURE 5–2   **Federal Budget Seasonally Adjusted Annual Rates (quarterly)**

Source: *1983 Historical Chart Book* (Washington, D.C.: Board of Governors of the Federal Reserve System, 1983).

is financed by the Treasury selling securities to the Federal Reserve, it is very expansive. The money supply will increase without having any significant short-run effects on interest rates. If the deficit is financed by selling securities to individuals, there is not the same expansion in the money supply, and short-term interest rates will rise unless the Federal Reserve intervenes with open-market trading.

A look at Figure 5–2 shows that surpluses have occurred very infrequently from 1950 to 1983, and that the annual deficit increased dramatically in the early 1980s. Surpluses have a tendency to reduce economic growth as the government slows its demand for goods and services relative to its income. In an analysis of fiscal policy, the important consideration for the investor is the determination of the flow of funds. In a deficit economy, the government usually stimulates GNP by spending on socially productive programs or by increasing spending on defense, education, highways, or other government programs. The Reagan administration instituted budget cuts in education, revenue sharing, and a rash of social programs at the same time that it reduced tax revenues through tax cuts. This strategy was one that attempted to shift GNP growth from the government sector into the private sector.

Monetary Policy

Monetary policy is conducted by the Federal Reserve Board of Governors through several methods of controlling the money supply and interest rates. There are lags in the effectiveness of monetary policy, but it can be implemented very quickly to reinforce fiscal policy or, when necessary, to offset the effects of fiscal policy.

The Federal Reserve has several ways to influence economic activity. First of all, it can raise or lower the reserve requirements on commercial bank time deposits or demand deposits. An increase in reserve requirements would contract the money supply. Why? The banking system would have to hold larger reserves for each dollar deposited and would not be able to loan as much money on the same deposit base. A reduction in reserve requirements would have the opposite effect. The Fed also changes the discount rate periodically to reflect its attitude toward the economy. This discount rate is the interest rate the Federal Reserve charges commercial banks on very short-term loans. The Fed does not make a practice of loaning funds to a single commercial bank for more than two or three weeks, and so this charge can influence an individual bank's willingness to borrow money for expansionary loans to industry. The Fed can also influence bank behavior by issuing policy statements, or jawboning.

Beyond these monetary measures, the tool most widely used is open-market operations in which the Fed buys and sells securities for its own portfolio. When the Fed sells securities in the open market, purchasers write checks to pay for their securities, and demand deposits fall, causing a contraction in the money supply. At the same time, the increase in the supply of Treasury bills sold by the Fed will force prices down and interest rates up to entice buyers to part with their money. The Fed usually accomplishes its adjustments by selling securities to commercial banks, government securities dealers, or individuals. If the Fed buys securities, exactly the opposite occurs; the money supply increases, and interest rates go down. As you will see in the next chapter on stock valuation, the interest rate is extremely important in determining the required rate of return, or discount rate for a stock. Many economists feel that Federal Reserve open-market activity and the resultant changes in the money supply and interest rates are good indicators of the policy position taken by the Fed. If the money supply increases and interest rates fall, the general consensus is that the Fed is encouraging economic expansion. As the money supply decreases or increases slowly and interest rates rise, the expectation is that the Fed is "tightening up" monetary policy to restrict economic growth and inflation. It should be pointed out that the Federal Reserve can not totally control the money supply. Money market funds, the resultant monetary expansion created by banks lending money, and changing spending patterns by the population all contribute to the difficulty in controlling the money supply.

   In the early 1980s, the Federal Reserve began to direct substantially more attention to controlling steady growth in the money supply rather than attempting to control interest rates. Historically, the policy has been the opposite. Thus the Fed, in recent times, has attempted to control the growth rate in the monetary aggregates of M1 (currency in circulation plus private checking deposits, including those in interest-bearing NOW accounts) and M2 (M1 plus savings accounts and money market mutual funds).

   Many "pure monetarists" (those who think that money growth is the major economic driving force) think that the desired growth rates for the monetary aggregates should be 3 to 5 percent for M1 and 8 to 10 percent for M2. This is a very narrow range. Politicians often argue for much greater flexibility. The Fed has taken a middle ground by allowing for moderate

FIGURE 5–3   Gross National Product Seasonally Adjusted Annual Rates (quarterly)

Source: *1983 Historical Chart Book* (Washington, D.C.: Board of Governors of the Federal Reserve System, 1983).

growth ranges. For example, in 1984 the desired annual target growth in M1 was 4 to 8 percent but the M2 target was 6 to 9 percent, which was 1 percent lower than the range in 1983. Because the Fed places more emphasis on controlling the growth rate in the money supply as opposed to simply stabilizing interest rates, investors can continue to expect more volatile interest rates than those experienced during most of the post–World War II period.

Government Policy, Real Growth, and Inflation

There is always the danger that fiscal or monetary policy can be too stimulative. This can cause rapid economic growth, demand for goods greater than supply, rising inflation, and eventually an economy that ends up in a recession.

Figure 5–3 depicts over 30 years of GNP in current dollars and in inflation-adjusted 1972 dollars. In the bottom portion of the figure, we see changes in the annual growth rate for real GNP.

Figure 5–4 shows the annual percentage change in the consumer price index and is used as a proxy for inflation. Notice the inverse relationship between real GNP in the bottom half of Figure 5–3 and inflation in Figure 5–4.

FIGURE 5–4   Consumer Price Index Change in Annual Rates, Seasonally Adjusted (quarterly)

Source: *1983 Historical Chart Book* (Washington, D.C.: Board of Governors of the Federal Reserve System, 1983).

(For example, observe the 1960 and 1980 periods.) Since real GNP is the "nominal" GNP adjusted for inflation, it stands to reason that the change in real GNP is inversely related to the rate of inflation. As inflation rises, real GNP falls (as indicated in 1980) and as inflation subsides, as in 1981–83, real GNP rises. Since real GNP is the measure of economic output in real physical terms, it does not do any good to stimulate the economy only to have all the gains eroded by inflation.

BUSINESS CYCLES AND CYCLICAL INDICATORS

The economy expands and contracts through a cyclical process, and by measuring GNP and other economic data we can develop a statistical picture of the economic growth pattern. The National Bureau of Economic Research (NBER) is the final authority in documenting cyclical turning points. The NBER defines recessions as two or more quarters of negative real GNP growth and documents the beginning and end of a recession. Table 5–1 presents an historical picture of business cycle expansions and contractions in the United States. While the modern day data may be more relevant, it is interesting to see that economic cycles have existed and been defined for over 130 years.

Table 5–1 measures each contraction and expansion and then presents summary data for all business cycles and for cycles in peacetime only. A trough represents the end of a recession and the beginning of an expansion, and a peak represents the end of an expansion and the beginning of a recession. In general, we see on page 143 that during peacetime cycles between 1945 and 1982 contractions (recessions) have lasted an average of 11 months, while

TABLE 5–1   Business Cycle Expansions and Contractions in the United States

Business cycle reference dates		Duration in months			
				Cycle	
		Contraction (trough from previous peak)	Expansion (trough to peak)	Trough from previous trough	Peak from previous peak
Trough	Peak				
December 1854	June 1857	—	30	—	—
December 1858	October 1860	18	22	48	40
June 1861	April 1865	8	46	30	54
December 1867	June 1869	32	18	78	50
December 1870	October 1873	18	34	36	52
March 1879	March 1882	65	36	99	101
May 1885	March 1887	38	22	74	60
April 1888	July 1890	13	27	35	40
May 1891	January 1893	10	20	37	30
June 1894	December 1895	17	18	37	35

TABLE 5–1   (*concluded*)

Business cycle reference dates		Duration in months			
		Contraction (trough from previous peak)	Expansion (trough to peak)	Cycle	
				Trough from previous trough	Peak from previous peak
Trough	*Peak*				
June 1897	June 1899	18	24	36	42
December 1900	September 1902	18	21	42	39
August 1904	May 1907	23	33	44	56
June 1908	January 1910	13	19	46	32
January 1912	January 1913	24	12	43	36
December 1914	August 1918	23	44	35	67
March 1919	January 1920	7	10	51	17
July 1921	May 1923	18	22	28	40
July 1924	October 1926	14	27	36	41
November 1927	August 1929	13	21	40	34
March 1933	May 1937	43	50	64	93
June 1938	February 1945	13	80	63	93
October 1945	November 1948	8	37	88	45
October 1949	July 1953	11	45	48	56
May 1954	August 1957	10	39	55	49
April 1958	April 1960	8	24	47	32
February 1961	December 1969	10	106	34	116
November 1970	November 1973	11	36	117	47
March 1975	January 1980	16	58	52	74
July 1980	July 1981	6	12	64	18
November 1982		16	—	28	—
Average, all cycles:					
1854–1982 (30 cycles)		18	33	51	51*
1854–1919 (16 cycles)		22	27	48	49†
1919–1945 (6 cycles)		18	35	53	53
1945–1982 (8 cycles)		11	45	56	55‡
Average, peacetime cycles:					
1854–1982 (25 cycles)		19	27	46	46‡
1854–1919 (14 cycles)		22	24	46	47§
1919–1945 (5 cycles)		20	26	46	45
1945–1982 (6 cycles)		(11)	(34)	46	44

Note: Underscored figures are the wartime expansions (Civil War, World Wars I and II, Korean war, and Vietnam war), the postwar contractions, and the full cycles that include the wartime expansions.
* 29 cycles.
† 15 cycles.
‡ 24 cycles.
§ 13 cycles.
Source: *Business Conditions Digest* (U.S. Department of Commerce Bureau of Economic Analysis, July 1984).

FIGURE 5–5   Cross-Classification of Cyclical Indicators by Economic Process and Cyclical Timing

A. Timing at business cycle peaks

Cyclical timing \ Economic process	(1) Employment and unemployment (18 series)	(2) Production and income (10 series)	(3) Consumption, trade, orders, and deliveries (13 series)	(4) Fixed capital investment (18 series)	(5) Inventories and inventory investment (9 series)	(6) Prices, costs, and profits (17 series)	(7) Money and credit (26 series)
Leading (L) indicators (62 series)	Marginal employment adjustments (6 series) Job vacancies (2 series) Comprehensive employment (1 series) Comprehensive unemployment (3 series)	Capacity utilization (2 series)	New and unfilled orders and deliveries (6 series) Consumption (2 series)	Formation of business enterprises (2 series) Business investment commitments (5 series) Residential construction (3 series)	Inventory investment (4 series) Inventories on hand and on order (1 series)	Stock prices (1 series) Commodity prices (1 series) Profits and profit margins (7 series) Cash flows (2 series)	Money flows (3 series) Real money supply (2 series) Credit flows (4 series) Credit difficulties (2 series) Bank reserves (2 series) Interest rates (1 series)
Roughly coincident (C) indicators (23 series)	Comprehensive employment (1 series)	Comprehensive output and real income (4 series) Industrial production (4 series)	Consumption and trade (4 series)	Backlog of investment commitments (1 series) Business investment expenditures (5 series)			Velocity of money (2 series) Interest rates (2 series)
Lagging (Lg) indicators (18 series)	Duration of unemployment (2 series)			Business investment expenditures (1 series)	Inventories on hand and on order (4 series)	Unit labor costs and labor share (4 series)	Interest rates (4 series) Outstanding debt (3 series)
Timing unclassified (U) (8 series)	Comprehensive employment (3 series)		Trade (1 series)	Business investment commitments (1 series)		Commodity prices (1 series) Profit share (1 series)	Interest rates (1 series)

B. **Timing at business cycle peaks**

Economic process / Cyclical timing	(1) Employment and unemployment (18 series)	(2) Production and income (10 series)	(3) Consumption, trade, orders, and deliveries (13 series)	(4) Fixed capital investment (18 series)	(5) Inventories and inventory investment (9 series)	(6) Prices, costs, and profits (17 series)	(7) Money and credit (26 series)
Leading (L) indicators (47 series)	Marginal employment adjustments (3 series)	Industrial production (1 series)	New and unfilled orders and deliveries (5 series) Consumption and trade (4 series)	Formation of business enterprises (2 series) Business investment commitments (4 series) Residential construction (3 series)	Inventory investment (4 series)	Stock prices (1 series) Commodity prices (2 series) Profits and profit margins (6 series) Cash flows (2 series)	Money flows (2 series) Real money supply (2 series) Credit flows (4 series) Credit difficulties (2 series)
Roughly coincident (C) indicators (23 series)	Marginal employment adjustments (2 series) Comprehensive employment (4 series)	Comprehensive output and real income (4 series) Industrial production (3 series) Capacity utilization (2 series)	Consumption and trade (3 series)	Business investment commitments (1 series)		Profits (2 series)	Money flow (1 series) Velocity of money (1 series)
Lagging (Lg) indicators (40 series)	Marginal employment adjustments (1 series) Job vacancies (2 series) Comprehensive employment (1 series) Comprehensive and duration of unemployment (5 series)		Unfilled orders (1 series)	Business investment commitments (2 series) Business investment expenditures (6 series)	Inventories on hand and on order (5 series)	Unit labor costs and labor share (4 series)	Velocity of money (1 series) Bank reserves (1 series) Interest rates (8 series) Outstanding debt (3 series)
Timing unclassified (U) (1 series)							Bank reserves (1 series)

Source: *Business Conditions Digest* (U.S. Department of Commerce Bureau of Economic Analysis, 1981).

expansions have averaged 34 months. Thus, one *complete* business cycle during modern *peacetimes* lasts almost four years whether measured from trough to trough or peak to peak. This has led many to call the cycle politically induced by the four-year presidential elections. While there may be some truth in this statement, there are many other theories about what causes the economy to cycle. However, if investors can make some forecast concerning the beginning and ending of the business cycle, they will be better able to choose what types of investments to hold over the various phases of the business cycle.

So far we have discussed the government's impact on the economy. Fiscal policy and monetary policy both provide important clues to the direction and magnitude of economic expansions and contractions. There are other measures used to evaluate the direction of the business cycle. These measures are called economic indicators, and they are divided into leading, lagging, and coincident indicators. The National Bureau of Economic Research classifies indicators relative to their performance at economic peaks and troughs.

Leading indicators change direction in advance of general business conditions and are of prime importance to the investor who wants to anticipate rising corporate profits and possible price increases in the stock market. Coincident indicators move roughly with the general economy, and lagging indicators usually change directions after business conditions have turned around.

The National Bureau of Economic Research publishes its indicators in the monthly publication, *Business Conditions Digest* (BCD). This publication includes moving averages, turning dates for recessions and expansions, cyclical indicators, composite indexes and their components, diffusion indexes,[1] and information on rates of change. Many of the series are seasonally adjusted and are maintained on a monthly or quarterly basis.

Figure 5–5 on page 144 and 145 presents a summary of cyclical indicators by economic process and cyclical timing with the first half (part A) of the figure presenting timing at business cycle peaks and the second half (part B) showing timing at business cycle troughs. Thus, in the first part we see the leading, coincident, and lagging indicators for business cycle peaks and in the second part, similar indicators for the bottoming out of business cycles (troughs). While we would not expect you to study or learn all the leading or lagging indicators for a cyclical peak or trough, it is important that you know that they are heavily relied upon by economists and financial analysts. Let's look more specifically at how they are used.

Leading Indicators

Of the 109 leading indicators shown in parts A and B of Figure 5–5, 62 lead at peaks and 47 lead at troughs. Of these, 12 basic indicators have been reasonably consistent in their relationship to the business cycle. These 12 leading

---

[1] A diffusion index shows the pervasiveness of a given movement in a series. If 100 units are reported in a series, the diffusion index will indicate what percentage followed a given pattern.

FIGURE 5–6   Composite Indexes (leading, lagging, and coincident indexes)

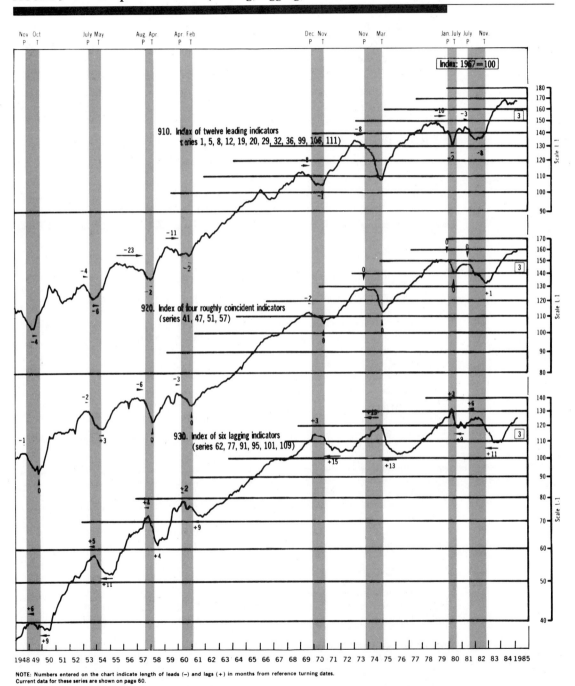

NOTE: Numbers entered on the chart indicate length of leads (−) and lags (+) in months from reference turning dates.
Current data for these series are shown on page 60.

Source: *Business Conditions Digest* (U.S. Department of Commerce Bureau of Economic Analysis, April 1985).

indicators have been standardized and used to compute a composite index that is widely followed. It is a much smoother curve than each individual component since erratic changes in one indicator are offset by movements in other indicators. The same can be said for a similar index of 4 coincident indicators and 6 lagging indicators.

Figure 5–6 shows the performance of the composite index of leading, lagging, and coincident indicators over several past business cycles. The bracketed areas are recessions as defined by the NBER. The minus figures indicate how many months the index preceded the economy. (For lagging indicators there are plus signs.)

TABLE 5–2   Components of the Leading, Coincident, and Lagging Indicators (series title and unit of measure)

LEADING INDICATORS

1.	Average workweek, production workers, manufacturing (hours)
5.	Average weekly initial claims, State unemployment insurance (thousands)
8.	New orders for consumer goods and materials in 1972 dollars (billion dollars)
32.	Vendor performance, companies receiving slower deliveries (percent)
12.	Net business formation (index: 1967 = 100)
20.	Contracts and orders for plant and equipment in 1972 dollars (billion dollars)
29.	New building permits, private housing units (index: 1967 = 100)
36.	Change in inventories on hand and on order in 1972 dollars, smoothed (annual rate, billion dollars)
99.	Change in sensitive materials prices, smoothed (percent)
19.	Stock prices, 500 common stocks (index: 1941–43 = 10)
106.	Money supply (M2) in 1972 dollars (billion dollars)
111.	Change in credit—business and consumer borrowing (annual rate, percent)
910.	Composite index of 12 leading indicators' (index: 1967 = 100)

COINCIDENT INDICATORS

41.	Employees on nonagricultural payrolls (thousands)
51.	Personal income less transfers in 1972 dollars (annual rate, billion dollars)
47.	Industrial production, total (index: 1967 = 100)
57.	Manufacturing and trade sales in 1972 dollars (million dollars)
920.	Composite index of 4 roughly coincident indicators (index: 1967 = 100)

LAGGING INDICATORS

91.	Average duration of unemployment (weeks)
77.	Ratio, constant-dollar inventories to sales, manufacturing and trade (ratio)
62.	Labor cost per unit of output, manufacturing—actual data as a percent of trend (percent)
109.	Average prime rate charged by banks (percent)
101.	Commercial and industrial loans outstanding in 1972 dollars (million dollars)
95.	Ratio, consumer installment credit to personal income (percent)
930.	Composite index of 6 lagging indicators (index: 1967 = 100)

Source: *Business Conditions Digest* (U.S. Department of Commerce Bureau of Economic Analysis, July 1984).

While the composite index of leading indicators (top of Figure 5–6) has been a better predictor than any single indicator, it has varied widely at peaks, with the longest lead time being 23 months before the peak in 1957 and the shortest being 3 months in 1981. At troughs, the longest lead has been 8 months before the bottom in 1982 and the shortest, one month in 1974–75. Table 5–2 presents the components for the 12 leading, 4 roughly coincident, and 6 lagging indicators.

Studies have found that the 12 leading indicators do not exhibit the same notice at peaks as they do at troughs. The notice prior to peaks is quite long, but the warning prior to troughs is very short, which means that it is very easy to miss a turnaround to the upside, but on the downside, you can be more patient waiting for confirmation from other indicators. It should also be noted that the indicators occasionally give false signals. Sometimes the indicators give no clear signal at all, and with the large variability of leads and lags versus the average lead time, an investor is lucky to get close to predicting economic activity within three or four months of peaks and troughs. It becomes clear that despite economic indicators and forecasting methods, investors cannot escape uncertainty in an attempt to manage their portfolios of assets.

One very important fact is that the stock market is the most reliable and accurate of the 12 leading indicators. This, of course, presents a very real problem for us because our initial objective is to forecast (as well as we are able) changes in common stock prices. In order to do this, we are constrained by the fact that the stock market is anticipatory and, in fact, has worked on a lead time of nine months at peaks and five months at troughs. Clearly, we need to find some variables that give longer leads than the stock market.

MONEY SUPPLY AND STOCK PRICES

One variable that has been historically popular as an indicator of the stock market is the money supply. The money supply is supposed to influence stock prices in several ways. Studies of economic growth and the money supply from 1867 to 1960 by Milton Friedman and Anna Schwartz found a long-term relationship between these two variables.[2]

Why does money matter? If you are a monetarist, money explains much of economic behavior. The quantity theory of money holds that as the supply of money increases relative to the demand for money, people will make adjustments in their portfolios of assets. If they have too much money, they will first buy bonds (a modification of the theory would now include Treasury bills or other short-term monetary assets), stocks, and, finally, real assets. This is the direct effect of money on stock prices sometimes referred to as the liquidity effect.

The indirect effect of money on stock prices would flow through the GNP's impact on corporate profits. As money influences economic activity, it

---

[2] Milton J. Friedman and Anna J. Schwartz, "Money and Business Cycles," *Review of Economics and Statistics,* Supplement, February 1963.

FIGURE 5–7   Money Supply, Stock Prices, and Corporate Profits Cyclical Indicators

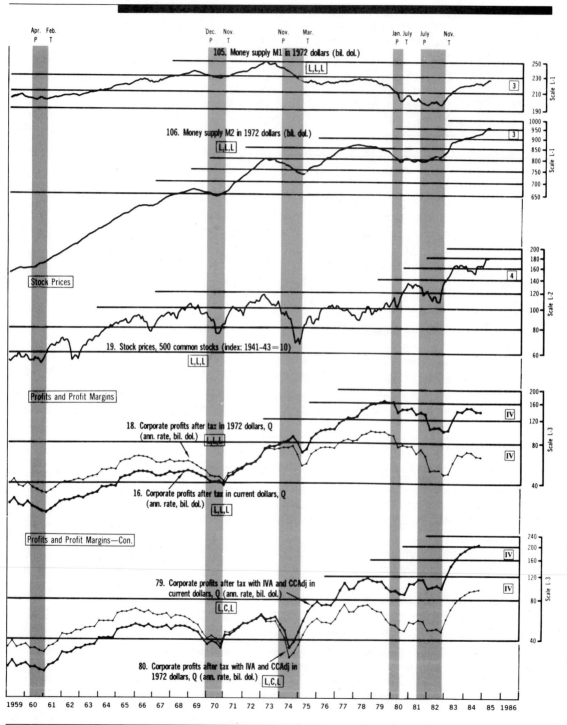

Source: *Business Conditions Digest* (U.S. Department of Commerce Bureau of Economic Analysis, April 1985).

will eventually influence corporate earnings and dividends and, thus, returns to the investors. Many studies have found that a significant relationship exists between the money supply variable and stock prices, but unfortunately, money supply growth and stock prices have turning points that are too similar to be really helpful to the investor.

Observe Figure 5–7, which includes the money supply, stock prices, and corporate profits on the same graph. It can be noted that in the 1969–70 and 1974–75 periods, the drop in the money supply did not lead the decline in stock prices enough to be helpful. In fact, during 1978–79 when the money supply began declining, stock prices continued to rise. This pattern of contrary movements is one that was of great interest to economists and financial analysts.

We question whether investors should react to short-term changes in the money supply. Present wisdom would suggest that the most positive long-term sign may simply be a *slow,* steady, predictable growth in the money supply— which will tend to moderate inflationary influences through restricted growth in the available dollars to purchase a limited supply of goods.

BUSINESS CYCLES AND INDUSTRY ANALYSIS

Each industry may be affected by the business cycle differently. Industries where the underlying demand for the product is consumer oriented will quite likely be sensitive to short-term swings in the business cycle. These industries would include durable goods, such as washers and dryers, refrigerators, electric and gas ranges, and automobiles. Changes in the automobile industry will also be felt in the tire and rubber industry as well as by auto glass and other automobile component suppliers. Figure 5–8 shows the automobile industry's sales from 1973 to mid-1984 relative to the real GNP's growth rate. Notice the similarity of the pattern. From the beginning of 1973 to the beginning of 1975, both GNP and automobile sales show steep declines. A recovery begins in 1975 and peaks in 1978 before declining again. This same type of pattern also continues into the 1980s. This close relationship is why it is often said that the United States lives in an automobile economy.

Not all industries are so closely related to the business cycle. Necessity-oriented industries, such as food and pharmaceuticals, are consistent performers since people do have to eat, and illness is not dependent upon the economy. Industries that have products with low price elasticities[3] that are habitual in nature, such as cigarettes and alcohol, do not seem to be much affected by business cycles either. In fact, there are some industries that do better during a recession. The movie industry prospers during a recession as more people substitute low-cost entertainment for more expensive forms. This is one pattern that may not remain the same, however. As cable television and pay TV come into their own with satellite hookups, people may find it even more convenient to stay at home than go to the movies when money is tight.

---

[3] Price elasticity represents the sensitivity of quantity purchased to price.

FIGURE 5–8   New Auto Sales and Real GNP, 1973–1984

Source: *Federal Reserve Quarterly Chart Book* (Washington, D.C.: Board of Governors of the Federal Reserve System, July 1981 and May 1984).

This is one thing that makes investments exciting—the ever changing environment.

Housing is another example of an industry that historically has done well in recessionary environments. As the economy comes to a standstill, interest rates tend to come down, and prospective home purchasers are once again able to afford mortgage rates on a home. In the period of extremely high mortgage rates in the early 1980s, it was felt that a precipitous drop in mortgage rate would be necessary to once again stimulate growth in the housing market.

The Federal Reserve tracks data on various types of consumer expenditures. In Figure 5–9, we see the pattern for personal consumption expenditures on durable goods, nondurables, and services. Durable goods have fared relatively poorly during this period (1976–84) and have been the most susceptible to downturns, while nondurables have done quite well, with services leading the growth for personal expenditures.

FIGURE 5–9   Personal Consumption Expenditures (services, nondurable goods, and durable goods)

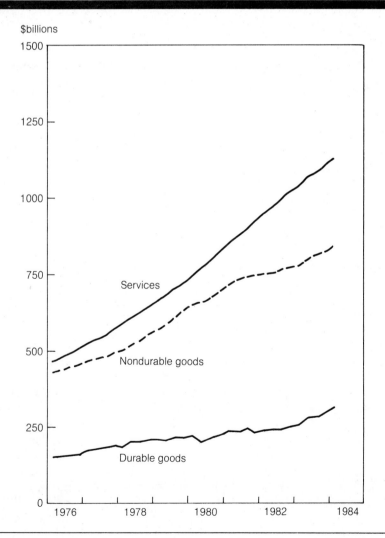

Source: *Federal Reserve Quarterly Chart Book* (Washington, D.C.: Board of Governors of the Federal Reserve Systems, May 1984).

Sensitivity to the business cycle may also be evident in industries which produce *capital* goods for other business firms (rather than consumer goods). Examples would be manufacturers of business plant and equipment, machine tools, or pollution control equipment. There often is a lag between the recovery from a recession and the increased purchase of capital goods, so that recoveries within these industries may be delayed. Computers and other high-technology industries tend to be less cyclical in nature and not as sensitive to the ups and down of the economy.

We do not mean to imply that cyclical industries are bad investments or that they should be avoided. We merely point out the cyclical influence of the economy. Often cyclical industries are excellent buys in the stock market because the market does not look far enough ahead to see a recovery and its impact on cyclical profits.

INDUSTRY LIFE CYCLES

Life cycles are created because of economic growth, competition, availability of resources, and the resultant market saturation by the particular goods and services offered. Life-cycle growth influences many variables considered in the valuation process. The particular phase of the life cycle that an industry or company is at determines the growth of earnings, dividends, capital expenditures, and market demand for products.

Figure 5–10 shows an industry life cycle (although it could very well be a company life cycle) and the corresponding dividend policy that is most likely to be found at each stage. A small firm in the initial stages of development (Stage I) pays no dividends because it needs all of its profits (if there are any) for reinvestment in new productive assets. If the firm is successful in the marketplace, the demand for its products will create growth in sales, earnings, and assets, and the industry will move into Stage II. At this stage, sales and returns on assets will be growing at an increasing rate, and earnings will still be reinvested. In the early part of Stage II, stock dividends (distributions of additional shares) may be instituted, and in the latter part of Stage II, *low* cash dividends may be started to inform investors that the firm is profitable.

Obviously, industries in Stage I or early Stage II are very risky, and the investor does not really know if growth objectives will be met or dividends will ever be paid. But if you want to have a chance to make an investment (after careful research) in a high-growth industry with large potential returns, then Stage I or II industries will provide you with opportunities for gains or losses. Since actual dividends are irrelevant in these stages, an investor will be purchasing shares for capital gains based on expected growth rather than current income. As the industry enters Stage III, the growth rate is still positive, but the rate of change starts declining. This is often the point where investors do not recognize that the growth rate has begun to decline, and they still pay large premiums over the regular market for stocks in these industries. However, when the market does realize that the growth rate in fact is diminishing, stock prices can take a sizable tumble.

FIGURE 5–10   Industry Life Cycle

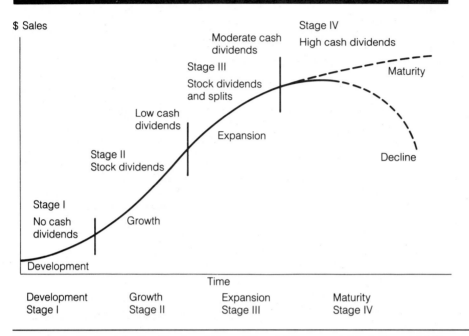

Source: Stanley Block and Geoffrey Hirt, *Foundations of Financial Management,* 3d ed. (Homewood, Ill.: Richard D. Irwin, 1984).

In Stage III, the expansion of sales continues but at a decreasing rate, and returns on investment may decline as more competition enters the market and attempts to take away market share from existing firms. The industry has expanded to the point where asset expansion slows in line with production needs, and the firms in the industry are more capable of paying cash dividends. Stock dividends and stock splits are still common in Stage III, and the dividend payout ratio usually increases from a low level of 5 to 15 percent of earnings to a moderate level of 25 to 40 percent of earnings. Finally, at Stage IV, maturity, the firm maintains a stable growth rate in sales similar to that of the economy as a whole, and when risk premiums are considered, its returns on assets level out to those of the economy. Automobiles might be a good example of a mature industry.

In unfortunate cases, industries suffer declines in sales (passenger rail-roads) if product innovation has not increased the product base over the years. In Stage IV, assuming maturity rather than decline, dividends might range from 40 to 60 percent of earnings. Of course, these percentages will be different from industry to industry depending on individual characteristics.

It is also important to realize that growth companies can exist in a mature industry and that not all companies within an industry experience the same growth path in sales, earnings, and dividends. Some companies are simply better managed, have better people, more efficient assets, and have put more money into productive research and development that has created new products or improved products.

For example, electric utilities are generally considered mature, but some utilities exist in states like Florida, Texas, and California that have undergone rapid population explosions over the last decade. These utilities would still have higher growth rates than the industry in general. Computer companies, such as IBM, were fast approaching maturity until technical innovations created new markets. Now personal computers and word processors have not only added vitality to older markets, but also created new industries of their own. You can trace the histories of many industries to see that this pattern repeats itself over and over.

The warning to the investor is to not become too enamored with a company just because it is in a "growth industry." Its time of glory may have passed. Other investors improperly ignore companies that are in the process of revitalization because they no longer carry the growth-stock tag. More will be said about growth stocks in the next chapter.

Other Industry Factors to Consider

There are other significant factors that a financial analyst may wish to evaluate for a given industry. For example, is the industry structure monopolistic like a regulated utility, oligopolistic like the automobile or steel industry, partially competitive like the drug industry, or very competitive like the market for farm commodities? Questions of industry structure are very important in analyzing pricing structures and price elasticities that exist because of competition or lack of it.

Questions of supply and demand relationships are very important as they affect the price structure of the industry and its ability to produce quality products at a reasonable cost. The cost variable can be affected by many factors. For example, high relative hourly wages in basic industries, such as steel, autos, rubber, and others, are somewhat responsible for the inability of the United States to compete in the world markets of these products. Availability of raw material is also an important cost factor. Industries like aluminum and glass have to have an abundance of low-cost bauxite and silicon to produce their products. Unfortunately, the aluminum industry uses very large amounts of electricity in the production process, and so the low cost of bauxite may be offset by the high cost of energy. Energy costs are of concern to all industries, but the availability of reasonably priced energy sources is particularly important to the airline and trucking industries. The list could go on and on, but as an analyst becomes familiar with a specific industry, he or she learns the crucial variables.

Most industries are also affected by government regulation. This applies to the automobile industry where safety and exhaust emmissions are regulated and to all industries where air, water, and noise pollution are of concern. Many industries engaged in interstate commerce, such as utilities, railroads, and telephone companies, are strongly regulated by the government. On the other hand, many industries, such as airlines, trucking, and natural gas production companies, are being deregulated, and these industries will be facing a new climate where the old game plan may no longer prove successful. Most industries are also affected by government expenditures; this is especially true for industries involved in defense, education, and transportation.

These are but a few examples to alert you to the importance of having a thorough understanding of your industry. This is why in many large investment firms, trust departments, and insurance companies, analysts are assigned to only one industry or to several related industries so that they may concentrate their attention on a given set of significant factors.

Chapter 6

VALUATION OF THE INDIVIDUAL FIRM

The analysis in Chapter 5 centered on economic activity and the resultant swings in the business cycle which affected industries and corporate profitability and influenced the purchase of common stocks. The valuation of the individual firm was depicted as the last major step of the valuation process (Figure 5–1).

Valuation is based upon economic factors, industry variables, and an analysis of the financial statements and the outlook for the individual firm. The purpose of valuation is to determine the long-run fundamental economic value of a specific company's common stock. In the process, we try to determine whether a common stock is undervalued, overvalued, or fairly valued relative to its market price. As will be indicated in Chapter 8, there is a continuing controversy in academic circles over the ability of security markets to correctly price securities. This has led to debate over the efficient market hypothesis, which states that all securities are correctly priced at any point in time (there is no secret information to be uncovered by the enterprising analyst). For purposes of this chapter, we shall not be fully bound by the limiting assumptions of the efficient market hypothesis—though they are carefully considered in Chapter 8. Furthermore, most of the orientation in this chapter is to long-run concepts of valuation rather than to the determination of short-term market pricing factors.

BASIC VALUATION CONCEPTS

There are several ways to approach the valuation of common stock. Some models rely solely on dividends expected to be received during the future, and these are usually referred to as dividend valuation models. A variation on the dividend model is the earnings model, which substitutes earnings as the main income stream for valuation. Earnings valuation models may also call for the determination of a price–earnings ratio, or multiplier of earnings, to determine value. Other methods may include the market value of assets, such as cash and liquid assets, replacement value of plant and equipment, and other hidden assets, such as undervalued timber holdings. For the first part of our discussion, we develop the dividend valuation model and then move to earnings-related approaches. We conclude with a consideration of asset values.

DIVIDEND VALUATION MODELS

The value of a share of stock may be interpreted by the shareholder as the present value of an expected stream of future dividends. Although in the short run, stockholders may be influenced by a change in earnings or other variables, the ultimate value of any holding rests with the distribution of earnings in the form of dividend payments. Though the stockholder may benefit from the retention and reinvestment of earnings by the corporation, at some point the

earnings must generally be translated into cash flow for the stockholder.[1]
While dividend valuation models are theoretical in nature and subject to many
limitations, they are the most frequently used models in the literature of
finance.

General Dividend Model

A generalized stock valuation model based on future expected dividends can
be stated as follows:

$$P_0 = \frac{D_1}{(1 + K_e)^1} + \frac{D_2}{(1 + K_e)^2} + \frac{D_3}{(1 + K_e)^3} + \cdots + \frac{D_\infty}{(1 + K_e)^\infty} \quad (6\text{--}1)$$

where:

P_0 = Present value of the stock price.
D_i = Dividend for each year.
K_e = Required rate of return (discount rate).

This model is a very general model and assumes that the investor can, in fact,
determine the right dividend for each and every year as well as the annualized
rate of return that an investor requires.

Constant Growth Model

Rather than predict the actual dividend each year, a more widely used model
includes an estimate of the growth rate in dividends. This model assumes a
constant growth rate in dividends to infinity.

If a constant growth rate in dividends is assumed, Formula (6–1) can be
expressed as:

$$P_0 = \frac{D_0(1 + g)^1}{(1 + K_e)^1} + \frac{D_0(1 + g)^2}{(1 + K_e)^2} + \frac{D_0(1 + g)^3}{(1 + K_e)^3} + \cdots + \frac{D_0(1 + g)^\infty}{(1 + K_e)^\infty} \quad (6\text{--}2)$$

where:

$D_0(1 + g)^1$ = Dividends in the initial year.
$D_0(1 + g)^2$ = Dividends in year 2, and so on.
g = Constant growth rate in the dividend.

The current price of the stock should equal the present value of the
expected stream of dividends. If we can correctly predict the growth of future
dividends and determine the discount rate, we can ascertain the value of the
stock.

For example, assume that we wanted to determine the present value of
ABC Corporation common stock based on this model. We shall assume that
ABC anticipates an 8 percent growth rate in dividends per share, and we use a

---

[1] Some exceptions to this principle are noted later in the chapter.

12 percent discount rate as the required rate of return. The required rate of return (discussed in Chapter 1) is intended to provide the investor with a minimum real rate of return, compensation for expected inflation, and a risk premium. Twelve percent is sufficient to fulfill that function in this example.

Rather than project out the dividends for an extremely long period of time and then discount them back to the present, we can reduce Formula (6–2) to a more usable form:

$$P_0 = D_1/(K_e - g) \qquad (6\text{--}3)$$

This formula is appropriate as long as two conditions are met. The first is that the growth rate must be constant in nature. For the ABC Corporation, we are assuming that to be the case. It is a constant 8 percent. Secondly, K_e (the required rate of return) must exceed g (the growth rate). Since K_e is 12 percent and g is 8 percent for the ABC Corporation, this condition is also met. Let's further assume D_1 (the dividend at the end of period 1) is $3.38.

Using Formula (6–3), we determine a stock value of:

$$
\begin{aligned}
P_0 &= D_1/(K_e - g) \\
&= \$3.38/(.12 - .08) \\
&= \$3.38/.04 \\
P_0 &= \$84.50
\end{aligned}
$$

This value, in theory, represents the present value of all future dividends. The meaning is further illustrated in Table 6–1, in which we take the present value of the first 20 years of dividends ($43.71) and then add in a figure of $40.79 to arrive at the present value of all future dividends of $84.50 as determined by Formula (6–3). The $40.79 value represents the present value of dividends occuring between 2006 and infinity (that is after the 20th year).

We must be aware that there are several things that could be wrong with our analysis. First, our expectations of dividend growth may be too high for an infinite period of time. Perhaps 6 percent is a more realistic estimate of expected dividend growth. If we substitute our new estimate into Formula (6–3), we can measure the price effect as dividend growth changes from an 8 percent rate to a 6 percent rate.

$$
\begin{aligned}
P_0 &= \$3.38/(.12 - .06) \\
&= \$3.38/.06 \\
&= \$56.33
\end{aligned}
$$

A 6 percent growth rate cuts the present value down substantially from the prior value of $84.50.

We could also misjudge our required rate of return, K_e, which could be higher or lower. A lower K_e would increase the present value of ABC Corporation, whereas a higher K_e would reduce its value. We have made these points to show how sensitive stock prices are to the basic assumptions of the model. Even though you may go through the calculations, the final value is only as accurate as your inputs. This is where a security analyst's judgment and expertise are important—in justifying the growth rate and required rate of return.

TABLE 6–1   Present Value Analysis of ABC Corporation

Year	Expected dividends g = 8%	Present value factor K_e = 12%*	Present value of dividends
1986	$ 3.38	.893	3.02
1987	3.65	.797	2.91
1988	3.94	.712	2.81
1989	4.26	.636	2.71
1990	4.60	.568	2.61
1991	4.97	.507	2.52
1992	5.37	.453	2.43
1993	5.80	.404	2.34
1994	6.26	.361	2.26
1995	6.76	.322	2.18
1996	7.30	.288	2.10
1997	7.88	.257	2.03
1998	8.51	.229	1.95
1999	9.19	.204	1.87
2000	9.93	.182	1.81
2001	10.72	.163	1.75
2002	11.58	.146	1.69
2003	12.51	.130	1.63
2004	13.51	.116	1.57
2005	14.59	.104	1.52

PV of dividends for years 1986–2005	43.71
PV of dividends for years 2006 to infinity	40.79
Total present value of ABC Common Stock	$84.50

* Figures are taken from Appendix B at the end of this book.

A Nonconstant Growth Model

Many analysts do not accept the premise of a constant growth rate in dividends or earnings. As we examined in Chapter 5, industries go through a life cycle in which growth is nonlinear. Growth is usually highest in the infancy and growth phases of the life cycle, and as expansion is reached, the growth rate slows until the industry reaches maturity. At maturity, a constant, long-run growth rate that approximates the long-run growth of the macro economy may be appropriate for a particular industry.

It should be remembered that some companies in an industry may not behave like the industry in general. Companies constantly try to avoid maturity or decline, and so they strive to develop new products and markets to maintain growth.

In situations where the analyst wants to value a company without the constant growth assumption, a variation on the constant growth model is possible. Growth is simply divided into several periods with each period having a present value. The present value of each period is summed to attain the total value of the firm's share price. An example of a two-period model may illustrate the concept. Assume that JAYCAR Corporation is expected to have the growth pattern shown in Figure 6–1.

FIGURE 6–1   JAYCAR Growth Pattern

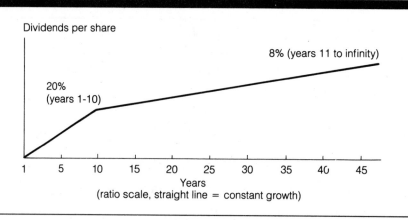

It is assumed that JAYCAR will have a dividend growth rate of 20 percent for the next 10 years of its life and an 8 percent perpetual growth rate after that. JAYCAR's dividend is expected to be $1 next year, and the appropriate required rate of return (discount rate) is 12 percent. Taking the present value for the first 10 years of dividends, and then applying the constant dividend growth model for years 11 through infinity, we can arrive at an answer. First, we find the present value of the initial 10 years of dividends.

Year	Dividends (20 percent growth)	PV factor (12 percent)*	Present value of dividends first 10 years
1	$1.00	.893%	$ .89
2	1.20	.797	.96
3	1.44	.712	1.03
4	1.73	.636	1.10
5	2.07	.567	1.17
6	2.48	.507	1.26
7	2.98	.452	1.35
8	3.58	.404	1.45
9	4.29	.361	1.55
10	5.15	.322	1.66
			$12.42

* Figures are taken from Appendix B at the end of this book.

We then determine the present value of dividends after the tenth year. The dividend in year 11 is expected to be $5.56 or $5.15 (for year 10) compounded at the new, lower 8 percent growth rate ($5.15 × 1.08). Since the rest of the dividend stream will be infinite, Formula (6–3) can provide the value of JAYCAR at the end of year 10, based on a discount rate of 12 percent and an expected growth rate of 8 percent.

$$P_{10} = D_{11}/(K_e - g)$$
$$P_{10} = \$5.56/(.12 - .08)$$
$$= \$5.56/.04$$
$$= \$139$$

An investor would pay $139 at the end of the 10th year for the future stream of dividends from year 11 to infinity. To get the present value of the 10th-year price, the $139 must be discounted back to the present by the 10-year PV factor for 12 percent from Appendix B (.322). This part of the answer is $139.00 × .322 or $44.76. The two parts of this analysis can be combined to get the current valuation per share of $57.18.

Present value of the dividends from years 1 to 10	$12.42
Present value of 10th year price ($139.00 × .322)	44.76
Total present value of JAYCAR common stock	$57.18

Do Dividends Really Matter?

Dividend valuation models estimate the present value from an expected future stream of dividends. If the predictions are correct, the valuation will probably be reasonably accurate, but if the forecast is off its target, such would not be the case.

If a firm fails to pay dividends, then dividend valuation makes little sense. If a firm were never to pay a dividend, would the company cease to have value? Probably not! As long as the expectation existed (borne out by reality) that retained earnings were being reinvested to increase the asset base of the company, the firm would have some value.

Dividends are currently taxed at 2½ times the rate for long-term capital gains. In this environment, many investors prefer to have capital gains from appreciating stock prices rather than dividends. Nevertheless, there has always been the "bird-in-the-hand theory" that dividends are worth more than earnings because, once paid to the stockholder, the company cannot take them away. While it is true that dividends do have information content and thus influence expectations, rising dividends are no guarantee that the common stock will also rise in the short run.

Fortune magazine compiled a list of companies with no dividends and with rising dividends for the period from 1970 to 1980. The results are not necessarily what one might expect. Table 6–2 shows 12 companies that paid no dividends over the entire 10-year period. The median annual return for these companies was 18.7 percent versus 9.4 percent for the Fortune 500 as a whole.

TABLE 6–2   A Dozen That Paid No Dividends

	Total return to investors, 1970–80	
Company	Annual average compounded (percent)	Rank in Fortune 500
NVF	41.7%	2
National Semiconductor*	33.3	7
Teledyne*	32.2	9
Tosco*	28.9	17
Data General*	25.3	34
Penn Central	19.9	78
Digital Equipment*	17.4	96
Lockheed	13.9	143
Median for 500	9.4	
LTV	6.9	284
Crown Cork & Seal	4.6	342
DPF*	(5.7)	451
Memorex*	(13.9)	463

* Company has never paid a cash dividend.
Source: "Fresh Evidence that Dividends Don't Matter," *Fortune,* May 4, 1981, p. 351. *Fortune* Magazine Art Department. © 1981 Time Inc. All rights reserved.

Table 6–3 presents 19 companies with rising dividends over this decade. The 19 companies with rising dividends performed rather poorly on the basis of total return because of declining stock prices.

While increased dividends generally increase common stock value, we see that this is not always the case. If a company's overall performance is questionable, then raising dividends may not encourage investors. Although the examples in Table 6–3 represent exceptions to the rule, they occur frequently enough to deserve investor caution.

EARNINGS VALUATION MODELS

Dividend valuation models are best suited for those companies that are in the expansion or maturity phase of their life cycle. Dividends of these companies are more predictable and usually make up a larger percentage of the total return than capital gains. Earnings-per-share models are also used for valuation. For example, the investor may take the present value of all future earnings to determine a value. This might be particularly appropriate where the firm pays no cash dividend and has no intention of paying one.

The Combined Earnings and Dividend Model

Another, more comprehensive valuation model relies on earnings per share (EPS) and a price-earnings ratio (earnings multiplier) combined with a finite

TABLE 6–3   Growing Dividends Didn't Save These Stocks

Company	Growth in cash dividends, average annual rate, compounded 1971–80 (percent)	Decline in stock price 1970–80 (percent)	Total return to investors, 1970–80	
			Annual average return, compounded (percent)	Rank in Fortune 500
Burroughs	26.6%	(1.4%)	1.2%	398
Brunswick	24.7	(17.3)	1.3	396
Economics Laboratory	16.7	(13.2)	.8	404
Jim Walter	16.3	(16.4)	1.9	386
Georgia-Pacific	14.0	(4.1)	2.4	381
Nashua	13.5	(16.8)	1.5	392
Coca-Cola	11.8	(21.2)	1.0	402
Brockway Glass	10.4	(36.4)	.7	411
Avon Products	10.0	(61.4)	(5.2)	449
Colgate-Palmolive	9.9	(8.1)	3.0	375
Quaker Oats	9.0	(6.4)	2.9	376
Warner-Lambert	8.7	(41.2)	(1.8)	432
ITT	8.5	(40.7)	.5	413
Owens-Illinois	8.4	(10.5)	3.3	370
Champion Spark Plug	8.0	(11.5)	4.2	350
Heublein	7.7	(38.3)	(1.3)	428
National Service Industries	7.3	(9.3)	5.0	324
Sybron	6.8	(45.4)	(1.7)	431
Squibb	4.9	(17.9)	.8	405

Source: "Fresh Evidence that Dividends Don't Matter" *Fortune,* May 4, 1981, p. 354. *Fortune* Magazine Art Department. © 1981 Time Inc. All rights reserved.

dividend model. The value of a common stock can be viewed as a dividend stream plus a market price at the end of the dividend stream. Using Procter & Gamble as an example, we develop a present value for the stock at the beginning of 1986 (the numbers are shown in Table 6–4).

The total present value (stock price) for Procter & Gamble is shown at the bottom of Table 6–4 to be $79.38. Note that Part A of Table 6–4 describes the present value of future dividends, while Part B is used to determine the present value of the future stock price. These are assumed to be the two variables that determine the current stock price under this model.

In Part A, earnings per share are first projected for the next five years. The earnings are then multiplied by the company's estimated payout ratio of 45 percent to determine anticipated dividends per share for the next five years. In this example, we are assuming investors have a 13 percent required rate of return, so that is used as the discount rate. The present value of five years of dividends is shown in column (5) of Part A of Table 6–4 as $13.11.

In Part B of the table, we multiply 1990 earnings per share of $10.17 by

TABLE 6–4   Procter & Gamble Present Value Analysis at Beginning of 1986

Part A: Present value of dividends for 5 years

	(1) Estimated earnings per share (growth = 10%) ×	(2) Estimated payout ratio =	(3) Estimated dividends per share ×	(4) PV factor (13%) =	(5) Present value
Year					
1986	$ 6.95	.45	3.13	.885	$ 2.77
1987	7.64	.45	3.44	.783	2.69
1988	8.41	.45	3.78	.693	2.62
1989	9.25	.45	4.16	.613	2.55
1990	10.17	.45	4.58	.543	2.48
					$13.11

Part B: Present value of common stock price   +

Year	EPS ×	P/E =	Price ×	PV factor	
1990	$10.17	12.0	$122.04	.543	66.27

A + B = Total present value of Procter & Gamble
common stock at the beginning of 1986 $79.38

the P/E multiple (earnings multiple) of 12 to arrive at an anticipated price five years into the future. This price of $122.04 is then discounted back for five years at 13 percent to arrive at a present value of $66.27.

The present value of the stock is equal to the present value of the dividend stream for five years ($13.11) plus the present value of the future stock price of ($66.27) for a total current value of $79.38 at the beginning of 1986.

The Pure, Short-Term Earnings Model

Often, investors/speculators take a very short-run view of the market and simply ignore using present value analysis with its associated long-term forecasts of dividends and earnings per share. Instead they only use earnings per share and apply an appropriate multiplier to compute the estimated value.

Applying this approach to Procter & Gamble's financial data initially presented in Table 6–4, we arrive at a value of $83.40, based on 1986 earnings and a price–earnings multiplier of 12.

$$P_0 = EPS \times P/E$$
$$= \$6.95 \times 12$$
$$P_{1986} = \$83.40$$

Of course, every method of valuation has its limitations. Although this method is simplified by ignoring dividends and present value calculations, earnings need to be correctly estimated, and the appropriate price–earnings (P/E) multiplier must be applied. Unfortunately, just as in the dividend models, even if the estimated EPS is correct, there is no assurance that the market will agree with your P/E ratio.

THE PRICE–EARNINGS RATIO

The price–earnings ratio is simply the price per share divided by earnings per share. The price–earnings ratio is ultimately set by investors in the market-place. In the previous section, we attempted to determine the value of a share of Procter & Gamble at the end of the year by estimating earnings per share and the likely P/E ratio. The P/E ratio may or may not turn out to equal our estimate. Any stock that has positive earnings may have its P/E ratio computed at any point in time. The current price of the stock is simply divided by 12 months of earnings per share.

Even though the current P/E ratio for a stock in the market is known, investors may or may not agree that it is appropriate. In fact, stockbrokers and investors probably spend more time examining P/E ratios and assessing their appropriate level than any other variable. Although the use of P/E ratios in valuation approaches lacks the theoretical underpinning of the present value-based dividend and earnings valuation models previously discussed in the chapter, P/E ratios are equally important. The well-informed student of invest-ments should have a basic understanding of both the theoretically based present-value approach and the more pragmatic, frequently used P/E ratio approach.

What determines whether a stock should have a high or low P/E ratio? Let's first talk about the market for stocks in general, and then we will look at individual securities.

Stocks generally trade at a relatively high P/E ratio (perhaps 13 or greater) when there are strong growth prospects in the economy. However, inflation also plays a key role in determining P/E ratios for the overall market.

It is interesting to note that the market was generally rising between 1973 and January of 1981 while price-earnings ratios were falling. This can be seen in Figure 6–2, in which stock prices are graphed on the upper portion of the figure and measured along the left-hand axis, and the range of annual P/E ratios is shown on the bottom portion of the figure, with values presented on the right-hand axis.

Why were P/E ratios declining between 1973 and early 1981? The year 1973 was the start of particularly high inflation, which continued into 1981 and finally was significantly reduced by 1984. To further illustrate the point, Figure 6–3 presents the relationship between the year-end Standard & Poor's 500 composite P/E ratio and the annual rate of inflation measured by the change in the consumer price index (CPI). The graphical relationship between these two variables shows that they are inversely related. The price–earnings ratio goes down when the change in the CPI goes up and the reverse is also true.

FIGURE 6–2   Standard & Poor's 500 Stock Index and Price–Earnings Ratios

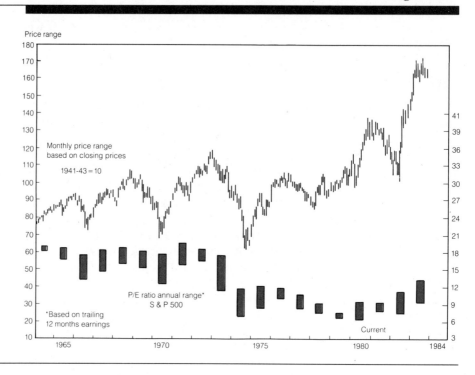

The dramatic drop in the P/E ratio in 1973–74 can be attributed to a large degree on the rate of inflation increasing from 3.41 percent in 1972 to 12.2 percent in 1974, or a change of more than three times its former level. For a brief period (1976) inflation decreased to an annual rate of less than 5 percent, only to soar to 13.3 percent by 1979. The average rate of inflation for 1982–83 was reduced to 3.84 percent and the market responded by paying higher share prices for one dollar of earnings (that is, higher P/E ratios). Perhaps if investors can be convinced that inflation will average less than 5 percent over the coming years, P/E ratios may again reach their former high levels. As was pointed out in Chapter 1, required rates of return are directly influenced by the rate of inflation. As inflation increases, the required rate of return on common stocks, K_e, rises, and prices decline. This is the basic mechanism that causes inflation to indirectly influence P/E ratios.

Of course, other factors besides the previously mentioned growth factor and the heavily emphasized inflationary considerations influence the P/E ratio for the market in general. Federal Reserve policy and interest rates, federal deficits, the government's leading indicators, the political climate, the mood and confidence of the population, international considerations, and many other factors have an influence on the P/E ratio for the overall market. The astute analyst is constantly studying a multitude of variables in analyzing the future outlook for P/E ratios.

FIGURE 6–3   Inflation and Price–Earnings Ratios

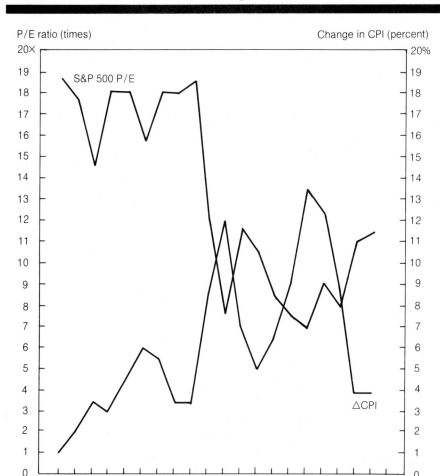

The P/E Ratio for Individual Stocks

Although the overall market P/E ratio is the collective average of individual P/Es, those factors that influence the market P/E do not necessarily impact P/E ratios of individual companies consistently from one industry to another. An individual firm's P/E ratio is heavily influenced by its growth prospects and the risk associated with its future performance. In Table 6–5, we see examples of growth rates and P/E ratios for different industries and firms. Generally, a strong future growth rate for 1984–89 (column 4) is associated with a reason-ably high P/E for mid-1984 (column 6). Obviously the relationship can be complicated by other considerations. For example, the brokerage firm, Merrill Lynch, shows an inordinately high P/E ratio of 60x in mid–1984. This is associated with a mere 7.0 percent expected growth rate for EPS in 1984–89.

TABLE 6–5   P/E and Growth in EPS

(1)	(2)	(3)	(4)	(5)	(6)	(7)
		5-year EPS growth	Expected growth	1979–83 median	P/E	Expected normal
Industry	Company	1979–83	EPS 1984–89	P/E	Mid-1984	P/E
Appliances	Maytag	5.0%	8.2%	9.8×	8.7×	10.0×
Newspaper	Dow Jones	19.0	19.5	14.0	19.5	27.0
Railroads	CSX	9.5	15.5	6.5	6.0	9.5
Drugs	Bristol Myers	13.5	15.0	12.0	13.7	15.0
Fast Foods	McDonald's	17.5	15.0	12.0	11.5	13.0
Trucking	Roadway	11.5	13.0	13.0	9.3	13.0
Tobacco	Reynolds	10.5	9.5	6.5	7.6	8.0
Brokerage	Merrill Lynch	26.0	7.0	7.5	60.0	10.0

Source: *Value Line Investment Survey,* selected issues (Value Line Inc.)

The reason behind this inconsistency is that Merrill Lynch's recent earnings are down sharply. Their slightly reduced price over an *unusually* low earnings base gives the appearance of a high P/E ratio. This high P/E ratio is phantom in nature and will work itself down as earnings improve, even if the stock price increases somewhat. Highly cyclical firms, such as those in the brokerage, auto, or housing industries, have temporarily misleading P/E ratios from time to time when their earnings are very low.

In addition to the future growth of the firm and the risk associated with that growth, investors and analysts also consider a number of other factors that influence a firm's P/E ratio. These cannot be easily quantified; nevertheless they have an impact on a broad range of stocks. Included in this category are the debt-to-equity ratio and the dividend policy of the firm. All things being equal, the less debt that a firm has, the more likely it is to be highly valued in the marketplace.

The dividend policy is a more elusive matter. For firms that show superior internal reinvestment opportunities, low cash dividends may be acceptable. On the other hand, maturing companies may be expected to pay a high cash dividend. For the latter group, a reduction in cash dividends may be associated with a lower P/E ratio.

Certain industries also traditionally command higher P/E ratios than others. Over the years, it would appear that investors have some preference for industries that have a high technology and research emphasis. Thus firms in computers, medical research and health care, and sophisticated telecommunications often have higher P/E ratios than the market in general. This does not mean that firms in these industries represent superior investments, but merely that investors value their earnings more highly.[2] There are also fads and other

----

[2] William Kittrell, Geoffrey A. Hirt, and Roger Potter, "Price-Earnings Multiples, Investors' Expectations, and Rates of Return: Some Analytical and Empirical Findings," paper presented at the 1984 Financial Management Association meeting.

factors that cause a shift in industry popularity from time to time. For example, because Ronald Reagan has emphasized military strength, defense-oriented stocks have been popular during his administration. Jimmy Carter stressed the need for environmental control, and stocks dealing in air and water pollution control traded at high P/E ratios during his tenure in office.

Another factor that influences a firm's P/E ratio is the quality of management as perceived by those in the marketplace. To the extent that management is viewed as being highly capable, clever, or innovative, the firm may carry a higher P/E ratio. Investors may look to magazines such as *Forbes* or *Business Week,* which highlight management strategies by various companies, or to management-oriented books such as *In Search of Excellence.*[3] Of course, it is entirely possible that today's trend setters may represent tomorrow's failures.

Not only is the quality of management important to investors in determining the firm's P/E ratio, but so is the quality of earnings. As, perhaps, you have studied in accounting and will observe further in the next chapter on financial statement analysis, there are many interpretations of a dollar's worth of earnings. Some companies choose to use very conservative accounting practices so that their reported earnings can be interpreted as being very solid by investors (in fact they may even be understated). Other companies use more liberal accounting interpretations in order to report maximum earnings to their shareholders, and they, at times, overstate their true performance. It is easy to see that a dollar's worth of conservatively reported earnings may be valued at a P/E ratio of 13 to 15 times, whereas a dollar's worth of liberally reported earnings should be valued at a much lower multiple.

All of these factors impact a firm's P/E ratio. Thus, investors will consider growth in sales and earnings, future risk, the debt position, the dividend policy, the quality of management and earnings, and a multitude of other factors in eventually arriving at the P/E ratio. The P/E ratio, like the price of the stock, is set by the interaction of the forces of demand and supply for the security. Those firms which are expected to provide returns greater than the overall economy, with equal or less risk, generally have superior P/E ratios.

Relating an Individual Stock's P/E Ratio to the Market—the General Signal Corporation

The General Signal Corporation is a leading producer of electronic and hydraulic control devices (pumps, valves, etc.). Table 6–6 provides a summary of earnings per share (EPS), the high-low stock price, and high-low P/E ratio for the company. Also shown is the average P/E ratio for the Standard & Poor's 500 Stock Index over a similar time period. In the last three columns, the high, average, and low P/E ratio for General Signal Corporation is compared to the average P/E ratio for the Standard & Poor's 500 Stock Index. For example, in 1976, General Signal's high P/E ratio is 14.20. The Standard & Poor's 500 Stock

---

[3] Thomas J. Peters and Robert H. Waterman, Jr., *In Search of Excellence* (New York: Harper & Row, 1982).

TABLE 6–6   General Signal Corporation—EPS, Price, P/E, and P/E Relative

Year	General Signal EPS	General Signal price		General Signal P/E			Standard & Poor's 500 P/E Average*	General Signal's P/E relative to S&P 500		
	EPS	High	Low	High	Average	Low	Average*	High	Ave.	Low
1976	2.00	28.40	17.10	14.20	11.36	8.6	11.25	1.26	1.01	.76
1977	2.43	29.50	22.70	12.14	9.28	9.3	9.28	1.31	1.16	1.00
1978	2.93	33.70	23.50	11.50	9.75	8.0	8.33	1.38	1.17	.96
1979	3.52	39.10	25.00	11.11	9.14	7.1	7.43	1.50	1.23	.96
1980	4.01	54.20	28.20	13.52	10.26	7.0	8.02	1.69	1.28	.87
1981	4.23	51.38	33.38	12.15	9.99	7.9	8.47	1.43	1.18	.93
1982	3.85	47.00	28.00	12.21	9.79	7.3	8.82	1.38	1.11	.83
1983	3.16	52.38	40.50	16.58	14.72	12.8	12.69	1.31	1.16	1.01
1984	4.15e									

Average high P/E for last five years for General Signal	13.11
Average low P/E for last five years for General Signal	8.42
Average P/E for last five years for General Signal	10.77
S&P's average P/E for last five years	9.09
Average P/E relative to S&P's 500 for last five years	1.19

e = Estimated.
* Quarterly average based on 12-month moving average EPS.

Index value is 11.25, and the relative (or ratio between the two) is 1.26. The same relationship can be derived for General Signal's average and low P/E ratios.

The second part of Table 6–6 provides average values over the last five years; for example, the average high P/E ratio over the last five years for General Signal is 13.11, the average low P/E is 8.42, etc.

Using the information from Table 6–6, we can derive a range of reasonable price predictions for General Signal based upon our estimates of future earnings per share. We indicate the following:

Year	Estimated EPS	P/E*			Anticipated stock price		
		High	Ave.	Low	High	Ave.	Low
1984e	$4.15	13.11	10.77	8.42	$54.41	$44.70	$34.94
1985e	4.73	13.11	10.77	8.42	62.01	50.94	39.83
1986e	5.39	13.11	10.77	8.42	70.66	58.05	45.38
1987e	6.15	13.11	10.77	8.42	80.63	66.24	51.78
1988e	7.01	13.11	10.77	8.42	91.90	75.50	59.02

e = Estimated.
* Taken from the second part of Table 6–6.

The earnings forecasts are based on an analysis of historical growth and future prospects. In September of 1984 General Signal was actually trading at

$48.75 per share. This price is a little higher than the average value of $44.70 shown above for 1984, but seems reasonable, given our analysis of historical P/E ratios. Furthermore, if earnings projections come through, higher stock values may be expected in the future.

What about a comparison of General Signal's P/E ratio to the Standard & Poor's 500? As indicated in the last line of the second part of Table 6–6, General Signal's average P/E carries a premium multiple of 1.19 times the average S&P 500. The Standard & Poor's Index was actually selling at 10.3 times earnings per share in late 1984. Based on the normal relationship to the S&P Index, General Signal should have a P/E ratio of 12.26 (10.3 × 1.19). This would imply a stock price of $50.88 (12.26 × $4.15) which is $2 higher than its current price. Whether this is reasonable or not would require much further analysis. The assumption of this kind of analysis is that by picking stocks selling at the low end of their P/E relative you have a better chance of outperforming the overall market.

FORECASTING EARNINGS PER SHARE

The other side of choosing an appropriate P/E is forecasting the earnings per share of a company with the proper growth rate. There are several ways investors can get earnings forecasts. They can rely on professional brokerage house research, investment advisory firms such as Value Line, financial magazines such as *Forbes* or *Business Week,* or they can do it themselves.

Investment Advisory Services

Standard & Poor's Earnings Forecaster is a service that provides estimated earnings per share data from several different sources. Table 6–7 shows a few forecasts from this S&P publication for GEO International and for Georgia Pacific. The company providing the forecast is listed as well as the date the forecast was made (i.e., Advest, September 15 for GEO International). There can be a wide difference of opinion for some companies, such as Georgia Pacific in the lumber-housing industry. The estimates for 1982 vary from $2.25 per share to $3.75 per share. Obviously, Bache has a different concept of interest rates and the housing industry than the other forecasters.

Least Squares Trendline

One of the most common ways of forecasting earnings per share is to use regression or least squares growth analysis. This involves a statistical method whereby a trendline is fitted to a time series of historical earnings. This trendline, by definition, is a straight line which minimizes the distance of the individual observations from the line. Figure 6–4 depicts a scattergram for the earnings per share of XYZ Corporation. The earnings of this company have been fairly consistent, and so we get a good trendline with a minimum of variation. The compounded growth rate for the whole 10-year period was 16.5

TABLE 6–7   Sample data from *Standard & Poor's Earnings Forecaster*

Company and fiscal year ending date	Stock price	Estimated date	P/E ratio	Earnings per share 1980*	1981	1982
GEO International (September)	34		8×	2.31		
Advest		September 15			4.00–4.25	—
Bacon, Whipple		September 16			4.20	—
A. G. Edwards		October 7			4.10	5.70
Howard, Weil, Labouisse, Freidrichs		October 14			4.00	5.75
Georgia Pacific (December)	20		9×	2.34		
Bache		September 3			1.65†	2.25
E. F. Hutton & Co.		September 20			1.60†	2.50
Shearson		August 1			2.75†	3.75
United Business Service		October 5			2.10†	—

* Actual.
† Fully diluted.
Source: *Standard & Poor's Earnings Forecaster,* October 23, 1981.

percent, with 9.8 percent for the first 5 years and 20.4 for the last 5 years. This shows up in Figure 6–4 as two distinct five-year trendlines. Most universities have statistical programs that run regression analysis, and even handheld calculators have the ability to compute a growth rate from raw data.

Whenever a mechanical forecast is made, subjectivity still enters the decision in choosing the data which will be considered in the regression plot.

FIGURE 6–4   Least Squares Trendline for EPS of XYZ Corporation

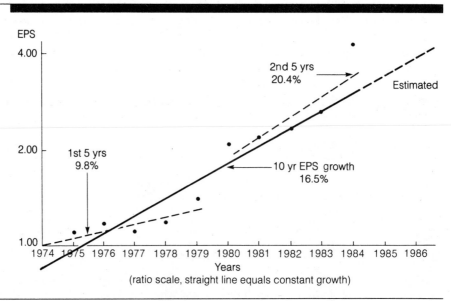

The analyst should be careful not to extrapolate a trend from a peak to a trough (bottom) or a trough to a peak. This can be extremely misleading for a cyclical industry. The analyst should also be sure to use enough data points to get a good line, and in cyclical industries, plot out the line for several business cycles to get a long-run average. Let's examine two actual companies to contrast different patterns of growth and the implications for forecasting.

Using Allied Corporation, a cyclical chemical stock, and Merck & Company, a consistently growing drug company, we compare earnings per share trends in Table 6–8. Both companies have achieved a similar overall growth over the time frame, but Allied Corporation is much more subject to ups and downs in the economy.

TABLE 6–8   Growth in Earnings per Share

Year	Earnings per share Allied Corporation (past 10-year EPS growth equals 12%)	Earnings per share Merck & Co. (past 10-year EPS growth equals 12%)
1972	1.59	1.99
1973	2.30	2.40
1974	3.62	2.79
1975	2.78	3.03
1976	3.01	3.38
1977	3.29	3.85
1978	2.83	4.07
1979	.13	5.06
1980	5.43	5.54
1981	6.11	5.36
1982	3.68	5.61
1983	4.17	6.10
1984e	5.20e	6.75e

e = Estimated.

The values are plotted in Figure 6–5. From that figure, it is clear that Merck & Company would provide the more reliable forecast based on past data. Its trendline is very consistent. While Merck has basically the same growth rate as Allied Corporation, it is much more stable with less deviation. In order to forecast Allied Corporation you would not start in 1982 and end in 1984 (trough to peak). Starting in 1977 would probably also not provide a "true" trendline because the line would begin at a cyclical peak. Clearly an Allied Corporation forecast based on 10 or 12 years of data is more reliable than a three- or five-year (based) forecast. With companies that follow economic cycles, the best forecasting period encompasses at least two peaks and two troughs or several business cycles. Remember that trendline earnings projected into the future, especially in the case of Allied Corporation, represent an average estimate and not an annual forecast.

FIGURE 6–5   Allied Corporation and Merck & Company EPS Trendlines

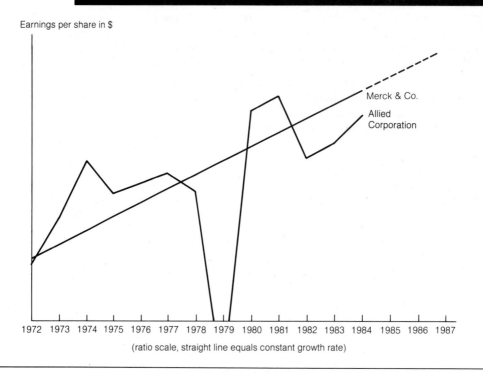

Earnings per share in $

Merck & Co.

Allied
Corporation

1972 1973 1974 1975 1976 1977 1978 1979 1980 1981 1982 1983 1984 1985 1986 1987

(ratio scale, straight line equals constant growth rate)

The Income Statement Method

A more process-oriented method of forecasting earnings per share is to start
with a sales forecast and create a standardized set of financial statements based
on historical relationships. Of course, the sales forecast must be accurate if the
earnings estimates are to have any significance. This method can be involved
and provides a student with a very integrated understanding of the relationships that go into the creation of earnings. For a firm such as Merck & Co. there
would not be much gained from an income statement forecast, but for Allied
Corporation the cyclical nature of profitability would be brought out.

Several important factors are included in this method of forecasting. The
analyst is forced to examine profitability and the resultant fluctuations in profit
margins before and after taxes. The impact of short-term interest expense and
any new bond financing can be factored into the analysis as well as any increase in shares of common stock from new equity financing.

Most analysts use an abbreviated method of forecasting earnings per
share. They use a sales forecast combined with aftertax profit margins. For
example, let us assume that the Hutchins Corporation has a sales and profit
margin history as set forth in Table 6–9. The sales have been growing at a 10
percent growth rate, and so the forecast is a simple extrapolation. However,

TABLE 6–9   Abbreviated Income Statement Method—Hutchins Corporation

Year	Sales ($000s)	Aftertax profit margin	Earnings ($000s)	Shares (000s)	Earnings per share
1980	$1,250,000	7.9%	$ 98,750	30,000	$3.29
1981	1,375,000	9.1	125,125	31,500	3.97
1982	1,512,500	8.5	128,562	33,200	3.87
1983	1,663,750	6.5	108,143	35,000	3.08
1984	1,830,125	8.3	151,900	35,200	4.31
1985	2,013,137	8.7	175,142	37,000	4.73
1986e	2,214,452	8.2	173,958	38,400	4.53
1987e	2,435,896	9.0	219,230	39,800	5.50

e = Estimated.

the profit margin has fluctuated between 6.5 percent and 9.1 percent, with 8.2 percent being the average. Common stock outstanding has also grown consistently by an average of 1.4 million shares per year. Given the cyclical nature of the profit margin, 8.2 percent was used for 1986, which is expected to be an average year. Nine percent was used for 1987, a year expected to be economically more robust. Multiplying the profit margin times the estimated sales produced an estimate of earnings which was divided by the number of shares outstanding to find the earnings per share. Once the EPS is found, it still must be plugged into a valuation model to determine a normal value.

GROWTH STOCKS AND GROWTH COMPANIES

In assessing the worth of an investment, stockbrokers, analysts, and investors often make reference to such terms as *growth stock* and *growth companies.* As part of the process of improving your overall valuation skills, you should have some familiarity with these terms.

A *growth stock* may be defined as the common stock of a company generally growing faster than the economy or market norm. These companies are usually predictable in their earnings growth. Many of the more popular growth stocks, such as 3M, Eastman Kodak, and McDonald's, are really in the middle-to-late stages of the expansion phase. They tend to be fully valued and recognized in the marketplace.

Growth companies, on the other hand, are those companies that exhibit rising returns on assets each year and sales that are growing at an increasing rate (growth phase of the life-cycle curve). Growth companies may not be as well known or recognized as growth stocks. Companies that may be considered to be growth companies might be in such industries as cable television, word processors, personal computers, medical electronics, and so on. These companies are growing very rapidly, and extrapolations of growth trends can be very dangerous if you guess incorrectly. There are many things that growth companies have in common. Usually, they have developed a proprietary product that is patented and protected from competition like the Xerox process (now other companies can use the dry process). This market protection allows a high rate of return and generates cash for new-product development.

One of the things that growth stocks and growth companies have in common is good research and development (R&D). Each company tries to prolong the growth and expansion phase of its life cycle as long as possible with new products or improved products. Value Line's November 13, 1981, issue of *Selection and Opinion* featured an article entitled "R&D: Key to Growth." Value Line took 409 companies over the 1978–80 period and measured research and development expenditures as a percentage of sales. They then ranked these 409 companies from the highest to lowest (R&D/sales) ratio. The top 10 R&D companies' average spending was 11 percent of sales dollars on research and development, which generated an earnings per share growth of 33.7 percent over the 10-year period. The bottom 10 companies spent less than .12 percent on average, and EPS grew at only 8.3 percent. A further test with the top 100 companies showed R&D/sales averaged 5.6 percent with a resultant 15.2 percent growth in EPS, while the bottom 100 companies' R&D/sales averaged .44 percent and increased earnings 11.3 percent.

Besides research and development, there are other indicators of growth potential. Companies should have sales growth greater than the economy by a reasonable margin. Increasing sales should be translated into similar earnings growth, which means consistently stable and high profit margins. Additionally, the earnings growth should show up in earnings per share growth (no dilution of earnings through unproductive stock offers). The firm should have a low labor cost as a percentage of total cost, since wages are prone to be inflexible on the downside but difficult to control on the upside.

The biggest error made in searching for growth-oriented companies is that the price may already be too high. By the time you identify the company, so has everyone else, and the price is probably inflated. If the company has one quarter where earnings do not keep up with expectations, the stock price could tumble. The trick, of course, is to find growth companies before they are generally recognized in the market, and this requires taking more risk in small companies trading over-the-counter.

ASSETS AS A SOURCE OF STOCK VALUE

Up until now, our emphasis has been primarily on earnings and dividends as the source of value. However, in certain industries, asset values may have considerable importance. These assets may take many forms—cash and marketable securities, buildings, land, timber, old movies, oil, and other natural resources. At times, any one of these assets may dominate a firm's value. Furthermore, companies with heavy cash positions are attractive merger and acquisition candidates because there is a possibility that a firm with highly

TABLE 6–10 Value from Energy Reserves

Company (1980 revenues in $ millions)	(1) Operating income (percent) Pipelines	(2) Operating income (percent) Oil and gas production	(3) Present value of proven reserves on 12/31/80 (per share)	(4) Stock price (early March)	(5) Price as multiple of estimated 1981 earnings*	(6) Yield (percent)
Interstate transmission:						
Texas Eastern ($4,272)	35%	54%	$178.17	$57.00	6.1	5.6%
United Energy Resources ($4,135)	91	9	14.49	42.75	6.3	3.6
Transco Companies ($2,628)	85	15	43.19	47.00	9.4	3.1
Panhandle Eastern Pipe Line ($2,472)	56	44	25.17	42.00	6.7	4.1
Southern Natural Resources ($1,798)	58†	8†	16.21	67.25	8.9	2.8
Intrastate transmission:						
ENSERCH ($2,695)	41	35	27.06‡	50.25	10.1	3.4
Houston Natural Gas ($2,358)	54	18	12.49§	49.50	8.5	2.6
Texas Oil & Gas ($1,191)	40‡	55‡	15.02 ‖	37.25	19.4	.5

* Source for earnings: Institutional Brokers Estimate System.
† Percent of net income.
‡ Estimate.
§ On July 31, 1980.
‖ On August 31, 1980.
Source: "There is Still a Glow in Gas Pipelines," *Fortune*, April 6, 1981, p. 96. *Fortune* Magazine Art Department.

liquid assets could be taken over and its own cash used to pay back debt incurred in the takeover.

In the 1970s and 1980s, natural resources have also had an important influence on value. Let's briefly examine this topic.

Natural Resources

Natural resources, such as timber, copper, gold, and oil, often give a company value even if the assets are not producing an income stream. This is because of the present value of the future income stream that is expected as these resources are used up. Companies like International Paper, Weyerhaeuser, and other forest-product companies have timberlands with market values far in excess of their book values and, in some cases, in excess of their common stock prices.

Oil companies with large supplies of oil under the ground may have to wait 20 years before some of it is pumped, but there may be substantial value there. In the case of natural-gas pipeline companies, increasing reserves have changed the way these companies are viewed by the market. They used to be considered similar to utilities because of their natural gas transmission system, but now they are also being valued based on their hidden assets (called energy reserves). Table 6–10 gives a list of pipeline companies and the present value of their proven reserves compared to the common stock price (in the third and fourth columns).

Investors should not overlook hidden assets because of naive extrapolation of past data or failure to understand an industry or company. Furthermore, assets do not always show up on the books of a company. They may be fully depreciated, like the movies *Sound of Music*, *Jaws*, or *Star Wars*, but still have substantial value in the television market.

Chapter 7

FINANCIAL STATEMENT ANALYSIS

Financial statements present a numerical picture of a company's financial and operating health. Since each company is different, an analyst needs to examine the financial statements for industry characteristics as well as for differences in accounting methods. The major financial statements are the balance sheet, income statement, and the sources-and-uses-of-funds statements. A very helpful long-term financial overview is usually provided by a 5- or 10-year summary statement found in the corporate annual report. One must remember that the footnotes to these statements are an integral part of the statements and provide a wealth of in-depth explanatory information. More depth can often be found in additional reports such as the 10K filed with the Securities and Exchange Commission and obtainable on request (free of charge) from most companies.

Fundamental analysis depends on variables internal to the company, and the corporate financial statements are one way of measuring fundamental value and risk. Financial statement analysis should be combined with economic and industry analysis before a final judgment is made to purchase or sell a specific security. Chapter 6 presented methods of valuation that used forecasts of dividends and earnings per share. Earnings per share combined with an estimated price–earnings ratio was also used to get a future price. Careful study of financial statements provides the analyst with much of the necessary information to forecast earnings and dividends, to judge the quality of earnings, and to determine financial and operating risk.

THE MAJOR FINANCIAL STATEMENTS

In the first part of this chapter, we examine the three basic types of financial statements—the income statement, the balance sheet, and the sources-and-uses-of-funds statement—with particular attention paid to the interrelationships among these three measurement devices. In the rest of the chapter, ratio analysis is presented in detail, and deficiencies of financial statements are discussed along with the impact of inflation and the role of the security analyst in interpreting financial statements.

Income Statement

The income statement is the major device for measuring the profitability of a firm over a period of time. An example of the income statement is presented in Table 7–1 for The Coca-Cola Company. First of all, note that the income statement is for a defined period of time, whether it be one month, three months, or a year. The statement is presented in a stair-step, or progressive, fashion so that we may examine the profit or loss after each type of expense item is deducted.

For 1983, The Coca-Cola Company had net operating revenues (sales) of $6,828,992,000. After subtracting the cost of goods sold and selling, administrative, and general expenses, the firm's operating income was $992,625,000. Because of a high level of cash and marketable securities during 1983, Coca-Cola had more interest income than interest expense (not a common occur-

TABLE 7–1   The Coca-Cola Company Income Statement

Consolidated Statements of Income		*The Coca-Cola Company and Subsidiaries*	
(In thousands except per share data)			
Year Ended December 31,	**1983**	1982	1981
Net Operating Revenues	**$6,828,992**	$6,021,135	$5,698,901
Cost of goods and services	**3,772,741**	3,310,847	3,187,924
Gross Profit	**3,056,251**	2,710,288	2,510,977
Selling, administrative and general expenses	**2,063,626**	1,830,527	1,724,925
Operating Income	**992,625**	879,761	786,052
Interest income	**82,912**	106,172	70,604
Interest expense	**72,677**	74,560	38,301
Other income (deductions)—net	**(2,528)**	6,679	(23,211)
Income From Continuing Operations			
Before Income Taxes	**1,000,332**	918,052	795,144
Income taxes	**442,072**	415,076	355,221
Income From Continuing Operations	**558,260**	502,976	439,923
Discontinued operations:			
Income from discontinued operations			
(net of applicable income taxes of			
$414 in 1983, $4,683 in 1982			
and $12,234 in 1981)	**527**	9,256	12,788
Gain on disposal of discontinued operations			
(net of applicable income taxes of $13,274)	**—**	—	29,071
Net Income	**$ 558,787**	$ 512,232	$ 481,782
Per Share:			
Continuing operations	**$ 4.10**	$ 3.88	$ 3.56
Discontinued operations	**—**	.07	.34
Net income	**$ 4.10**	$ 3.95	$ 3.90
Average Shares Outstanding	**136,222**	129,793	123,610

Source: The Coca-Cola Company Annual Report, 1983.

ance) and reported income from continuing operations before taxes of slightly over $1.0 billion. Income after taxes from continuing operations is $558,260,000. Notice that The Coca-Cola Company has been disposing of some assets for the last three years and that income from discontinued operations is listed separately. While income from discontinued operations was not material in all years, the analyst still needs this information. The income statement shows two earnings-per-share patterns. It is the earnings per share from continuing operations that are relevant in making forecasts of expected growth.

Are these good income figures or bad? As we shall see later, the analyst's interpretation of the numbers will depend on historical figures, industry data, and on the relationship of income to balance sheet items such as assets and net worth.

Balance Sheet

The balance sheet indicates what the firm owns, and how these assets are financed in the form of liabilities or ownership interest. While the income statement purports to show the profitability of the firm, the balance sheet delineates the firm's holdings and obligations. Together these statements are intended to answer two questions: How much did the firm make or lose, and what is a measure of its worth? A balance sheet for The Coca-Cola Company is presented in Table 7–2.

TABLE 7–2   The Coca-Cola Company Consolidated Balance Sheet

Consolidated Balance Sheets (In thousands except per share data)	*The Coca-Cola Company and Subsidiaries* December 31.	
Assets	1983	1982
Current		
Cash	$ 319,385	$ 177.530
Marketable securities, at cost (approximates market)	292,084	83.381
Trade accounts receivable, less allowances of		
$20,160 in 1983 and $21,336 in 1982	779,729	751.775
Inventories and unamortized film costs	744,107	808.799
Prepaid expenses and other assets	195,009	255.080
Total Current Assets	2,330,314	2.076.565
Investments, Film Costs and Other Assets		
Investments, at cost	241,780	221.909
Unamortized film costs	252,612	211.460
Other assets	240,880	241.395
	735,272	674.764
Property, Plant and Equipment		
Land	128,642	126.201
Buildings and improvements	618,586	602.475
Machinery and equipment	1,412,697	1.383.668
Containers	341,597	333.472
	2,501,522	2.445.816
Less allowances for depreciation	940,716	907.250
	1,560,806	1.538.566
Goodwill and Other Intangible Assets	601,430	633.415
	$5,227,822	$4.923.310
Liabilities and Shareholders' Equity	1983	1982
Current		
Loans and notes payable	$ 85,913	$ 70.561
Current maturities of long-term debt	20,783	50.623
Accounts payable and accrued expenses	910,951	792.250
Participations and other entertainment obligations	154,213	154.803
Accrued taxes—including income taxes	219,240	258.574
Total Current Liabilities	1,391,100	1.326,811
Participations and Other Entertainment Obligations	226,129	190.408
Long-Term Debt	513,202	462.344
Deferred Income Taxes	176,635	165.093
Shareholders' Equity		
Common stock, no par value—		
Authorized: 180,000,000 shares		
in 1983 and 140,000,000 shares		
in 1982;		
Issued: 136,653,676 shares in 1983		
and 136,099,741 shares in 1982	68,704	68.427
Capital surplus	500,031	478.308
Retained earnings	2,494,215	2.300.217
Foreign currency translation adjustment	(130,640)	(54.486)
	2,932,310	2.792.466
Less treasury stock, at cost (300,588 shares		
in 1983; 359,338 shares in 1982)	11,554	13,812
	2,920,756	2.778.654
	$5,227,822	$4.923.310

Source: The Coca-Cola Company Annual Report, 1983.

Note that the balance sheet is given at one point in time, in this case December 31, 1983. It does not represent the result of transactions for a specific month, quarter, or year, but rather is a cumulative chronicle of all transactions that have affected the corporation since its inception. This is in contrast to the income statement, which measures results only over a short, quantifiable period of time. Generally, balance sheet items are stated on an original cost basis rather than at market value.

The Coca-Cola Company was chosen for analysis because of its product diversification, international scope, and its well-known soft drinks such as Coca-Cola, Tab, Sprite, Diet Coke, etc. Its food division accounted for almost 19 percent of sales and 12 percent of operating income in 1983. This division includes Minute Maid orange juice, Hi-C fruit drinks, Maryland Club and But-ter-Nut coffees, Ronco household consumer products, and Presto pasta prod-ucts as well as institutional food service products.

During 1982 Coca-Cola purchased Columbia Pictures Industries as a diversification move. In 1983 this division accounted for 12.5 percent of reve-nues and 9 percent of operating income. Columbia produces the television series "Fantasy Island," and the daytime "soaps" "Days of Our Lives" and "The Young and the Restless." Some of the big-name movies produced by Columbia were *Tootsie, The Big Chill, The Natural, The Karate Kid,* and one of the biggest movies of all time, *Ghostbusters.*

Sources-and-Uses-of-Funds Statements

The third major financial statement is the sources-and-uses-of-funds statement (statement of changes in financial position). This statement supplements the income statement and balance sheet. As indicated in Figure 7–1, the sources-and-uses-of-funds statement allows us to measure how changes in the balance sheet were financed over a period of time. While the balance sheet is nothing more than a snapshot of the firm at a point in time, if we put together two such snapshots, we can ascertain significant changes.

In the case of Coca-Cola's sources-and-uses-of-funds statement (Table 7–3), the emphasis is on changes in the amount of working capital available to the firm. Working capital represents net short-term assets (current assets mi-nus current liabilities). Only the *noncurrent* changes in the balance sheet are listed individually in the major portions of Table 7–3. If we look at the differ-ence between long-term sources of funds and long-term uses of funds, the difference will tell us by how much working capital went up or down.[1]

Sources of working capital include increases in stockholders' equity, decreases in long-term assets, and increases in long-term liabilities. Applica-tions or uses of working capital include decreases in stockholders' equity, increases in long-term assets, and decreases in long-term liabilities. Changes in

---

[1] Other firms may use a cash approach, where the emphasis is on changes in every single account, rather than merely net working capital.

FIGURE 7–1   Relationship of Funds Statement to Balance Sheet

stockholders' equity are caused by profits or losses, cash dividends, and the retirement of securities, as well as accounting adjustments.

In the Coca-Cola example, sources of working capital totaled $1,107,027,000 in 1983. The primary contributions came from income from continuing operations ($558 million) and the adding back of depreciation, amortization, and deferred income tax charges that represented noncash deductions on the income statements. There were also contributions from the reduction of assets from discontinued operations, the sale of stock, the increases in long-term debt, and a number of other items.

The applications or uses of working capital were primarily in the form of cash dividends ($365 million), additions to property plant and equipment ($376 million), and additions to noncurrent film costs ($115 million). The total applications of working capital were $917,567,000.

Sources of working capital exceeded the *applications* of working capital by $189,460,000.

Source	$1,107,027,000
Application	917,567,000
Difference	$ 189,460,000

The allocation of the increased working capital is shown in the bottom part of Table 7–3.

In analyzing a sources and uses statement, the analyst must examine how the buildup (or reduction) in long-term assets was accomplished. For example, are increases in long-term assets being supported by profits and long-term borrowing, or are they being financed by the more dangerous route of short-term borrowing? Also, what is the source of funding for cash dividends? In the

TABLE 7–3   The Coca-Cola Company Sources and Uses of Funds

Consolidated Statements of Changes in Financial Position (In thousands)	The Coca-Cola Company and Subsidiaries		
Year Ended December 31,	1983	1982	1981
Source of Working Capital			
From operations:			
Income from continuing operations	$ 558,260	$ 502,976	$439,923
Add charges not requiring outlay of working capital during the year:			
Depreciation	153,655	143,549	132,713
Amortization:			
Goodwill	16,468	10,101	3,796
Noncurrent film costs	57,167	43,495	—
Deferred income taxes	12,220	48,702	23,169
Other	25,460	24,111	57,134
Total From Continuing Operations	823,230	772,934	656,735
Discontinued operations (excludes provisions for depreciation, amortization and deferred income taxes of $8,219 in 1983, $7,504 in 1982 and $7,186 in 1981)	8,746	16,760	49,045
Total From Operations	831,976	789,694	705,780
Net long-term assets of discontinued operations (including property, plant and equipment)	89,990	1,851	8,303
Common stock issued	22,000	370,152	1,090
Increase in long-term debt	50,398	249,392	4,057
Increase in participations and other entertainment obligations	35,721	—	—
Transfer of noncurrent film costs to current	16,987	93,909	—
Disposals of property, plant and equipment	34,972	44,467	64,023
Decrease in investments and other assets	—	21,836	—
Decrease in goodwill (purchase accounting adjustment)	20,547	—	—
Other	4,436	3,302	—
	1,107,027	1,574,603	783,253
Application of Working Capital			
Cash dividends	364,789	321,557	286,787
Acquisitions of purchased companies excluding net current assets:			
Property, plant and equipment—net	7,439	56,739	9,814
Other assets net of other liabilities	(583)	89,693	103
Goodwill	7,480	516,115	10
Additions to property, plant and equipment	376,197	325,016	319,792
Additions to noncurrent film costs	115,306	95,804	—
Increase in investments and other assets	19,361	—	86,284
Foreign currency translation	27,299	21,693	—
Other	279	28,153	11,215
	917,567	1,454,770	714,005
Increase in Working Capital	$ 189,460	$ 119,833	$ 69,248
Increase (Decrease) in Working Capital by Component			
Cash and marketable securities	$ 350,558	$ (78,631)	$108,456
Trade accounts receivable	27,954	268,284	(39,632)
Inventories and unamortized film costs	(64,692)	58,080	(59,516)
Prepaid expenses and other current assets	(60,071)	192,586	4,685
Loans and notes payable	(15,352)	19,086	(2,060)
Current maturities of long-term debt	29,840	(45,108)	2,013
Accounts payable and accrued expenses	(118,701)	(120,201)	60,974
Participations and other entertainment obligations	590	(154,803)	—
Accrued taxes—including income taxes	39,334	(19,460)	(5,672)
Increase in Working Capital	$ 189,460	$ 119,833	$ 69,248

Source: The Coca-Cola Company Annual Report, 1983.

case of Coca-Cola, there was strong funding from profits and depreciation/ amortization add-back to help meet these needs. Many companies are not so fortunate. For example, a number of hard-pressed firms in the energy industry in the 1980s had insufficient earnings to pay dividends or maintain or expand long-term asset commitments. In such cases short-term borrowing is required to meet long-term needs. This leads to a reduction in working capital and a dangerous operating position.

KEY FINANCIAL RATIOS FOR THE SECURITY ANALYST

We have just summarized the three major financial statements that will be the basis of your analysis in this section emphasizing financial ratios. Ratio analysis brings together balance sheet and income statement data to permit a better understanding of the firm's past and current health which will aid you in forecasting the future outlook.

Ratio Analysis

Ratios are used in much of our daily life. We buy cars based on miles per gallon; we evaluate baseball players by earned run averages and batting averages; basketball players by field goal and foul-shooting percentages, and so on. These are all ratios constructed to judge comparative performance. Financial ratios serve a similar purpose, but you must know what is being measured in order to construct a ratio and to understand the significance of the resultant number.

Financial ratios are used to weigh and evaluate the operating performance and capital structure of the firm. While an absolute value such as earnings of $50,000 or accounts receivable of $100,000 may appear satisfactory, its acceptability can only be measured in relation to other values.

For example, are earnings of $50,000 actually good? If a company earned $50,000 on $500,000 of sales (10 percent "profit margin" ratio), that might be quite satisfactory, whereas earnings of $50,000 on $5,000,000 could be disappointing (a meager 1 percent return.) After we have computed the appropriate ratio, we must compare our firm's results to the achievements of similar firms in the industry as well as to our own firm's past performance. Even then, this "number crunching" process is not always adequate because we are forced to supplement our financial findings with an evaluation of company management, physical facilities, and numerous other factors.

Ratio analysis will not discover "gold mines" for the analyst. It is more like a physical exam at the doctor's office. You hope you are all right but if not, you may be content to know what is wrong and what to do about it. Just as with medical illness some diseases are easier to cure than others, the same is true of financial illness. The analyst is the doctor. He or she determines the illness and keeps track of management to see if they can administer the cure. Sometimes ailing companies can be very good values. Penn-Central went into bankruptcy and its common stock could have been purchased at $2 per share for several years. In 1984, Penn Central stock traded in the $35–50 range. Chrysler and Lockheed were both on the brink of bankruptcy until the government made guaranteed loans available. Chrysler could have been bought at $3 per share and Lockheed at $1 per share, but by 1984 Chrysler traded in a price range of $20–32 and Lockheed $30–47. These were sick companies that got repaired, and any investor willing to take a risk would have profited nicely but albeit at great risk.

Bankruptcy Studies

In a sense, ratio analysis protects an investor from picking losers more so than it guarantees picking winners. Several studies have used ratios as predictors of financial failure. The most notable studies are by William Beaver and Edward Altman. Beaver found that ratios of failing firms signal failure as much as five years ahead of bankruptcy, and as bankruptcy approaches, the ratios deteriorate more rapidly, with the greatest deterioration in the last year. The Beaver studies also found that (*a*) "Investors recognize and adjust to the new solvency positions of failing firms and (*b*) the price changes of the common stocks act as if investors rely upon ratios as a basis for their assessments, and impound the ratio information in the market prices."[2]

The first Altman[3] research study indicated that five ratios combined were 95 percent accurate in predicting failure one year ahead of bankruptcy and were 72 percent accurate two years ahead of failure, with the average lead time for the ratio signal being 20 months. Altman developed a Z score which was an index developed through multiple discriminate analysis that could predict failure. Altman modified and improved his model's accuracy even further by increasing the number of ratios to seven.[4] This service is currently sold to institutional investors by Zeta Services Inc. The Z (zeta) score relies upon the following variables:

1. Retained earnings/total assets (cumulative profitability).
2. Standard deviation of operating income/total assets (measure of earnings stability during last 10 years).
3. Earnings before interest and taxes/total assets (productivity of operating assets).
4. Earnings before interest and taxes/Interest (leverage ratio, interest coverage).
5. Current assets/current liabilities (liquidity ratio).
6. Market value of common stock/book value of equity (a leverage ratio).
7. Total assets (proxy for size of the firm).

---

[2] Beaver, William H. "Market Prices, Financial Ratios, and the Prediction of Failure," *Journal of Accounting Research,* Autumn 1968, p. 192.

[3] Altman, Edward I. "Financial Ratios, Discriminant Analysis and the Prediction of Corporate Bankruptcy," *Journal of Finance,* September 1968, pp. 589–609.

[4] Altman, Edward I. *Corporate Financial Distress,* New York: John Wiley & Sons, 1983.

The greater the firm's bankruptcy potential, the lower its Z score. The ratios were not equally significant, but together they separated the companies into a correct bankruptcy group and nonbankruptcy group a high percentage of the time. Retained earnings/total assets has the heaviest weight in the analysis and leverage is also very important. In the next section we present six classifications of ratios that ought to be helpful to the analyst. Many more could be used, but these represent the most widely used measures.

Classification System

We divide 20 significant ratios into six primary groupings:

A. Profitability ratios:
   1. Operating margin.
   2. Aftertax profit margin.
   3. Return on assets.
   4. Return on equity.
B. Asset utilization ratios:
   5. Receivables turnover.
   6. Inventory turnover.
   7. Fixed asset turnover.
   8. Total asset turnover.
C. Liquidity ratios:
   9. Current ratio.
   10. Quick ratio.
   11. Net working capital to total assets.
D. Debt utilization ratios:
   12. Long-term debt to equity.
   13. Total debt to total assets.
   14. Times interest earned.
   15. Fixed charge coverage.
E. Price ratios:
   16. Price to earnings.
   17. Price to book value.
   18. Dividends to price (dividend yield).
F. Other ratios:
   19. Average tax rate.
   20. Dividend payout.

The interpretation of ratios is as much a science as an art, and one can compare ratio analysis to putting together a puzzle. It takes all the pieces of a puzzle to make a complete picture, but a skillful analyst can often get a good picture of the company with only 5 or 10 ratios. Whether the picture is in focus depends upon the interpretive skill of the analyst.

The users of financial statements will attach different degrees of importance to the six categories of ratios. To the potential investor, the critical consideration is profitability and debt utilization. For the banker or trade creditor, the emphasis shifts to the firm's current ability to meet debt obligations. The bondholder, in turn, may be primarily influenced by debt to total assets— while also eyeing the profitability of the firm in terms of its ability to cover interest payments in the short term and principal payments in the long term. Of course, the shrewd analyst looks at all the ratios, with different degrees of attention.

A. Profitability ratios.   The profitability ratios allow the analyst to measure the ability of the firm to earn an adequate return on sales, total assets, and invested capital. The profit margin ratios (1, 2) relate to income statement items, while the two return ratios (3, 4) relate the income statement (numerator) to the balance sheet (denominator). Many of the problems related to profitability can be explained, in whole or in part, by the firm's ability to effectively employ its resources. We shall apply these ratios to Coca-Cola's income statement and balance sheet for 1983 which were previously presented in Tables 7–1 and 7–2. The values are further rounded for ease of computation (dollars in millions).

Profitability ratios (Coca-Cola, 1983; in millions)

1. Operating margin $= \dfrac{\text{Operating income}}{\text{Sales (revenue)}} = \dfrac{\$\ 993}{\$6,829} = 14.54\%$

2. Aftertax profit margin $= \dfrac{\text{Net income}}{\text{Sales (revenue)}} = \dfrac{\$\ 559}{\$6,829} = 8.19\%$

3. Return on assets

   (a) $\dfrac{\text{Net income}}{\text{Total assets}} = \dfrac{\$\ 559}{\$5,228} = 10.69\%$

   (b) $\dfrac{\text{Net income}}{\text{sales}} \times \dfrac{\text{Sales}}{\text{Total assets}}$

   $\quad\quad 8.19\% \quad \times \quad 1.306 \quad\quad\quad = 10.69\%$

4. Return on equity

   (a) $\dfrac{\text{Net income}}{\text{Stockholder's equity}^5} = \dfrac{\$\ 559}{\$2,921} = 19.14\%$

   (b) $\dfrac{\text{Return on assets}}{(1 - \text{Debt/Assets})} = \dfrac{10.69\%}{1 - .441} = 19.14\%$

The profitability ratios indicate that Coca-Cola's aftertax profit margin, in comparison to the operating margin, is slightly higher than one would expect, given a 46 percent corporate tax rate for the year. This leads us to suspect that investment tax credits or other tax benefits reduced the tax rate.

---

[5] A working definition of stockholders' equity is the common stock accounts plus retained earnings. Coca-Cola also has a few other adjustments.

Du Pont Analysis—Notice that the return on assets and return on equity have parts (*a*) and (*b*), or two ways to determine the ratio. The methods employed in (*b*), which arise from the Du Pont Company's financial system, help the analyst see the relationship between the income statement and the balance sheet. The return on assets is generated by multiplying the aftertax profit margin (income statement) by the asset turnover ratio (combination income statement–balance sheet ratio).

The Du Pont Company was a forerunner in stressing that satisfactory return on assets may be achieved through high profit margins or rapid turnover of assets, or a combination of both. The Du Pont system causes the analyst to examine the sources of a company's profitability. Since the profit margin is an income statement ratio, a high profit margin indicates good cost control, whereas a high asset turnover ratio demonstrates efficient use of the assets on the balance sheet. Different industries have different operating and financial structures. For example, in the heavy capital goods industry the emphasis is on a high profit margin with a low asset turnover—while in food processing the profit margin is low and the key to satisfactory returns on total assets is a rapid turnover of assets.

Du Pont analysis further stresses that the return on equity stems from the return on assets adjusted for the amount of financial leverage by using the total debt-to-asset ratio. About 44 percent of The Coca-Cola Company's assets are financed by debt, and the return on equity reflects a high level of debt financing because return on equity (19.14 percent) is almost twice as large as return on assets (10.69 percent). As a detective, the financial analyst can judge how much debt a company employs by comparing these two measures of return. Of course, you will want to check this clue with the debt utilization ratios. The total relationship between return on assets and return on equity under the Du Pont system is depicted in Figure 7–2.

FIGURE 7–2   Du Pont Analysis

In computing return on assets and equity, the analyst must also be sensitive to the age of the assets. Plant and equipment purchased 15 years ago may be carried on the books far below its replacement value in an inflationary economy. A 20 percent return on assets that were purchased in the late 60s or early 70s may be inferior to a 15 percent return on newly purchased assets.

B. Asset utilization ratios.   Under this heading, we measure the speed at which the firm is turning over accounts receivable, inventory, and longer-term assets. In other words, asset utilitization ratios measure how many times per year a company sells its inventory or collects its accounts receivable. For long-term assets, the utilization ratio tells us how productive the fixed assets are in terms of sales generation.

Asset utilization ratios (Coca-Cola, 1983; in millions)

5.   Receivables turnover $= \dfrac{\text{Sales}}{\text{Receivables}} = \dfrac{\$6,829}{\$\ \ 780} = 8.76\times$

6.   Inventory turnover $= \dfrac{\text{Sales}}{\text{Inventory}} = \dfrac{\$6,829}{\$\ \ 744} = 9.18\times$

7.   Fixed asset turnover $= \dfrac{\text{Sales}}{\text{Fixed assets}} = \dfrac{\$6,829}{\$1,561} = 4.37\times$

8.   Total asset turnover $= \dfrac{\text{Sales}}{\text{Total assets}} = \dfrac{\$6,829}{\$5,228} = 1.30\times$

The asset utilization ratios relate the income statement (numerator) to the various assets on the balance sheet. Given that Coca-Cola's primary products are soft drinks and food, the receivable turnover and inventory turnover ratios reflect high turnover. Since most of the company's consumable products are not perishable, these ratios seem satisfactory. However the large amount of cash and marketable securities, as seen on the balance sheet, reduces the total asset turnover. We can also tell from comparing fixed asset turnover to total asset turnover that a sharp reduction in the ratios occurs. This does not seem to be totally warranted with such high receivables and inventory turnover even in light of the high cash position. Closer scrutiny of the balance sheet shows that the Investments, Film Costs, and Other Assets category accounts for $735 million in assets not included in fixed asset turnover, and the same is true of $600 million of goodwill. These factors create a lower total asset turnover without directly influencing fixed asset turnover.

C. Liquidity ratios.   The primary emphasis of the liquidity ratios is a determination of the firm's ability to pay off short-term obligations as they come due. These ratios can be related to receivables and inventory turnover in that a faster turnover creates a more rapid movement of cash through the company and improves liquidity. Again remember that each industry will be different. A jewelry store chain will have much different ratios than a grocery store chain.

Liquidity ratios (Coca-Cola, 1983; in millions)

9. Current ratio $= \dfrac{\text{Current assets}}{\text{Current liabilities}} = \dfrac{\$2,330}{\$1,391} = 1.675$

10. Quick ratio

$$\dfrac{\text{Current assets} - \text{inventories}}{\text{Current liabilities}} = \dfrac{\$2,330 - \$744}{\$1,391} = 1.14$$

11. Net working capital to total assets

$$\dfrac{\text{Current assets} - \text{Current liabilities}}{\text{Total assets}} = \dfrac{\$2,330 - \$1,391}{\$5,228} = .180$$

The first two ratios (current and quick) indicate whether the firm can pay off its short-term debt in an emergency by liquidating its current assets. The quick ratio looks only at the most liquid assets which include cash, marketable securities, and receivables. Cash and securities are already liquid but receivables usually will be turned into cash during the collection period. If there is concern about the firm's liquidity, the analyst will want to cross check the liquidity ratios with receivable turnover and inventory turnover to determine how fast the current assets are turned into cash during an ordinary cycle.

The last liquidity ratio is a measure of the percentage of current assets (after short-term debt has been paid) to total assets. This indicates the liquidity of the assets of the firm. The higher the ratio, the greater the short-term assets relative to fixed assets and the safer a creditor.

Coca-Cola seems to be in reasonable shape. Coke syrup is not that perishable and the raw ingredients such as sugar are readily marketable. This makes the current ratio of 1.675 quite safe when compared to a quick ratio of over 1.1.

D. Debt utilization ratios.   The debt utilization ratios provide an indication of the way the firm is financed between debt (lenders) and equity (owners) and therefore helps the analyst determine the amount of financial risk present in the firm. Too much debt can not only impair liquidity with heavy interest payments but can also damage profitability and the health of the firm during an economic recession or industry slowdown.

Debt utilization ratios (Coca-Cola, 1983; in millions)

12. Long-term debt to equity

$$\dfrac{\text{Long-term liabilities}}{\text{Stockholder's equity}} = \dfrac{\$\,513}{\$2,921} = .176$$

13. Total debt to total assets

$$\dfrac{\text{Total debt}}{\text{Total assets}} = \dfrac{\$2,307}{\$5,228} = .441$$

14. Times interest earned

$$\dfrac{\text{Income before interest and taxes}}{\text{Interest}} = \dfrac{\$\,993}{\$\,73} = 13.60\times$$

15.   Fixed charge coverage[6]

$$\frac{\text{Income before fixed charges and taxes}}{\text{Fixed charges}} = \frac{\$ \ 993}{\$ \ \ \ 73} = 13.60\times$$

We have already discussed the impact of financial leverage on return on equity, and the first two ratios in this category indicate to the analyst how much financial leverage is being used by the firm. The more debt, the greater the interest payments and the more volatile the impact on the firm's earnings. Companies with stable sales and earnings, such as utilities, can afford to employ more debt than those in cyclical industries, such as automobiles or airlines. Ratio 12, long-term debt to equity, provides information concerning the long-term capital structure of the firm. In the case of Coca-Cola, long-term liabilities represent 17 percent of the stockholders' equity base provided by the owners of the firm. Ratio 13, total debt to total assets, looks at the total assets and the use of borrowed capital. Each firm must consider its optimum capital structure, and the analyst should be aware of industry fluctuations in assessing the firm's proper use of leverage. Coca-Cola seems quite safe, given that its business is not subject to large swings in sales.

The last two debt utilization ratios indicate the firm's ability to meet its cash payments due on fixed obligations such as interest, leases, licensing fees, or sinking fund charges. The higher these ratios, the more protected the creditor's position. Use of the fixed charge coverage is more conservative than interest earned since it includes all fixed charges. Now that leases are capitalized and show up on the balance sheet it is easier to understand that lease payments are similar in importance to interest expense. Charges after taxes such as sinking fund payments must be adjusted to before-tax income. For example, if a firm is in the 40 percent tax bracket and must make a $60,000 sinking fund payment, the firm would have had to generate $100,000 in before-tax income to meet that obligation. The adjustment would be as follows:

$$\text{Before-tax income required} = \frac{\text{Aftertax payment}}{1 \ - \ \text{tax rate}}$$

$$= \frac{\$60,000}{1 \ - \ .40}$$

$$= \quad \$100,000$$

Coca Cola's fixed charge coverage is the same as its interest earned ratio because it has no fixed charges other than interest expense.

E. Price ratios.   Price ratios relate the internal performance of the firm to the external judgment of the marketplace in terms of value. What is the firm's

---

[6] Coca-Cola had no lease expense or sinking fund payments in 1983; therefore ratios 14 and 15 are the same.

end result in market value? The price ratios indicate the expectations of the market relative to other companies. For example, a firm with a high price-to-earnings ratio has a higher market price relative to $1 of earnings than a company with a lower ratio.

Price ratios (Coca-Cola, March 26, 1984; in millions)

16. Price to earnings

$$\frac{\text{Common stock price}}{\text{Earnings per share}} = \frac{\$54.375}{\$4.10} = 13.26\times$$
(fully diluted)

17. Price to book value

$$\frac{\text{Common stock price}}{\text{Book value per share}} = \frac{\$54.375}{\$21.55} = 2.52\times$$

18. Dividends to price (dividend yield)[7]

$$\frac{\text{Dividends per share}}{\text{Common stock price}} = \frac{\$2.68}{\$54.375} = 4.93\%$$

Coca-Cola's price–earnings ratio indicates that the firm's stock price represents $13.26 for every $1 of earnings. This number can be compared to that of other companies in the soft-drink industry and/or related industries. As indicated in Chapter 6, the price–earnings ratio (or P/E ratio, as it is commonly called) is influenced by the earnings and the sales growth of the firm; also, the risk (or volatility in performance), the debt–equity structure of the firm, the dividend payment policy, the quality of management, and a number of other factors. The P/E ratio indicates expectations about the future of a company. Firms which are expected to provide greater returns than those for the market in general, with equal or less risk, often have P/E ratios higher than the overall market P/E ratio.

Expectations of returns and P/E ratios do change over time, as Table 7–4 illustrates. Price–earnings ratios for a selected list of U.S. firms in 1975, 1981, and 1984 show that during this nine-year period price–earnings ratios fell for those companies during the first two periods and recovered for most between 1981 and 1984. A change in investor philosophy may have substantially lowered the P/E ratio of many of the traditional growth stocks, such as IBM, Upjohn, McDonald's, and Texas Instruments from their high values in 1975.

The price-to-book-value ratio relates the market value of the company to the historical accounting value of the firm. In a company that has old assets this ratio may be quite high, but in one with new, undepreciated fixed assets the ratio might be lower. This information needs to be combined with your knowledge of the company's assets and of industry norms.

---

[7] Dividends annualized at most recent quarterly rate.

TABLE 7–4   Price–Earnings Ratios for Selected U.S. Corporations

Corporation	Industry	P/E ratio		
		December 31, 1975	December 10, 1981	September 28, 1984
Exxon	International oil	8	5	7
Texas Utilities	Public utility	9	6	6
Union Carbide	Chemical	9	5	17
Bank America	Banking	10	7	10
CBS	Broadcasting	11	7	11
Halliburton	Oil service	12	11	11
Winn-Dixie	Retail	14	8	11
IBM	Computers	17	9	13
Upjohn	Ethical drugs	18	10	9
McDonald's	Restaurant franchises	26	10	12
Texas Instruments	Semiconductors	34	15	23
S&P 500	Market index	11	8	11

The dividend yield is part of the total return that an investor receives along with capital gains or losses. It is usually calculated by annualizing the current quarterly dividend, since that is the cash value a current investor would receive over the next year.

F. Other ratios.   The other ratios presented in category F are to help the analyst spot special tax situations that impact the profitability of an industry or company, and to determine what percentage of earnings are being paid to the stockholder and what is being reinvested for internal growth.

Other ratios (Coca-Cola, 1983; in millions)

19.   Average tax rate

$$\frac{\text{Income tax}}{\text{Taxable income}} = \frac{\$ \ 442}{\$1000} = 44.2\%$$

20.   Dividend payout*

$$\frac{\text{Dividends per share}}{\text{Earnings per share}} = \frac{\$2.68}{\$4.10} = 65.4\%$$

These other ratios are calculated to provide the analyst with information that may indicate unusual tax treatment or reinvestment policies. For example, the tax ratio for forest products companies will be low because of the capital gains treatment given timber cuttings. A company's tax rate may decline in one year due to heavy capital expenditures and the resultant investment tax credits. Earnings per share may rise, but we need to know if it is from operations or from favorable tax treatment. If it is from operations, we will be more sure of next year's forecast, but if it is from tax benefits we can not normally count on the benefits being continued into the future.

The dividend payout ratio provides data concerning the firm's reinvestment strategies. A high payout ratio tells the analyst that the stockholder is receiving a large part of the earnings and that the company is not retaining much income for investment in new plant and equipment. High payouts are usually found in industries that do not have great growth potential, while low payout ratios are associated with firms in growth industries.

USES OF RATIOS

The previous section presented 20 ratios that may be helpful to the analyst in evaluating a firm. How can we further use the data we have gathered to check the health of companies we are interested in analyzing?

One way is to compare the company to the industry. This is becoming more difficult as companies diversify into several industries. Twenty years ago firms competed in one industry and ratio comparisons were more reliable. Now companies have a wide range of products and markets. Coca-Cola is becoming more diversified all the time. Table 7–5 presents the business segments in which Coca-Cola operates.

Coca-Cola has three principal business segments: Soft Drinks, Entertainment, and Foods. This additional data adds a new dimension to our analysis. The soft-drink segment is by far the largest segment, accounting for almost 69 percent of total revenues and 86.5 percent of operating income. This is accomplished with only 51 percent of the firm's assets. Entertainment (Columbia Pictures) has almost 27 percent of the assets and yet produces the smallest percentage of revenues (12.4 percent) and even less operating profit (9 percent). We know from previous reading that Coca-Cola is redeploying its assets by selling off certain operations and acquiring new ones such as Columbia. The analyst must be able to forecast Coca-Cola with Columbia Pictures as an integral part. By looking at the business segments, we can tell that recently acquired Columbia Pictures does not match Coca-Cola's traditional return requirements or its asset turnover ratio. Is this because of poor management at Columbia or simply industry characteristics? More comments about this a bit later in the chapter.

Other data drawn from Table 7–5 are summarized in Table 7–6. In the first line of Table 7–6, we see that each dollar invested in assets in the food segment produces the most revenue ($2.97), with the soft-drink division in second place ($1.76) and the entertainment segment well behind ($.61). The ratio of operating income to assets places the soft drink division in first place, with the food segment close behind. The entertainment division is once again a distant third. It is only in the area of operating income to sales that the entertainment division is able to achieve a second-place finish.

After examining Table 7–5 and Table 7–6, an analyst realizes that Coca-Cola's ratios reflect a composite of several industries. Familiarity with all seg-

TABLE 7–5 Business Segments for the Coca-Cola Company

Notes to Consolidated Financial Statements (continued)

13. Lines of Business (1). The Company operates principally in the soft drink industry. In June 1982, the Company acquired Columbia Pictures Industries, Inc., which operates in the entertainment industry. Citrus, Hi-C fruit drinks, coffee and pasta products are included in the Foods Business Sector. Plastic products are not material and are also included in the Foods Business Sector. Inter-company transfers between Sectors are not material. Information concerning operations in different lines of business is as follows (in millions):

Year Ended December 31,	1983	1982	1981
Net operating revenues:			
Soft drinks	**$4,694.6**	$4,413.8	$4,558.6
Entertainment	**849.5**	457.3	—
Foods	**1,284.9**	1,150.0	1,140.3
Consolidated net operating revenues	**$6,829.0**	$6,021.1	$5,698.9
Operating income:			
Soft drinks	**$ 858.6**	$ 800.0	$ 752.0
Entertainment	**90.6**	35.8	—
Foods	**121.3**	117.9	106.7
General expenses	**(77.9)**	(73.9)	(72.6)
Consolidated operating income	**$ 992.6**	$ 879.8	$ 786.1
Identifiable assets at year-end:			
Soft drinks	**$2,670.6**	$2,521.4	$2,472.5
Entertainment	**1,394.0**	1,309.8	—
Foods	**431.9**	380.4	379.0
Corporate assets (principally marketable securities, investments and fixed assets)	**731.3**	476.2	452.7
Discontinued operations	**—**	235.5	260.6
Consolidated assets	**$5,227.8**	$4,923.3	$3,564.8
Capital expenditures (including fixed assets of purchased companies):			
Soft drinks	**$ 237.6**	$ 249.5	$ 251.5
Entertainment	**72.9**	53.9	—
Foods	**45.1**	53.7	58.4
Corporate	**28.0**	24.6	19.6
Consolidated capital expenditures	**$ 383.6**	$ 381.7	$ 329.5
Depreciation and amortization of goodwill:			
Soft drinks	**$ 120.4**	$ 117.6	$ 109.0
Entertainment	**15.7**	7.6	—
Foods	**25.2**	20.8	18.7
Corporate	**8.8**	7.6	8.8
Consolidated depreciation and amortization of goodwill	**$ 170.1**	$ 153.6	$ 136.5

(1) Operating results for 1982 and 1981 have been restated to exclude the results of the Company's wine business, which was sold in 1983 and has been accounted for as a discontinued operation. In addition, certain amounts for 1982 and 1981 have been reclassified on a comparable basis with 1983.

Source: The Coca-Cola Company Annual Report, 1983.

TABLE 7–6 Selected Values by Industry Segment, The Coca-Cola Company

	Soft drink	Entertainment	Food
Revenue/Assets	1.76×	.61×	2.97×
Operating income/Assets	32.2%	6.5%	28.1%
Operating income/Sales	18.3%	10.7%	9.4%

ments makes the analyst more capable of interpreting the significance of these ratios. It may be that the analyst will compare the Coca-Cola ratios with two or three industries rather than one. Table 7–7 compares selected Coca-Cola ratios with the soft drink, recreation, and food industries.

Table 7–7   Selected Ratio Comparisons for the Coca-Cola Company, 1983

	Coca-Cola	Industries		
		Soft drinks	Recreation	Food
Operating margin	14.54%	14.5%	15.0%	9.5%
Aftertax profit margin	8.19%	5.6%	.6%	3.6%
Return on equity	19.14%	17.5%	1.5%	13.5%
Long-term debt to equity	17.60%	30.5%	42.0%	33.3%
Price to earnings	13.26×	10.9×	12.1×	9.0×
Dividend yield	4.93%	5.2%	2.5%	5.1%
Average tax rate	44.2%	40.0%	38.0%	44.0%
Dividend payout	65.4%	54.0%	35.0%	45.0%

Industry source: *Value Line Investment Survey* (Arnold Bernhard & Co., March 1984).

In comparing Coca-Cola with the industry ratios in Table 7–7, it is important to know that five companies (Coca-Cola, Pepsi, Dr Pepper, MEI, and Royal Crown) make up the soft drinks industry ratios and by the time you read this page, Dr Pepper will be privately held and Royal Crown will be merged. Secondly, the recreation industry ratios include manufacturing companies such as Brunswick and AMF as well as firms like Disney and MGM. Additionally, the 1983 data is not fully representative because MGM took a large loss write-off ($418 million) on its Atari division, which distorted the whole industry picture. So you see, even with industry ratios, truth is hard to find and the analyst must have a perspective on the industry over time.

The most important set of ratios is for the soft drink industry, since that is Coca-Cola's major market. Coca-Cola's operating profit margins are on the same level as its competitors, but its aftertax margins are superior. This, most likely, is because Coca-Cola has relatively little long-term debt (17.6 percent) compared to the rest of the soft drink industry. This allows the firm to bring more operating profit down to aftertax income.

Return on equity is the highest of all three industries. The company does seem to be retaining less income than other companies (dividend payout of 65.4%), but it did note in its annual report that investors should expect slower growth in dividends as the company increases its internal spending. This reflects an unwillingness on management's part to expand by increasing the amount of debt in the firm's capital structure. Evidently the market thinks that Coca-Cola's earnings merit a higher value compared to the three industries since it has a superior price–earnings ratio.

TABLE 7–8   International Diversification

Notes to Consolidated Financial Statements (continued)

14. Operations in Geographic Areas (1). Information about the Company's operations in different geographic areas is presented below (in millions). Inter-company transfers between geographic areas are not material.

Year Ended December 31,	1983	1982	1981
Net operating revenues:			
United States	$4,071.4	$3,351.5	$3,048.5
Latin America	401.3	516.3	608.1
Europe and Africa	1,225.6	1,155.6	1,096.3
Canada and Pacific	1,130.7	997.7	946.0
Consolidated net operating revenues	$6,829.0	$6,021.1	$5,698.9
Operating income:			
United States	$ 498.7	$ 403.2	$ 322.3
Latin America	69.4	123.2	156.1
Europe and Africa	295.4	249.5	235.6
Canada and Pacific	207.0	177.8	144.7
General expenses	(77.9)	(73.9)	(72.6)
Consolidated operating income	$ 992.6	$ 879.8	$ 786.1
Identifiable assets at year-end:			
United States	$2,996.5	$2,773.2	$1,431.5
Latin America	420.9	435.9	436.2
Europe and Africa	606.5	582.0	583.0
Canada and Pacific	472.6	420.5	400.8
Corporate assets (principally marketable securities, investments and fixed assets)	731.3	476.2	452.7
Discontinued operations	—	235.5	260.6
Consolidated assets	$5,227.8	$4,923.3	$3,564.8

(1) Operating results for 1982 and 1981 have been restated to exclude the results of the Company's wine business, which was sold in 1983 and has been accounted for as a discontinued operation.

Identifiable liabilities of operations outside the United States were $652 million, $627 million and $637 million at December 31, 1983, 1982 and 1981, respectively.

Source: The Coca-Cola Company Annual Report, 1983.

In general one could conclude that Coca-Cola is in good shape, but that the profitability of its entertainment division could be increased with more productive use of Columbia's assets. Movie companies have a low, distorted, balance sheet figure for assets since most of their films are fully depreciated after a three-year run. This should inflate returns on assets so we can assume that Columbia, with its *low* returns, has had some problems and expect that Coca-Cola will turn the company around over time. That is certainly Coca-Cola's intention.

It is important to realize that Coca-Cola is an international company that may be impacted by political and economic events abroad. Devaluation of the Mexican peso, revolts, and the rising dollar can all have an impact on Coca-Cola's reported earnings. Table 7–8 shows the breakdown of the company's worldwide sales and profitability by region. While the United States accounts for about 60 percent of sales, the two regions "Europe and Africa," and "Canada and Pacific" account for 18 and 16 percent of sales, respectively, but a much larger share of income. Europe and Africa account for almost 30 percent of income while Canada and Pacific account for 20 percent. We can see that the trouble spot is Latin America. Sales and profits have been declining for three years, while assets have stayed about the same. High inflation and deflating currencies in Latin America are part of the problem. Just a return to 1982 profitability for Latin America would boost earnings per share $.40 and have a significant positive effect on the profitability ratios.

COMPARING LONG-TERM TRENDS

Over the course of the business cycle, sales and profitability may expand and contract, and ratio analysis for any one year may not present an accurate picture of the firm. Therefore, we look at trend analysis of performance over a number of years.

First examine the 10-year summary of selected financial data for Coca-Cola in Table 7–9. One can see the overall growth in net operating revenues since 1974. The firm has a higher level of cash and marketable securities than usual. An increase in the amount of long-term and total debt over the last two years is apparent, but the level is still not high. Over the last two years the company has issued common stock, which combined with the increased debt, shows up in a large increase in total capital since 1981. In terms of income from continuing operations to net operating revenues, the years 1980 and 1981 seem to have been low points for the company due to competition from Pepsi and the effects of the recession. 1982 and 1983, however, indicate that Coca-Cola is back to its historical average performance. The payout ratio has been rising, but management intends to reduce this ratio.

A GENERAL STUDY OF INDUSTRY TRENDS

In this section we expand the horizon by shifting our attention to four very different industries, and look at their comparative trends over time based on the ratios of return on equity and long-term debt to equity. The specially picked industries are airlines, brewing, chemicals, and drugs. By studying these important industries, the analyst develops a feel for comparative performance in our economy.

The return on equity for the four separate industries shown in Table 7–10 exhibits some wide differences in profitability. Table 7–10 is graphed in Figure 7–3 and the trends are more visible. It is clear that the drug industry has the highest and most consistent returns on equity, with very little variation due to industry or economic effects. The brewing industry has the next highest returns but more volatility than drugs. The chemical industry is next, followed by airlines, which show a cyclical character and very low returns.

Although it may be easy to generalize about industries and their relationship to economic cycles, individual companies within each industry seem to stand out. The benefit of looking at companies in the industry together is that the best and worst become apparent to the trained analyst.

TABLE 7–9

Selected Financial Data
(In millions except per share data)

Year Ended December 31,	1983	1982	1981
Summary of Operations (a,b)			
— Net operating revenues	$6,829	$6,021	$5,699
Cost of goods and services	3,773	3,311	3,188
Gross profit	3,056	2,710	2,511
Selling, administrative and			
general expenses	2,063	1,830	1,725
Operating income	993	880	786
Interest income—net	10	31	32
Other income (deductions)—net	(3)	7	(23)
Income from continuing operations			
before income taxes	1,000	918	795
Income taxes	442	415	355
Income from continuing operations	$ 558	$ 503	$ 440
Year-End Position			
— Cash and current marketable securities	$ 611	$ 261	$ 340
Property, plant and equipment—net	1,561	1,539	1,409
Total assets	5,228	4,923	3,565
— Long-term debt	513	462	137
— Total debt	620	583	232
Shareholders' equity	2,921	2,779	2,271
— Total capital (c)	3,541	3,362	2,503
Per Share Data (e)			
Income from continuing operations	$ 4.10	$ 3.88	$ 3.56
Net income	4.10	3.95	3.90
Dividends	2.68	2.48	2.32
Financial Ratios			
— Income from continuing operations			
to net operating revenues	8.2%	8.4%	7.7%
Income from continuing operations			
to average shareholders' equity	19.6%	19.9%	20.2%
Long-term debt to total capital	14.5%	13.7%	5.5%
Total debt to total capital	17.5%	17.3%	9.3%
— Dividend payout	65.3%	62.8%	59.5%
Other Data			
Average shares outstanding (e)	136	130	124
Capital expenditures	$ 384	$ 382	$ 330
Depreciation	154	144	133

Notes:
(a) Operating results for 1974-1982 have been restated to exclude the results of the Company's wine business which was sold in November 1983 and accounted for as a discontinued operation.
(b) In June 1982, the Company acquired Columbia Pictures Industries, Inc. in a purchase transaction.

In 1982, the Company adopted Statement of Financial Accounting Standards No. 52, "Foreign Currency Translation." See Note 10 to the Consolidated Financial Statements.

In the brewing industry, Heileman stands head and shoulders over the others in terms of return on equity even though it uses very little long-term debt. Pabst was recently acquired, and Coors has been struggling in this very competitive industry. The chemical industry had a difficult time dealing with the recession in 1981–82 and the effects lingered into 1983. Monsanto is perhaps the most consistent company in terms of profitability and the industry on the whole seems not to have any real losers. Again, the drug industry has consistent winners changing positions from year to year. Historically, Lilly Pfizer, and Merck have been the premier companies in the industry for high returns. The airline industry truly lacks any consistent performers among the major carriers.

				The Coca-Cola Company and Subsidiaries		
1980	1979	1978	1977	1976	1975	1974
$5,475	$4,588	$4,013	$3,328	$2,928	$2,773	$2,425
3,103	2,521	2,203	1,836	1,614	1,633	1,462
2,372	2,067	1,810	1,492	1,314	1,140	963
1,635	1,378	1,167	922	806	693	616
737	689	643	570	508	447	347
5	26	28	23	23	16	15
(9)	(3)	(14)	(9)	(4)	(8)	5
733	712	657	584	527	455	367
329	318	300	268	245	218	170
$ 404	$ 394	$ 357	$ 316	$ 282	$ 237	$ 197(d)
$ 231	$ 149	$ 321	$ 350	$ 364	$ 389	$ 241
1,341	1,284	1,065	887	738	647	601
3,406	2,938	2,583	2,254	2,007	1,801	1,610
133	31	15	15	11	16	12
228	139	69	57	52	42	69
2,075	1,919	1,740	1,578	1,434	1,302	1,190
2,303	2,058	1,809	1,635	1,486	1,344	1,259
$ 3.27	$ 3.18	$ 2.89	$ 2.56	$ 2.29	$ 1.93	$ 1.60(d)
3.42	3.40	3.03	2.68	2.38	2.02	1.65(d)
2.16	1.96	1.74	1.54	1.325	1.15	1.04
7.4%	8.6%	8.9%	9.5%	9.6%	8.5%	8.1%
20.2%	21.5%	21.6%	21.0%	20.6%	19.0%	17.1%
5.8%	1.5%	.8%	.9%	.7%	1.2%	1.0%
9.9%	6.8%	3.8%	3.5%	3.5%	3.1%	5.5%
63.2%	57.6%	37.4%	57.5%	55.7%	56.9%	63.0%
124	124	124	123	123	123	123
$ 293	$ 381	$ 306	$ 264	$ 191	$ 145	$ 154
127	106	88	77	67	64	57

(c) Includes shareholders' equity and total debt.
(d) In 1974, the Company adopted the last-in, first-out (LIFO) accounting method for certain major categories of inventories. This accounting change caused a reduction in net income of $31.2 million ($.25 per share) in 1974.
(e) Adjusted for a two-for-one stock split in 1977.

Source: The Coca-Cola Company Annual Report, 1983.

In Table 7–11 and Figure 7–4 the same four industries' long-term debt to equity ratios are given, which might explain the impact of financial leverage on the return on equity and possibly explain why some companies and industries are more volatile than others. In general the airline industry has the most debt, followed by the chemical, brewing, and drug industries.

The basic business of airlines requires a large capital commitment in terms of airplanes, and therefore a large amount of debt is needed to finance them because profitability is not sufficient to provide enough internal funds. Delta traditionally has had a low level of long-term debt but in 1983 the firm increased its borrowing dramatically. Currently, Northwest is the only airline that is almost entirely without long-term debt (in 1983 long-term debt was 11

TABLE 7–10   Return on Equity (selected companies; in percent)

	1974	1975	1976	1977	1978	1979	1980	1981	1982	1983
Airline (industry)	6.6	NMF	7.3	11.9	16.6	6.8	1.0	NMF	NMF	NMF
AMR (American)	3.6	NMF	9.2	10.2	16.2	9.8	NMF	2.0	NMF	14.9
Delta	20.4	10.2	13.0	14.9	17.8	16.0	10.1	14.1	2.0	NMF
Eastern	2.3	NMF	10.4	9.1	15.3	11.8	NMF	NMF	NMF	NMF
Northwest	11.0	7.0	7.8	12.4	7.8	8.5	.8	1.3	.6	5.9
UAL (United)	12.7	NMF	2.4	0.1	25.6	NMF	1.8	NMF	1.0	8.9
Brewing (industry)	10.0	8.8	11.7	11.1	10.3	12.7	12.8	11.6	11.9	15.6
Anheuser-Busch	11.9	4.3	9.0	13.5	14.7	15.8	16.6	18.0	15.1	17.0
Carling O'Keefe	NMF	NMF	3.1	1.2	8.8	10.4	10.4	11.1	16.1	19.5
Coors	11.3	4.1	15.4	12.2	9.2	10.4	9.1	6.9	5.1	10.4
Heileman	12.3	3.3	21.7	22.8	23.2	27.4	27.3	25.3	23.5	23.8
Pabst	8.2	8.8	12.6	8.1	4.1	3.5	4.5	NMF	1.1	ACQ
Chemical (industry)	16.9	3.2	14.1	12.9	13.6	15.0	13.0	11.9	7.1	8.5
Allied	14.9	1.1	11.3	11.6	9.5	.8	15.0	14.0	6.6	13.1
Dow	29.8	5.1	21.4	17.8	16.9	20.1	18.1	11.5	4.4	5.8
Du Pont	10.8	7.1	11.4	12.8	16.5	17.7	12.6	10.3	8.5	9.3
Monsanto	18.4	5.5	16.3	11.5	11.7	11.9	5.3	13.4	9.4	10.6
Union Carbide	21.2	3.9	14.4	11.3	10.8	13.8	14.1	12.3	6.0	4.3
Drug (industry)	19.4	8.5	18.1	16.6	19.2	20.0	19.5	17.9	19.0	19.7
Lilly	21.1	8.9	18.6	18.1	20.1	21.0	19.7	19.8	20.0	21.6
Merck	25.6	4.1	23.2	22.8	21.1	22.9	22.3	19.9	18.8	18.5
Pfizer	15.9	5.9	15.7	25.6	16.5	16.8	16.2	13.0	16.9	20.5
Searle(G.D)	21.3	0.2	14.1	NMF	16.9	18.0	17.9	18.2	21.1	16.2
Upjohn	17.1	5.1	15.8	16.7	20.2	20.1	19.7	18.8	13.0	15.2

NMF = not meaningful due to loss; ACQ = Acquired.
Source: *Value Line Investment Survey* (Arnold Bernhard & Co., selected issues).

FIGURE 7–3   Return on Equity—Airlines, Brewing, Chemicals, and Drugs

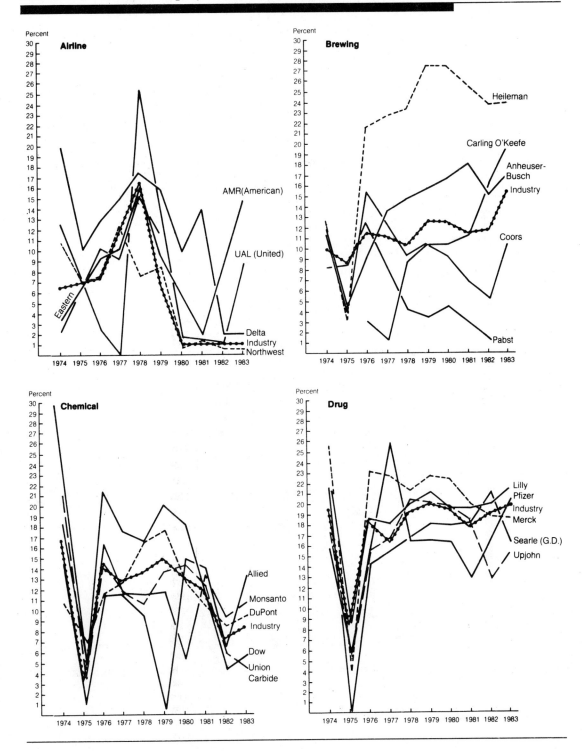

TABLE 7–11   Long-Term Debt to Equity (selected companies; in percent)

	1974	1975	1976	1977	1978	1979	1980	1981	1982	1983
Airline (industry)	130.3	136.0	111.0	91.4	106.0	118.6	140.0	150.8	180.2	139.2
AMR (American)	84.3	83.4	68.2	59.7	119.3	131.0	158.2	180.3	160.2	98.8
Delta	77.7	82.2	64.7	38.3	22.7	14.7	16.0	19.1	35.5	121.8
Eastern	204.0	214.5	167.0	116.0	213.0	256.6	250.9	340.7	484.0	732.3
Northwest	36.3	39.4	18.3	13.4	12.6	11.8	7.5	1.5	0.0	11.7
UAL (United)	117.7	125.8	116.6	89.6	97.2	106.3	100.0	107.35	160.1	82.1
Brewing (industry)	29.5	39.0	35.5	31.7	32.0	32.7	39.4	37.0	38.7	35.6
Anheuser-Busch	35.9	57.6	53.7	48.6	55.7	55.2	71.0	67.7	53.5	46.8
Carling O'Keefe	19.1	17.9	15.1	17.1	13.3	10.9	7.7	5.2	3.3	2.9
Coors	—	—	—	—	—	—	—	—	—	—
Heileman	38.2	40.2	29.0	22.2	21.2	31.5	35.8	33.9	87.8	40.0
Pabst	—	—	—	7.3	9.5	7.	5.2	5.2	15.3	ACQ
Chemical (industry)	38.3	43.2	44.7	51.2	50.0	46.6	45.3	56.3	47.4	42.6
Allied	43.3	59.0	57.3	69.4	74.6	66.7	46.0	34.4	18.5	42.2
Dow	66.2	63.8	65.6	76.1	86.5	78.6	77.7	81.3	69.5	55.5
Du Pont	21.1	23.2	31.7	30.0	23.1	20.8	19.4	70.1	54.1	41.3
Monsanto	33.4	42.8	40.6	42.9	47.4	43.2	48.8	33.3	28.7	25.6
Union Carbide	35.7	46.5	51.5	47.0	40.7	43.9	38.9	39.9	47.1	48.4
Drug (industry)	16.6	24.9	25.8	23.8	22.5	20.2	18.9	18.3	17.1	15.7
Lilly	.6	1.2	1.8	—	.3	.2	1.9	2.8	2.4	4.3
Merck	5.2	23.0	19.7	16.7	14.5	12.8	11.3	12.0	15.3	15.8
Pfizer	29.9	50.7	45.7	41.2	42.8	40.0	37.1	40.7	26.3	22.2
Searle(G.D)	60.5	87.0	78.8	90.2	80.2	50.3	16.5	33.3	30.8	24.4
Upjohn	14.3	41.0	46.0	41.2	33.6	29.8	35.3	47.5	47.4	51.9

— = No long-term debt.
Source: *Value Line Investment Survey* (Arnold Bernhard & Co., selected issues).

FIGURE 7–4   Total Debt to Equity—Airlines, Brewing, Chemicals, and Drugs

percent of equity). This industry in general is burdened with debt and the cyclical nature of the industry compounds earnings swings.

All the other industries are in safe territory. Coors has no long-term debt while Anheuser-Busch is declining after having a rising debt ratio during its rapid expansion in the last half of the 1970s. Dow leads chemicals with the highest long-term debt to equity ratio but has made a concerted effort to reduce its debt load over the last three years. Du Pont traditionally had the lowest debt ratio, but the purchase of Conoco Oil in 1981 caused long-term debt to rise significantly. The company has been reducing its debt burden. The drug industry, in general, has low levels of debt, mostly because their consistently high returns allow internal generation of funds and little reliance on the debt markets.

These tables only cover two ratios but they should get across the point that industry comparisons allow one to pick the quality companies and find the potential losers. These two ratios can be extremely important when making risk-return choices between common stocks.

DEFICIENCIES OF FINANCIAL STATEMENTS

Several differences occur between companies and industries, and inflation has additionally clouded the clarity of accounting statements. Some of the more important difficulties occur in the area of inflation-adjusted accounting statements, inventory valuation, depreciation methods, pension funds liabilities, research and development, deferred taxes, and foreign exchange accounting. We do not have space to cover all of them, but we will touch on the most important ones.

Inflation

Inflation causes phantom sources of profit that may mislead even the most alert analyst. The major problem is that revenue is almost always stated in current dollars, whereas plant and equipment or inventory may have been purchased at lower price levels. Thus, profit may be more a function of increasing prices than of satisfactory performance.

Much of the distortion of inflation shows up on the balance sheet since most of the values on the balance sheet are stated on a historical or original cost basis. This may be particularly troublesome in the case of plant and equipment and inventory, which may now be worth two or three times the original cost or—from a negative viewpoint—may require many times the original cost for replacement.

The accounting profession has been groping with this problem for decades, and the discussion becomes particularly intense each time inflation rears its ugly head. In October 1979, the Financial Accounting Standards Board (FASB) issued a ruling that required about 1,300 large companies to disclose inflation-adjusted accounting data in their annual reports. The ruling was extended for five more years in 1984. This information is disclosed in addition to the traditional historical cost data.

Inflation-adjusted accounting is a relatively new concept in accounting practice, and most likely it will undergo many modifications over time. Initially, the FASB required the use of two separate methods. The first, called the constant-dollar method, adjusts statements by using the consumer price index. The second, called the current-cost method (sometimes referred to as replacement cost), requires assets to be revalued at their current cost. It now appears that the second method is the most widely accepted, and in 1984 the FASB said that the constant-dollar reporting requirement will be dropped for those companies using current-cost information. Overall, these adjustments will affect inventory and plant and equipment the most, thus affecting overall balance sheet accounts and the total asset value of the firm. The revaluation will also affect inflation-adjusted profits through adjustments to depreciation expense and cost of goods sold, and profits will be smaller than they would be on a historical-cost basis. The appendix at the end of this chapter presents The Coca-Cola Company's 1983 inflation-adjusted data provided to the stockholders in the annual report.

Many financial executives think that the new data will simply confuse most investors, but others see benefits. One problem seems to be that many analysts do not know exactly how to use these statements for comparative purposes, and the SEC and FASB hope that another five years will increase use and the analysts' adaptability to these statements. The most important benefit could be the ability to determine if a company is generating enough cash flow from internal operations to replace worn-out equipment and maintain the existing level of production. Another benefit to investors will come from being able to measure dividends, income, and stock prices in dollars adjusted for inflation.

From a study of 10 chemical firms and 8 drug companies using current-cost (replacement-cost) data found in the financial 10K statements that these companies filed with the Securities and Exchange Commission, it was found that the changes shown in Table 7–12 occurred in their assets, income, and other selected ratios.

The comparison of replacement-cost and historical-cost accounting methods shows that replacement cost increases assets but at the same time reduces income. This increase in asset lowers the debt-to-assets ratio, since debt is a monetary asset that is not revalued because it is paid back in nominal dollars.

TABLE 7–12   Comparison of Replacement-Cost Accounting to Historical-Cost Accounting

	Ten chemical companies		Eight drug companies	
	Replacement cost	Historical cost	Replacement cost	Historical cost
Increase in assets	28.4%	—	15.4%	—
Decrease in net income before taxes	(45.8%)	—	(19.3%)	—
Return on assets	2.8%	6.2%	8.3%	11.4%
Return on equity	4.9%	13.5%	12.8%	19.6%
Debt-to-assets ratio	34.3%	43.8%	30.3%	35.2%
Interest coverage ratio (times interest earned)	7.1×	8.4×	15.4×	16.7×

Note: Replacement cost is but one form of current cost. Nevertheless, it is widely used as a measure of current cost.
Source: Jeff Garnett and Geoffrey A. Hirt, "Replacement Cost Data: A Study of the Chemical and Drug Industry for Years 1976 through 1978" (working paper).

The decreased debt-to-assets ratio would indicate that the financial leverage of the firm is decreased, but a look at the interest coverage ratio tells a different story. Because the interest coverage ratio measures the operating income available to cover interest expense, the declining income penalizes the ratio, and the firm shows a decreased ability to cover its interest cost.

As long as prices continue to rise in an inflationary environment, profits appear to feed on themselves. The main objection is that when prices do level off, there is a rude awakening for management and unsuspecting stockholders as expensive inventory is charged against softening retail prices. A 15 to 20 percent growth rate in earnings may be little more than an "inflationary illusion." Industries most sensitive to inflation-induced profits are those with cyclical products, such as lumber, copper, rubber, and food products, as well as those in which inventory is a significant percentage of sales and profits. Reported profits for the lumber industry have been influenced as much as 50 percent by inventory pricing, and a number of other industries' profits have been influenced by 15 to 20 percent.[8]

Inventory Valuation

The income statement can show considerable differences in earnings, depending upon the method of inventory valuation. The two basic methods are FIFO (first-in, first-out) and LIFO (last-in, first-out). In an inflationary economy, a firm could be reporting increased profits even though no actual increase in physical output took place. The example of the Rhoades Company will illustrate this point. We first observe their income statement for 1985 in Table 7–13. They sold 1,000 units for $20,000 and show earnings after taxes of $4,200 and an operating margin and aftertax margin of 35 percent and 21 percent, respectively.

Assume that in 1986 the number of units sold remains constant at 1,000 units. However, inflation causes a 10 percent increase in price, from $20 to $22 per unit. Total sales will go up to $22,000, but with no actual increase in physical volume. Further assume the firm uses FIFO inventory pricing, so that inventory first purchased will be written off against current sales. We will assume that 1,000 units of 1985 inventory at a cost of $10 per unit are written off against 1986 sales revenue. If Rhoades used LIFO inventory, and cost of goods sold went up 10 percent also, to $11 per unit, income will be less than under FIFO. Table 7–14 shows the 1986 income statement of Rhoades under both inventory methods.

Table 7–14 demonstrates the difference between FIFO and LIFO inventory methods. Under FIFO, Rhoades Corporation shows higher profit margins and more income even though no physical increase in sales occurs. This is because FIFO costing lags behind current prices, and the company generates

---

[8] Ronald M. Copeland, Joseph F. Wojdak, and John K. Shank, "The Use of LIFO to Offset Inflation," *Harvard Business Review*, May–June 1971, pp. 91–100.

TABLE 7–13

RHOADES CORPORATION
First-Year Income Statement
Net income for 1985

Sales	$20,000	(1,000 units at $20)
Cost of goods sold	10,000	(1,000 units at $10)
Gross profit	10,000	
Selling and administrative expense	2,000	
Depreciation	1,000	
Operating profit	7,000	
Taxes (40 percent)	2,800	
Earnings after taxes	$ 4,200	
Operating margin	$7,000/20,000 = 35%	
Aftertax margin	$4,200/20,000 = 21%	

"phantom profits" due to capital gains on inventory. Unfortunately, this inventory will need to be replaced next period at higher costs. When and if prices turn lower in a recessionary environment, FIFO will have the opposite effect and show a more negative performance. LIFO inventory costing, on the other hand, relates current costs to current prices, and although profits rise in dollar terms from 1985, the margins stay basically the same. The only problem with LIFO inventory accounting is that low-cost layers of inventory build up on the balance sheet of the company and understate inventory. This will cause inventory turnover to appear higher than under FIFO.

TABLE 7–14

RHOADES CORPORATION
Second-Year Income Statement Using FIFO and LIFO
Net income for 1986

	FIFO		LIFO	
Sales	$22,000	(1,000 at $22)	$22,000	(1,000 at $22)
Cost of goods sold	10,000	(1,000 at $10)	11,000	(1,000 at $11)
Gross profit	12,000		11,000	
Selling and administrative expense	2,200	(10% of sales)	2,200	(10% of sales)
Depreciation	1,000		1,000	
Operating profit	8,800		7,800	
Taxes (40 percent)	3,520		3,120	
Earnings after taxes	$ 5,280		4,680	
Operating margin	$8,800/22,000 = 40%		$7,800/22,000 = 35.4%	
Aftertax margin	$5,280/22,000 = 24%		$4,680/22,000 = 21.2%	

Extraordinary Gains and Losses

Nonrecurring gains or losses may occur from the sale of corporate fixed assets, lawsuits, or similar events that would not be expected to occur often, if ever again. Some analysts argue that such extraordinary events should be included in computing the current income of the firm, while others would leave them off in assessing operating performance. The choice can have a big impact on ratios that rely on earnings or earnings per share. Extraordinary gains can inflate returns and lower payout ratios if they are included in earnings. The analyst concerned about forecasting should only include those earnings from continuing operations; otherwise, the forecast will be seriously off its mark. Unfortunately, there is some inconsistency in the manner in which nonrecurring losses are treated in spite of determined attempts by the accounting profession to ensure uniformity of action.

Pension Fund Liabilities

One area of increasing concern among financial analysts is the unfunded liabilities of corporate pension funds. These funds eventually will have to pay workers their retirement income from the pension fund earnings and assets. If the money is not available from the pension fund, the company is liable to make the payments. These unfunded pensions may have to come out of earnings in future years, which would penalize shareholders and limit the corporation's ability to reinvest in new assets.

Other Distortions

There are other problems in accounting statements and methods of reporting earnings. Space does not permit us to cover each and every area of potential earnings distortion, but a mention of some of them might provide you with areas that require further investigation. Some other areas for detective work are in accounting methods for the following: research and development expenditures, deferred taxes, investment tax credits, foreign exchange currency translations, merger accounting, intangible drilling and development costs, and percentage depletion allowances. As you can see, there are many issues that cause analysts to dig further and to be cautious about accepting bottom-line earnings per share.

Chapter 8

A BASIC VIEW OF TECHNICAL ANALYSIS AND MARKET EFFICIENCY

In the preceding three chapters, we have followed a fundamental approach to security analysis. That is, we have examined the fundamental factors that influence the business cycle, the performance of various industries, and the operations of individual firms. We have further examined the financial statements and tools of measurement that are available to the security analyst. In following a fundamental approach, one attempts to evaluate the appropriate worth of a security and perhaps ascertain whether it is under- or overpriced.

In this chapter, we shall examine a technical approach to investment timing. In this approach, analysts and market technicians examine prior price and volume data, as well as other market-related indicators, to determine past trends in the belief that they will help forecast future ones. Technical analysts place much more emphasis on charts and graphs of *internal market data* than on such fundamental factors as earnings reports, management capabilities, or new product development. They believe that even when important fundamental information is uncovered, it may not lead to profitable trading because of timing considerations and market imperfections.

We shall also devote much time and attention in this chapter to the concept of market efficiency; that is, the ability of the market to adjust very rapidly to the supply of new information in valuing a security. This area of study has led to the efficient market hypothesis, which states that all securities are correctly priced at any point in time.

At the outset, be aware that there are many disagreements and contradictions in the various areas that we will examine. As previously implied, advocates of technical analysis do not place much emphasis on fundamental analysis, and vice versa. Even more significant, proponents of the efficient market hypothesis would suggest that neither technical nor fundamental analysis is of any great value in producing superior returns.

In light of the various disagreements that exist, we feel it is important that the student be exposed to many schools of thought. For example, we devote the first part of the chapter to technical analysis and then later offer research findings that relate to the value of the technical approach as well as the fundamental approach. Our philosophy throughout the chapter is to recognize that there is a gap between practices utilized by brokerage houses (and on Wall Street) and beliefs held in the academic community, yet the student should be exposed to both.

TECHNICAL ANALYSIS

Technical analysis is based on a number of basic assumptions:

1. Market value is determined solely by the interaction of demand and supply.
2. Demand and supply are governed by both rational and irrational factors.
3. It is assumed that though there are minor fluctuations in the market, stock prices tend to move in trends that persist for long periods of time.
4. Reversals of trends are caused by shifts in demand and supply.

5.   Shifts in demand and supply can be detected sooner or later in charts.

6.   Many chart patterns tend to repeat themselves.[1]

For our purposes, the most significant items to note are the assumptions that stock prices tend to move in trends that persist for long periods and that these trends can be detected in charts. The basic premise is that past trends in market movements can be used to forecast or understand the future. The market technician generally assumes that there is a lag between the time he perceives a change in the value of a security and when the investing public ultimately assesses this change.

In developing the tools of technical analysis, we shall divide our discussion between the *(a)* use of charting, and *(b)* key indicator series to project future market movements.

THE USE OF CHARTING

Charting is often linked to the development of the Dow theory in the late 1890s by Charles Dow.[2] Mr. Dow was the founder of the Dow Jones Company and editor of *The Wall Street Journal.* Many of his early precepts were further refined by other market technicians, and it is generally believed that the Dow theory was successful in signaling the market crash of 1929.

Essential Elements of the Dow Theory

The Dow theory maintains that there are three major movements in the market: daily fluctuations, secondary movements, and primary trends. According to the theory, daily fluctuations and secondary movements (covering two weeks to a month) are only important to the extent that they reflect on the long-term primary trend in the market. Primary trends may be characterized as either bullish or bearish in nature.

In Figure 8–1 we look at the use of the Dow theory to analyze a market trend. Note that the primary movement in the market is positive in spite of two secondary movements that are downward. The important facet of the secondary movements is that each low is higher than the previous low and each high is higher than the previous high. This tends to confirm the primary trend, which is bullish.

Under the Dow theory, it is assumed that this pattern will continue for a long period, and the analyst should not be confused by secondary movements. However, the upward pattern must ultimately come to an end. This is indicated by a new pattern in which a recovery fails to exceed the previous high (abortive recovery) and a new low penetrates a previous low as indicated in the top part of Figure 8–2. For a true turn in the market to take place, the new

---

[1] R. D. Edwards and John Magee, Jr., *Technical Analysis of Stock Trends* (Springfield, Mass: John Magee, 1958).

[2] *The Wall Street Journal,* December 19, 1900.

FIGURE 8–1   Presentation of the Dow Theory

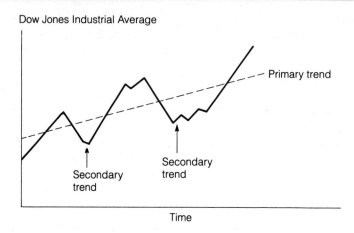

pattern of movement in the Dow Jones Industrial Average must also be confirmed by a subsequent movement in the Dow Jones Transportation Average as indicated on the bottom part of Figure 8–2.

A subsequent change from a bear to a bull market would require similar patterns of confirmation. While the Dow theory has proved helpful to market technicians, there is always the problem of false signals. For example, not

FIGURE 8–2   Market Reversal and Confirmation

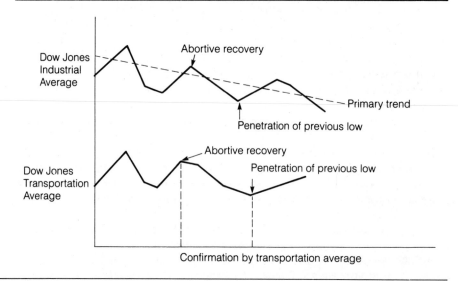

every abortive recovery is certain to signal the end of a bull market. Furthermore, the investor may have to wait a long time to get full confirmation of a change in a primary trend. By the time the Transportation Average confirms the pattern in the Industrial Average, important market movements may have already taken place.

Support and Resistance Levels

Chartists attempt to define trading levels for individual securities (or the market) where there is a likelihood that price movements will be challenged. Thus, in the daily financial press or on television, the statement is often made that the next barrier to the current market move is at 1350 (or some other level). This assumes the existence of support and resistance levels. As indicated in Figure 8–3, a support level is associated with the lower end of a trading range and a resistance level with the upper end.

FIGURE 8–3   Support and Resistance

Support may develop each time a stock goes down to a lower level of trading because investors who previously passed up a purchase opportunity may now choose to act. It is a signal that new demand is coming into the market. When a stock reaches the high side of the normal trading range, resistance may develop because some investors who bought in on a previous wave of enthusiasm (on an earlier high) may now view this as a chance to get even. Others may simply see this as an opportunity to take a profit.

A breakout above a resistance point (as indicated in Figure 8–3) or below a support level is considered significant. The stock is assumed to be

trading in a new range, and higher (lower) trading values may now be expected.

Volume

The amount of volume supporting a given market movement is also considered significant. For example, if a stock (or the market in general) makes a new
high on heavy trading volume, this is considered to be bullish. Conversely, a
new high on light volume may indicate a temporary move that is likely to be
reversed.

A new low on light volume is considered somewhat positive because of
the lack of investor participation. On the other hand, when a new low is
established on the basis of heavy trading volume, this is considered to be quite
bearish.

In the mid-1980s, the New York Stock Exchange has been averaging a
volume of 80 to 90 million shares daily. When the volume jumps to 130 to 140
million shares, analysts take a very strong interest in the trading pattern of the
market.

Types of Charts

Up until now, we have been using typical line charts to indicate market patterns. Technicians also use bar charts and point and figure charts. We shall
examine each.

Bar chart.   A bar chart shows the high and low price for a stock with a dash
along the line to indicate the closing price. An example is shown in Figure 8–4.

FIGURE 8–4   Bar Chart

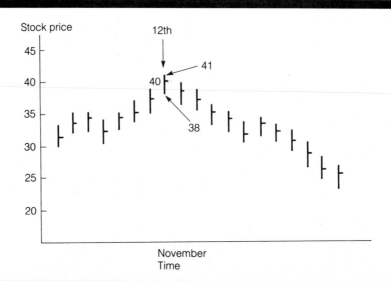

FIGURE 8–5   Bar Chart of Market Averages

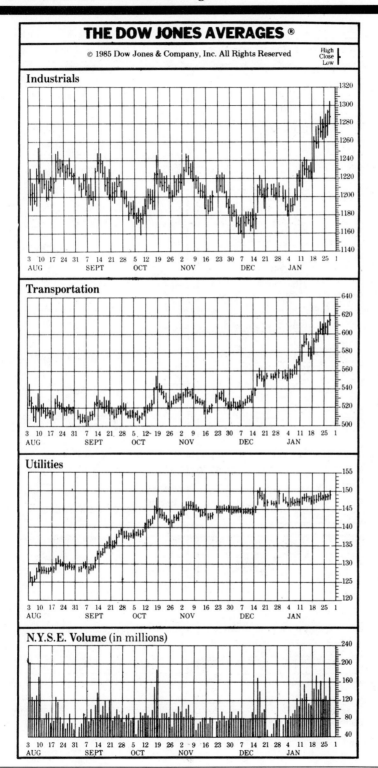

FIGURE 8–6   Chart Representation of Market Bottoms and Tops

Source: Irwin Shishko, "Techniques of Forecasting Commodity Prices," *Commodity Yearbook* (New York: Commodity Research Bureau, 1965), p. 4.

We see on November 12 the stock traded between a high of 41 and a low of 38 and closed at 40. Daily information on the Dow Jones Averages are usually presented in the form of a bar chart, with daily volume shown at the bottom as indicated in Figure 8–5.

Trendline, published through a division of Standard & Poor's, provides excellent charting information on a wide variety of securities traded on the major exchanges and is available at many libraries and brokerage houses. Market technicians carefully evaluate the charts, looking for what they perceive to be significant patterns of movement. For example, the pattern in Figure 8–4 on page 242 might be interpreted as a head and shoulder pattern (note the head in the middle) with a lower penetration of the neckline to the right indicating a sell signal. In Figure 8–6, we show a series of price movement patterns presumably indicating market bottoms and tops.

Though it is beyond the scope of this book to go into interpretation of chart formations in great detail, special books on the subject are suggested at the end of our discussion of charting.

Point and Figure Chart

A point and figure chart (PFC) emphasizes significant price changes and the reversal of significant price changes. Unlike a line or bar chart, there is no time dimension. An example of a point and figure chart is presented in Figure 8–7.

FIGURE 8–7   Point and Figure Chart

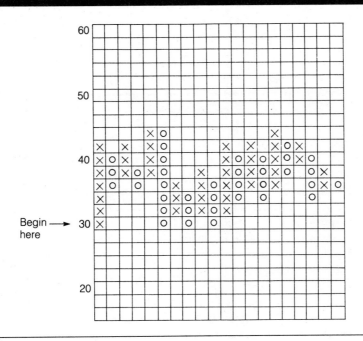

The assumption is that the stock starts out at 30. Only moves of two points or greater are plotted on the graph (some may prefer to use one point). Advances are indicated by X's and declines are shown by O's. A reversal from an advance to a decline or vice versa calls for a shift in columns. Thus, the stock initially goes from 30 to 42 and then shifts columns in its subsequent decline to 36 before moving up again in column 3. A similar pattern persists throughout the chart.

Chartists carefully read point and figure charts to observe market patterns (where there is support, resistance, breakouts, congestion, etc.). Students with a strong interest in charting may consult such books as Edwards and Magee, *Technical Analysis of Stock Trends*[3] and Zweig, *Understanding Technical Forecasting.*[4] The problem in reading charts has always been to analyze patterns in such a fashion that they truly predict stock market movements before they unfold. In order to justify the effort, one must assume that there are discernible trends over the long term.

KEY INDICATOR SERIES

In the television series, "Wall Street Week," host Louis Rukeyser has a number of technical indicators that he watches on a weekly basis. He refers to them as his elves and compares the bullish and bearish indicators to determine what the next direction of the market might be.

In this section, we will examine similar bullish and bearish technical indicator series. We will first look at contrary opinion rules, then smart money rules, and finally overall market indicators.

Contrary Opinion Rules

The essence of a contrary opinion rule is that it is easier to figure out who is wrong than who is right. If you know your neighbor has a terrible sense of direction and you spot him taking a left at the intersection, you automatically take a right. In the stock market, there are similar guidelines.

Odd-lot theory. An odd-lot trade is one of less than 100 shares, and only small investors tend to engage in odd-lot transactions. The odd-lot theory suggests that you watch very closely what the small investor is doing and then do the opposite. *The Wall Street Journal* reports odd-lot trading on a daily basis, and *Barron's* reports similar information on a weekly basis. It is a simple matter to construct a ratio of odd-lot purchases to odd-lot sales. For example, on July 18, 1984, 195,357 odd-lot shares were purchased, and 392,164 shares were sold, indicating a ratio of .498. The ratio generally fluctuates between .40 and 1.60.

---

[3] R. D. Edwards and John Magee, Jr., *Technical Analysis of Stock Trends,* 5th ed. (Springfield, Mass: Stock Trends Service, 1966).

[4] Matin E. Zweig, *Understanding Technical Forecasting* (Princeton, N.J.: Dow Jones, 1978).

The odd-lot theory actually suggests that the small trader does all right most of the time but badly misses on key market turns. As indicated in Figure 8–8, the odd-lot trader is on the correct path as the market is going up; that is, selling off part of the portfolio in an up market (the name of the game is to buy

FIGURE 8–8   Comparing Standard & Poor's 500 Index and the Odd-lot Index

low and sell high). This net selling posture is reflected by a declining odd-lot index (purchase/sales ratio). However, as the market continues upward, the odd-lot trader suddenly thinks he or she sees an opportunity for a killing in the market and becomes a very strong net buyer. This precedes a fall in the market.

The odd-lot trader is also assumed to be a strong seller right before the bottom of a bear market. Presumably, when the small trader finally gets grandfather's 50 shares of AT&T out of the lockbox and sells them in disgust, it is time for the market to turn upward.

As if to add injury to insult, there is a corollary to the odd-lot theory that says one should be particularly sensitive to what odd-lot traders do on Monday because odd-lotters tend to visit with each other over the weekend, confirm each others opinions or exchange hot tips, and then call their brokers on Monday morning. The assumption is that their chatter over the barbeque pit or in the bowling alley is even more suspect than their own individual opinions.

While the odd-lot theory appeared to have some validity in the 1950s and 1960s, it has not been a particularly valuable tool in the 1970s and early 1980s. For one thing, the odd-lotters outguessed many of the professional money managers in selling off before the stock market debacle of the mid-1970s, and they began buying in advance of a recovery. Another problem is that odd-lotters have been fairly consistent net sellers since the late 1960s, so there is not a balanced movement in the index.

Short sales position.   A second contrary opinion rule is based on the volume of short sales in the market. As you will recall from Chapter 3, a short sale represents the selling of a security you do not own with the anticipation of purchasing the security in the future to cover your short position. An investor would only engage in a short sale transaction if he believed the security would, in fact, be going down in price in the near future so that he could buy back the security at a lower price to cover his short sale. When the aggregate number of short sellers is large (that is they are bearish), this is thought to be a bullish signal.

The contrary opinion stems from two sources: first, that short sellers are sometimes emotional and may overreact to the market; second and more important, that there now is a built-in demand for stocks that have been sold short by investors who will have to repurchase the shares to cover their short positions.

Daily short sale totals for the New York Stock Exchange are recorded in *The Wall Street Journal.* Also once a month (around the 20th), *The Wall Street Journal* provides a report on total short sale figures for the two major exchanges, as well as securities traded on those exchanges (based on mid-month data). This feature usually contains comments about current trends in the market.

Technical analysts compute a ratio of the total short sales positions on an exchange to average daily exchange volume for the month. The normal ratio is between 1.00 and 1.75. A ratio of 1.00 would indicate that the current short sales position is equal to one day's average trading volume.

As the short sales ratio (frequently called the short interest ratio) approaches the higher end of the normal trading range, this would be considered bullish (remember this is a contrary opinion trading rule). As is true with many other technical trading rules, its use in predicting future performance has produced mixed results.[5]

Investment advisory recommendations.   A further contrary opinion rule states that you should watch the predictions of the investment advisory services and do the opposite. This has been formalized by Investors Intelligence (an investment advisory service itself) into the Index of Bearish Sentiment. Abraham W. Cohen, president of Investors Intelligence, suggests that when 42 percent or more of the advisory services are bearish, you should expect a market upturn. Conversely, when only 17 percent or fewer are bearish, you should expect a decline.[6]

Lest one take investment advisory services too lightly, however, observe the market impact of a recommendation by Joseph Granville, publisher of the *Granville Market Letter.* On Tuesday, January 6, 1981, Mr. Granville issued a late evening warning to his subscribers to "sell everything." He helped cause a

[5] Randall Smith, "Short Interest and Stock Market Prices," *Financial Analysts Journal,* November–December, 1968, pp. 151–54. Barton M. Briggs, "The Short Interest—A False Proverb," *Financial Analysts Journal,* July–August, 1966, pp. 111–16.

[6] How to Read Stock Market Indicators," *Business Week,* December 8, 1980, p. 14.

next-day decline in the Dow Jones Industrial Average of 23.80 points. Forty billion ($40,000,000,000) in market value was chopped off the total value of stocks traded on U.S. security exchanges and the over-the-counter market.

Although market events did not immediately confirm Mr. Granville's pessimism (and brought much criticism), the fact that one man could trigger such a reaction is an indication of the number of people that are influenced by the suggestion of an advisory service.

Greed Index. A final contrary opinion rule is represented by the Greed Index. The index measures how greedy investors are, and is prepared by Lee H. Idleman, research director at Neuberger and Berman. Greed, as measured by the index, is synonymous with bullish sentiment, or optimism. The more greedy or optimistic investors are, the more likely the market is to fall under this contrary opinion rule. The Greed Index comprises 10 different factors that are assigned a value from 1 to 10. Among these factors are portfolio aggressiveness (high technology versus defensive stocks), acceptance of new ideas, ratio of positive to negative comments by investment analysts, willingness to invest in untested issues and so on.

When the Greed Index exceeds 60, this is considered to be bearish. It got up to 69 in March 1983 before a market sell-off began. It got to an all-time high of 89 in December 1968 during the go-go days of a long-forgotten bull market. When the Greed Index goes below 30, this is interpreted as a buy signal. For example, the index was at 28 before the great market upturn of June 1982. While the Greed Index may provide some market clues, it is less than exacting. For example, the investor who began to go short when the index hit 60 in 1968, would have suffered large losses before the index got up to 89.

Smart Money Rules

Market technicians have long attempted to track the pattern of sophisticated traders in the hope that they might provide unusual insight into the future. We shall briefly observe theories related to bond market traders and stock exchange specialists.

Barron's Confidence Index. The *Barron's* Confidence Index is used to observe the trading pattern of investors in the bond market. The theory is based on the premise that bond traders are more sophisticated than stock traders and will pick up trends more quickly. The theory would suggest that if one can figure out what bond traders are doing today, he may be able to determine what stock market investors will be doing in the near future.

Barron's Confidence Index is actually computed by taking the yield on 10 top-grade corporate bonds and dividing by the yield on 10 intermediate grade bonds, and multiplying by 100.

$$\begin{array}{c}\textit{Barron's} \\ \text{Confidence} \\ \text{Index}\end{array} = \frac{\text{Yield on 10 top grade corporate bonds}}{\text{Yield on 10 intermediate grade bonds}}(100) \qquad (8\text{--}1)$$

The bonds in this index are presented in Table 8–1.

TABLE 8–1   Issues in *Barron's* Confidence Index

Best (Top) Grade

Industrials
  AT&T 3⅞s 90
  Exxon 6s 97
  Gen. Elec. 8½s 04
  U.S. Steel 4½s 86

Transports
  Atchison 4s 95
  Ches. and Ohio 4½s 92
  Nort. and Western 4s 96
  Union Pac. 2½s 91

Utilities
  Consumer Pwr. 5⅞s 96
  Ill. Bell 2¾s

Intermediate Grade

Industrials
  Beth. Steel 6⅞s 99
  Ford Motor 8⅛s 90
  Pfizer 9¼s 00

Transports
  Louis. Nash. 7⅜s 93
  Missouri Pac. 4¼s 05
  St. L. SF. 4s 97

Utilities
  Alabama Pwr. 9¾s 04
  Detroit Ed. 9s 99
  Pacific G.&E. 7¼s 05
  Phil. Elec. 7⅜s 01

The index is published weekly in the "Market Laboratory" section of *Barron's* magazine. What does it actually tell us? First of all, we can observe that the top-grade bonds in the numerator will always have a smaller yield than the intermediate grade bonds in the denominator. The reason is that the higher-quality issues can satisfy investors with smaller returns. The bond market is very representative of a risk-return trade-off environment in which less risk requires less return and higher risk necessitates a higher return.

With top-grade bonds providing smaller yields than intermediate-grade bonds, the Confidence Index will always be less than 100 (percent). The normal trading range is between 80 and 95, and it is within this range that technicians look for signals on the economy. If bond investors are bullish about future economic prosperity, they will be rather indifferent between holding top-grade bonds and intermediate-grade bonds, and the yield differences betwen these two categories will be relatively small. This would indicate that the Confidence Index may be close to 95. An example is presented below in which top-grade bonds are providing 11.4 percent and intermediate-grade bonds are yielding 12 percent.

$$\begin{array}{l}\text{\textit{Barron's}} \\ \text{Confidence} \\ \text{Index}\end{array} = \frac{\text{Yield on 10 top-grade corporate bonds}}{\text{Yield on 10 intermediate-grade bonds}}(100)$$

$$= \frac{11.4\%}{12\%}(100) = 95(\%)$$

Now let us assume that investors become quite concerned about the outlook for the future health of the economy. If events go poorly, some weaker corporations may not be able to make their interest payments, and thus, bond market investors will have a strong preference for top-quality issues. Some investors will continue to invest in intermediate- or lower-quality issues but only at a sufficiently high yield differential to justify the risk. We might assume that the *Barron's* Confidence Index will drop to 84 because of the increasing spread between the two yields in the formula.

$$\begin{array}{l}\text{\textit{Barron's}} \\ \text{Confidence} \\ \text{Index}\end{array} = \frac{\text{Yield on 10 top grade corporate bonds}}{\text{Yield on 10 intermediate grade bonds}}(100)$$

$$= \frac{11.6\%}{13.8\%}(100) = 84(\%)$$

The yield on the intermediate-grade bonds is now 2.2 percent higher than that on the 10 top-grade bonds, and this is reflected in the lower Confidence Index reading. Of course, as confidence in the economy is once again regained, the yield spread differential will narrow, and the Confidence Index will go up.

Market technicians assume that there is a few months of lead time between what happens to the Confidence Index and what happens to the economy and stock market. As is true with other such indicators, it has a mixed record of predicting future events. One problem is that the Confidence Index is only assumed to consider the impact of investors' attitudes on yields (their demand pattern). We have seen in the late 1970s and 1980s that the supply of new bond issues can also influence yields. Thus, a very large bond issue by AT&T or General Motors may drive up high-grade bond yields even though investor attitudes indicate they should be going down.

Short sales by specialists.   Another smart money index is based on the short sales positions of specialists. Recall from Chapter 2 that one of the roles that specialists perform is to make markets in various securities listed on the organized exchanges. Because of the uniquely close position of specialists to the action on Wall Street, market technicians ascribe unusual importance to their decisions. One measure of their activity that is frequently monitored is the ratio of specialists' short sales to the total amount of short sales on an exchange.

When we previously mentioned short sales in this chapter, we suggested that a high incidence of short selling might be considered bullish because short sellers often overreact to the market and provide future demand potential to cover their short position. In the case of market specialists, this is not necessarily true. These sophisticated traders keep a book of limit orders on their securities so that they have a close feel for market activity at any given point in time, and their decisions are considered important.

The normal ratio of specialist short sales to short sales on an exchange is about 55 percent. When the ratio goes up to 65 percent or more, market technicians interpret this as a bearish signal. A ratio under 40 percent is considered bullish.

Overall Market Rules

Our discussion of key indicator series has centered on both contrary opinion rules and smart money rules. We now briefly examine two overall market indicators; the breadth of the market indicator series and the cash position of mutual funds.

Breadth of the market.   A breadth of the market indicator attempts to measure what a broad range of securities are doing as opposed to merely examining a market average. The theory is that market averages, such as the Dow Jones Industrial Average of 30 stocks or the Standard & Poor's 500 Stock Average, are weighted toward large firms and may not be representative of the entire market. In order to get a broader perspective of the market, an analyst may examine all stocks on an exchange. In Figure 8–9, we see an example of daily advances and declines for all stocks on the New York Stock Exchange.

The technician often compares the advance-declines with the movement of a popular market average to determine if there is a divergence between the two. Advances and declines usually move in concert with the popular market averages but may move in the opposite direction at a market peak or bottom.

FIGURE 8–9   Advance–Decline Data on the New York Stock Exchange

MARKET DIARY

	Tue.	Mon.	Fri.	Thu.	Wed.	Tue.
Issues traded	1,977	1,945	1,965	1,950	1,967	1,994
Advances	884	705	887	502	421	694
Declines	628	790	625	942	1,098	796
Unchanged	465	450	453	506	448	504
New highs	16	8	11	4	4	15
New lows	98	99	104	140	99	70

One of the possible signals for the end of a bull market is when the Dow Jones Industrial Average is moving up but the number of daily declines consistently exceeds the number of daily advances. This indicates that conservative investors are investing in blue chip stocks but that there is a lack of broad-based confidence in the market. In Table 8–2, we look at an example of divergence between the advance–decline indicators and the Dow Jones Industrial Average (DJIA).

TABLE 8–2   Comparing Advance–Decline Data and the Dow Jones Industrial Average

Day	(1) Advances	(2) Declines	(3) Unchanged	(4) Net advances or declines	(5) Cumulative advances or declines	(6) DJIA
1	850	750	350	+100	+100	+7.09
2	800	810	340	− 10	+ 90	+4.52
3	792	821	337	− 29	+ 61	+3.08
4	780	828	342	− 48	+ 13	+5.21
5	719	890	341	−171	−158	−2.02
6	802	812	336	− 10	−168	+5.43
7	783	824	343	− 41	−209	+3.01
8	692	912	340	−226	−435	+ .52

In column 4, we see the daily differences in advances and declines. In column 5, we look at the cumulative pattern by adding or subtracting each new day's value from the previous total. We then compare the information in column 4 and column 5 to the Dow Jones Industrial Average (DJIA) in column 6. Clearly, the strength in the Dow Jones Industrial Average is not reflected in the advance-decline data, and this may be interpreted as signaling future weakness in the market.

Breadth of the market data can also be used to analyze upturns in the market. When the Dow Jones Industrial Average is going down but advances consistently lead declines, the market may be positioned for a recovery. Some market technicians develop sophisticated weighted averages of the daily advance-declines to go along with the data in Table 8–2.

While a comparison of advance-decline data to market averages can provide important insights, there is also the danger of false signals. Not every divergence between the two signals a turn in the market, so the analyst must be careful in his or her interpretation. The technical analyst generally looks at a wide range of variables.

Mutual fund cash position.   Another overall market indicator is the cash position of mutual funds. This measure indicates the buying potential of mutual funds and is generally representative of the purchasing potential of other large institutional investors. The cash position of mutual funds, as a percentage of their total assets, generally varies between 5 percent and 20 to 25 percent.[7]

At the lower end of the boundary, it would appear that mutual funds are fully invested and can provide little in the way of additional purchasing power. As their cash position goes to 15 percent or higher, market technicians assess this as representing significant purchasing power that may help to trigger a market upturn. While the overall premise is valid, there are problems in identifying just what is a significant cash position for mutual funds in a given market cycle. It may change in extreme market environments.

EFFICIENT MARKET HYPOTHESIS

We shift our attention from technical analysis to that of examining market efficiency. As indicated at the beginning of the chapter, we shall now view any contradictions between the assumptions of fundamental or technical analysis and findings of the efficient market hypothesis.

We previously said that an efficient market is one in which new information is very rapidly processed so that securities are properly priced at any given point in time. An important premise of an efficient market is that there are a large number of profit-maximizing participants concerned with the analysis and valuation of securities. This would seem to describe the security market environment in the United States. Any news on IBM, AT&T, an oil embargo, or tax legislation is likely to be absorbed and acted upon very rapidly by profit-maximizing individuals. For this reason, the efficient market hypothesis (EMH) assumes that no stock price can be in disequilibrium or improperly priced for very long. There is almost instantaneous adjustment to new information. The efficient market hypothesis applies most directly to large firms trading on the major security exchanges.

The efficient market hypothesis further assumes that information travels in a random, independent fashion and that prices are an unbiased reflection of all currently available information.

More generally, the efficient market hypothesis is stated and tested in three different forms: the weak form, the semi-strong form, and the strong form. We shall examine each of these and the related implications for technical and fundamental analysis.

WEAK FORM OF THE EFFICIENT
MARKET HYPOTHESIS

The weak form of the efficient market hypothesis suggests that there is no relationship between past and future prices of securities. They are presumed to be independent over time. Because the efficient market hypothesis maintains that current prices reflect all available information and that information

---

[7] The cash dollars are usually placed in short-term credit instruments, as opposed to stocks and bonds.

travels in a random fashion, it is assumed that there is little or nothing to be gained from studying past stock prices.

The weak form of the efficient market hypothesis has been tested in two different ways. First, researchers have attempted to determine the actual independence of price changes over time.

Tests of Independence

Tests of independence have examined the degree of correlation between stock prices over time and have found the correlation to be consistently small (between +.10 and −.10) and not statistically significant. This would indicate stock price changes are independent.[8] A further test is based on the frequency and extent of runs in stock price data. A run occurs when there is no difference in direction between two or more price changes. An example of a series of data and some runs is presented below.

Runs can be expected in any series of data through chance factors, but an independent data series should not produce an unusual amount of runs. Statistical tests have indicated that security prices generally do not produce any more runs that would be expected through the process of random number generation.[9] This would also tend to indicate that stock price movements are independent over time.

Trading Rule Tests

A second method of testing the weak form of the efficient market hypothesis (that past trends in stock prices are not helpful in predicting the future) is through trading rule tests. Because practicing market technicians maintain that tests of independence (correlation studies and runs) are too rigid to test the assumptions of the weak form of the efficient market hypothesis, additional tests by academic researchers have been developed. These are known as trading rule or filter tests. The purpose of these tests is to determine whether a given trading rule based on past price data, volume figures, etc. can be used to beat a naive buy-and-hold approach. The intent is to simulate the conditions under which a given trading rule is used and then determine if superior returns were produced after consideration of transaction costs and the risks involved.

---

[8] Sidney S. Alexander, "Price Movements in Speculative Markets: Trends or Random Walks," *Industrial Management Review,* May 1961, pp. 7–26. Eugene F. Fama, "The Behavior of Stock Market Prices," *Journal of Business,* January 1965, pp. 34–105.

[9] Sidney S. Alexander, "Price Movements in Speculative Markets: Trends or Random Walks," *Industrial Management Review,* May 1961, pp. 7–26. Eugene F. Fama, "The Behavior of Stock Market Prices," *Journal of Business,* January 1965, pp. 34–105.

As an example of a trading rule, if a stock moves up 5 percent or more, the rule might be to purchase it. The assumption is that this represents a breakout and should be considered bullish. Similarly, a 5 percent downward movement would be considered bearish and call for a sell strategy (rather than a buy-low/sell-high strategy, this is a follow-the-market-trend strategy). Other trading rule tests might be based on advance-decline patterns, short sales figures, and similar technical patterns. Research results have indicated that in a limited number of cases, trading rules may produce slightly positive returns, but after commission costs are considered, the results are neutral and sometimes negative in comparison to a naive buy-and-hold approach.[10]

Implications for Technical Analysis

The results of the *tests of independence* and *trading rules* would seem to uphold the weak form of the efficient market hypothesis. Security prices do appear to be independent over time or, more specifically, move in the pattern of a random walk.

Some challenge the research on the basis that academic research in this area does not capture the personal judgment that an experienced technician brings forward in reading his charts. There is also the fact that there are an infinite number of trading rules, and not all of them can or have been tested.[11] Nevertheless, research on the weak form of the efficient market hypothesis would seem to suggest that prices move independently over time, that past trends cannot be used to predict the future, and that charting and technical analysis may have limited value.

SEMI-STRONG FORM OF THE EFFICIENT MARKET HYPOTHESIS

The semi-strong form of the efficient market hypothesis maintains that all public information is already impounded into the value of a security, and therefore, one cannot use fundamental analysis to determine whether a stock is under- or overvalued.

Basically, the semi-strong form of the efficient market hypothesis would support the notion that there is no learning lag in the distribution of public information. When a company makes an announcement, investors across the country assess the information with equal speed. Also, a major firm listed on the New York Stock Exchange could hardly hope to utilize some questionable accounting practice that deceptively leads to higher reported profits and not

---

[10] Eugene F. Fama and Marshall Blume, "Filter Rules and Stock Market Trading Profits," *Journal of Business,* supplement, January 1966, pp. 226–41. George Pinches, "The Random Walk Hypothesis and Technical Analysis," *Financial Analysts Journal,* March–April 1970, pp. 104–10.

[11] It has even been suggested that an investor observe the winning team in the Super Bowl and invest accordingly. If a National Football Conference team (or an original National Football League team such as the Steelers) wins, this is assumed to be bullish. If an American Football Conference team wins, this is considered bearish.

expect sophisticated analysts to pick it up. (This may not be equally true for a lesser known firm that trades over-the-counter and enjoys little investor attention.)

Researchers have tested the semi-strong form of the efficient market hypothesis by determining whether investors who have acted on the basis of newly released public information have been able to enjoy superior returns. If the market is efficient in a semi-strong sense, this information is almost immediately impounded in the value of the security, and there would be little or no trading profits available. The implications would be that one could not garner superior returns by trading on public information about stock splits, earnings reports, or other similar items.

Tests on the semi-strong form of the efficient market hypothesis have generally been on the basis of risk-adjusted returns. Thus, the return from a given investment strategy must be compared to the performance of popular market indicators with appropriate risk adjustments. As will be described in Chapter 19, the risk measurement variable is usually the beta. After such adjustments are made, the question becomes, Are there abnormal returns that go beyond explanations associated with risk? If the answer is yes and can be shown to be statistically significant, then the investment strategy may be thought to refute the semi-strong form of the efficient market hypothesis. The investor must also cover transaction costs in determining that a given strategy is superior.

The risk adjustment measure may be viewed as:

$$K_i = a_i + b_i k_M + e_i$$

| Actual return | Inter-cept | Risk variable | Market return | Random error term |

Each of these items will receive further attention in Chapter 19. For now, our concern is whether our investment strategy can produce consistently superior, abnormal returns.

Tests examining the impact of such events as stock splits and stock dividends, earnings announcements, and changes in accounting policy have generally indicated that the market is efficient in a semi-strong sense. For example, a study by Fama, Fisher, Jensen, and Roll indicated that almost all of the market impact of a stock split takes place before public announcement.[12] There is little to be gained from acting on the announcement.

Other studies have indicated that favorable or unfavorable earnings reports have generally been considered prior to public announcement, and there is little or no price change after announcement (unless there is a very large deviation from expected results).[13]

---

[12] Eugene F. Fama, Lawrence Fisher, Michael G. Jensen, and Richard Roll, "The Adjustment of Stock Prices to New Information," *International Economic Review,* February 1969, pp. 2–21.

[13] Ray Ball and Philip Brown, "An Empirical Evaluation of Accounting Income Numbers," *Journal of Accounting Research,* Autumn 1968, pp. 159–78.

According to the semi-strong form of the efficient market hypothesis, investors not only digest information very quickly, but they are able to see through mere changes in accounting information that do not have economic consequences. For example, the switching from accelerated depreciation to straight-line depreciation for financial reporting purposes (but not tax purposes) would tend to make earnings per share look higher but would provide no economic benefit for the firm. Research studies indicate this would have no positive impact on valuation.[14]

Similarly, investors are not deceived by mere accounting changes related to inventory policy, reserve accounts, exchange translations, or other items that appear to have no economic benefits. The corporate treasurer who switches from LIFO to FIFO accounting to make earnings look better in an inflationary economy will probably not see his or her firm's stock price rise as investors look at the economic consequences of higher taxes associated with the action and disregard the mere financial accounting consequences of higher reported profits.[15] Under this circumstance, the effect on stock may be neutral or negative.

Implications for Fundamental Analysis

If stock values are already based on the analysis of all available public information, it may be assumed that there is little to be gained from additional fundamental analysis. Under the semi-strong form of the efficient market hypothesis, if General Motors is trading at $70, the assumption is that every shred of public information about GM has been collected and evaluated by thousands of investors, and they have determined an equilibrium price of $70. The assumption is that anything you read in *The Wall Street Journal* or *Standard & Poor's* publications has already been considered many times over by others and is currently impounded in the value of the stock. If you were to say that you think GM is really worth $73 because of some great new product, proponents of the semi-strong form of the efficient market hypothesis would suggest that your judgment cannot be better than the collective wisdom of the marketplace in which everyone is trying desperately to come out ahead.

Ironically, although many would suggest that fundamental analysis may not lead to superior profits in an efficient market environment, it is fundamental analysis itself which makes the market so efficient. Because everyone is doing fundamental analysis, there is little in the way of unabsorbed or undigested information. Therefore, one extra person doing fundamental analysis is unlikely to achieve superior insight.

---

[14] T. Ross Archibald, "Stock Market Reaction to Depreciation Switch-Back," *Accounting Review*, January 1972, pp. 22–30. Robert S. Kaplan and Richard Roll, Investor Evaluation of Accounting Information: Some Empirical Evidence," *Journal of Business*, April 1972, pp. 225–57.

[15] Shyam Sunder, "Stock Price and Risk Related to Accounting Changes in Inventory Valuation," *Accounting Review*, April 1975, pp. 305–15.

Although the semi-strong form of the efficient market hypothesis has strong research support and would generally be considered valid, there are exceptions. For example, Basu has found that stocks with low P/E ratios consistently provide better returns than stocks with high P/E ratios on both a nonrisk-adjusted and risk-adjusted basis.[16] Since a P/E ratio is publicly available information that may be used to generate superior returns, this flies in the face of the more common conclusions on the semi-strong form of the efficient market hypothesis. Banz[17] and Reinganum's[18] research indicates that small firms tend to provide higher returns than larger firms even after considering risk. Perhaps fewer institutional investors in smaller firms make for a less efficient market and superior potential opportunities. Oppenheimer and Schlarbaum have also shown that investors can generate superior risk-adjusted returns by following widely disseminated rules by Graham and Dodd on such factors as dividends, capitalization, firm size and P/E ratios, and by using only public information.[19] Additional evidence of this nature continues to accumulate, and in Chapter 14, on special situations, we present an extended discussion of some of the above items and other possible contradictions to the majority viewpoint of the semi-strong version of the efficient market hypothesis. We also comment on measurement problems in that chapter.

Thus, even if the semi-strong form of the efficient market hypothesis appears to be generally valid, exceptions can be noted. Also, there is the possibility that while most analysts may not be able to add additional insight through fundamental analysis, there are exceptions to every rule. It can be assumed that some analysts have such *extraordinary* insight and capability in analyzing publicly available information that they can perceive what others cannot. Also, if you take a very long-term perspective, the fact that a stock's value is in short-term equilibrium may not discourage you from taking a long-term position or attempting to find long-term value.

STRONG FORM OF THE EFFICIENT MARKET HYPOTHESIS

The strong form of the efficient market hypothesis goes beyond the semi-strong form to state that stock prices reflect not only all public information,

---

[16] S. Basu, "Investment Performance of Common Stocks in Relation to Their Price-Earnings Ratios: A Test of the Efficient Market Hypothesis," *Journal of Finance,* June 1977, pp. 663–82. Also, S. Basu, "The Information Content of Price-Earnings Ratios," *Financial Management,* Summer 1975, pp. 53–64.

[17] Rolf W. Banz, "The Relationship between Returns and Market Value of Common Stocks," *Journal of Financial Economics,* March 1981, pp. 3–18.

[18] Marc R. Reinganum, "Misspecification of Capital Asset Pricing—Empirical Anomalies Based on Earnings Yield and Market Values," *Journal of Financial Economics,* March 1981, pp. 19–46.

[19] Henry Oppenheimer, R. Oppenheimer, and Gary G. Schlarbaum, "Investing with Ben Graham: An Ex Ante Test of the Efficient Markets Hypothesis," *Journal of Financial and Quantitative Analysis,* September 1981, pp. 341–60.

but *all* information. Thus, it is hypothesized that insider information is also immediately impounded into the value of a security. In a sense, we go beyond the concept of a market that is highly efficient to one that is perfect.

The assumption is that no group of market participants or investors has monopolistic access to information. If this is the case, then no group of investors can be expected to show superior risk-adjusted returns under any circumstances.

Unlike the weak and semi-strong form of the efficient market hypothesis, major test results are not generally supportive of the strong form of the hypothesis. For example, specialists on security exchanges have been able to earn superior rates of return on invested capital.[20] The book they keep on unfilled limit orders would appear to provide monopolistic access to information. An SEC study actually found that specialists typically sell above their latest purchase 83 percent of the time and buy below their latest sell 81 percent of the time.[21] This implies wisdom that greatly exceeds that which would be available in a perfect capital market environment. Likewise, an institutional investor study, also sponsored by the SEC, indicated that specialists average return on capital was over 100 percent.[22]

Another group that appears to use nonpublic information to garner superior returns is corporate insiders. As previously described, an insider is considered to be a corporate officer, member of the board of directors, or substantial stockholder. The SEC requires that insiders report their transactions to that regulatory body. A few weeks after reporting to the SEC, the information becomes public. Researchers can then go back and determine whether investment decisions made by investors appeared, on balance, to be wise. Did heavy purchases by insiders precede strong upward price movements, and did sell-offs precede poor market performance? The answer appears to be yes. Research studies indicate insiders consistently achieve higher returns than would be expected in a perfect capital market.[23] Although inside traders are not allowed to engage in short-term (of six months or less) or illegal transactions to generate trading profits, they are allowed to take longer-term positions, which may well prove to be profitable. It has even been demonstrated that investors who follow the direction of inside traders after information on their

---

[20] Victor Niederhoffer and M. F. M. Osborne, "Market-Making and Reversal on the Stock Exchange," *Journal of the American Statistical Association,* December 1966, pp. 897–916.

[21] Securities and Exchange Commission, *Report of the Special Study of the Security Markets,* part 2 (Washington, D.C.: U.S. Government Printing Office, 1965).

[22] Securities and Exchange Commission, *Institutional Investor Study Report* (Washington D.C.: U.S. Government Printing Office, 1971).

[23] James H. Lorie and Victor Niederhoffer, "Predictive Statistical Properties of Insider Trading," *Journal of Law and Economics,* April 1966, pp. 35–53. Joseph E. Finnerty, "Insiders and Market Efficiency," *Journal of Finance,* September 1976, pp. 1141–48. Jeffrey Jaffe, "Special Information and Insider Trading," *Journal of Business,* July 1974, pp. 410–28. Shannon P. Pratt and Charles W. DeVere, "Relationship between Insider Trading and Rates of Return for NYSE Common Stocks, 1960–1966," in *Modern Developments in Investment Management,* ed. James H. Lorie and Richard Beasley (New York: Praeger Publishers, 1972), pp. 268–79.

activity becomes public may enjoy superior returns.[24] (This, of course, represents contrary evidence to the semi-strong form of the efficient market hypothesis as well.)

Even though there is evidence on the activity of specialists and insiders that would cause one to reject the strong form of the efficient market hypothesis (or at least not to accept it), the range of participants with access to superior information is not large. For example, tests on the performance of mutual fund managers have consistently indicated that they are not able to beat the market averages over the long term.[25] Although mutual fund managers may get the first call when news is breaking, that is not fast enough to generate superior returns.

While the strong form of the efficient market hypothesis suggests more opportunity for superior returns than the weak or semi-strong form, the premium is related to monopolistic access to information rather than other factors.

Part Three

FIXED INCOME AND LEVERAGED SECURITIES

We now shift our attention from stocks to fixed-income and leveraged securities. Fixed-income securities include bonds, preferred stock, certificates of deposit, and even money market funds. In the high interest rate environment of the last decade, many investors have increased their emphasis on fixed-return investments. However, we shall see that fixed-income securities are not without risk or uncertainty as to outcome.

In Chapter 9 we look at the organization of the debt markets and the elements that define the basic debt instrument. The functions of the bond rating agencies are also explored, along with the perceived efficiency of the bond market. In Chapter 10 we assume the role of the bond investor and examine a number of strategy considerations for optimizing return on investment. Chapter 11 moves to a discussion of duration, or weighted average life, of a bond. Since professional investors use duration concepts in designing their strategies, the student is given a basic description of these considerations. (The chapter is optional in nature and may be skipped without loss of continuity.)

The second half of this section covers leveraged securities, that is, securities in which there is a magnified return or loss potential for a given level of investment ("maximum bang for the buck"). The discussion begins with convertibles and warrants in Chapter 12. We examine the valuation of these securities and the existence of speculative premiums (the difference between market value and intrinsic value). We also look at the advantages and disadvantages of convertibles and warrants to the investor as well as to the corporation. A recurring question is, are we dealing with fool's gold? While the answer is no, it is a qualified no that can only be fully understood after you have examined the ins and outs of investing in these securities.

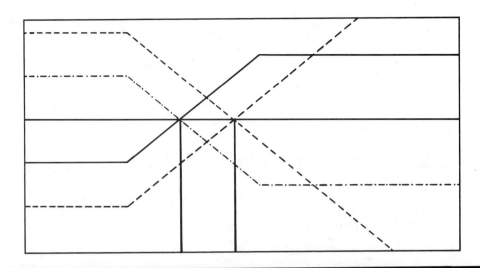

The stock option became highly popular with the founding of the Chicago Board Options Exchange in 1973. Options allow the investor to buy and sell stock at a specified future price, and they may be used as a form of speculation or as a defensive tool. In Chapter 13, we examine the basic types of options (puts and calls), the operations of the options market, how option prices are established, and the use of leverage in the option contract. We also examine how "option plays" can be tailored to the overall objectives of the portfolio. We conclude with a discussion of some of the more sophisticated option strategies.

Chapter 9
BOND AND FIXED-INCOME FUNDAMENTALS

Chapter 10
PRINCIPLES OF BOND VALUATION AND INVESTMENT

Chapter 11
DURATION AND REINVESTMENT CONCEPTS

Chapter 12
CONVERTIBLE SECURITIES AND WARRANTS

Chapter 13
PUT AND CALL OPTIONS

Chapter 9

Bond and Fixed-Income Fundamentals

THE BOND CONTRACT

SECURED AND UNSECURED BONDS

THE COMPOSITION OF THE BOND MARKET
U.S. Government Securities
Federally Sponsored Credit Agency Issues
State and Local Government Securities
Corporate Securities

BOND MARKET INVESTORS

BOND RATINGS
Actual Rating System

BOND QUOTES

BOND MARKETS, CAPITAL MARKET THEORY, AND EFFICIENCY

OTHER FORMS OF FIXED-INCOME SECURITIES

PREFERRED STOCK AS AN ALTERNATIVE TO DEBT
Features of Preferred Stock

As the reader will observe in various sections of this chapter, bonds actually represent a more substantial portion of new offerings in the capital markets than common stock. Some of the most financially rewarding jobs on Wall Street go to sophisticated analysts and dealers in the bond market.

In this chapter, we will examine the fundamentals of the bond instrument for both corporate and government issuers, with an emphasis on the debt contract and security provisions. We will also look at the overall structure of the bond market and the ways in which bonds are rated. The question of bond market efficiency is also considered. While most of the chapter deals with corporate and government bonds, other forms of fixed-income securities also receive attention. Thus, there is a brief discussion of short-term, fixed-income investments (such as certificates of deposit and commercial paper) as well as preferred stock.

In Chapter 10 we will shift the emphasis to actually evaluating fixed-income investments and devising strategies that attempt to capture profitable opportunities in the market. In Chapter 11 we will look at the interesting concept of *duration*. We begin our present discussion by considering the key elements that go into a bond contract.

THE BOND CONTRACT

A bond normally represents a long-term contractual obligation of the firm to pay interest to the bondholder as well as the face value of the bond at maturity. The major provisions in a bond agreement are spelled out in the *bond indenture,* a complicated legal document often over 100 pages in length, administered by an independent trustee (usually a commercial bank). We shall examine some important terms and concepts associated with a bond issue.

Par value—the face value of a bond. Most corporate bonds are traded in $1,000 units, while many federal, state, and local issues trade in units of $5,000 or $10,000.

Coupon rate—the actual interest rate on the bond, usually payable in semiannual installments. To the extent that interest rates in the market go above or below the coupon rate after the bond is issued, the market price of the bond will change from the par value. A bond initially issued at a rate of 8 percent will sell at a substantial discount from par value when 14 percent is the currently demanded rate of return. We will eventually examine how the investor makes and loses substantial amounts of money in the bond market with the swings in interest rates. A few corporate bonds are termed *variable rate notes* or *floating rate notes,* meaning that the coupon rate is only fixed for a short period of time and then varies with a stipulated short-term rate, such as the rate on U.S. government Treasury bills. In this instance, the interest payment varies up and down rather than the price of the bond, and most of the bonds can be redeemed at par early in the life of the issue at the option of the holder. This type of issue is likely to become increasingly popular in the future. In recent times, zero-coupon bonds have also been issued at values substantially below maturity value. The investor receives his or her return in the form of capital appreciation over the life of the bond since no semiannual cash interest payments are received.

Maturity date—the date on which final payment is due at the stipulated par value.

Methods of repayment—repayment of the bond can take place under many different arrangements. Some bonds are never paid off, such as selected *perpetual* bonds issued by the Canadian and British governments, in which there are no maturity dates. A more normal procedure would simply call for a single-sum lump payment at the end of the obligation. Thus, the issuer may make 40 semiannual interest payments over the next 20 years plus one lump-sum payment of the par value of the bond at maturity. There are three other significant means of repayment.

The first is the *serial* payment, in which bonds are paid off in installments over the life of the issue. Each serial bond has its own predetermined date of maturity and receives interest only to that point. Although the total bond issue may span over 20 years, 15 to 20 maturity dates are assigned. Municipal bonds are often issued on this basis. Second, there may be a *sinking fund* provision in which semiannual or annual contributions are made by a corporation into a fund administered by a trustee for purposes of debt retirement. The trustee takes the proceeds and goes into the market to purchase bonds from willing sellers. If no sellers are available, a lottery system may be used to repurchase the required number of bonds from among outstanding bondholders.

Finally, debt may be retired under a *call provision*. A call provision allows the corporation to call or force in all of the debt issue prior to maturity. The corporation usually pays a 5 percent to 10 percent premium over par value as part of the call provision arrangement. The ability to call is often *deferred* for the first five years of an issue (it can only take place after this time period). There are exceptions. An investor recently related buying a Michigan-Wisconsin Pipeline bond in 1981 having a 17.75 percent coupon with a deferred call to November 1, 1988. To his surprise the bond was called in less than three years when rates declined substantially. The fine print stated that the bond could not be called by a refunding (selling a new issue to replace the old bond) but could be retired at any time before maturity with cash from other sources. It pays to read the fine print rather than taking your broker's word for it.

SECURED AND UNSECURED BONDS

We have discussed some of the important features related to interest payments and retirement of outstanding issues. At least of equal importance is the nature of the security provision for the issue. Bond market participants have a long-standing practice of describing certain issues by the nature of asset claims in liquidation. In actuality, only infrequently are pledged assets sold off and the proceeds distributed to bondholders. Typically, the defaulting corporation is reorganized, and existing claims are partially satisfied by issuing new securities to the participating parties. Of course, the stronger and *better secured* the initial claim, the higher the quality of the security to be received in a reorganization.

There are a number of terms used to denote collateralized or secured debt. Under a *mortgage* agreement, real property (plant and equipment) is pledged as security for a loan. A mortgage may be *senior* or *junior* in nature, with the former requiring satisfaction of claims before payment is given to the latter. Bondholders may also attach an *after-acquired property clause* requiring that any new property be placed under the original mortgage.

A very special form of a mortgage or collateralized debt instrument is the *equipment trust certificate.* It is used by firms in the transportation industry (railroads, airlines, etc.). Proceeds from the sale of the certificate are used to purchase new equipment, and this new equipment in turn serves as collateral for the trust certificate.

Not all bond issues are secured or collateralized by assets. Certainly, most federal, state, and local government issues are unsecured. A wide range of corporate issues also are unsecured. There is a set of terminology referring to these unsecured issues. A corporate debt issue that is unsecured is referred to as a *debenture.* Even though the debenture is not secured by a specific pledge of assets, there may be priorities of claims among debenture holders. Thus, there are senior debentures and junior, or subordinated, debentures.

If liquidation becomes necessary because all other avenues for survival have failed, secured creditors are paid off first out of the disposition of the secured assets. The proceeds from the sale of the balance of the assets are then distributed among unsecured creditors, with those holding a senior ranking being satisfied before those holding a subordinate position (subordinated debenture holders).[1]

Unsecured corporate debt may provide slightly higher yields because of the greater suggested risk. However, this is partially offset by the fact that many unsecured debt issuers have such strong financial statements that security pledges may not be necessary.

Companies with less favorable prospects may issue *income bonds.* These bonds specify that interest is to be paid only to the extent that it is earned in current income. There is no legally binding requirement to pay interest on a regular basis, and failure to make interest payments cannot trigger bankruptcy proceedings. These issues appear to offer the corporation the unusual advantage of paying interest as a tax-deductible expense (as opposed to dividends) combined with freedom from the binding contractual obligation of most debt issues. But any initial enthusiasm for these issues is quickly reduced by recognition of the fact that they have very limited appeal to investors. The issuance of income bonds is usually restricted to circumstances where new corporate debt is issued to old bondholders or preferred stockholders to avoid bankruptcy or where a troubled corporation is being reorganized.

---

[1] Those secured creditors that are not fully satisfied by the disposition of secured assets may also participate with the unsecured creditors in the remaining assets.

THE COMPOSITION OF THE BOND MARKET

Having established some of the basic terminology relating to the bond instrument, we now are in a position to take a more comprehensive look at the bond market.

While there may be a tendency to think of corporate issues as making up a large percentage of the bond market, this is simply not the case. Corporate issues must vie with offerings from the U.S. Treasury, federally sponsored credit agencies, and state and local governments (municipal offerings). The relative importance of the four types of issues is indicated in Figure 9–1. Over

FIGURE 9–1   Long-Term Funds Raised by Business and the Government

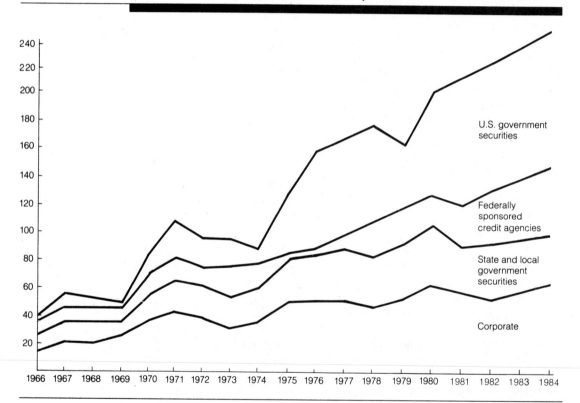

Source: *Federal Reserve Bulletin* (Washington D.C.: Federal Reserve Board of Governors, selected issues).

the 18-year period, new issues of corporate securities averaged only 30 percent of the total, while government securities (federal, state, and local) made up the other 70 percent. It is interesting to note the dramatic recent rise in long-term U.S. government securities (top portion of Figure 9–1). Large deficits, beginning in the mid-1970s, have steadily increased the U.S. government's portion of new financing. In the 1984 fiscal year, the U.S. deficit was in excess of $200 billion and economists were concerned that the U.S. government's need for funds would "crowd out" smaller corporate borrowers, keeping them from being able to raise capital for needed plant and inventory expansion.

In the following section, we will briefly discuss the various forms of debt instruments available to the investor.

U.S. Government Securities

U.S. government securities take the form of Treasury bills, Treasury notes, and Treasury bonds (only the latter two are considered in the top part of Figure 9–1). The distinction between the three categories relates to the life of the obligation.

Treasury bills (T-bills) are short-term in nature, with a maximum maturity of one year and common maturities of 91 and 182 days. Treasury bills are unique in that they trade on a discount basis—meaning that the yield the investor receives takes place as a result of the difference between the price paid and the maturity value (and no actual interest is paid). Thus, a $10,000 Treasury bill quoted to pay 10 percent annualized interest over a six-month period will initially sell for $9,500. The investor receives $500 on the $10,000 face amount, or 5 percent for six months, which is translated into a 10 percent annualized rate. Actually, the true rate is slightly higher than the 10 percent quoted rate. The investor is receiving $500 interest on the $9,500 discounted price ($500/%9,500) or 5.26 percent, which translates into 10.52 percent.

Treasury bills trade in minimum units of $10,000, and there is an extremely active secondary, or resale, market for these securities. Thus, an investor buying a Treasury bill from the government with an initial life of approximately six months would have no difficulty in selling it to another investor after two or three weeks. Since the T-bill now has a shorter time to run, its market value would be a bit closer to par.

A second type of U.S. government security is the *Treasury note,* which is considered to be of intermediate term and generally has a maturity of 1 to 7 years. Finally, *Treasury bonds* are long-term in nature and mature in 7 to 25 years or longer. Unlike Treasury bills, Treasury notes and bonds provide direct interest and trade in units of $1,000 and higher. Because there is no risk of default (unless the government stops printing money or the ultimate bomb explodes), U.S. government securities provide lower returns than other forms of credit obligations. Interest on U.S. government issues is fully taxable for IRS purposes but is exempt from state and local taxes.

Some Treasury notes and bonds have been repackaged into zero-coupon bonds by major brokerage firms and investment bankers such as Merrill Lynch, Goldman Sachs, A. G. Becker, and others. These firms buy U.S. "governments" and put these securities in trust (usually a commercial bank acts as trustee). A security is divided into two parts—one generating a cash flow from the interest payments and the other providing principal at maturity. These two parts are then sold separately to investors with specific needs. The principal payment part is generically called a "zero-coupon Treasury bond" but each investment banker labels their own product, with names such as TIGRs (for Merrill Lynch's Treasury Investment Growth Receipts); COUGARs (for A. G. Becker's

Zero-Coupon Certificates on Government Receipts); and RATs, CATs, and GATORs for other firms. For example, Merrill Lynch's TIGRs are called Principal TIGRs (the zero-coupon part) and Serial TIGRs, which pay interest at six-month intervals for 40 payments. Serial TIGRs are annuities with, of course, no principal at maturity. In 1985, the U.S. treasury also began trading zero-coupon bonds directly on its own.

Since zero-coupon bonds pay no interest, all returns to the investor come in the form of increases in the value of the investment. For example, 15-year zero-coupon bonds might initially sell for 18 percent of par value. You might buy a $1,000 instrument for $180.[2]

The Internal Revenue Service taxes zero-coupon bonds as if interest were paid semi-annually even though no cash flow is received until maturity. The tax is based on amortizing the built-in gain over the life of the instrument. For tax reasons, zero-coupons are usually only appropriate for nontaxable accounts such as Individual Retirement Accounts, Keogh plans or other non-taxable pension funds.

Federally Sponsored Credit Agency Issues

Referring back to Figure 9–1, observe the rapid growth in securities issued by federal agencies. New issues have been running at the rate of approximately $20–$30 billion per year. These issues represent obligations of various agencies of the government, such as the Federal Home Loan Bank, the Federal National Mortgage Association (FNMA), and the Federal Housing Administration (FHA). Although these issues are authorized by an act of Congress and are used to finance federal projects, they are not direct obligations of the Treasury but rather of the agency itself.

Though the issues are essentially free of risk (there is always the implicit standby power of the government behind the issues), they carry a slightly higher yield than U.S. government securities simply because they are not directly issued by the Treasury. Agency issues have been particularly active as a support mechanism for the housing industry. The issues generally trade in denominations of $5,000 and up. They have varying maturities of from 1 to 40 years, with an average life of approximately 15 years. Examples of some agency issues are presented below.

	Minimum denomination	Life of issue
Federal Home Loan Bank	$10,000	12–25 years
Federal Intermediate Credit Banks	5,000	Up to 4 years
Federal Housing Administration	50,000	1–40 years
Export-Import Bank	5,000	Up to 7 years
U.S. Postal Service	10,000	25 years

[2] On zero-coupon bonds the yield to maturity is a true rate over the life of the security, since the price paid includes the assumption of continuous compounding at the yield to maturity. Zero-coupon securities are the most price-sensitive to a change in interest rates of any bond having the same maturity. This is fine when interest rates decline, but can be disastrous when rates rise. A good deal more will be said about zero-coupon bonds in Chapter 11.

Interest on agency issues is fully taxable for IRS purposes and is generally taxable for state and local purposes although there are exceptions. (For example, interest on obligations issued by the Federal Housing Administration are subject to state and local taxes, but those of the Federal Home Loan Bank are not.)

One agency issue that is of particular interest to the investor because of its unique features is the GNMA ("Ginnie Mae") pass-through certificate. These certificates represent an undivided interest in a pool of federally insured mortgages. Actually, GNMA, the Government National Mortgage Association, buys a pool of mortgages from various lenders at a discount and then issues securities to the public against these mortgages. Security holders in GNMA certificates receive monthly payments that essentially represent a pass through of interest and principal payments on the mortgages. These securities come in minimum denominations of $25,000, are long-term in nature, and are fully taxable for federal, state, and local income tax purposes. A major consideration in this investment is that the investor has fully consumed his or her capital at the end of the investment. (Not only has interest been received monthly, but all principal has been returned over the life of the certificate, and therefore there is no lump-sum payment at maturity.)

State and Local Government Securities

Debt securities issued by state and local governments are referred to as municipal bonds. Examples of issuing agencies include states, cities, school districts, toll roads, or any other type of political subdivision. The most important feature of a municipal bond is the tax-exempt nature of the interest payment. Dating back to the United States Supreme Court opinion of 1819 in *McCullough* v. *Maryland,* it was ruled that the federal government and state and local governments do not possess the power to tax each other. An eventual by-product of the judicial ruling was that income from municipal bonds cannot be taxed by the IRS. Furthermore, income from municipal bonds is also exempt from state and local taxes if bought within the locality in which one resides. Thus, a Californian buying municipal bonds in that state would pay no state income tax on the issue. However, the same Californian would have to pay state or local income taxes if the originating agency were in Texas or New York.

We cannot overemphasize the importance of the federal tax exemption that municipal bonds enjoy. The consequences are twofold. First of all, individuals in high tax brackets may find highly attractive investment opportunities in municipal bonds.[3] Some have referred to municipal bond investments as "welfare for the rich." The formula used to equate interest on municipal bonds to other investments is:

---

[3] It should be noted, however, that any capital gain on a municipal bond is taxable as would be the case with any investment.

$$Y = \frac{i}{(1 - t)} \qquad (9\text{--}1)$$

where:

y = Equivalent before-tax yield on a taxable investment.
i = Yield on the municipal obligation.
t = Marginal tax rate of the investor.

If an investor has a marginal tax rate of 45 percent and is evaluating a municipal bond paying 10 percent interest, the equivalent before-tax yield on a taxable investment would be:

$$\frac{10\%}{(1 - .45)} = \frac{10\%}{.55} = 18.18\%$$

Thus, the investor could choose between a *non*-tax-exempt investment paying 18.18 percent and a tax-exempt municipal bond paying 10 percent and be indifferent between the two. Table 9–1 presents examples of trade-offs between tax-exempts and non-tax-exempt (taxable) investments at various interest rates and marginal tax rates. Clearly, the higher the marginal tax rate, the greater the advantage of tax-exempt municipal bonds.

TABLE 9–1   Marginal Tax Rates and Return Equivalents

Yield on municipal (percent)	Comparable yield on taxable investment (in percent for each marginal tax bracket)			
	35 percent bracket	40 percent bracket	45 percent bracke	50 percent bracket
8.0%	12.3%	13.3%	14.5%	16.0%
9.0	13.8	15.0	16.4	18.0
10.0	15.4	16.6	18.2	20.0
11.0	16.9	18.3	20.0	22.0
12.0	18.5	20.0	21.8	24.0
13.0	20.0	21.7	23.6	26.0
14.0	21.5	23.3	25.5	28.0

A second significant feature of municipal bonds is that the yield that the issuing agency pays on municipal bonds is lower than the yield on taxable instruments. Of course, a municipal bond paying 10 percent may be quite competitive with taxable instruments paying considerably more. Average differentials are presented in Table 9–2.

TABLE 9–2   Comparable Yields on Long-Term Municipals and Taxable Corporates (yearly averages)

Year	Municipals Aa	Corporates Aa	Yield difference
1984	9.95	12.25	2.30
1983	9.20	12.42	3.22
1982	11.39	14.41	3.02
1981	10.89	14.75	3.86
1980	8.06	12.50	4.44
1979	6.12	9.94	3.82
1978	5.68	8.92	3.24
1977	5.39	8.24	2.85
1976	6.12	8.75	2.63
1975	6.77	9.17	2.40
1974	6.04	8.84	2.80
1973	5.11	7.66	2.55
1972	5.19	7.48	2.29
1971	5.36	7.78	2.42

Sources: *Moody's Municipal & Government Manual, Moody's Industrial Manual, Moody's Bond record* (published by Moody's Investors Service, Inc., New York, N.Y., selected issues).

The difference is of a 2 to 4.5 percent magnitude, and this is extremely important to issuing agencies. The ability of a city, state, or political subdivision to save 2 to 4.5 percent from normal bond market yields is critically important to municipal issuers. During those time periods when an overly aggressive Congress has attempted to propose legislation that might overturn the tax-exempt features of municipals, the cries of anger from mayors and governors is loud and clear. A major distinction that is also important to the bond issuer and investor is whether the bond is of a general obligation or revenue nature.

General obligation versus revenue bonds.   A general obligation issue is backed by the full faith, credit, and "taxing power" of the governmental unit. For a revenue bond, on the other hand, the repayment of the issue is fully dependent on the revenue-generating capability of a specific project or venture, such as a toll road, bridge, or municipal colosseum.

Because of the taxing power behind most general obligation (GO) issues, they tend to be of extremely high quality. Approximately three fourths of all municipal bond issues are of the general obligation variety, and very few failures have taken place in the post–World War II era. Revenue bonds tend to be of more uneven quality, and the economic soundness of the underlying revenue-generating project must be carefully examined (though most projects are quite worthwhile).

One special form of revenue bond that has gained popularity in the late 1970s and 80s is the pollution and environmental control revenue bond. A political subdivision offers the issue with the backing of a long-term pledge or guarantee from an industrial firm that will use the proceeds. Essentially, the political subdivision serves as a funneling device for the corporate entity and, through this approach, allows for the utilization of tax-exempt funds by the corporation. Well over 1,000 such issues are currently in existence. Examples of pollution and environmental control bonds are presented in Table 9–3.

TABLE 9–3   Pollution and Environmental Control Revenue Bonds

Amount	State/municipality	Lessee/guarantor
$ 35,000,000	Escambia County, Fla.	St. Regis Paper Co.
60,000,000	Gary, Ind.	Standard Oil of Indiana
110,000,000	East Baton Rouge, La.	Exxon Corp.
40,000,000	Ohio Air Quality Authority	Republic Steel Corp.
60,000,000	Gulf Coast Waste Disposal	Shell Oil Co.
75,000,000	Allegeheny County—Pennsylvania	U.S. Steel Corp.

Source: *Moody's Bond Record* (published by Moody's Investors Service, Inc., New York, N.Y., selected issues).

Congress has been generally supportive of this activity as a means of providing less expensive financing for low-dollar return projects that provide benefits to society. In an earlier era, industrial revenue bonds (tax-exempt issues used to attract industry into a given area through low-cost financing) enjoyed a similar popularity. However, since the net benefit to society of one city stealing another city's factory and payroll is nil, many restrictions have been put on industrial revenue bonds.

Municipal bond guarantee.   A growing factor in the municipal bond market is the third-party guarantee. Whether dealing with a general obligation or revenue bond, a fee may be paid by the originating governmental body to a third party insurer to guarantee that all interest and principal payments will be made. A number of states, including California and Michigan, now have provisions to guarantee payments on selected issues. There are also two large private insurers. The first is a consortium of four insurance companies that market their product under the name of the Municipal Bond Insurance Association (MBIA). The second is the American Municipal Bond Assurance Corporation (AMBAC). Both will insure general obligation or revenue bonds.

A bond that carries a guarantee will have a slightly lower yield and a better secondary, or resale, market. This may be important because municipal bonds, in general, do not provide as strong a secondary market as U.S. government issues. The market for a given municipal issue is often small and fragmented, and there are high indirect costs associated with reselling the issue.

Corporate Securities

While corporate bonds represent only 30 percent of the total bond market (which also includes U.S. government securities, federally sponsored credit agencies, and municipal bonds), they are still the dominant source of new financing for the U.S. corporation. That is, corporate bonds have been the most significant form of new financing for U.S. corporations, as indicated in Figure 9–2.

FIGURE 9–2   Long-Term Corporate Financing, 1964–1983

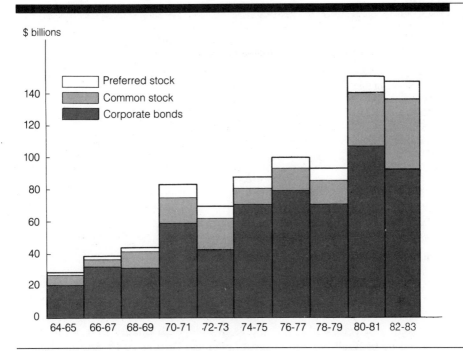

Source: *Federal Reserve Bulletin* (Washington, D.C.: Federal Reserve Board of Governors, *SEC Monthly Statistical Review* (U.S. Securities and Exchange Commission, selected issues).

Between 1964 and 1983, corporate bonds represented 77 percent of the total volume of long-term corporate securities sold. In tight money periods, such as 1974–75, the ratio approached 87 percent. However, during 1982–83 when the stock market reached new highs, corporations took advantage of lofty stock prices, using common stock to raise 29 percent of external funds. Bond financing was only 62.5 percent during this period.

The corporate market may be broken down into a number of subunits, including *industrials, public utilities, rails* and *transportation,* and *financial issues* (banks, finance companies, etc.). The industrials are a catchall category that includes everything from high technology companies to discount chain stores. Public utilities represent the largest segment of the market and have issues that run up to 40 years in maturity. Because public utilities are in constant need of funds to meet ever expanding requirements for power generation, telephone services, and other essentials, they are always in the bond market to raise new funds. The needs associated with rails and transportation as well as financial issues tend to be less than those associated with public utilities or industrials. In Table 9–4, we see the comparative yields from three of the categories and for all corporations.[4]

TABLE 9–4 Comparative Yields on Aa Bonds among Corporate Issuers (percent)

(January)	Industrial	Public utility	Rails and transportation	All corporations
1984	12.39%	13.02%	12.22%	12.71%
1983	11.94	12.74	11.24	12.35
1982	15.01	16.48	13.52	15.75
1981	13.01	14.03	11.40	13.52
1980	11.16	11.95	9.99	11.56
1979	9.24	9.70	8.33	9.48
1978	8.42	8.76	7.93	8.59
1977	7.90	8.41	7.52	8.16
1976	8.87	9.39	8.45	9.13
1975	8.81	9.45	8.70	9.13
1974	7.85	8.15	7.92	8.00

Source: *Moody's Bond Record* (published by Moody's Investors Service, Inc., New York, N.Y., selected issues).

The higher yields on public utility issues represent a supply–demand phenomenon more than anything else. A constant stream of new issues to the market can only be absorbed by a higher yield pattern. In other cases the higher required return also may be associated with quality deterioration as measured by profitability and interest coverage. During 1983–84, the default of the Washington State Power Authority on bonds issued to construct power-generating facilities sent waves through the bond market. Again in 1984 when Public Service of Indiana canceled construction of a partially complete nuclear power plant, nuclear utility issues (both stocks and bonds) suffered severe price erosion and the bond market demanded high risk premiums on bonds of almost all nuclear utilities.

Corporate bonds of all types generally trade in units of $1,000, and this is a particularly attractive feature to the smaller investor who does not wish to purchase in units of $5,000 to $10,000 (which is necessary for many Treasury, federally sponsored credit agency issues, and municipals). Because of higher risk relative to government issues, the investor will generally receive higher yields on corporates as well. All income from corporates is taxable for federal, state, and local purposes. Finally, corporate issues have the disadvantage of being subject to calls. When buying a bond during a period of high interest rates, the call provision must be considered a negative feature because the

[4] Financial issues are generally not broken out of the published data.

high-yielding bonds may be called in for early retirement as interest rates go down.

BOND MARKET INVESTORS

Having considered the issuer or supply side of the market, we now comment on the investor, or demand, side. The bond market is dominated by large institutional investors (insurance companies, banks, pension funds, mutual funds) even more than the stock market. Institutional investors account for 90 to 95 percent of the trading in key segments of the bond market.[5] However, the presence of the individual investor is partially felt in the corporate and municipal bond market where the incentives of low denomination ($1,000) corporate bonds or tax-free municipal bonds have some attraction.

Institutional investors' preferences for various sectors of the bond market are influenced by their tax status as well as the nature of their obligations or liabilities to depositors, investors, or clients. For example, banks traditionally have been strong participants in the municipal bond market because of their substantial tax obligations. Their investments tend to be in short- to intermediate-term assets because of the short-term nature of their deposit obligations (the funds supplied to the banks). One problem that banks find in their bond portfolios is that such investments are often preferred over loans to customers when the economy is weak and loan demand is sluggish. Not so coincidentally, this happens to be the time period when interest rates are low. When the economy improves, interest rates go up, and so does loan demand. In order to meet the loan demand of valued customers, banks liquidate portions of their bond portfolio. The problem with this recurring process is that banks are buying bonds when interest rates are *low* and selling them when interest rates are *high*. This can cause losses in the value of the bank portfolio.

The bond market investor must be prepared to deal in a relatively strong primary market (new issues market) and a relatively weak secondary market (resale market). While the secondary market is active for many types of Treasury and agency issues, such is not the case for corporate and municipal issues. Thus, the investor must look well beyond the yield, maturity, and rating to determine if a purchase is acceptable. The question that must be considered is: How close to the going market price can I dispose of the issue if that should be necessary? If a 5 or 10 percent discount is involved, that might be unacceptable. Unlike the stock market, the secondary market in bonds tends to be dominated by over-the-counter transactions (although there are listed bonds traded as well).

In February of 1982, the Securities and Exchange Commission began allowing a process called shelf registration under SEC Rule 415. Shelf registration permits large companies to file one comprehensive registration statement, which outlines the firm's plans for future long-term financing. Then, when

---

[5] Sidney Homer, "Historical Evolution of Today's Bond Market," *Journal of Portfolio Management,* Spring 1975, pp. 6–11.

market conditions seem appropriate, the firm can issue the securities without further SEC approval. Future issues are said to be sitting on the shelf, waiting for the most advantageous time to appear. Shelf registration has been most frequently used with debt issues and other fixed income securities. Table 9–5 from *Moody's Bond Survey* of May 1984 shows a sample of the various shelf offerings outstanding at that time. The largest is the $2 billion offering of notes by Citicorp. While only 30–40 percent of corporate bonds are sold through shelf registration, this process is becoming increasingly popular in the 1980s.

TABLE 9–5   Prospective Offerings—Shelf Registrations under SEC Rule 415

Date of registration	Original amount ($millions)	Registrants	Types of securities	Prospective ratings
6/07/1982	150.0	ACF Industries, Inc.	Equity Trust Certificates	A2
2/17/1984	1,000.0	Alliance Mortgage Acceptance Corp.	GNMA Obligations	—
10/11/1983	500.0	American Express Credit Corp.	Senior Unsecured Debt Securities	Aa2
1/17/1983	250.0	Carolina Power & Light	First Mortgage Bonds	A2
3/14/1983	50.0	Central Power & Light	Cumulative Preferred Stock	"aa3"
3/09/1983	2,000.0	Citicorp	Notes	Aa1
8/04/1983	150.0	Continental Illinois Corp.	Adjusted Rate Preferred Stock	"ba2"

Private Placement.   A number of bond offerings are sold to investors as a private placement. That is, they are sold privately to investors rather than through the public markets. Historically, private placements have equaled 30 to 35 percent of new debt issues. Private placements are most popular with such investors as insurance companies and pension funds. They are primarily offered in the corporate sector by industrial firms rather than public utilities. The lender can generally expect to receive a slightly higher yield than on public issues to compensate for the extremely limited or nonexistent secondary market and the generally smaller size of the borrowing firm in a private placement.

BOND RATINGS

Bond investors tend to place much more emphasis on independent analysis of quality than do common stock investors. For this reason, both corporate financial management and institutional portfolio managers keep a very close eye on bond rating procedures. The difference between an AA and an A rating may mean the corporation will have to pay ¼ percent more interest on the bond issue (perhaps 12½ percent rather than 12¼ percent). On a $100 million, 20-year issue, this represents $250,000 per year (before tax), or a total of $5 million over the life of the bond.

The two major bond rating agencies are Moody's Investors Service (a subsidiary of Dun & Bradstreet, Inc.) and Standard & Poor's (a subsidiary of McGraw-Hill, Inc.). They rank thousands of corporate and municipal issues as well as a limited number of private placements, commercial paper, and preferred stock issues, and offerings of foreign companies and governments. U.S. government issues tend to be free of risk and therefore are given very little attention by the bond rating agencies. Moody's, founded in 1909, is the older of the two bond rating agencies and covers twice as many securities as Standard & Poor's (particularly in the municipal bond area). Other less well-known bond rating agencies include Fitch Investors Service, Inc. (an old-line rating agency that specializes in bank securities), and Duff & Phelp, Inc.

The bond ratings, generally ranging from an AA to a D category, are decided on a committee basis at both Moody's and Standard & Poor's.[6] There are no fast and firm quantitative measures that specify the rating that a new issue will receive. Nevertheless, measures pertaining to cash flow and earnings generation in relationship to debt obligations are given strong consideration. Of particular interest are coverage ratios that show the number of times that interest payments, as well as all annual contractual obligations, are covered by earnings. A coverage of two or three may contribute to a low rating, while a ratio of 5 to 10 may indicate the possibility of a strong rating. Operating margins, return on invested capital, and returns on total assets are also evaluated along with debt-to-equity ratios.[7] Financial ratio analysis makes up perhaps 50 percent of the evaluation. Other factors of importance are the nature of the industry in which the firm operates, the relative position of the firm within the industry, the pricing clout that the firm has, and the quality of management.

Decisions are not made in a sterile, isolated environment. Thus, it is not unusual for corporate management or the mayor to make an actual presentation to the rating agency, and on-sight visitations to plants or cities may take place. Corporations or municipalities have been known to change their operating or financial policies in order to satisfy people at the rating agencies. Perhaps the size of the issue will be pared down to provide for better interest coverage, or an increase in cash dividends will be delayed to strengthen the internal financing position of the firm.

The overall quality of the work done by the bond rating agencies may be judged by the agencies' acceptance in the business and academic community. In truth, their work is very well received. Although Paine, Webber and some other investment houses have established their own analysts to shadow the activities of the bond rating agencies and look for imprecisions in their classifi-

---

[6] Irwin Ross, "Higher Stakes in the Bond Rating Game," *Fortune*, April 1976, pp. 133–42.

[7] Similar appropriate measures can be applied to municipal bonds, such as debt per capita or income per capita within a governmental jurisdiction.

cations (and thus potential profits), the opportunities are not great. Academic researchers have generally found that accounting and financial data were well considered in the bond ratings and that rational evaluation appeared to exist.[8]

One item lending credibility to the bond rating process is the frequency with which the two major rating agencies arrive at exactly the same grade for a given issue (and this occurs well over 50 percent of the time). When "split ratings" do occur (different ratings by different agencies), they are invariably of a small magnitude. A typical case might be AAA versus AA rather than AAA versus BBB. While one can question whether one agency is looking over the other's shoulder or "copying its homework," this is probably not the case in this skilled industry.

Nevertheless, there is room for criticism. While initial evaluations are quite thorough and rational, the subsequent monitoring process may not be wholly satisfactory. Subsequent changes in corporate or municipal government events may not trigger a rating change quickly enough in all cases. One sure way that a corporation or municipal government will get a reevaluation is for them to come out with a new issue. This tends to generate a review of all existing issues.

Actual Rating System

In Table 9–6, we see an actual listing of the designations used by Moody's and Standard & Poor's. Note that Moody's combines capital letters and small *a*'s, and Standard & Poor's uses all capital letters.

The first four categories are assumed to represent investment-grade quality (high or medium grades). Large institutional investors (insurance companies, banks, pension funds) generally confine their activities to these four categories. The next two B grades are considered speculative in nature, while C and D rated issues are generally in default and may trade flat (without interest). Moody's also modifies their basic ratings with numerical values for categories Aa through B: 1 is the highest in a category, 2 is the mid-range, and 3 is the lowest. Thus a Aa2 rating means the bond is in the mid-range of Aa. Standard & Poor's has a similar modification process with plusses and minuses applied. Thus AA+ would be on the high end of a AA rating, AA would be in the middle and AA− would be on the low end.

It is also possible for a corporation to have issues outstanding in more than one category. For example, highly secured mortgage bonds of a corporation may be rated AA, while unsecured issues carry an A rating.

The level of interest payment on a bond is inverse to the quality rating. If a bond rated AAA by Standard & Poor's pays 12 percent, an A-quality bond

[8] James O. Horrigan, "The Determination of Long-Term Credit Standing with Financial Ratios," *Empirical Research in Accounting: Selected Studies,* supplement to *Journal of Accounting Research,* 4 (1966), pp. 44–62. Thomas F. Pogue and Robert M. Soldofsky, "What's in a Bond Rating?" *Journal of Financial and Quantitative Analysis,* June 1969, pp. 201–8. George E. Pinches and Kent A. Mingo, "A Multivariate Analysis of Industrial Bond Ratings," *Journal of Finance,* March 1973, pp. 1–18.

TABLE 9–6   Description of Bond Ratings

Quality	Moody's	Standard & Poor's	Description
High-grade	Aaa	AAA	Bonds that are judged to be of the best quality. They carry the smallest degree of investment risk and are generally referred to as "gilt edge." Interest payments are protected by a large or exceptionally stable margin, and principal is secure.
	Aa	AA	Bonds that are judged to be of high quality by all standards. Together with the first group, they comprise what are generally known as high-grade bonds. They are rated lower than the best bonds because margins of protection may not be as large.
Medium-grade	A·	A	Bonds that possess many favorable investment attributes and are to be considered as upper medium-grade obligations. Factors giving security to principal and interest are considered adequate.
	Baa	BBB	Bonds that are considered as medium-grade obligations, i.e., they are neither highly protected nor poorly secured.
Speculative	Ba	BB	Bonds that are judged to have speculative elements; their future cannot be considered as well assured. Often the protection of interest and principal payments may be very moderate.
	B	B	Bonds that generally lack characteristics of the desirable investment. Assurance of interest and principal payments or of maintenance of other terms of the contract over any long period of time may be small.
Default	Caa	CCC	Bonds that are of poor standing. Such issues may be in default, or there may be elements of danger present with respect to principal or interest.
	Ca	CC	Bonds that represent obligations which are speculative to a high degree. Such issues are often in default or have other marked shortcomings.
	C		The lowest rated class in Moody's designation. These bonds can be regarded as having extremely poor prospects of attaining any real investment standing.
		C	Rating given to income bonds on which interest is not currently being paid.
		D	Issues in default with arrears in interest and/or principal payments.

Sources: *Moody's Bond Record* (published by Moody's Investors Service, Inc., New York, N.Y.) and *Bond Guide* (Standard & Poor's).

might pay 13 percent; a BB, 13.75 percent; and so on. The spread between these yields changes from time to time and is watched closely by the financial community as a barometer of future movements in the financial markets. A relatively small spread between two rating categories would indicate investors generally have confidence in the economy. As the yield spread widens between higher and lower rating categories, this may indicate some loss of confidence. Investors are demanding increasingly higher yields for lower-rated bonds. Their loss of confidence indicates they will demand progressively higher returns for taking risks.

The relative positioning of different types of corporate bonds within the various rating categories is presented in Table 9–7. We see the predominance of bonds ranked in the top four categories, with one exception being the transportation industry (rails, airlines).

TABLE 9–7   Percentage Distribution of Corporate Bonds by Rating Categories (based on par value outstanding)

	Total corporate	Utilities	Industrial	Finance	Transportation
AAA	23%	26%	21%	19%	7%
AA	26	25	26	33	10
A	33	32	34	34	27
BBB	13	16	10	5	18
BB	2	1	3	1	8
B	1	—	2	1	8
CCC and lower	2	—	4	7	22
	100%	100%	100%	100%	100%

Source: Salomon Brothers.

BOND QUOTES

The Wall Street Journal and a number of other sources publish bond values on a daily basis. In Table 9–8, we see an excerpt from the daily quote sheet for corporate bonds.

In the first column, note the company name followed by the annual coupon rate and the maturity date. For example, the sixth entry in the Table shows Alabama Power with a coupon rate of 7¾ percent maturing in 02 (the year 2002). The current yield (Cur Yld) represents the annual interest or coupon payment divided by the price and is 12 percent (rounded). The volume (Vol) is indicated to be 3 bonds traded, and the closing price is 64-⅞. The bond quote does not represent actual dollars, but percent of par value. Since corporate bonds trade in units of $1,000 par value, 64.875 percent represents $648.75. Other issues of Alabama Power also trade at different prices.

A student interested in further information on a bond could proceed to *Moody's Bond Record,* published by Moody's Investors Service, or the *Bond Guide,* published by Standard & Poor's. For example, using the aforementioned *Moody's Bond Record,* the reader could determine, in Table 9–9, that the Avco 7½s of 1993 are subordinated debentures with a Moody's bond rating of Ba2 and a current call price of 100 percent of par, or $1,000 (no premium in this case). The *Moody's Bond Record* further indicates that the bonds were initially issued on January 1, 1969, and interest is payable on March 31 and November 30 of each year (first column, Interest Dates).

In Table 9–10 we turn our attention to quotes on U.S. government securities (as opposed to corporate issues). Treasury notes and bonds are traded on a price basis as a percentage of par value, similar to corporate bonds. Historically, price changes in the market have been rather small and bonds are quoted in ⅟₃₂ of a percentage point. For example, the price for the 10½

TABLE 9-8 Daily Quotes on Corporate Bonds

TABLE 9-9 Background Data on Bond Issues

Issue	Interest Dates	Current Call Price	Moody's Rating	Current Price		Yield to Mat	Price Range 1984 High / Low	Price Range 1946-83 High / Low	Amt Outst Mil $	Sink Fund Prov	Legal Status	Fed Tax	Issued	Price	Yld
Autotote Systems Inc. sr.deb.11.50 1996	J&D1	100.00	— r	80	bid	15.20	81 50	84 53	13.6	Yes	—	N	6-2-81		
• AVCO CORP. sr.nts.12.00 1990	J&D15	* 100.00	Baa3 r	90¼	sale	14.58	97¾ 85¼	102 72¾	75.0	No	—	N	6-19-80	100.00	12.00
• do sub.deb. 7.50 1993 "	M31&N30	100.00	Ba2 r	64	bid	14.76	71 61¾	94½ 30¼	66.8	No	—	N	Jan.1969		
• Avco Finan. Ser Inc. sr.nts.14.125 1985	J&D15	N.C.	A3 r	100	sale	14.12	104¼ 100	107 99¾	100	No	—	1 N	8-17-82	99.63	14.25

TABLE 9–10   Daily Quotes on Government Issues

Treasury Issues/ Bonds, Notes & Bills

Thursday, May 31, 1984

Representative mid-afternoon Over-the-Counter quotations supplied by the Federal Reserve Bank of New York City, based on transactions of $1 million or more.

Decimals in bid-and-asked and bid changes represent 32nds; 101.1 means 101 1/32. a-Plus 1/64. b-Yield to call date. d-Minus 1/64. n-Treasury notes.

Treasury Bonds and Notes

Rate	Mat.	Date	Bid	Asked	Bid Chg.	Yld.
8⅞s,	1984	Jun n	99.27	99.31+	.1	8.97
14⅜s,	1984	Jun n	100.6	100.10−	.1	9.39
13⅛s,	1984	Jul n	100.13	100.17	....	9.25
6⅜s,	1984	Aug	99.4	99.20	....	8.14
7¼s,	1984	Aug n	99.10	99.14	....	9.93
11⅝s,	1984	Aug n	100.6	100.10	....	9.97
13¼s,	1984	Aug n	100.17	100.21	....	9.49
12⅛s,	1984	Sep n	100.8	100.12−	.1	10.69
9¾s,	1984	Oct n	99.10	99.14−	.1	11.10
12⅜s,	1987	Nov n	97.31	98.3 +	.5	13.33
11¼s,	1987	Dec n	94.1	94.5 +	.9	13.36
12⅜s,	1988	Jan n	97.2	97.6 +	.7	13.38
10⅛s,	1988	Feb n	90.11	90.15+	.10	13.48
12s,	1988	Mar n	95.15	95.17+	.7	13.52
13⅛s,	1988	Apr n	99.14	99.18+	.13	13.40
8¼s,	1988	May n	84.14	84.22+	.11	13.37
9⅞s,	1988	May n	89	89.4 +	.9	13.52
14s,	1988	Jul n	101.16	101.24+	.9	13.43
10½s,	1988	Aug n	90.5	90.9 +	.7	13.61
15¾s,	1988	Oct n	105.18	105.26+	.2	13.56
8¾s,	1988	Nov n	84.18	84.26+	.12	13.39
11¾s,	1988	Nov n	93.26	93.30+	.10	13.61
14¾s,	1989	Jan n	102.30	103.2 +	.11	13.71
11¾s,	1989	Feb n	92.3	92.7 +	.10	13.67
14⅜s,	1989	Apr n	102.3	102.7 +	.9	13.73
9¼s,	1989	May n	84.26	85.2 +	.10	13.49
11¾s,	1989	May n	93.2	93.6 +	.9	13.69
14½s,	1989	Jul n	102.17	102.21+	.7	13.76
11⅞s,	1989	Oct n	93.2	93.10+	.9	13.68
10¾s,	1989	Nov n	88.19	88.23+	.7	13.76
→ 10½s,	1990	Jan n	87.9	87.17+	.9	13.76
3½s,	1990	Feb	89.8	90.8 +	.2	5.51
10½s,	1990	Apr n	86.31	87.7 +	.11	13.75
8¼s,	1990	May	78.20	79.4 +	.12	13.46
10¾s,	1990	Jul n	87.14	87.18+	.9	13.84
10¾s,	1990	Aug n	87.13	87.21+	.9	13.77
11½s,	1990	Oct n	90.13	90.17+	.10	13.78
13s,	1990	Nov n	96.21	96.25+	.9	13.77
11¾s,	1991	Jan n	91	91.4 +	.10	13.84
12⅜s,	1991	Apr	93.18	93.22+	.11	13.83
14½s,	1991	May n	102.27	103.3 +	.6	13.79
14⅞s,	1991	Aug n	104.16	104.24+	.8	13.81
14¼s,	1991	Nov n	101.20	101.28+	.8	13.84
14⅝s,	1992	Feb n	103.8	103.16+	.9	13.87
13¾s,	1992	May n	99.9	99.17+	.12	13.85
4¼s,	1987-92	Aug	89.18	90.18+	.2	5.71
7¼s,	1992	Aug	68.19	69.3 +	.8	13.62
10½s,	1992	Nov n	83.14	83.18+	.10	13.86
4s,	1988-93	Feb	89.16	90.16	....	5.38
6¾s,	1993	Feb	66.6	66.22+	.14	13.34
7⅞s,	1993	Feb	70.8	70.16+	.16	13.81
10⅞s,	1993	Feb n	85	85.4 +	.12	13.87

U.S. Treas. Bills

Mat. date	Bid	Asked	Yield Discount	Mat. date	Bid	Asked	Yield Discount
-1984-				-1984-			
6- 7	8.39	8.29	8.41	10- 4	10.16	10.10	10.60
6-14	9.65	9.57	9.73	10-11	10.25	10.21	10.75
6-21	10.17	10.11	10.30	10-18	10.32	10.28	10.84
6-28	7.74	7.58	7.72	10-25	10.33	10.27	10.86
7- 5	9.22	9.16	9.36	11- 1	10.59	10.55	11.19
7-12	9.48	9.40	9.63	11- 8	10.58	10.52	11.18
7-19	9.43	9.37	9.61	11-15	10.41	10.35	11.01
7-26	9.31	9.23	9.49	11-24	10.58	10.52	11.23
8- 2	9.77	9.69	9.98	11-29	10.58	10.54	11.27
8- 9	9.76	9.70	10.01	12-27	10.58	10.52	11.31
8-16	9.73	9.67	10.00				
8-23	9.71	9.65	10.00	-1985-			
8-30	9.75	9.73	10.10	1-24	10.39	10.33	11.14
9- 6	9.82	9.78	10.18	2-21	10.79	10.73	11.60
9-13	9.70	9.64	10.05	3-21	10.86	10.80	11.74
9-20	9.96	9.90	10.35	4-18	10.96	10.90	11.93
9-27	9.95	9.89	10.35	5-16	10.99	10.97	12.09

Treasury note due January 1990 is quoted at 87.9 bid and 87.17 asked. These prices translate into 87-9/32 and 87-17/32 percent of $1,000. The bid price on a $1,000 bond would be $872.8125 and the asked price $875.3125, for a total spread between the bid and asked price of $2.50 per $1,000 bond. This small spread is customary in the very liquid government bond market. Note that while Treasury notes and bonds are quoted on the basis of price, Treasury bills are quoted on the basis of yield. Looking at the Treasury bills in the right-hand part of Table 9–10, notice that the bid and asked prices are quoted as a discount from the $10,000 par value. A $10,000 Treasury bill quoted at 10 percent, with one year to maturity, would provide $1,000 in interest and would sell on a discount basis for $9,000. The effective yield would be 11.1 percent ($1,000/ $9,000). The same 10 percent bond with six months to maturity would provide $500 in interest and sell for $9,500. The effective yield would be 10.53 percent ($500/ $9,500 times 2).

BOND MARKETS, CAPITAL MARKET THEORY, AND EFFICIENCY

In many respects, the bond market appears to demonstrate a high degree of rationality in recognition of risk and return. Corporate issues promise a higher yield than government issues to compensate for risk, and furthermore, federally sponsored credit agencies pay a higher return than Treasury issues for the same reason. Also, lower-rated bonds consistently trade at higher yields than quality bonds, to provide a risk premium.

Taking this logic one step further, bonds should generally pay a lower return than equity investments. Why? The reason is that the equity holder is in a riskier position because of the absence of a contractual obligation to receive payment. As was pointed out in Chapter 1, Ibbotson and Sinquefield[9] and Fisher and Lorie[10] have attributed superior returns to equity investments relative to debt over the long term.

However, in the highly inflationary, high-interest rate periods of the 1970s and 80s the aforementioned researchers as well as others have indicated a reversal of this pattern; that is, "lower-risk" debt investments have at times provided a higher return (for example, virtually riskless bank CDs have paid as much as 18 percent).

A number of studies have also investigated the efficiency of the bond market. A primary item under investigation was the extent of price change that was associated with a change in a bond rating. If the bond market is efficient, much of the information that led to the rating change was already known to the public and should have been impounded into the value of the bond before the rating change. Thus, the rating change should not have led to major price movements. Major research has generally been supportive of this hypothesis.[11]

---

[9] *Stocks, Bonds, Bills and Inflation, 1984 Yearbook,* (Chicago: R. G. Ibbotson and Associates, Inc., 1984).

[10] Lawrence Fisher and James H. Lorie, *A Half Century of Returns on Stocks and Bonds,* (Chicago: University of Chicago Graduate School of Business, 1977). Also, James H. Lorie and Lawrence Fisher, "Rates of Return on Investment in Common Stock," *Journal of Business,* January 1964, pp. 1–17. Lawrence Fisher and James H. Lorie, "Rates of Return on Investment in Common Stock: The Year-by-Year Record 1926–1965," *Journal of Business,* July 1968, pp. 219–316.

[11] Steven Katz, "The Price Adjustment Process of Bonds to Rating Classifications: A Test of Bond Market Efficiency," *Journal of Finance,* May 1974, pp. 551–59. George W. Hettenhouse and William S. Sartoris, "An Analysis of the Informational Content of Bond Rating Changes," *Quarterly Review of Economics and Business,* Summer 1976, pp. 65–78.

Nevertheless, there is evidence that the bond market may still be less efficient than the stock market (as viewed in terms of short-term trading profits).[12] The reason behind this belief is that the stock market is heavily weighted toward being a secondary market in which *existing* issues are constantly traded back and forth between investors. The bond market is more of a primary market, with the emphasis on new issues. Thus, bond investors are not constantly changing their portfolio with each new action of the corporation. Many institutional investors, such as insurance companies, are not active bond traders in existing issues but instead buy and hold bonds to maturity.

OTHER FORMS OF FIXED-INCOME SECURITIES

Our interest so far in this chapter has been on fixed-income securities, primarily in the form of bonds issued by corporations and various sectors of the government. There are other significant forms of debt instruments from which the investor may choose, and they are primarily short-term in nature.

Certificates of deposit (CDs).   These instruments are used by commercial banks and savings and loans (or other thrift institutions) and have traditionally been issued in small amounts such as $1,000 or $10,000, or large amounts such as $100,000 (jumbo CDs). The procedure is that the investor provides the funds and receives an interest-bearing certificate in return. The smaller CDs usually have a maturity of anywhere from six months to five years, and the jumbo CDs 30 to 90 days.

The jumbo CDs are usually sold to corporate investors, money market funds, pension funds, etc., while the small CDs are sold to individual investors. One main difference between the two CDs, besides the dollar amount, is that there is a secondary market for the jumbo CDs which allows these investors to maintain their liquidity without suffering an interest penalty. Investors in the small CDs have no such liquidity. Their only option is to redeem the certificate before maturity to the borrowing institution and suffer the interest penalty.

Small CDs have been traditionally regulated by the government, with federal regulatory agencies specifying the maximum interest rate that can be paid and the life of the CD. By 1986, all such interest rate regulations and ceilings will be phased out, and the free market will determine return. Any financial institution will be able to offer whatever it desires.

Commercial paper.   Another form of a short-term credit instrument is commercial paper, which is issued by large business corporations to the public. Commercial paper usually comes in minimum denominations of $25,000 and represents an unsecured promissory note. Commercial paper will carry a higher yield than small CDs or government Treasury bills and will be in line

---

[12] George E. Pinches and Clay Singleton, "The Adjustment of Stock Prices to Bond Rating Changes," *Journal of Finance,* March 1978, pp. 29–44.

with the yield on jumbo CDs. The maturity is usually 30, 60, or 90 days (though up to six months is possible).

Bankers' acceptance.   This instrument often arises from foreign trade. The acceptance is a draft which is drawn on a bank for approval for future payment and is subsequently presented to the bank for payment. The investor buys the bankers' acceptance from an exporter (or other third party) at a discount with the intention of presenting it to the bank at face value at a future date. Bankers' acceptances provide yields comparable to commercial paper and jumbo CDs and have an active secondary or resale market.

Money market funds.   These funds, previously discussed in Chapter 3, are not a direct form of fixed-income security, but rather represent a vehicle for individuals to buy short-term fixed-income securities through a mutual fund arrangement. An individual with a small amount to invest may pool his or her funds with others to buy high-yielding jumbo CDs and other similar instruments indirectly through the fund. There is a great deal of flexibility in withdrawing funds through check-writing privileges (usually in minimums of $500). As also mentioned in Chapter 3, individuals may get money market returns by depositing funds at a bank or savings and loan into a money market account. This account allows the individual to write three checks per month without penalty and presently requires a minimum balance of $1,000.

PREFERRED STOCK AS AN ALTERNATIVE TO DEBT

Finally, we look at preferred stock as an alternative to debt because some investors may elect to purchase preferred stock to satisfy their fixed-income needs. A $50 par value preferred stock issue paying $6.40 in annual dividends would provide an annual yield of 12.80 percent.

Preferred stock as an investment falls somewhere between bonds and common stock as far as protective provisions for the investor. In the case of debt, the bondholders have a contractual claim against the corporation and may force bankruptcy proceedings if interest payments are not forthcoming. Common stockholders have no such claim but are the ultimate owners of the firm and may receive dividends and other distributions after all prior claims have been satisfied. Preferred stockholders, on the other hand, are entitled to receive a stipulated dividend and must receive the dividend prior to any payment to common stockholders. However, the payment of preferred stock dividends is not compelling to the corporation as is true in the case of debt. In bad times, preferred stock dividends may be omitted by the corporation.

While preferred stock dividends are not tax deductible to the corporation, as would be true with interest on bonds, they do offer certain investors unique tax advantages. The tax law provides that any corporation which receives *preferred* or common stock dividends from another corporation must add only 15 percent of such dividends to its taxable income. Thus, if a $5 dividend is received, only 15 percent of the $5, or 75 cents, would be taxable to the corporate recipient.[13]

Because of this tax feature, preferred stock may carry a slightly lower yield than corporate bond issues of similar quality. As indicated in Table 9–11 (since the early 1960s) preferred stock has actually carried a yield of ¼ to 1 percent below comparable corporate bond issues. As interest rates rose in the late 1970s and 1980s, the spread in favor of corporate bonds became even larger, peaking at over 3 percent.

TABLE 9–11   Yields on Corporate Bonds and High-Grade Preferred Stock

Year	(1) High-grade bonds (percent)	(2) High-grade preferred stock (percent)	(2) − (1) Spread
1983	12.42%	10.55%	−1.87%
1982	14.41	11.68	−2.73
1981	14.75	11.64	−3.11
1980	12.50	10.11	−2.39
1979	9.94	8.54	−1.40
1978	8.92	7.76	−1.16
1977	8.24	7.12	−1.12
1972	7.49	6.56	−.93
1967	5.66	5.13	−.53
1962	4.47	4.21	−.26
1957	4.03	4.36	.33
1952	3.04	3.75	.71
1947	2.70	3.51	.81

Source: *Moody's Industrial Manual* and *Moody's Bond Record* (published by Moody's Investor Service, selected issues).

Features of Preferred Stock

Preferred stock may carry a number of features that are similar to a debt issue. For example, a preferred stock issue may be *convertible* into common stock. Also, preferred stock may be *callable* by the corporation at a stipulated price, generally slightly above par. The call feature of a preferred stock issue may be of particular interest in that preferred stock has no maturity date as such. If the corporation wishes to take preferred stock off the books, it must call in the issue or purchase the shares in the open market at the going market price.

---

[13] An individual investor does not enjoy the same tax benefit. The purpose of the corporate exemption is to avoid triple corporate taxation (that is, the issuing corporation is taxed once, and the receiving corporation's stockholders are taxed on subsequent dividend distributions, but the receiving corporation itself is only lightly taxed).

An important feature of preferred stock is that the dividend payments are usually *cumulative* in nature. That is, if preferred stock dividends are not paid in any one year, they accumulate and must be paid before common stockholders can receive any cash dividends. If preferred stock carries a $6.40 dividend and dividends are not paid for three years, the full $19.20 must be paid before any dividends go to common stockholders. This provides a strong incentive for the corporation to meet preferred stock dividend obligations on an annual basis even though preferred stock does not have a fixed, contractual obligation as is true of bonds. If the corporation gets behind in preferred stock dividends, it may create a situation that is quite difficult to get out of in the future. Being behind or in arrears on preferred stock dividends can make it almost impossible to sell new *common stock* because of the preclusion of common stock dividends until the preferred stockholders are satisfied.

An example of existing preferred stock issues is presented in Table 9–12. The issues are listed in *Moody's Bond Record,* and the daily price quotes may be found in the NYSE Composite Stock Transactions section of the *The Wall Street Journal* or other newspapers.

TABLE 9–12   Examples of Outstanding Preferred Stock Issues, August 1984

Issuer	Moody's rating*	Par value	Call price	Market price	Yield (percent)
American Telephone & Telegraph $3.64 cumulative preferred	aa1	$ 50	$102.50	33⅞	10.8
Gulf States Utilities Co. $8.80 cumulative preferred	baa3	100	105.88	62	13.0
Tenneco $7.40 cumulative preferred	baa2	100	101.00	66½	11.1

* Lowercase letters are used by Moody's to rate preferred stock.
Sources: *Moody's Bond Record* (Moody's Investor Service, Inc., New York, N.Y.) and *The Wall Street Journal.*

Chapter 10

PRINCIPLES OF BOND VALUATION AND INVESTMENT

The old notion that a bond represents an inherently conservative investment can be quickly dispelled. A $1,000, 10 percent coupon rate bond with 25 years to maturity could rise $214.80 or fall $157.60 in response to a 2 percent change in interest rates in the marketplace. According to a study by Ibbotson and Sinquefield, investors enjoyed a total return of 43.79 percent on long-term corporate bonds in 1982 and a return of over 18 percent in 1970 and 1976. By contrast, the same investor would have lost 8.09 percent on his bond portfolio in 1969.[1] While bond prices may not normally be as volatile as those of stocks, there are still many opportunities for wide fluctuations in value.

In this chapter, we will examine the valuation process for bonds, the relationship of interest rate changes to the business cycle, and various investment and speculative strategies related to bond maturity, quality, and pricing.

FUNDAMENTALS OF THE BOND VALUATION PROCESS

The price of a bond at any point in time represents the present value of future interest payments plus the present value of the par value of the bond at maturity. We say that:

$$V = \sum_{t=1}^{n} \frac{C_t}{(1 + i)^t} + \frac{P_n}{(1 + i)^n} \qquad (10-1)$$

where:

V = Market value or price of the bond.
n = Number of periods.
t = Each period.
C_t = Coupon or interest payment for each period, t.
P_n = Par or maturity value.
i = Interest rate in the market.

We can use logarithms and various mathematical calculations to find the value of a bond or simply use Table 10–1 and Table 10–2 to determine the present value of C_t and P_n and add the two together. (Expanded versions of these two tables are presented in appendixes at the end of the text.)

Assume a bond pays 10% interest or $100 ($C_t$) for 20 years ($n$) and has a par ($P_n$) or maturity value of $1,000. The interest rate (i) in the marketplace is assumed to be 12 percent. The present value of the bond, using annual compounding, is shown to be $850.90 as follows:

Present value of coupon payments (C_t) (from Table 10–1)	Present value of maturity value (P_n) (from Table 10–2)
$n = 20, i = 12\%$	$n = 20, i = 12\%$
$100 × 7.469 = $746.90	$1,000 × .104 = $104.00

Present value of coupon payments	= $746.90
Present value of maturity value	= 104.00
Value of bond	= $850.90

---

[1] *Stocks, Bonds, Bills and Inflation, 1984 Yearbook* (Chicago: A. G. Ibbotson and Associates, Inc., 1984).

TABLE 10–1   Present Value of an Annuity of $1 (coupon payments ($C_t$)

Number of periods (n)	Interest rate (i)					
	4 percent	5 percent	6 percent	8 percent	10 percent	12 percent
1	.962	.952	.943	.926	.909	.893
2	1.886	1.859	1.833	1.783	1.736	1.690
3	2.775	2.723	2.673	2.577	2.487	2.402
4	3.630	3.546	3.465	3.312	3.170	3.037
5	4.452	4.329	4.212	3.993	3.791	3.605
10	8.111	7.722	7.360	6.710	6.145	5.650
20	13.590	12.462	11.470	9.818	8.514	7.469
30	17.292	15.373	13.765	11.258	9.427	8.055
40	19.793	17.160	15.046	11.925	9.779	8.244

Because the bond pays 10 percent of the par value when the competitive market rate of interest is 12 percent, investors will only pay $850.90 for the issue. This bond is said to be selling at a discount of $149.10 from the $1,000 par value. The discount is determined by several factors, such as the years to maturity, spread between the coupon and market rates, and the level of the coupon. While the $850.90 price was calculated using annual compounding, coupon payments on most bonds are paid semiannually. To adjust for this, we *divide* the annual coupon payment and required interest rate in the market by two and *multiply* the number of periods by two. Using the same example as before but with the appropriate adjustments for semiannual compounding, we show a slightly lower price of $849.30 as follows:

Present value of coupon payments (C_t) (from Table 10–1)	Present value of maturity value (P_n) (from Table 10–2)
$n = 40, i = 6\%$	$n = 40, i = 6\%$
$\$50 \times 15.046 = \$752.30$	$\$1,000 \times .097 = \$97.00$

Present value of coupon payments	= $752.30
Present value of maturity value	= 97.00
Value of bond	= $849.30

We see a minor adjustment in price as a result of using the more exacting process. To check our answer, in Table 10–3 we present an excerpt from a bond table indicating prices for 10 percent and 12 percent annual coupon rate bonds at various market rates of interest (yields to maturity) and time periods. Though the values are quoted on an annual basis, the assumption is that semiannual discounting, such as that shown in our second example, was utilized. Note that for a bond with a 10 percent coupon rate, a 12 percent market rate (yield to maturity), and 20 years to run, the value in the table is 84.93. This is assumed to represent 84.93 percent of par value. Since the par value of the bond in our example was $1,000, the answer would be $849.30 ($1,000 × 84.93%). This is precisely the answer we got in our second example. A typical

TABLE 10–2   Present Value of a Single Amount of $1 (par or maturity value P_n)

Number of periods (n)	Interest rate (i)					
	4 percent	5 percent	6 percent	8 percent	10 percent	12 percent
1	.962	.952	.943	.926	.909	.893
2	.925	.907	.890	.857	.826	.797
3	.889	.864	.840	.794	.751	.712
4	.855	.823	.792	.735	.683	.636
5	.822	.784	.747	.681	.621	.567
10	.676	.614	.558	.463	.386	.322
20	.456	.377	.312	.215	.149	.104
30	.308	.231	.174	.099	.057	.033
40	.208	.142	.097	.046	.022	.011

modern bond table may be 1,000 pages long and cover time periods up to 30 years and interest rates from ¼ to 30 percent. For professionals working with bonds on a continual basis, financial calculators and computers are replacing these tables, with quicker response time.

TABLE 10–3   Excerpts from Bond Value Table

Yield to maturity (percent)	Coupon rate (10 percent)				Coupon rate (12 percent)				Yield to maturity (percent)
	1 year	5 years	10 years	20 years	1 year	5 years	10 years	20 years	
8%	101.89%	108.11%	113.50%	119.79%	103.77%	116.22%	127.18%	139.59%	8%
9	100.94	103.96	106.50	109.20	102.81	111.87	119.51	127.60	9
10	100.00	100.00	100.00	100.00	101.86	107.72	112.46	117.16	10
11	99.08	96.23	94.02	91.98	100.92	103.77	105.98	108.02	11
12	98.17	92.64	88.53	84.93	100.00	100.00	100.00	100.00	12
13	97.27	89.22	83.47	78.78	99.09	96.41	94.49	92.93	13
14	96.38	85.95	78.81	73.34	98.19	92.98	89.41	86.67	14

Source: Reprinted by permission from the *Thorndike Encyclopedia of Banking and Financial Tables*, 1981, Copyright © 1981, Warren Gorham and Lamont Inc., 210 South Street, Boston, Mass. All rights reserved.

RATES OF RETURN

Bonds are evaluated on a number of different types of returns, including current yield, yield to maturity, yield to call, and anticipated realized yield.

Current Yield

The current yield, which is shown in *The Wall Street Journal* and many daily newspapers, is the annual interest payment divided by the price of the bond.

An example might be a 12 percent coupon rate $1,000 par value bond selling for $900. The current yield would be:

$$\frac{\$120}{\$900} = 13.3\%$$

The 13.3 percent indicates the annual cash rate of return an investor would receive in interest payments on the $900 investment, but does not include any adjustments for capital gains or losses as bond prices change in response to new market interest rates. Another problem with current yield is that it does not take into consideration the maturity date of a debt instrument. A bond with 1 year to run and another with 20 years to run would have the same current yield quote if interest payments were $120 and the price were $900. Clearly, the one-year bond would be preferable under this circumstance because the investor would not only get $120 in interest, but also a gain in value of $100 ($1000 − $900) within a one-year time period.

Yield to Maturity

Yield to maturity takes into consideration annual interest received, the difference between the current bond price and its maturity value, and the number of years to maturity. Returning to our earlier example, if a bond pays $100 in annual interest and sells for $849.30 with 20 years to maturity, the investor would be receiving $100 annually plus the $150.70 differential, spread over 20 years, or $7.54 per year. This would indicate a total annual return of $107.54. We would also think of the investor's average investment as being approximately the mid-point between the initial investment of $849.30, and the ending value of $1,000. Thus, the average investment would be $924.65. The yield to maturity is the total return an investor would receive from income plus capital appreciation assuming the bond is held to maturity. The *approximate* yield to maturity would be:

$$\frac{\$107.54}{\$924.65} = 11.63\%$$

The preceding calculations can be summarized into a formula in which we show:

$$Y' = \frac{\text{Coupon payment } (C_t) + \dfrac{\text{Par value } (P_n) - \text{Market value } (V)}{\text{Number of periods } (n)}}{\dfrac{\text{Market value } (V) + \text{Par value } (P_n)}{2}} \qquad (10\text{--}2)$$

On an annual basis, we indicate:

Y' = Approximate yield to maturity.
Coupon payment = $100.
Par or maturity value = $1,000.

Market value = $849.30.
Number of periods = 20.

$$Y' = \frac{\$100 + \dfrac{\$1,000 - \$849.30}{20}}{\dfrac{\$849.30 + \$1,000}{2}}$$

$$= \frac{\$100 + \dfrac{\$150.70}{20}}{\$924.65}$$

$$= \frac{\$107.54}{\$924.65}$$

$$= 11.63\%$$

This answer is merely an approximation of exact yield to maturity. The precise answer can only be found mathematically by returning to Formula (10–1) and determining the precise interest rate (i) that allows us to discount back all future coupon payments (C_t) and the par or maturity value (P_n) at the end of n periods to arrive at the current price. The yield to maturity may be thought of as the internal rate of return or yield on the bond. Since computing the exact yield to maturity is a very involved, trial-and-error process, bond tables are readily available to allow us to determine this value. As a matter of fact, all we have to do is return to Table 10–3, the bond value table, and use it in a slightly different fashion. We pick our coupon rate, read across the table for number of years, into the table for price, and then read to the outside column to determine yield. A 10 percent coupon rate bond with 20 years to run, selling at $849.30 (84.93 in the table), provides the investor with a yield to maturity of 12 percent.[2]

Note the exact answer in this case is .37 percent above the approximation (12 percent versus 11.63 percent). In the jargon of bond trading, each 1/100th of 1 percent is referred to as a basis point, so we say the difference is 37 basis points. The approximate-yield-to-maturity method tends to understate exact yield to maturity for issues trading at a discount (in this case, the bond is priced at $849.30). The opposite effect takes place for bonds trading at a premium (above par value). The extent of the discrepancy is directly related to the magnitude of the discount or premium and the life span on the bond. For a $950 bond with five years to maturity, the difference between approximate yield and exact yield is a mere .03 percent, or three basis points.[3]

The concept of *yield to maturity* is used interchangeably with the term *market rate of interest.* When we say the market rate of interest is 12 percent, it is the equivalent of saying the required yield to maturity is 12 percent.

---

[2] Interpolation may also be used to find intermediate values in the table.

[3] It should be pointed out that in all our bond problems, we are assuming that we are buying the bond at the beginning of an interest payment period. To the extent there is accrued interest, we would have to modify our calculations slightly.

Yield to Call

As discussed in the preceding chapter on bond fundamentals, not all fixed-income securities are held to maturity. To the extent a debt instrument may be called in prior to maturity, a separate calculation is necessary to determine yield to the call date. Assume a 20-year bond was initially issued at a 13.5 percent interest rate, and after two years, rates have dropped. Let us assume the bond is currently selling for $1,180 and the yield to maturity on the bond is 11.15 percent. However, the investor who purchases the bonds for $1,180 may not be able to hold the bonds for the remaining 18 years because the issue can be called. Under these circumstances yield to maturity may not be the appropriate measure of return over the expected holding period.

In the present case we shall assume the bonds can be called in five years after issue at $1,090. Thus, the investor who buys the bonds two years after issue can have his bonds called back after three more years at $1,090. To compute yield to call, we determine the approximate interest rate that will equate an $1,180 investment today with $135 (13.5 percent) per year for the next three years plus a payoff or call price value of $1,090 at the end of three years. We can adjust Formula (10–2) (approximate yield to maturity) to Formula (10–3) (approximate yield to call).

$$Y_c' = \frac{\text{Coupon payment } (C_t) + \dfrac{\text{Call price } (P_c) - \text{Market price } (V)}{\text{Number of periods to call } (n_c)}}{\dfrac{\text{Market value } (V) + \text{Call price } (P_c)}{2}} \quad (10–3)$$

On an annual basis, we show:

Y_c' = Approximate yield to call.
Coupon payment = $135.
Call price = $1,090.
Market value = $1,180.
Number of periods to call = 3.

$$Y_c' = \frac{\$135 + \dfrac{\$1,090 - \$1,180}{3}}{\dfrac{\$1,180 + \$1,090}{2}}$$

$$= \frac{\$135 + \dfrac{-\$90}{3}}{\$1,135}$$

$$= \frac{\$135 - \$30}{\$1,135}$$

$$= \frac{\$105}{\$1,135}$$

$$= 9.25\%$$

The yield to call figure of 9.25 percent is 238 basis points less than the yield to maturity figure of 11.63 percent. Clearly, the investor needs to be aware of the differential. Generally speaking, any time the market price of a bond is equal to or greater than the call price, the investor should do a separate calculation for yield to call.[4]

In the case where market interest rates are much lower than the coupon, there is always the chance that the company will call the bond. Because of this possibility, the call price often serves as an upper price limit and further reductions in market interest rates will not cause this callable bond to increase in price. In other words, investors' capital gain potential may be quite limited with bonds selling at a premium.

Anticipated Realized Yield

Finally, we have the case where the investor purchases the bond with the intention of holding the bond for a period that is different from either the call date or the maturity date. Under this circumstance, we examine the anticipated realized yield for the holding period.

Assume an investor buys a 12.5 percent coupon bond for $900. Based on his forecasts of lower interest rates, he anticipates the bond will go to $1,050 in three years. The formula for the approximate realized yield is:

$$Y_r' = \frac{\text{Coupon payment } (C_t) + \dfrac{\text{Realized price } (P_r) - \text{Market price } (V)}{\text{Number of periods to realization } (n_r)}}{\dfrac{\text{Market value } (V) + \text{Realized price } (P_r)}{2}}$$

$$(10\text{–}4)$$

The terms are:

Coupon payment = $125.
Realized price = $1,050.
Market price = $900.
Number of periods to realization = 3.

$$Y_r' = \frac{\$125 + \dfrac{\$1,050 - \$900}{3}}{\dfrac{\$900 + \$1,050}{2}}$$

$$= \frac{\$125 + \dfrac{\$150}{3}}{\$975}$$

$$= \frac{\$125 + \$50}{\$975}$$

$$= \frac{\$175}{\$975}$$

$$= 17.95\%$$

---

[4] Bond tables may also be used to find the exact value for yield to call. A source is *Thorndike Encyclopedia of Banking and Financial Tables* (Boston: Warren, Gorham & Lamont, 1981).

The anticipated return of 17.95 percent would not be unusual in periods of falling interest rates such as 1970, 1976, and 1982.

Reinvestment Assumption

Throughout our analysis, when we have talked about yield to maturity, call, or realization, we have assumed that the determined rate also represents an appropriate rate for reinvestment of funds. If yield to maturity is 11 percent or 12 percent, then it is assumed that coupon payments, as they come in, can also be reinvested at that rate. To the extent that this is an unrealistic assumption, the investor will wish to temper his thinking. For example, if it is anticipated that returns can be reinvested at a higher rate in the future, this increases true yield, and the opposite effect would be present for a decline in interest rates.

The reinvestment topic is more fully developed in Chapter 11, and the interested student can also consult *Inside the Yield Book: New Tools for Bond Market Strategy*[5] for a more complete development of the reinvestment assumption.

THE MOVEMENT OF INTEREST RATES

In developing our discussion of bond valuation and investments, we have observed that lower interest rates bring higher bond prices and profits. A glance back at Table 10–3 (right-hand portion) indicates that a 20-year, 12 percent coupon bond will sell for $1,171.60 if yields to maturity on competitive bonds decline to 10 percent and to $1,276.00 when yields decline to 9 percent. The maturity of the bond is also important, with the impact on price being much greater for longer-term obligations.

The investor who wishes to make a substantial profit in the bond market must make an attempt to anticipate the turns and directions of interest rates. While much of the literature on efficient markets would indicate this is an extremely difficult task,[6] Wall Street economists, bank economists, and many others rely upon interest rate forecasts to formulate financial strategies. The fact that short-term and long-term rates do not necessarily move in the same direction or move with the same magnitude makes the task even more formidable. Nevertheless, some historical analysis and knowledge of interest rate patterns over the business cycle is useful in making investment decisions.

Interest rates have long been viewed as a coincident indicator in our economy; that is to say, they are thought to move in concert with industrial

[5] S. Homer and M. L. Leibowitz, *Inside the Yield Book: New Tools for Bond Market Strategy* (Englewood Cliffs, N.J.: Prentice-Hall, 1972).

[6] Michael J. Prell, "How well do the Experts Forecast Interest Rates?" Federal Reserve Bank of Kanses City, *Monthly Review,* September–October, 1973, pp. 3–13. Oswald D. Bowlin and John D. Martin, "Extrapolations of Yields over the Short Run: Forecast or Folly?" *Journal of Monetary Economics* (1975), pp. 275–88. Richard Roll. *The Behavior of Interest Rates* (New York: Basic Books, 1970).

production, gross national product, and similar measures of general economic health. This is generally true, although in the recessions of 1969–70, 1973–75, and 1980–81 interest rates actually lagged behind the decline in industrial production.

This pattern of lag between interest rate changes and the business cycle, witnessed since the mid-1960s, can be explained in terms of inflationary expectations. In earlier time periods, the occurrence of a recession tended to immediately break off inflationary expectations. Since the mid-60s, a decline in inflationary rates has only taken place well into the recession, deferring the drop-off of interest rates.

While inflationary expectations have their greatest influence on long-term rates, a number of other factors also influence overall interest rates. The demand for funds by individuals, business, and the government represent one side of the equation, with the desire for savings and Federal Reserve policy influencing the supply side. A classic study by Feldstein and Eckstein found that bond yields were inversely related to the money supply (the slower the growth, the higher the interest rates) and directly related to economic activity, the demand for loanable funds by the government, the level of inflation, and changes in short-term interest rate *expectations.*[7]

Term Structure of Interest Rates

Of general importance to understanding the level of interest rates is the development of an appreciation for the relationship between the level of interest rates and the maturity of the debt obligation. There is no one single interest rate, but rather a whole series of interest rates associated with the given maturity of bonds.

The term structure of interest rates depicts the relationship between maturity and interest rates. It is sometimes called a yield curve because yields on existing securities having maturities from 3 months to 30 years are plotted on a graph to develop the curve. In order to eliminate any business risk consideration, the securities analyzed are usually U.S. Treasury issues. Examples of four different types of term structures are presented in Figure 10–1.

In panel (a) we see an ascending term structure pattern in which interest rates increase with the lengthening of the maturity dates. When the term structure is in this posture, it is a general signal that interest rates will rise in the future. In panel (b) we see a descending pattern of interest rates, with this pattern generally predictive of lower interest rates. Panel (c) is a variation of panel (b), with the hump indicating intermediate-term interest rates. This particular configuration is an even stronger indicator that interest rates may be declining in the future. Finally, in panel (d) we see a flat-term structure indicating investor indifference between debt instrument maturity. This generally indicates there is no discernible pattern for the future of interest rates. There

---

[7] Martin Feldstein and Otto Eckstein, "The Fundamental Determinants of the Interest Rate," *The Review of Economics and Statistics,* November 1970, pp. 363–75.

FIGURE 10–1   Term Structure of Interest Rates

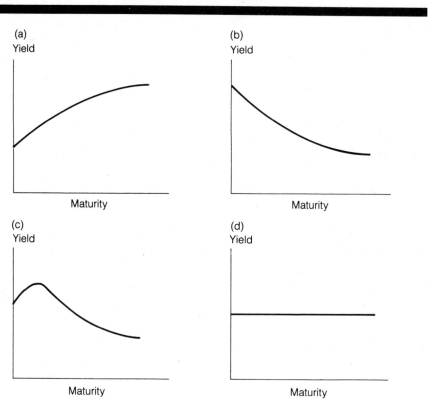

are several theories of interest rates that are used to explain the particular shape of the yield curve. We shall review three of these theories.

Expectations hypothesis.   The dominant rationale for the shape of the term structure of interest rates rests on a phenomenon called the expectations hypothesis. The hypothesis is that any long-term rate is an average of the expectations of future short-term rates over the applicable time horizon. Thus, if lenders expect short-term rates to be continually increasing in the future, they will demand higher long-term rates. Conversely, if they anticipate short-term rates to be declining, they will accept lower long-term rates. An example may be helpful. Suppose that the interest rate on a one-year Treasury bill is 10 percent, and that after one year it is assumed a new one-year Treasury bill may be bought to yield 12 percent. At the end of year two it is assumed that a third one-year Treasury bill may be bought to yield 14 percent. In other words, the investor can buy (this is sometimes called "roll over") three one-year Treasury bills in yearly succession, each with an expected one-year return.

But what about the investor who buys a one-, two-, or three-year security today? The yield he will require will be based on expectations about the future. For the one-year security, there is no problem. The 10 percent return will be acceptable. But the investor who buys a two-year security now will want the average of the 10 percent he could expect in the first year and the 12 percent expected in the second year, or 11 percent.[8] An investor who buys a three-year security will demand an average of 10, 12, and 14 percent, or a 12 percent return. Higher expected interest rates in the future will mean that longer maturities will carry higher yields than will shorter maturities. The reverse would be true if interest rates were expected to go down.

The expectations hypothesis tends to be reinforced by lender/borrower strategy. If investors (lenders) expect interest rates to increase in the future, they will attempt to lend short-term and avoid long-term obligations so as to diminish losses on long maturity obligations when interest rates go up. Borrowers have exactly the opposite incentive. When interest rates are expected to go up, they will attempt to borrow long-term now to lock in the lower rates. Thus the desire of lenders to lend short term (and avoid the long-term) and the desire of borrowers to borrow long-term (and avoid short-term) accentuates the expected pattern of rising interest rates. The exact opposite motivations are in effect when interest rates are expected to decline.

Liquidity preference theory.   The second theory used to explain the term structure of interest rates is called the liquidity preference theory. The shape of the term structure curve tends to be upward sloping more than any other pattern. This reflects a recognition of the fact that long maturity obligations are subject to greater price change movements when interest rates change. Because of the increased risk of holding longer-term maturities, investors demand a higher return to hold long-term securities relative to short-term securities. This is called the liquidity preference theory of interest rates. Since short-term securities are more easily turned into cash without the risk of large price changes, investors will pay a higher price for short-term securities and thus receive a lower yield.

Market segmentation theory.   The third theory related to the term structure of interest rates is called the market segmentation theory and focuses on the demand side of the market. There are several large institutional participants in the bond market, each with his own maturity preferences. Banks tend to prefer short-term liquid securities to match the nature of their deposits, whereas life insurance companies prefer long-term bonds to match their long-run obligations. The behavior of these two institutions, as well as of savings and loans, often creates pressure on short-term or long-term rates but very little in the intermediate market of 5–7 year maturities. This theory helps to focus on

---

[8] The expectations hypothesis actually uses the geometric mean (compound growth rate) rather than the arithmetic mean (simple average) used in the example. For a short number of years, the two means would be quite similar.

the accumulation or liquidation of securities by institutions during the different phases of the business cycle and the resultant impact on the yield curve.

As stated earlier, the expectations hypothesis is probably the most dominant theory, but all three theories have some part in the creation of the term structure of interest rates. Also, as we discussed, the curve takes on many different shapes over time. For example, in May of 1981 the yield curve had reached new high levels and was steeply downsloping in anticipation of lower interest rates, as viewed in Figure 10–2. Lower rates came, and by May of

FIGURE 10–2   Yield Curve Patterns

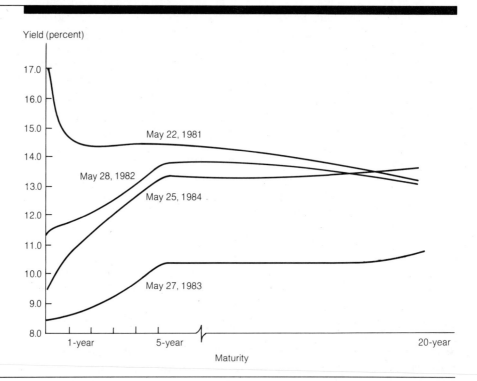

1982, short-term rates had fallen sharply, but long-term rates were still relatively high, as investors had fears of high continued inflation. The term structure at this point was slightly humped, but by May 1983 the curve had shifted down significantly for all maturities, and was now presenting a more normal upsloping yield curve. Over the two-year period from May of 1981 to May of 1983, three-month Treasury bills dropped from 16.99 percent to 8.48 percent, for a total decline of 851 basis points. Long-term Treasuries went from 13.26 percent to 10.75 percent over the same two-year period, for a decline of only

251 basis points. One year later, by May 25, 1984, interest rates had started to rise on fears that large government deficits would rekindle rampant inflation. What happened between May 1983 and May 1984 was that long-term rates rose to 13.49 percent, or a change of 274 basis points, more than wiping out the previous decrease since 1981. Obviously, investors in long-term bonds suffered large capital losses between May 1983 and May 1984. This pattern of interest rate advances and declines and yield curve changes no doubt will take place many times throughout the 1980s.

Before concluding our discussion of the term structure of interest rates and proceeding to the development of investment strategies, one final observation is significant. Short-term rates, which are most influenced by Federal Reserve policy in attempting to regulate the money supply and economy, are much more volatile in nature than long-term rates. An examination of Figure 10–3 indicates that *short-term* prime commercial paper rates move much more widely than *long-term,* high-grade corporate bond rates.

FIGURE 10–3   Relative Volatility of Short-Term and Long-Term Interest Rates

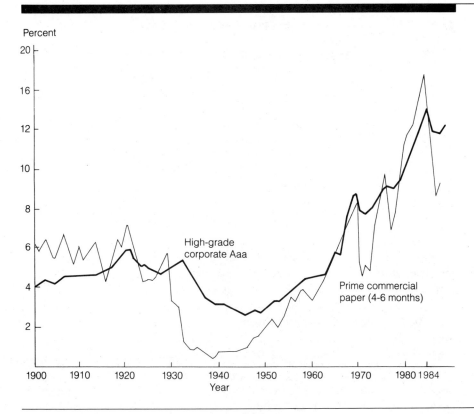

Source: *Federal Reserve Historical Chart Book* (Washington, D.C.: Federal Reserve Board of Governors).

INVESTMENT STRATEGY—INTEREST RATE CONSIDERATIONS

Thus far in this chapter, we have examined the different valuation procedures for determining the price or yield on a bond and the methods for evaluating the future course of interest rates. We now bring this knowledge together in the form of various investment strategies.

When the bond investor believes that interest rates are going to fall, he will take a long position in the market by buying long-term bonds and try to maximize the price movement pattern associated with a change in interest rates. He can do this by considering the *maturity, coupon rate,* and *quality* of the issue.

Because the impact of an interest rate change is much greater on long-term securities, the investor will generally look for extended maturities. The impact of various changes in yields on bond prices for a 12 percent coupon rate bond can be examined in Table 10–4. For example, looking at the second line from the bottom, we see a 2 percent drop in interest rates would cause a 1.86 percent increase in value for a bond with one year to maturity, but an 18.93 percent increase in value for a bond with 30 years to maturity.

TABLE 10–4   Change in Market Prices of Bonds for Shifts in Yields to Maturity (12 percent coupon rate)

Yield change (percent)	Maturity (years)				
	1	5	10	20	30
+3%	−2.69%	−10.30%	−15.29%	−18.89%	−19.74%
+2	−1.81	− 7.02	−10.59	−13.33	−14.04
+1	− .91	− 3.57	− 5.01	− 7.08	− 7.52
−1	+ .92	+ 3.77	+ 5.98	+ 8.02	+ 8.72
−2	+1.86	+ 7.72	+12.46	+17.16	+18.93
−3	+2.81	+11.87	+19.51	+27.60	+30.96

We can also observe that the effect of interest rate changes is not symmetrical. Drops in interest rates will cause proportionally greater gains than increases in interest rates will cause losses, particularly as we expand the maturity. An evaluation of the 30-year column running from −19.74 percent to +30.96 percent will confirm this point.[9]

---

[9] A sophisticated investor would also consider the concept of *duration.* Duration is defined as the weighted average time to recover interest and principal. For a bond that pays interest (which includes most cases except zero-coupon bonds), duration will be shorter than maturity, in that interest payments start almost immediately. Portfolio strategy may call for maximizing duration rather than maturity in order to achieve maximum movement.

Though we have emphasized the need for long maturities in maximizing price movement, the alert student will recall that short-term interest rates generally move up and down more than long-term interest rates as was indicated in Figure 10–3. What if short-term rates are more volatile—even though long-term rates have a greater price impact—which then do we choose? The answer is fairly direct. The mathematical impact of long maturities on price changes far outweighs the more volatile feature of short-term interest rates. A one-year debt instrument would need to have an interest rate *change* of almost *10 percent* to have the equivalent impact of a 1 percent change in a 30-year debt obligation.

Another consideration in maximizing price movement is the coupon rate level of the bond. Assume two bonds have "roughly" the same yield to maturity and that one possesses a 13.5 percent coupon rate and is trading well above par while the other has a 5 percent coupon rate and is trading substantially below par. The price of the lower coupon rate bond is more sensitive to interest rate changes. For example, a 5 percent coupon rate, 30-year bond will advance 30.42 percent as a result of a 2 percent decline in interest rates, whereas the 13.5 percent coupon rate bond will move only 16.71 percent.[10] This is an important point if the investor expects to trade bonds actively over the interest rate cycle. The next chapter on duration provides a more comprehensive analysis of price sensitivity, coupon rates, maturity, market rates, and their combined impact on bond prices.

A final consideration is the quality of the offering. High-quality securities are more sensitive to *pure* interest rate changes than are lower-quality issues. Most of the movement in Treasury securities or Aaa utilities is a function of interest rates, whereas lower-grade corporates may also be influenced by GNP, industry projections, and corporate profits. To take advantage of a perceived interest rate move, quality should be stressed. For other investment strategies related to a perceived improvement in business conditions, lower-quality corporates may be an ideal investment outlet.

Actually some investment managers put together portfolios of high-risk, low-grade bonds. The headline in a *Wall Street Journal* article of May 16, 1984, read "Merrill Lynch Seeks 'Junk-Bond' Buyers for Cash to Finish Seabrook Nuclear Unit." These so-called junk bonds are extremely speculative and carry high yields with a relatively high risk of default. These bonds may behave more like common stock than bonds and rally on good news, actual interest payments, or improving business conditions. Several institutions such as Merrill Lynch, Fidelity Investments, and Drexel Burnham Lambert Inc. manage a mutual fund with a junk-bond emphasis. One such manager is James R. Caywood of Security Pacific Corporation. He uses a large amount of junk-bonds, a small amount of convertible bonds, and financial futures or options to hedge his funds risk.[11] During the last half of 1983 and first half of 1984 his

---

[10] Tax benefits and protection from call provisions are other advantages of low coupon rate bonds and are discussed in a subsequent section.

[11] Financial futures and bond options are covered in Chapter 15.

fund increased by over 8 percent while the Salomon Bros. High-Grade Bond Index fell 6.8 percent. Junk bonds can be fun to play with, but for now let's return to a more conventional approach.

Example of Interest Rate Change

Let's look at an actual example of an interest rate change. Assume we buy 20-year, Aaa utility bonds at par providing a 12 percent coupon rate. Further assume that interest rates on these bonds in the market fall to 10 percent.[12] Based on Table 10–5, the new price on the bonds would be $1,171.60 ($1,000 × 117.16).

TABLE 10–5   Bond Value Table (coupon rate 12 percent)

Yield to maturity (percent)	Number of years		
	10	20	30
8%	127.18%	139.59%	145.25%
10	112.46	117.16	118.93
12	100.00	100.00	100.00
14	89.41	86.55	85.96

Source: Reprinted by permission from the *Thorndike Encyclopedia of Banking and Financial Tables*, 1981, copyright © 1981, Warren, Gorham and Lamont Inc., 210 South Street, Boston, Mass. All rights reserved.

Though we have assumed the gain in price from $1,000 to $1,171.60 took place very quickly, even if the time horizon were one year, the gain is still 17.16 percent annually. This is only part of the picture. An integral part of many bond interest rate strategies is the use of margin or borrowed funds. For government securities, it is possible to margin as low as 5 percent, and on high-quality utility or corporate bonds, the requirement is generally 30 percent. In the above case, if we had put down 30 percent and borrowed the balance, the rate of return on invested capital would have been 57.2 percent.

$$\frac{\text{Return}}{\text{Investment}} = \frac{\$171.60}{\$300.00} = 57.2\%$$

Though we would have had to pay interest on the $700 we borrowed, the interest on the bonds (which belongs to the borrower/investor) would have partially or fully covered this expense. Also if interest rates drop down further to 8 percent, our leveraged return could be over 100 percent on our original investment.

---

[12] Buying bonds at a lower coupon rate, that are trading at a discount from par, would provide greater price volatility as previously indicated, but would complicate our analysis unnecessarily. We will also not worry about calls for now; this matter will be given attention in the next section.

Lest the overanxious student sell all his or her worldly possessions to participate in this impressive gain, there are many admonitions. Even though we think interest rates are going down, they may do quite the opposite. A 2 percent *increase* in interest rates would cause a $134.50 loss or a negative return on a leveraged investment of $300 of 44.8 percent. At the very time it appears that interest rates should be falling due to an anticipated or actual recession, the Federal Reserve may generate the opposite effect by tightening the money supply as an anti-inflation weapon as it did in 1970, 1974, 1979, and 1981. Having now given adequate warning, the authors would summarize the discussion of interest rate plays by saying there are opportunities for unusually large profits with the anticipated risks.

INVESTMENT STRATEGY—DEEP DISCOUNT VERSUS PAR BONDS

Another feature in analyzing a bond is the current pricing of the bond in regard to its par value. Bonds that were previously issued at interest rates significantly lower than current market levels may trade at deep discounts from par. The long-term secular upward trend in interest rates since World War II has made the deep discount bond very common. As an example, consider the pricing pattern for a number of American Telephone and Telegraph bonds in mid-1984.

Coupon rate (percent)	Maturity year	Price
3.875%	1990	$718.75
7.000	2001	562.50
7.125	2003	558.75
8.800	2005	661.25
8.625	2007	642.50

Deep discount bonds generally trade at a lower yield to maturity than bonds selling at close to par. There are two reasons for this. One is that a deep discount bond has almost no chance to be called away. Even if prices go up because of falling interest rates, the price is still likely to be below par value. Because of this protection against a caller and the associated risk of having to reinvest principal at a lower interest rate, the investor in deep discount bonds accepts a lower yield. Secondly, the deep discount bond offers the investor certain tax advantages; namely, that part of the return will represent capital gains as opposed to being subject to the ordinary income tax provision associated with pure interest income. We are assuming that the capital gain is long-term (bond owned for more than six months) and therefore is taxed at a maximum of 20 percent. For this reason, also, the investor is willing to accept a lower yield to maturity on a before-tax basis.[13]

---

[13] Zero-coupon bonds, discussed in Chapter 10, do not ordinarily receive favorable capital gains treatment. The investor's ordinary income tax rate is applied to the annual amortized increase in value over the life of the bond.

Let us examine how the tax feature might influence an investment deci-sion. Assume we are evaluating three bonds that each have 20 years to run. Their coupon rates, price, and yield to maturity are presented in Table 10–6.

TABLE 10–6   Characteristics of Potential Bond Investments

Bond	Coupon rate (percent)	Price	Yield to maturity (percent)[55]
A	6%	$ 612.60	10.75%
B	10	866.20	11.75
C	12	1,000.00	12

Our first inclination may be to invest in bond C because it provides the highest yield to maturity. But in bonds A and B, we get both interest income and capital appreciation by holding the bond to maturity. As an approximate measure, in bond A we are getting 6 percent per year in interest and the balance in capital gains. Let us assume that interest on ordinary income is taxed at 50 percent and capital gains at 20 percent. In Table 10–7, we evaluate each bond on an aftertax basis to see which provides the highest yield.

TABLE 10–7   Total Aftertax Yield (percent)

Bond	(1) Yield to maturity	(2) Coupon portion of yield	(3) (1) − (2) Capital gains portion of yield	(4) Aftertax yield on coupon (50% tax)	(5) Aftertax yield on capital gains (20% tax)	(6) (4) + (5) Total aftertax yield
A	10.75%	6.00%	4.75%	3.00%	3.80%	6.80%
B	11.75	10.00	1.75	5.00	1.40	6.40
C	12.00	12.00	–0–	6.00	–0–	6.00

As indicated in the table, we have divided the yield to maturity (1) between the coupon portion (2) and the capital gains portion (3) and then examined aftertax return in columns 4 and 5. The coupon payment in column 2 is assumed to be taxed at 50 percent, providing the value in column 4, while the capital gains portion in column 3 is assumed to be taxed at 20 percent, providing the figures in column 5. Total aftertax return is presented in column 6. In the measures utilized, the lowest yield-to-maturity bonds actually provide the highest aftertax yields.

INVESTMENT STRATEGY—YIELD SPREAD CONSIDERATIONS

As discussed in the previous chapter, different types or grades of bonds provide different yields. For example, the yield on Baa corporate bonds is always above that of corporate Aaa obligations, to compensate for risk. Similarly, Aaa corporates pay a higher yield than long-term government obligations. In Figure 10–4, we observe the actual yield spread between Moody's corporate Baa's, Moody's Corporate Aaa's, and long-term government securities.

Let's direct our attention to total spread between corporate Baa bonds and government securities (corporate Aaa's fall somewhere in between). Over the long term, the spread appears to be between 75 and 100 basis points. For example, in 1973, corporate Baa's were yielding 8 percent, while government

FIGURE 10–4   Yield Spread Differentials on Long-Term Bonds

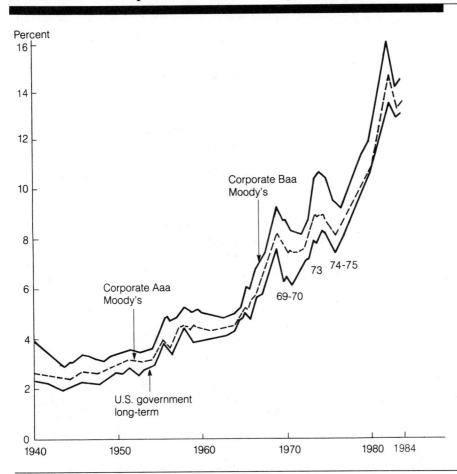

securities provided a return of 7.25 percent. Nevertheless, at certain phases of the business cycle, the yield spread changes. For example, in the early phases of a recession, confidence tends to be at a low ebb, and as a consequence, investors will attempt to shift out of low-grade securities into stronger instruments. The impact on the yield spreads can be observed in the recessions of 1969–70, 1974–75, and 1981–82. In all cases, the yield spread between corporate Baa's and government securities went over 200 basis points, only to narrow again during the recovery. Remember that in Chapter 8, on technical analysis, one of the market indicators was the Barron's Confidence Index which measured the ratio of high-grade bonds to medium-grade bonds. The closer the confidence index is to 1.00, the smaller the spread between rates and the more optimistic investors are about the economy. The further the index is below 1.00, the greater the spread in yields and the less the confidence.

The individual investor must determine how the yield spread affects his strategy. If he does not need to increase the quality of his portfolio during the low-confidence periods of a recession, he can enjoy unusually high returns on lower-grade instruments relative to higher grades.

INVESTMENT STRATEGY—SWAPS

The term swap refers to the procedure of selling out of a given bond position and immediately buying into another one with similar attributes in an attempt to improve overall portfolio return or performance.

Often there are bonds that appear to be comparable in every respect with the exception of one characteristic. For example, newly issued bonds that are the equivalent in every sense to outstanding issues generally trade at a slightly higher yield. The rationale behind this phenomenon is discussed further in Chapter 14 under a general discussion of special situations.

Swaps may also be utilized for tax adjustment purposes and are very popular at the end of the year. Assume that you own a AAA rated AT&T bond that you bought five months ago and are currently sitting on a 20 percent capital loss because of rising interest rates. You can sell the bond and claim the loss (up to $3,000) against ordinary income.[14] This will save you taxes equal to the loss times your marginal tax rate. You can then take the proceeds from the sale and reinvest in a bond of equal risk, and you will have increased your total cash returns because of tax benefits. If interest rates turn down, you may be able to eventually claim a long-term capital gain.

Another common swap is the pure pickup yield swap where a bond owner thinks that he can increase the yield to maturity by selling a bond and buying a different bond of equal risk. The key to this swap is that the bond price of one or both bonds has to be in disequilibrium. This, of course, assumes the market is less than totally efficient. By selling the bond that is overpriced and purchasing the bond that is underpriced the investor is increasing the yield on his investment. If by chance the true quality and risk of the two bonds

---

[14] Losses above $3,000 can be carried forward to future years.

are different, the bond trader may have swapped for nothing or may even end up losing on the trade. Other types of swaps exist for arbitrages associated with interest payment dates, call transactions, conversion privileges, or any quickly changing factor in the market.

Chapter 11

DURATION AND REINVESTMENT CONCEPTS

REVIEW OF BASIC BOND VALUATION CONCEPTS

In Chapter 10 we discussed the principles of bond valuation. The value of a bond was established in Formula (10–1) as follows:

$$V = \sum_{t=1}^{n} \frac{C_t}{(1 + i)^t} + \frac{P_n}{(1 + i)^n}$$

(10–1)

where:

V = Market value or price of the bond.
n = Number of periods.
t = Each period.
C_t = Coupon or interest payment for each period, t.
P_n = Par or maturity value.
i = Interest rate in the market.

Based on this equation, as interest rates in the market rise the price of the bond will decline, because the present value of the cash flows is worth less at a higher discount rate. The opposite is true if interest rates decline. We also demonstrated in Table 10–4 that bonds with long-term maturities were generally more sensitive to changes in interest rates than were short-term bonds. In the reproduction of Table 10–4 below, it can be seen that a 30-year bond

(Reproduction of Table 10–4)   **Change in Market Prices of Bonds for Shifts in Yields to Maturity (12 percent coupon rate)**

Yield change (percent)	Maturity (years)				
	1	5	10	20	30
+3%	−2.69%	−10.30%	−15.29%	−18.89%	−19.74%
+2	−1.81	− 7.02	−10.59	−13.33	−14.04
+1	− .91	− 3.57	− 5.01	− 7.08	− 7.52
−1	+ .92	+ 3.77	+ 5.98	+ 8.02	+ 8.72
−2	+1.86	+ 7.72	+12.46	+17.16	+18.93
−3	+2.81	+11.87	+19.51	+27.60	+30.96

exhibits larger price changes in response to a change in yield than do shorter-term obligations. For example, a 2 percent drop in interest rates would cause a 1.86 percent increase in value for a bond with one year to maturity, but an 18.93 percent increase in value for a bond with 30 years to maturity. Given the relationship between the life of a bond and the price sensitivity just described, it is particularly important that we have an appropriate definition of the life or term of a bond.

The first inclination is to say the term of a bond is an easily determined matter. One supposedly merely needs to look up the maturity date (such as

1995 or 2004) in a bond book and the matter is settled. However, the notion of effective life of a bond is more complicated than this. The situation is somewhat analogous to the quoted coupon rate on the bond not really conveying the true yield on the obligation. Similarly, the maturity date on a bond may not convey all important information about the life of a bond.

In studying the true characteristics about the life of a bond, not only must the final date and amount of the maturity payment be considered, but also the pattern of coupon payments that take place in the interim. If you were to receive $1,000 after 20 years and no interest payments during the term of the obligation, clearly the effective life is 20 years. But suppose in addition to the $1,000, you were also to receive $100 per year for the next 20 years. Part of the payment is coming early and part of the payment is coming late, and the weighted average term of the payout is certainly less than 20 years. The higher the coupon payments relative to the maturity payment, the shorter the weighted average life of the payout. In the next section, we shall go through the simple mathematics of computing the weighted average life of the payout; for now it is enough to know that such a concept exists.

The important consideration is that bond price sensitivity can be more appropriately related to weighted average life than to just the maturity date. While many bond analysts simply relate price sensitivity to maturity, (and we did that also in Chapter 10), there is a more sophisticated approach related to weighted average life.

Before we move on to determining weighted average life, there is an investment decision we wish you to consider. Assume you have to decide whether to invest in an 8 percent coupon rate bond with a 20-year maturity or a 12 percent coupon rate bond with a 25-year maturity. Which bond will have the larger increase in price if interest rates decline? You may choose the 25-year, 12 percent coupon rate bond because it has the longer maturity, but don't answer too quickly on this. Let's consider weighted average life, and then eventually come back to this question of price sensitivity.

DURATION

The concept of weighted average life of a bond falls under the general topic of duration. We shall first of all do a simple example of weighted average life, and then more formally look at duration. Assume that we have a five-year bond that provides $80 per year for the next five years, plus $1,000 at the end of five years. For ease of calculation, we are using annual coupon payments in our analysis. Semiannual analysis would change the answer only slightly. An approach to computing weighted average life is presented in Table 11–1.

First of all, we see the weighted average life of the bond, based on the annual cash flows, is 4.4290 years. Let's see how this is calculated. In column (1) is the year in which each cash flow falls, and in column (2) is the size of the cash flow for each year plus the total cash flow. Column (3) calls for dividing the annual cash flow in column (2) by the total cash flow at the bottom of column (2) to determine what percentage of the total it represents. For example, the annual cash flow of $80 on the first line of column (2) represents .0571

TABLE 11–1   Simple Weighted Average Life

(1)	(2)	(3) Annual cash flow (2) ÷ by total cash flow	(4) Year × weight (1) × (3)
Year, t	Cash flow		
1	$ 80	.0571	.0571
2	80	.0571	.1142
3	80	.0571	.1713
4	80	.0571	.2284
5	80	.0571	.2855
5	1,000	.7145	3.5725
Total cash → flow	$1,400	1.0000	4.4290

of the total cash flow of $1,400. ($80 ÷ $1,400 = .0571.) The same basic procedure is followed for all subsequent years. In column *(4)*, each year is multiplied by the weights (percentages) developed in column *(3)*. For example, year 1 is multiplied by .0571 to arrive at .0571 in column *(4)*. Year 2 is multiplied by .0571 to arrive at .1142 in column *(4)*. This procedure is followed for each year and each weight. The final answer is 4.4290 for the weighted average life of the bond.

If you can understand the approach presented in Table 11–1, you should have no difficulty in following a more formal and appropriate definition of weighted average life called duration. Duration represents the weighted average life of a bond where the weights are based on the *present value* of the individual cash flows relative to the *present value* of the total cash flows (previously we did not discount the cash flows in determining weights, but merely used stated values). An example of duration is presented in Table 11–2. Present value calculations are based on the market rate of interest (yield to maturity) for the bond, which in this case, we shall assume to be 12 percent.

The only difference between Table 11–1 and Table 11–2 is that in Table 11–2 the cash flows are present valued before the weights are determined. Thus the cash flows *(2)* are multiplied by the present value factors at 12 percent *(3)* to arrive at the present value of cash flows *(4)*. The total present value of cash flows at the bottom of column *(4)* is also the same concept as the price of the bond. In column *(5)*, weights for each year are determined by dividing the present value of each annual cash flow *(4)* by the total present value of cash flows (bottom of column *4*). For example in year 1, the present value of the cash flow is $71.44, and this is divided by the total present value of cash flows of $855.40 to arrive at .0835 in column *(5)*. Similarly, the weight in year 2, as shown in column *(5)*, is determined by dividing $63.76 by $855.40 to arrive at .0745. In column *(6)*, each year is multiplied by the weights developed in column *(5)*. For example, year 1 is multiplied by .0835 to arrive at .0835 in column *(6)*. Year 2 is multiplied by .0745 to arrive at .1490. This procedure is followed for each year, and the values are then summed. The final

TABLE 11–2   Duration Concept of Weighted Average Life

(1)	(2)	(3)	(4)	(5)	(6)
Year, t	Cash flow (CF)	PV factor at 12 percent	PV of cash flow (CF)	PV of annual cash flow (4) ÷ by total PV of cash flows	Year × weight (1) × (5)
1	$ 80	.893	$ 71.44	.0835	.0835
2	80	.797	63.76	.0745	.1490
3	80	.712	56.96	.0666	.1998
4	80	.636	50.88	.0595	.2380
5	80	.567	45.36	.0530	.2650
5	$1,000	.567	567.00	.6629	3.3145
		Total PV of → cash flows (V)	$855.40	1.0000	4.2498 ↑ Duration

answer for duration (the weighted average life based on present value) is 4.2498. Duration, once determined, is the most representative value for effective bond life, and the measure against which bond price sensitivity should be evaluated.

The formula for duration can be formally stated as:

$$\text{Duration} = \underbrace{\frac{PV\ CF}{V}}_{\text{Weight}}\underbrace{(1)}_{\text{Year}} + \underbrace{\frac{PV\ CF}{V}}_{\text{Weight}}\underbrace{(2)}_{\text{Year}} + \underbrace{\frac{PV\ CF}{V}}_{\text{Weight}}\underbrace{(3)}_{\text{Year}}$$

$$+ \cdots + \underbrace{\frac{PV\ CF}{V}}_{\text{Weight}}\underbrace{(n)}_{\text{Year}} \quad (11\text{–}1)$$

where:

    PV = The present value factor for each time period (from Appendix B at the end of the book).

    CF = The yearly cash flow for each time period.

    V = The total present value or market price of the bond.

    n = number of periods to maturity.[1]

---

[1] Using the symbols from Formula (10–1), duration can also be stated as:

$$\text{Duration} = \sum_{t=1}^{n} \frac{C_t \dfrac{1}{(1+i)^t}}{V}(t) + \frac{P_n \dfrac{1}{(1+i)^n}}{V}(n)$$

If semiannual analysis is used throughout the calculation, the answer should be divided by two to convert the figure to annual terms.

TABLE 11–3   Duration for an 8 Percent Coupon Rate Bond with Maturities of 1, 5, and 10 Years Discounted at 12 Percent

1-Year bond

(1)	(2)	(3)	(4)	(5)	(6)
				PV of annual cash flow (4) ÷ by total PV	Year × weight
		PV factor	PV of cash		
Year, t	Cash flow (CF)	at 12 percent	flow (CF)	of cash flows	(1) × (5)
1	$ 80	.893	$ 71.44	.0741	.0741
2	1,000	.893	893.00	.9259	.9259
		Total PV of → cash flows	$964.44	1.0000	1.0000 ↑ Duration

5-Year bond

(1)	(2)	(3)	(4)	(5)	(6)
				PV of annual cash flow (4) ÷ by total PV	Year × weight
		PV factor	PV of cash		
Year, t	Cash flow (CF)	at 12 percent	flow (CF)	of cash flows	(1) × (5)
1	$ 80	.893	$ 71.44	.0835	.0835
2	80	.797	63.76	.0745	.1490
3	80	.712	56.96	.0666	.1998
4	80	.636	50.88	.0595	.2380
5	80	.567	45.36	.0530	.2650
5	1,000	.567	567.00	.6629	3.3145
		Total PV of → cash flows	$855.40	1.0000	4.2498 ↑ Duration

10-Year bond

(1)	(2)	(3)	(4)	(5)	(6)
				PV of annual cash flow (4) ÷ by total PV	Year × weight
		PV factor	PV of cash		
Year, t	Cash flow (CF)	at 12 percent	flow (CF)	of cash flows	(1) × (5)
1	$ 80	.893	$ 71.44	.0923	.0923
2	80	.797	63.76	.0824	.1648
3	80	.712	56.96	.0736	.2208
4	80	.636	50.88	.0657	.2628
5	80	.567	45.36	.0586	.2930
6	80	.507	40.56	.0524	.3144
7	80	.452	36.16	.0467	.3269
8	80	.404	32.32	.0418	.3344
9	80	.361	28.88	.0373	.3357
10	80	.322	25.76	.0333	.3330
10	1,000	.322	322.00	.4160	4.1600
		Total PV of → cash flows	$774.08	1.0000	6.8381 ↑ Duration

In Table 11–3 on page 329, we observe durations for an 8 percent coupon rate bond with maturities of 1, 5, and 10 years. The discount rate is 12 percent. The procedure used to compute duration in Table 11–3 is precisely the same as that employed in Table 11–2. Although many calculations are involved, you should primarily direct your attention to the last value presented in the last column (6) for each of the three bonds. This value, of course, represents the duration of the issue.

We see in Table 11–3 that the duration for a one-year bond is 1.0. Since all cash flows are paid at the end of year 1, duration equals the maturity.[2] As maturity increases (to 5 and 10 years) duration increases but less than the maturity of the bond. With a 5-year bond, duration is 4.2498, and with a 10-year bond, duration is 6.8381. Duration is increasing at a decreasing rate because the principal repayment in the last year becomes a smaller percentage of the total present value of cash flow, and the annual coupon payments become more important.[3]

DURATION AND PRICE SENSITIVITY

Once duration is computed, its most important use is in determining the price sensitivity of a bond. In Table 11–4, we consider the maturity, duration, and percentage price change for an 8 percent coupon rate bond based on a 2 percent decrease and of a 2 percent increase in interest rates. The *market* rate of interest for computing duration in Table 11–4 is 8 percent. One quick point before examining Table 11–4. Duration is related not only to maturity, but also to coupon rate and market rate of interest. For example, in Table 11–3, the coupon rate of interest was 8 percent and the market rate of interest was 12 percent. In the calculations in Table 11–4, the coupon rate is 8 percent and the market rate of interest is assumed to be 8 percent. Because of the different market rates of interest in Tables 11–3 and 11–4, the duration for a given maturity (such as 5 and 10 years) will be different. The point just discussed will be further clarified later in the chapter, so even if you do not fully understand it, you should still continue to read on.

We see in Table 11–4 that the longer the maturity or duration, the greater the impact of a 2 percent change in interest rates on price. However, we shall also observe how much more closely the percentage change in price parallels the change in duration as compared to maturity. For example, between 25 and 50 years, duration increases very slowly (column 2) and the same can be said for the increase in the percentage impact that a 2 percent decline in interest rates has on price (column 3). This is true in spite of the fact that the maturity period has increased by 100 percent, from 25 to 50 years.

As a rough measure of price sensitivity, one can multiply duration times

---

[2] If semiannual analysis were used, the duration would be slightly less than the maturity in the first year.

[3] A sinking fund provision can also have an effect on duration, causing the weighted average life of the bond to be shorter.

TABLE 11–4   Duration and Price Sensitivity (8 percent coupon rate bond)

(1)	(2)	(3) Impact of a 2 percent decline in interest rates on price	(4) Impact of a 2 percent increase in interest rates on price
Maturity	*Duration*		
1	1.0000	+ 1.89%	− 1.81%
5	4.3121	+ 8.42	− 7.58
10	7.2470	+14.72	−12.29
20	10.6038	+22.93	−17.03
25	11.5290	+25.57	−18.50
30	12.1585	+27.53	−18.85
40	12.8787	+30.09	−19.55
50	13.2123	+31.15	−19.83

the change in interest rates to determine the percentage change in the value of a bond.

$$\begin{array}{c}\text{Percentage}\\ \text{change in the}\\ \text{value of a}\\ \text{bond}\end{array}\;\dots\;\begin{array}{c}\text{Approximately}\\ \text{equals}\end{array}\to\text{Duration}\times\begin{array}{c}\text{Change in}\\ \text{interest rates}\end{array}$$

The sign in the final answer is reversed because interest rate changes and bond prices move in opposite directions. For example, if a bond has a duration of 7.2470 years, and interest rates go down by 2 percent, a rough measure of bond value appreciation is +14.494 percent (7.2470 × 2). Columns *(2)* and *(3)* in Table 11–4, across from 10 years maturity, indicate that this is a reasonably good approximation. That is, when duration was 7.2470, a 2 percent drop in interest rates produced a 14.72 percent increase in bond prices (not too many basis points away from our projected value of +14.494 percent). The approximation gets progressively rougher as the term of the bond is extended.[4] It is also a less valid measure for interest rate increases (and the associated price decline). Even with these qualifications, one can observe a more useful relationship between price changes and duration than between price changes and maturity.

It is for this reason that the analyst must have a reasonable feel for the factors that influence duration. It is apparent that the length of the bond affects duration, but, as previously mentioned, it is not the only variable. Duration is

---

[4] The approximation can be slightly improved by using modified duration instead of actual duration. Modified duration is defined as: Duration ÷ (1 + market rate of interest/the number of coupon payments per period). For more information, see Michael H. Hopewell and George C. Kaufman, "Bond Price Volatility and Term to Maturity: A Generalized Respecification," *American Economic Review,* September 1973, pp. 749–53.

also influenced by market rate of interest and the coupon rate on the bond. In fact, it is theoretically possible for these two factors to outweigh maturity in determining duration. That is to say, it is possible that a bond with a shorter maturity than another bond may actually have a longer duration and be more price-sensitive to interest rate changes.

Duration and Market Rates

Market rates of interest (yield to maturity) and duration are inversely related. The higher the market rate of interest, the lower the duration. This is because of the present valuing effect that is part of duration. Higher market rates of interest mean lower present values. For example, in Table 11–2, if the market rate of interest in column (3) had been 16 percent instead of 12 percent, the final answer for duration would have been 4.1859. The new value is actually computed in Table 11–5. Clearly, it is less than the 4.2498 duration value in Table 11–2.

TABLE 11–5   Duration of an 8 Percent Coupon Rate Bond with a 16 Percent Market Rate of Interest

(1)	(2)	(3)	(4)	(5)	(6)
				PV of annual cash flow (4)	Year ×
		PV factor	PV of cash	÷ by total PV	weight
Year, t	Cash flow (CF)	at 16 percent	flow (CF)	of cash flows	(1) × (5)
1	$ 80	.862	$ 68.96	.0935	.0935
2	80	.743	59.44	.0806	.1612
3	80	.641	51.28	.0695	.2085
4	80	.552	44.16	.0598	.2392
5	80	.476	38.08	.0516	.2580
5	1,000	.476	476.00	.6451	3.2255
		Total PV of → cash flows	$737.92	1.0000	4.1859 ↑ Duration

To expand our analysis, in Table 11–6 we see the duration values for an 8 percent coupon rate bond at different market rates of interest. As market rates of interest increase, duration decreases. This can be easily seen in the 20-year row (reading across). At a 4 percent market rate of interest, duration for the 8 percent coupon rate bond is 12.3995. At 8 percent it is 10.6038, and at 12 percent, 8.9390.

Also note in Table 11–6 that an equal change in market rates of interest will have a bigger impact on duration when rates move down than when they move up. For example, in the 50-year row, a 4 percent decrease in market rates of interest (say, from 8 percent to 4 percent) causes duration to increase by

TABLE 11–6   Duration Values at Varying Market Rates of Interest (based on 8 percent coupon rate bond)

Maturity (years)	Market rates of interest				
	4 percent	6 percent	8 percent	10 percent	12 percent
1	1.00	1.00	1.00	1.00	1.00
5	4.3717	4.3423	4.3121	4.2814	4.2498
10	7.6372	7.4450	7.2470	7.0439	6.8381
→20	12.3995	11.4950	10.6038	9.7460	8.9390
25	14.2265	12.8425	11.5290	10.3229	9.2475
30	15.7935	13.8893	12.1585	10.6472	9.3662
40	18.3274	15.3498	12.8787	10.9176	9.3972
50	20.2481	16.2494	13.2123	10.9896	9.3716

7.0358 years, from 13.2123 to 20.2481 years. A similar increase of 4 percent from 8 percent to 12 percent would only cause duration to decrease by 3.8407 years, from 13.2123 to 9.3716 years.

Duration and Coupon Rates

In the previous section, we learned that duration is inversely related to market rate of interest. We now look at the relationship between duration and the coupon rate on a bond. As the coupon rate rises, duration decreases. Why? The answer is that high coupon rate bonds tend to produce higher annual cash flows prior to maturity, and thus tend to weight duration toward the earlier to middle years. On the other hand, low coupon rate bonds produce less annual cash flows prior to maturity and have less influence on duration. Duration is weighted more heavily toward the final payment at maturity, and duration tends to be somewhat closer to the actual maturity on the bond. At the extreme, on a zero-coupon bond, maturity and duration are the same.

The relationship between duration and coupon rates can be seen in Table 11–7. Here three different coupon rate bonds are presented. Each bond

TABLE 11–7   Duration and Coupon Rates (25-year bonds)

Market rate of interest	Coupon rates		
	4 percent	8 percent	12 percent
4%	16.2470	14.2265	13.3278
6	14.7455	12.8425	12.0407
8	13.2459	11.5290	10.8396
10	11.8112	10.3229	9.7501
12	10.4912	9.2475	8.7844

is assumed to have a maturity of 25 years. The best way to read the table is to pick a market rate of interest in the first column and then read across the table to determine the duration at various coupon rates. For example, at an 8 percent market rate of interest, duration is 13.2459 at a 4 percent coupon rate, 11.5290 at an 8 percent coupon rate, and 10.8396 at a 12 percent coupon rate. Clearly, the higher the coupon rate, the lower the duration (and vice versa).

The impact of coupon rates on duration is also demonstrated in Figure 11–1. Note that with a zero-coupon bond the line is at a 45-degree angle; that is, duration and years to maturity are always the same value. There is only one payment, and it is at maturity.

FIGURE 11–1   The Effect of Coupon Rates on Duration

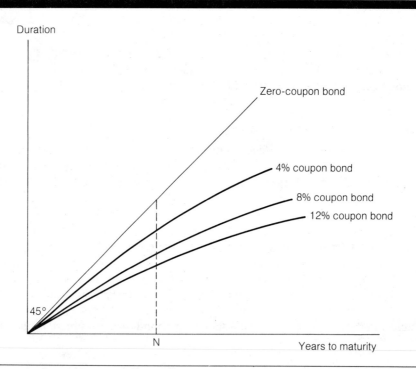

You can also observe in Figure 11–1 that progressively higher coupon rates lead to a lower duration. As an example, go to point N on the horizontal axis, and observe duration for 4 percent, 8 percent, and 12 percent interest. Clearly the higher the coupon rate, the lower the duration value.

Because the higher the duration the greater the price sensitivity, it follows that an investor desiring maximum price movements will look toward lower coupon rate bonds. As previously demonstrated, low coupon rate and high duration go together, and high duration leads to maximum price sensitivity. The relationship of low coupon rates to price sensitivity was briefly discussed in Chapter 10 under investment strategy. We now see that the unnamed explanatory variable at that point was duration.

BRINGING TOGETHER THE INFLUENCES ON DURATION

The three factors that determine the value of duration are maturity of the bond, market rate of interest, and the coupon rate. Duration is positively correlated with maturity, but moves in the opposite direction of market rates of interest and coupon rates, i.e., the higher the coupon rate, the lower the duration. Earlier in this chapter, you were asked to consider whether you should invest in an 8 percent coupon rate, 20-year bond or a 12 percent coupon rate, 25-year bond. Since we were assuming interest rates were going to go down, you were looking for maximum price volatility. Had you not studied duration, you probably would have selected the bond with the longest maturity. This would generally be a valid assumption as indicated in Chapter 10. However, the primary emphasis to the sophisticated bond investor when assessing price volatility, or sensitivity, is duration.

Note that the bond with the longer maturity (25 years versus 20 years) also has a higher coupon rate (12 percent versus 8 percent). The first factor (longer maturity) would indicate higher duration, but the second factor (higher coupon rate) would indicate a lower duration. What is the net effect? The answer can be found in earlier tables in this chapter. Let's assume that the market rate of interest is 12 percent for both bonds. Table 11–6 presented information on 8 percent coupon rate bonds for varying maturities and market rates of interest. To determine the duration on the 8 percent coupon rate, 20-year bond, assuming a 12 percent market rate of interest, we read across the 20-year row to the last column in the table and see the answer is 8.9390. (Note that all bonds in Table 11–6 have an 8 percent coupon rate, so we must identify the value associated with 20 years and a 12 percent market rate of interest.)

To determine the duration for the 12 percent coupon rate, 25-year bond with a 12 percent market rate of interest, we must go to Table 11–7. Note that all bonds in this table have a 25-year maturity, so read down to a market rate of interest of 12 percent and across to a coupon rate of 12 percent. The value for duration on this bond is 8.7844.

Based on the above analysis, the answer to the question posed earlier in the chapter is that the bond with the shorter maturity (8 percent coupon rate for 20 years) has a longer duration than the bond with the greater maturity (12 percent for 25 years), and thus is the most price-sensitive.[5]

---

[5] As previously indicated, if we vary the market rate of interest, we can also influence the outcome to our question.

Bond	*Duration*
8%, 20 years	8.9390 ← greater price sensitivity
12%, 25 years	8.7844

In actuality, if interest rates went down by 2 percent, the 8 percent, 20-year bond would go up by 18.5 percent, while the 12 percent, 25-year bond would only increase by 17.9 percent.

DURATION AND ZERO-COUPON BONDS

Characteristics of zero-coupon bonds were briefly described in Chapter 9. As previously mentioned, Figure 11–1 depicts the duration of zero-coupon bonds as a 45-degree line relative to years to maturity. This graphically indicates that the duration of a zero-coupon bond equals the number of years it has to maturity. For all bonds of equal risk and maturity, the zero-coupon bond has the greatest duration and therefore the greatest price sensitivity. This price risk is one that is often lost in the image of safety that CATs, RATs, TGRs, COUGARs, and other zero-coupons have when backed by U.S. government securities.

A headline in *The Wall Street Journal* on June 1, 1984, appeared as follows: "Zero-Coupon Bonds' Price Swings Jolt Investors Looking for Security."[6] It was reported that between March 31, 1983, and March 31, 1984, Salomon Brothers' 30-year CATs declined 25 percent in price, while returns on conventional 30-year government bonds declined only a few percentage points. The article cited one client buying $100,000 of zero coupons, thinking they were similar to short-term Treasury bill investments, only to find out four weeks later that his zero-coupon bonds had declined in value by $24,000.

To put the volatility of a zero-coupon bond into better perspective, we compare the duration of a zero-coupon bond to that of an 8 percent coupon bond for several maturities in Table 11–8.

The far right column in Table 11–8 indicates the ratio of duration between zero-coupon and 8 percent coupon rate bonds. As stressed throughout the chapter, duration represents a measure of price sensitivity. Thus for a 10-year maturity period, a zero-coupon bond is almost 1½ times as price sensitive as an 8 percent coupon rate bond (the ratio in the last column is 1.4625). For a 20-year maturity period, it is over two times more price-sensitive (2.2374), and for 50 years the duration, or price sensitivity, ratio is over 5 times greater (5.3353). This might explain why zero-coupons were much more sensitive to rising interest rates during 1983–84 as described in the story in *The Wall Street Journal.* Of course, tremendous profits can be made in zero-coupon bonds when there is a sharp drop in interest rates as in early 1985.

---

[6] Randall Smith, "Zero-Coupon Bonds' Price Swings Jolt Investors Looking for Security," *The Wall Street Journal,* June 1, 1984, p. 19.

TABLE 11–8   Duration of Zero-Coupon versus 8 Percent Coupon Bonds (market rate of interest is 12 percent)

Years to maturity	Duration of zero-coupon bond	Duration of 8 percent coupon bond	Relative duration of zero-coupon to 8 percent coupon bonds
10	10	6.8374	1.4625
20	20	8.9390	2.2374
30	30	9.3662	3.2030
40	40	9.3972	4.2566
50	50	9.3716	5.3353

THE USES OF DURATION

Duration is primarily used as a measure to judge bond price sensitivity to interest rate changes. Since duration includes information on several variables (maturity, coupon rate, and market rate of interest), it captures more information than any one of them. It therefore allows more accurate decisions for complex bond strategies. One such strategy involves the timing of investment inflows to provide a needed cash outlay at a known future date. Perhaps $1,000,000 is needed after five years. Everything is tailored to this five-year time horizon. If interest rates go up, there will be a decline in the value of the portfolio, but a higher reinvestment rate opportunity for inflows. Similarly, if interest rates go down, there will be capital appreciation for the portfolio, but a lower reinvestment rate opportunity. By tying all the investment decisions to a duration period, the portfolio manager can take advantage of these counter forces to ensure a necessary outcome. This strategy is called immunization, and is used by insurance companies, pension funds, and other institutional money managers to protect their portfolios against swings in interest rates. For a more comprehensive discussion of immunization strategies, an article by Fisher and Weil is an appropriate source.[7] For an excellent criticism of duration and immunization strategy, see Yawitz and Marshall.[8] One of the problems with duration analysis is that it often assumes a parallel shift in yield curves. Although long-duration bonds are clearly more price-sensitive than shorter-duration bonds, there is no assurance that long- and short-term interest rates will move by equal amounts.

---

[7] Lawrence Fisher and Roman L. Weil, "Coping with Risk of Interest Rate Fluctuations: Returns to Bondholders from Naive and Optimal Strategies," *Journal of Business,* October 1971, pp. 408–31.

[8] Jess B. Yawitz and William J. Marshall, "The Shortcomings of Duration as a Risk Measure for Bonds," *The Journal of Financial Research,* Summer 1981, pp. 91–101.

BOND REINVESTMENT ASSUMPTIONS AND TERMINAL WEALTH ANALYSIS

Reinvestment Assumptions

As indicated in the previous section, one concern an investor may have when purchasing bonds is that the interest income will not be reinvested to earn the same return that the coupon payment represents. This may not be a problem for an individual consuming the interest payments, but it could be a serious concern for individuals building a retirement portfolio or a pension fund manager accumulating funds for future payout to retirees. The crucial issue is the amount of money accumulated at the time the retirement fund will be used to cover living expenses. And, of course, one major determinant of the ending value of a retirement fund is the rate of return on coupon payments as they are reinvested.

Since the late 1960s, interest rates have been much higher and more volatile than during the previous 30 years. This has caused more emphasis on the management of fixed-income securities, not only in the selection of maturity but also in the switching from short- to long-term securities. These volatile high rates have caused more emphasis on concepts like duration to measure bond price sensitivity and on total return as a measure of bond management success. Given that interest rates change daily and by large amounts over the period of a year, what impact would a lower or higher reinvestment assumption have on the outcome of your retirement nest egg?

First let us look at a small part of Appendix A (reproduced in Table 11–9 for compound sums). Appendix A assumes that all interest is reinvested at the same rate as the coupon rate in order to find the ending value of one dollar invested at a given rate for a set maturity. For our current analysis, we are assuming annual interest (though the answer only changes slightly if we use semiannual interest).

TABLE 11–9   Compound Sum of $1.00 (from Appendix A)

Period	7 percent	8 percent	9 percent	10 percent	11 percent	12 percent
10	1.967	2.159	2.367	2.594	2.839	3.106
20	3.870	4.661	5.604	6.727	8.062	9.646
30	7.612	10.063	13.268	17.449	22.892	29.960
40	14.974	21.725	31.409	45.259	65.001	93.051

The table values are given in $1 amounts, so for a $1,000 bond we would just move the decimal three places to the right. A $1,000 bond having a 12 percent coupon rate with interest being reinvested at 12 percent would compound to $93,051 over 40 years, while a 7 percent coupon bond reinvested at

7 percent would only compound to $14,974 over a similar time period. A difference of 5 percent in the rates creates a total difference of $78,077. This is quite a large difference. Notice that the longer the compounding period, the larger the difference. From further inspection of Table 11–9, other comparisons can be made between years and total ending values.

The importance of the reinvestment assumption can also be viewed from the perspective of its contribution to total wealth. For example, an investor in a 40-year bond at a 12 percent coupon rate and assumed reinvestment rate of 12 percent will have an accumulated value of $93,051. In terms of payout, $4,800 (40 × $120) comes directly from 40 years of 12 percent interest payments, $1,000 comes from principal, and the balance of $87,251 comes from interest that is earned on the annual interest payments. In this case, interest on interest represents 93.8 percent of the overall return ($87,251/ $93,051).

Terminal Wealth Analysis

Now we will assume a reinvestment assumption different from the coupon rate. Take the two extreme values from Table 11–9 of 12 percent and 7 percent. Assume that you buy a bond having a 12 percent coupon rate, but that the interest can only be reinvested at 7 percent. To find the ending value of this investment we will need to use a terminal wealth table.

Table 11–10 is called a terminal wealth table because it generates the ending value of the investment at the end of each year, assuming that the bond has a *maturity* date corresponding to that year. Let's use 10 years as an example in examining Table 11–10. If the bond matures in 10 years, the $1,000 principal in column (2) will be recovered. Also the investor will receive $120 in annual interest (12 percent of $1,000) in year 10 as indicated in column (3). In column (4) the accumulated interest up to the beginning of year 10 is shown. The reinvestment rate on this previously accumulated interest is a mere 7 percent as indicated in column (5). The interest on the previously accumulated interest is $100.62 (.07 × $1,437.38). Finally, the total interest for year 10 is shown in column (7). This consists of the coupon interest of $120 and the interest on interest of $100.62 and totals to $220.62. The total ending value of the portfolio is shown in column (8). The ending value consists of the recovered principal of $1,000, plus the accumulated interest of $1,437.38 up to the beginning of year 10, plus the total interest paid in year 10 of $220.62. The ending wealth value (portfolio sum) thus shown in column (8) is $2,658.00. The value is summarized below.

–Recovered principal	$1,000.00	Column (2)
–Accumulated interest (beginning of year 10)	1,437.38	Column (4)
–Total annual interest (during year 10)	220.62	Column (7)
Ending wealth value (portfolio sum)	$2,658.00	Column (8)

TABLE 11–10   Terminal Wealth Table (12 percent coupon with 7 percent reinvestment rate on interest)

(1) Years to maturity	(2) Principal	(3) Annual coupon interest	(4) Accumulated interest*	(5) Reinvestment rate on interest	(6) Interest on interest	(7) Total annual interest	(8) Portfolio sum	(9) Compound sum factor	(10) Annual percentage return
0.0	$1,000.00								
1.0	1,000.00	$120.00	$ 0.00			$ 120.00	$ 1,120.00	1.12000	12.00
2.0	1,000.00	120.00	120.00	.07	$ 8.40	128.40	1,248.40	1.24840	11.73
3.0	1,000.00	120.00	248.40	.07	17.39	137.39	1,385.79	1.38579	11.48
4.0	1,000.00	120.00	385.79	.07	27.01	147.01	1,532.80	1.53280	11.26
5.0	1,000.00	120.00	532.80	.07	37.30	157.30	1,690.10	1.69010	11.06
6.0	1,000.00	120.00	690.10	.07	48.31	168.31	1,858.41	1.85841	10.86
7.0	1,000.00	120.00	858.41	.07	60.09	180.09	2,038.50	2.03850	10.71
8.0	1,000.00	120.00	1,038.50	.07	72.70	192.70	2,231.20	2.23120	10.55
9.0	1,000.00	120.00	1,231.20	.07	86.18	206.18	2,437.38	2.43738	10.40
10.0	1,000.00	120.00	1,437.38	.07	100.62	220.62	2,658.00	2.65800	10.26
11.0	1,000.00	120.00	1,658.00	.07	116.06	236.06	2,894.06	2.89406	10.14
12.0	1,000.00	120.00	1,894.06	.07	132.58	252.58	3,146.64	3.14664	10.02
13.0	1,000.00	120.00	2,146.64	.07	150.26	270.26	3,416.90	3.41690	9.91
14.0	1,000.00	120.00	2,416.90	.07	169.18	289.18	3,706.08	3.70608	9.80
15.0	1,000.00	120.00	2,706.08	.07	189.43	309.43	4,015.51	4.01551	9.71
16.0	1,000.00	120.00	3,015.51	.07	211.09	331.09	4,346.60	4.34660	9.61
17.0	1,000.00	120.00	3,346.60	.07	234.26	354.26	4,700.86	4.70086	9.54
18.0	1,000.00	120.00	3,700.86	.07	259.06	379.06	5,079.92	5.07992	9.44
19.0	1,000.00	120.00	4,079.92	.07	285.59	405.59	5,485.51	5.48551	9.37
20.0	1,000.00	120.00	4,485.51	.07	313.99	433.99	5,919.50	5.91950	9.29
21.0	1,000.00	120.00	4,919.50	.07	344.37	464.37	6,383.87	6.38387	9.22
22.0	1,000.00	120.00	5,383.87	.07	376.87	496.87	6,880.74	6.88074	9.16
23.0	1,000.00	120.00	5,880.74	.07	411.65	531.65	7,412.39	7.41239	9.09
24.0	1,000.00	120.00	6,412.39	.07	448.87	568.87	7,981.26	7.98126	9.04
25.0	1,000.00	120.00	6,981.26	.07	488.69	608.69	8,589.95	8.58995	8.98
26.0	1,000.00	120.00	7,589.95	.07	531.30	651.30	9,241.25	9.24125	8.92
27.0	1,000.00	120.00	8,241.25	.07	576.89	696.89	9,938.14	9.93814	8.87
28.0	1,000.00	120.00	8,938.14	.07	625.67	745.67	10,683.81	10.68381	8.82
29.0	1,000.00	120.00	9,683.81	.07	677.87	797.87	11,481.68	11.48168	8.78
30.0	1,000.00	120.00	10,481.68	.07	733.72	853.72	12,335.40	12.33540	8.73
31.0	1,000.00	120.00	11,335.40	.07	793.48	913.48	13,248.88	13.24888	8.69
32.0	1,000.00	120.00	12,248.88	.07	857.42	977.42	14,226.30	14.22630	8.65
33.0	1,000.00	120.00	13,226.30	.07	925.84	1,045.84	15,272.14	15.27214	8.61
34.0	1,000.00	120.00	14,272.14	.07	999.05	1,119.05	16,391.19	16.39119	8.57
35.0	1,000.00	120.00	15,391.19	.07	1,077.38	1,197.38	17,588.57	17.58857	8.53
36.0	1,000.00	120.00	16,588.57	.07	1,161.20	1,281.20	18,869.77	18.86977	8.50
37.0	1,000.00	120.00	17,869.77	.07	1,250.88	1,370.88	20,240.65	20.24065	8.46
38.0	1,000.00	120.00	19,240.65	.07	1,346.85	1,466.85	21,707.50	21.70750	8.43
39.0	1,000.00	120.00	20,707.50	.07	1,449.53	1,569.53	23,277.03	23.27703	8.40
40.0	1,000.00	120.00	22,277.03	.07	1,559.39	1,679.39	24,956.42	24.95642	8.37

* At beginning of year.

A $1,000 investment that grows to $2,658.00 after 10 years is the equivalent of a $1 investment that grows to 2.65800 as indicated in column *(9)*. The annual percentage return for a $1 investment that grows to 2.65800 after 10 years is 10.26 percent as indicated in column *(10)*.

A similar analysis can be done for all other maturity periods running from 1 to 40 years. One thing to notice from Table 11–10 is that the longer the maturity period of the bond, the greater the effect the low 7 percent reinvestment rate has on the bond. For 5 years, the annual percentage return (column 10) is 11.06 percent, for 15 years 9.71 percent, and for 40 years 8.37 percent.

What is the actual difference between the ending value for a 40-year, 12 percent coupon rate bond assuming a *12 percent* reinvestment rate and the 40-year, 7 *percent* reinvestment rate just presented in Table 11–10? Earlier in this section we saw in Table 11–9 that a 12 percent coupon rate bond with an assumed 12 percent reinvestment rate for 40 years would grow to $93,051. In Table 11–10, we see a 12 percent coupon rate bond with a 7 percent reinvestment rate will only grow to $24,956.42 after 40 years. It should be evident that it is not only the coupon rate that matters, but the reinvestment rate as well.

If the bond were not held to maturity in our analysis, then we would have to rely upon the realized rate of return analysis developed in Chapter 10. The realized rate of return approach would assume that the bond is not held to maturity and that it is sold at either a gain or loss. In the case of the bond analyzed in the terminal wealth table (11–10), we know that since interest rates declined, any sale of the bond before maturity should result in a capital gain. How large that capital gain would be will be dependent upon its duration. Terminal wealth analysis is a way of analyzing the reinvestment assumption when bonds are held to maturity, while the realized yield approach assumes that bonds are actively traded to take advantage of interest rate swings.

Zero-Coupon Bonds and Terminal Wealth

One of the benefits of zero-coupon bonds is that they lock in a compound rate of return (or reinvestment rate) for the life of the bond *if held to maturity.* There are no coupon payments during the life of the bond to be reinvested, so the originally quoted rate holds throughout if held to maturity. If a $1,000 par value, 15-year zero-coupon bond is quoted at a price of $183 to yield 12 percent, you truly have locked in a 12 percent reinvestment rate. Some would say you have not only locked in 12 percent, but have thrown away the key. In any event, zero-coupon bonds allow you to predetermine your reinvestment rate.

Of course, if a zero-coupon bond is sold before maturity, there could be large swings in the sales price of the bond because of its high duration characteristics. Under this circumstance, the locked-in reinvestment concept for the zero-coupon bond loses much of its meaning. It is only valid when the zero-coupon bond is held to maturity.

Chapter 12

CONVERTIBLE SECURITIES AND WARRANTS

An investment in convertible securities or warrants offers the market participant special opportunities to meet investment objectives. For conservative
investors, convertible securities can offer regular income and potential downside protection against falling stock prices. Convertibles also offer capital gains
opportunities for an investor desiring the appreciation potential of an equity
investment. Warrants are more speculative securities and offer the chance for
leveraged returns.

These securities have been used as financing alternatives for corporations
in periods of high interest rates or tight money. Also, convertibles have been
utilized as a medium of exchange for acquiring other companies' stock in
mergers and acquisitions. Convertibles and warrants have advantages to the
corporation and to the owner of the security. It is important to realize as we go
through this chapter that what is an advantage to the corporation is often a
disadvantage to the investor, and vise versa. These securities involve trade-offs
between the buyer and the corporation that are taken into consideration in the
pricing of each security.

CONVERTIBLE SECURITIES

A convertible security is a bond or share of preferred stock that can be converted into common stock at the option of the holder. Thus, the owner has a
fixed-income security that can be transferred to common stock if and when the
affairs of the firm indicate that such a conversion is desirable. For purposes of
our discussion, we will use a Tandy Corporation 6½ percent convertible bond
(debenture) rated Aa by Moody's.

While this bond was called for redemption on September 10, 1980, it still
serves as one of the best examples of the benefits and perils of owning convertible bonds. In general, the best time to buy convertible bonds is when interest
rates are high (bond prices are depressed) and when stock prices are relatively
low. Purchase at times like these increases the probability of a successful
investment because rising stock prices and falling interest rates both exert
upward pressure on the price of a convertible security. This will become more
apparent as we proceed through the chapter.

CONVERSION PRICE AND CONVERSION RATIO

The following quote from the footnotes to Tandy's 1979 Annual Report indicates the kind of information available to the bond- or stockholder.

> On October 31, 1978, the Company issued $100,000,000 of 6½ percent con-
> vertible subordinated debentures due 2003. These debentures are convertible at
> the option of the holder into common stock of the Company at $29 per share,
> unless previously redeemed. The debentures may be redeemed, at the Compa-
> ny's option, at any time in whole or in part on not less than 30 nor more than 60
> days notice at 106.50 percent of their principal amount on or before December
> 31, 1979. The redemption price declines annually to 100.00 in 1998. Mandatory
> sinking fund payments are required, beginning in 1989, sufficient to redeem on
> December 31 of each year $5,000,000 principal amount of debentures at par.

Most of the terms contained in the quote are simply a review of your knowledge on bonds. However, one question is not answered directly. How many shares of common stock are you entitled to receive upon conversion? Notice that the debentures are convertible at $29 per share. This is called the *conversion price*. The face value ($1,000) or par value never changes (the market price does), so by dividing the face value by the conversion price, we get the number of shares received upon conversion of one $1,000 bond. This is called the *conversion ratio*.

$$\frac{\text{Face value}}{\text{Conversion price}} = \text{Conversion ratio} \qquad (12\text{--}1)$$

For the Tandy convertible bond, an investor would receive 34.4827 shares for each bond.

$$\frac{\$1000 \text{ (face value)}}{\$29/\text{share (conversion price)}} = \frac{34.4827 \text{ shares}}{\text{(conversion ratio)}}$$

Value of the Convertible Bond

Let us follow the October 31, 1978, issue of Tandy's $6\frac{1}{2}$ percent convertible bond through conversion on September 10, 1980. The bond was originally sold at $1,000, and the common stock price on the day of this offering closed at $23\frac{1}{8}$ on the New York Stock Exchange. If the bondholder converted the bond into 34.48 shares of common stock, what would be the market value of the common stock received? We can find this by multiplying the conversion ratio by the market price per share of the common stock, and we get a value of $797.35.

Conversion ratio × Common stock price = Conversion value (12–2)
  34.48 shares × $23.125 = $797.35 (round to $797)

This value is called the *conversion value* and represents the value of the underlying shares of common stock each bond represents.

The convertible bond also has what is called a *pure bond value*. This represents its value as a straight bond (nonconvertible). In the case of Tandy Corporation there was also a straight debenture outstanding, carrying a coupon rate of 10 percent and a market price of $960. Based on this information, the yield to maturity on a nonconvertible Tandy bond would be 10.45 percent at the time the convertible bond was issued. If the $6\frac{1}{2}$ percent Tandy bond were valued as a straight debenture at this 10.45 percent yield to maturity, it would have a pure bond value of $654.[1] This is considered the floor price or minimum value of the bond. The conversion value and the pure bond value can be seen in Figure 12–1, which depicts the Tandy convertible bond. As a

---

[1] Using present value procedures from Chapter 10, the interest payment of $65 per year for 25 years would have a present value at 10.45 percent of $570.17, and the principal of $1,000 would have a present value of 83.34 for a total value of $653.51. We round to $654.

FIGURE 12–1   Tandy Convertible Bond on Day of Issue, October 31, 1978

side point, the reader should be aware that it is possible for the pure bond value to change if interest rates in the market change. This point, of course, is not reflected in Figure 12–1.

Bond Price and Premiums

You may wonder how a company can originally sell a bond for $1,000 when the conversion value is $797 and the pure bond value is $654. Let's examine these values. The difference between the bond's market price ($1,000) and the conversion value ($797) is a premium of $203; it is usually expressed as a percentage of the conversion value and thus is called the *conversion premium.* In this case, the conversion premium at issue was 25.47 percent.

$$\text{Conversion premium} = \frac{\text{Market price of bond} - \text{Conversion value}}{\text{Conversion value}} \quad (12\text{--}3)$$

$$= \frac{\$1000 - \$797}{\$797} = \frac{\$203}{\$797}$$

$$= 25.47 \text{ percent}$$

The $203 premium indicates the extra amount paid for the 34.48 shares of stock. Remember, in essence you paid $29 per share for 34.48 shares by purchasing the bond, but you could have had the same number of shares purchased on the NYSE for 23⅛.

    There are several reasons why people pay the conversion premium. In the case of Tandy's bond, the premium is somewhat larger than the usual 15 to

20 percent. First, Tandy common stock pays no dividend, while the bond pays $65 per year in interest. If the bondholder owns the bond for a little over three years, he recovers almost all the premium through the $65 yearly differential between dividend and interest income. Many companies do pay dividends on their common stock, and an analysis of interest income versus dividend income is always important in comparing a stock purchase to a convertible bond purchase.

Additionally, the bond price will rise as the stock price rises because of the convertible feature, but there is a downside limit if the stock should decline in price. This downside limit is established by the pure bond value, which in this case is $654. This downside protection is further justification for the conversion premium. One way to compute this downside protection is to calculate the difference between the market price of the bond and the pure bond value as a percentage of the market price.

$$\text{Downside risk} = \frac{\text{Market price of bond} - \text{Pure bond value}}{\text{Market price of bond}} \qquad (12-4)$$

$$= \frac{\$1000 - \$654}{\$1000} = \frac{\$346}{\$1000}$$

$$= 34.6 \text{ percent}$$

In the case of Tandy, there is a downside limit of 34.6 percent. This is the maximum percentage the bond will decline in value if the stock price falls. One important warning is necessary—the pure bond value is sensitive to market interest rates. As competitively rated Aa bond interest rates rise, the pure bond value will decline. Therefore, downside risk can vary with changing interest rates.

The conversion premium is also affected by several other variables. The more volatile the stock price as measured by beta or standard deviation of returns, the higher the conversion premium. This occurs because the potential for capital gains is larger than on less volatile stocks. The longer the term to maturity, the higher the premium—because there is a greater chance that the stock price could rise, making the bond more valuable.

Figure 12–2 presents a graph of the Tandy convertible bond and depicts the conversion premium in Panel (a) and the downside risk in Panel (b). Point P in both panels represents the parity point where the conversion value equals the pure bond value. Notice that the market price follows the conversion value to the right of point P and is more influenced by the pure bond value to the left of point P. As the common stock price rises, the conversion value rises accordingly, and the bond market price also rises. Furthermore, the conversion premium shrinks and the downside risk increases, which gives the bondholder less downside protection should the stock decline. As the stock declines, the conversion value falls and the conversion premium increases, but the downside risk declines as the pure bond value acts as a "floor value."

Let us track the Tandy bond from issue to conversion. As previously mentioned, Tandy Corporation also had a debenture (nonconvertible) out-

FIGURE 12–2   Tandy Convertible Bond—6½ Percent, 2003 Maturity (convertible into 34.4827 shares of common stock as of October 31, 1978)

standing with a 10 percent coupon. The debenture maintained a relatively stable price, and the yield to maturity hovered around 10.45 percent during the 22 months the convertible bond was outstanding. Given that the convertible bond would have approximately the same yield to maturity as the debenture, we assume that the pure bond value of the convertible bond stayed the same in all three panels in Figure 12–3. In Panel (a) we see the original information on the convertible issue. Approximately seven months later, as

FIGURE 12–3   Tandy 6½ Convertible Bond Closing Prices

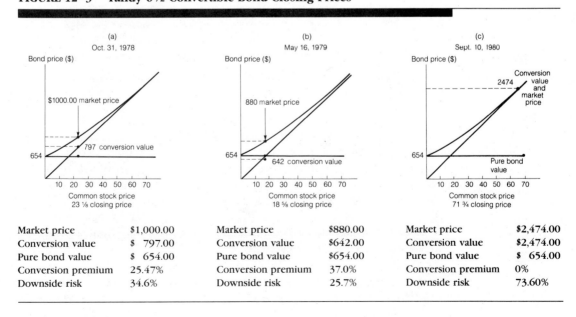

	(a) Oct. 31, 1978	(b) May 16, 1979	(c) Sept. 10, 1980
Market price	$1,000.00	$880.00	$2,474.00
Conversion value	$ 797.00	$642.00	$2,474.00
Pure bond value	$ 654.00	$654.00	$ 654.00
Conversion premium	25.47%	37.0%	0%
Downside risk	34.6%	25.7%	73.60%

shown in Panel (b), Tandy common stock had declined to 18⅝ and the bond to $880, creating a conversion value of $642 and a conversion premium of 37 percent. The downside risk had declined from 34.6 percent on October 31, 1978, to 25.7 percent by May 16, 1979. In retrospect, this would have been a good price at which to buy the bond. By September 10, 1980, we see in Panel (c) that the stock skyrocketed to 71¾ and the bond had a conversion value of $2,474. This was exactly equal to the market price, as there was no conversion premium. On this date, the Tandy Corporation also called the bond at $1,061.60. Thus, the investor could allow the bond to be redeemed at a mere $1,061.60 or convert it into common shares worth $2,474.[2]

Comparison to Common Stock

Would you have been better off putting $1,000 in Tandy stock on October 31, 1978, or $1,000 into the convertible bond? One thousand dollars in Tandy stock at 23⅛ would have purchased 43.24 shares, while $1,000 invested in the bond got the investor 34.48 shares. On the day of redemption (September 10, 1980), a stock investment would have been worth $3,103 and the convertible bond, $2,474 plus $128 in interest over the life of the issue, or $2,602. The common stock investor would have been better off, but if the stock had gone down sharply, then the convertible with its floor value would have been the better investment. Table 12–1 shows the comparison between a stock investment and a convertible bond investment.

TABLE 12–1   Comparative Tandy Corporation Investments

	Amount invested, October 31, 1978	Shares	Stock prices, September 10, 1980	Ending value	Total dividends	Total interest	Total value
Stock	$1,000	43.24	71¾	$3,103	$0	—	$3,103
Convertible bond	1,000	34.48	71¾	2,472	—	$128	2,602

Actually, we have picked one of the more successful convertible bond offerings in recent years. If the convertible bondholder had taken common shares on the call date, these 34.48 shares would have increased to 137.93 shares by June 1981, through several 2-for-1 stock splits. During 1983 Tandy common stock reached $64.50 per share, which would have created a total value of $8,896.00 on the original $1,000 investment. However, by July of 1984 the shares fell to $25.25 ($3,482), which shows that timing is important. The danger in using such a good example is that you may think convertible bonds are always a good investment.

---

[2] As the third alternative, the investor might immediately sell the bonds and allow another investor to convert.

Table 12—2 is a page from the Shearson/American Express January 1984 issue of *Selected Convertibles*. A glance down the fourth column of the top portion of the table for bond prices will point out that many bonds were above $1,000.00 (remember that bond prices are quoted in percentages of par value). Examples include American General, Bank of New York, and Barnett Banks. Notice that the conversion premiums (seventh column) for these bonds are quite low, which would indicate that the stock price is close to the conversion price. However, several of the convertibles, such as Burnup & Sims, Digicon, Hughes Tool, Oak Industries, and Storage Technology have conversion premiums of 100 percent, which means that the bond price is twice the conversion value. This indicates that these bonds are selling based on their interest-paying ability rather than on the underlying stock price. Notice that most of the bonds and preferred stock listed in Table 12—2 have ratings below an S&P category of A. This is quite common for convertibles.

Disadvantages to Convertibles

It has been said that everything has a price, and purchasing convertible securities at the wrong price can eliminate one of its main advantages. For example, once convertible debentures begin going up in value, the downside protection becomes pretty meaningless. In the case of Tandy Corporation, in our earlier example, the floor price is at $654. If an investor were to pay $1,400 for the convertible bond, he or she would be exposed to $746 in potential losses (hardly adequate protection for a true risk averter). Also, don't forget if interest rates in the market rise, the floor price, or pure bond value, could fall, thus creating greater downside risk.

Another drawback with convertible bonds is that the purchaser is invariably asked to accept below-market rates on the debt instrument. The interest rate on convertibles is generally one third below that for instruments in a similar risk class (e.g., 8 percent instead of 12 percent). In the sophisticated environment of the bond and stock markets, one seldom gets an additional benefit without having to suffer a corresponding disadvantage.

The student will also recall that the purchaser of a convertible bond pays a premium over the conversion value. For example, if a $1,000 bond were convertible into 20 shares of common at $45 per share, a $100 conversion premium would be involved initially. If the same $1,000 were invested directly in common stock at $45 per share, 22.2 shares could be purchased. If the shares go up in value, we have 2.2 more shares on which to garner a profit.

From the institutional investor's standpoint many convertible securities lack liquidity because of small trading volume or even the small amount of convertibles issued by one company. The institutions tend to stick with convertible issues of $100 million or more when they can be found.

When to Convert into Common Stock

Convertible securities generally have a call provision, such as the Tandy bond had (see earlier description), which gives the corporation the option of re-

TABLE 12–2

Selected Convertible Bonds–January 1984

Issue	Coupon	Maturity	S&P Rating	Approx. Price	Current Yield	Conversion $ PX/#Shs.	Conv. Prem.	Yield Advan. Over Common	Call Price	Quotron Symbol
Amer General	11%	2/ 8/07	A +	133	8.2%	$18.3/54.6	6.0%	4.7%	110.0	AGW.F
American Medical Int'l*	8¼	4/ 1/08	A –	88	9.4	40.0/25.0	47	7.4	107.4	AMV.F
Avnet*	8	10/ 1/13	A +	111	7.2	52.0/19.2	25	6.1	106.4	AVI.F
Bank of New York	12	12/ 1/06	A	132	10.0	24.6/40.6	1	4.4	109.6	BKQ.F
Barnett Banks†	12¼	12/15/06	A –	140	8.8	31.0/32.3	11	5.7	108.6	BBF.F
Big Three Ind.	8½	4/15/06	A	82	10.4	43.5/23.0	61	6.7	106.7	BIH.F
Boeing Co.*	8⅞	6/15/06	A	123	7.2	42.2/23.7	18	4.0	106.5	BAH.F
Burnup & Sims	12	11/15/01	B +	80	15.0	19.3/52.0	100	14.0	107.2	—
Comserv (OTC)†† †	11	7/ 1/02	CCC	65	16.9	14.5/69.0	55	16.9	108.8	—
Digicon†	10½	11/15/01	B	67	15.7	32.8/30.5	100	15.7	107.4	DGCA.A
Dreyfus Corp.	7⅜	6/1/08	BBB +	83	8.9	37.0/27.0	28	6.8	105.9	DRY.F
Eastman Kodak*	8¼	12/15/07	AAA	101	8.2	102.3/9.8	35	4.3	107.4	EKA.F
General Cinema (RJR)*	10	3/15/08	BBB	112	8.9	62.8/15.9	14	3.4	107.0	GCN.F
Graphic Scanning	10	12/ 1/01	B	82	12.2	10.6/94.1	33	12.2	107.0	—
Great Western Fincl.*	8⅞	12/01/07	BBB –	99	9.0	30.5/32.8	37	5.0	107.7	GWF.F
GTE Corp.*	10½	11/ 1/07	BBB	117	8.9	46.0/21.7	21	2.0	107.6	GTV.F
Hughes Tool*	9½	12/15/06	A	86	11.0	47.2/21.2	100	7.0	107.8	HTB.F
InterNorth(MOB)*	10½	6/ 1/08	BBB +	101	10.4	40.0/25.0	39	3.4	100.0	INZ.F
LIN Broadcasting (OTC)††	8¾	12/15/07	BB –	122	7.2	20.3/49.4	11	7.2	107.9	LINB.G
M/A Com*	9¼	5/15/06	BB +	92	10.1	36.5/27.4	67	9.0	107.4	MAI.F
Mapco*	10	5/15/05	BBB –	88	11.4	45.7/21.9	63	7.3	107.3	MDX.F
MCI Comm.†† †	7¾	3/15/03	BB +	82	9.5	26.1/38.4	46	9.5	106.2	MCICG
Oak Industries*	10½	2/15/02	B	66	15.9	33.7/29.7	100	15.9	108.4	OAB.F
Pacific Scientific	7¾	6/15/03	B	75	10.3	38.0/26.3	60	8.0	106.2	PSX.F
PNC Financial (OTC) †† †	8¼	5/15/08	AA	106	7.8	46.0/21.7	17	2.9	106.6	—
Pogo Producing*	8	12/31/05	BB –	74	10.8	39.5/25.3	40	7.9	106.8	PPP.F
Quaker State	8⅞	3/15/08	BBB +	100	8.9	20.8/48.2	19	4.3	107.1	KSG.F
Research Cottrell	10½	10/31/06	BBB –	106	9.9	17.0/58.8	19	7.8	108.9	RCT.F
Seagram Co.*	8¼	6/ 1/08	A	107	7.7	37.8/26.5	11	5.8	106.6	SEG.F
Storage Technology*	9	5/15/01	BBB –	72	12.5	36.8/27.2	100	12.5	106.3	STV.F
Storer Communications*	8½	12/31/05	BB –	108	7.9	40.0/25.0	14	6.8	107.2	SCII.F
Sun Co. (BDX)	10¾	4/ 1/06	AA –	97	11.1	59.9/16.7	56	8.0	109.1	SUU.F
Texas Industries*	9	1/15/08	B +	99	9.1	43.1/23.2	22	6.8	107.2	TXP.F
Wang Lab*	7¾	6/ 1/08	BBB	97	8.0	52.2/19.2	41	7.7	106.7	WANI.A

Selected Convertible Preferred Stocks–January 1984

Issue	Dividend	S&P Rating	Approx. Price	Current Yield	Conversion Ratio	Conversion Premium	Yield Advan. Over C/S	Call Price	Quotron Symbol	Ex-Div Schedule
Allied Corp*	6.74	BBB	64	10.5%	.786	45%	6.2%	57.0	ALD.PrC	JAJO
Anheuser Busch*	3.60	NR	49	7.4	.645	22	4.7	40.0	BUD.PrA	FMAN
Barnett Banks†	2.375	NR	42	5.7	1.042	2	2.6	25.0	BBF.PrA	MJSD
Castle & Cooke	2.50	NR	32	7.8	1.553	14	7.8	27.5	CKE.Pr	FMAN
Cigna*	2.75	NR	29	9.5	.422	52	3.9	27.1	CI.PrA	MJSD
City Investing*	2.875	BB –	25	11.5	.500	32	6.5	27.9	CNV.PrE	MJSD
Crown Zellerbach*	4.625	BB –	50	9.3	1.058	28	6.7	53.2	ZB.PrA	MJSD
Fruehauf	2.00	BB –	37	5.4	.758	6	4.5	27.0	FTR.Pr	JAJO
Georgia Pacific*	2.24	BBB +	35	6.4	1.00	45	4.0	39.0	GP.PrA	FMAN
LTV Corp*	3.06	BB –	30	10.2	1.3	25	8.8	28.1	LTV.PrB	FMAN
RCA Corp*	2.125	BB	28	7.6	.714	12	5.1	26.1	RCA.PrC	MJSD
Signal Co.*	4.125	A +	57	7.2	1.471	18	4.5	53.3	SGN.PrA	JAJO
UAL Inc.*	2.40	BB –	28	8.6	.585	29	8.6	26.1	UAL.PrB	FMAN
United Technologies*	2.55	A	33	7.7	.393	15	4.1	29.0	UTX.PrD	FMAN
Weyerhaeuser*	4.50	A	49	9.2	1.111	30	5.3	53.0	WY.PrA	FMAN

*Listed Options Available
†Shearson/American Express has an investment banking relationship.
††Shearson/American Express maintains an Over-the-Counter market in the underlying common stocks.

Special Note: The call provisions of convertible bonds and preferreds can be very complex. When in question, please call for complete details. The call price and date may not be complete as described in a summary guide.

deeming the bond at a specified price before maturity. The call price is usually at a premium over par value ($1,000) in the early years of callability, and it generally declines over time to par value. We know that as the price of the common stock goes up, the convertible security will rise along with the stock so that the investor has no incentive to convert his bonds into stock. However, the corporation may use the call privilege to force conversion before maturity. Companies usually force conversion when the conversion value is well above the call price, like the Tandy offer which forced conversion on September 10, 1980, when the conversion value was $2,474 and the call price was $1,061.60. Investors will take the shares rather than the call price since the shares are worth more. This enables the company to turn debt into equity on its balance sheet and makes new debt issues a better risk for future lenders because of higher interest coverage and a lower debt-to-equity ratio.

Corporations may also encourage voluntary conversion by using a step-up in the conversion price over time. When the bond is issued, the contract may specify the following conversion provisions.

	Conversion price	Conversion ratio
First five years	$40	25.0 shares
Next three years	45	22.2 shares
Next two years	50	20.0 shares
Next five years	55	18.2 shares

At the end of each time period, there is a strong inducement to convert rather than accept an adjustment to a higher conversion price and a lower conversion ratio. This is especially true if the bond's conversion value is the dominating influence on the market price of the bond. In the case where the conversion value is below the pure bond value and where the interest income is greater than the dividend income, an investor will most likely not be induced to convert through the step-up feature.

About the only other reason for voluntarily converting is if the dividend income received on the common stock is greater than the interest income on the bond. Even in this case, investors who are risk-averse may want to hold the bond because interest is guaranteed, whereas dividends may be reduced. As with most investment decisions, investors must consider their expectations of future corporate and market conditions. Hard and fast rules are difficult to find, and different investors may react according to their own risk aversion and objectives.

ADVANTAGES AND DISADVANTAGES TO THE ISSUING CORPORATION

Having established the fundamental characteristics of the convertible security from the investor viewpoint, let us now turn the coin over and examine the factors a corporate financial officer must consider in weighing the advisability of a convertible offer for the firm.

Not only has it been established that the interest rate paid on convertible issues is lower than that paid on a straight debt instrument, but also the convertible feature may be the only device for allowing smaller corporations access to the bond market. In this day of debt-ridden corporate balance sheets, investor acceptance of new debt may be contingent upon a special sweetener, such as the ability to convert to common stock.

Convertible debentures are also attractive to a corporation that feels its stock is currently undervalued. For example, assume a corporation's $1,000 bonds are convertible into 20 shares of common stock at a conversion price of $50. Also assume the company's common stock has a current price of $45, and new shares of stock might be sold at only $44.[3] Thus, the corporation will effectively receive $6 over current market price, assuming future conversion. Of course, one can also argue that if the firm had delayed the issuance of common stock or convertibles for a year or two, the stock might have gone up from $45 to $60 or $65, and new common stock might have been sold at this lofty price.

To translate this to overall numbers for the firm, if a corporation needs $10 million in funds and offers straight stock now at a new price of $44, it must issue 227,272 shares ($10 million/$44). With convertibles, the number of shares potentially issued is only 200,000 shares ($10 million/$50). Finally, if no stock or convertible bonds are issued now and the stock goes up to a level at which new shares can be offered at a price of $60, only 166,667 will be required ($10 million/$60).

Another matter of concern to the corporation is the accounting treatment accorded to convertibles. In the funny-money days of the 1960s conglomerate merger movement, corporate management often chose convertible securities over common stock because the convertibles had a nondilutive effect on earnings per share. As is indicated in the following section on reporting earnings for convertibles, the rules were changed in 1969, and this practice is no longer followed.

ACCOUNTING CONSIDERATIONS WITH CONVERTIBLES

Prior to 1969, the full impact of the conversion privilege as it applied to convertible securities, warrants (long-term options to buy stock), and other dilutive securities was not adequately reflected in reported earnings per share. Since all of these securities may generate additional common stock in the future, the potential effect of dilution should be considered. Let us examine the unadjusted (for conversion) financial statements of the XYZ Corporation in Table 12–3.

---

[3] There is always a bit of underpricing to ensure the success of a new offering.

TABLE 12–3   XYZ Corporation

1. Capital section of balance sheet
   Common stock (1 million shares at $10 par) $10,000,000
   4.5% convertible debentures (10,000 deben-
     tures of $1,000; convertible into 40 shares
     per bond, or a total of 400,000 shares)   10,000,000
   Retained earnings   20,000,000
   Net worth $40,000,000

2. Condensed income statement
   Earnings before interest and taxes $ 2,450,000
   Interest (4.5% of $10 million of convertibles)   450,000
   Earnings before taxes   2,000,000
   Taxes (50%)   1,000,000
   Earnings after taxes $ 1,000,000

3. Earnings per share (unadjusted)

$$\frac{\text{Earnings after taxes}}{\text{Shares of common stock}} = \frac{\$1,000,000}{1,000,000} = \$1$$

An analyst would hardly be satisfied in accepting the unadjusted earnings per share figure of $1 for the XYZ Corporation. In computing earnings per share, we have not accounted for the 400,000 additional shares of common stock that could be created by converting the bonds. How then do we make this full disclosure? According to Accounting Principles Board *Opinion No. 15,* issued by the American Institute of Certified Public Accountants in 1969, we need to compute earnings per share using two different methods when there is potential dilution of a material nature.

1. Primary earnings per share

$$= \frac{\text{Adjusted earnings after taxes}}{\text{Shares outstanding} + \text{Common stock equivalents}} \qquad (12\text{–}5)$$

Common stock equivalents include warrants, other options, and any convertible securities that paid less than two thirds of the going interest rate at time of issue.[4]

2. Fully diluted earnings per share

$$= \frac{\text{Adjusted earnings after taxes}}{\begin{array}{c}\text{Shares outstanding} + \text{Common stock equivalents} \\ + \text{All convertibles regardless of the interest rate}\end{array}} \qquad (12\text{–}6)$$

The intent in computing both primary and fully diluted earnings per share is to consider the effect of potential dilution. Common stock equivalents

---

[4] The going interest rate was initially defined as the prime interest rate in Accounting Principles Board *Opinion No. 15* (1969). In 1982 the Financial Accounting Standards Board defined the going interest rate as the average Aa bond yield at the time of issue.

represent those securities that are capable of generating new shares of common stock in the future. Note that convertible securities may or may not be required in computing primary earnings per share depending on rates, but they must be included in computing fully diluted earnings per share.

In the case of the XYZ Corporation in Table 12–3 the convertibles pay 4.5 percent interest. We assume that the going interest rate was 9 percent at the time they were issued, so they are considered as common stock equivalents and are included in both primary and fully diluted earnings per share.

We get new earnings per share for the XYZ Corporation by assuming that 400,000 new shares will be created from potential conversion, while at the same time allowing for the reduction in interest payments that would take place as a result of the conversion of the debt to common stock. Since beforetax interest payments on the convertibles are $450,000, the aftertax interest cost ($225,000) will be saved and can be added back to income. Making the appropriate adjustments to the numerator and denominator, we show adjusted earnings per share.

$$\frac{\text{Primary earnings}}{\text{per share}^5} = \frac{\text{Adjusted earnings after taxes}}{\text{Shares outstanding} + \text{Common stock equivalents}}$$

$$= \frac{\overset{\text{Reported}}{\underset{\text{earnings}}{\$1,000,000}} + \overset{\text{Interest}}{\underset{\text{savings}}{\$225,000}}}{1,000,000 + 400,000} = \frac{\$1,225,000}{1,400,000} = \$.875$$

We see a 12½-cent reduction from the earnings per share figure of $1 in Table 12–4. The new figure is the value that a sophisticated security analyst would utilize.

SPECULATING THROUGH WARRANTS

A warrant is an option to buy a stated number of shares of stock at a specified price over a given time period. For example, Eastern Airlines has a number of issues of warrants outstanding. One warrant due in the late 1980s, allows the holder to buy one share of common stock at $10 per share. Eastern has been struggling to stay alive in the airline competition and the stock price as of July 23, 1984, was $4.125. If Eastern Airlines can return to profitability, the common stock could rise above $10 per share and the warrants could become quite valuable. If the stock does not eventually rise to $10 per share, it is possible that Eastern Airlines could extend the expiration date of the warrant. One advantage of the warrants to the company is that when exercised, they bring in cash for new shares of common stock. A firm like Eastern might want to increase equity under its current heavy debt load.

Warrants are usually issued as a sweetener to a bond offering, and they may enable the firm to issue debt when this would not be feasible otherwise.

---

[5] Same as fully diluted in this instance.

TABLE 12-4   Selected Warrants as of July 23, 1984

(1) Firm, warrant, listing stock listings	(2) Warrant price	(3) Per share stock price	(4) Per share option price	(5) Intrinsic value (3) − (4)	(6) Premium (2) − (5)	(7) Percent stock must rise to break even	(8) Number of shares per warrant	(9) Due date
American General, NY, NY	6.25	20.125	24.25	−4.125	10.375	52%	1.00	1/4/89
Atlas Corp., AM, NY	3.75	15.25	31.25	−16.00	19.75	130%	1.00	Perpetual
Computers Horizons, OTL, OTL	1.75	6.50	15.25	−4.375*	6.125	168%	.5	9/20/88
Eastern Airlines, NY, NY	1.50	4.125	10.00	−5.875	7.375	179%	1.00	6/1/87
Fuqua Industries, OTL, NY	30.00	25.00	11.75	30.34*	−.34	−1%	2.29	6/30/88
International Harvester, NY, NY	4.75	6.50	5.00	1.50	3.25	50%	1.00	12/15/93
Kidde, AM, NY	3.375	29.125	40.00	−10.875	14.25	49%	1.00	11/15/87

* For these two companies, we use column (3) − column (4) times the value in column (8).

AM = American Stock Exchange, NY = New York Stock Exchange, OTL = Over-the-Counter. The first abbreviation indicates where the warrant trades, and the second abbreviation indicates where the common stock trades.

The warrants allow the bond issue to carry a lower coupon rate and are usually detachable from the bond after the issue date. After being separated from the bond, warrants have their own market price and are primarily traded on the American Stock Exchange or over-the-counter, with a few issues traded on the New York Stock Exchange. After the warrants are exercised, the initial debt with which they were sold remains in existence.

The financial company Bache Group (Bache Halsey Stuart Shields), which is known for its retail brokerage business, had a bond offering October 30, 1980. They offered 35,000 units of $1,000 debentures due in the year 2000 with a coupon interest rate of 14 percent. To each bond, 30 warrants were attached. Each warrant allowed the holder to buy one share of stock at $18.50 until November 1, 1985. At the time of issue, the warrant had no true value since the common stock was selling below $18.50. During 1981, however, the stock went up as several merger offers were made for retail brokerage companies.[6] On May 29, 1981, Bache common stock was selling at $31\frac{1}{2}$, and each warrant traded at $13\frac{5}{8}$. The 30 warrants received with each bond were now worth $408.75 and provided the sweetener every bondholder had hoped for.

Because a warrant is dependent on the market movement of the underlying common stock and has no "security value" as such, it is highly speculative in nature. If the common stock of the firm is volatile, the value of the warrants may change dramatically.

Tri-Continental Corporation warrants went from $\frac{1}{32}$ to $75\frac{3}{4}$ between 1942 and 1969, while United Airlines warrants moved from $4\frac{1}{2}$ to 126 in the 1962–66 time span. Of course, this is not a one-way street, as holders of LTV warrants will attest when they saw their holdings dip from 83 to $2\frac{1}{4}$ in the 1968–70 bear market.

Valuation of Warrants

Because the value of a warrant is closely tied to the underlying stock price, we can develop a formula for the minimum or intrinsic value of a warrant.

$$I = (M - OP) \times N \qquad\qquad (12\text{–}7)$$

where:

I = The intrinsic or minimum value of the warrant.
M = The market value of the common stock.
OP = The option or exercise price of the warrant.
N = The number of shares each warrant entitles holder to purchase.

Assume that the common stock of the Graham Corporation is $25 per share, and each warrant carries an option to purchase one share at $20 over the next 10 years. Using Formula (12–7) the minimum value is $5. [($25 – $20) × 1]. Since the warrant has 10 more years to run and is an effective vehicle for speculative trading, it may well trade for over $5. If the warrant

---

[6] Bache was subsequently acquired by Prudential Insurance Company.

were selling for $9, we would say that it had an intrinsic or formula value of $5 and a premium of $4.

Even if the stock were trading at less than $20 (the option price on the warrant), the warrant might still have some value in the market. Speculators might purchase the warrant in the hope that the common stock value would increase sufficiently in the future to make the option provision valuable. If the common stock were selling for $15 per share, thus giving the warrant a negative intrinsic value of $5, the warrant might still command a value of $1 or $2 in anticipation of increased common stock value. In Table 12–4 on page 359, we see warrant prices in column (2) and intrinsic values in column (5) for a number of warrants. In column (6) we see the premium (warrant price minus intrinsic value).

In several cases the intrinsic value is negative according to the formula but in practice when the intrinsic value is negative, we generally say it is zero or has no value. Since the owner of the warrant has the option to purchase stock at a set price, the only money the warrant holder can lose is the purchase price of the warrant. Therefore, a negative intrinsic value is meaningless except for determining the premium in column (6) and the break-even percentage in column (7).

As an example of an extreme case, Atlas Corporation's common stock was trading $16.00 below the exercise price on the warrant, and yet the warrant still traded for $3.75. Atlas warrants are perpetual, however, and even though the stock had to increase 130 percent for a warrant purchaser to break even, there is no expiration date to worry about. Actually the Eastern Airlines warrant is even more speculative than Atlas, which can be seen by its high break-even percentage and short time to expiration.

The typical relationship between the market price and the intrinsic value of a warrant is depicted in Figure 12–4. We assume the warrant entitles the holder to purchase one new share of common stock at $20.

Although the intrinsic value of the warrant is theoretically negative at a common stock price between 0 and $20, the warrant still carries some value in the market. Also, observe that the difference between the market price of the warrant and its intrinsic value is diminished at the upper ranges of value. Two reasons may be offered for the declining premium.

First, the speculator loses the ability to use leverage to generate high returns as the price of the stock goes up. When the price of the stock is relatively low, say, $25, and the warrant is in the $5 to $10 range, a 10-point movement in the stock could mean a 200 percent gain in the value of the warrant, as indicated in Part (A) of Table 12–5. At the upper levels of stock value, much of this leverage is lost, as indicated in Part (B) of the same table. At a stock value of $50 and a warrant value of approximately $30, a 10-point movement in the stock would produce only a 33 percent gain in the warrant.

Another reason why speculators pay a very low premium at higher stock prices is that there is less downside protection. A warrant selling at $30 when the stock price is $50 is more vulnerable to downside movement than is a $5 to $10 warrant when the stock is in the 20s.

FIGURE 12–4   Market Price Relationships for a Warrant

Premiums are also influenced by the same factors that affect convertible bond premiums. More volatile common stocks will have greater potential to create short-run profits for warrant speculators, so the higher the price volatility the greater the premium. Also, the longer the option has before expiration, the higher the premium will be. This "time premium" is worth more the longer the common stock has to reach and surpass the option price of the warrant.

Use of Warrants by Corporations

As previously indicated, warrants may allow for the issuance of debt under difficult circumstances. While a straight debt issue may not be acceptable or may be accepted only at extremely high rates, the same security may be well received because detachable warrants are included. Warrants may also be included as an add-on in a merger or acquisition agreement. A firm might offer $20 million in cash plus 10,000 warrants in exchange for all the outstanding shares of the acquisition candidate.

The use of warrants has traditionally been associated with such aggressive, "high-flying" firms as real estate investment trusts, airlines, and conglomerates. However, in 1970, American Telephone and Telegraph came out with a $1.57 billion debt offering sweetened by the use of warrants.

As a financing device for creating new common stock, warrants may not be as desirable as convertible securities. A corporation with convertible debentures outstanding may force the conversion of debt to common stock through a call, while no similar device is available to the firm with warrants.

TABLE 12–5   Leverage in Valuing Warrants

(A)	(B)
Stock price, $25; warrant price, $5* + 10-point movement in stock price. New warrant price, $15 (10-point gain)	Stock price, $50; warrant price, $30 + 10-point movement in stock price. New warrant price, $40 (10-point gain)
$$\text{Percentage gain in warrant} = \frac{\$10}{\$5} \times 100 = 200\%$$	$$\text{Percentage gain in warrant} = \frac{\$10}{\$30} \times 100 = 33\%$$

* The warrant price would, of course, be greater than $5 because of a premium. Nevertheless, we use $5 for ease of computation.

The only possible inducement might be a step-up in the option price—whereby the warrant holder may pay a progressively higher option price if he does not exercise by a given date.

The capital structure of the firm after the exercise of a warrant is somewhat different from that created after the conversion of a debenture. In the case of a warrant, the original debt outstanding remains in existence after the detachable warrant is exercised, whereas the conversion of a debenture extinguishes the former debt obligation.[7]

ACCOUNTING CONSIDERATIONS WITH WARRANTS

As with convertible securities, the potential dilutive effect of warrants must be considered. Warrants are generally included in computing both primary and fully diluted earnings per share.[8] The accountant must compute the number of new shares that could be created by the exercise of all warrants, with the provision that the total can be reduced by the assumed use of the cash proceeds to purchase a partially offsetting amount of shares at the market price. Assume that warrants to purchase 10,000 shares at $20 are outstanding and that the current price of the stock is $50. We show the following:

1. New shares created   10,000
2. Reduction of shares from cash proceeds (computed below)   4,000

    Cash proceeds—10,000 shares at $20 = $200,000
    Current price of stock—$50
    Assumed reduction in shares outstanding from cash proceeds =
      $200,000/$50 = 4,000
3. Assumed net increase in shares from exercise of warrants
    (10,000 − 4,000)   6,000

---

[7] It should be pointed out that a number of later financing devices can blur this distinction. See Jerry Miller, "Accounting for Warrants and Convertible Bonds," *Management Accounting,* January 1973, pp. 36–38.

[8] Under most circumstances, if the market price is below the option price, dilution need not be considered (APB *Opinion No. 15*).

In computing earnings per share, we will add 6,000 shares to the denominator with no adjustment to the numerator, which will lower earnings per share. If earnings per share had previously been $1 based on $100,000 in earnings and 100,000 shares outstanding, EPS would not be reduced to $.943.

$$\frac{\text{Earnings}}{\text{Shares}} \frac{\$100,000}{106,000} = \$.943$$

With warrants included in computing both primary and fully diluted earnings per share, their impact on reported earnings is important from both the investor and corporate viewpoints.

Chapter 13

PUT AND CALL OPTIONS

The word *option* has many different meanings, but most of them include the ability or right to choose a certain alternative. One definition provided by *Webster's* is "the right, acquired for a consideration, to buy or sell something at a fixed price within a specified period of time." This definition is very general and applies to puts, calls, warrants, real estate options, or any other contracts entered into between two parties where a choice of action or decision can be put off for a limited time at a cost. The person acquiring the option pays an agreed-upon sum to the person providing the option. For example, someone may want to buy your house for its sale price of $75,000. The buyer does not have the money but will give you $2,000 in cash if you give him the right to buy the house for the next 60 days at $75,000. If you accept, you have given the buyer an option and have agreed not to sell the house to anyone else for the next 60 days. If the buyer raises $75,000 within the 60-day limit, he may buy the house, giving you the $75,000. Perhaps he finds the $75,000 but also finds another house he likes better for $72,000. He will not buy your house, but you have $2,000 and must now find someone else to buy your house. By selling the option, you tied up the sale of your house for 60 days, and if the option is unexercised, you have foregone an opportunity to sell the house to someone else.

Puts and calls are options on common stock. A put is an option to sell 100 shares of common stock at a specified price for a given period of time. Calls are the opposite of puts and allow the owner the right to buy 100 shares of common stock from the option seller (writer). Contracts on listed puts and calls have been standardized at date of issue for periods of three, six, and nine months, although as these contracts approach expiration, they may be purchased with a much shorter life.

OPTIONS MARKETS

Before the days of options trading on exchanges, puts and calls were traded over-the-counter by the Put and Call Dealers Association. These dealers would buy and sell puts and calls for their own accounts for stocks traded on the New York Stock Exchange and then try to find an investor, hedger, or speculator to take the other side of the option. For example, if you owned 1,000 shares of General Motors and you wanted to write a call option giving the buyer the right to buy 1,000 shares of General Motors at $70 per share for six months, the dealer might buy the calls and look for someone who would be willing to buy them.

There were several disadvantages to this system. Dealers had to have contact with the buyers and sellers, and the financial stability of the option writer had to be endorsed (guaranteed) by a brokerage house. The option writer either had to keep the shares on deposit with the brokerage firm or put up a cash margin. Options in the same stock could exist in the market at various strike prices (price at which the option could be exercised) and scattered expiration dates. This meant that when an option buyer wanted to exercise or terminate the contract before expiration, he or she would have to deal directly with the option writer. This does not make for an efficient, liquid market. Unlisted options also reduced the striking price of a call by any dividends paid during the option period, which did not benefit the writer of the call.

Listed Options Exchanges

The Chicago Board Options Exchange was established in 1973 as the first exchange for call options. The market response was overwhelming, and within three years, the American, Pacific, and Philadelphia exchanges were also trading call options. By 1984, the list of stocks with available option contracts increased dramatically from the original list of 20 companies to 390 companies, and puts as well as calls were traded for many companies. Appendix 13A at the end of the chapter presents a comprehensive list of available options as well as the principal trading exchange for the option. On many days the number of underlying shares of stock represented by options traded on the option exchanges is greater than the number of actual shares traded on the NYSE in those same issues.

Table 13–1, from the *Chicago Board Option Exchange's 1983 Fact Book,* shows the growth in options trading since 1973. Besides the Chicago Board Options Exchange (CBOE), the American Exchange (AMEX), the Philadelphia Exchange (PHLX), and the Pacific Coast Exchange (PSE) all continue to trade options. The New York Stock Exchange began trading options in 1985.

The options market has recently been expanded to include options not only on individual stocks, but options on stock market indexes as well. Thus, by the mid-1980s one could buy an option to purchase the equivalent of the Standard & Poor's 500 Stock Index or other indexes. This, of course, is different from the traditional option to purchase options on individual stocks such as General Motors. This chapter will concentrate on options on individual stocks, while Chapter 16 will cover stock index options and futures.

There are several reasons why the listed options markets are so desirable compared to the previous method of over-the-counter trading for options. The contract period was standardized with three-, six-, and nine-month expiration dates on three calendar cycles.

Cycle 1: January/April/July/October.
Cycle 2: February/May/August/November.
Cycle 3: March/June/September/December.

As one month's expiration date comes up, another month in the cycle is added. For example, as the January option expires, the October nine-month option is added, and the cycle is continued. The use of three cycles spreads out the expiration dates for the options so that not all contracts come due on the same day. Each contract expires at 11:59 P.M. Eastern time on the Saturday immediately following the third Friday of the expiration month. For all practical purposes, any closing out of positions must be done on that last Friday while the markets are open.

The exercise price (striking price) is also standardized. This is the price at which the contract specifies for a buy or sell. For all stocks under $100 per

TABLE 13–1 Historical Stock Options Contract Volume on All Exchanges (for individual stocks)

Time period	CBOE	AMEX	PHLX	PSE	MSE*	Total	CBOE share of options contract volume	Reported NYSE volume (millions of shares)	Options volume in shares as % of NYSE volume CBOE	Options volume in shares as % of NYSE volume All options
1983	71,695,563	36,199,701	16,607,806	11,155,906	—	135,658,976	52.8	21,589.6	33.2	62.8
1982	75,721,605	38,766,996	13,466,652	9,309,563	—	137,264,816	55.2	16,458.0	46.0	83.4
1981	57,584,175	34,859,475	10,009,565	6,952,567	—	109,405,782	52.6	11,853.7	48.6	92.3
1980	52,916,921	29,048,323	7,758,101	5,486,590	1,518,611	96,728,546	54.7	11,352.3	46.6	85.2
1979	35,379,600	17,467,018	4,952,737	3,856,344	2,609,164	64,264,863	55.1	8,155.9	43.4	78.8
1978	34,277,350	14,380,959	3,270,378	3,289,968	2,012,363	57,231,018	59.9	7,205.1	47.6	79.4
1977	24,838,632	10,077,578	2,195,307	1,925,031	600,780	39,637,328	62.7	5,273.8	47.1	75.2
1976	21,498,027	9,035,767	1,274,702	550,194	15,237	32,373,927	66.4	5,360.1	40.1	60.4
1975	14,431,023	3,530,564	140,982	—	—	18,102,569	79.7	4,693.4	30.7	38.6
1974	5,682,907	—	—	—	—	5,682,907	100.0	3,517.7	16.2	16.2
1973	1,119,177	—	—	—	—	1,119,177	100.0	4,053.2	2.8	2.8

* The Midwest Stock Exchange options program was consolidated with the CBOE on June 2, 1980.

Source: *Chicago Board Options Exchange Fact Book* (Chicago: Chicago Board Options Exchange, 1983).

share, the striking price changes by $5 intervals, and for stocks selling over $100 per share, the strike price changes by $10 a share. As the underlying stocks change prices in the market, options with new striking prices are added. For example, a stock selling at $30 per share when the January option is added will have a striking price of $30, but if the stock gets to 32½ (half way to the next striking price), the exchange may add another option (to the class of options) with a $35 strike price.

An example of an actual call option is presented in Table 13–2 for Exxon. Note the different strike prices (35, 40, 45, 50) and expiration months (January, April, July). Exxon common stock is selling for 44¼. The values within the table, such as 9⅜ or 4⅜, reflect the price of the various option contracts. Much of this type of information will take on greater meaning as we go through the chapter.

TABLE 13–2   November 1, 1984, Exxon Calls

Stock price close Exxon	Strike price	Calls—last		
		January	April	July
44¼	35	9⅜	9⅝	Not traded
44¼	40	4⅜	4⅞	5
44¼	45	⅞	1⁹⁄₁₆	2
44¼	50	⅛	⁵⁄₁₆	Not traded

This standardization of expiration dates and strike prices creates more certainty when buying and selling options in a changing market and allows more efficient trading strategies because of better coordination between stock prices, strike prices, and expiration dates. Dividends no longer affect the option contract as they did in the unlisted market. Transactions occur at arm's length between buyer and seller without any matchmaking needed on the part of the broker. The ultimate result of these changes in the option market is a highly liquid, efficient market where speculators, hedgers, and arbitrageurs all operate together.

THE OPTIONS CLEARING CORPORATION

Much of the liquidity and ease of operation of the option exchanges is due to the role of the Options Clearing Corporation, which functions as the issuer of all options listed on the five exchanges—the CBOE, the AMEX, the Pacific Coast Exchange, the Philadelphia Exchange, and the NYSE. Investors who want to trade puts and calls need to have an approved account with a member brokerage firm; upon opening an account, they receive a prospectus from the Options Clearing Corporation detailing all aspects of option trading.

Options are bought and sold or written through a member broker the same as other securities. The exchanges allow special orders, such as limit, market, and stop orders, as well as orders used specifically in options trading, like spread orders and straddle orders. The order process originates with the broker and is transacted on the floor of the exchange. Remember that for every order there must be a buyer and seller (writer) so that the orders can be "matched." Once the orders are matched, they are filed with the Options Clearing Corporation, which then issues the necessary options or closes the position. There are four basic transactions handled:

Opening purchase transaction—A transaction in which an investor intends to become the holder of an option.

Opening sale transaction—A transaction in which an investor intends to become the writer of an option.

Closing purchase transaction—A transaction in which an investor who is obligated as a writer of an option intends to terminate his obligation as a writer. This is accomplished by "purchasing" an option in the same series as the option previously written. Such a transaction has the effect, upon acceptance by the Options Clearing Corporation, of canceling the investor's preexisting position as a writer.

Closing sale transaction—A transaction in which an investor who is the holder of an outstanding option intends to liquidate his position as a holder. This is accomplished by "selling" an option in the same series as the option previously purchased. Such a transaction has the effect, upon acceptance by the Options Clearing Corporation, of liquidating the investor's preexisting position as a holder of the option.

What occurs in a transaction is that holders and writers of options are not contractually linked together but are committed to the Options Clearing Corporation. Since there are no certificates issued for options, a customer must maintain a brokerage account as long as he or she holds an option position and must liquidate the option through the broker originating the transaction unless a brokerage transfer is completed before an ensuing transaction. If an option is traded on more than one exchange, it may be bought, sold, or closed out on either exchange and cleared through the Options Clearing Corporation. Basically, the aggregate obligation of the option holders is backed up by the aggregate obligation of the option writers. If holders choose to exercise their options, they must do so through the Clearing Corporation, which randomly selects a writer from all Clearing member accounts in the same option series.[1]

---

[1] Actually very few option holders choose to exercise their option and take possession of securities. Data for 1983 indicate that only 15.1 percent of all call options were exercised while only 6.9 percent of all put options were exercised. Assuming that the option holder does not want to exercise her option, she may choose to close her position on the open market through a closing sale transaction. An investor would do this whenever the value of the option after commissions is positive. During 1983, 63 percent of all call contracts were closed out (not necessarily at a profit) and 22 percent of call contracts expired worthless.

This would be true whether the holder chooses to exercise early or at expiration. Upon notice from the Options Clearing Corporation, a call writer must sell 100 shares of the underlying common stock at the exercise price, while the put writer must buy 100 shares from the holder exercising the put.

All option contracts are adjusted for stock splits, stock dividends, or other stock distributions. For example, a 2-for-1 stock split for a stock selling at 60, with options available at 70, 60, and 50 strike prices, would cause the stock to trade at 30 and the strike prices to be 35, 30, and 25. Now the option holder would have two puts or calls at the adjusted price.

OPTION PREMIUMS

Before one can understand various option strategies, an investor or speculator must be able to comprehend what creates option premiums (prices). Look at Table 13–3. Using Eastman Kodak (EK) as an example, we can see that the common stock closed at $70 per share on the NYSE and that puts and calls are available at the following strike prices—55, 60, 65, 70, 75, 80. The October 70 call closed at 3¾ ($375.00 for one call on 100 shares), while the October 80 call closed at ⁹⁄₁₆. The 65 call is said to be "in-the-money" because the market price (70) is above the strike (or purchase) price (65), but the 80 call is "out-of-the-money" since the strike price is above the market price. The 70 call is said to be "at-the-money" because the strike price and the market price are equal.

In-the-money options have an intrinsic value equal to the market price minus the strike price. In the case of the EK October 65 call, the intrinsic value is $5 as indicated by Formula (13–1). Options that are out of the money have no positive intrinsic value.

$$\text{Intrinsic value}_{call} = \text{Market price} - \text{Strike price} \quad (13\text{–}1)$$
$$\text{Intrinsic value}_{EK\ 65\ October\ call} = \$70 - \$65$$
$$= \$5$$

The EK October 80 call would have a negative $10 intrinsic value derived by Formula (13–1). When the market price minus the strike price is negative, the negative value represents the amount the stock price must increase to have the option at-the-money where the strike price and market price are equal.

Returning to the Eastman Kodak 65 October call, we see in Table 13–3 that the total premium is 7⅛, while the previously computed intrinsic value is $5. This call option has an additional premium of 2⅛ due to other factors. The total premium (option price) is a combination of the intrinsic value plus a speculative premium which is a function of common stock volatility and risk, time to expiration, dividend yield on the underlying common stock, potential leverage, and market expectations.

$$\text{Total premium} = \text{Intrinsic value} + \text{Speculative premium} \quad (13\text{–}2)$$
$$\$7\tfrac{1}{8} = \$5 + \$2\tfrac{1}{8}$$

TABLE 13–3

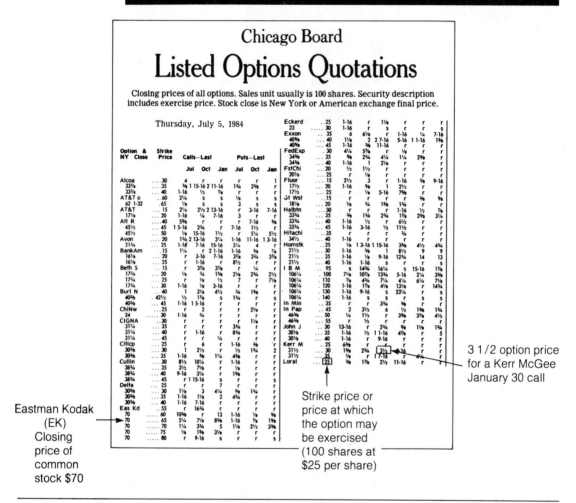

Eastman Kodak (EK) Closing price of common stock $70

Strike price or price at which the option may be exercised (100 shares at $25 per share)

3 1/2 option price for a Kerr McGee January 30 call

Generally, the higher the volatility of the common stock—as measured by its stock price's standard deviation or by its beta—and the lower the dividend yield, the greater the speculative premium. The longer the exercise period, the higher the speculative premium, especially if market expectations over the duration of the option are positive. Finally, the deeper the option is in-the-money, the smaller the leverage potential and therefore the smaller the speculative premium. Most often, we examine the speculative premium separately to see if it is a reasonable premium to pay for the possible benefits.

The speculative premium can be expressed in dollars or as a percentage of the common stock price. A speculative premium expressed in percent

TABLE 13–4   Speculative Premiums on July 5, 1984, for Eastman Kodak Options

Market price	Eastman Kodak strike price	Total premium	−	Intrinsic value	=	Speculative premium	Speculative premium as % of common stock price
$70	$55 October call	$16¾		$15		$ 1¾	2.33%
70	65 October call	7⅛		5		2⅛	2.83
70	70 October call	3¾		0		3¾	5.00
70	75 October call	1⅝		(5)		6⅝	8.83
70	80 October call	⁹⁄₁₆		(10)		10⁹⁄₁₆	14.08

indicates the increase in the stock price needed for the purchaser of a call option to break even on the expiration date. Table 13–4 shows this point. Notice that the Eastman Kodak October 55 call option, which is deep in-the-money, has the lowest speculative premium, while the 80 option has the highest. Realize that the 80 option only has a cash value of ⁹⁄₁₆ (the total premium) and that the other $10 represents the required increase in the stock price for the strike price and market price to be equal. The 14.08 percent premium, however, does represent the percentage movement in stock price by the expiration date for a break-even position. Remember that at expiration there will be no speculative premium. The option will only reflect the intrinsic value and possibly even a discount because of commission expenses incurred upon exercise.

Table 13–5 provides a look at premiums for in-the-money and out-of-the-money options with varying times to expiration. Since the quotes are as of July 5, the July options will expire first, then the October options and finally the January options. You should notice how the option premiums increase with more time to expiration.

Eastman Kodak's speculative premiums are not very high due to a low beta, high dividend yield, and an uninspired stock market in July 1984. Several relationships in Table 13–5 are evident, however. The speculative premiums increase with time for all strike prices but are very low for the 55 and 60 calls because of low leverage potential and a chance of being exercised on the expiration date. The 75 and 80 calls have high speculative premiums, but an option writer would *not reap much cash inflow.* Generally speaking, out-of-the-money call options have high speculative premiums, but little of the premium may be in the form of cash. A $50 stock with a $55 strike price may have a $2 total premium and a speculative premium of $7. Note that only a small part of the speculative premium is in cash. This, or course, is an important consideration for an option writer.

Table 13–6 demonstrates the relationship of betas and dividend yields to the speculative premium. The three options listed are all October calls from Table 13–3, and they are either at-the-money or slightly in-the-money. Notice that the speculative premiums (in percent) rise as the betas increase and

TABLE 13–5 Speculative Premiums over Time (Eastman Kodak calls, July 5, 1984, Beta .85)

Market price	Strike price	July total premium*	Speculative premium Dollars	Speculative premium Percent	October total premium†	Speculative premium Dollars	Speculative premium Percent	January total premium‡	Speculative premium Dollars	Speculative premium Percent
$70	$55	Not traded	—	—	$16¾	$ 1¾	2.50	Not traded	—	—
70	60	$10⅜	$ ⅜	.54%	Not traded	—	—	$13	$3	4.29%
70	65	5¼	¼	.36	7⅛	2⅛	3.04	8⅜	3⅜	4.82
70	70	1¼	1¼	1.79	3¾	3¾	5.36	5	5	7.14
70	75	⅛	5⅛	7.32	1⅝	6⅝	9.46	3⅛	8⅛	11.61
70	80	Not traded	—	—	⁹⁄₁₆	10⁹⁄₁₆	15.09	Not offered	—	—

* July—16 days to expiration.

† October—107 days to expiration.

‡ January—198 days to expiration.

TABLE 13–6   **Speculative Premiums Related to Betas and Dividend Yields**

Stock	October strike	Market price	Total premium	Speculative premium Dollars	Speculative premium Percent	Beta	Expected dividend yield
Eastman Kodak	$70	$70	$3¾	$3¾	5.36%	.85	5.6%
Citicorp	30	30⅜	2½	2⅛	7.00	1.05	6.1
Delta Airlines	30	30⅜	3	2⅝	8.64	1.10	1.8

dividend yields fall. This, of course, is not always true since other factors, such as market attitudes, can have a strong bearing on the speculative premium in addition to other influences mentioned previously. In fact, Citicorp's higher dividend yield is associated with a higher speculative premium relative to Eastman Kodak because the banking industry was considered to be quite risky with the Continental Illinois Bank's loan loss problems and Citicorp's large international loan portfolio. Normally, higher dividend yields are associated with lower speculative premiums.

Premiums can be deceiving. The novice may attempt to write the options with the highest total premium or speculative premium, while the buyer may think the smallest investment provides the greatest leverage. These are not usually true if we look at speculative premiums on a per-day basis. For example, the EK 70 calls have the following speculative premiums per day. Note the speculative premium (in percent) is divided by the number of days to expiration.

Speculative premiums
until expiration

July	70	1.79%/16 days =	.1119% per day
October	70	5.36%/107 days =	.0501% per day
January	70	7.14%/198 days =	.0361% per day

An examination of daily premiums would suggest that call writers should write short-lived calls and then roll them over if they don't get exercised. On the other hand, call buyers get more time for less premium by purchasing long-lived calls.

Although this section has examined call premiums, puts have most of the same relationship except for the definitions of in-the-money and out-of-the-money. Since puts allow the owner to sell stock at the strike price, in-the-money put options exist where the strike price is above the market price of the stock. Out-of-the-money puts have market values for common stock above the strike price. Since the owner of the stock can sell the stock for more in the market than by exercising a put, the put has no intrinsic value. The speculative premium of a put as a percentage of the stock price then represents the percentage decline in the stock price necessary to break even.

Understanding option premiums is important in order to make sense out of options strategies. Various strategies involving puts and calls are covered in the next section. Do not go on unless you are reasonably comfortable with this section on option premiums. Appendix 13–B presents the Black-Scholes option pricing model, a much more sophisticated way of analyzing option prices and their time premiums and speculative premiums. This model puts all the variables together in a model to demonstrate the relationships and determinants of option prices. This appendix is primarily designed for those who wish to achieve a more advanced understanding of the theoretical basis for option pricing and is not essential for the standard reading of the text.

BASIC OPTION STRATEGIES

Option strategies can be very aggressive and risky, or they can be quite conservative and used as a means of reducing risk. Option buyers and writers both attempt to take advantage of the option premiums discussed in the preceding section. In theory many option strategies can be created, but in practice the market must be liquid in order to execute these strategies. After a decade of explosive growth, option volume declined slightly in 1984–85 while trading on the underlying stocks went up. Because of the introduction of index options, trading in individual equity options may have been affected. A reduction of individual option trading reduces the ability to create workable strategies for specific companies. For example, the lack of a liquid market can keep institutional investors from executing hedging strategies involving several hundred thousand shares. Even with these limitations in mind, the average investor can still find many opportunities for option strategies. In this section, we discuss the possible uses of puts and calls to achieve different investment goals. Table 13–7 provides option quotes at three separate time periods for our examples. We have ignored commissions in most examples, but we do advise that commissions can be a significant hidden cost in some types of option strategies.

Buying Call Options

The leverage strategy.   Leverage is a very common reason for buying call options when the market is expected to rise during the exercise period. The use of calls in this way is similar to warrants discussed in Chapter 12, but calls have shorter lives and lower premiums. The call option is priced much lower than the common stock, and the leverage is derived from a small percentage change in the price of the common stock that can cause a large percentage change in the price of the call option. For example, on July 5, 1984, Federal Express common stock closed at 34⅜, and the 40 October call closed at 1 (see Table 13–7). Two months later in September, the stock closed at 42⅞ for an 8½ point gain of 24.7 percent. The 40 October call option closed at 4¼ for

TABLE 13-7

Chicago Board
Listed Options Quotations

Closing prices of all options. Sales unit usually is 100 shares. Security description includes exercise price. Stock close is New York or American exchange final price.

Thursday, July 5, 1984   Thursday, September 6, 1984   Thursday, November 1, 1984

Option & NY Close	Strike Price	Calls—Last			Puts—Last		
		Jul	Oct	Jan	Jul	Oct	Jan

(July 5, 1984 section — quotations for Alcoa, AT&T o, AT&T, Atl R, Avon, BankAm, Beth S, Burl N, ChiNw, CIGNA, Citicp, Cullin, Delta, Eas Kd, Eckerd, Exxon, FedExp, FstChi, Fluor, Gt Wst, Halbtn, Hitachi, Homstk, B M, In Min, In Pap, John J, Kerr M, Loral)

Option & NY Close	Strike Price	Calls—Last			Puts—Last		
		Oct	Jan	Apr	Oct	Jan	Apr

(September 6, 1984 section — quotations for Alcoa, AT&T, Atl R, Avon, BankAm, Beth S, Burl N, ChiNw, CIGNA, Citicp, Cullin, Delta, Dig Eq, Eas Kd, Eckerd, Engelh, Exxon, FedExp, FstChi, Fluor, Gt Wst, Halbtn, Homstk, I B M, In Min, In Pap, John J, Kerr M, Loral)

Option & NY Close	Strike Price	Calls Last			Puts-Last		
		Jan	Apr	Jul	Jan	Apr	Jul

(November 1, 1984 section — quotations for Alcoa, AT&T, Atl R, Avon, BankAm, Beth S, Burl N, ChiNw, CIGNA, Citicp, Cullin, Delta, Eas Kd, Eckerd, Engelh, Exxon, FedExp, FstChi, Fluor, Gt Wst, Halbtn, Hitachi, Homstk, I B M, In Min, In Pap, John J, Kerr M, Loral)

a 3¼ point gain of 325 percent. The option increased by more than 13 times the percentage move in the common stock. The relationship is indicated below.

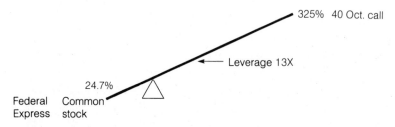

Figure 13–1 depicts the relationship between profit and loss opportunities for the Federal Express 40 October call option, given the market price at expiration (no speculative premium exists at expiration).

As long as the common stock closes under 40, the call buyer loses the whole premium of 1 (or 100 times $1 equals $100). At a price of 41, the call buyer breaks even as the option is worth an intrinsic value of 1. As the stock increases past 41, the profit starts accumulating. If the option is sold before expiration, a speculative premium may alter the profit potential.

FIGURE 13–1   Federal Express 40 October Call Buy 1 Option (excludes commissions)

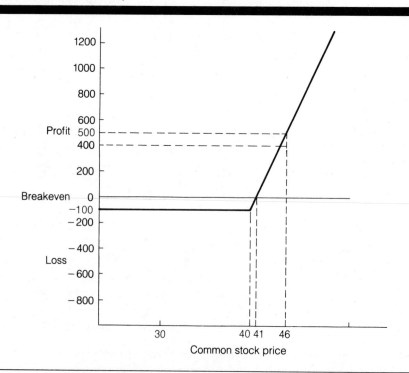

An investor striving for maximum leverage will generally buy options that are out-of-the-money or only slightly in-the-money. Buying high-priced options for $10 or $15 that are well in-the-money definitely limits the potential for leverage. You may have to invest almost as much in the options as you would have in the stocks.

Playing the leverage game doesn't always work out. If a speculator had assumed that Federal Express would continue its rapid price rise, he might have purchased an in-the-money January 40 call on September 6, 1984 for 6. While the stock declined 4⅜ from 42⅞ to 38½ by November 1, 1984, the call option declined from 6 to 2¼ (−62.5 percent). Since the stock decline from 42⅞ to 38½ represents only a 10.2 percent loss, the 62.5 percent loss on the option is significant. It is not hard to lose all your money under these circumstances—leverage works in reverse too.

Call options instead of stock.   Many people do not like to risk losing large amounts of money and view call options as a way of controlling 100 shares of stock without a large dollar commitment. For example, using Table 13–7 for the September 6, 1984, prices, International Paper common stock could have been purchased at 55½ or $5,550 plus commission for 100 shares. A January 55 call could also be bought for 4¼ ($425), which would leave $5,125 leftover cash ($5,550 − $425) for an investment elsewhere while still maintaining the opportunity to buy 100 shares at 55.

Assume the call is purchased for $425 and $5,125 is left to be invested in a money market fund at 10 percent until November 1, 1984. The interest income would be about $85 for two months.

During this time the stock declined from 55½ to 50⅞. That's a loss of 4⅝, or $462.50. This was partially offset by a $60 dividend payment, for a net loss of $402.50 on the 100 shares of stock. As would be expected, the call option also went down from 4¼ ($425) to 1 ($100). That's a loss of $325, which was partially offset by the $85 of interest income from the investment of leftover cash in a money market fund. The net loss associated with the call option is $240 ($325 − $85). The net loss on the call option of $240 is certainly less than the net loss of $402.50 on the stock purchase. The overall effect is demonstrated in Table 13–8. An additional unspecified, cost consideration is that the investor probably saved another $25 to $50 in commissions since stock trading is more expensive than option trading.

Had the stock really declined in value, say, to $30, the advantage of the limited dollar loss exposure of the option would be even more apparent. The purchaser of 100 shares of stock would have lost $2,550 as the stock declined from 55½ to 30. This loss is only slightly reduced by the receipt of $60 in dividends. On the other hand, the purchaser of the option cannot lose more than the initial purchase price of $425 (100 × 4¼). Even this loss is slightly offset by the $85 of interest from the investment of leftover cash in a money market account.

Of course, if the stock does the opposite and goes way up to $70 or $80, both the stock purchaser and option buyer will show substantial profits.

TABLE 13–8   Comparison of Call Option to Stock Purchase (International Paper)

Buy call; Draw interest	*Buy stock*
September 6, 1984	September 6, 1984
$425.00 (100 × 4¼)	$5,550.00 (100 × 55½)
November 1, 1984 value	November 1, 1984 value
$100.00 (100 × 1)	$5,087.50 (100 × 50⅞)
+ 85.00 Interest income	+ 60.00 Dividend income
$185.00	$5,147.50
$240.00 Loss	$402.50 Loss

Protecting a short position.   Calls are often used to cover a short sale against the risk of rising stock prices. This is called hedging your position; by purchasing a call, the short seller guarantees a loss of no more than a fixed amount while at the same time reducing any potential profit by the total premium paid for the call. Again refer to Table 13–7 and assume you had sold 100 shares of Delta Airlines short at 30⅜ on July 5, 1984, and had bought a January 30 call for 4¼ as protection against a rise in the price of the stock. By November 1, the stock has risen to 39⅛ for an 8¾ loss on the short position. This loss has been partially offset by an increase in the call option price to 9¾, or a 5½ gain. Instead of losing 8¾, the short position is only out 3¼ so far (8¾ − 5½). This is the loss of 8¾ on the short position less the gain of 5½ on the call option. This strategy has locked in a maximum loss potential of 3⅞ plus commissions. The 3⅞ is the *speculative* premium paid for the January 30 call; as the stock rises, the speculative premium evaporates at expiration, but otherwise the call goes up dollar for dollar with the stock. If the investor thinks Delta is a good short at 39⅛ on November 1, he may sell the call for 9¾ on November 1 and be left with an unprotected short position with the stock at 39⅛, hoping for an eventual decline in the stock price.

Consider the initial 4¼ call premium insurance. If the stock goes up, it limited your loss, but if the stock goes down, your profit on the short position is reduced by the call premium. In the case of Delta, the stock would have to reach 26⅛ (30⅜ − 4¼) before the short seller with call protection would break even. A decline of more than 14 percent in the stock price would have to occur before the short seller would begin to profit, and this ignores commissions. As is true of most option plays, there are advantages and disadvantages to most strategies.

Guaranteed price.   Often an investor thinks a stock will rise over the short-term and long-term, but does not currently have the cash available to purchase the stock. The important point for this strategy is that the investor wants to own this stock eventually but does not want to miss out on a good buying opportunity now (based on his or her expectations). Perhaps the oil stocks are depressed or semiconductors have hit bottom. A call option can be utilized. The investor could be anticipating a cash inflow at a specific time in the future when he plans to exercise the call option with a tax refund, a book royalty, or even the annual Christmas bonus.

For example, on July 5, 1984, Mrs. Harris buys a January 70 Eastman Kodak call option for 5, which is a 5 speculative premium since Eastman Kodak is selling at 70 per share. By September, she has received her $7,000 anticipated check and exercises the option when the stock is selling at 75¾. For tax purposes, the cost or basis of this 100 shares of Eastman Kodak is the strike price (70) plus the option premium (5), or 75 per share. Since most investors will not pursue this strategy if they expect prices to fall, they will usually seek out the deepest in-the-money option that they can afford because it is likely to have the lowest speculative premium. For example, Mrs. Harris could have used a January 60 call with a price of 13 and the final cost would be 73 rather than 75 per share. If she does not initially have the $1,300 for the 60 call, she might consider the 65 call for 8⅜ as the next best alternative.

Writing Call Options

Writers of call options take the opposite side of the market from the buyers. The writer is similar to a short seller in that he or she expects the stock to decline or stay the same. In order for short sellers to profit, prices must decline, but since writers of call options receive a premium, they can make a profit if prices stay the same or even rise less than the speculative premium. Option writers can write covered options, meaning they own the underlying common stock, or they can write naked call options, meaning they do not own the underlying stock.

Writing covered call options is often considered a hedged position because, if the stock price declines, the writer's loss on the stock is partially offset by the option premium. A writer of a covered call must decide if he is willing to sell the underlying stock if it closes above the strike price and the option is exercised. He also must consider any adverse tax consequences, such as short-term capital gains.

Returning to Table 13–7 for another set of option quotes, find Atlantic Richfield (Atl R) options. The market price of the common stock is 49⅞ on September 6 (middle of table), and the writer for an October call option can choose from the strike prices reprinted in Table 13–9.

TABLE 13–9   Atlantic Richfield October Strike Prices

September 6, 1984	Strike	October premiums	Market price
Atl R	45	5⅜	49⅞
Atl R	50	1½	49⅞
Atl R	55	¼	49⅞

Remember, the writer agrees to sell 100 shares at the strike price for the consideration of the premium. The 45 strike price has the highest premium and would be a good write if the stock closed at less than 45 because the call would not get exercised and the writer would profit by the amount of the premium, 5⅜. If the stock closed above 45, then the call could get exercised, and the writer would have to deliver 100 shares at 45. More likely, the option writer would buy back the option for its price in the market to avoid having the option exercised. For example, if the ending value of the stock were 48, the option writer could buy back the 45 option for 3. If the stock closed at more than 50⅜, the call writer would be at a loss and could buy back the option at a loss. Figure 13–2 shows this relationship between profit and loss and the common stock price.

By October 20, the date of expiration, Atlantic Richfield stock closed at 46⅜, and the option was worth 1⅜. Both a covered writer and a naked writer would have made a profit. The covered writer would have collected a dividend, repurchased the call option at 1⅜ and still have had possession of 100

FIGURE 13–2   Atlantic Richfield October Calls Write 1 Call (excludes commissions)

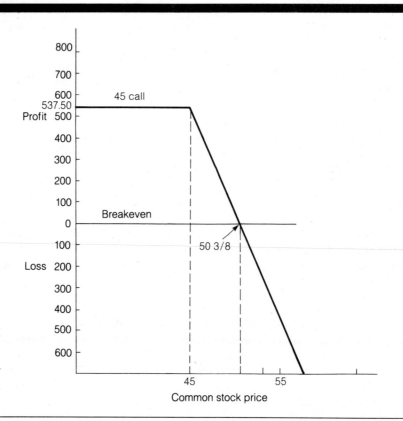

shares of stock now valued at $4,637.50 instead of $4,987.50. The following is an analysis of how the two types of call writers fared.

Covered writer		*Naked writer*	
−Initial investment			
(100 @ 49⅞)	($4,987.50)	−Margin (30 percent of	
+Option premium (5⅜)	537.50	stock price)	($1,496.25)
+Dividend	75.00	+Option premium (5⅜)	537.50
+Ending value stock	4,637.50	+Ending value margin	1,496.25
−Repurchase of option (1⅜)	(137.50)	−Repurchase of option (1⅜)	(137.50)
Profit	$ 125.00	Profit	$ 400.00
Percent return on		Percent return on	
initial investment	2.55%	initial margin investment	26.7%

The covered writer hedged the losses on his stock by collecting an option premium. In spite of a declining stock price, he still managed a positive return. Our naked writer was required to put up margin on 30 percent of the value of the stock to ensure her ability to close out the option write if the stock should rise significantly. The capital was returned to her when it was no longer needed as collateral, and she profited with almost a 27 percent return. To avoid exercise of the option, the call writer in both cases is assumed to enter the market with a closing transaction to repurchase the 45 call at 1⅜ before expiration. If the stock price had risen, the naked writer was exposed to unlimited risk as she either had to close out her position at a loss or purchase the stock above the strike price and deliver it at a loss. The covered writer had limited risk because he locked in the cost of his stock and can deliver it or close out his position before it is called.

Another critical decision for a call writer is the choice of months. In the section on option premiums, we examined percentage premiums per day and found that the shortest expiration dates provided the highest daily speculative premium. In most cases, the call writer will choose the shorter-term options and, as they expire, write another short-term option. Annualized returns of 20 percent are not uncommon for continuously covered writing strategies.

Buying Put Options

The owner of a put may sell 100 shares of stock to the put writer at the strike price. The strategy behind a put is similar to selling short or writing a call except losses are limited to the total investment (premium), and no more risk exposure is possible if the stock rises. Buying a put in anticipation of a price decline is one method of speculating on market price changes. The same factors influencing call premiums also apply to put premiums except that expectations for the direction of the market are the opposite.

On September 6, 1984, Eastman Kodak's common stock price was 75¾, and a 75 January put could be purchased for 2½ (see Table 13–7 and remember to look for put prices rather than call prices). The put was out-of-the-money by ¾. Four and one half months remained until expiration. The buyer of the put would expect a price decline with the idea that the intrinsic value of the put would increase. By November 1, 1984, Eastman Kodak had declined to 71¼ with the 75 January put at 4¾. The intrinsic value was now 3¾ (75 − 71¼) and the speculative premium was 1. At this point in time, the owner of the put had a 2¼ gain on a 2½ investment or a 90 percent return while the stock was declining only 6 percent.

Puts can make money in a down market and also possibly help offset a large loss in the value of the common stock. In the latter case, an owner of 100 shares of Eastman Kodak could have bought a put to hedge against a loss in the value of the stock. Eastman Kodak dropped 4½ (74¾ − 71¼), and the gain of 2¼ on the put offset some of the loss suffered on the common stock.

Hedges do not always work out as expected. For example, on September 6, 1984, assume the owner of 100 shares of IBM anticipated a price decline because of expectations of rising interest rates, but he did not want to sell the stock and pay a capital gains tax on these shares held for many years. Instead he bought a January 120 put for 3⅞ when the stock was at 123¼. By November 1, 1984, IBM stock was up 2¾ (the decline never materialized), and the January 120 put was worth 1⅜, providing a loss of $250 on the put. Of course, one can think of the $250 loss as insurance against a price decline that never happened—much like auto insurance, we pay a premium for something we hope never happens.

USING OPTIONS IN COMBINATIONS

Spreads

Now that you have a basic understanding of puts and calls from both the buyer's and writer's perspective, we proceed with a discussion of spreads. Most combinations of options are called spreads and consist of buying one option (going long) and writing an option (going short) on the same underlying stock. Spreads are for the sophisticated investor and involve many variations on a theme. Vertical spreads involve buying and writing two contracts at different striking prices with the same month of expiration. Horizontal spreads consist of buying and writing two options with the same strike price but different months, and a diagonal spread is a combination of the vertical and horizontal spread. These spreads are constructed using call options. Table 13–10 presents an example of XYZ Corporation demonstrating the options, months, and strike prices involved in each type of spread. There are more complicated spreads than these, such as the butterfly spread, variable spread, and domino spread. We cannot attempt to explain all of these spreads in the space available and so we will concentrate on vertical bull spreads and vertical bear spreads.

Since spreads require the purchase of one call and the sale of another call, a speculator's account will have either a debit or credit balance. If the cost of the long call is greater than the revenue from the short position, the speculator has a net cash outflow and a debit in his account. When your spread is put on with a debit, it is said that you have "bought the spread." You have "sold the

TABLE 13–10   Spreads (call options)

Vertical Spreads			Option Prices		
	Mkt. Price	Strike Price	Oct.	Jan.	April
XYZ	36⅜	35	4	6	6½
	36⅜	40	2	3⅜	4
	36⅜	45	11/16	1½	6

Horizontal Spread (Time Spread)					
	Mkt. Price	Strike Price	Oct.	Jan.	April
XYZ	36⅜	35	4	6	6½
	36⅜	40	2	3⅜	4
	36⅜	45	11/16	1½	6

Diagonal Spread					
	Mkt. Price	Strike Price	Oct.	Jan.	April
XYZ	36⅜	35	4	6	6½
	36⅜	40	2	3⅜	4
	36⅜	45	11/16	1½	6

spread" if the receipt from writing the call is greater than the cost of the long call and you have a credit balance. For example, the difference between the option prices for a vertical spread on XYZ Corporation in Table 13–10 with October strike prices of 35 and 40 is $2 ($4 − $2). The $2 difference between these two option prices is sometimes called the price spread and could be either a debit or credit, depending on whether a bull or bear spread is used. In either case, the profit or loss from a spread position results in the change between the two option prices over time as the price of the underlying stock goes up or down.

Vertical bull spread.   Being a bull spread, the expectation is that the common stock price will rise. The speculator can buy the common stock outright, or if he wants to profit from an expected price increase but reduce his risk of loss, he can enter into a bull spread. Vertical bull spreads limit both the maximum gain and maximum loss available. They are usually debit positions because the spreader buys the higher-priced, in-the-money option and shorts (writes) an inexpensive, out-of-the-money option. Using Table 13–10 for an

XYZ October bull spread, we would buy the October 35 at 4 and sell the October 40 at 2 for a debit of 2 (price spread). This represents a $200 investment. Assume that three weeks later, XYZ stock rises from 36⅜ to 42 with the October 35 selling at 7½ (previously purchased at 4) and the October 40 at 4½ (previously sold at 2). Table 13–11 shows the result of closing out the spread.

TABLE 13–11   Profit on Vertical Bull Spread

	XYZ October 35		XYZ October 40		Price spread
Bought at	4	Sold at	2		2
Sold at	7½	Bought at	4½		3
Gain	3½	(Loss)	(2½)		1
		Net gain	$100		
		Investment	$200		
		Return	50%		

Because the investment was only $200, the total return of $100 provided a 50 percent return. However, returns on spreads can be greatly altered by commissions. If the following spread incurred commissions of $50 in and out, the percentage return could be cut in half to 25 percent.

The maximum profit at expiration is equal to the difference in strike prices ($5 in this case) minus the initial price spread ($2 in this case). For the XYZ bull spread, the maximum profit is $300, and the maximum loss is the original debit of $200. At expiration, all speculative premiums are gone, and each option sells at its intrinsic value. Table 13–12 shows maximum profit and loss at various closing market prices at expiration. Remember, our initial investment is $200.

TABLE 13–12   XYZ Vertical Bull Spread

XYZ stock price at expiration 35				XYZ stock price at expiration 40				XYZ stock price at expiration 45			
October 35		October 40		October 35		October 40		October 35		October 40	
Bought at	4	Sold at	2	Bought at	4	Sold at	2	Bought at	4	Sold at	2
Expired at*	0	Expired at*	0	Sold at*	5	Expired at*	0	Sold at*	10	Bought at*	5
(Loss)	(4)	Gain	2	Gain	1	Gain	2	Gain	6	Loss	(3)
(Net loss) (2)				Net gain 3				Net gain 3			
$(200) 100 percent loss				$300 150 percent gain				$300 150 percent gain			

* All call options on date of expiration equal their intrinsic value.

As Table 13–12 shows, profit does not increase after the stock moves through the $40 call price. The stock price must increase from 36⅜ to 40 (10 percent) to generate a 150 percent spread profit. Every dollar of increased profit on the long position is offset by $1 of loss on the short position after the stock passes a price of 40. One of the important but difficult aspects of spreading is forecasting a range of prices rather than just the direction prices will move. If a speculator is bullish, he or she may buy a call instead of spreading. The potential loss is higher with the call but still limited, while the possible gain is unlimited. The relationship between long calls and bull spreads starts in the bottom of Figure 13–3. Note the maximum loss with the bull spread is

FIGURE 13–3   Profit and Loss Relationships on Spreads and Calls

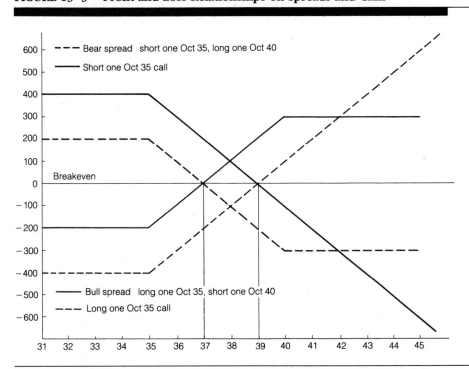

$200 and $400 with a long call. The break-even point is also $2 less for the bull spread ($37 versus $39). However, the long call has unlimited profit potential, and the bull spread is locked in at $300 at a stock price of $40 or higher. The spread position lowers the break-even point by $2 per share but also limits potential returns—a classic case of risk-return trade-off.

Vertical bear spread.   The speculator enters a bear spread anticipating a decline in stock prices. Instead of selling short or writing a call with both having unlimited risk, he spreads by selling short the call with the lower strike price (highest premium) and covers the upside risk with the purchase of a call having a higher strike price. This creates a credit balance. In a sense, the bear spread does the opposite of the vertical bull spread as seen in Table 13–13, in which we show profits and losses from the strategy if XYZ ends up at $35 or at $40. With a bear spread, the price spread of 2 is the maximum gain if the stock closes at $35 or less at expiration, while the maximum loss equals 3, the difference between the exercise prices minus the price spread. The relation-ships between bear spreads and writing a call option was also demonstrated in Figure 13–3 (the comparison starts at the top of the figure).

TABLE 13–13   XYZ Vertical Bear Spread

XYZ stock price at expiration 35				XYZ stock price at expiration 40			
October 35		October 40		October 35		October 40	
Sold at	4	Bought at	2	Sold at	4	Bought at	2
Expired at	0	Expired at	0	Bought at	5	Expired at	0
Gain	4	(Loss)	(2)	(Loss)	1	(Loss)	2
	Net gain 2				(Net loss) (3)		
	$200				$(300)		

Straddles

A straddle is a combination of a put and call on the same stock with the same strike price and expiration date. It is used to play wide fluctuations in stock prices and is usually applied to individual stocks with high betas and a history of large, short-term fluctuations in price. The speculator using a straddle may be unsure of the direction of the price movement but may be able to make a large enough profit on one side of the straddle to cover the cost of both options even if one option expires worthless.

For example, assume a put and a call can be bought for $5 apiece on an ABC October 50 when ABC Corporation is selling at 50 with six months to expiration. The total investment is 10 ($1,000). If the stock should rise from 50 to 65 at expiration, the call would provide a profit of 10 (15 value − 5 cost), and the put would be left to expire worthless for a loss of 5. This would provide a net gain of 5, or $500. The same type of example can be drawn if the price goes way down. Some who engage in spreads or straddles might attempt to close out one position before the other. This expands the profit potential but also increases the risk.

OTHER OPTION CONSIDERATIONS

Many factors have not been covered in detail because of their changing nature over time. Tax laws relating to options are constantly changing, and some items, such as capital gains holding periods for determination of long-term and short-term tax treatment, have been revised several times in the last several years. We do know that tax laws have a significant impact on spread positions and also on the long-term tax treatment where put options are involved. The best advice we can give is to check the tax consequences of any option strategy with your accountant or stockbroker.

Commissions vary between different brokerage houses and are not easy to pinpoint for option transactions since quantity discounts exist. We can assure you that because many option positions involve small dollar outlays, commissions of $25 to $50 for buying and selling can significantly alter your returns and even create losses. Commissions on exercising common stock through options are higher than the transaction costs of options, and these are a motivating force in causing closing option transactions before expiration. Overall, commissions on options tend to be more significant than commissions on commodities or other highly leveraged investments.

APPENDIX 13–A: Options Available on Companies' Common Stock

Company Name/Ticker Symbol/Exchange

Company	Exch.
Abbott Labs (ABT)	PH
Advanced Micro Devices (AMD)	P
Aetna Life (AET)	A
Air Products & Chemicals (APD)	PH
Alcan Aluminum (AL)	A
Alexander & Alexander Srv. (AAL)	C
Allied (ALD)	PH
Allied Stores (ALS)	C
Allis-Chalmers (AH)	PH
Aluminum Co. of America (AA)	C
Amax (AMS)	A
Amdahl (AMH)	C
Amerada Hess (AHC)	PH
American Brands (AMB)	C
American Broadcasting (ABC)	P
American Can (AC)	A
American Cyanamid (ACY)	A
American Electric Power (AEP)	C
American Express (AXP)	C,A
American Home Products (AHP)	A
American Hospital Supply (AHS)	C
American Intl. Group (AIG)	C
American Medical Intl. (AMI)	C
AT&T (T)	C
AMF (AMF)	A
AMP (AMP)	C
AMR (AMR)	A
Anheuser-Busch (BUD)	PH
Apache (APA)	C
Archer-Daniels-Midland (ADM)	PH
Arkla (ALG)	A
Armco (AS)	PH
ASA, Ltd. (ASA)	A
Asarco (AR)	A
Ashland Oil (ASH)	PH
Atlantic Richfield (ARC)	C
Automatic Data Proc. (AUD)	PH
Avco (AV)	PH
Avnet (AVT)	A
Avon (AVP)	C
Baker International (BKO)	P
Bally Mfg. (BLY)	C,A
Bank America (BAC)	C
Bard C.R. (BCR)	PH
Bausch & Lomb (BOL)	A
Baxter Travenol Labs (BAX)	C
Beatrice Foods (BRY)	A
Becton Dickinson (BDX)	PH
Bell South Corp. (BLS)	A
Bethlehem Steel (BS)	C
Beverly Enterprises (BEV)	P
Black & Decker (BDK)	C
Boeing (BA)	C
Boise Cascade (BCC)	C
Bristol-Myers (BMY)	C
Browning Ferris Ind. (BFI)	A
Brunswick (BC)	C
Bucyrus-Erie (BY)	A
Burlington Northern (BN)	C
Burroughs (BGH)	C,A
Campbell Red Lake (CRK)	PH
Capital Cities Comm. (CCB)	C
Carter Hawley Hale (CHH)	P
Caterpillar (CAT)	A
CBS (CBS)	C
Celanese (CX)	C
Cessna Aircraft (CEA)	C
Champion Intl. (CHS)	C
Chase Manhattan (CNB)	A
Chemical New York (CHL)	A
Chevron Corp. (CHV)	A
Chicago & Northwestern (CNW)	C
Chrysler (C)	C
Church's Fried Chicken (CHU)	PH
CIGNA (CI)	C
Cincinnati Milacron (CMZ)	PH
Citicorp (FNC)	C
City Investing (CNV)	PH
Clorox (CLX)	PH
Coastal (CGP)	C,A
Coca-Cola (KO)	C
Coleco (CLO)	PH
Colgate Palmolive (CL)	C
Colt Industries (COT)	PH
Combustion Eng. (CSP)	P
Comdisco (CDO)	P
Commodore Intl. (CBU)	PH
Commonwealth Edison (CWE)	C
Communication Satellite (CQ)	PH
Community Psych. Ctrs. (CMY)	C
Computer Sciences (CSC)	C
Computervision (CVN)	PH
Consolidated Edison (ED)	A
Continental Telecom (CTC)	A
Control Data (CDA)	C
Cooper Industires (CBE)	A
CooperVision (EYE)	A
Corning Glass (CLW)	C
Cray Research (CRY)	P
Crown Zellerbach (ZB)	A
CSX (CSX)	P
Cullinet (CUL)	C
Dart & Kraft (DK)	A
Data General (DGN)	P
Datapoint (DPT)	C
Dataproducts (DPC)	P
Dayton-Hudson (DH)	C
Deere (DE)	A
Delta Air Lines (DAL)	C
Denny's (DEN)	P
Diamond Shamrock (DIA)	P
Diebold (DBD)	C
Digital Equipment (DEC)	C,A
Disney (DIS)	C,A
Dome Mines (DM)	PH
Dominion Resources (D)	PH
Dow Chemical (DOW)	C
Dresser (DI)	PH
Duke Power (DUK)	PH
Dun & Bradstreet (DNB)	A
duPont (DD)	C,A
E-Systems (ESY)	P
Eastern Gas & Fuel (EFU)	PH
Eastman Kodak (EK)	C
Eckerd, Jack (ECK)	C
Edwards A.G. (AGE)	C
EG & G (EGG)	PH
Emerson Electric (EMR)	A
Emery (EAF)	PH
Engelhard (EC)	C
Enserch (ENS)	P
Enstar (EST)	PH
Exxon (XON)	C
Federal Express (FDX)	C
Fed. Natl. Mort. Assoc. (FMN)	PH
Financial Corp. (FIN)	PH
Firestone (FIR)	A
First Boston (FBC)	C
First Chicago (FBC)	C
First Mississippi (FRM)	A
Fleetwood Ent. (FLE)	A
Fluor (FLR)	C
Ford Motor (F)	C
Foster Wheeler (FWC)	P
Freeport-McMoRan (FTX)	C
GAF (GAF)	PH
GCA (GCA)	A
General Dynamics (GD)	C
General Electric (GE)	C
General Foods (GF)	C
General Instrument (GRL)	PH
General Motors (GM)	C
Genuine Parts (GPC)	P
Genrad (GEN)	PH
GEO International (GX)	A
Georgia-Pacific (GP)	PH
Gerber Scientific (GRB)	AH
Gillette (GS)	A
Global Marine (GLM)	A
Golden Nugget (GNG)	A
Golden West Fin. (GDW)	PH
Goodyear Tire (GT)	A
Gould (GLD)	A
Grace W.R. (GRA)	A
Great Western Fin. (GWF)	C
Greyhound (G)	A
GTE (GTE)	A
Gulf + Western (GW)	C
Gulf Canada Ltd. (GOC)	PH
Frank B. Hall & Co. (FBH)	A
Halliburton (HAL)	C
Harris (HRS)	C
Hecla (HL)	A
Hercules (HPC)	A
Hewlett-Packard (HWP)	C
Hilton Hotels (HLT)	P
Hitachi (HIT)	C
Holiday Inns (HIA)	C
Homestake Mining (HM)	C
Honeywell (HON)	C
Hospital Corp. of Amer. (HCA)	P
Household International (HI)	A
Houston Natural Gas (HNG)	P
Hughes Tool (HT)	A
Humana (HUM)	C
Hutton E.F. (EFH)	A
Inexco Oil (INX)	PH
IBM (IBM)	C
Intl. Flavors & Frag. (IFF)	C
Intl. Minerals & Chem. (IGL)	C
International Paper (IP)	C
ITT (ITT)	C
Johnson & Johnson (JNJ)	C
Joy Manufacturing (JOY)	PH
Kaneb Services (KAB)	A
Kerr-McGee (KMG)	C
Key Pharmaceuticals (KPH)	P
K Mart (KM)	C
Lear Siegler (LSI)	PH
Lehman (LEM)	P
Levi Strauss (LVI)	PH
Lilly, Eli (LLY)	A
Limited (LTD)	C
Litton Industries (LIT)	C
Lockheed (LK)	P
Loews Corp. (LTR)	C
Loral (LOR)	C

A – AMEX;   C – CBOE;   P – Pacific;   PH – Philadelphia

March 1, 1985

Company Name/Ticker Symbol/Exchange

Company	Exch	Company	Exch	Company	Exch
Louisiana Land & Expl. (LLX)	PH	Quaker Oats (OAT)	PH	Trans World (TW)	P
Louisiana Pacific (LPX)	A	Ralston Purina (RAL)	C	Travelers (TIC)	P
LTV (LTV)	A	Raychem Corp. RYC)	P	Tri-Continental (TY)	PH
M/A Com (MAI)	A	Raytheon (RTN)	C	TRW (TRW)	A
R.H. Macy (MZ)	A	RCA (RCA)	C	UAL (UAL)	C
Manufacturers Hanover (MHC)	A	Reading & Bates (RB)	P	Union Carbide (UK)	A
MAPCO (MDA)	P	Resorts Intern'l Cl. A (RT.A)	P	Union Pacific (UNP)	PH
Marriott (MHS)	PH	Revco D.S. (RDS)	A	United States Steel (X)	A
Martin Marietta (ML)	PH	Revlon (REV)	C	United Technologies (UTX)	C
Mary Kay Cosmetics (MKY)	C	Reynolds Metals (RLM)	P	Unocal (UCL)	P
MCA (MCA)	PH	Reynolds R.J. Ind. (RJR)	C	Upjohn (UPJ)	C
McDermott (MDR)	PH	Rockwell International (ROK)	A	U.S. Air (U)	P
McDonald's (MDC)	C	Rowan (RDC)	PH	Valero Energy (VLO)	A
McDonald Douglas (MD)	P	Royal Dutch Petroleum ((RD)	A	Varian (VAR)	A
Medtronic (MDT)	C	Ryder Systems (RDR)	P	Veeco (VEE)	P
Merck (MRK)	C	Sabine (SAB)	C	Verbatim (VRM)	P
Merrill Lynch (MER)	C,A	Safeway Stores (SA)	C	Viacom International (VIA)	C
Mesa Petroleum (MSA)	A	St. Regis Corp. (SRT)	PH	Wal-Mart Stores (WMT)	C
MGM/UA (MGM)	C	Sanders Associates (SAA)	PH	Walter, Jim (JWC)	C
Middle South Utilities (MSU)	C	Santa Fe Southern Pac. (SFX)	A	Wang Labs B (WAN.B)	P
Minnesota Mining & Mfg. (MMM)	C	Schering-Plough SGP)	A	Warner Communications (WCI)	C
Mitchell Energy & Devel. (MND)	P	Schlumberger Ltd. (SLB)	C	Warner-Lambert (WLA)	A
Mobil (MOB)	C	Scientific Atlanta (SFA)	P	Waste Management (WMX)	PH
Mohawk Data Sciences (MDS)	P	Scott Paper (SPP)	PH	Wendy's International (WEN)	P
Monsanto (MTC)	C	Seagram (VO)	P	Western Co. of N. Amer. (WSN)	A
Morgan J.P. (JPM)	PH	Searle G.D. (SRL)	A	Western Union (WU)	PH
Motorola (MOT)	A	Sears & Roebuck (S)	C	Westinghouse (WX)	A
Murphy Oil (MUR)	P	Security Pacific (SPC)	PH	Weyerhaeuser (WY)	C
National Distillers (DR)	A	SEDCO (SED)	A	Whittaker (WKR)	A
National Medical Ent. (NME)	A	Shaklee (SHC)	A	Williams (WMB)	C
National Patent (NPD)	P	Shell Oil (SUO)	P	Winnebago (WGO)	C
National Semiconductor (NSM)	C,A	Signal Cos. (SGN)	P	Woolworth F.W. (Z)	PH
NBI (NBI)	C	Singer (SMF)	A	Xerox (XRX)	C,P
Newmont Mining (NEW)	PH	Skyline (SKY)	C	Zapata (ZOS)	P
NL Industries (NL)	PH	Smith International (SII)	P	Zenith Radio (ZE)	A
Noble Affiliates (NBL)	A	Smith Kline (SKB)	P		
Norfolk Southern (NSC)	C	Sony (SNE)	P		
Northern Telecom (NT)	C	Southern Co. (SO)	C	**Index Options**	
Northrop (NOC)	C	Southland (SLC)	PH		
Northwest Airlines (NWA)	C	Southland Royalty (SRO)	P	S & P 100 Index (OEX)	C
Northwest Industires (NWT)	C	Southwest Airlines (LUV)	C	S & P 500 Index (SPX)	C
Novo Industry A/S (NVO)	A	Sperry (SY)	C	S & P Trans. Index (OTN)	C
Occidental Petroleum (OXY)	C	Squibb (SQB)	C	AMEX Market Value Ind. (XAM)	A
Ocean Drilling & Expl. (ODR)	A	Standard Oil of Ind. (SN)	C	Computer Tech. Index (XCI)	A
Owens-Corning Fiber (OCF)	PH	Standard Oil of Ohio (SOH)	A	Gold/Silver Index (XAU)	PH
Owens-Illinois (OI)	C	Sterling Drug (STY)	A	Major Market Index (XMI)	A
Paine Webber (PWJ)	C	Storage Technology (STK)	P	NYSE Double Index (NDX)	NY
Paradyne (PDN)	C	Storer Communications (SCI)	A	NYSE Options Index (NYA)	NY
Parker Drilling (PKD)	P	Sun Co. (SUN)	PH	NYSE Telephone Index (NTI)	NY
Penn Central (PC)	PH	Sybron (SYB)	A	Oil Index (XOI)	A
Penney J.C. (JCP)	A	Syntex (SYN)	C	Oil & Gas Index (XOZ)	A
Pennzoil (PZL)	C	Tandy (TAN)	C,A	Technology Index (PSE)	P
Pepsi Co. (PEP)	C	Tektronix (TEK)	C	Transportation Index (XTI)	A
Perkin-Elmer (PKN)	P	Teledyne (TDY)	C,P	Value Line Comp. Index (XVL)	PH
Pfizer (PFE)	A	Telex (TC)	A		
Phelps Dodge (PD)	A	Tenneco (TGT)	A		
Phibro-Salomon (PSB)	PH	Teradyne (TER)	P		
Philip Morris (MO)	A	Tesoro Petroleum (TSO)	PH		
Phillips Petroleum (P)	A	Texaco (TX)	A		
Pioneer (PNA)	PH	Texas Instruments (TXN)	C		
Pitney Bowes (PBI)	A	Texas Oil & Gas (TXO)	PH		
Pittston (PCO)	PH	Textron (TXT)	PH		
Pogo Producing (PPP)	P	Thrifty (TFD)	A		
Polaroid (PRD)	C,P	Tidewater (TDW)	C		
PPG Industries (PPG)	PH	TIE Communications (TIE)	P		
Prime Computer (PRM)	A	Time (TL)	PH		
Procter & Gamble (PG)	A	Toys "R" Us (TOY)	C		
Pulte Homes (PHM)	PH	Transamerica (TA)	PH		

A – AMEX;   C – CBOE;   P – Pacific;   PH – Philadelphia;   NY – NYSE

Part Four

BROADENING THE INVESTMENT PERSPECTIVE

In this section, we expand the investment horizon to consider many different types of investment strategies.

We begin in Chapter 14 with a consideration of "special situations" that at times exist in the stock and bond markets. Empirical research has indicated that some of these investment alternatives may provide superior returns on a risk-adjusted basis. Topics for consideration include investing in mergers and acquisitions, in new stock or bond issues, in securities that are initially listed on major exchanges, and in firms that are repurchasing their own shares in the market. Also, the possible advantage of investing in small firms or those with low P/E ratios is considered.

Another consideration for the investor expanding the investment horizon is that of commodity and financial futures (discussed in Chapter 15). Commodities include such items as wheat, copper, and pork bellies, whereas financial futures include such categories as currencies and Treasury securities. In the chapter, we consider the mechanics of various trading and hedging strategies and the risks that are involved.

As a follow-up to Chapter 15, we expand the discussion to stock index futures and options in Chapter 16. It is currently possible to hedge the risk of an entire stock portfolio by going short (selling futures or writing options) on such indexes as the S&P 500, S&P 100, NYSE Index, etc. Speculative strategies for upward markets are also considered.

The emphasis in Chapter 17 is on real assets, which include real estate, gold and silver, precious gems, collectibles, and many other forms of tangible assets. Real assets are thought to represent a strong inflation hedge; however, they also have drawbacks in terms of illiquidity and high transaction costs. In

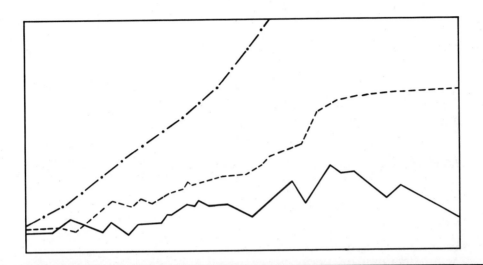

this chapter, we also go through a detailed analysis of a real estate investment project.

For those who might wish to add an international dimension to their investment strategy, Chapter 18 may be of interest. Not only are there risk reduction benefits through international diversification, but, in some cases, superior return potential as well. After pointing out some of the difficulties of foreign investments, the authors indicate how most of these can be overcome by investing in internationally oriented mutual funds or in securities called ADR's (American Depository Receipts).

Chapter 14
INVESTMENTS IN SPECIAL SITUATIONS

Chapter 15
COMMODITIES AND FINANCIAL FUTURES

Chapter 16
STOCK INDEX FUTURES AND OPTIONS

Chapter 17
INVESTMENTS IN REAL ASSETS

Chapter 18
INTERNATIONAL SECURITIES MARKETS

Chapter 14

INVESTMENTS IN SPECIAL SITUATIONS

In a previous discussion of market efficiency in Chapter 8, we suggested that while the security markets were generally efficient in the valuing of securities, there were still opportunities for special returns in a limited number of circumstances. Just what these circumstances are is subject to debate as not all researchers agree.

In most instances, special or abnormal returns refer to gains beyond what the market would normally provide after adjustment for risk. In this chapter, we will explore such topics as market movements associated with mergers and acquisitions, the underpricing of new stock issues, the impact of an exchange listing on a stock's valuation, the stock market impact of a firm repurchasing its own shares, and the small-firm effect. Additionally, in the bond market, we will look at a special situation associated with interest rate premiums on new bond issues.

We will attempt to separate some of the market folklore from significant analysis. Furthermore, when a valid investment opportunity is perceived to exist, we attempt to suggest under what circumstances it is most likely to prove profitable. Let's begin our analysis with a discussion of investment opportunities in mergers and acquisitions.

MERGERS AND ACQUISITIONS

Many stocks that were leaders in daily volume and price movement in the late 1970s and 1980s represented firms that were merger candidates; that is, companies that were being acquired or anticipated being acquired by other firms. The stocks of these acquisition candidates often increased by 60 percent or more over a relatively short period of time. The list of acquired companies included such well-known names as Conoco, Gulf Oil, Avis, EDS, Seven-Up, and Anaconda Copper.

Premiums for Acquired Companies

The primary reason for the upward market movement in the value of the acquisition candidate is the high premium that is offered over current market value in a merger or acquisition. The premium represents the difference between the offering price per share and the market price per share for the candidate (before the impact of the offer). For example, a firm that is selling for $25 per share may attract a purchase price of $40 per share. Quite naturally, the stock will go up in response to the offer and the anticipated consummation of the merger.

As expected, researchers have consistently found that there are abnormal returns for acquisition candidates.[1] A study has indicated that the aver-

---

[1] Gershon Mandelker, "Risk and Return: The Case of Merging Firms," *Journal of Financial Economics*, December 1974, pp. 303–35; Donald R. Kummer and J. Ronald Hoffmeister, "Valuation Consequences of Cash Tender Offers," *Journal of Finance*, May 1978, pp. 505–16; and Peter Dodd, "Merger Proposals, Management Discretion and Stockholder Wealth," *Journal of Financial Economics*, December 1980, pp. 105–38.

age premium paid in a recent time period was approximately 60 percent, and there was an associated upward price movement of a similar magnitude.[2] This is a much larger average premium than in prior time periods and may be attributed to the recognition of high replacement value in relationship to current market value. The premium was based on the difference between the price paid and the value of the acquisition candidate's stock *three months* before announcement of the merger. Some examples of premiums paid are presented in Table 14–1.

TABLE 14–1   Premiums Paid in Mergers and Acquisitions

Acquiring firm	Acquired firm	Price paid in cash for acquiring company's stock	Value of acquired firm three months before announcement	Premium paid (percent)
Beatrice Food Co	Harmon International Industries	$35.25	$20.00	76.25%
Parker Pen Co.	Manpower, Inc.	15.20	11.50	32.18
Colt Industries	Menaso Man.	26.60	15.00	77.33
Pepsico, Inc.	Pizza Hut, Inc.	38.00	22.375	69.83
Walter Kidde & Co.	Victor Comptometer	11.75	7.375	59.32
Dana Corporation	Weatherford Co.	14.00	9.375	49.33
Allis Chalmers Corporation	American Air Filter	34.00	19.50	74.36
Time, Inc.	Inland Containers	35.00	20.75	68.67

The only problem from an investment viewpoint is that approximately two thirds of the price gain related to large premiums takes place before public announcement. It is clear that people close to the situation are trading on information leaks. The highly prestigious investment banking house of Morgan Stanley was actually embarrassed by charges brought by the U.S. Attorney's Office that two of its former merger and acquisition specialists were conspiring to use privileged information on takeovers to make profits on secret trading accounts.[3]

Those who attempt to legitimately profit by investing in mergers and acquisitions can follow a number of routes. First of all, there are investors who try to identify merger candidates before public announcement to capture maximum profits. This is a difficult process. While researchers have attempted to identify financial and operating characteristics of acquisition candidates, the

---

[2] Henry Oppenheimer and Stanley Block, "An Examination of Premiums and Exchange Ratios Associated with Merger Activity during the 1975–78 Period" (Financial Management Association Meeting, 1980).

[3] "Two Former Morgan Stanley Executives Accused of Plot Involving Takeover Data," *The Wall Street Journal*, February 4, 1981, p. 2.

information is often contradictory and may even change over time.[4] In prior time periods (such as the 1960s), aquisition candidates were often firms with sluggish records of performance, whereas many of the current acquirees are high-quality companies that have unusually good records of performance (Alcon Labs, Coca Cola Bottling of Los Angeles, Steak and Ale, EDS).

Some alert analysts do keep a close eye on such sources as the *Financial Weekly's* "Stocks in the Spotlight," which pinpoints securities that are undergoing unusual volume or pricing patterns (of course, this could be for any number of reasons). Other investors identify industries where companies are being quickly absorbed and attempt to guess which firm will be the next to be acquired. Prime examples of such industries in recent times were natural resource firms being acquired by multinational oil companies, and brokerage houses being absorbed by insurance companies or other firms in the financial services industry.

While trying to guess an acquisition candidate prior to public announcement can be potentially profitable, it requires that an investor tie up large blocks of capital in betting on an event that may never come to pass. Others prefer to invest at the time of announcement of a merger or acquisition. A gain of the magnitude of 20 percent or more may still be available (over a few months' time period). Perhaps a stock that was $25 before any consideration of merger is up to $34 on announcement. If the actual purchase price is $40, there may still be a nice profit to be made. The only danger is that the announced merger may be called off, in which case the stock may sharply retreat in value, perhaps all the way back down to $25 (that is, assuming another potential acquiring company does not come into the picture). Examples of price drops associated with merger cancellations are shown in Table 14–2.

The wise investor must carefully assess the likelihood of cancellation. Special attention must be given to such factors as the possibility of antitrust action, the attitude of the target company's management toward the merger,

TABLE 14–2   Stock Movement of Potential Acquirees in Cancelled Mergers

Acquirer-potential acquiree	Preannouncement	One day after announcement	One day after cancellation
Mead Corporation—Occidental Petroleum	20⅜	33¼	23¼
Olin Corp.—Celanese	16	23¾	16¾
Chicago Rivet—MITE	20¾	28⅛	20¾

---

[4] Robert J. Monroe and Michael A. Simkowitz, "Investment Characteristics of Conglomerate Targets: A Discriminant Analysis," *Southern Journal of Business,* November 1971, pp. 1–15. Donald J. Stevens, "Financial Characteristics of Merger Firms: A Multivariate Analysis," *Journal of Financial and Quantitative Analysis,* March 1973, pp. 149–58.

the possibility of unhappy stockholder suits, and the likelihood of poor earnings reports or other negative events. In a reasonably efficient market environment, the potential price gain that exists at announcement may be well correlated with the likelihood of the merger being successfully consummated. That is to say, if it appears that the merger is almost certain to go through, the stock may be up to $37.50 at announcement based on an anticipated purchase price of $40. If a serious question remains, the stock may only be at $31. When a merger becomes reasonably certain, arbitrageurs come in and attempt to lock in profits by buying the acquisition candidate at a small spread from the purchase price.

One of the most interesting features of the current merger movement has been the heavy incidence of unfriendly takeovers; that is, the bidding of one company for another against its will. This strategy has occurred in 20 to 25 percent of announced mergers.[5] Such events often lead to the appearance of a third company on the scene, referred to as a "white knight," whose function is to save the target company by buying them out, thus thwarting the undesired suitor. The new suitor is generally deemed to be friendly to the interests of the target company and may be specifically invited by it to partake in the process. Examples of white knights occurred when Gulf Oil thwarted an offer from Mesa Petroleum and went with Standard Oil of California (renamed Chevron) in 1984. Similarly, Marathon Oil rejected an offer from Mobil to merge with U.S. Steel in 1982, and Babcock and Wilcox rejected an offer from United Technologies, choosing to go with J. Ray McDermott in the late 1970s.

As one might guess, these multiple-suitor bidding wars often lead to unusually attractive offers. A 40 to 60 percent premium may ultimately parlay into an 80 to 100 percent gain or more. For example, the bidding for Gulf Oil sent the stock from 38 to 80.

Acquiring Company Performance

What about the acquiring company's stock in the merger and acquisition process? Is this a special situation; that is, does this stock also show abnormal market gains associated with the event? A study by Mandelker has indicated that it does not.[6] Long-term economic studies have indicated that many of the anticipated results from mergers may be difficult to achieve.[7] There is often an initial feeling of optimism that is not borne out in reality. The synergy, or "2 + 2 = 5," effect associated with broadening product lines or eliminating overlapping functions may be offset by the inability of management to mesh divergent

---

[5] Anna Merjos, "Costly Propositions—Some Big Mergers Have Lately Fallen Through," *Barron's,* May 14, 1979, p. 9.

[6] Gershon Mandelker, "Risk and Return: The Case of Merging Firms," *Journal of Financial Economics,* December 1974, pp. 303–35.

[7] T. Hogarty, "The Profitability of Corporate Managers," *Journal of Business,* July 1970, pp. 317–27.

philosophies. However, companies do appear to be more adept at the process than in prior time periods; now conservatively managed firms, such as General Motors, Du Pont, and Atlantic Richfield, are replacing the funny-money conglomerate gunslingers of the 1960s. Nevertheless, most investors would prefer to position themselves with the acquired firm, which is certain to receive a high premium, rather than with the acquiring firm, which has to pay it.

Form of Payment

A final consideration in a merger is the form of payment. Cash offers usually carry a slightly higher premium than stock offers because of the immediate tax consequences to the acquired firm's shareholders. When stock is offered, the tax obligation usually may be deferred by the acquired company's stockholders until the stock of the acquiring firm is actually sold. This may occur relatively soon or many years in the future.

The merger movement of the late 1970s and the 1980s has seen a much heavier utilization of cash as a medium of payment than in prior time periods (in the 50 percent range as opposed to 25 percent in the 1960s).[8] Many of the old accounting advantages associated with stock or residual stock items (convertibles, warrants) in mergers have been diminished by accounting rule changes. Most financial management texts have whole chapters covering mergers and acquisitions, which could further expand your knowledge of the subject.

NEW STOCK ISSUES

Another form of a special situation is the initial issuance of stock by a corporation. There is a belief in the investment community that securities may be underpriced when they are issued to the public for the first time. That is to say, when a company goes public by selling formerly privately held shares to new investors in the over-the-counter market, the price may not fully reflect the value of the security.

Why does this so-called underpricing take place, and what is the significance to the investor? The underpricing may be the result of the firm commitment to buy the shares that an investment banker makes in distributing the issue. That is, the investment banker agrees to buy the stock from company A at a set price and then resells it to the public (along with other investment bankers, dealers, and brokers). The investment banker must be certain that the issue will be fully subscribed to at the initial public market price or he (and others) will absorb losses or build up unwanted inventory. In order to protect his position, the investment banker may underprice the issue by 5 to 10 percent to ensure adequate demand.

---

[8] 1978 Merger Survey (Chicago: W. T. Grimm and Co., 1978).

Studies by Reilly,[9] McDonald and Fisher,[10] and Ibbotson[11] have indicated there are positive abnormal returns in the new issues market for one week and one month after issue. Reilly, for example, observed positive excess returns of 10.9 percent one week after issue and 11.6 percent one month after issue. However, the efficiency of the market comes into play after the stock is actively trading on a regular basis, and any excess returns begin to quickly disappear. The lesson to be learned here is that, on average, the best time to buy a new, unseasoned issue is on initial distribution from the underwriting syndicate (investment bankers, dealers, brokers), and the best time to sell is in the first few weeks of trading.

Participating in the distribution of a new issue is not always as easy as it sounds. A really hot new issue may be initially oversubscribed, and only good customers of a brokerage house may be allocated shares. Such was the case in the feverish atmosphere that surrounded the initial public trading of Apple Computer and Genentech. Genentech actually went from $35 to $89 in the first 20 minutes of trading (only to quickly come back down). For the most part, customers with a regular brokerage account and a desire to participate in the new-issues market can find adequate opportunities for investment, though perhaps in less spectacular opportunities than those described above.

Performance of Investment Bankers

Research studies indicate that large, prestigious investment banking houses do not generally provide the highest initial returns to investors in the new issues they underwrite.[12] The reason for this is that the upper tier investment bankers tend to underwrite the issues of the strongest firms coming into the market. These firms generally shop around among the many investment bankers that are interested in their business and eventually negotiate terms that would allow for very little underpricing when they reach the market. (They want most of the benefits to go to the corporation, not to the initial stockholders.)

Factors to Consider in a New Issue

First of all, the investor should consider the management of the firm and their prior record of performance. In most cases, a firm that is going public will have

[9] Frank K. Reilly, "New Issues Revisited," *Financial Management,* Winter 1977, pp. 28–42.

[10] J. G. McDonald and A. K. Fisher, "New Issue Stock Price Behavior," *Journal of Finance,* March 1974, pp. 97–102.

[11] Roger G. Ibbotson, "Price Performance of Common Stock New Issues," *Journal of Financial Economics,* September 1975, pp. 235–72.

[12] Brian M. Neuberger and Carl T. Hammond, "A Study of Underwriters' Experience with Unseasoned New Issues," *Journal of Financial and Quantitative Analysis,* March 1974, pp. 165–74. Also, see Dennis E. Logue, "On the Pricing of Unseasoned New Issues, 1965–1969," *Journal of Financial and Quantitative Analysis,* January 1973, pp. 91–103, and Brian M. Neuberger and Chris A. La Chapelle, "Unseasoned New Issue Price Performance on Three Tiers: 1975–1980," *Financial Management,* Autumn 1983, pp. 23–28.

past sales and profit figures that can be compared to others in the industry. In one study the average sales volume for a firm approaching the new issues market was $22.9 million with $1.8 million in aftertax profits and $14.6 million in assets.[13]

The investor also should take a close look at the intended use of funds from the public distribution. There are many legitimate purposes, such as the construction of new plant and equipment, the expansion of product lines, or the reduction of debt. The investor should be less enthusiastic about circumstances in which funds are being used to buy out old stockholders or to acquire property from existing shareholders.

The investor should also be sensitive to the industry and nature of the product involved. Examples of changing industry patterns for new issues are presented in Table 14–3.

TABLE 14–3   Industry Groupings for New Public Issues (based on samples)

Lines of business	1969–1972	1974–1978
Computers	8	18
Electronics	5	9
Retailing	7	3
Wholesaling	2	0
Financial services	11	11
Energy	3	9
Health care	6	8
Light manufacturing	21	6
Heavy manufacturing	7	12
Entertainment	4	1
Restaurants	1	1
Construction	7	1
Transportation	0	2
Food processing	4	4
Other	16	17
	102	102

Source: Stanley Block and Marjorie Stanley, "The Financial Characteristics and Price Movement Patterns of Companies Approaching the Unseasoned Securities Market in the Late 1970's," *Financial Management,* Winter 1980, p. 36.

Wall Street West

A discussion of the market for new issues would not be complete without a few comments on the "Denver Stock Exchange." This is a special market for low-priced, untested securities that are somewhat different in character from

---

[13] Stanley Block and Marjorie Stanley, "The Financial Characteristics and Price Movement Patterns of Companies Approaching the Unseasoned Securities Market in the Late 1970's," *Financial Management,* Winter 1980, pp. 30–36.

the issues previously discussed. They are often referred to as "penny" stocks. Investors may be looking for a gamble here, and there is plenty of opportunity. Of the 270 new issues taking place between January 1, 1979, and January 30, 1980, 199 were initially offered for $1 or less.[14] Many of these infant, wildcatter companies provided astronomical returns for investors shortly after trading, while others were hardly ever heard of again.

EXCHANGE LISTINGS

A special situation of some interest to investors is an exchange listing, in which a firm trading over-the-counter now lists its shares on an exchange (such as the American or New York Stock Exchange). Another version of a listing is for a firm to step up from an American Stock Exchange listing to a New York Stock Exchange listing.

An exchange listing may well generate interest in a security (particularly in reference to moving up from the over-the-counter market to an organized exchange). The issue will now be assigned a specialist who has responsibility for maintaining a continuous and orderly market.[15] Furthermore, there may be greater marketability for the issue as well as more readily available price quotes (particularly in small-town newspapers). An exchange listing may also make the issue more acceptable for margin trading and short selling. Large institutional investors and foreign investors may also consider a listed security more appropriate for inclusion in their portfolio.

Listed firms must meet certain size and performance criteria provided in Table 14–4 (and previously mentioned in Chapter 2 for the NYSE). Although the criteria are not highly restrictive, meeting these standards may still signal a favorable message to investors.

A number of research studies have specifically examined the stock market impact of exchange listings. As might be expected, there is a strong upward movement associated with securities that are to be listed, but there is also a strong sell-off after the event has taken place. Research by Van Horne,[16] Fabozzi,[17] and others[18] indicates that the total effect may be neutral. Research by

---

[14] Penny Stocks, "New Issues Are Still the Rage; Risks, Fraud Charges Don't Deter Investors," *The Wall Street Journal,* March 30, 1981, p. 42.

[15] This is not always a superior arrangement to having multiple market makers in the over-the-counter market. It depends on how dedicated the specialist is to maintaining the market. Some banks and smaller industrial firms may choose the competitive dealer system in the over-the-counter market in preference to the assigned specialist.

[16] James C. Van Horne, "New Listings and Their Price Behavior," *Journal of Finance,* September 1970, pp. 783–94.

[17] Frank J. Fabozzi, "Does Listing on the AMEX Increase the Value of Equity?" *Financial Management,* Spring 1981, pp. 43–50.

[18] Richard W. Furst, "Does Listing Increase the Market Value of Common Stock?" *Journal of Business,* April 1970, pp. 174–80. Waldemar M. Goulet, "Price Changes, Managerial Accounting and Insider Trading at the Time of Listing," *Financial Management,* Spring 1974, pp. 303–6.

TABLE 14–4   Minimum Requirements for Exchange Listing

1. Demonstrated earning power under competitive conditions of: *either* $2.5 million before Federal income taxes for the most recent year and $2 million pre-tax for each of the preceding two years, *or* an aggregate for last three fiscal years of $6.5 million *together with* a minimum in the most recent fiscal year of $4.5 million. (All three years must be profitable.)

2. Net tangible assets of $16 million, but greater emphasis is placed on the aggregate market value of the common stock.

3. Market value of publicly held shares, subject to adjustment depending on market conditions, within the following limits:

Maximum	$18,000,000
Minimum	$ 9,000,000
Present (2/13/84)	$18,000,000

4. A total of 1,100,000 common shares publicly held.

5. *Either* 2,000 holders of 100 shares or more, *or* 2,200 total stockholders *together with* average monthly trading volume (for the most recent six months) of 100,000 shares.

Ying, Lewellen, Schlarbaum, and Lease (YLSL) would tend to indicate an overall gain.[19]

The really significant factor is that regardless of whether a stock has a higher net value a few months after listing as opposed to a few months before listing, there still may be profits to be made. This would be true if the investor simply bought the stock four to six weeks before listing and sold it upon listing. Because an application approval for listing is published in the weekly bulletin of the American Stock Exchange or the New York Stock Exchange well before the actual date of listing, this is often possible. The study by YLSL, sighted above, indicates there may be an opportunity for abnormal returns on a risk-adjusted basis in the many weeks between announcement of listing and actual listing (between 4.40 percent and 16.26 percent over normal market returns, depending on the time period involved). In this case, YLSL actually reject the semi-strong form of the efficient market hypothesis by suggesting there are substantial profits to be made even after announcement of a new listing. The wise investor may wish to sell on the eventual date of listing because sometimes a loss in value may take place at that point.

The reader should also be aware of the potential impact of delisting on a security; that is, the formal removal from New York Stock Exchange or American Stock Exchange listing, and a resumption of trading over-the-counter. This may take place because the firm has fallen substantially below the require-

---

[19] Louis K. W. Ying, Wilbur G. Lewellen, Gary G. Schlarbaum, and Ronald C. Lease, "Stock Exchange Listing and Securities Returns," *Journal of Financial and Quantitative Analysis,* September 1977, pp. 415–32.

ments of the exchange.[20] As you would expect, this has a large negative effect on the security. Merjos found that 48 of the 50 firms in her study declined between the last day of trading on an exchange and the resumption of trading over-the-counter.[21] The average decline was 17 percent. While the value was not risk adjusted, it is large enough to indicate the clear significance of the event.

STOCK REPURCHASE

The repurchase by a firm of its own shares provides for an interesting special situation. The purchase price is generally over current market value and tends to increase the demand for the shares while decreasing the effective supply. Before we examine the stock market effects of a repurchase, we will briefly examine the reasons behind the corporate decisions.

Reasons for Repurchase

In some cases, management believes their stock is undervalued in the market. Prior research studies have indicated that repurchased securities have generally underperformed the popular market averages before announcement of repurchase.[22] Thus, management or the board of directors may perceive this to be an excellent opportunity because of depressed prices. Others, however, might see the repurchase as a sign that management is not creative or that it lacks investment opportunities for the normal redeployment of capital.[23] Empirical study indicates that firms that engage in repurchase transactions often have lower sales and earnings growth and lower return on net worth than other, comparable firms.[24] There also tends to be a concentration of these firms in the lower-growth areas, such as apparels, steel, food products, tobacco, and aerospace.

Tax factors may also play a role in the repurchase decision. In the literature of finance, it is suggested that a stock repurchase will put a stockholder in a better aftertax position than the direct payment of cash dividends.[25] Assume a corporation has $2 million in excess cash, with 1 million shares of stock

---

[20] Firms may also be delisted because they have been acquired in a merger or acquisition, in which case the shares are no longer traded.

[21] Anna Merjos, "Stricken Securities," *Barron's,* March 4, 1963, p. 9.

[22] Richard Norgaard and Connie Norgaard, "A Critical Evaluation of Share Repurchase," *Financial Management,* Spring 1974, pp. 44–50. Larry Y. Dann, "Common Stock Repurchases: An Analysis of Returns to Bondholders and Stockholders," *Journal of Financial Economics,* June 1981, pp. 113–38.

[23] Charles D. Ellis and Allen E. Young, *The Repurchase of Common Stock* (New York: The Ronald Press, 1971), p. 61.

[24] Norgaard and Norgaard, "A Critical Evaluation."

[25] Harold Bierman, Jr., and Richard West, "The Acquisition of Common Stock by the Corporate Issuer," *Journal of Finance,* December 1966, pp. 687–96.

outstanding. One strategy would be to pay the stockholders a $2 cash dividend. An alternate strategy, however, would be to repurchase a portion of the outstanding shares in the market. Through reducing the shares outstanding, earnings per share would increase, and with an assumed constant P/E ratio, the market price would increase. Thus, corporate management may determine that stockholders could receive additional value either in the form of dividends, which are taxable as ordinary income, or appreciation in value, which is taxable at a lower capital gains tax rate. The lower capital gains rate may therefore provide support for a repurchase strategy. This line of reasoning is largely theoretical; the market may or may not provide the appreciation in value associated with an increase in earnings per share in each individual case.

Another reason for the repurchase of shares is the acquisition of treasury stock to be used in future mergers and acquisitions or to fulfill obligations under an employee stock option plan. Shares may also be acquired to reduce the number of voting shares outstanding and thus diminish the vulnerability of the corporation to an unwanted or unsolicited takeover attempt by another corporation. Finally, the repurchase decision may be closely associated with a desire to reduce stockholder servicing cost; that is, to eliminate small stockholder accounts that are particularly unprofitable for the corporation to maintain.

Actual Market Effect

From the viewpoint of a special situation, the key question is, What is the stock market impact of the repurchase? Is there money to be made here or not? Much of the earlier research said no.[26] However, recent research would tend to indicate there might well be positive returns to investors in a repurchase situation.[27] Most of the higher returns are confined to formal tender offers to repurchase shares (perhaps 10 to 20 percent of the shares outstanding) rather than the use of informal, unannounced, open-market purchases. Under a formal tender offer, the corporation will specify the purchase price, the date of purchase, and the number of shares it wishes to acquire.

Of particular interest is the fact that most of the positive market movement comes *on* and *after* the announcement rather than before it. The implications are that there may be trading profits to be made here.

---

[26] A good example is Charles D. Ellis and Allen E. Young, *The Repurchase of Common Stock* (New York: Ronald Press, 1971), p. 156.

[27] Terry E. Dielman, Timothy J. Nantell, and Roger L. Wright, "Price Effects of Stock Repurchasing: A Random Coefficient Regression Approach," *Journal of Financial and Quantitative Analysis,* March 1980, p. 175–89. Larry Y. Dann, "Common Stock Repurchases: An Analysis of Returns to Bondholders and Stockholders," *Journal of Financial Economics,* June 1981, pp. 113–38. Theo Vermaelen, "Common Stock Repurchases and Market Signaling: An Empirical Study," *Journal of Financial Economics,* June 1981, pp. 139–83. R. W. Masulis, "Stock Repurchase by Tender Offer: An Analysis of the Causes of Common Stock Price Changes," *Journal of Finance,* May 1980, pp. 305–19.

TABLE 14–5   Summary Statistics for the Tender Offer Sample, 1962–1976 (143 observations)

Characteristic of offers	Mean (percent)	Median (percent)
Tender offer premium relative to closing market price one *day* prior to announcement	22.46%	19.40%
Tender offer premium relative to closing market price one *month* prior to announcement	20.85	18.83
Percentage of outstanding shares sought	15.29	12.57
Percentage of outstanding shares acquired	14.64	11.93
Percentage of outstanding shares tendered	18.04	14.27
Number of shares tendered ÷ number of shares sought	142.30	115.63
Number of shares acquired ÷ number of shares sought	111.35	100.00
Value of proposed repurchase relative to pre-offer market value of equity	19.29	15.28
Value of actual repurchase relative to pre-offer market value of equity	18.63	13.90
Duration of offer	22 days	20 days

Source: Larry Y. Dann, "Common Stock Repurchases: An Analysis of Returns to Bondholders and Stockholders," *Journal of Financial Economics,* June 1981, p. 122.

Dann determined that the average premium paid over the stock price (the day prior to announcement) was 22.46 percent as indicated on the top line of Table 14–5.

This high premium helps to generate a return of 8.946 percent on the day of announcement and 6.832 percent one day after announcement. This represents a two-day return of approximately 15.8 percent.[28] Dann further indicated that the price movements shortly *before* announcement were negligible, as indicated in Table 14–6.

The predominant argument for the beneficial effects of the repurchase is that management knows what they are doing when they purchase their *own* shares. In effect, they are acting as insiders for the benefit of the corporation, and we previously observed in Chapter 8 that insiders tend to be correct in their investment decisions. This factor, combined with the high premium, may provide positive investment results. Of course, these are merely average results over many transactions, and not all tender offers will prove to be beneficial events. The investor must carefully examine the premium offered, the number of shares to be repurchased, the reasons for repurchase, and the future impact on earnings and dividends per share.

[28] Professor Dann's observations are based on raw data rather than normalized returns. However, they are of sufficient magnitude to be important.

TABLE 14–6   Common Stock Rates of Return over a 121-Day Period Around Announcement of Common Stock Repurchase Tender Offer

Trading day	Mean rate of return (percent)	Trading day	Mean rate of return (percent)
−60	.217%	0	8.946%
−50	−.034	1	6.832
−40	.058	2	.908
−30	−.562	3	−.041
−25	−.125	4	.133
−20	−.071	5	.158
−19	.026	6	.230
−18	−.346	7	.129
−17	−.317	8	.051
−16	−.413	9	−.211
−15	.377	10	.213
−14	−.228	11	.172
−13	−.738	12	−.024
−12	.051	13	.181
−11	−.424	14	−.143
−10	−.578	15	.497
− 9	.188	16	−.105
− 8	−.391	17	−.236
− 7	.107	18	.148
− 6	.417	19	.141
− 5	−.169	20	−.057
− 4	.943	25	−.003
− 3	.239	30	−.025
− 2	.490	40	.133
− 1	.959	50	−.069
		60	.161

Source, Larry Y. Dann, "Common Stock Repurchases: An Analysis of Returns to Bondholders and Stockholders," *Journal of Financial Economics,* June 1981, p. 124.

THE SMALL-FIRM EFFECT

Two University of Chicago doctoral studies in the early 1980s have contended that a true key to superior risk-adjusted rates of return rests with investing in firms with small market capitalizations. (Market capitalization refers to shares outstanding times stock price.) In a study of New York Stock Exchange firms, covering from 1936 to 1975, Banz indicates that the lowest quintile (one fifth) firms in terms of market capitalization provide the highest returns even after adjusting for risk. Banz suggests that, "on average, small NYSE firms have had significantly larger risk-adjusted returns than larger NYSE firms over a 40-year period."[29]

---

[29] Rolf W. Banz, "The Relationship between Returns and Market Value of Common Stocks,' *Journal of Financial Economics,* March 1981, pp. 3–18.

Some criticized Banz for using only NYSE firms in his analysis and for using a time period that included the effects of both a depression and a major war. Small firms had incredibly high returns following the depression. A similar type study, produced by Reinganum[30] at about the same time, overcame these criticisms. Reinganum examined 2,000 firms that were traded on the New York Stock Exchange or American Stock Exchange between 1963 and 1980. He annually divided the 2,000 firms up into 10 groupings based on size, with the smallest category representing less than $5 million in market capitalization and the largest grouping representing a billion dollars or more.

A synopsis of the results from the Reinganum study are presented in Table 14–7.

TABLE 14–7   Synopsis of Results—Reinganum Study

(1) Grouping*	(2) Median market value (capitalization, in millions)	(3) Median share price	(4) Average annual return
MV 1	$ 4.6	$ 5.24	32.77%
MV 2	10.8	9.52	23.51
MV 3	19.3	12.89	22.98
MV 4	30.7	16.19	20.24
MV 5	47.2	19.22	19.08
MV 6	74.2	22.59	18.30
MV 7	119.1	26.44	15.64
MV 8	209.1	30.83	14.24
MV 9	434.6	34.43	13.00
MV 10	1,102.6	44.94	9.47

* MV = market value.
Source: Marc R. Reinganum, "Portfolio Strategies Based on Market Capitalization," *The Journal of Portfolio Management,* Winter 1983, pp. 29–36.

Column (2) indicates the median value of the market capitalization for the firms in each group. Column (3) is the median stock price for firms in each group, while column (4) indicates average annual return associated with that category.

As observed in column (4), the smallest capitalization group (MV 1)

[30] Marc R. Reinganum, "Misspecification of Capital Asset Pricing—Empirical Anomalies Based on Earnings Yield and Market Values," *Journal of Financial Economics,* March 1981, pp. 19–46. Also, "A Direct Test of Roll's Conjecture on the Firm Size Effect," *Journal of Finance,* March 1982, pp. 27–35, and "Portfolio Strategies Based on Market Capitalization," *The Journal of Portfolio Management,* Winter 1983, pp. 29–36.

outperformed the largest capitalization group (MV 10) by over 23 percent per year. Although not included in the table, in 14 out of the 18 years under study, the MV 1 group showed superior returns to the MV 10 group. In a similar analysis, Reinganum found that $1 invested in the smallest capitalization group would have grown to $46 between 1963 and 1980, while the same dollar invested in the largest capitalization group would have only grown to $4. As did Banz, Reinganum adjusted his returns for risk and continued to show superior risk-adjusted returns.

Such superior return evidence drew criticisms from different quarters. Roll sugested that small-capitalization studies underestimate the risk measure (beta) by failing to account for the infrequent and irregular trading patterns of stocks of smaller firms.[31] Stoll and Whaley maintained that transaction costs associated with dealing in smaller capitalization firms might severely cut into profit potential.[32] They indicated that the average buy-sell spread on small capitalized, low-priced stocks might be four or five times that of large capitalization firms. Reinganum has maintained that even after accounting for these criticisms, small capitalization firms continue to demonstrate superior risk-adjusted returns.[33]

Given that there might be advantages to investing in smaller firms, why haven't professional money managers picked up on the strategy. This, in part, is a Catch-22. Part of the reason for the inefficiency in this segment of the market that allows for superior returns is the absence of institutional traders. This absence means that there is less information generated on the smaller firms, and the information that is generated is reacted to in a less immediate fashion. Studies suggest there is an important linkage between the absence of organized information and superior return potential.[34]

For the institutional investor who wishes to participate in the small-firm segment of the market there is, of course, the problem of positioning. A large purchase may only be possible at well in excess of the current market price and a sell at well below the market. While market critics may well have us believe that it is the smaller investor who has difficulty in competing with the large, market-dominating institutional investor, the opposite may, in fact, be true. Historically, the 100 share investor has been able to explore segments of the market that are effectively closed to the institutional money manager.

In response to the small-firm effect, indirect doors are being opened up

---

[31] Richard Roll, "A Possible Explanation of the Small Firm Effect," *Journal of Finance,* September 1981, pp. 879–88.

[32] H. A. Stoll and R. E. Whaley, "Transaction Costs and the Small Firm Effect," Working paper, Owen Graduate School of Management, Vanderbilt University, January 1982.

[33] Marc R. Reinganum, "A Direct Test of Roll's Conjecture on the Firm Size Effect," *Journal of Finance,* March 1982, pp. 27–35, and "Portfolio Strategies Based on Market Capitalization," *The Journal of Portfolio Management,* Winter 1983, pp. 29–36.

[34] Avner Arbel and Paul Strebel, "Pay Attention to Neglected Firms," *The Journal of Portfolio Management,* Winter 1983, pp. 37–42.

to institutional investors through newly formed money management groups. The institutional investor can place his money with these groups. An example is Dimensional Fund Advisors (DFA). Market Researcher Rex Sinquefield serves as executive vice president of the fund, which specializes in investments in small capitalization firms. The fund only invests in the fifth quintile (lowest 20 percent) of NYSE firms in terms of market capitalization. DFA buys stocks without engaging in significant analysis, but rather relies on the small-firm effect to hopefully produce long-term positive effects.

Advocates of the small-firm effect argue that it is this phenomenon alone, rather than others, such as the low P/E ratio effect, that leads to superior risk-adjusted returns. Peavy and Goodman would argue that the low P/E ratio effect is also important,[35] and others maintain that the dividend yield must also be taken into consideration.[36] No doubt debate will continue on these points for many years to come.

A SPECIAL SITUATION IN THE BOND MARKET—NEW BOND ISSUES

The student should be aware of the situation that exists in the new issues market for bonds. As indicated in Figure 14–1, new bond issues are often priced to provide higher yields than existing (seasoned) issues of the same quality, maturity, and other similar features. The lines descending from the dots on the graph represent the difference between the yield on old issues and new issues. This yield differential provides a special-situation opportunity for higher returns to the investor.

What is the reason for the gap in yields between new and seasoned issues? It could be that investment bankers choose to overprice the yield (underprice the bond) in order to ensure the successful distribution of the issue and reduce the risk. Investment bankers are particularly vulnerable to taking losses on new bond issues when interest rates are rising rapidly. A new issue they thought was attractively priced when interest rates were 12 percent may prove to be almost unmarketable if interest rates shoot up. For this reason, it is hypothesized that investment bankers may garner an extra margin of protection by overpricing yields on new issues in relation to seasoned issues, particularly when interest rates are moving upward. The danger of getting trapped into too low a rate is illustrated by what happened to the securities firm of Salomon Brothers in its distribution of a high-quality IBM offering in October of 1979. Federal Reserve Board Chairman Paul Volcker announced an unexpected, extreme credit tightening policy during the distribution process, and bond prices fell dramatically, leaving Salomon Brothers and other investment bankers with approximately $10 million in losses.

---

[35] John W. Peavy III and David A. Goodman, "The Significance of P/Es for Portfolio Returns," *The Journal of Portfolio Management,* Winter 1983, pp. 43–47.

[36] Solveig Jansson, "The Big Debate over Little Stocks," *Institutional Investor,* June 1982, pp. 141–48.

FIGURE 14–1   Yields on Corporate Bonds—New Issues versus Seasoned Issues

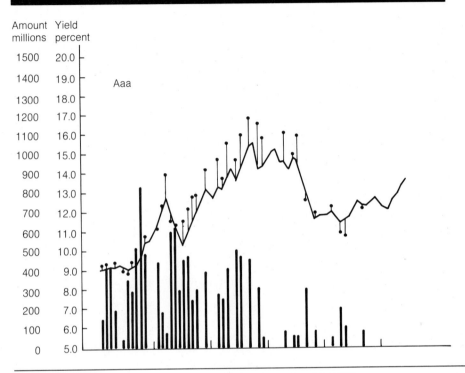

Source: *Moody's Bond Record* (New York: Moody's Investor's Service, Inc., July 1984).

One important piece of research has taken a slightly different approach to explain the gap between yields on new and existing issues of the same quality. Lindvall has suggested that dealers or market makers in the existing bond market are slow to change the value of their inventory to reflect current market conditions.[37] Because trading in existing bond issues is not as intense as similar trading in the stock market, dealers are more arbitrary in setting prices. This may be particularly true when interest rates are going up and dealers do not wish to mark down the value of their inventory. The essence of the Lindvall argument is that, in the bond market, new offerings may come closer to reflecting current market conditions than seasoned issues do.

Regardless of the reasoning, it is clear that new issues tend to carry a higher yield than existing issues of the same quality most of the time. The consequences are twofold. First, investors should prefer new issues to seasoned issues, other things being equal. Second, there may be short-term arbitrage or swap possibilities between old and new issues.

---

[37] John R. Lindvall, "New Issue Corporate Bonds, Seasoned Market Efficiency and Yield Spreads," *Journal of Finance,* September 1977, pp. 1057–67.

Chapter 15

COMMODITIES AND FINANCIAL FUTURES

What do pork bellies, soybeans, Japanese yen, and Treasury bills have in common? They are all items on which contracts may be traded in the commodities and financial futures markets.

A futures contract is an agreement that provides for the delivery of a specific amount of a commodity at a designated time in the future at a given price. An example might be a contract to deliver 5,000 bushels of corn in September of 1985 at $3.00 per bushel. The person who sells the contract does not need to have actual possession of the corn, nor does the purchaser of the contract need to plan on taking possession of the corn. Almost all commodity futures contracts are closed out or reversed before the actual transaction is to take place. Thus, the seller of a futures contract for the delivery of 5,000 bushels of corn may simply buy back a similar contract for the purchase of 5,000 bushels and close out his position. The initial buyer also reverses his position. Over 97 percent of all contracts are closed out in this fashion rather than through actual delivery.[1] The commodities futures market is similar to the options market in that there is a tremendous volume of activity but very few actual items ever change hands.

The futures markets were originally set up to allow grain and livestock producers and processors to hedge their positions in a given commodity. For example, a wheat producer might have a five-month lead time between the planting of his crop and the actual harvesting and delivery to the market. While the current price of wheat might be $4.00 a bushel, there is a tremendous risk that the price might change before delivery to the market. The wheat producer can hedge his position by offering to sell futures contracts for the delivery of wheat. Even though he will probably close out or reverse these futures contracts prior to the call for actual delivery, he will still have effectively hedged his position. Let's see how this works. If the price of wheat goes down, he will have to sell his crop for less than he anticipated when he planted the wheat, but he will make up the difference on the wheat futures contracts. That is, he will be able to buy back the contracts for less than he sold them. Of course, if the price of the wheat goes up, the extra profit he makes on the crop will be lost on the futures contracts as he now has to buy back the contracts at a higher price.[2]

A miller who uses wheat as part of his processing faces the opposite dilemma in terms of pricing. The miller is afraid the price of wheat might go up and ultimately cut into his profit margin when he takes actual delivery of his product. He can hedge his position by buying futures contracts in wheat. If the actual price of wheat does go up, the extra cost of producing his product will be offset by the profits he makes on his futures contracts.

---

[1] "Speculating on Inflation: Futures Trading in Interest Rates, Foreign Currencies and Precious Metals," Merrill Lynch, Pierce, Fenner & Smith, July 1979.

[2] The hedger not only reduces risk of loss but also eliminates additional profit opportunities. This may be appropriate for farmers since they are not in the risk-taking business but rather in agriculture.

FIGURE 15–1

353

COMMODITY RESEARCH BUREAU FUTURES PRICE INDEX
(1967 = 100)
(Weekly High, Low & Close)

27 MARKETS

BARLEY — WPG.
BROILERS — CHI.
CATTLE (LIVE) — CHI.
COCOA — N.Y.
COFFEE "C" — N.Y.
COPPER — N.Y.
CORN — CHI.
COTTON "2" — N.Y.
EGGS "SHELL" — CHI.
FLAXSEED — WPG.
GREASEWOOL — N.Y.
HOGS (LIVE) — CHI.
OATS — CHI.
ORANGE JUICE — N.Y.

PLATINUM — N.Y.
PLYWOOD — CHI.
PORK BELLIES — CHI.
POTATOES — N.Y.
RAPESEED — WPG.
RYE — WPG.
SILVER — N.Y.
SOYBEAN MEAL — CHI.
SOYBEAN OIL — CHI.
SOYBEANS — CHI.
SUGAR "11" — N.Y.
WHEAT — CHI.
WHEAT — MPLS.

CRB Futures Price Index, Monthly High, Low & Close 1967 = 100

Year		Jan.	Feb.	Mar.	Apr.	May	June	July	Aug.	Sept.	Oct.	Nov.	Dec.	Range
1980	High	290.4	297.4	296.9	263.7	271.8	286.4	303.2	308.4	329.0	329.9	337.6	329.0	337.6
	Low	276.8	287.5	258.0	256.3	259.4	269.4	289.5	301.9	310.4	316.8	321.8	295.1	256.3
	Close	289.6	288.4	258.0	258.1	270.1	286.4	302.3	308.4	319.4	327.1	334.8	308.5	—
1981	High	314.5	306.9	298.4	300.7	290.0	286.0	279.7	279.7	276.0	274.0	269.8	264.8	314.5
	Low	299.2	296.7	287.5	287.7	280.7	263.9	266.6	268.1	266.8	266.6	260.7	250.5	250.5
	Close	300.1	296.7	298.4	289.1	287.5	263.9	279.3	269.4	268.6	268.9	262.2	254.9	—
1982	High	267.2	268.6	257.5	257.3	253.3	242.0	242.4	238.4	239.8	234.3	236.3	235.7	268.6
	Low	256.0	256.5	248.7	252.5	244.9	231.5	233.2	227.1	227.9	225.8	231.2	231.1	225.8
	Close	267.2	256.5	250.1	253.1	244.9	239.3	233.7	235.4	227.9	229.9	235.7	234.0	—
1983	High	242.7	245.1	242.1	247.3									
	Low	234.8	232.1	232.8	244.7									
	Close	242.7	232.1	242.1	246.7									

Source: *Commodity Yearbook* (New York: Commodity Research Bureau, 1983), p. 6.

The commodities market allows the many parties in need of hedging opportunities to acquire contracts. While some of this could be accomplished on a private basis (one party in Kansas City calls another party in Chicago on the advice of his banker), this would be virtually impossible to handle on a large-scale basis. Liquid, fluid markets, such as those provided by the commodity exchanges, are necessary to accomplish this function.

While the hedgers are the backbone and basic reason for existence of the commodity exchanges, they are not the only significant participants. We also have the speculators who take purely long or short positions without any intent to hedge actual ownership. Thus, there is the speculator in wheat or silver who believes that the next major price move can be predicted to such an extent that a substantial profit can be made. Because commodities are purchased on the basis of a small investment in the form of margin (usually running 5 to 10 percent of the value of the contract), there is substantial leverage on the investment, and percentage returns and losses are greatly magnified. The typical commodities trader often suffers many losses with the anticipation of a few very substantial gains. Commodities speculation, as opposed to hedging, represents somewhat of a gamble, and stories have been told of reformed commodities speculators who gave up the chase to spend the rest of their days merely playing the slot machines.

The volatility of commodity prices can be seen in Figure 15–1 on page 435. While the price trend for the 27 commodities in the index has been upward, note the up and down patterns, particularly in the mid-1970s and early 1980s.

TYPES OF COMMODITIES AND EXCHANGES

Commodities and financial futures can be broken down into a number of categories based on their essential characteristics. As indicated in Table 15–1, there are six primary categories. In each case, we show representative items that fall under the category.

The first five categories represent traditional commodities, but category 6 came into prominence in the 1970s, with foreign exchange futures originating in 1972, interest rate futures beginning in 1975, and stock index futures in 1982. Because financial futures have tremendous implications for financial managers, we will give them special attention in a later section of this chapter. We will defer discussion of stock index futures to Chapter 16, so that they can be given complete coverage as a separate topic.

The commodities listed in Table 15–1 trade on various commodity exchanges in the United States and Canada (see Table 15–2). While the exchanges are well organized and efficient in their operation, they are still run by an open auction complete with outcries of bids and various hand-signal displays.

The largest commodity exchange is the Chicago Board of Trade (CBT) with the Chicago Mercantile Exchange (CME) in second place. While some exchanges are highly specialized, such as the New York Cotton Exchange,

TABLE 15–1 Categories of Commodities and Financial Futures

(1)	(2)	(3)
Grains and oilseeds:	Livestock and meat:	Food and fiber:
Corn	Cattle—feeder	Cocoa
Oats	Cattle—live	Coffee
Soybeans	Hogs—live	Cotton
Wheat	Pork bellies	Orange juice
Barley	Turkeys	Potatoes
Rye	Broilers	Sugar
		Rice
		Butter

(4)	(5)	(6)
Metals and petroleum:	Wood:	Financial futures:
Copper	Lumber	*a.* Foreign exchange
Gold	Plywood	(pound, yen, franc,
Platinum		etc.)
Silver		*b.* Interest rate futures
Mercury		GNMA certificates
Heating oil no. 2		Treasury bonds
		Treasury bills
		Certificates of deposit
		Commercial paper
		Eurodollars
		c. Stock index futures
		S&P 500
		Value Line

TABLE 15–2 Major United States and Canadian Commodity Exchanges

American Commodities Exchange (ACE)
Chicago Board of Trade (CBT)
Chicago Mercantile Exchange (CME)
  Also controls International Monetary Market (IMM)
Commodity Exchange (CMX)
Kansas City Board of Trade (KC)
Minneapolis Grain Exchange (MPLS)
New Orleans Commodity Exchange
New York Coffee, Sugar, and Cocoa Exchange (CSCE)
New York Cotton Exchange (CTN)
New York Futures Exchange (NYFE)
  Subsidiary of the New York Stock Exchange
New York Mercantile Exchange (NYM)
Pacific Commodities Exchange (PCE)
Winnipeg Grain Exchange (WPG)

most exchanges trade in a wide number of securities. For example, the Chicago Board of Trade deals in such diverse products as corn, oats, soybeans, wheat, plywood, GNMA certificates, and Treasury bonds.

The American Commodities Exchange (ACE), part of the American Stock Exchange, and the New York Futures Exchange (NYFE), part of the New York Stock Exchange, are rather new in the game and specialize in financial futures. As the Chicago Board of Trade and Chicago Mercantile Exchange moved into this territory with financially oriented securities (such as GNMA futures and Treasury bill futures), members of Wall Street felt compelled to get into the financial futures game as well.

The activities of the commodity exchanges are primarily regulated by the Commodity Futures Trading Commission (CFTC), a federal regulatory agency established by Congress in 1975. The CFTC has had a number of jurisdictional disputes with the SEC over the regulation of financial futures.

Types of Commodities Contracts

The commodity contract lists the type of commodity and the denomination in which it is traded (bushels, pounds, troy ounces, metric tons, percentage points, etc.). The contract will also specify the standardized unit for trade (5,000 bushels, 30,000 pounds, etc.). A further designation will indicate the month in which the contract ends, with most commodities having a whole range of months from which to choose. Typically, contracts run as far as a year into the future, but some interest rate futures contracts extend as far as three years.

Examples of the sizes of futures contracts are presented in Table 15–3. Be aware that there may be many different forms of the same commodity (such as spring wheat or amber/durum wheat).

TABLE 15–3   Size of Commodity Contracts

Contract	Trading units	Size of contract based on mid-1984 prices
Corn	5,000 bushels	$ 16,200
Oats	5,000 bushels	9,500
Wheat	5,000 bushels	20,000
Pork bellies	38,000 pounds	26,500
Coffee	37,500 pounds	53,250
Cotton	50,000 pounds	42,500
Sugar	112,000 pounds	6,720
Copper	25,000 pounds	17,500
Gold	100 troy ounces	35,000
Silver	5,000 troy ounces	40,000
Treasury bonds	$100,000	59,150
Treasury bills	$1,000,000	878,200

ACTUAL COMMODITIES CONTRACT

To examine the potential gain or loss in a commodities contract, let's go through a hypothetical investment. Assume we are considering the purchase of a December wheat contract (it is now May 1). The price on the futures contract is $4.00 per bushel. Since wheat trades in units of 5,000 bushels, the total price is $20,000. As we go through our example, we will examine many important features associated with commodity trading—beginning with margin requirements.

Margin Requirements

Commodity trading is based on the use of margin rather than on actual cash dollars. Margin requirements are typically 5 to 10 percent of the value of the contract and may vary over time or even from exchange to exchange for a given commodity. For our example, we will assume a $1,500 margin requirement. This would represent 7.5 percent of the value of the contract ($20,000).

Margin requirements on commodities contracts are much lower than those on stock transactions, where 50 percent of the purchase price has been the requirement since 1974. Furthermore, in the commodities market, the margin payment is merely considered to be a good-faith payment against losses. There is no actual borrowing or interest to be paid.[3]

In addition to the initial margin requirements, there are also margin maintenance requirements (minimum maintenance standards) that run 70 to 80 percent of the value of the initial margin. In the case of the wheat contract, the margin maintenance requirement might be $1,200 (80% $\times$ $1,500). If our initial margin of $1,500 is reduced by $300 due to losses on our contract, we will be required to replace the $300 to cover our margin position. If we do not do so, our position will be closed out and we will take our losses.

The margin requirement, relative to size, is even less for financial futures. For example, on a $1 million Treasury bill contract, the investor generally must only post an initial margin of $1,500. Similar requirements exist for other types of financial futures.

Note that the high risk inherent in a commodities contract is not so much a function of volatile price movements as it is the impact of high leverage made possible by the low initial margin requirements. A 10 percent price move may equal or exceed the size of our initial investment in the form of the margin deposit. This is similar to the type of leverage utilized in the options market as described in Chapter 13. However, the action in the commodities market is much quicker. You can be asked to put up additional margin within hours after you establish your initial position.

---

[3] It should also be pointed out that we may need a minimum account balance of $5,000 or greater to open a commodity account.

Market Conditions

Because the price of every commodity moves in response to market conditions, each investor must determine the key market variables that influence the value of his or her contract. In the case of wheat, the investor may be particularly concerned about such factors as weather and crop conditions in the Midwest, the price of corn as a substitute product, the carryover of wheat supply from the previous year, and the potential wheat sales to the Soviet Union and other foreign countries. A rumor about an impending transaction with the Soviet Union has often caused market prices to change radically.

Gains and Losses

In the present example, assume we guessed right in our analysis of the wheat market; we purchased a December futures contract for $4.00 per bushel, and the price goes to $4.35 per bushel (recall that the contract was for 5,000 bushels). With a 35-cent increase per bushel, we have established a dollar gain of $1,750 (5,000 bushes × $.35 per bushel profit). With an initial margin requirement of $1,500, we have made a percentage profit of 116.7 percent.[4]

$$\frac{\text{Dollar gain}}{\text{Amount of margin deposit}} = \frac{\$1,750}{\$1,500} \times 100 = 116.7\%$$

If this transaction took place over a one-month time period, the annualized gain would be 1,400 percent (116.7% × 12 = 1,400.4%). Note that this was all accomplished by a 35-cent movement in the price of a December wheat contract from $4.00 to $4.35, a percentage change of 8.7 percent ($.35/$4.00).

Actually, the investor may choose to close out his contract or attempt to let his profits run. He also may use his profits to establish the basis for margin on additional futures contracts. A paper gain of $1,750 is more than enough to provide the $1,500 margin on another wheat contract. Actually, a gain of only 30 cents per bushel would have accomplished this by providing $1,500 in profits (5,000 bushels × $.30).

The investor is now in a position to use an inverse pyramid to expand his position. With two contracts outstanding, a mere 15-cent price change will provide $1,500 in profits.

$$\begin{array}{rl}
\$ & .15 \text{ Price change} \\
\times & \underline{10,000} \text{ Bushels (two contracts)} \\
& \$1,500 \text{ Profits (can be applied} \\
& \text{to third contract)}
\end{array}$$

The $1,500 in profits can be used to purchase a third contract, and now with 15,000 bushels under control, a 10-cent price change will generate enough profits for a fourth contract.

---

[4] This does not include commissions, which are generally less than $60 to $70 for a complete transaction (buy and sell).

$ .10 Price change
× 15,000 Bushels (three contracts)
$1,500 Profits (can be applied
to fourth contract)

The process of inverse pyramiding begins to sound astounding since eventually a 1-cent or ½-cent change in the price of wheat will trigger off enough profits for a new contract. Of course, there are great risks associated with such a process. It is like building a house with playing cards. If one card tumbles, the whole house comes down. The investor can become so highly leveraged that any slight reversal in price can trigger off tremendous margin calls. While it is often wise to let profits run and perhaps do some amount of pyramiding, prudence must be exercised.

Our primary attention up to this point has been on contracts that are making money. What are the implications if there is an immediate price reversal after we have purchased our December wheat contract? You will recall there was a margin maintenance requirement of $1,200 based on our initial margin of $1,500. In this case, a $300 loss would call for an additional deposit to bring our margin position up to $1,500. How much would the price of wheat have to decline for us to get this margin call to increase our deposit? With a 5,000-bushel contract, we are talking about a mere decline of 6 cents per bushel.

$$\frac{\$300 \text{ loss}}{5,000 \text{ bushels}} = \$.06 \text{ per bushel}$$

This could happen in a matter of hours or days after our initial purchase. When we get the margin call, we can either elect to put up the additional $300 and continue with the contract or tell our commodities broker to close out our contract and take our losses. If we put up the $300, our broker could still be on the phone two hours later asking for more margin because the price has shown further deterioration. Because investors often buy multiple contracts, such as 10 December wheat contracts, the process can be all the more intense. In the commodities market, the old adage of "cut your losses short and let your profits run" probably has its greatest significance. Even a seasoned commodities trader might determine that he is willing to lose 80 percent of the time and only win 20 percent of the time, but those victories will represent home runs and the losses mere outs.

Price Movement Limitations

Because of the enormous opportunities for gains and losses in the commodities markets, the commodity exchanges do place some broad limitations on maximum daily price movements in a commodity. Some examples are shown in Table 15–4.

These daily trading limits obviously must affect the efficiency of the market somewhat. If market conditions indicate the price of wheat should

TABLE 15–4   Maximum Daily Price Changes

Commodity	Exchange	Normal price range	Maximum daily price change (from previous close)*
Corn	CBT	$2.30–$4.00	$.10 per bushel
Oats	CBT	$1.25–$2.40	$.06 per bushel
Wheat	CBT	$3.00–$5.50	$.20 per bushel
Pork bellies	CBT	$.40–$.80	$.02 per pound
Copper	CME	$.60–$1.50	$.03 per pound
Silver	CMX	$6.00–$50.00	$.50 per ounce
Treasury bills	IMM of CME	85% of par and up	50 basis points

* These values may change slightly from exchange to exchange and are often temporarily altered in response to rampant speculation.

decline by 30 cents and the daily limit is 20 cents, then obviously the price of wheat is not in equilibrium as it opens the following morning. However, the desire to stop market panics tends to override the desire for total market efficiency in the commodity markets. Nevertheless, the potential intraday trading range is still large. Recall, for example, that a 20-cent change in the price of wheat, which is the daily limit, is more than enough to place tremendous pressure on the investor to repeatedly increase his margin position. On the typical 5,000-bushel contract, this would represent a daily loss of $1,000.

READING MARKET QUOTES

We now turn our attention to interpreting market quotes in the daily newspaper. In Figure 15–2, we show an excerpt from the June 1, 1984, edition of *The Wall Street Journal* covering 18 different types of contracts (this represents about one third of the contracts reported for that day).

In each case, we see there is a wide choice of months for which a contract may be purchased. For example, oats, which trade on the Chicago Board of Trade (CBT), have futures contracts for July, September, December, and March. Some commodities offer a contract for virtually every month. In order to directly examine some of the terms in Figure 15–2, we reproduce the portion related to the oats contract (CBT) in Table 15–5.

We initially read the second line in the table that indicates we are dealing in oats traded on the Chicago Board of Trade (CBT). We then note that oats are traded in 5,000-bushel units and quoted in cents per bushel. Quotations in cents per bushel require some mental adjustment. For example, 200 cents per bushel would actually represent two dollars ($2) per bushel. We generally move the decimal point two places to the left and read the quote in terms of dollars. For example, the July 1984 opening price was 188, or $1.88 per bushel.

Futures Prices

Thursday, May 31, 1984

Open Interest Reflects Previous Trading Day.

—GRAINS AND OILSEEDS—

	Open	High	Low	Settle	Change	Lifetime High	Low	Open Interest
CORN (CBT) 5,000 bu.; cents per bu.								
July	353¾	354¼	349¾	350½	− 3¼	388	288¼	81,567
Sept	328	329¼	325½	325¾	− 2¾	356½	295½	23,685
Dec	304¼	306¼	303	303	− 2	330	279¾	41,936
Mar85	313	314½	312	312¼	− 1¼	319	289¾	7,188
May	317¼	319	316¼	316½	− 1	322	295½	1,498
July	320¼	320½	318½	318½	− 1	323¼	307½	603
Sept	311½	311½	311½	311½	− 1	315	311	8

Est vol 35,900; vol Wed 34,771; open int 156,486, +807.

	Open	High	Low	Settle	Change	Lifetime High	Low	Open Interest
CORN (MCE) 1,000 bu.; cents per bu.								
July	354	354¼	349⅝	350½	− 3¼	388⅛	288½	6,092
Sept	327¾	329	325¾	325¾	− 2¾	355	298½	1,019
Dec	304¼	306	302¾	303	− 2	330	281¼	5,428
Mar85	313	313¾	312½	312¼	− 1¼	319	292¼	303
May	....	....	....	316½	− 1	321	292	46
July	320	320	320	318½	− 1	323¼	309¾	21

Est vol 1,150 vol Wed 1,123; open int 12,909, +89.

	Open	High	Low	Settle	Change	Lifetime High	Low	Open Interest
OATS (CBT) 5,000 bu.; cents per bu.								
July	188	188½	187	188½	+ 1½	226	166¼	2,017
Sept	183¾	184	182	182½	− ½	219	164¾	915
Dec	187½	187½	186	186¼	− ¾	193¼	168½	906
Mar85	189¼	189¾	189¼	189¾	− 1½	196½	181¾	267

Est vol 600; vol Wed 864; open int 4,105, +236.

	Open	High	Low	Settle	Change	Lifetime High	Low	Open Interest
SOYBEANS (CBT) 5,000 bu.; cents per bu.								
July	867	868¼	846	847	− 19	992½	639½	58,102
Aug	861	863	842	843	−17½	956¾	640	15,846
Sept	791	798½	786	786¼	− 5	860	705½	8,980
Nov	745	755	742	745½	+ 1	772¼	661	24,609
Jan85	756	765½	753	754¼	− 1¼	765½	676	5,698
Mar	767	776	764	766¾	+ ¼	776	692	1,916
May	775	784	773	777	+ 2	784	729½	608
July	781½	781½	781½	781½	+ 2	784	742	111

Est vol 85,300; vol Wed 67,668; open int 115,870, −79.

	Open	High	Low	Settle	Change	Lifetime High	Low	Open Interest
SOYBEANS (MCE) 1,000 bu.; cents per bu.								
July	886	867	845	847	− 19	992½	645	20,291
Aug	861	863	841	843	−17½	955	646	2,061
Sept	801	797½	784½	786¼	− 5	853	708	560
Nov	746	755	742	745½	+ 1	772¼	661	4,181
Jan85	753	766	752½	754¼	− 1¼	766	678	747
Mar	767	776	763	766¾	+ ¼	776	722	386
May	773	783	772	777	+ 2	783	733	92
July	777	777	777	781½	+ 2	777	754	30

Est vol 5,280; vol Wed 5,513; open int 28,348, − 5.

	Open	High	Low	Settle	Change	Lifetime High	Low	Open Interest
SOYBEAN MEAL (CBT) 100 tons; $ per ton.								
July	200.50	200.90	195.20	195.40	− 4.70	267.50	188.00	30,597
Aug	202.50	203.00	197.50	197.80	− 4.40	251.00	190.30	10,866
Sept	200.00	200.00	196.50	196.50	− 3.20	243.00	188.00	6,674
Oct	190.00	192.50	189.00	189.50	− .30	240.00	182.00	9,680
Dec	191.50	194.00	190.50	192.50	+ 1.30	227.00	182.50	13,197
Jan85	193.00	196.10	192.50	194.30	+ 1.60	208.00	184.00	2,645
Mar	195.80	198.00	194.00	195.70	+ 2.20	209.00	188.50	750
May	....	....	....	198.00	− 2.50	205.00	191.00	63

Est vol 27,600; vol Wed 14,330; open int 74,473, −29.

	Open	High	Low	Settle	Change	Lifetime High	Low	Open Interest
SOYBEAN OIL (CBT) 60,000 lbs.; cents per lb.								
July	37.10	37.70	36.75	36.90	− .38	39.75	20.00	26,429
Aug	36.15	36.80	35.90	35.95	− .35	38.45	20.30	10,398
Sept	34.50	34.75	34.10	34.15	− .52	36.15	23.45	6,680
Oct	31.55	31.85	31.15	31.18	− .62	33.05	23.50	10,637
Dec	29.70	29.85	29.30	29.33	− .58	30.80	23.45	8,804
Jan85	29.55	29.55	29.00	29.05	− .45	30.25	24.05	2,213
Mar	29.10	29.10	28.90	28.90	− .30	30.25	25.25	864
May	....	....	....	28.88	− .30	29.90	28.20	4
July	....	....	....	28.88	− .30	30.25	29.50	0

Est vol 24,200; vol Wed 28,307; open int 66,029, −932.

	Open	High	Low	Settle	Change	Lifetime High	Low	Open Interest
WHEAT (CBT) 5,000 bu.; cents per bu.								
July	363	363¾	356	356	− 7½	427	322	25,380
Sept	367	367¾	360	360¼	− 7¼	432	325	11,966
Dec	382½	383¾	375½	375¾	− 7¾	418	337½	12,395
Mar85	393	393¾	386	386¼	− 8	404	344	3,032
May	396	396	390½	390½	− 7¼	405	367¼	119
July	382	382	376	376	− 7	390	376	12

Est vol 20,400; vol Wed 14,168; open int 52,904, −359.

	Open	High	Low	Settle	Change	Lifetime High	Low	Open Interest
WHEAT (KC) 5,000 bu.; cents per bu.								
July	370	370¼	365½	365½	− 5	419	339¼	9,212
Sept	376	376	371½	371½	− 4¾	417	343½	5,100
Dec	388	388¼	383½	383½	− 5	397	355	2,501
Mar85	392½	392½	392½	392½	− 6	407½	377¼	173

Est vol 4,379; vol Wed 3,383; open int 16,986, +52.

	Open	High	Low	Settle	Change	Lifetime High	Low	Open Interest
WHEAT (MPLS) 5,000 bu.; cents per bu.								
July	413¾	414	409	409¼	− 4½	430	372½	2,342
Sept	405	405¼	400	400¼	− 4¾	408½	364½	1,915
Dec	410½	410¾	405½	406	− 5	414	366½	798
Mar85	....	....	409	409	− 3¼	413½	392½	168

Est vol 1,080; vol Wed 1,212; open int 5,222, −47.

	Open	High	Low	Settle	Change	Lifetime High	Low	Open Interest
WHEAT (MCE) 1,000 bu.; cents per bu.								
July	362½	363¼	355	356	− 7½	428	322⅜	14,186
Sept	367	367	359½	360¼	− 7¼	430	327	232
Dec	383	383¼	375	375¾	− 7¾	408¾	340	3,015
Mar85	392½	392½	392¼	386¼	− 8	397½	348	88
May	....	....	....	390½	− 7¼	401½	368	5
July	381	381	381	376	− 7	387	381	2

Est vol 680; vol Wed 450; open int 17,528, +106.

	Open	High	Low	Settle	Change	Lifetime High	Low	Open Interest
COTTON (CTN)—50,000 lbs.; cents per lb.								
July	84.96	85.17	84.50	84.62	− .34	86.25	71.50	10,416
Aug	....	....	....	81.00	− 1.25	80.80	79.90	1
Oct	80.96	80.96	80.21	80.25	− .89	82.09	72.19	3,556
Dec	77.66	77.75	77.05	77.08	− .61	78.40	70.72	14,623
Mar85	78.75	78.75	78.20	78.15	− .70	79.35	72.50	1,996
May	....	....	....	78.60	− .70	79.20	73.74	128
July	79.32	79.32	79.32	78.71	− .70	79.85	75.75	146
Oct	....	....	....	76.60	− .70	77.50	77.00	7

Est vol 6,000; vol Wed 5,883; open int 30,873, −86.

	Open	High	Low	Settle	Change	Lifetime High	Low	Open Interest
ORANGE JUICE (CTN)—15,000 lbs.; cents per lb.								
May	....	....	....	....	....	....	....	64
July	179.25	181.90	178.50	181.55	+ 1.30	190.50	101.00	3,484
Sept	179.10	180.25	177.50	180.10	+ .10	188.90	103.80	3,008
Nov	178.25	178.95	177.10	178.50	− .65	185.65	107.50	1,387
Jan85	178.50	179.05	178.00	179.00	− .40	183.60	109.00	1,639
Mar	179.00	179.00	178.50	178.75	− .35	182.70	118.50	1,124
May	179.00	179.00	178.50	178.65	− .35	181.50	151.00	168
July	177.25	177.25	177.25	178.50	....	181.00	155.00	156
Sept	178.25	178.50	178.25	178.50	....	181.00	171.50	52

Est vol 1,500; vol Wed 546; open int 11,042, +38.

	Open	High	Low	Settle	Change	Lifetime High	Low	Open Interest
SUGAR—WORLD (CSCE)—112,000 lbs.; cents per lb.								
July	5.72	5.88	5.70	5.88	+ .13	14.95	5.48	27,239
Sept	5.99	6.14	5.97	6.14	+ .14	14.93	5.80	3,829
Oct	6.17	6.35	6.16	6.35	+ .16	15.30	6.03	41,855
Jan85	6.77	6.90	6.77	6.85	+ .07	13.10	6.60	535
Mar	7.32	7.51	7.31	7.45	+ .09	13.60	7.19	12,433
May	7.59	7.76	7.57	7.71	+ .10	10.50	7.54	3,591
July	7.87	8.00	7.86	8.00	+ .12	9.95	7.86	1,646
Sept	8.20	8.20	8.20	8.26	+ .07	9.75	8.10	84
Oct	8.40	8.48	8.40	8.47	+ .07	9.05	8.30	67

Est vol 6,066; vol Wed 4,045; open int 91,289, +747.

	Open	High	Low	Settle	Change	Lifetime High	Low	Open Interest
SUGAR—DOMESTIC (CSCE)—112,000 lbs.; cents per lb.								
July	22.10	22.10	22.05	22.05	− .02	22.65	21.35	3,770
Sept	22.10	22.14	22.05	22.08	− .04	22.58	21.50	2,063
Nov	21.80	21.83	21.80	21.82	+ .02	22.19	21.65	2,399
Jan85	21.76	21.76	21.76	21.76	− .07	22.20	21.66	477
Mar	21.86	21.86	21.85	21.85	− .02	22.30	21.70	2,066
May	21.90	21.90	21.90	21.90	− .02	22.40	21.75	996
July	21.98	21.98	21.98	21.98	− .02	22.43	21.90	617

Est vol 438; vol Wed 215; open int 12,388, −36.

—METALS & PETROLEUM—

	Open	High	Low	Settle	Change	Lifetime High	Low	Open Interest
COPPER (CMX)—25,000 lbs.; cents per lb.								
June	63.25	63.25	63.25	63.35	− .15	72.10	63.25	1
July	63.80	64.20	63.35	63.95	− .20	89.80	62.35	39,985
Aug	....	....	....	64.65	− .20	....	....	0
Sept	65.25	65.55	64.70	65.35	− .20	90.80	63.75	21,530
Dec	67.40	67.60	66.80	67.45	− .15	92.70	65.70	13,212
Jan85	....	....	....	68.15	− .15	92.00	66.55	257
Mar	69.35	69.60	69.20	69.55	− .10	93.20	67.50	7,352
May	70.65	70.65	70.60	70.95	− .10	92.50	69.10	4,444
July	72.10	72.10	72.10	72.40	− .10	88.25	70.35	2,268
Sept	73.50	73.50	73.50	73.80	− .10	82.10	72.25	957
Dec	75.60	75.60	75.60	76.00	....	84.25	74.05	1,514
Jan86	....	....	....	76.75	....	84.20	70.00	56
Mar	....	....	....	78.30	+ .05	80.00	76.55	424

Est vol 9,000; vol Wed 9,747; open int 92,000, +451.

	Open	High	Low	Settle	Change	Lifetime High	Low	Open Interest
GOLD (CMX)—100 troy oz.; $ per troy oz.								
June	383.00	388.50	383.00	386.80	+ 2.30	580.00	370.00	8,281
July	387.00	391.00	387.00	390.10	+ 2.10	388.80	378.80	7
Aug	390.50	395.50	390.30	393.60	+ 2.00	588.00	377.00	42,102
Oct	399.00	403.50	399.00	401.70	+ 1.90	597.00	385.50	12,165
Dec	408.00	412.50	407.00	410.40	+ 2.00	608.00	386.80	20,184
Feb85	416.00	420.50	416.00	419.30	+ 2.00	522.00	402.50	22,028
Apr	426.00	429.50	425.80	428.30	+ 1.90	514.50	410.00	20,816
June	436.50	439.50	436.20	437.90	+ 1.80	510.00	415.50	13,960
Aug	447.00	447.00	447.00	447.90	+ 1.70	485.00	422.00	3,019
Oct	455.50	455.50	455.50	457.80	+ 1.60	493.00	434.00	703
Dec	466.50	470.00	466.50	468.40	+ 1.50	489.50	450.00	1,589
Feb86	....	....	....	478.70	+ 1.50	479.00	459.00	168
Apr	....	....	....	489.10	+ 1.40	....	....	0

Est vol 34,000; vol Wed 43,629; open int 145,022, +101.

	Open	High	Low	Settle	Change	Lifetime High	Low	Open Interest
GOLD (IMM)—100 troy oz.; $ per troy oz.								
June	383.00	386.20	383.00	386.20	+ 3.40	574.60	372.90	287
Sept	394.70	397.50	394.70	397.50	+ 3.60	436.00	386.00	27
Dec	406.50	409.50	406.50	409.50	+ 4.70	444.50	397.20	181

Est vol 25; vol Wed 211; open int 495, −61.

TABLE 15–5   Price Quotes for Oat Contracts

(1)	Open	High	Low	Settle	Change	Lifetime high	Low	Open interest
(2) **Oats (CBT)—5,000 bu.; cents per bu.**								
July	188	188½	187	188½	+1½	226	166¼	2,017
Sept	183¾	184	182	182½	– ½	219	164¾	915
Dec	187½	187½	186	186¼	– ¾	193¼	168½	906
Mar 85	189¼	193¾	189¼	193¾	–1½	196½	181¾	267

Source: *Reprinted by permission of The Wall Street Journal.* © Dow Jones & Company, Inc., June 1, 1984, p. 25.

Across the top of the table we observe that we are given information on the open, high, low, settle (close), and change from the previous day's close as well as the lifetime high and low for that particular contract. The last column represents the open interest, or the number of actual contracts presently outstanding for that delivery month.

THE CASH MARKET AND THE FUTURES MARKET

Many commodity futures exchanges provide areas where buyers and sellers can negotiate cash (or spot) prices. The cash price is the actual dollar value paid for the immediate transfer of a commodity. Unlike a futures contract, there must be a transfer of the physical possession of the goods. Prices in the cash market are somewhat dependent on prices in the futures market. Thus, it is said that the futures markets (12 in the United States and 1 in Canada) provide an important service as a price discovery mechanism. By cataloging price trends in everything from corn to cattle, the producers, processors, and handlers of over 40 commodities are able to observe price trends in categories of interest.

THE FUTURES MARKET FOR FINANCIAL INSTRUMENTS

The major event in the commodities markets for the last decade has been the development of financial futures contracts. With the great volatility in the foreign exchange markets and in interest rates, corporate treasurers, investors, and others have felt a great need to hedge their positions. Financial futures also have an appeal to speculators because of their low margin requirements and wide swings in value.

Financial futures may be broken down into three major categories, currency futures, interest rate futures, and stock index futures (the latter is covered in Chapter 16). Trading in currency futures began in May of 1972 on the International Monetary Market (part of the Chicago Mercantile Exchange).

Interest rate futures started trading on the Chicago Board of Trade in October of 1975 with the GNMA certificate.[5] Trading in financial futures, regardless of whether they are currency or interest rate futures, is very similar to trading in traditional commodities, such as corn, wheat, copper, or pork bellies. There is a stipulated contract size, month of delivery, margin requirement, and so on. We will first look at currency futures and then shift our attention to interest rate futures.

CURRENCY FUTURES

These futures are generally available in eight different currencies. They include the following:

British pound	West German mark
Canadian dollar	French franc
Japanese yen	Mexican peso
Swiss franc	Dutch guilder

The futures market in currencies provides many of the same functions as the older and less formalized market in "foreign exchange" operated by banks and specialized brokers, who maintain communication networks throughout the world. In either case, one can speculate or hedge. The currency futures market, however, is different in that it provides standardized contracts and a strong secondary market.

Let's examine how the currency futures market works. Assume you wish to purchase a currency futures contract in Japanese yen. The standardized contract is 12.5 million yen. The value of the contract is quoted in cents per yen. Assume that you purchase a December futures contract in May, and the price on the contract is .4342 cents per yen. The total value of the contract is $54,275 (12.5 million yen × $.004342). The typical margin on a yen contract is $3,000.

We will assume that the yen strengthens relative to the dollar. This might happen because of decreasing U.S. interest rates, declining inflation in Japan, or any number of other reasons. Under these circumstances, the currency might rise to .4530 cents per yen (the yen is now equivalent to more cents than it was previously). The value of the contract has now risen to $56,625 (12.5 million × $.004530). This represents an increase in value of $2,350.

$$\begin{array}{r} \$56,625 \\ -54,275 \\ \hline \$\ 2,350 \end{array}$$

[5] A GNMA (Ginnie Mae) certificate represents an interest in a pool of federally insured mortgages. Actually, GNMA (the Government National Mortgage Association) buys a pool of mortgages from various lenders at a discount and then issues securities to the public against the mortgages. They are pass-through in nature in that the holder of a GNMA certificate receives the interest and principal payment on the mortgages on a monthly basis.

With an original margin requirement of $3,000, this represents a return of 78.3 percent.

$$\frac{\$2,350}{\$3,000} \times 100 = 78.3\%$$

On an annualized basis, it would even be higher. Of course, the contract could produce a loss if the yen weakens against the dollar as a result of higher interest rates in the United States or increasing inflation in Japan. With a normal margin maintenance requirement of $2,400, a $600 loss on the contract will call for additional margin beyond the original $3,000.

Corporate treasurers often try to hedge an exposed position in their foreign exchange dealings through the currency futures market. Assume a treasurer closes a deal today to receive payment in two months in Japanese yen. If the yen goes down relative to the dollar, he will have less value than he anticipated. One solution would be to sell a yen futures contract (go short). If the value of the yen goes down, he will make money on his futures contract that will offset the loss on the receipt of the Japanese yen in two months.

In Table 15–6, we see the typical size of contracts for four other foreign currencies that trade on the International Monetary Market (part of the Chicago Mercantile Exchange).

TABLE 15–6   Contracts in Currency Futures

Currency	Trading units	Size of contract based on mid-1984 prices
British pound	25,000	$35,000
Canadian dollar	100,000	77,250
Swiss franc	125,000	56,250
West German mark	125,000	46,300

INTEREST RATE FUTURES

Since the inception of the interest rate futures contract with GNMA certificates in October of 1975, the market has been greatly expanded to include Treasury bonds, Treasury bills, Treasury notes, commercial paper, certificates of deposits, and Eurodollars. There is almost unlimited potential for futures contracts on interest-related items.

Interest rate futures trade on a number of major exchanges, including the Chicago Board of Trade, the International Monetary Market of the Chicago Mercantile Exchange, the New York Futures Exchange, and the American Commodities Exchange. As we mentioned earlier, there is competition between Chicago and New York on interest rate futures. Among the most popularly traded contracts in the 1980s were Treasury bonds and GNMA certificates traded on the Chicago Board of Trade, and Treasury bills traded on the

International Monetary Market of the Chicago Mercantile Exchange. The New York Futures Exchange was coming on strong with their Treasury bond and certificates of deposit futures, and the American Commodities Exchange was also moving into various Treasury futures, such as Treasury bonds and Treasury bills.

Figure 15–3 shows examples of quotes on interest rate futures. Direct your attention to the second category, Treasury bonds (CBT), trading on the Chicago Board of Trade.

FIGURE 15–3 Examples of Price Quotes on Interest Rate Futures

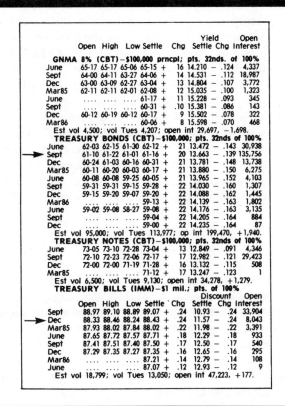

The bonds trade in units of $100,000, and the quotes are in percent of par taken to 32ds of a percentage point. Although it is not shown in this data, the bonds on which the futures are based are assumed to be new, 15-year instruments paying 8 percent interest. Since long-term rates tend to be above 8 percent, the quoted price is usually at a discount from $100,000. In the first column for the September contract for Treasury bonds, we see a price of 61–

10. This indicates a value of 61¹⁰⁄₃₂ percent of par. We thus show a contract value of $61,312.50 (61¹⁰⁄₃₂ × $100,000). This represents the opening value. The entire line in Figure 15–3 would read as follows:

	Open	High	Low	Settle	Chg.	Yield Settle	Chg.	Open Interest
Sept	61–10	61–22	61–01	61–16	+20	13.663	−.139	135,756

We see the settle, or closing, price is 61–16, which represents a change (chg.) of ²⁰⁄₃₂ from the close from the previous day. The reader should be aware that the close for the previous day is not necessarily the same as the open for the current day.[6] We also see what yield the settle (closing) price represents on a 15-year bond paying an 8 percent coupon rate. In this case, it is 13.663 percent, which is a decline in yield from the previous day of .139 percent. The decline in yield is consistent with the increase in settle price (and vice versa). Finally, we see there is an open interest of 135,756 indicating the number of contracts that are presently outstanding for September.

Assume we buy a September futures contract for 61–16 or $61,500 (61¹⁶⁄₃₂ × $100,000). The margin requirement for this contract on the Chicago Board of Trade is $2,000 with a $1,600 margin maintenance requirement. In this case, it may be that we have bought the futures contract because we anticipate easier monetary policy by the Federal Reserve, which will trigger a decline in interest rates and an increase in bond prices. If interest rates decline by .3 percent (30 basis points), Treasury bond prices will increase by approximately 1³⁰⁄₃₂.[7] On a $100,000 par value futures contract, this would represent a gain of $1,937.50 as indicated below.

$$\begin{array}{r} \$100,000 \\ \times \quad 1^{30}/_{32}\% \ (1.9375\%) \\ \hline \$1,937.50 \end{array}$$

With a $2,000 initial margin, the $1,937.50 profit represents an attractive return. Note, however, that if interest rates go up by even a small amount, our Treasury bond futures contract value will fall, and there will be a margin call.

As is true of other commodities, when we trade in interest rate futures, we do not take actual title or possession of the commodity unless we fail to reverse our initial position. The contract merely represents a bet or hedge on the direction of future interest rates and bond prices.

Quotes on Treasury Bill Futures

One type of interest rate future that requires special attention is the Treasury bill future. Particular reference in this case is made to the 90-day, $1 million, T-bill futures contract that trades on the International Monetary Market of the

[6] A number of overnight events can cause the difference. In this case, we can assume the close for the previous day was 60–96 based on the change of +20.

[7] This is derived from a standard bond table and not explicitly calculated in their example.

Chicago Mercantile Exchange and is shown on the bottom portion of Figure 15–3 on page 447. We reproduce the second line below.

	Open	High	Low	Settle	Chg.	Yield Settle	Chg.	Open Interest
Dec	88.33	88.46	88.24	88.43	+.24	11.57	−.24	8,043

The items of particular interest are the settle price of 88.43 and the settle discount of 11.57 percent. Unlike other interest rate futures, such as Treasury bonds or GNMA certificates, we cannot simply multiply the settle price of 88.43 (percent) times par value of $1 million to get the value of the contract. Why? Because this Treasury bill represents a 90-day instrument, and the annual yield of 11.57 percent must be converted to a 90-day rate in order to determine value. We thus take the annual rate of 11.57 percent and multiply it by $90/360$ to get an equivalent 90-day yield of 2.89%.

$$11.57 \times \frac{90}{360} = 2.89\%$$

We then subtract this value from 100 percent to get the appropriate percentage to multiply times par value to get the value of the contract. For the $1 million Treasury bill, the actual converted price is:

$$(100\% - 2.89\%) \times \$1,000,000$$
$$97.11\% \times \$1,000,000 = \$971,100$$

Each time the yield on a Treasury bill changes by .01 percent ($1/100$ of 1 percent or 1 basis point), the price of the T-bill future will change by $25 as indicated in the two steps below:

$$.01\% \text{ of } \$1,000,000 = \$100$$

we convert this from an annual rate to a 90-day rate by multiplying by $90/360$.

$$\$100 \times {}^{90}\!/_{360} = \$25$$

Thus, if you buy a Treasury bill futures contract and interest rates on Treasury bills change by .50 percent (50 basis points), you will gain or lose $1,250.

$25 For each .01% or basis points
× 50 Basis points
———
$1,250

The initial margin requirement for a $1 million Treasury bill on the International Monetary Market of the Chicago Mercantile Exchange is only $1,500, with a $1,200 margin maintenance requirement. The daily trading limit is 50 basis points, so a $1,250 change in value is possible in one day.[8]

---

[8] The American Commodity Exchange and other markets have even smaller margin requirements and larger daily limits for price movements, so there is plenty of opportunity for action.

Hedging with Interest Rate Futures

Interest rate futures have opened up opportunities for hedging that can only be compared to the development of the traditional commodities market over a century ago. Consider the following potential hedges against interest rate risks.

a. A corporate treasurer is awaiting a new debt issue that will take place in 60 days. The underwriters are still putting the final details together. The great fear is that interest rates will rise between now and then. The treasurer could hedge his or her position in the futures market by selling a Treasury bond, Treasury bill, GNMA certificate, or other similar security short. If interest rates go up, the price to buy back the interest rate futures will go down, and a profit will be made on the short position. This will partially or fully offset the higher interest costs on the new debt issue.

b. A corporate treasurer is continually reissuing commercial paper at new interest rates or borrowing under a floating prime agreement at the bank. He or she fears that interest rates will go up and make a big dent in projected profits. By selling (going short) on commercial paper, certificates of deposit, or other interest rate futures, the corporate treasurer can make enough profit on interest rate futures if interest rates go up to compensate for the higher costs of money.

c. A mortgage banker has made a forward commitment to provide a loan at a set interest rate one month in the future. If interest rates go up, the resale value of the mortgage in the secondary market will go down. He or she can hedge the position by selling or going short on a GNMA certificate futures contract or other interest rate futures contract.

d. A pension fund manager has been receiving a steady return of 12.5 percent on his short-term portfolio in 90-day Treasury bills. He is afraid that interest rates will go down and he will have to adjust to receiving lower returns on the managed funds. His strategy might be to buy (go long) on a Treasury bill futures contract. If interest rates go down, he will make a profit on his futures contract that will partially or fully offset his decline in interest income. Of course, if he is heavily invested in long-term securities and fearful of an interest rate rise, a sell or short position that would provide profits on an interest rate rise would be advisable. This, of course, would offset part of the loss in the portfolio value due to increasing interest rates.

e. A commercial banker has most of his loans on a floating prime basis, meaning that the rate that he charges will change with the cost of funds. However, some of the loans have a fixed rate associated with them. If the cost of funds go up, the fixed-rate loans will become unprofitable. By selling or going short in interest rate futures, the danger of higher interest rates can be hedged away by the profits he will make on the interest rate futures. Similarly, a banker may make a commitment to pay a set amount of interest on certificates of deposit for the next six months. If interest rates go down, the banker may have to loan the funds at a lower rate than he is currently paying. If he buys a futures contract in certificates of deposit, then lower interest rates will increase the value of the contract and provide a profit. This will offset the possible negative profitability spread described above.

An Actual Example

Assume an industrial corporation has a $10 million, 15-year bond to be issued in 60 days. Long-term rates for such an issue are currently 12.75 percent, and there is concern that interest rates will go up by ¼ percent by the time of the issue. The corporate treasurer has figured out that the extra ¼ percent would have a present value cost of $161,550 over the life of the issue (on a before-tax basis).

$10,000,000
¼%
―――――――
$25,000
6.462   Present value factor for 15 years at 13 percent
―――――――
$161,550   Present value of futures costs

To establish a hedge position, he sells 154 Treasury bond futures short. We assume they are currently selling at 65 (65 percent of $100,000), equaling $65,000 each. The total value of the hedge would be $10,010,000. This is roughly the equivalent to the $10 million size of the corporate bond issue. If interest rates go up by ¼ percent, the profit on the Treasury bond futures contract (due to falling prices with a short position) will probably offset the present value of the increased cost of the corporate bond issue.

Of course, we do not suggest that both rates (on Treasury bonds and corporate bonds) would move exactly together. However, the general thrust of the example should be apparent. We are actually establishing a *cross-hedging* pattern by using one form of security (Treasury bonds) to hedge another form of security (corporate bonds). This is often necessary. Even when the same security is used, there may be differences in maturity dates or quality characteristics so that a perfect hedge is difficult to establish.

Many financial managers prefer partial hedges to complete hedges. They are willing to take away part of the risk but not all of it. Others prefer no hedge at all because it locks in their position. While a hedge ensures them against loss, it precludes the possibility of an abnormal gain.

Nevertheless, in a risk-averse financial market environment, most financial managers can gain by hedging their position as described in the many examples in this section. Companies such as Burlington Northern, Esmark, and Stauffer Chemical have established reputations for just such actions.[9] Others have not yet joined the movement because of a lack of appreciation or understanding of the highly innovative financial futures market. Much of this will change with the passage of time.

―――――――

[9] "Hedging with Interest Rate Futures," *Business Week,* December 8, 1980, p. 96.

OPTIONS AS WELL AS FUTURES

In late 1982 many exchanges began offering options on financial instruments and commodities. For example, the Chicago Board Options Exchange began listing put and call options on Treasury bonds. Also, the American Stock Exchange started trading options on Treasury bills and Treasury notes, and the Philadelphia Exchange offered foreign currency options. The Chicago Board of Trade, the Chicago Mercantile Exchange and the Comex have also attached options to commodity plays. The relationship, similarities, and dissimilarities between option contracts and futures contracts is given much greater attention in the following chapter, Stock Index Futures and Options. For now it will suffice to say that the futures contract requires an initial margin, which can be parlayed into large profits or immediately wiped out, whereas an option requires the payment of an option premium, which represents the full extent of an option purchaser's liability.

Chapter 16

STOCK INDEX FUTURES AND OPTIONS

In February of 1982, the Kansas City Board of Trade began trading futures on a stock index, the Value Line Index. This event ushered in a whole new era of futures and options trading.

A future or option on an index allows the investor to participate in the movement of an entire index rather than an individual security. There are currently futures and options relating to such indexes as the Standard & Poor's 500 Stock Index, the New York Stock Exchange Composite Index, the American Stock Exchange Index, the Value Line Index, and many other old and new market measures.[1]

If an investor purchases a futures contract on a stock market index, he puts down the required margin, and gains or losses on the transaction based on the movement of the index. For example, an investor may purchase a futures contract on the Standard & Poor's 500 Stock Index with $6,000 in margin. The actual contract value is based on the index value times 500. If the S&P 500 Futures Index were at 160, the initial contract value would be $80,000 (500 × 160). If the index went up or down by 2 points, the investor would gain or lose $1,000 (500 × ±2). Since the initial investment is only $6,000 in margin, we see a fairly large percentage gain or loss for a small movement in the index (16.7% = $1,000/$6,000).

An "option" on the Standard & Poor's 500 Stock Index can also be purchased. Such an option is traded on the Chicago Board Options Exchange. If the S&P 500 Stock Index were 161 at a given point in time, an option to purchase the index at a strike price of 160, may carry a premium (price) of $3. The premium is multiplied by 100 to get a total value for the option of $300 (100 × $3). If the Standard & Poor's 500 Stock Index closed out at 167 at expiration, the premium value will be $7 and a profit of $400 will be achieved.

Final value	100 × $7 =	$700
Purchase price	100 × $3 =	$300
Profit		$400

As we go further into the chapter, you will see there are not only futures and options on stock market indexes, but also "options to purchase futures" on stock market indexes.

Stock index futures have grown faster than any new futures trading outlet in history. In their first six months of trading, the average daily volume was 4.5 times as great as the volume on Treasury bill and Treasury bond futures during a comparable period of infancy. Volume figures on the Standard & Poor's 500 Futures Index are presented in Figure 16–1. While stock index futures in general only began trading in 1982, they now make up over 10 percent of the total volume on the 135-year-old U.S. commodity futures markets.[2] The under-

---

[1] To date, there is no contract on the Dow Jones Industrial Average because Dow Jones & Company has resisted having their venerable index used for this purpose.

[2] This market is composed of traditional commodities futures, financial futures, and stock index futures. It should be noted that the term *financial futures* is sometimes considered to be a very broad term, covering currency, interest rate, and stock index futures.

FIGURE 16–1

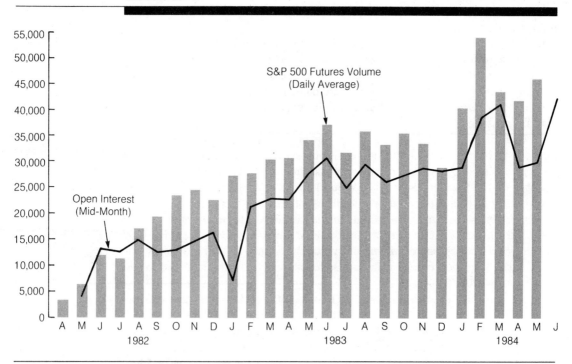

Source: *Standard & Poor's Stock Guide,* July 1984.

lying value of the stocks traded in index futures often equals the entire volume on the New York Stock Exchange on a daily basis. Stock index options are enjoying a similar popularity. In time, they may equal or exceed stock index futures in investor acceptance.

Before we go into a deeper discussion of futures and options on stock market indexes, the student should have read Chapter 13 on put and call options and Chapter 15 on Commodities and Financial Futures.

TRADING STOCK INDEX FUTURES

As indicated in Table 16–1, there are four key stock index futures contracts. The S&P (Standard & Poor's) 500 Futures Index traded on the Chicago Mercantile Exchange (CME), the S&P 100 Futures Index traded on the same exchange, the NYSE (New York Stock Exchange) Composite Futures traded on the New York Futures Exchange (NYFE),[3] and the KC Value Line Futures traded on the Kansas City Board of Trade.

---

[3] The NYFE is a division of the New York Stock Exchange.

TABLE 16–1   Stock Index Futures (April 19, 1984, prices)

	Open	High	Low	Settle	Change	Lifetime High	Low	Open Interest
S&P 500 FUTURES INDEX (CME) 500 Times Index								
June	158.45	159.85	158.40	159.20 +	.10	177.10	155.00	27,779
Sept	160.90	162.15	160.85	161.55 +	.10	178.15	156.80	1,689
Dec	163.30	164.15	163.15	163.95 +	.30	179.20	158.60	155
Mar85	165.90	165.90	164.85	165.70 +	.35	180.25	160.50	19
June	167.60	167.60	166.50	167.40 +	.35	180.70	161.75	6
Sept	169.30	169.30	168.25	169.70 +	.35	171.75	165.70	5

Est vol 33,741; vol Wed 43,480; open int 29,653, + 159.

S&P 500 STOCK INDEX (Prelim)
157.30 158.02 157.10 158.02 + .12

S&P 100 FUTURES INDEX (CME) 200 Times Index								
Apr	154.80	155.40	154.60	155.78 +	.78	158.90	151.00	841
May	155.30	155.60	155.25	155.95 +	.40	158.65	153.10	1
June	155.70	157.00	155.55	156.60 +	.40	177.80	152.20	2,473
July	....	....	....	157.10 +	.40	157.90	154.05	1
Sept	....	....	....	158.85 +	.30	162.00	154.30	6

Est vol 399; vol Wed 755; open int 3,322, −224.

S&P 100 STOCK INDEX (Prelim)
154.60 155.78 154.35 155.78 + .58 ....

NYSE COMPOSITE FUTURES (NYFE) 500 Times Index								
June	91.45	92.15	91.30	91.80 +	.15	103.00	82.30	6,419
Sept	92.60	93.25	92.60	93.00 +	.15	103.10	89.25	999
Dec	93.75	93.90	93.75	94.15 +	.15	103.55	91.35	637
Mar85	94.90	95.10	94.90	95.30 +	15	103.80	93.00	208
June	96.05	96.05	96.05	96.45 +	.15	105.00	94.25	65
Sept	97.20	97.20	97.20	97.60 +	.15	99.00	96.00	14

Est vol 8,299; vol Wed 13,794; open int 8,342, + 277.

NYSE COMPOSITE STOCK INDEX
90.83 90.92 90.44 90.89 + .06

KC VALUE LINE FUTURES (KC) 500 Times Index								
June	179.60	181.10	179.35	180.45 +	.60	212.00	176.15	3,442
Sept	181.70	183.40	181.70	182.80 +	.80	213.50	178.45	99
Dec	....	....	....	185.10 +	.80	210.00	182.20	4

Est vol 2,825; vol Wed 3,422; open int 3,545, − 88.

KC VALUE LINE COMPOSITE STOCK INDEX
179.05 179.05 178.54 179.02 + .04

You will note in Table 16–1 that the title line for each contract (such as S&P 500 Futures Index) indicates an appropriate multiple times the index. For example, 500 times the index for the S&P 500, NYSE Composite Futures, and KC Value Line Futures. For the S&P 100 Futures Index, the multiplier is 200 times. Looking at the June settle prices in each of the four indexes, we see the value of the contracts in Table 16–2.

TABLE 16–2   Value of Contracts

	June settle price	Multiplier	Contract value
S&P 500 Futures	159.20	500	$79,600
S&P 100 Futures	156.60	200	31,320
NYSE Composite Futures	91.80	500	45,900
KC Value Line Futures	180.45	500	90,225

With a margin of from 5 to 10 percent of the value of the contract, the investor can establish a position. If the investor thinks the market is going up, he will purchase a futures contract. If he thinks the market is going down, he will sell a futures contract and hope that the market will decline so that the contract can be closed out (repurchased) at a lower value than the sales price. Selling futures contracts can also be used to hedge a large stock portfolio. If the market goes down, what you lose on your portfolio you recoup in your futures contract.

In the example in Table 16–2, the investor has four indexes from which to choose. (Stock market indexes were covered in Chapter 3). You should be aware that the S&P 500, S&P 100, and NYSE indexes are heavily influenced by large corporations (IBM, Exxon, etc.). The indexes are weighted in proportion to the total market values of the firms in the index. The larger the firm, the more heavily it is weighted. The Value Line Index is an equal-weighted index, which means that IBM has no greater price influence than a smaller firm trading on the American Stock Exchange or over-the-counter.

Also note the relative size of the contracts in Table 16–2. If you wish to deal in smaller values, you may prefer the S&P 100 contract. If you are attempting to hedge a large dollar portfolio, however, your preference might be for the S&P 500 contract or the KC Value Line contract (which you might use in multiples).

We shall direct our attention for now to the S&P 500 Futures Index contract (though the same basic principles would apply to other contracts). Part of the material from Table 16–1 that pertains to the S&P 500 Futures Index is reproduced in Table 16–3 so that we can examine a number of key features related to the contract.

TABLE 16–3   S&P 500 Futures Index (CME) 500 Times Index (April 19, 1984, prices)

Contract month	Open	High	Low	Settle	Change
June 84	158.45	159.85	158.40	159.20	+.10
Sept	160.90	162.15	160.85	161.55	+.10
Dec	163.30	164.15	163.15	163.95	+.30
March 85	165.90	165.90	164.85	165.70	+.35
June	167.60	167.60	166.50	167.40	+.35
Sept	169.30	169.30	168.25	169.70	+.35

Value of S&P 500 Stock Index (April 19, 1984) = 158.02

Trading Cycle

The trading cycle is made up of the four months of June, September, December, and March. The last day of trading for a contract is the third Thursday of the ending month. The reader will observe that the contracts in Table 16–3 extend out nearly a year and a half in the future.

Margin Requirement

As previously mentioned, the basic margin requirement for buying or selling an S&P 500 Futures Index contract is $6,000. Based on the June 1984 contract settle value of $79,600 (found in Table 16–2), this represents a margin requirement of 7.54 percent ($6,000 ÷ $79,600). There is also a margin maintenance requirement of $2,500. Thus if the initial margin or equity in the account falls to this level, the investor will be required to supply sufficient cash or securities to bring the account back up to the $6,000 level. Since the contract trades at 500 times the index, a decline of 7 points in the S&P contract value would cause a loss of $3,500. In this instance, the margin position would be reduced from $6,000 to $2,500, and the investor would be called upon to supply $3,500 in funds to bring the margin up to the initial $6,000 balance.

Actually, if the investor can prove that he is hedging a long position, the margin requirement will be less. For example, if an investor owns a portfolio of stocks that roughly equates the value of the index futures contract ($79,600 in this case), the initial margin requirement is only $2,500 and the margin maintenance requirement is $1,500. Since a hedged position is not as risky as a speculative position, less margin is required. Of course, it is sometimes difficult to prove that a truly hedged position is in place.[4]

Minimum Price Change

The minimum price change for the S&P 500 Futures Index contract is .05. Thus if the June futures contract is at 159.20, the smallest possible price move would be down to 159.15 or up to 159.25. Since the index is multiplied times 500 to determine value, an index movement of .05 represents $25 (500 × .05 = $25). Thus the smallest possible price change is $25. Unlike many traditional commodities, there is no limit to daily price movements on the S&P Futures Index contract (or any other of the stock index futures contracts).

Cash Settlement

In traditional commodity futures markets, the potential for physical delivery exists. One who is trading in wheat or Treasury bonds could actually decide to deliver the commodity to close out the contract. As discussed in Chapter 15, this only happens a very small percentage of the time, but it is possible. The stock index futures market, on the other hand, is purely a cash settlement market. There is never the implied potential for future delivery of the Standard & Poor's 500 Stock Index. An investor simply closes out (or reverses) his position prior to the settlement date. If he does not, his account is automati-

---

[4] For an investor initiating a spread position (buying and selling comparable but somewhat different contracts at the same time), the margin requirement is even lower ($400 initial, $200 maintenance).

cally credited with his gains or debited with his losses and the transaction is completed.[5]

One of the advantages of a cash settlement arrangement is that it makes it impossible for a "short squeeze" to develop. A short squeeze takes place when one attempts to corner a market in a commodity, such as silver, so that it is not possible for those who have short positions to make physical delivery. Clearly, with a cash settlement position, this can never happen.

Basis

The term *basis* represents the difference between the stock index futures price and the value of the actual underlying index.[6] We can now turn back to Table 16–3 to see a numerical example of basis. On April 19, 1984, the S&P 500 Futures contract for June was quoted at a settle (closing) price of 159.20 (2d item from the right in the first row). The actual S&P 500 Stock Index, as shown at the bottom of Table 16–3, closed at 158.02. The basis, or difference, between the futures price and the actual underlying index was 1.18.

Stock index futures price	159.20
Actual underlying index	158.02
Basis	1.18

Moving to the December 1984 contract in Table 16–3, the basis is the difference between the December contract settle value of 163.95 and the value of the underlying index which, of course, is still 158.02. The difference is 5.93. For the data in Table 16–3, the basis indicates a premium is being paid over the actual underlying index value and, furthermore, the premium expands with the passage of time. This is generally thought to be a positive sign. If the index futures price is below the actual underlying index, there is a negative basis.

For an excellent discussion of the ability of stock index futures to forecast the actual underlying index, the reader may wish to consult an article by Zeckhauser and Niederhoffer in the January–February 1983 issue of the *Financial Analysts Journal*.[7] A part of their thesis is that futures contracts move instantaneously to reflect market conditions, whereas the actual underlying index moves more slowly. If the market makes an important move, some of the stocks that are part of the actual underlying index will not yet have traded. Thus, initial, significant, and potentially predictive information may be found in the futures market quotes.

Also, at times, futures or options markets stay open later or begin trading earlier than the actual underlying stock markets. For example, stock futures

---

[5] Actually the account is adjusted daily to reflect the gains and losses. This is known as marking the customer's position to market.

[6] The same concept can be applied to other types of futures contracts.

[7] Richard Zeckhauser and Victor Niederhoffer, "The Performance of Market Index Futures Contracts," *Financial Analysts Journal*, January–February 1983, pp. 59–65.

trade for three minutes after the Federal Reserve releases money supply data at 4:12 P.M. Eastern time. The stock market has already closed at 4 P.M. Eastern time. Market watchers pay particular attention to what happens in the futures market in anticipation of what might happen in the stock market the next day. Also, in July of 1984, the Chicago Board of Trade began trading options on the American Exchange Major Market Index 15 minutes before the actual stock market opened.[8]

Overall Features

Many of the important features related to stock index futures on the various exchanges are presented in Table 16–4. This table can serve as a ready reference guide to trading commodities in various markets.

TABLE 16–4   Specifications for Stock Index Futures Contracts

NYSE Composite Index

Exchange	*Trading hours*	*Index*	*Trading symbol*	*Contract size and value*	*Contract months*
New York Futures Exchange (NYFE) of the New York Stock Exchange	10:00 AM to 4:15 PM (NYT)*	Total Value of NYSE Market: 1505 listed common stocks, weighted to reflect market value of issues	YX	$500 X the NYSE Composite Index	March, June, September, December

S&P 500 Index

Index and Options Market (IOM) of Chicago Mercantile Exchange (CME)	10:00 AM to 4:15 PM (NYT)*	Value of 500 selected stocks traded on NYSE, AMEX and OTC, weighted to reflect market value of issues	SP	$500 X the S&P 500 Index	March, June, September, December

Value Line Index

Kansas City Board of Trade (KCBT)	10:00 AM to 4:15 PM (NYT)*	Equally weighted average of 1683 NYSE, AMEX, OTC and Regional stock prices expressed in index form	KV	$500 X the VLA Index	March, June, September, December

* NYT = New York time.

---

[8] A brief description of this index is given in the stock index options section of this chapter.

USE OF STOCK INDEX FUTURES

There are a number of actual and potential users of stock index futures. As is true of most commodity futures contracts, the motivation may be either speculation or the opportunity to hedge.

Speculation

The speculator may use stock index futures in an attempt to profit from major movements in the market. He or she may have developed a conviction about the next move in the market through utilizing fundamental or technical analysis. For example, those who utilize fundamental analysis may determine that P/E ratios are at a 10-year low or that earnings performance should be extremely good in the next two quarters, so they wish to bet on the market moving upward. Market technicians might observe that a resistance or support position in the market is being penetrated, and that it is time to take a position based on the anticipated consequences of that penetration.

While the market participant could put his or her money in individual stocks, it might be more efficient and less time-consuming to simply invest in stock index futures. In buying futures on the S&P 500 Index, you are capturing the performance of 500 securities, with the New York Stock Exchange Index over 1,500 securities, and with the Value Line Index approximately 1,700 securities.

As discussed in Chapter 1, there are two types of risks associated with investments: systematic, or market-related, risks and unsystematic, or firm-related, risks. Since only systematic risk is assumed to be rewarded in an efficient capital market environment (unsystematic risk can be diversified away), the investor may only wish to be exposed to systematic risk. Stock index futures represent an efficient approach to only taking systematic, market-related risk.

Another advantage of stock index futures is that there is less manipulative action and insider trading than with individual securities. While it is possible (though not legal) for "informed" insider trading to cause an individual stock to move dramatically in the short-term, such activity is not as likely for an entire index. This advantage, however, should not be overstated. Trading activity on the S&P 100 Index did come under scrutiny of the major exchanges in April of 1984.[9]

Stock index futures also offer maximum leverage potential. As previously indicated, the margin is only 5 to 10 percent of the investment that is being controlled. An $80,000 S&P index futures contract can be established for $6,000 in margin, and there is no interest on the balance.[10] If you were invest-

---

[9] "CBOE, Big Board Join to Formally Probe Unusual Trading in Stock-Index Option," *The Wall Street Journal,* April 26, 1984, p. 3.

[10] As mentioned in Chapter 15, margin on futures contracts merely represents good-faith money and there is never any interest on the balance.

ing $80,000 in actual stocks through margin, you would have to put up a minimum of $40,000 (50%) in margin and pay interest on the balance. Also, the commissions on a stock index futures contract are miniscule in comparison to commissions on securities of comparable value.

One of the key questions an investor must consider is the relative volatility of the various indexes. This will give him some feel for the profit or wipeout potential for a given investment. In Table 16–5, you can observe the mean (average) daily price movements on the Standard & Poor's 500 Stock Index over a number of years. The mean appears to be approximately .50 (½ of a point) per day. Since stock index futures contracts trade in multiples of 500, a .50 movement would lead to a profit or loss of $250. With a margin requirement of $6,000, that's a fairly good daily move on your money. By contrast, if $6,000 were invested in a certificate of deposit at a 10 percent annualized return, only $1.67 in interest would accrue on a daily basis. The difference here, of course, is that the $250 related to the index may be up or down, whereas the $1.67 is only up.

TABLE 16–5   **Absolute Values of Daily Changes* in the S&P 500 Stock Index (by year)**

Year	Mean	Maximum
1968	.32	1.71
1969	.37	1.90
1970	.44	3.48
1971	.35	1.73
1972	.36	2.26
1973	.65	3.07
1974	.69	3.27
1975	.54	2.14
1976	.47	1.60
1977	.37	1.72
1978	.47	3.70
1979	.41	3.25
1980	.74	3.63
1981	.64	3.24
1982†	.59	3.18

* Daily changes are defined as the difference between the closing price for the S&P 500 Index on one day and the closing price on the next day.
† Through March 31, 1982.
Source: *Inside S&P 500 Stock Index Futures* (Chicago: Index and Option Market Division of Chicago Mercantile Exchange, 1983).

As further indicated in the last column of Table 16–5, the maximum (largest) *daily* price change taking place in any given year is in the 2 to 3.5 point range, indicating maximum potential daily moves of $1,000 to $1,750 (2 × 500 to 3.5 times 500).

The reader should be aware that the price moves reported in Table 16–5 relate to the actual underlying index rather than to the index futures contract. Nevertheless, one tends to move parallel to the other, so the approximations are reasonably valid.

A more detailed presentation of movements in the major indexes can be seen in Figure 16–2. Panel (a) shows price changes for the S&P 500 Index, Panel (b) for the Value Line Index, and Panel (c) for the NYSE Composite Index. Each line represents the high and low for a month with the dot along the middle representing the closing price for that period. For example, as indicated in Panel (a), the S&P 500 in January of 1978 (first observation on the graph) had a high of approximately 94, a low of approximately 88½ and a close of 89. You should note that the year is set at the middle of the time period rather than at the beginning.

Let's examine the consequences of some of the price movements in Figure 16–2. In looking at the S&P 500 Index in Panel (a), for 1982, we see the index was as low as 102 in mid-1982 and as high as 143 in late 1982. Assuming the price of the index futures contract parallels that of the underlying index, a

FIGURE 16–2   Movements in Stock Market Indexes

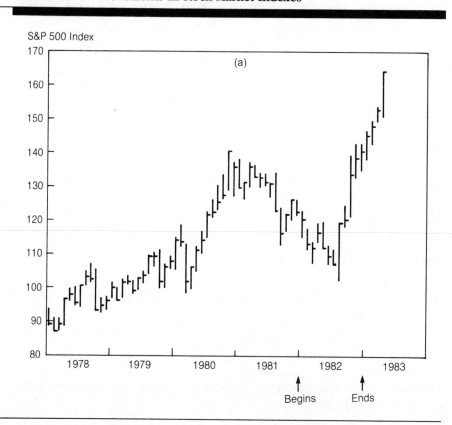

FIGURE 16–2 (*concluded*)   **383**

Value Line Index

NYSE Composite Index

Source: These charts are reprinted from *The Merrill Lynch Guide to Stock Index Futures* by permission of
Merrill Lynch, Pierce, Fenner & Smith Incorporated. © Copyright 1983 Merrill Lynch, Pierce, Fenner & Smith
Incorporated.

41 point increase would translate into a $20,500 gain ($41 \times 500$). On an initial margin of $6,000, this represents a 342 percent gain ($20,500/ $6,000). If you had merely held a portfolio of stocks that performed as well as the S&P 500 Index, your return would be 40.2 percent (a gain of 41 on a base value of 102). The gain on the index futures was over eight times greater.

As is true of all leveraged investments, this is a two-edged sword. You may recall from our earlier discussion that if your margin declines from $6,000 to $2,500 on an S&P index futures contract, you will be required to put up more margin to cover your position. This $3,500 decline in margin would occur if the value of your contract went down by seven points (500×7). The call for more margin puts tremendous pressure on the investor. One must decide whether to liquidate a position and close out a $3,500 loss or put up an additional $3,500 in cash (which could possibly generate another $3,500 loss). In once again examining Panel (a) of Figure 16–2, you can see many time periods where seven-point declines were commonplace.

The investment strategy we have discussed up to this point was in anticipation of an upward market. Quite obviously, you can also speculate that the market will go down. You simply sell a contract with the anticipation of repurchasing it at a lower price at a later point in time. There are similar margin requirements, and gains come from a declining market and losses from an increasing market. If the index futures price goes up by seven points, you will be called upon to put up more margin.

Hedging

Up to now our discussion of stock index futures has mainly related to speculating (or anticipating the next major move in the market). Perhaps the most important use of stock index futures is for hedging purposes. One who has a large diversified portfolio may feel the market is about to decline. A portfolio manager who suffers a 20 percent decline in his or her portfolio actually requires a 25 percent gain from the newly lower base just to break even.

A portfolio manager faced with the belief that a declining market is imminent may be inclined to sell off part or all of the portfolio.[11] The question becomes, is this realistic? First of all, there are large transaction costs associated with selling off part or all of a portfolio and then repurchasing it at a later point in time. Secondly, it may be difficult to liquidate a position in certain securities that are thinly traded. For example, a mutual fund or pension fund that tries to sell 10,000 shares of a small over-the-counter stock may initially find a price quote of $25, but only be able to close out its relatively large position at $23.50. A $15,000 loss would be suffered. Furthermore, there may be the same type of problem in reacquiring the stock after the overall market decline is over. This problem could be multiplied by 25 or 50 times, depending on the number of securities in the portfolio. Though larger, more liquid,

---

[11] While the authors are not necessarily recommending this as a prudent strategy, it is often a way of life among money managers.

holdings would be easier to trade there are still significant transactions costs involved.

A more easily executed defensive strategy would be to sell one or more stock index futures as a hedge against the portfolio. If the stock market does go down, the loss on the portfolio will be partially or fully offset by the profit on the stock index futures contract(s) because they are bought back at a lower price than the initial sales price.

As an example, assume a corporate pension fund has $20,000,000 in stock holdings. The investment committee for the fund is very bearish in its outlook. There is a fear that the overall market could go down by 20 percent in the next few months and a $4,000,000 loss would be suffered. The pension fund decides to fully hedge its position.

The fund is going to use S&P Index futures for the hedge. We shall assume the futures can be sold for 162, with a settlement date in three months. Before the number of contracts for execution is determined, the portfolio manager must consider the relative volatility of his portfolio. If the portfolio is more volatile than the market, this must be factored into the decision-making process. As discussed in Chapter 1, the beta coefficient indicates how volatile a stock is relative to the market. If a stock has a beta of 1.20, it is 20 percent more volatile than the market (or market index). We shall assume the $20,000,000 portfolio discussed above has a weighted average beta of 1.15 (that is, the portfolio is 15 percent more volatile than the market).

In order to determine the number of contracts necessary to hedge the position, we use the following formula:

$$\frac{\$ \text{Value of portfolio}}{\$ \text{Value of contract}^{12}} \times \frac{\text{Weighted beta}}{\text{of portfolio}} = \frac{\text{Number of}}{\text{contracts}} \qquad (16\text{--}1)$$

In the example under discussion, we would show:

$$\frac{\$20,000,000}{162 \times 500} \times 1.15 = \frac{\text{Number of}}{\text{contracts}}$$

In the first term, the numerator is the size of the portfolio being hedged. The denominator is the size of each contract. It is found by multiplying the S&P futures contract value of 162 by 500. The first term is then multiplied by the beta value of 1.15. The answer works out as:

$$\frac{\$20,000,000}{\$81,000} \times 1.15 = 246.91 \times 1.15 = 284 \text{ contracts}$$

The portfolio can be effectively hedged with 284 contracts.

Assume the market does go down, but only by 10 percent instead of the 20 percent originally anticipated. Let's demonstrate that the hedge has worked. Since the portfolio has a beta of 1.15, its decline would be 11.5 percent (10 percent × 1.15). With a $20,000,000 portfolio, the loss would be

---

[12] Based on the particular contract being analyzed.

$2,300,000. To offset this loss, we will have a gain on 284 contracts. The gain is shown as follows:

S&P Index futures contract (sales price)	= 162.0
Decline in price on the futures contract[13] (10% × 162)	16.2
Ending value (purchase price)	= 145.8

The 16.2 point decline on the index futures indicates the profit made on each contract. They were sold for 162.0 and repurchased for 145.8. With 284 contracts, the profit on the stock index futures contracts comes out as $2,300,400.

Profit per contract (16.2 × 500) =	$8,100
Number of contracts	284
Total profit =	$2,300,400

The gain of $2,300,400 on the stock index futures contracts offsets the loss of $2,300,000 on the portfolio. The difference of $400 between the two values represents a rounding procedure. Actually executing a perfect hedge may be further complicated by a number of other factors such as the lack of an appropriate index to match against the portfolio and the change in basis over time. Also, the portfolio may not move exactly in accordance with the beta. There are no doubt many real-world factors that can complicate any hedge.

While a stock index futures hedge offers the advantage of protecting against losses, it, of course, takes away the upside potential. If the market goes up by 10 percent instead of down, the gain on the portfolio may be wiped out by the loss on the stock index futures contracts. The investor could be forced to buy back the futures for 10 percent more than the selling price. Because some portfolio managers are afraid of losing all their upside potential in a hedged position, they may only wish to hedge a fourth or a half of their position.

Other uses of hedging.   There are a number of other uses of hedging with stock index futures besides protecting the position of a long-term investment portfolio. These include:

Underwriter hedge.   As described in Chapter 14, the investment banker or underwriter has a risk exposure from buying stock from the issuing corporation with the intention of reselling it in the public markets. If there is weakness during the distribution period, the potential resale price could fall below the purchase price, and the underwriter's profit would be wiped out. In order to protect against this market risk, the underwriter could sell stock index futures contracts. If the market goes down, presumably the loss on the stock will be compensated for by the gain on the stock index futures contract as a result of

---

[13] Note that the futures contract is assumed to move on a one-to-one basis with the market. The actual relationship may not be this precise.

being able to repurchase it at a lower price. This, of course is not a perfect hedge. It is entirely possible that the stock could go down while the market is going up, and losses on both the stock and stock index futures contract would take place (writing options directly against the stock might be more efficient, but in many cases such options are not available).

Specialist or dealer hedge. As indicated in Chapter 2, a specialist on an exchange or a dealer in the over-the-counter market buys and sells stocks for his own inventory for temporary holding. He may, at times, assume a larger temporary holding than desired, with all the risks associated with that exposure. Stock index futures can reduce the market (or systematic) risk, although the futures can not reduce the specific risk associated with a security.

Retirement or estate hedge. As we move into the next two or three decades, large retirement funds will be accumulated from voluntary retirement plans. A retirement plan participant who has accumulated a large sum in an equity fund may feel a need to hedge his or her position in certain time periods in the economy (where liquidation is either not legal or possible). A futures contract may provide that hedge. Also, one with responsibility for an estate may be locked into a portfolio during the period of probate (validation of the will process), and wish to hedge his or her position with a stock index futures contract.

Tax hedge. An investor may have accumulated a large return on a diversified portfolio in a given year. In order to maintain the profitable position, but defer the taxable gains until the next year, futures contracts may be employed.

TRADING STOCK INDEX OPTIONS

Stock index options also allow the market participant to speculate or hedge against major market movements. Stock index options are similar in many respects to the standard put and call options on individual stocks discussed in Chapter 13. The purchaser of an option pays an initial premium, and then closes out the option at a given price in the future. One essential difference between stock index options and options on individual securities is that in the former case there is only a cash settlement of the position, whereas in the latter case (individual securities), you can force the option writer to deliver the securities.

Examples of stock index options are presented in Table 16–6.

The major option contracts are the S&P 100 Index and S&P 500 Index (traded on the Chicago Board Options Exchange), the American Exchange Major Market Index (a price-weighted index of 20 large firms),[14] the Amex

---

[14] Somewhat surprising is the fact that 15 out of 20 firms in the Index are part of the Dow Jones Industrial Average. The index is not meant to represent the American Stock Exchange, but large firms. An option contract on the American Exchange Major Market Index also began trading on the Chicago Board of Trade in July of 1984.

TABLE 16–6   Stock Index Options (April 19, 1984)

Index Options

Chicago Board

S&P 100 INDEX

Strike Price	Calls–Last Apr	May	June	Puts–Last Apr	May	June
140	....	....	1/4	....	1/16	....
145	10	10½	10⅞	....	3/16	⅝
150	5¾	6⅝	7⅜	1/16	⅞	1½
155	¾	3¼	4½	1/16	2⅜	3⅛
160	1/16	1⅛	2¼	4⅛	5⅜	6
165	1/16	¼	¾	10	10½	10¾
170	....	1/16	¼	15	15¼	....
175	....	1/16	⅛	20½	....	....

Total call volume 106,701. Total call open int. 358,892.
Total put volume 76,071. Total put open int. 415,339.
The index: High 155.78; Low 154.34; Close 155.78, +0.58.

S&P 500 INDEX

Strike Price	Calls–Last June	Sept	Puts–Last June	Sept
155	....	....	1½	....
160	2 13/16	....	....	....
165	#1⅛	....	....	....

Total call volume 12.   Total call open int. 122.
Total put volume 2.   Total put open int. 219.
The index: High 158.02; Low 157.10; Close 158.02, +0.12.

COMPUTER/BUSINESS EQUIPMENT INDEX
(No Trades)

Total call volume 0.   Total call open int. 1353.
Total put volume 0.   Total put open int. 29.
The index: High 162.09; Low 160.80; Close 161.79, +0.23.

American Exchange

MAJOR MARKET INDEX

Strike Price	Calls–Last Apr	May	June	Puts–Last Apr	May	June
105	....	....	....	....	⅛	7/16
110	2 7/16	3⅞	4⅜	1/16	¾	1 5/16
115	1/16	1 1/16	1 13/16	2⅛	3⅛	3⅜
120	....	⅛	½	7¾	....	....

Total call volume 7029   Total call open int. 41,812
Total put volume 5343   Total put open int. 42,389
The index: High 112.84; Low 111.63; Close 112.84, +0.52

AMEX MARKET VALUE INDEX

Strike Price	Calls–Last Apr	May	June	Puts–Last Apr	May	June
200	8¼	8¾	....	....	¾	1¼
205	2⅞	....	6⅞	....	1⅞	2⅝
210	....	2⅜	4⅛	2⅛	....	4⅞
215	....	¾	....	....	....	....

Total call volume 199   Total call open int. 2435
Total put volume 233   Total put open int. 2447
The index: High 208.21; Low 207.58; Close 207.93, −0.18

N.Y. Stock Exchange

NYSE OPTIONS INDEX

Strike Price	Calls–Last Apr	May	Jun	Puts–Last Apr	May	Jun
85	5⅝	5⅝	6½	....	⅛	¼
90	⅞	2 1/16	2 13/16	1/16	1	1¼
95	....	¼	11/16	4⅜	4¼	4¾
100	....	....	⅛	....	....	....

Total call volume 7631.   Total call open int. 67,933.
Total put volume 3,397.   Total put open int. 68,917.
The index: High 90.92; Low 90.44; Close 90.89, +0.06

The multiplier times the premium is 100.

Market Value Index (based on that exchange's index), and the NYSE Options Index (based on the New York Stock Exchange Composite Index). For closer inspection, we reproduce part of the Chicago Board Options Exchange S&P 100 Index quotations in Table 16–7.

TABLE 16–7   S&P 100 Index Stock Options (Chicago Board Options Exchange) (April 19, 1984, prices)

	Calls			Puts		
Strike price	April	May	June	April	May	June
140	—	—	¼	—	¹⁄₁₆	—
145	10	10 ½	10 ⅞	—	³⁄₁₆	⅝
150	5 ¾	6 ⅝	7 ⅜	¹⁄₁₆	⅞	1 ½
155	¾	3 ¼	4 ½	¹⁄₁₆	2 ⅜	3 ⅛
160	¹⁄₁₆	1 ⅛	2 ¼	4 ⅛	5 ⅜	6
165	¹⁄₁₆	¼	¾	10	10 ½	10 ¾
170	—	¹⁄₁₆	¼	15	15 ¼	—
175	—	¹⁄₁₆	⅛	20 ½	—	—

The multiplier times the premium is 100.
Value of the S&P 100 Index (April 19, 1984) = 155.78.

Options related to the S&P 100 Index have been the most popular of the stock index options. The S&P 100 Index represents a market-value-weighted index of 100 of the stocks currently listed for option trading on the Chicago Board Options Exchange (CBOE). The movement of the S&P 100 Index closely parallels that of the S&P 500 Index.

Note at the bottom of Table 16–7 that the S&P 100 Index closed on April 19, 1984, at 155.78. With this value in mind, we can examine the strike price and premiums for the various contracts. The premium in each case is multiplied times 100 to determine the total cash involved.[15] Let's read down to the 150 strike price and across to the June call option (3rd month column). The premium is 7⅜ (7.375).

Assume an investor bought a June 150 contract for a 7.375 premium on April 19, 1984, and that when the June contract expired, the S&P 100 Index was 165 under our optimistic assumption; and that under our pessimistic assumption it was 145. At a value of 165, the option valve is 15 (165 − 150). The ending or expiration price is 15 points higher than the strike price. Keep in mind the option cost 7.375. The profit is shown to be $762.50. At an ending value of 145, the option is worthless, and there is a loss of $737.50.

---

[15] The 100 multiplier applies to all the other option contracts listed in Table 16–6 as well.

	165 Optimistic Assumption	145 Pessimistic Assumption
Final value (100×15) =	1,500.00	0
Purchase price (100×7.375) =	737.50	737.50
Profit or loss =	+ \$762.50	− \$737.50

We have been working with call options; let's shift our attention to put options. If a 150 June put option (the option to sell at 150 rather than buy at 150) had been purchased on April 19th, we can see in the third row of the last *put* column of Table 16–7 that the initial price of the June put option would have been 1½. Let's assume that when the June put contract expired, the S&P 100 Index was 165 under what is now our pessimistic assumption and 145 under what is now our optimistic assumption.

At a final value of 165, there is no value associated with a put option that allows you to sell at 150. Since the put option costs 1½, there is a \$150 loss. At a final value of 145, the put option to sell at 150 has a value of 5. With a cost of 1½, a \$350 profit takes place.

The profits and losses are indicated below:

	165 Pessimistic Assumption	145 Optimistic Assumption
Final value (0) =	0	(100×5) = 500
Purchase price ($100 \times 1½$) =	150	($100 \times 1½$) = 150
Profit or loss =	− \$150	+ \$350

Hedging with Stock Index Options

The discussion of stock index options thus far has pertained to straight investments. Stock index options can also be used for hedging. Like stock index futures, stock index options can be used to protect a portfolio, or for special purposes by underwriters, specialists, dealers, tax planners, and others.

At times options may offer a hedging advantage over futures to investors who are limited by law from purchasing futures contracts. On the other hand, futures generally allow for a more efficient hedge than options. If the market goes down by 20 or 25 percent, chances are good that a completely hedged short futures position (selling futures contracts) will compensate fully, or to a reasonable degree, losses in a portfolio. An option write, used to hedge a portfolio, may prove to be inadequate. Perhaps the option premium income represents 10 percent of the portfolio, but the market goes down by 25 percent. Fifteen percent of the loss will be unprotected. Buying a put option may overcome this problem, but the cash outflow to purchase the put option could involve substantial funds. Clearly, both futures and options have their advantages and disadvantages.

STOCK INDEX OPTIONS FOR INDUSTRIES

There are also option contracts tailor-designed for industries. Thus, one who wishes to speculate on a given industry's performance, or hedge against holdings in that industry, can use industry index options. The options are similar to those previously discussed in that put and call options are traded at various strike prices. The industry index options trade at a value equal to 100 times the premium.

Examples of industry index options are presented in Table 16–8. We will briefly examine the first two industry indexes.

TABLE 16–8   Industry Index Options

Index	Exchange
1. S&P Computer and Business Equipment Index	Chicago Board Options Exchange
2. S&P Integrated International Oil Index	Chicago Board Options Exchange
3. S&P Telephone Index	Chicago Board Options Exchange
4. S&P Transportation Index	Chicago Board Options Exchange
5. NY Telephone Index	New York Stock Exchange
6. Computer Technology Index	American Stock Exchange
7. Oil and Gas Index	American Stock Exchange
8. Transportation Index	American Stock Exchange
9. Gaming/Hotel Index	Philadelphia Stock Exchange
10. Technology Index	Pacific Stock Exchange

S&P Computer and Business Equipment Index.   This S&P industry index is made up of 12 firms. It is a market-value-weighted index. The participating firms and weights in 1983 are shown in Table 16–9.

TABLE 16–9   S&P Computer and Business Equipment Index

Company	Weight
Burroughs Corporation	2.3
Control Data	2.1
Data General	.8
Datapoint	.5
Digital Equipment	5.8
IBM	73.0
NCR Corporation	3.3
Pitney-Bowes	.9
Sperry Corporation	2.3
Storage Technology	.7
Wang Labs	4.2
Xerox Corporation	4.2
	100.0

Source: *S&P Computer and Business Equipment Index (OBE): A Preview* (Chicago: Chicago Board Options Exchange, 1983).

FIGURE 16-3

S&P Computer and Business Equipment Index (OBE): Comparison of Weekly Values
January 1981 through August 1983

Source: *S&P Computer and Business Equipment Index (OBE): A Preview* (Chicago: Chicago Board Options Exchange, 1983).

A three-year history of the index is presented in Figure 16-3. As you can see, the price movements are quite volatile.

The S&P Integrated International Oil Index.   This market-value-weighted index comprises six firms. The firms and their weights in 1983 are shown in Table 16-10.

In Figure 16-4, we can observe a three-year history of the index that indicates even greater price volatility than that shown in Figure 16-3 for the Computer and Business Equipment Index.

A purchaser of an S&P Integrated International Oil Index option might buy an option with a 120 strike price for a premium of 3 ($300 in total). The option will move up and down in value with the underlying index just as all other options do.

TABLE 16–10   S&P Integrated International Oil Index

Company	Weight
Exxon Corporation	37.3
Gulf Oil	8.0
Mobil Corporation	15.1
Royal Dutch Petroleum	14.3
Standard Oil of California	14.4
Texaco, Inc.	10.9
	100.0

Source: *S&P Integrated International Oil Index (OIO): A Preview* (Chicago: Chicago Board Options Exchange, 1983).

FIGURE 16–4

S&P International Oil Index (OIO): Comparison of Weekly Values
January 1980 through August 1983

Source: *S&P Integrated International Oil Index (OIO): A Preview* (Chicago: Chicago Board Options Exchange, 1983).

OPTIONS ON STOCK INDEX FUTURES

We have discussed *stock index futures* and *stock index options,* so a natural extension of our discussion is to consider the third form of stock index trading, *options on stock index futures.* The three forms of index trading are listed below for future reference.

a. Stock index futures.
b. Stock index options.
c. Options on stock index futures.

An option on a stock index future (item c) gives the holder the right to purchase the *stock index future* at a specified price over a given time period. This is slightly different from the stock index option (item b) that gives the holder the right to purchase the *underlying index at a specified price over a given time period.*[16] *The contrast is shown in Figure 16–5.*

The primary topic for discussion in this section is represented by the left-hand column in Figure 16–5, an option on a stock index future. The value of an option to purchase a stock index future will depend on the outlook for the

FIGURE 16–5   Comparison of Option Contracts

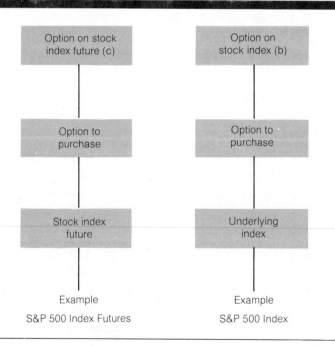

Option on stock index future (c)	Option on stock index (b)
Option to purchase	Option to purchase
Stock index future	Underlying index
Example S&P 500 Index Futures	Example S&P 500 Index

---

[16] Because of cash settlement procedures, the actual index will never actually be purchased, and the gain or loss will be settled for cash.

TABLE 16–11   Options on Stock Index Futures (April 19, 1984)

Chicago Mercantile Exchange

S&P 500 STOCK INDEX – Price = $500 times premium.

Strike Price	Calls – Settle			Puts – Settle		
	Jun	Sep	Dec	Jun	Sep	Dec
135	....	....	....	....	....	
140	....	....	....			
145	...	....	....	.15	....	
150	9.60	....	....	.50	1.50	
155	5.60	....	....	1.45	2.70	
160	2.65	5.85	....	3.40	4.55	
165	1.00	3.80	....	6.70	7.00	7.50
170	.30	2.15	....	11.00	....	
175	.10	1.25	....	....	....	
180	.05	.70	....	....	....	
185	.05	....	....	....	....	

Estimated total vol. 1,268
Calls: Wed. vol. 426; open int. 11,456
Puts: Wed. vol. 547; open int. 13,326

N.Y. Futures Exchange

NYSE Composite Index – Price = $500 times premium.

Strike Price	Calls – Settle			Puts – Settle		
	Jun	Sep	Dec	Jun	Sep	Dec
88	4.40	6.25	8.05	.60	1.25	1.90
90	2.95	4.85	6.60	1.15	1.85	2.45
92	1.85	3.65	5.35	2.05	2.65	3.20
94	1.10	2.60	4.20	3.30	3.60	4.05
96	.55	1.90	3.30	4.75	4.90	5.15
98	.25	1.30	2.55	6.45	6.30	6.40
100	.10	.85	1.90	8.30	7.85	7.75
102	.05	.55	....	10.20	9.55	....
104	.05	.35	....	12.20	11.35	....

Estimated total vol. 122
Calls: Wed. vol. 85; open int. 4611
Puts: Wed. vol. 75; open int. 1565

futures contract. Quotes on options to purchase stock index futures are shown in Table 16–11.[17]

As indicated in Table 16–11, options on stock index futures trade on the Chicago Mercantile Exchange (based on S&P 500 stock index futures) and the New York Futures Exchange (based on NYSE composite index futures). Let's look at sample quotes on the Chicago Mercantile Exchange at the top of the table. A call option to buy a June S&P 500 stock index futures contract at a strike price of 160 has a premium of 2.65. On these option contracts, the premium is multiplied times *500* to get the value of the contract. Thus the cost of the contract is $1,325 (500 × 2.65).

In examining Table 16–11, note that the premiums on the call options increase substantially with the passage of time from June to September. This gain in value is not only a function of the extended time period associated with the option, but also of the fact that the S&P 500 futures contract has a higher

---

[17] These quotes generally appear in the futures section of *The Wall Street Journal* rather than the options section. This can be potentially confusing to the reader.

value in September than June. On April 19, 1984, the June S&P 500 futures contract traded at 159.20, while the September contract traded at 161.55. Thus options on stock index futures not only have a time premium (as all options do), but may also have an additional premium (or discount) depending on the relationship of the far-term futures market to the near-term futures market.

Options on stock index futures may be settled on a cash basis, or the holder of a call option may actually exercise the option and force the option writer to produce a specified futures contract.

Although options on *stock index futures* preceded options on *stock indexes* in the marketplace, they are not currently as popular. Nevertheless, they continue to trade on major exchanges in Chicago and New York.

Chapter 17

INVESTMENTS IN REAL ASSETS

In this chapter, we turn our attention to real assets; that is, tangible assets that may be seen, felt, held, or collected. Examples of such assets are real estate, gold, silver, diamonds, coins, stamps, and antiques. This is no small area from which to consider investments. For example, the total market value of all real estate holdings in the United States in the mid-1980s was in excess of $4.5 trillion as compared to $3 trillion in stocks and bonds.

As further evidence of value, in the 1980s, Rubens's painting, *Samson and Delilah,* sold for $5.4 million, and a 132-carat diamond earring set sold for $6.6 million. Coins and stamps also sold for values well into the hundreds of thousands.

A number of the traditional stock brokerage houses have moved into the area of real assets with such firms as Merrill Lynch participating in real estate and Thomson McKinnon Securities managing a diamond fund. Likewise, Citicorp of New York has an art investment program. No less than 25 million people in the United States are stamp collectors, and 8 million collect and invest in coins.

As was pointed out in Chapter 1, in inflationary environments, real assets have at times outperformed financial assets (such as stocks and bonds). With this in mind, the reader is well advised to become familiar with these investment outlets—not only to take advantage of the investment opportunities, but to be well aware of the pitfalls. A money manager who is challenged by clients to include real assets in a portfolio (such as real estate or precious metals) must be conversant not only with the opportunities, but also with the drawbacks.

ADVANTAGES AND DISADVANTAGES OF REAL ASSETS

As previously mentioned, real assets may offer an opportunity as an inflation hedge. This is because inflation means higher replacement costs for real estate, precious metals, and other physical items. Real assets also serve as an investment hedge against the unknown and feared. When people become concerned about world events, gold and other precious metals may be perceived as the last, safe haven for investments.

Real assets also may serve as an effective vehicle for portfolio diversification. Since financial and real assets at times move in opposite directions, some efficient diversification may take place. A study by Robichek, Cohn, and Pringle in the *Journal of Business* actually indicates that movements between various types of real and monetary assets are less positively correlated than are those for monetary assets alone.[1] The general findings indicate that enlarging the universe of investment alternatives would benefit the overall portfolio construction in terms of risk-return alternatives. The reader who wishes to follow the performance of a wide range of investments can consult the monthly investment scorecard of *Money* magazine as a source. An example for mid-1984 is presented in Table 17–1.

---

[1] Alexander A. Robichek, Richard A. Cohn, and John J. Pringle, "Return on Alternative Media and Implications for Portfolio Construction," *Journal of Business,* July 1972, pp. 427–43.

TABLE 17–1   **Investment Scorecard**

	Mid-May	A month earlier	A year earlier	One-month change (percent)	12-month change (percent)
Stocks					
Dow Jones Industrial Average	1157	1157	1214	0%	− 4.7%
Over-the-counter Index	251	243	302	+3.3	−16.9
Semiconductor stocks	56	51	46	+9.8	+21.8
Construction machinery stocks	338	369	319	−8.4	+ 6.0
Interest-bearing securities (prices)					
Long-term corporate	63.1	64.6	74.5	−2.3	−15.3
Long-term Treasury	63.65	65.0	75.7	−2.2	−16.0
Interest-bearing securities (yields)					
Long-term corporate	13.9%	13.6%	11.5%	+2.2	+20.9
Long-term Treasury	12.8%	12.5%	10.5%	+2.4	+21.9
Municipal bonds	10.0%	9.9%	8.9%	+1.0	+12.4
Money market certificates	10.1%	10.1%	8.6	0	+ 1.7
Money market funds	9.3%	9.0%	7.9%	+3.3	+17.7
Metals and gems					
Gold (ounce)	$372	$382	$440	−2.6	−15.5
Silver (ounce)	$8.63	$9.10	$12.90	−5.2	−33.1
Diamond (one-carat D-flawless)	$14,500	$14,500	$17,000	0	−14.7
Real estate					
Median single-family house	$72,400	$71,800	$68,900	+0.8	+ 5.1
REIT index	3.68	3.59	3.94	+2.5	− 6.6
Collectibles					
Sotheby art index	289	—	257	—	+12.5
Coin portfolio	$24,735	—	$19,910	—	+24
U.S. stamp index	568.6	—	628.3	—	− 9.5

Notes and cautions: House price is for March. Sources: National Association of Securities Dealers, Standard & Poor's, Shearson Lehman/American Express, the Bond Buyer, Federal Reserve, Donoghue's Money Fund Report, Handy & Harman, the Diamond Registry, National Association of Realtors, Numismatic Professionals, Linn's Stamp News.

A final advantage of an investment in real assets is the psychic pleasure that may be provided. One can easily relate to a beautiful painting in the living room, a mint gold coin in a bank lockbox, or an attractive real estate development.

There are many disadvantages to consider as well. Perhaps the largest drawback is the absence of large, liquid, and relatively efficient markets. Whereas stocks or bonds can generally be sold in a few minutes at a value close to the latest quoted trade, such is not likely to be the case for real estate, diamonds, art, and other forms of real assets. It may take many months to get the desired price for a real asset, and even then, there is an air of uncertainty about the impending transaction until it is consummated.

Furthermore, there is the problem of dealer spread or middleman commission. Whereas in the trading of stocks and bonds, spreads or commissions are very small (usually 1 or 2 percent), dealer spreads for real assets can be as large as 20 to 25 percent or more. This is particularly true for small items that do not have great value. On more valuable items, such as rare paintings, valuable jewels, or mint gold coins, the dealer spread tends to be smaller (perhaps 5 to 10 percent) but still more than that on securities.

The investor in real assets generally receives no current income (with the possible exception of real estate) and may in fact incur storage and insurance costs. Furthermore, there may be the problem of high unit cost for investments. You cannot easily acquire multiple art masterpieces.

A final drawback or caveat in real assets is the hysteria or overreaction that tends to come into the marketplace from time to time. Gold, silver, diamonds, and coins may be temporarily bid all out of proportion to previously anticipated value. The last buyer, who arrives too late, may end up owning a very unprofitable investment. The trick is to get into the recurring cycle early enough to take advantage of the large capital gains opportunities that regularly occur for real assets. Also, you should buy items of high enough quality so that you can ride out the setbacks if your timing is incorrect.

In the remainder of this chapter, we will examine real estate, gold, silver, diamonds, and other collectibles as investment outlets. Because real estate lends itself more directly to analytical techniques familiar to students of finance, it will receive a proportionately larger share of our attention.

REAL ESTATE AS AN INVESTMENT

Approximately one half of the households in the United States own real estate as a home or investment. Also, many firms in the brokerage and investment community have also moved into the real estate sector. As examples, Merrill Lynch and Shearson Lehman/American Express have acquired real estate affiliates to broker property, conduct mortgage banking activities, or package real estate syndications. While only 2.3 percent of pension fund assets are currently in real estate, predictions indicate that the number may grow to 10 percent by the end of the current decade.[2]

Some insight into changing real estate values may be gained from viewing Figure 17–1. We see the gain for a dollar invested in 1946 (as compared to fixed-income investments).

---

[2] "Soaring Real Estate Values Are Enticing Big Securities Concerns into the Field," *The Wall Street Journal,* August 6, 1980, p. 32.

FIGURE 17–1   Growth in Value, 1946–1980 ($1 of investment)

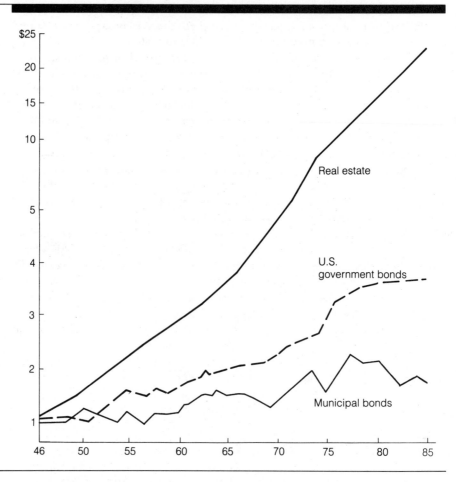

In Table 17–2, we see the change in conventional mortgage rates and median home prices in the United States. The gain in home prices is well over threefold.

Real estate investments may include such outlets as your own home, duplexes and apartment buildings, office buildings, shopping centers, industrial buildings, hotels and motels, as well as raw land. The investor may participate as an individual, as part of a limited partnership real estate syndicate, or through a real estate investment trust. These forms of ownership will receive further coverage toward the end of this section.

We have already talked generally about the advantages and disadvantages of real assets (on the positive side, an inflation hedge and the associated psychic value, and on the negative side, illiquidity and high transaction costs).

TABLE 17–2   Mortgage Rates and Home Prices

Year	Average conventional mortgage rate	Median price of a new home*
1970	8.40	$23,258
1971	7.71	24,998
1972	7.56	27,110
1973	7.98	30,823
1974	8.97	34,055
1975	9.11	37,237
1976	9.05	42,200
1977	8.80	47,900
1978	9.30	55,100
1979	10.48	64,000
1980	12.25	72,700
1981	14.16	78,000
1982	14.47	80,400
1983	12.20	82,500
1984	13.75	86,300

* There are a number of different definitions of "average new home." The value may change somewhat between data collectors.
Sources: Federal Home Loan Bank Board (Washington, D.C.); National Association of REALTORS® (Chicago); Moody's (New York), Jim Kaden, economist; U.S. League of Savings Associations (Chicago); and Federal Reserve System (Washington, D.C.).

Over and above these considerations, real estate also has some unique features of its own. A major advantage of real estate relates to tax considerations. Accelerated depreciation and interest payments can provide substantial tax benefits.[3] Also, real estate provides for a high degree of leverage with a cash down payment of 20 to 25 percent supporting a large asset base. Most other forms of real assets do not serve so readily as collateral. An issue associated with real estate is the high degree of government regulation (particularly at the local level). Thus, the investor must be prepared to deal with zoning regulations, building codes, and the incidence of relatively high property taxes. On the other hand, the government also serves in a positive role by providing guarantees for FHA and VA loans and a secondary market for mortgages (the original lender can dispose of the initial mortgage).

Throughout the rest of this section on real estate, we will evaluate a typical real estate investment and the related tax aspects, consider new methods of real estate financing, and examine limited partner syndicates and real estate investment trusts.

---

[3] In the tax reform package developed by the Treasury Department in 1984–85, the tax benefits related to real estate would be reduced somewhat by extending the depreciation period. It is still problematical as to whether the proposed reform package will become law. The examples in this chapter are based on the tax laws in existence in mid-1985.

INVESTMENT EXAMPLE

Assume we are considering investing $170,000 in a new fourplex (four-unit apartment housing project). Our land costs will be $30,000, and the actual physical structure will cost $140,000. This latter amount will be the value to be depreciated. Though we are dealing with relatively small numbers for ease of computation, the same types of considerations would apply to a multimillion-dollar shopping center or office building. Before we actually evaluate our cash inflows and outflows, we will consider tax and accounting factors related to depreciation in real estate.

Depreciation Effects

In the present case, we can write off depreciation on real estate over 18 years. The appropriate annual depreciation schedule is presented in Table 17–3.[4]

Applying the depreciation schedule in Table 17–3 to our $140,000 physical structure (fourplex building), we show the depreciation schedule in Table 17–4. The $30,000 land value cannot be written off for depreciation purposes.

TABLE 17–3   Accelerated Depreciation Allowance on Real Estate under the 1981 Economic Recovery Tax Act and 1984 Deficit Reduction Act (approximates 175 percent declining balance depreciation with an eventual shift to straight-line)

Year of depreciation	Percentage depreciation
1–2	9%
3	8
4–5	7
6	6
7–12	5
13–18	4

Most real estate investors prefer the most rapid depreciation possible in the early years because it provides a tax shelter for other income. However, there are two issues here. One is that a rapid rate of depreciation in the early life of the asset dictates a slower rate in the later years as depreciation runs out.

A second issue related to accelerated depreciation is that of *recaptured depreciation,* which can take place upon selling the property. When accelerated depreciation is taken and the property is sold at a profit, part of the profit may be taxed as ordinary income rather than capital gains. This part of the profit is considered to be recaptured depreciation.

---

[4] Low-income rental property can be written off over 15 years. The present project would not qualify for such treatment.

TABLE 17–4   Accelerated Depreciation Schedule for Investment

Year	Percentage depreciation	Initial unit value	Dollar depreciation
1	9%	$140,000	$12,600
2	9		12,600
3	8		11,200
4	7		9,800
5	7		9,800
6	6		8,400
7	5		7,000
8	5		7,000
9	5		7,000
10	5		7,000
11	5		7,000
12	5		7,000
13	4		6,600
14	4		5,600
15	4		5,600
16	4		5,600
17	4		5,600
18	4		5,600

Cash Flow Considerations

The only aspect of our investment we have considered so far is depreciation. We have established the fact that on a $170,000 investment with $30,000 in land and $140,000 in the building, we could take 9 percent in first-year depreciation or $12,600 (see Table 17–4).[5] Depreciation is a noncash, tax-deductible item. We now must consider various cash flow items, such as the receipt of rent and the payment of interest, property taxes, insurance, maintenance expenses, and so on. An example of overall cash flow analysis is presented in Table 17–5.

We see in Table 17–5 that we have a loss of $12,270 for federal income tax purposes and that this provides a tax shelter benefit of $6,135 against other income. We also add depreciation back in to get cash flow because it was previously subtracted out but is really a noncash item. The negative and two positive values provide a positive cash flow figure of $6,465 at the bottom of Table 17–5.

We should point out that in considering the cost of the loan in Table 17–5, we have only evaluated interest payments. We might wish to consider repayment of principal as well. In the present case, we are assuming that in the first year we are paying 12 percent interest on a loan balance of $127,500, or $15,300 (as shown in Table 17–5). Assuming a 20-year loan (it is not unusual

---

[5] We are assuming the real estate is purchased at the first of the year so that the full 9 percent depreciation can be taken.

TABLE 17–5   Cash Flow Analysis for an Apartment (Fourplex) Investment

Gross annual rental (4 units at $425 per month/$5,100 per year each)		$20,400
Less 5 percent vacancy		1,020
Net rental income		$19,380
Interest expense on a loan of 75 percent of property value at 12 percent interest:		
(75%) × $170,000 = $127,500		
(12%) × $127,500 = $15,300	$15,300	
Property taxes	2,000	
Insurance	750	
Maintenance	1,000	
Depreciation	$12,600	
Total expenses		$31,650
Before-tax income or (loss)		(12,270)
Tax shelter benefit assumes 50 percent tax rate		6,135
Depreciation		12,600
Cash flow		$6,465

for the life of the loan to be different from the depreciation period), the total first-year payment for interest and principal is actually $17,070, indicating that $1,770 is applied toward the repayment of principal.

$$\text{Payment} - \text{Interest} = \text{Repayment of principal}$$
$$\$17,070 - \$15,300 = \$1,770$$

On this basis, our cash flow figure will be reduced to $4,695.

$$\text{Cash flow} - \text{Repayment of principal} = \text{Net cash flow}$$
$$\$6,465 - \$1,770 = \$4,695[6]$$

Of course, this value only applies to the first year. Rental income, interest, depreciation, and many other expense items will change each year. (For example, we will eventually run out of depreciation.)

In terms of investor return in the first year, the initial cash investment is $42,500. This is based on the total value of the property of $170,000 minus the initial loan amount of $127,500, requiring the investor to put up $42,500 in cash. With a *net* cash inflow of $4,695 in the first year, the cash on cash investor return in the first year is 11.05% ($4,695/$42,500). This represents the cash return on the investment divided by the actual "cash" investment.

---

[6] One could argue that we are building up equity or ownership interest through the repayment of principal. However, our focus for now is simply on the amount of cash flow going in and out. We will consider buildup in equity in a subsequent discussion.

The investor will also build up his or her equity or ownership interest by the amount of repayment toward principal as well as any increase in property value resulting from inflation. If the property increases by 8 percent in the first year, this represents an added benefit of $13,600 (8 percent times the $170,000 value of the property). Actually, return benefits associated with price appreciation may exceed all other considerations. An investor may be willing to accept little or no cash flow if he or she can enjoy inflation-related gains. Note that in the present case, the $13,600 gain from price appreciation alone would represent a first-year return on cash investment of 32 percent ($13,600/$42,500).

You can readily see the twin factors that make real estate attractive are depreciation write-off and appreciation in value due to price appreciation. Apartments, office buildings, warehouses, and shopping centers have served particularly well as good performers in inflationary environments. In low-inflationary environments, the benefits of real estate are substantially reduced as there is less price appreciation potential. The investor must also be sensitive to the possibility of new tax legislation that could reduce early depreciation write-off benefits. Nevertheless, the previous example clearly shows some of the key factors to examine in real estate investments.

FINANCING OF REAL ESTATE

One of the essential considerations in any real estate investment analysis is the cost of financing. In the prior example, we said a loan for $127,500 over 20 years at 12 percent interest would have yearly payments of $17,070. Note, in Table 17–6, the effects of various interest rates on annual payments.

TABLE 17–6 Interest Rates and Annual Repayment Obligations for a 20-Year Loan (principal amount equals $127,500)

	8 percent	10 percent	12 percent	14 percent	16 percent
Annual payment	$ 12,986	$ 14,975	$ 17,070	$ 19,251	$ 21,504
Total interest over the life of the loan	132,220	172,000	213,900	257,520	302,580

We see the difference in annual payments ranges from $12,986 at 8 percent up to $21,504 at 16 percent. Even more dramatic is the increase in total interest paid over the life of the loan; it goes from $132,220 at 8 percent to $302,580 at 16 percent. (Keep in mind that the total loan was only $127,500.)

An investor who has the unlikely opportunity to shift out of the loan at 16 percent into one at 8 percent might be willing to pay as much as $83,692.72 for the privilege. (Tax effects are not specifically considered here.)

$$16 \text{ percent interest} - 8 \text{ percent interest} = \text{Dollar difference in annual payments}$$

$$\$21,504 \quad - \quad \$12,986 \quad = \quad \$8,518$$

Present value of $8,518 over 20 years assuming an 8 percent discount rate (see Appendix D at the end of the book):

$$\$8,518 \times 9.818 = \$83,629.72$$

Thus, it is easy to appreciate the role of interest rates in a real estate investment decision. No industry is more susceptible to the impact of changing interest rates than real estate. Each time the economy overheats and interest rates skyrocket, the real estate industry comes to a standstill. With the eventual easing of interest rate pressures, the industry once again enjoys a recovery.

This pattern has continued into the 1980s. It is within this environment that many traditional lenders have hesitated to commit themselves to long-term lending on a fixed interest rate basis. A 20-year loan commitment at a fixed rate of 10 percent can be both embarrassing and expensive to the lender when interest rates advance to 14 or 15 percent.

New Types of Mortgages

In actuality, a whole new set of mortgage arrangements have appeared as alternatives to the fixed interest rate mortgage (particularly for home mortgages). The borrower must now be prepared to consider such alternative lending arrangements as the *variable rate mortgage,* the *graduated payment mortgage,* and the *shared appreciation mortgage.*

Adjustable rate mortgage (ARM).   Under an adjustable rate mortgage, the interest rate is adjusted regularly. Recent pronouncements by federal regulatory authorities have indicated a tendency to allow the rate to *float* more and more with market conditions (originally there were many restrictions). If interest rates go up, borrowers may either increase their normal payments or extend the maturity date of the loan at the same, fixed-payment level to fully compensate the lender. Similar downside adjustments can also be made if interest rates fall. Generally, adjustable rate mortgages are initially made at rates 1 to 2 percent below fixed-interest rate mortgages because the lender enjoys the flexibility of changing interest rates and is willing to share the benefits with the borrower. Adjustable rate mortgages currently account for over half of the residential mortgage market. Although adjustable rate mortgages usually have an upper boundary (such as 15 or 18 percent), there is a real possibility of default for many borrowers if interest rates reach high levels.

Graduated payment mortgage (GPM).   Under this type of financial arrangement, the payments start out on a relatively low basis and increase over the life of the loan. This type of mortgage may be well suited to the young borrower who has an increasing repayment capability over the life of the loan.

An example would be a 30-year, $50,000 loan at 12 percent which would normally require monthly payments of $503.20 under a standard fixed-payment mortgage. With a graduated payment mortgage, monthly payments might start out as $350 or $400 and eventually progress to over $600. The GPM plan has been referred to by a few of its critics as the "gyp em" plan, in that early payments may not be large enough to cover interest and therefore later payments must cover not only the amortization of the loan, but also interest on the accumulated, unpaid, early interest. This is not an altogether fair criticism but merely an interpretation of what the graduated payment stream represents.

Shared appreciation mortgage (SAM).   Perhaps the newest and most innovative of the mortgage payment plans is the shared appreciation mortgage. This provides the lender with a direct hedge against inflation because he directly participates in any increase in value associated with the property being mortgaged. The lender may enjoy as much as 30 to 40 percent of the appreciation in value over a specified time period, such as 10 years. The lender may take his return from the selling of the property or from the refinancing of the appreciated property value with a new lender. In return for this appreciation potential privilege, the lender may advance funds at well below current market rates (perhaps at three quarters of current rates). The shared appreciation mortgage is not yet legal in all states.

Other forms of mortgages.   Somewhat similar to the shared appreciation mortgage is the concept of *equity participation* that is popular in commercial real estate. Under an equity participation arrangement, the lender not only provides the borrowed capital, but part of the equity or ownership funds as well. A major insurance company or savings and loan thus may acquire an equity interest of 10 to 25 percent (or more). This financing arrangement becomes popular each time inflation rears its head. Some lenders are simply unwilling to commit capital for long time periods without a participation feature.

Borrowers may also look toward a *second mortgage* for financing. Here a second lender provides additional financing beyond the first mortgage in return for a secondary claim or lien. The second mortgage is generally for a shorter period of time than the initial mortgage. Primary suppliers of second mortgages in the 1980s have been sellers of property. Quite often, in order to consummate a sale, it is necessary for the seller to supplement the financing provided by a financial institution. Sellers providing second mortgages generally advance the funds at rates below the first mortgage rate to facilitate the sale, whereas other second mortgage lenders (nonsellers) will ask for a few percentage points above the first mortgage rate to compensate for the extra risk of being in a secondary claim position.

In some cases, sellers may actually provide all the financing to the buyer. Usually the terms of the mortgage are for 20–30 years, but the seller has the right to call in the loan after three to five years if he so desires. The assumption is that the buyer may have an easier time finding his own financing at that point in time. This may or may not turn out to be true.

FORMS OF REAL ESTATE OWNERSHIP

Ownership of real estate may take many forms. The investor may participate as an individual, in a regular partnership, through a real estate syndicate (generally a limited partnership), or through a real estate investment trust (REIT).

Individual or Regular Partnership

Investing as an individual or with two or three others in a regular partnership offers the simplest way of getting into real estate from a legal viewpoint. The investors pretty much control their own destinies and can take advantage of personal knowledge of local markets and changing conditions to enhance their returns.

As is true with most smaller and less complicated business arrangements, there is a well-defined center of responsibility that often leads to quick corrective action. However, there may be a related problem of inability to pool adequate capital to engage in large-scale investments as well as the absence of expertise to develop a wide range of investments. Furthermore, there is unlimited liability to the investor(s).

Syndicate or Limited Partnership

In order to expand the potential for investor participation, a syndicate or limited partnership may be formed.[7] The purpose of the limited partnership is to combine the limited liability protection of a *corporation* with the tax provisions of a *regular partnership*. The limited partnership works as follows: a general partner forms the limited partnership and has unlimited liability for the partnership liabilities. The general partner then sells participation units to the limited partners whose liability is generally limited to the extent of their initial investment (such as $5,000 or $10,000). Limited liability is particularly important in real estate because mortgage debt obligations may exceed the net worth of the participants.

The other significant feature of the limited partnership (or any partnership) is that all profits or losses are directly assigned to the partners rather than accounted for in the business unit. Thus, there is avoidance of double taxation as would be true in a corporation. The direct assignment of tax losses in the early years of a project may be particularly attractive as a tax shelter device for a wealthy individual. As we showed in Table 17–5, a typical investment might be an apartment project that has a $12,270 first-year tax loss, in spite of the fact that there was a positive cash flow of $6,465 and perhaps another $13,600

---

[7] A syndicate may take the form of a corporation, but this is not common. The term *real estate syndicate* has become virtually synonymous with the limited partnership form of operation.

appreciation in value due to inflation. Investors can claim the tax losses directly rather than have them go through business or corporate taxation first. Thus, we see the limited partnership offers the dual benefits of (a) limited liability to limited partners (similar to a corporation) as well as (b) the avoidance of double taxation and therefore the direct assignment of losses as tax shelters (similar to individuals or regular partnerships).

As previously indicated, the limited partnership allows the investor to participate in much larger, more diversified holdings than the individual or normal partnership could hope to achieve. A wealthy investor in Connecticut can acquire an interest in apartments in Dallas, shopping centers in Phoenix, and so on. Furthermore, he or she will have full-time managers to look after the holdings.

As is true in almost any form of investment, there are also drawbacks to the limited partnership. As implied by the title, the *limited* partner has very little to say in the operations of the partnership. It is the general partner who represents the operation and makes the day-to-day decisions. This is fine as long as the general partner is operating in a prudent and effective manner. However, it is quite difficult for limited partners to replace the general partner when other forms of behavior appear.

Furthermore, the limited partners must be particularly sensitive to the front-end fees and commissions that the general partner might charge. These can vary anywhere from 5 to 10 percent to as large as 20 to 25 percent.[8] The investor must also be sensitive to any double-dealing that the general partner might be doing. An example would be selling property back and forth between different syndicates that the general partner has formed and taking a commission each time. The inflated paper profits may prove quite deceptive and costly to the uninformed limited partner.

In assessing a general partner and his associated real estate deal, the investor should look at a number of items. First of all, prior record of performance should be reviewed. Is this the 1st or 10th deal that the general partner has put together? The investor will also wish to be sensitive to any lawsuits against the general partner that might exist. The investor might also wish to ascertain whether he or she is investing in a *blind pool* arrangement where funds are provided to the general partner to ultimately select properties for investment or if specific projects have already been identified and analyzed.

Finally the investor may have to decide whether to invest in a limited partnership/syndication that is either *public* or *private* in nature. A public offering generally involves much larger total amounts and has gone through the complex and rigorous process of SEC registration. Of course, SEC registration only attempts to ensure that full disclosure has taken place—it does not judge the prudence of the venture. A private offering of a limited partnership syndication is usually local in scope and restricted to a maximum of 35 investors.

---

[8] Kenneth R. Harvey, *Beating Inflation with Real Estate* (New York: Random House, 1980), p. 230.

FIGURE 17–2   Data Sheet for an REIT

SOUTHMARK CORP. NYSE-SM | RECENT PRICE **10** | P/E RATIO **6.7** (Trailing: 5.7 Median: NMF) | EARN'S YLD **15.0%** | DIV'D YLD **1.6%** | **675**

High	Low
16.8	14.5
30.8	18.6
31.1	23.2
32.9	21.9
26.3	1.6
5.0	0.9
4.1	1.0
1.5	NA
1.3	NA
2.1	0.9
3.9	1.0
4.8	2.8
6.5	3.7
12.5	5.1

Target Price Range
1986 1987 1988 1989

Jan. 20, 1984 Value Line

Insider Decisions 1983
A S O N D J F M A M J J A S O
to Buy 0 0 0 0 0 1 0 0 0 0 2 0 2 0
to Sell 0 0 2 2 1 1 0 0 0 0 0 0 0 0

1.0 × Book Value
10.0 × "Cash Flow" p sh
10% div'd
10% div'd

TIMELINESS 1 Highest
Relative Price Performance Next 12 Mos. **5** Lowest
SAFETY 3 (Scale: 1 Highest to 5 Lowest)
BETA 1.15 (1.00 = Market)

10
(Continued from Capital Structure)
Common Stock 29,062,450 shs (34% of Cap'l)
Warrants
3.21 mill. Series C warrants each exercisable until 2-1-87 for 1.21 common share for a total price of $7.50, callable at $2.50. (Called effective 2-1-84).

NYSE trading suspended
3-16-77 to 11-8-78

Relative Price Strength

1986-88 PROJECTIONS
	Price	Gain	Ann'l Total Return
High	30	(+200%)	32%
Low	17	(+70%)	16%

Institutional Decisions
	3Q'82	4Q'82	1Q'83	2Q'83	3Q'83
to Buy	3	2	3	3	11
to Sell	1	4	5	4	1
Hldg's(000)	1341	1338	1329	1329	3656

Percent 15.0
shares 10.0
traded 5.0

© Value Line, Inc.

1968	1969	1970	1971	1972	1973	1974	1975	1976	1977	1978	1979	1980	1981	1982	1983	1984	1985		86-88E
--	--	--	15.11	15.35	16.19	15.75	2.73	d6.97	d2.98	d1.25	1.69	1.88	3.26	5.47	8.32	10.25		Book Value per sh (A)	18.00
--	--	--	1.50	2.20	2.51	1.78	d12.59	d10.75	d7.68	d1.06	d.02	.35	.32	1.63	1.81	2.00		"Cash Flow" per sh	2.30
--	--	--	1.52	2.15	2.56	1.71	d12.85	d10.79	d.77	d1.53	d.31	.04	.19	1.19	1.34	1.50		Earnings per sh (B)	2.00
--	--	--	1.51	2.05	2.50	2.15	.37	--	--	--	--	.04	.05	.16				Div'ds Decl'd per sh (C)	.50
--	--	--	35.83	54.63	82.94	93.18	103.70	108.91	61.29	36.72	15.65	13.08	6.77	21.61	31.50	22.85		Loans & Real Est per sh	29.35
--	--	--	3.40	4.11	4.62	4.63	4.63	4.63	4.63	4.63	7.79	8.31	18.17	18.10	19.63	35.00		Common Shs Outst'g	37.50
--	--	--	43%	74%	82%	7%	-72%	205%	--	--	10%	-10%	-30%	-5%				Premium over Book	35%
--	--	--	14.5	12.7	11.3	10.0	--	--	--	--	--	NMF	16.0	3.4	4.2	Bold figures are Value Line estimates		Avg Ann'l P/E Ratio	12.0
--	--	--	6.9%	7.9%	8.9%	10.0%	--	--	--	--	--	NMF	6.2%	3.0%	24.0%			Avg Ann'l Earn's Yield	8.3%
--	--	--	6.9%	7.5%	8.6%	12.5%	11.3%							1.0%	.8%			Avg Ann'l Div'd Yield	2.1%

CAPITAL STRUCTURE as of 9/30/83
ST Debt $53.5 mill. (7% of Cap'l)
LT Debt $381.3 mill. (49% of Cap'l)
Due in 5 Yrs 240.0 mill. **LT Interest** $45.0 mill.
(Total long and short-term interest coverage in fiscal 1983: 2.4x)
Pfd Stock $80.3 mill. **Pfd Div'd** See below
1,606,024 shs. Series D cum. adj. rate dividend (floats at 175 basis points above the highest rate on three Treasury securities, between 8% and 17%) with $50 liq. value.
(Continued on Chart)

60.2	39.8	25.2	19.0	28.5	20.5	23.0	26.1	99.1	161.6	240	Gross Income ($mill) (A)	350
7.9	d58.6	d50.0	d35.8	d7.1	d2.5	.4	3.5	26.4	37.7	75.0	Net Profit ($mill)	95.0
13.2%	NMF	NMF	NMF	NMF	NMF	1.7%	13.4%	26.7%	23.3%	31.0%	Net Profit Margin	27.0%
121.7	490.5	504.6	394.0	179.4	121.8	108.6	123.1	391.0	618.5	800	Loans & Real Est ($mill)	1100
5.7	53.9	91.4	55.0	33.5	21.0	15.3	12.4	1.8	1.8	1.5	Loss Reserve ($mill)	1.0%
11.3%	9.3%	1.8%	1.2%	2.1%	2.1%	2.2%	5.5%	13.1%	13.2%	11.5%	Avg Interest Paid	11.0%
303.5	365.9	361.4	193.0	157.6	76.7	63.3	1.8	31.9	61.9	35.0	Short-Term Debt ($mill)	50.0
85.0	56.6	91.0	62.6	28.9	19.4	17.7	54.5	241.3	311.1	380	Long-Term Debt ($mill)	300
73.0	12.7	d32.3	d13.8	d5.8	13.2	15.6	59.3	149.8	293.1	490	Net Worth ($mill)	875
25.6%	13.3%	3.0%	6.4%	9.0%	14.2%	19.4%	51.9%	45.0%	53.9%	61.5%	% Cap Funds to Tot Cap	75.0%
.8%	7%	1.1%	1.5%	2.6%	4.4%	2.9%	3.5%	4.9%	3.8%	3.0%	% Expenses to Assets	2.5%
11.2%	NMF	NMF	NMF	NMF	NMF	1.3%	5.9%	15.3%	11.3%	11.0%	% Earned Total Cap'l	9.5%
10.3%	NMF	NMF	NMF	NMF	NMF	2.8%	11.3%	27.1%	19.3%	15.5%	% Earned Net Worth	11.0%

FUNDS FLOW
	1981	1982	1983
Net Profit Plus			
Noncash Charges	6.7	50.9	48.3
Investments Repaid	17.0	86.3	192.7
Net New Debt	(14.1)	32.7	(15.5)
New Equity	23.0	47.8	79.3
Investments Funded	35.8	219.8	281.3
Dividends Declared	--	2.2	8.6

FINANCIAL POSITION
	9/30/82	9/30/83
Senior Debt	$284.4 mill.	$368.8 mill.
Subordinated Debt	$40.8 mill.	$66.0 mill.
Sr Debt/Cap'l Funds	1.3:1	.9:1
Total Debt/Equity	2.7:1	1.3:1

PORTFOLIO CONDITION
	Year Ago	Latest
Mtges Repaid in Quarter	$28.2 mill.	$47.4 mill.
Loss Reserve—% of Invests	4%	.2%
Non-Earn Assets—% of Invests	NA	NA

LOANS & REAL ESTATE ($mill.) (A)
Fiscal Year Ends	Sept. 30	Dec. 31	Mar. 31	June 30
1980	120.9	120.3	112.8	108.6
1981	105.8	104.2	102.1	123.1
1982	141.8	225.0	234.5	391.0
1983	449.1	476.0	473.8	618.5
1984	730.9	750	775	800

EARNINGS PER SHARE (A) Full Fiscal Year
Fiscal Year Ends	Sept. 30	Dec. 31	Mar. 31	June 30	(B) Full Year
1980	.01	--	.03	--	.04
1981	.07	--	.06	.11	.19
1982	.30	.37	.47	.05	1.19
1983	.06	.18	.38	.72	1.34
1984	.26	.40	.40	.44	1.50

QUARTERLY DIVIDENDS PAID (C) Full Year
Calendar	Mar. 31	June 30	Sept. 30	Dec. 31	Full Year
1980	NO DIVIDENDS PAID 1976-80				
1981	--	--	.04	--	.04
1982	--	--	--	.05	.05
1983	--	--	.04	.04	.08
1984					

(A) Fisc. yr. ends June 30th of cal. yr. Ended Sept. 30 thru fiscal '76. Fiscal '77 = 9 mos. Portfolio growth from June quarter '81 mostly from acquisitions. (B) Fully-diluted egs. beg. in '81, primary in '80 and before. Next egs. rep't due late Jan. Excl. extra. gains: '76, $1.09; mos. to 6/30/77, $11.71; '78, $3.41. '79, $1.95; '80, 9¢; '81, 92¢; '82, $1.04; '83, 96¢; '84, 24¢. (C) Next div'd meet'g about Feb. 1. Goes ex about Feb. 13. Div'd paym'ts: 3/15,6/15,9/15,12/15.

BUSINESS: Southmark Corp. (formerly Citizens and Southern Realty Investors) acquires real estate assets, seeks to enhance their value and then to realize a profit on their disposition. At 6/30/83, 34% of investments were in real estate of which apartments comprised 33%; shopping centers, 11%; condominiums, 9%; land, 24%; office buildings, 6%; hotels/motels, 7%; other, 10%. Owns 92% of North American Mortgage, 50% of American Realty Trust and interests in other real estate cos. Has 5,719 shareholders. Chrmn. & Pres. Gene E. Phillips and William S. Friedman have 41% of voting control. Inc.: Ga. Address: 1601 LBJ Freeway, Suite 800, Dallas, TX 75234.

The Series C warrants have been called, effective February 1st. Each warrant can be exchanged for 1.21 Southmark common shares until January 25th upon payment of $7.50 per warrant. At the recent common stock quotation of $10, the warrants have a value of $4.60, well above the $2.50 call price. As long as the common price remains above 8¼, the warrants should be exercised rather than permitted to be called.

Common shares outstanding will have increased by more than 75% in fiscal '84, which ends June 30th. The call for redemption and subsequent conversion of the Series A preferred stock added 10.5 million shares in the September and December quarter. The warrant exercise will add another 4.8 million shares in the March quarter. In order to give more meaningful year-to-year comparisons, the accompanying statistics now show fully diluted earnings from '81 forward.

Earnings comparisons remain strong, but the stock's price has weakened. The weakness relates in part to a negative article on real estate syndications, which appeared in a national magazine. Such syndications are Southmark's bread and butter business (probably 35% or more of combined September- and December-quarter profits). Management reports that its syndication business is strong and that it has never had a syndication go awry. But when the bubble some syndicators appear to be building bursts, Southmark could experience negative fallout. There's also a measure of uncertainty that stems from the ambitious pace of acquisitions in '81-'83 and from the complexity that's been introduced into financial reporting by the resulting rapid growth of disparate financial entities. Thus, only venturesome investors will want to hold these shares on the expectation that fundamentals will be strong enough to support superior relatively price action over the next year.

Most future acquisitions will be designed to fill out present business lines. As the life insurance business and the S&L operations grow, they will reduce the relative importance of real estate transactions and thereby tend to smooth the income statement's bottom line. The lower interest rates that we think will unfold over the 3- to 5-year pull will be conducive to profitable growth of both of these new activities. Lower rates will also help contain the cost of the $130 million floating rate preferred. _D.L.H/N.R.W_

Company's Financial Strength C+
Stock's Price Stability 5
Price Growth Persistence 60
Earnings Predictability 30

Factual material is obtained from sources believed to be reliable but cannot be guaranteed.

Real Estate Investment Trusts

Another form of real estate investment is the real estate investment trust (REIT). REITs are similar to mutual funds or investment companies and trade on organized exchanges or over-the-counter. They pool investor funds, along with borrowed funds, and invest them directly in real estate or use them to make construction or mortgage loans to investors.

The advantage to the investor of an REIT is that he or she can participate in the real estate market for as little as $5 to $10 per share. Furthermore, this is the most liquid type of real estate investment because of the large secondary market for the shares.

REITs were initiated under the Real Estate Investment Trust Act of 1960. Like other investment companies, they enjoy the privilege of single taxation of income (only the stockholder pays and not the trust). In order to qualify for the tax privilege of a REIT, a firm must pay out at least 90 percent of its income to shareholders, have no less than 75 percent of its assets in real estate, and concurrently obtain at least 75 percent of its income from real estate.

REITs may take any of three different forms or combinations thereof. *Equity trusts* buy, operate, and sell real estate as an investment; *construction and development trusts* make short-term loans to developers during their construction period; and *mortgage trusts* make long-term loans to real estate investors. REITs are generally formed and advised by affiliates of commercial banks, insurance companies, mortgage bankers, and other financial institutions. Representative issues include Bank America Realty, Continental Illinois Property, and Connecticut General Mortgage.

Although REITs were enormously popular investments during the 1960s and early 1970s, the bottom fell out of the REIT market in the mid-1970s. Many had made questionable loans that came to the surface in the tight money, recessionary period of 1973–75. Nevertheless, REITs have now regained some of their earlier popularity. Many investors look at the equity trust, which owns real estate directly, as a hedge against inflation. Somewhat less popular are the construction and development trusts and mortgage trusts (many REITs combine these various functions). The investor in REITs hopes to receive a reasonably high yield because 90 percent of income must be paid out in the form of dividends plus a modest capital appreciation in stock value. In some cases, outside investors have taken over REIT's with the intention of liquidating assets at higher than current stock market values.

There are over 200 REITs from which the investor may choose. Further information on REITs may be acquired from the National Association of Real Estate Investment Trusts, 1101 17th St., N.W., Washington, D.C. 20036. In Figure 17–2, a Value Line data sheet is presented for Southmark Corporation, an example of a reasonably successful REIT.

GOLD AND SILVER

We now examine a number of other forms of real asset investments. Precious metals represent the most volatile of the investment alternatives. Gold and

FIGURE 17–3   Dollar per Troy Ounce

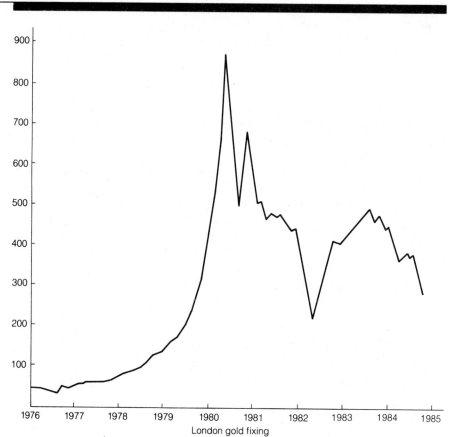

London gold fixing

silver tend to move up in troubled times and show a decline in value during stable, predictable periods. Observe the movement in the price of gold between January 1976 and December 1984 in Figure 17–3.

Gold

Major factors that tend to drive up gold prices are fear of war, political instability, and inflation (these were particularly evident in 1979 with the takeover of U.S. embassies and double-digit inflation). Conversely, moderation in worldwide tensions and lower inflation cause a decline in gold prices. High interest rates are also a negative influence on gold prices. When interest rates are high, it may be very expensive to carry gold as an investment.

Gold may be owned in many different forms, and a survey by *Changing Times* indicated that 30 percent of the United States population with incomes over $30,000 per year owned gold or other forms of precious metals. Let's examine the different forms of gold ownership.

Gold bullion. Gold bullion includes gold bars or wafers. The investor may own anywhere from 1 troy ounce to 10,000 troy ounces (valued at approximately $3 million in 1985). Smaller bars generally trade at a 6 to 8 percent premium over pure gold bullion value, with larger bars trading at a 1 to 2 percent premium. Gold bullion may provide storage problems, and unless the gold bars remain in the custody of the bank or dealer who initially sells them, they must be reassayed before being sold.

Gold coins. Many of the storing and assaying costs associated with gold bullion can be avoided by investing directly in gold coins. There are three basic outlets for investing in gold coins. First, there are *gold bullion coins,* such as the South African Kruggerand, the Mexican 50 peso, and the Austrian or Hungarian 100 korona. These coins trade at a small premium of 2 to 3 percent over pure bullion value and afford the investor an excellent outlet for taking a position in the market. A second form is represented by *common date gold coins* that are no longer minted, such as the United States double eagle, the British sovereign, or the French Napoleon. These coins may trade at as much as 50 to 100 times their pure gold bullion value. Finally, there are gold coins that are *old* and *rare* and that may trade at a numismatic value into the thousands or hundreds of thousands of dollars.

Gold stocks. In addition to gold bullion and gold coins, the investor may choose to take a position in gold by simply buying common stocks that have heavy gold mining positions. Examples of companies listed on U.S. exchanges include Campbell Red Lake (Canadian based), Dome Mines (Canadian based), and Homestake Mining (U.S. based). Because these securities often move in the opposite direction of the stock market as a whole, they may provide excellent portfolio diversification. The investor may also examine closed-end investment companies with heavy gold mining positions (such as ARA Limited).

Gold futures contracts. Finally, the gold investor may consider trading in futures contracts. Gold futures are traded on five different U.S. exchanges and on many foreign exchanges.[9]

Silver

Silver has many of the same investment characteristics as gold in terms of being a hedge against inflation and a safe haven for investment during troubled times. Silver has moved from $4 a troy ounce in 1976 to over $50 an ounce in early 1980 and then back to $6 an ounce in 1985.

---

[9] There are also options on gold futures on the Comex.

More so than gold, silver has heavy industrial and commercial applications. Areas of utilization include photography, electronic and electrical manufacturing, electroplating, dentistry, and silverware and jewelry. It is estimated that industrial uses of silver exceed annual production by 150 million ounces per year. Furthermore, supply of silver does not necessarily increase with price because silver is a byproduct of copper, lead, zinc, and gold. Because of the undersupply factor, many consider silver to be appropriate for long-term holding.

Investment in silver can also take many different forms. Some may choose to buy *silver bullion* in the form of silver bars. Because the price of silver generally is 1/20th to 1/40th the price of gold and larger bulk is involved for an equivalent dollar size investment, the storage and carrying costs can be quite high. Secondly, *silver coins* may be bought in large bags or as rare coins for their numismatic value. Keep in mind that dimes, quarters, and half-dollars minted during and prior to 1965 were 90 percent pure silver. As a third outlet, the investor may wish to consider *silver futures contracts.* Finally, the investor may purchase *stocks* of firms that have interests in silver mining, such as Callahan Mining, Hecla Mining, or Rosario Resources.

PRECIOUS GEMS

Precious gems include diamonds, rubies, sapphires, and emeralds. Diamonds and other precious gems have appeal to investors because of their small size, easy concealment, and great durability. They are particularly popular in Europe because of a long-standing distrust of paper currencies as a store of value.

The reason diamonds are so valuable can be best understood by considering the production process. It is estimated that 50 to 200 *tons* of rock or sand is required to uncover one carat (1/142 of an ounce) of quality diamonds.

The distribution of diamonds is under virtual monopolistic control by De Beers Consolidated Mines of South Africa, Ltd. They control the distribution of approximately 80 percent of the world's supply and have a stated policy of maintaining price control. Diamonds have generally enjoyed a steady, somewhat spectacular movement in price. For example, the price of a "D" color, one-carat, flawless, polished diamond increased over 10-fold between 1974 and 1980.

Of course, not all diamonds have done so well. Furthermore, there have been substantial breaks in the market, such as in 1974 and 1980–82 when diamond prices declined by one fourth and more. Even with large increases in value, the diamond investor does not automatically come out ahead. There may be dealer markups anywhere from 10 percent to 100 percent so that three to five years of steady gain may be necessary to show a substantial profit.

In no area of investment is product and market knowledge more important. Either you must be an expert yourself or know that you are dealing with an "honest" expert. Diamonds are judged on the basis of the four *c*'s (color, clarity, carat weight, and cut), and the assessment of any stone should be certified by the Gemological Institute of America. As is true of most valuable items, the investor is well advised to purchase the highest quality possible. You are considerably better off using the same amount of money to buy a higher-quality, smaller-carat diamond than a lesser-quality, high-carat diamond.

OTHER COLLECTIBLES

A listing of other collectibles for investment might include art, antiques, stamps, Chinese ceramics, rare books, sports memorabilia, and other items that appeal to various sectors of our society. Each offers psychic pleasure to the investor as well as the opportunity for profit.

Anyone investing in a collectible should have some understanding of current market conditions and of the factors that determine the inherent worth of the item. Otherwise, you may be buying someone else's undesirable holding at a premium price. It is important not to get swept away in a buying euphoria. The best time to buy art, antiques, or stamps is when the bloom is off the market and dealers are overburdened with inventory, not when there is a weekly story in *The Wall Street Journal* or *Business Week* about overnight fortunes being made. There seems to be a pattern or cycle in the collectibles market the same as in other markets (arts, antiques, and stamps actually do move together). The market was very strong in the 1970s with a pause in the mid-1970s caused by the recession. The market gained tremendous momentum from 1975 to 1980, with a sell-off in late 1980 and early 1981. Only a moderate recovery has taken place in the mid-1980s.

As is true of other markets, the wise investor in the collectibles market must be sensitive to dealer spreads. A price guide that indicates a doubling in value every two or three years may be meaningless if the person with whom you are dealing sells for $100 and buys back for $50. The wise investor/collector can best maintain profits by dealing with other collectors or investors and eliminating the dealer or middleman from the transaction where possible.

Such periodicals as *Money* magazine and the *Collector/Investor* provide excellent articles on the collectibles market. Specialized periodicals, such as *American Arts and Antiques, Coin World, Linn's Stamp News, The Sports Collectors Digest,* and *Antique Monthly,* also are helpful. The interested reader can find books on almost any type of collectible in a public library or large bookstore.

Chapter 18

INTERNATIONAL SECURITIES MARKETS

In Chapter 1, we discussed the advantage of diversification in terms of risk reduction. In order to reduce risk exposure, the investor may desire a broad spectrum of securities from which to choose. An investor who lives in California would hardly be expected to limit all his investments to that geographic boundary. The same might be said for an investor living in the United States or Germany or Japan. The advantages of crossing international boundaries may be substantial in terms of diversification benefits. While energy-importing nations such as France or Japan may temporarily suffer from high energy prices, energy-exporting nations are benefiting. The same can be said about the effects of crop failures, wars, tariffs, and many other factors. Furthermore, in spite of the alternating up and down markets in the United States, there is almost certain to be a bull market somewhere in the world for the investor who likes to keep his chips on the table at all times.

The main drawback to investing in international securities would appear to be the more complicated nature of the investment. Currently, one cannot simply pick up the phone and ask his broker to buy 100 shares of Banco Bilbao on the Spanish Stock Exchange (this may change some day in the future). Nevertheless, the difficulties of participating in international securities are not as great as one might initially expect. As will be later suggested in this chapter, there are a number of feasible and easily executed routes to follow in participating in the international markets.

The primary attention in this chapter is in international equities, although investments may certainly include fixed-income securities and real assets.

In the chapter, we shall examine the composition of world equity markets, the diversification and return benefits that can be derived from foreign investments, the obstacles that are present, and finally, the methods of participating in foreign investments, directly and indirectly.

THE WORLD EQUITY MARKET

In the early 1970s, U.S. securities represented 75 percent of the total market value of equities around the world. In the 1980s that value has declined to close to 50 percent as security markets in other countries have become more important. In Figure 18–1 we see a percentage breakdown of approximately a trillion dollars of equity securities in major exchanges outside of the United States. One can quickly see the importance of the Tokyo Stock Exchange in Japan as well as of a number of other key exchanges. The U.S. equity market, of course, is equal to the full size of this graph.

DIVERSIFICATION BENEFITS

As previously mentioned, not all foreign markets move in the same direction at any point in time. In Table 18–1, we see the stock market movements for a number of key countries over a 21-year period. Sharply contrasting movements are noted in such years as 1973 and 1977. In 1973 U.S. equities were

FIGURE 18–1   Market Values of Non-U.S. Equities at the End of 1980 (in billions of U.S. dollars; non-U.S. equity total = $1,049.3 billion)

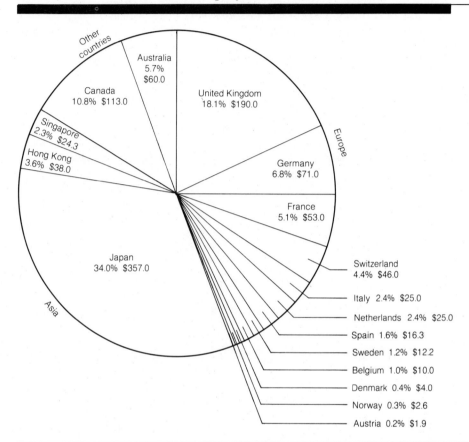

Source: Roger G. Ibbotson, Richard C. Carr, and Anthony W. Robinson, "International Equity and Bond Returns," *Financial Analysts Journal,* July–August 1982, p. 63.

down by 18.68 percent, while equities in Norway gained 128.52 percent, those in Austria appreciated by 25.09 percent, and those in Spain gained 24.03 percent. In 1977 U.S. equities showed a slightly bearish posture with a 3.03 percent decline, while equities in the United Kingdom were up 56.49 percent and stocks in Switzerland appreciated 25.49 percent.

Another way to consider diversification benefits is to measure the extent of correlation of stock movements. Such a measure is presented in Table 18–2, in which stock movements of a number of foreign countries are compared to those of the United States.

The average correlation is approximately .30, which is low. The best risk reduction benefits can be found by combining U.S. securities with those from such countries as Spain (−.115), Austria (−.076), and Norway (.009); and the least benefits can be found in combinations with Hong Kong (.814), the Neth-

TABLE 18–1 World Equities: Year-by-Year Adjusted Total Returns (in percent)*

		Europe																
Year	U.S. total	Austria	Belgium	Denmark	France	Germany	Italy	Netherlands	Norway	Spain	Sweden	Switzerland	United Kingdom	Hong Kong	Japan	Singapore	Canada	Australia
1960	0.83	52.28	−7.99	3.77	6.72	42.32	46.18	3.24	12.24	10.14	5.51	43.82	0.13		38.50		−1.16	−0.07
1961	27.52	41.14	22.84	3.81	13.62	2.14	14.73	12.49	18.14	36.42	5.57	54.89	12.56		−13.03		39.03	14.86
1962	−9.29	−12.76	−1.99	8.12	11.38	−21.70	−10.44	−5.39	−15.43	19.65	12.47	−8.51	4.76		4.68		−6.84	0.95
1963	21.04	−4.28	18.06	17.77	−14.77	14.87	−12.71	17.71	0.42	0.15	12.92	−14.49	22.80		8.78		14.39	24.92
1964	16.71	3.78	8.04	11.88	−1.17	4.70	−26.43	9.61	10.22	10.44	23.17	−7.16	−5.14		10.93		24.36	5.17
1965	15.26	−1.16	−2.65	11.93	−4.10	−12.63	30.16	−10.00	0.37	16.12	11.00	−11.74	12.66		21.39		4.81	−9.75
1966	−8.21	−4.88	−15.82	5.63	−8.18	−15.06	8.89	−14.54	−7.61	11.87	−23.93	−12.91	−2.07		9.04		−9.24	−4.87
1967	30.45	0.97	13.35	−11.88	0.46	51.80	−2.51	38.97	1.09	−8.48	7.69	52.39	16.57		−4.85		7.18	44.70
1968	14.95	2.95	13.63	17.81	14.81	13.61	4.23	37.58	21.55	31.42	45.52	30.44	51.34		26.43		26.61	28.62
1969	−9.86	6.90	7.18	3.36	18.39	23.42	15.19	−4.42	24.75	46.87	1.75	5.05	−12.52		34.15		3.21	16.10
1970	−1.00	13.49	9.66	−6.47	−5.14	−23.76	−17.52	−6.50	39.53	−3.68	−18.92	−13.17	−5.72	21.31	−6.35	−5.43	15.81	−19.14
1971	18.16	8.44	25.00	10.18	1.66	24.61	−12.34	1.76	14.13	26.26	36.12	27.41	47.99	59.52	46.55	65.52	14.13	−1.59
1972	17.71	37.65	32.69	112.20	24.83	18.54	15.33	29.56	9.03	42.30	16.82	28.61	3.93	161.66	126.56	211.04	33.12	21.06
1973	−18.68	25.00	18.16	5.44	3.83	−4.44	10.18	−4.74	28.52	24.03	2.86	−3.75	−23.44	−39.01	−20.13	−34.58	−3.11	−12.06
1974	−27.77	15.00	−11.74	−10.74	−22.43	17.20	−33.43	−15.56	−39.98	−8.49	11.72	−12.37	−50.33	−60.33	−15.65	−46.69	−26.52	−32.97
1975	37.49	−2.90	17.45	23.96	45.08	30.09	−8.69	50.23	−15.14	0.05	21.00	41.18	115.06	99.56	19.84	63.57	15.07	50.71
1976	26.68	15.58	13.00	7.23	−20.03	6.57	−26.55	16.94	14.98	−36.00	6.37	10.42	−12.55	40.55	25.80	13.83	9.71	−10.00
1977	−3.03	−3.76	11.02	1.74	5.07	23.08	−18.92	14.65	−23.83	−19.66	−21.64	25.49	56.49	−11.58	15.70	4.60	−1.37	11.25
1978	8.53	15.68	33.27	9.47	73.19	26.96	46.37	20.83	6.81	7.86	23.96	21.82	14.63	18.61	53.33	45.31	20.55	22.24
1979	24.18	19.43	21.08	−2.18	28.90	−1.93	17.39	19.95	183.01	5.51	2.64	12.21	22.20	83.50	−11.69	28.58	52.26	43.44
1980	33.22	−11.90	−11.40	15.80	−1.30	−8.20	78.40	11.90	−17.30	4.60	21.00	−7.10	38.80	69.90	29.70	61.20	22.00	52.20

* U.S.-dollar-adjusted.
Source: Roger G. Ibbotson, Richard C. Carr, and Anthony W. Robinson, "International Equity and Bond Returns," *Financial Analysts Journal,* July–August 1982, p. 69.

TABLE 18–2   Correlation of Foreign Stock Movements with U.S. Stock Movement (1960–1980)

U.S.	1.000
Hong Kong	.814
Netherlands	.730
Canada	.710
Australia	.699
United Kingdom	.617
Singapore	.579
Switzerland	.454
Sweden	.398
Belgium	.389
Denmark	.243
Japan	.216
France	.214
Germany	.210
Italy	.208
Norway	.009
Austria	−.076
Spain	−.115

Source: Roger G. Ibbotson, Richard C. Carr, and Anthony W. Robinson, "International Equity and Bond Returns," *Financial Analysts Journal,* July–August 1982, p. 71.

erlands (.730), and Canada (.710). Somewhat attractive is the relatively low correlation with Japan (.216). According to one researcher, a well-diversified international portfolio can achieve the same risk reduction benefits as a pure U.S. portfolio that is twice the size in terms of securities.[1] In Chapter 19, there is a much more detailed discussion on the importance of correlation considerations to risk reduction. We have merely touched the surface for now.

RETURN POTENTIAL IN INTERNATIONAL MARKETS

Actually, risk reduction through effective international diversification is only part of the story. Not only does the investor have less risk exposure, but there is also the potential for higher returns in many foreign markets. Why? A number of countries have had superior growth rates to that of the United States in terms of real GNP. These would include Japan, Norway, Singapore, and Hong Kong. Secondly, many countries have become highly competitive in traditional U.S. products such as automobiles, steel, and consumer electronics. A classic example is, once again, Japan. Thirdly, many nations (Germany, Japan, France, Canada) enjoy higher individual savings than does the United States and this leads to capital formation and potential investment opportunity. This, of course, is not to imply that the United States does not have the strongest

---

[1] Bruno H. Solnik, "Why Not Diversify Internationally Rather than Domestically?" *Financial Analysts Journal,* July–August 1974, pp. 48–54.

security markets in the world. It clearly does. However, it is a more mature market than many others, and there may be abundant opportunities for superior returns in a number of foreign markets.

In Table 18–3 we can see the compound rate of return for 18 different countries over a long time period. While the return for U.S. equities during this time frame was 8.7 percent (column one, second item from the bottom), Hong Kong, Japan, and Singapore enjoyed annualized returns of between 15 and 25 percent. If you examine the next to last column in Table 18–3, you can observe the value that a one-unit investment would have grown to over this

TABLE 18–3   World Equities: Summary Statistics, 1960–1980

Asset	Annual returns in U.S. dollars			Year-end wealth index (1959 = 1.00)	1980 Year-end value in billions U.S. $
	Compound return (percent)	Arithmetic mean (percent)	Standard deviation (percent)		
Non-U.S. equities:					
Europe					
Austria	9.1%	10.3%	16.9%	6.23	$ 1.9
Belgium	9.2	10.1	13.8	6.39	10.0
Denmark	9.5	11.4	24.2	6.72	4.0
France	6.2	8.1	21.4	3.56	53.0
Germany	8.3	10.1	19.9	5.32	71.0
Italy	2.4	5.6	27.2	1.63	25.0
Netherlands	9.3	10.7	17.8	6.45	25.0
Norway	10.3	17.4	49.0	7.81	2.6
Spain	8.4	10.4	19.8	5.49	16.3
Sweden	8.4	9.7	16.7	5.40	12.2
Switzerland	10.2	12.5	22.9	7.74	46.0
United Kingdom	10.0	14.7	33.6	7.39	190.0
Europe total	8.4	9.6	16.2	5.47	457.0
Asia					
Hong Kong*	24.6	40.3	61.3	11.24	38.0
Japan	15.6	19.0	31.4	20.86	357.0
Singapore*	23.2	37.0	66.1	9.96	24.3
Asia total	15.9	19.7	33.0	22.29	419.3
Other					
Australia	9.8	12.2	22.8	7.12	60.0
Canada	10.7	12.1	17.5	8.47	113.0
Other total	10.6	11.9	17.1	8.24	173.0
Non-U.S. total equities	10.6	11.8	16.3	8.23	1049.3
U.S. total equities	8.7	10.2	17.7	5.78	1380.6
World total equities	9.3	10.5	15.8	6.47	2429.9

* 1970–1980.
Source: Roger G. Ibbotson, Richard C. Carr, and Anthony W. Robinson, "International Equity and Bond Returns," *Financial Analysts Journal*, July–August 1982, p. 65.

21-year period. If it had been invested in U.S. equities, the ending value would be 5.78. The same one-unit investment in Asian securities (referred to as "Asia total," and including Hong Kong, Japan, and Singapore) would have grown to 22.29. If invested in the category of "Other" securities (including Australia and Canada), the accumulation is to 8.24.

It should be pointed out that Table 18–3 represents a relatively long-term prospective. There are, of course, time periods when the United States outperforms foreign markets. A diagram of the accumulated values previously discussed is prsented in Figure 18–2.

We bring together two main points of this chapter in Table 18–4 on p. 526. Here we see a listing of a number of foreign countries whose returns are superior to those of the United States and whose correlation values with U.S. equity markets are less than .5 (providing high returns and risk reduction at

FIGURE 18–2   U.S.-Dollar-Adjusted Cumulative Wealth Indexes of World Equities, 1960–1980 (year-end 1959 = 1.00)

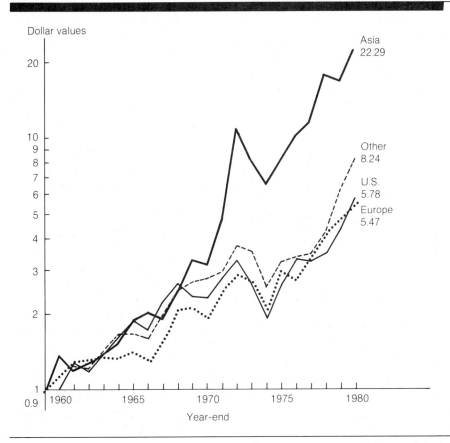

Source: Roger C. Ibbotson, Richard C. Carr, and Anthony W. Robinson, "International Equity and Bond Returns," *Financial Analysts Journal,* July–August 1982, p. 66.

TABLE 18–4   Annual Compound Returns and Correlation Values with U.S. Security Markets (1960–1980)

Country	Compound (percent) return	Correlation with U.S. security market
Japan	15.6%	.216
Norway	10.3	.009
Switzerland	10.2	.454
Denmark	9.5	.243
Belgium	9.2	.389
Austria	9.1	−.076
United States	8.7	1.000

the same time). Japan with its strong returns and low correlation appears particularly attractive.

Current Quotations on Foreign Market Performance

In order to track the current performance of selected world markets, *The Wall Street Journal* provides daily quotes of price movement activity. The closing quotes of May 23, 1984, are presented in Table 18–5.

TABLE 18–5   Daily *Wall Street Journal* Quote

	May 23	May 22	% This Year
U.S.	143.7	144.4	− 8.1
Britain	305.6	308.2	+ 8.4
Canada	242.5	243.5	−12.6
Japan	452.2	453.2	+ 7.5
France	183.8	184.5	+11.2
Germany	124.6	125.1	− 2.4
Hong Kong	617.4	620.3	+ 6.4
Switzerland	114.7	116.3	− 1.7
Australia	125.9	126.9	−13.1
World Index	177.6	177.9	− 3.4

The quotes assume a base period value of each country's index of 100 for 1969. As reflected in the index quotes of May 23, it is plain that Hong Kong (617.4) and Japan (452.2) have substantially outperformed the United States (143.7) over the 15-year period. Also in the year-to-date performance for 1984 (last column), Hong Kong and Japan are up while the United States is down. Of the 9 countries shown in Table 18–5, 4 have an increase in value for the year, while 5 have a decline. This once again provides evidence of the differing movements in foreign markets.

The last item at the bottom of Table 18–5, the World Index, is a value-weighted index of the performance in 19 major countries as compiled by Capital International, S.A., of Geneva, Switzerland. The United States alone makes up approximately 50 percent of the index because it is value-weighted by market size. Similar type information on global stock markets can also be found in the "International Trades" section of *Barron's*.

The *Institutional Investor,* a magazine used by professional portfolio managers, also tracks the performance of world markets on a regular basis. Quotes for December 31, 1983 (from the February 1984 issue) are shown in Table 18–6.

Table 18–6 is of interest because it shows price–earnings ratios and yields, as well as price changes, for foreign markets. Note the extremes in

TABLE 18–6   World Stock Markets

Here's a recap of the performance of 19 stock markets in leading countries around the world as of December 30, 1983, based upon data supplied by Capital International Perspective of Geneva. It should be noted that the percentage changes are in local currencies and are calculated from Capital International's market indexes.

Rank		3 Months % change	6 Months % change	9 Months % change	12 Months % change	Price–earnings ratio	Yield
1	Mexico	16.2%	56.4%	125.0%	188.1%	4.8	5.5%
2	Hong Kong	16.0	−9.0	−12.1	9.7	9.0	5.8
3	Switzerland	14.8	15.8	19.5	26.7	12.6	2.5
4	Germany	11.4	9.7	15.8	38.3	15.0	3.7
5	France	10.4	23.4	33.1	58.4	63.8	4.7
6	Australia	9.3	28.9	51.9	63.0	15.1	3.6
7	Japan	6.3	12.2	18.3	21.3	25.1	1.3
8	United Kingdom	4.9	1.6	15.2	24.5	10.4	4.8
9	Belgium	4.6	7.7	19.3	36.1	10.4	10.6
10	Singapore/Malaysia	4.2	0.5	11.0	30.1	28.2	1.8
11	Norway	4.2	19.3	49.5	91.5	12.9	3.3
12	Netherlands	4.0	7.6	22.4	52.1	6.4	5.0
13	Denmark	3.6	29.8	48.3	95.5	17.2	1.7
14	Austria	2.2	0.4	3.7	9.5	272.2	2.7
15	Canada	2.0	4.2	19.0	29.5	27.5	3.2
16	United States	−0.6	−1.6	7.4	16.6	12.2	4.5
17	Sweden	−1.5	6.9	15.6	61.2	15.2	2.1
18	Italy	−2.2	0.5	−8.8	22.3	Loss	3.1
19	Spain	−4.0	−7.7	−3.2	4.1	7.0	14.2
	The World Index	2.2	2.7	11.7	21.6	13.9	3.8

Source: *Institutional Investor,* February 1984, p. 50.

price–earnings ratios for certain countries such as Austria (272.2) and France (63.8). Also note in the price-earning ratio column that the average firm in Italy actually had a loss.

Less Developed Countries

Our discussion thus far has primarily centered on what are considered as developed countries (DCs). While many of these countries are considerably smaller than the United States, they still have reasonably well-organized economies and financial markets. There are also potential investment opportunities in less developed countries that have not been previously mentioned. These include such nations as Chile, Jordan, Korea, Thailand, and Zimbabwe. A number of these less developed countries may represent superior investment opportunities in terms of return and risk reduction opportunities. In fact, most have low or negative correlations with the U.S. While this chapter will not explicitly cover the less developed markets, the reader who has an interest in this subject is encouraged to read an article by Vihang Errunza in the September–October 1983 issue of the *Financial Analysts Journal*—"Emerging Markets: A New Opportunity for Improving Global Portfolio Performance."[2]

CURRENCY FLUCTUATIONS AND RATES OF RETURN

Up until now, we have been talking about rates of returns in foreign countries without specifying whether they were in terms of foreign exchange of that country or of U.S. dollars. For example, assume an investment in France produces a 10 percent return. But suppose at the same time the French franc declines in value by 5 percent against the U.S. dollar. The French franc profits are thus worth less in dollars. In the present case, the gain on the investment would be shown as follows:

110%	(Investment with 10% profit)
× .95	(Adjusted value of French franc relative to U.S. dollar)
104.5%	Percent of original investment

The actual return in U.S. dollars would be 4.5 percent instead of 10 percent. Of course, if the French franc appreciated by 5 percent against the dollar, the French franc profits converted to dollars would be worth considerably more than 10 percent. The values are indicated below.

110%	(Investment with 10% profit)
× 1.05	(Adjusted value of French franc relative to U.S. dollar)
115.5%	Percent of original investment

---

[2] Vihang R. Errunza, "Emerging Markets: A New Opportunity for Improving Global Portfolio Performance," *Financial Analysts Journal,* September–October 1983, p. 51–58.

The 10 percent gain in the French franc investment has produced a 15.5 percent gain in U.S. dollars. It is apparent that a U.S. investor in foreign securities must not only consider the potential trend of security prices, but also the trend of foreign currencies against the dollar. A consideration of this point becomes more apparent in examining Table 18–7.

TABLE 18–7   Return on World Stock Markets (through March 1983)

	Return in each currency (percent)			Currency valuation (percent)			Return in U.S. dollars (percent)		
	3-month	*1-year*	*5-year*	*3-month*	*1-year*	*5-year*	*3-month*	*1-year*	*5-year*
New York	8.8%	36.6%	11.4%	0.0%	0.0%	0.0%	8.8%	36.6%	11.4%
Tokyo	4.0	15.7	8.7	−2.0	3.5	−1.7	1.9	19.8	6.8
London	9.8	15.2	7.2	−8.3	−16.9	−4.5	0.6	−4.3	2.4
Toronto	10.1	36.6	15.2	−0.7	−0.8	−1.7	9.3	35.5	13.2
Frankfurt	19.1	26.5	2.7	−2.2	−0.7	−3.9	16.5	25.6	−1.3
Sydney	5.6	11.0	10.8	−11.9	−17.7	−5.4	−6.9	−8.7	4.8
Paris	20.5	10.8	8.6	−7/4	−13.9	−9.1	11.6	−4.5	−1.3
Zurich	9.0	22.4	1.3	−3.7	−7.2	−2.6	5.0	13.7	−1.3
Hong Kong	27.1	14.6	17.3	−3.7	−13.0	−7.2	22.4	−25.7	8.8
Milan	28.5	4.8	28.5	−5.3	−8.4	−10.1	21.7	−4.0	15.6
Amsterdam	29.4	49.9	7.1	4.0	−2.0	−4.6	24.1	47.0	2.2
Singapore	18.5	19.3	24.9	1.1	2.3	2.1	19.8	22.0	27.5

Although the foreign exchange impact in Table 18–7 is not significant in some countries, its effect can be clearly seen for London. In this instance, the one-year return in the local currency was 15.2 percent (column 2), but the currency (British pound) declined 16.9 percent against the U.S. dollar for the one-year period, causing an overall *loss* on the investment of 4.3 percent (second column from the right for London). The values are computed as follows:

> 115.2%   (Investment with 15.2% profit)
>   Adjusted value of British pound to the U.S. dollar
> × .831   (1.000 − .169 decline in currency)
> 95.7%   Percent of original investment

The ending value of 95.7 percent indicates a loss of 4.3 percent from the initial value of 100 percent.[3] If one were to merely subtract the foreign cur-

---

[3] Due to rounding and other statistical adjustments, not all values adjusted to U.S. dollars come out as precisely as this.

rency loss of 16.9 percent from the 15.2 percent profit, the answer would be a loss of 1.7 percent, but this is not the correct procedure. The reason is that the gain of 15.2 percent was on an initial base of 100 percent, but the foreign currency loss of 16.9 percent was on an ending value of 115.2 percent (which comes out to an actual loss in currency value of 19.5 percent). The difference between 19.5 percent and 15.2 percent is 4.3 percent.

Actually those who track the performance in foreign markets usually make adjustments so that the reported returns are in U.S. dollars that have already been adjusted for foreign currency effects. For example, all the returns in Tables 18–1, 18–3, and 18–4 of this chapter have already been adjusted for the foreign currency effect. However, the material in Table 18–6 is an example of returns specifically reported in unadjusted local currencies.

One might justifiably ask, how important is the foreign currency effect in relation to the overall return performance in the foreign currency? Do events in foreign exchange markets tend to overpower actual returns achieved in specific investments in foreign countries? Normally, the foreign currency effect is only about 10–20 percent as significant as the actual return performance in the foreign currency.[4] However, when the dollar is rising or falling rapidly over a short period of time, the impact can be much greater.

In a well-diversified international portfolio, the changes in foreign currency values in one part of the world normally tend to cancel out changes in other parts of the world. Also, those who do not wish to have foreign currency exposure of any sort may use forward exchange contracts, futures market contracts, or put options on foreign currency to hedge away the risk. Finally, there are those who believe in parity theories that suggest that one should get additional compensation in local returns to make up for potential losses in foreign currency values. This latter point is a purely theoretical matter that provides little comfort in the short run.

The authors would suggest that those considering international investments be sensitive to the foreign currency effect, but not be overly discouraged by it. The superior return potential from foreign investments shown in Figure 18–2 (and most other places in this chapter) are constructed *after* taking into consideration the foreign exchange effect on U.S. dollar returns. While foreign currency swings have been *wider* in recent times, they are still not a major deterrent to an internationally diversified portfolio.

OTHER OBSTACLES TO INTERNATIONAL INVESTMENTS

There are some other problems that are peculiar to international investments. Let us consider some of these.

---

[4] Betrand Jacquillat and Bruno Solnik, "Multinationals are Poor Tools for Diversification," *Journal of Portfolio Management,* Winter 1978, pp. 8–12.

Political Risks

Many firms operate in foreign political climates that are more volatile than that of the United States (such as Mexico). There is the danger of nationalization of foreign firms or the blockage of capital flows to investors. There also may be the danger of a violent overthrow of the political party in power. Furthermore, many countries have been unable to meet their foreign debt obligations, and this has important political implications.

The informed investor must have some feel for the political/economic climate of the foreign country in which he or she invests. Of course, problems sometimes create opportunities. It is entirely possible that local investors may overreact to political changes that are taking place in their environment. Because all their eggs are in one basket, they may engage in an "overkill" or oversell in regard to political changes. It is possible that a less impassioned outside investor may actually identify an opportunity for profit.

Nevertheless, political risk represents a potential deterrent to foreign investment. The best solution for the investor is to be sufficiently diversified around the world so that a political or economic development in one foreign country does not have a major impact on his or her portfolio (this can be accomplished through a mutual fund or through other means discussed later in the chapter).

Tax Problems

Many major foreign countries may impose a 7.5 percent to 15 percent withholding tax against the dividends or interest paid to nonresident holders of equity or debt securities. However, it is often possible for *tax-exempt* U.S. investors to secure an exemption or rebate on part or all of the withholding tax. Also, taxable U.S. investors can normally claim a U.S. tax credit for taxes paid in foreign countries. The problem is more likely to be one of inconvenience and paper shuffling rather than loss of funds.[5]

Lack of Market Efficiency

U.S. capital markets tend to be the most liquid and efficient in the world. Therefore, an investor who is accustomed to trading on the New York Stock Exchange may have some difficulties in adjusting to foreign markets. There is likely to be a larger spread between the bid (sell) and ask (buy) price in foreign countries. Also, there may be more difficulty in handling a large transaction (the seller may have to absorb a larger discount in executing the trade). Furthermore, as a general rule, commission rates are higher in foreign markets than in the United States.

---

[5] Gary L. Bergstrom, John K. Koeneman, and Martin J. Siegel, "International Securities Market" in *Readings in Investment Management,* ed. Frank J. Fabozzi (Homewood, Ill.: Richard D. Irwin, 1983).

Administrative Problems

There can also be administrative problems in dealing in foreign markets in terms of adjusting to the various local systems. For example, in the Hong Kong, Swiss, and Mexican stock markets, you must settle your account one day after the transaction; in London there is a two week settlement procedure; and in France there are different settlement dates for cash and forward markets. The different administrative procedures of foreign countries simply add up to an extra dimension of difficulty in executing trades (as implied throughout this chapter, there are ways to avoid most of these difficulties by going through mutual funds and other investment outlets).

Information Difficulties

The U.S. security markets are the best in the world at providing investment information. The Securities and Exchange Commission, with its rigorous requirements for full disclosure, is the toughest national regulator of investment information. Also, the United States has the Financial Accounting Standard Board (FASB) continually providing pronouncements on generally accepted accounting principles for financial reporting. Publicly traded companies are required to provide stockholders with fully audited annual reports. In the United States we are further spoiled by the excellent evaluative reports and ratings generated by Moody's, Standard & Poor's, Value Line, and other firms. We also have extensive economic data provided by governmental sources such as the Department of Commerce and the Federal Reserve System.

Many international firms, trading in less sophisticated foreign markets, simply do not provide the same quantity or quality of data. This would be particularly true of firms trading in some of the smaller foreign markets. Even when the information is available, there may be language problems for the analyst who does not speak German, French, Portuguese, etc.

Also, the analyst must be prepared to analyze the firm in light of the standards that are generally accepted in the foreign market in which the company operates. For example, Japanese companies often have much higher debt ratios than U.S. firms. A debt-to-equity ratio of three times is not unusual in Japan, whereas in the United States the standard is closer to one to one. The uninformed analyst may be inclined to "mark down" the Japanese firm for high debt unless he or she realizes the different features at play in the Japanese economy. For example, in Japan there are normally very close relationships between the lending bank and the borrower, with the lender perhaps having an equity position in the borrower and with interlocking boards between the two. This diminishes the likelihood of the lender calling in the loan in difficult economic periods. Also, the Japanese make extensive use of reserve accounts which tend to give the appearance of a smaller asset or equity base than actually exists. This pattern of understatement is further aided by a strict adherence to historical cost valuation even though Japanese land values have increased more rapidly than almost anywhere else in the world. When appropriate adjustments are made for these effects on financial reporting, a Japanese debt-to-equity ratio of three to one may not be a matter of any greater concern than a U.S. debt-to-equity ratio of one to one.

METHODS OF PARTICIPATING IN FOREIGN INVESTMENTS

The avenues to international investment include investing in firms in their own foreign markets, purchasing the shares of foreign firms trading in the United States, investing in mutual funds and closed-end funds with a global orientation, buying the shares of multinational corporations, and entrusting funds to private money managers who specialize in international equities. We shall examine each of these alternatives.

Direct Investments

The most obvious, but least likely alternative, would be to directly purchase the shares of a firm in its own foreign market through a foreign broker or an overseas branch of a U.S. broker. The investor might consider such firms as Toshiba or Fanuc on the Tokyo Stock Exchange, Consolidated Rutile on the Sydney Stock Exchange, or Hoechst on the Frankfort Stock Exchange. This approach is hampered with all the difficulties and administrative problems associated with international investments. There could be information-gathering problems, tax problems, stock delivery problems, capital transfer problems, and communication difficulties in executing orders. Only the most sophisticated money manager would probably follow this approach (though this may change somewhat in the future as foreign markets become better coordinated).

A more likely route to direct investment would be to purchase the shares of foreign firms that actually trade in U.S. security markets. There are actually hundreds of foreign firms that actively trade their securities in the United States. A listing of some key participants is presented in Table 18–8.

TABLE 18–8   Foreign Firms Trading on the New York Stock Exchange

Country	Company	Industry
Bahamas	Commodore International Ltd.	Integrated microcomputer systems
Bermuda	Sea Containers Ltd. (3 Pfd. issues)	Cargo container leasing
Canada	Alcan Aluminum Ltd.	Aluminum
	AMCA International Limited	Industrial prods.; construct.; engineer.
	Bell Canada Enterprises Inc.	Telecommunication services & equip.
	Campbell Red Lake Mines Ltd.	Gold mining
	Campbell Resources Inc. (2 issues)	Holding co.—coal; oil & gas interests
	Canadian Pacific Enterprises Ltd.	Iron & steel production; mining
	Canadian Pacific Limited	Integrated transportation system
	Carling O'Keefe Limited	Breweries

TABLE 18–8   (*concluded*)

Country	Company	Industry
	Dome Mines Limited	Gold mining
	Genstar Limited (2 issues)	Land, building development
	Hiram Walker Resources Ltd.	Distilleries; gas utility
	Inco Ltd.	Nickel & copper production
	Inspiration Resources Corporation	Metals mining; petroleum
	MacMillan Bloedel Ltd.	Forest products, pulp & paper
	Massey-Ferguson Ltd.	Farm equipment
	McIntyre Mines Ltd.	Coal mining
	Mitel Corporation	Electronic telecomm. equip.
	Moore Corporation Ltd.	Business forms
	Northern Telecom Ltd.	Telecommunications equip.
	Northgate Exploration Limited	Holding co.—explor.; mining; invest.
	Ranger Oil Limited	Oil & gas exploration, production
	Seagram Co. Ltd.	Distilleries
	Westcoast Transmission Co., Ltd.	Natural gas transmission
Denmark	Novo Industri A/S	Industrial enzymes; drugs
Great Britain	British Petroleum Company Ltd.	Holding co. integrated oil company
	Imperial Chemical Industries PLC	Diversified chemicals
	Plessey Company Ltd.	Telecommun. and electronic equip.
	"Shell" Transport and Trading Public Ltd. Co.	Holding co.,—integrated oil company
	Tricentrol PLC	Oil & gas prod., oil trading
	Unilever PLC	Foods; consumer goods
Japan	Hitachi, Ltd.	Indust. equip., consumer products
	Honda Motor Co., Ltd.	Motor vehicles and parts
	Kubota, Ltd.	Agricultural equipment; piping
	Kyocera Corp.	Ceramic electronic products
	Matsushita Electric Industrial Co., Ltd.	Consumer electronic products
	Pioneer Electronic Corporation	Consumer electronic products
	Sony Corporation	Consumer electronic products
	TDK Corporation	Electronic components; magnetic tapes
Netherlands	KLM Royal Dutch Airlines	Air transportation
	Royal Dutch Petroleum Co.	Holding company-integrated oil co.
Netherlands Antilles	Erbamont N.V.	Pharmaceuticals
	Schlumberger, Ltd.	Oilfield serv.; electronics
	Unilever, N.V.	Foods; consumer goods
Panama	Norlin Corporation	Organs, pianos, guitars
	Syntex Corporation	Pharmaceuticals
Philippines	Benguet Corporation	Mining; construction
South Africa	ASA Limited	Investment company
Spain	Banco Central, S.A.	Holding company—bank

Source: *New York Stock Exchange Fact Book* (New York: New York Stock Exchange, 1984), p. 40.

Firms such as Alcan Aluminum Ltd., Massey-Ferguson Ltd., and Hitachi, Ltd., trade their stocks directly on the New York Stock Exchange. Most of the other firms on the list (as well as other large foreign firms) trade their shares in the United States through American Depository Receipts (ADRs). These ADRs represent the ownership interest in a foreign company's common stock. The process is as follows: The shares of the foreign company are purchased and put in trust in a foreign branch of a New York bank. The bank, in turn, receives and can issue depository receipts to the American shareholders of the foreign firm. These ADRs (i.e., depository receipts) allow foreign shares to be traded in the United States.

When you call your broker and ask to purchase Sony Corporation or Honda Motor Co., Ltd. (which are represented by ADRs), you will notice virtually no difference between this transaction and buying shares of General Motors or Eastman Kodak. You can receive a certificate that looks very much like a U.S. stock certificate. You'll receive your dividends in dollars and get your reports about the company in English. Generally, you will pay your normal commission rates.

In Table 18–9, you see a page from *Standard & Poor's Stock Guide* that includes Sony Corporation's ADRs. Note the financial information is basically the same as that for other U.S. corporations trading on a major exchange or over-the-counter. The Sony ADRs also receive coverage from *Value Line* and other reporting services. There are daily quotes in *The Wall Street Journal* just as there would be for any company. Since these ADRs trade on the New York Stock Exchange, the quote would be found in that section of the paper.

The *Standard & Poor's Stock Guide* is a good place to start in determining whether a foreign company has ADRs trading in the United States or not. As previously indicated, there are hundreds of ADRs trading in U.S. markets.

Indirect Investments

The forms of indirect investments in the international securities include *(a)* purchasing shares of multinational corporations, *(b)* purchasing mutual funds or closed-end investment funds specializing in worldwide investments, and *(c)* engaging the services of a private firm specializing in foreign investment portfolio management.

Purchasing shares of multinational corporations. Multinational corporations, that is, firms with operations in a number of countries, represent an opportunity for international diversification. For example, the major oil companies have investments and operations throughout the world. The same can be said for large banking firms and mainframe computer manufacturers. When one buys Exxon, to some extent he or she is buying exposure to the world economy (71.4 percent of sales are foreign for this firm). A list of the 20 largest U.S. multinational firms is presented in Table 18–10. Of particular interest is the second column from the left, which represents foreign revenue as a percentage of total revenue, and the fourth column from the right, which represents foreign profit as a percentage of total profit.

TABLE 18–9   Sample Page from Standard & Poor's Stock Guide

200 Smu-Sou

Standard & Poor's Corporation

↑S&P 500 ◆Options Index	Ticker Symbol	Name of Issue (Call Price of Pfd. Stocks)	Market	Com. Rank. & Pfd. Rating	Par Val.	Inst. Hold Cos	Inst. Hold Shs. (000)	Principal Business	Price Range 1971-82 High	Price Range 1971-82 Low	1983 High	1983 Low	1984 High	1984 Low	Apr. Sales in 100s	Last Sale Or Bid High	Last Sale Or Bid Low	Last	%Div. Yield	P-E Ratio
1	SJM	Smucker (J.M.)	NY,M	A–	No	22	1084	Preserves; jellies & fillings	37½	7%	46¼	30¾	44½	33½	483	38¼	36¼	37¾	2.5	13
2	SNA	Snap-on Tools	NY,M	A	1	127	8995	Hand tools; auto/ind'l maint	31½	8½	34½	24½	33¾	27	4603	28½	24½	25	3.1	13
3	SOI	Snyder Oil Partners²⁴	AS	NR	No		82	Mgmt of oil & gas prop.			16¾	14¾	16¼	14¾	303	15¾	14¾	15	13.3	7
4	SOCI	Society Corp	OTC	NR	12½	21	1084	Multi-bank hldg:Cleveland	24½	7	33	21½	33	28½	686	31	29¾	30B	5.7	7
5	SOFT	SofTech Inc	OTC	NR	10¢	13	412	Devel software svcs & p'od	22	7	25½	13	15½	9	1284	8½	7	7¾B		15
6	SAGA	Software AG Sys Gr	OTC	NR	1¢	14	864	Computer sys software pkgs	22¼	5½	13	7⅞	14	10⅜	3502	14	11¾	12⅜B		15
7	SSD	Solid State Scient'l	AS,B,M,P,Ph	C	40¢	17	137	Semiconductor devices	18¾	3%	11¼	6	8¼	5¾	1334	8%	6½	8%		26
8	SNT	Sonet, Inc		B	3¾	270	114	Semiconductors-microwave	10½	6%	39½	23½	37½	23⅛	10091	37½	34½	36½	4.2	
10	SONO	Sonoco Products	NY,B,C,M,P,Ph	A+	No	53	2339	Industrial paper products	32¾	4½	47	28¾	46½	39½	1879	43½	39½	43⅜	12.9	12
11	SNMA	Sonoma Vineyards	OTC	C	25¢	6		Premium wines; mach tools	41	3%	11¾	5½	7¼	4¾	2586	6⅜	5¼	5¾B		d
12	SNE	Sony Corp ADR	NY,B,C,M,P,Ph,To,Mo	NR	50⅓	153	31246	Color TV sets,tape rec,radio	26½	3%	16½	12½	17¾	14¾	80878	16¾	15½	16⅜	1.0	21
13	SOOL	Soo Line RR	NY,M	NR	1	26	1072	Railroad contr by Canad Pac	33¾	5%	36½	26¾	29½	23¼	3670	25½	23¼	25¼	4.8	42
14	SPOK	South Cal Pet E&G	NY,M	B+	1	20	472	Savings & loan in Oklahoma	34¾	5½	35¾	28	37	30½	906	12½	10	11B	12	4
15	SORG	Sorg Printing	OTC		No			Fin'l & corporate printing	15½	4⅞	24½	23¼	23¼	10						
16	SOR	Source Capital	NY,M	NR	1	14	191	Closed-end invest divers	30	5%	31¼	27½	31⅜	28⅛	608	30⅜	28¾	30%	10.2	
17	Pr	$2.40 cm Pfd(27.50)vtg	NY	A–	3¾	140	9144		26½	16¾	21¼	19½	20½	19½	140	20¾	19¾	19½	12.3	
18	SCG	South Carolina E&G	NY,B,C,M,Ph	A–	4½			Utility: electric & gas	31¾	8¾	20¼	19	19	19	9907	19¼	17¾	18%	12.5	7
20	SCNC	South Carolina Nat'l	OTC	A	50	36	1447	Bank hldg: South Carolina	33½	9¼	45	30½	43	35	454	43¾	40	43B	4.1	7
21	SJI	South Jersey Indus	NY,Ph	A–	2½	14	287	Hldg co. gas, fuel oil, sand	29	9⅛	25½	19¾	26¾	22	430	25	22½	24½	10.0	7
22	SDR	South Texas Drill & Ex	NY,M	NR	2½	1	100	On Shore contract drill gr o&g	13%	2¼	14	2½	4	2	521	2½	2	2½		9
23	SDW	Southdown, Inc	NY,B,M,Ph	B+	2½	27	1117	Cement mfr & dstr: oil & gas	45¾	8%	43¾	28¾	42	38¼	696	42½	40½	41%	4.8	10
25	SCNC	Southeastern Capital		NR	1	68	4555	Multiple bank hldg:Miami	13%	6	13	9	11	10	5042	10%	22%	10%	10.4	33
26	SMGS	Southeast'n Mich Gas Ent.	OTC	B+	10	2	84	Integrated natural gas sys	13%	7%	14¼	10½	14⅛	13⅛	235	14⅛	13⅛	14⅜	s10.7	6
27	STBN	Southern Pub Sv S.C.	NY,M,OtC	NR	2½	7	181	Util flow'y svrei Carolina	18¼	7½	14	10½	14¼	10¾	965	20½	18¼	18½	$4.8	9
28	SCE	Southern Bancorp S.C.	NY,B,C,M,Ph	A	8⅓	414	300	Bank hldg:South Carolina	19¼	4¼	40¼	34½	40¼	34¼	28000	37½	34¼	37½	s4.3	13
29	Pr A	5% Orig Pfc (NC) vtg	AS,¹⁰),P	AA	8⅓	1	57	Util: primar'y engaged in supply electric energ	34½	16½	39¾	33	38½	33	55	34¾	34¼	10%	11.1	16
31	Pr D	4.32% cm Pfd (28¼)vtg	AS,P	AA	25	1		in portions of central&south-ern California, excluding the City of Los Angeles & certain other cities. Fuel mix: oil & gas 32%,coal 15%,renew-ables includ'g all hydro 10%, nuclear 1% purchased power: 42%	17	4	10	8%	9%	8½	177	8%	8%	8%	12.3	
32	Pr C	4.24% cm Pfd (25.80) vtg	AS,P	AA	25	1			16⅛	4	10	8	9½	8¼	841	8%	7%	7%	12.7	
33	Pr E	4.08% cm Pfd (25½)vtg	AS,P	AA	25	1			16½	6½	9½	8	9¼	8	1518	8½	7¾	8%	12.7	
34	Pr G	4.78% cm Pfd (25.80)vtg	AS,P	AA	25				16⅛	6¼	11¼	8	12	8	349	11½	11	11	13.0	
35	Pr F	5.80% cm Pfd (25¼)vtg	AS,P	AA	25	2	4		22¼	8	13¼	11¾	12	11					13.2	
36	Pr H	8.96% cm Pfd (¹¹107)vtg	AS,P	AA	100	1	3		117	56¾	80½	69%	77	66%	74	66½	65%	65½	13.7	
37	Pr J	8.70% cm Pfd (¹¹102)vtg	AS,P	AA	100	1			115½	54%	80%	68	72%	65½	70	65%	58¾	65%	13.4	
38	Pr L	7.58% cm Pfd (¹¹102½)vtg	AS,P	AA	25	1	6		105¾	47%	70%	60	62%	56½	37	59¼	56%	58%	12.9	
39	Pr M	8.85% cm Pfd (¹¹26.75)vtg	AS,P	AA	25	1	2		28¾	14½	20¾	18½	19	18¼	301	17½	16%	17%	13.0	
40		9.20% cm Pfd (25¼)vtg	NY,B,C,M,P,Ph	AA	25	1			28¾	14½	21	18¾	20	17¼	1215	18%	17%	17%		
41	Pr H	8.54% cm Pfd(¹¹108.54:$F100)vtg	AS,P	AA	100	2	19	Subsid of Pacific Lighting Water supply;some elec Elec util hldg/Southeast	100	59	88½	73	77	70	271	75¾	75¾	73¾	11.6	
42	Pr Pr	12% cm Pfd(¹¹112:$F100)vtg	AS,P	AA	25	3	30		106½	81½	109	92½	105½	99½	203	102¾	99½	99½	12.1	
43	Pr	5.20% cm Cv Pref (25)vtg	AS,P	AA	25		2		29	9¾	32½	11½	30¾	27¼	102	30½	27¼	27¾	4.4	
44	SWTR	South'n Cal Gas cm6%PfrdA(NC)vtg	AS,P	AA–	25				23¼	9¾	16	11¾	12½	11¾	47	11¾	11¾	11½B		8
46	SO	Southern Co	NY,B,C,M,P,Ph	A	5	260	38115		28¾	7%	17¼	14½	17¼	14¾	297	16	15¼	15¾B	10.6	5
							167								58885				11.6	

Uniform Footnote Explanations—See Page 1. Other: ¹P:Cycle 2. ²AS,P. ³P "CBOE:Cycle 2. ⁴P △$0.04,'80. ⁵△$0.06,'80. ⁶**100% nontaxable'83. ⁷⁺Units Ltd Partnership:Int.
**Vote May 14 Penn Central acq.$8.65. ¹¹CBOE:Cycle 2. ¹⁰$0.16,'80. ¹²$0.27,'83. ¹⁴Approx. △$0.15,'83. ¹H.F.Ahmanson plans mgr $40. ¹²$0.15,'83. ¹⁹Subsid Pfd. ²⁰Mo Dec.'80. ²¹$0.48,'80.
**$3.96,'83. ¹⁴△$0.22,'82. ¹⁸$0.52,'93,'83. ¹⁹$1.65,'83 ¹⁹$34.91,'81. ¹To 2-28-85, scale to $101 in'90. ¹To 9-30-85, scale to $101 in'87, then $101. ¹⁹Subsid. Pfd M$.
¹⁴To 5-1-88:scale to $25¾ in'89. ¹⁴To 7-1-85:scale to $25¾ in'90. ¹⁹To 4-29-84, scale to 101 in'94. ¹⁹To 9-29-85, scale to 101 in'95. ¹⁹⊗$1.75,'83. ¹⁹⊗$1.5,'83. ²⁰Subsid. Pfd M$.

Source: *Standard & Poor's Stock Guide*, May 1984.

TABLE 18–10 Large U.S. Multinational Corporations

Rank	Company	Foreign revenue (millions)	Total revenue (millions)	Foreign as % of total	Foreign operating profit* (millions)	Total operating profit* (millions)	Foreign as % of total	Foreign assets (millions)	Total assets (millions)	Foreign as % of total
1	Exxon	$69,386	$97,173	71.4%	$2,208	$4,343	50.8%	$29,914	$62,289	48.0%
2	Mobil	37,778[1]	60,969[1]	62.0	880[2]	1,380[2]	63.8	18,802	36,439	51.6
3	Texaco	31,118	46,986	66.2	833[2]	1,281[2]	65.0	12,956	27,114	47.8
4	Standard Oil California	16,957	34,362	49.3	404[2]	1,377[2]	29.3	8,861	23,465	37.8
5	Phibro-Salomon	16,600	26,703	62.2	218[2]	337[2]	64.7	4,600	39,669	11.6
6	Ford Motor	16,526	37,067	44.6	460[2]	−658[2]	P/D	14,327	21,956	65.3
7	IBM	15,336	34,364	44.6	1,646[2]	4,409[2]	37.3	14,122	32,541	43.4
8	General Motors	14,376	60,026	23.9	−107[2]	963[2]	D/P	12,288	41,363	29.7
9	Gulf Oil	11,513	28,427	40.5	300[2]	900[2]	33.3	7,625	20,436	37.3
10	E I du Pont de Nemours	11,057	33,223	33.3	488[6]	1,491[6]	32.7	5,911	24,343	24.3
11	Citicorp	10,865	17,814	61.0	448[2]	723[2]	62.0	73,316[4]	121,482[4]	60.4
12	Intl Tel & Tel[3]	9,824	21,922	44.8	851	1,194	71.3	9,914	29,172	34.0
13	BankAmerica	8,051	14,955	53.8	253[5]	389[5]	65.0	54,847[4]	119,869[4]	45.8
14	Chase Manhattan	6,207	10,171	61.0	215[2]	307[2]	70.0	41,387	80,863	51.2
15	Dow Chemical	5,544	10,618	52.2	143	356	40.2	5,260	11,807	44.5
16	General Electric	5,490[1]	27,192[1]	20.2	395[2]	1,817[2]	21.7	5,373	21,615	24.9
17	Sun Co	4,901[1]	15,739[1]	31.1	54[6]	706[6]	7.7	2,399	12,019	20.0
18	Standard Oil Indiana	4,862[1]	28,389[1]	17.1	618[2]	1,826[2]	33.8	6,470	24,289	26.6
19	Occidental Petroleum	4,715[1]	18,527[1]	25.4	345[6]	548[6]	63.0	3,502	15,773	22.2
20	Safeway Stores	4,380	17,633	24.8	84[2]	160[2]	52.5	1,052	3,891	27.0

* Unless otherwise indicated. [1] Includes other income. [2] Net income. [3] Includes proportionate interest on unconsolidated subsidiaries or investments. [4] Average assets. [5] Income before security gains or losses. [6] Profit before interest and after taxes.

Source: Excerpt from "100 Largest Multinationals," *Forbes*, July 4, 1983, p. 114.

Although buying shares in a U.S. multinational firm is an easy route to take in order to experience worldwide economic effects, some researchers maintain that multinationals do not provide the major *investment* benefits that are desired. Jacquillat and Solnik found that multinationals provide very little risk reduction over and above purely domestic firms (perhaps only 10 percent).[6] The prices of multinational shares tend to move very closely with U.S. financial markets in spite of their worldwide investments. Thus U.S. multinationals may not do well in a U.S. bear market even if they have investments in strong markets in other countries. This leaves us to turn to mutual funds and closed-end investment companies as potential international investments.

Mutual funds and closed-end investment companies.   As will be described in Chapter 20, mutual funds offer the investor an opportunity for diversification as well as professional management. Nowhere is the mutual fund concept more important than in the area of international investments. Those who organize the funds usually have extensive experience in investing overseas and are prepared to deal with the administrative problems. This, of course, does not necessarily lead to superior returns, but the likelihood for inexperienced blunders is reduced. An example of an international fund, the Scudder International Fund, Inc., is presented in Table 18–11. A description of the fund's international holdings is presented in the upper part of the table.

The Scudder Fund is an open-end mutual fund and trades at its net asset value. The net asset value is equal to the market value of the portfolio minus liabilities divided by the total number of shares outstanding in the mutual fund. It is also a no-load fund.

One may also invest in closed-end investment companies specializing in international equity investments. As described in Chapter 20, a closed-end investment company has a fixed supply of shares outstanding and trades on a national exchange or over-the-counter, much as an individual company does it may trade at a premium or discount from its net asset value. An example is the Japan Fund.

A listing of internationally oriented funds is provided in Table 18–12. The address for these funds can be found in *Wiesenberger Investment Companies Service,* a publication found in most libraries.

Specialists in international securities.   The large investor may consider the option of engaging the services of selected banks and investment counselors with specialized expertise in foreign equities. Major firms include Morgan Guaranty Trust Co., State Street Bank and Trust Co., Batterymarch Financial Management, and Fidelity Trust Company of New York. These firms provide a total range of advisory and management services. However, they often require a minimum investment well in excess of $100,000 and are tailored to the needs of the large institutional investor.

---

[6] Bertrand Jacquillat and Bruno Solnik, "Multinationals Are Poor Tools for Diversification," *Journal of Portfolio Management,* Winter 1978, pp. 8–12.

TABLE 18–11

SCUDDER INTERNATIONAL FUND, INC.

The primary objective of the fund is long-term growth of capital, through investments in companies which, without limitation to any particular country, have their principal activities and interests outside the United States. Under normal conditions, the fund expects to maintain a portfolio consisting primarily of a diversified list of equity securities. The fund may purchase restricted issues up to five percent of invested assets.

At the end of 1983, the fund had 81% of its assets in common stocks, of which the substantial proportion was in five industrialized countries: Japan (20.1% of assets), Netherlands (11.8%), Germany (8.9%), Canada (7.9%) and Switzerland (6.7%). The five largest individual common stock investments were Siemens, A.G. (2.6% of assets), Philips Gloeilampenfabricken (2.3%), Société Générale de Surveillance and Daimler Benz (2.2% each) and Ciba-Geigy (2%). The rate of portfolio turnover in the latest fiscal year was 38.9% of average assets. Unrealized appreciation at the calendar year-end was 27% of total net assets.

Statistical History

	———AT YEAR-ENDS———								**———ANNUAL DATA———**				
			Net Asset Value			— % of Assets in —			Income Div-	Capital Gains			
	Total Net Assets	Number of Share-	Per Share	Yield	Cash & Equiv-	Bonds & Pre-	Com- mon		idends	Distribu-	Expense Ratio	Offering Price ($)	
Year	($)	holders	($)	(%)	alent	ferreds	Stocks		($)	tion ($)	(%)	High	Low
1983	133,482,471	6,578	22.15	1.4	8	11	81		0.31	—	1.13	22.15	17.10
1982	79,112,561	3,940	17.33	3.1	12	22	66		0.54	—	1.16	17.92	14.06
1981	59,814,118	3,233	17.84	2.3	18	18	64		0.404	0.034	1.10	19.26	15.78
1980	49,088,930	2,773	18.81	2.9	18	11	71		0.572	1.231*	1.15	19.32	14.80
1979	25,927,381	2,184	16.35	2.8	18	12	70		0.493	1.356*	1.25	17.00	14.78
1978	18,058,078	2,108	15.37	1.8	2	—	98		0.286	0.497*	1.41	16.69	12.95
1977	14,454,457	2,175	13.30	2.1	9	—	91		0.277	—	1.28	13.72	12.72
1976	16,157,645	2,462	13.65	1.1	10	—	90		0.148	—	1.35	13.65	12.22
1975	17,992,758	2,725	13.01	2.7	12	2	86		0.35	—	1.48	13.14	10.33
1974	15,527,507	2,943	10.33	1.5	30	1	69		0.156	0.257	1.26	14.40	9.56
1973	24,012,278	3,136	13.89	0.1	21	—	79		0.022	1.757	1.38	19.42	13.16

* Includes $0.008 short-term capital gains in 1978; $0.303 in 1979; $0.104 in 1980.

An assumed investment of $10,000 in this fund, with capital gains accepted in shares and income dividends reinvested, is illustrated below. The explanation on Page 163 must be read in conjunction with this illustration.

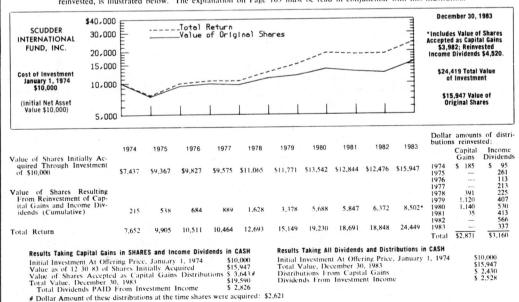

SCUDDER INTERNATIONAL FUND, INC.

Cost of Investment January 1, 1974 $10,000

(Initial Net Asset Value $10,000)

December 30, 1983

*Includes Value of Shares Accepted as Capital Gains $3,982; Reinvested Income Dividends $4,520.

$24,419 Total Value of Investment

$15,947 Value of Original Shares

	1974	1975	1976	1977	1978	1979	1980	1981	1982	1983		Dollar amounts of distributions reinvested:	
												Capital Gains	Income Dividends
Value of Shares Initially Acquired Through Investment of $10,000	$7,437	$9,367	$9,827	$9,575	$11,065	$11,771	$13,542	$12,844	$12,476	$15,947	1974	$ 185	$ 95
											1975	—	261
											1976	---	113
											1977	---	213
											1978	391	225
Value of Shares Resulting From Reinvestment of Capital Gains and Income Dividends (Cumulative)	215	538	684	889	1,628	3,378	5,688	5,847	6,372	8,502*	1979	1,120	407
											1980	1,140	530
											1981	35	413
											1982	—	566
Total Return	7,652	9,905	10,511	10,464	12,693	15,149	19,230	18,691	18,848	24,449	1983	—	337
											Total	$2,871	$3,160

Results Taking Capital Gains in SHARES and Income Dividends in CASH

Initial Investment At Offering Price, January 1, 1974	$10,000
Value as of 12 30 83 of Shares Initially Acquired	$15,947
Value of Shares Accepted as Capital Gains Distributions	$ 3,643#
Total Value, December 30, 1983	$19,590
Total Dividends PAID From Investment Income	$ 2,826

Dollar Amount of these distributions at the time shares were acquired: $2,621

Results Taking All Dividends and Distributions in CASH

Initial Investment At Offering Price, January 1, 1974	$10,000
Total Value, December 30, 1983	$15,947
Distributions From Capital Gains	$ 2,430
Dividends From Investment Income	$ 2,528

TABLE 18–12   Internationally Oriented Funds

Name of fund	Open- or closed-end	Load (L) no-load (NL)	Where invested
Canadian Fund, Inc.	Open	L	Canada
International Investors Incorporated	Open	L	Gold mines
G. T. Pacific Fund, Inc.	Open	NL	Asia (Japan, Hong Kong, etc.)
Kemper International Fund, Inc.	Open	L	Worldwide
Merrill Lynch Pacific	Open	L	Far East
Merrill Lynch International Holdings	Open	L	Worldwide
Putnam International Equities Fund	Open	L	Worldwide
Research Capital Fund, Inc.	Open	L	Foreign mining
T. Rowe Price International Fund, Inc.	Open	NL	Worldwide
Scudder International Fund, Inc.	Open	NL	Worldwide
Strategic Investments Fund, Inc.	Open	L	South African gold mines
Templeton World Fund, Inc.	Open	L	Worldwide
Transatlantic Fund, Inc.	Open	NL	Worldwide
United International Growth Fund	Open	L	Worldwide
ASA Limited	Closed	Commission	South African gold mines
Japan Fund	Closed	Commission	Japan
U.S. and Foreign Securities	Closed	Commission	Worldwide

The average investor, with an international interest, is probably better-advised to consider the ADR alternative or the mutual fund or closed-end investment company.

Part Five

INTRODUCTION TO PORTFOLIO MANAGEMENT

The contemporary portfolio manager is continually called on to assess the nature of his or her performance over a period of time. A couple of decades ago, an analysis that merely indicated the extent of gains and losses would have been sufficient. This is no longer the case. There are at least two dimensions to every modern portfolio evaluation: the rate of return that was earned and the amount of risk that was taken. Many of the earlier concepts related to risk, introduced in Chapter 1, will now be more formally developed.

In Chapter 19 we evaluate the risk measurement tools for an individual asset as well as a portfolio of assets. We also review the concept that most investors are risk-averse. This implies that higher returns will have to be expected in order to induce investors to accept higher risks.

If we accept the concept of a premium return for risk we must then consider what type of risk should be rewarded. Portfolio theory suggests that much of the risk in individual assets can be diversified away in a cross section or portfolio of investments, and that only risk that cannot be diversified is likely to receive a higher return in a competitive marketplace. We examine the performance of institutional investors at the end of Chapter 19.

Chapter 20 is devoted to mutual funds as an alternative way to manage money. Mutual funds provide a diversified portfolio of investments that are professionally managed to achieve the investor's desired investment objectives. The chapter discusses the details of mutual funds and describes basic terms such as load, no-load, open, closed, net asset value and more. Additionally this chapter presents the risk-return experience for several basic groups of funds covering aggressive growth stocks, growth-income stocks, bonds,

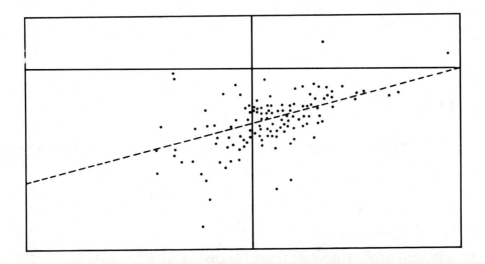

balanced funds, and Treasury bills. Finally, we end with a discussion of share-holder services provided by the management company and a presentation of some investment strategies available to mutual investors.

Chapter 19
PORTFOLIO MANAGEMENT

Chapter 20
MUTUAL FUNDS

Chapter 19

PORTFOLIO MANAGEMENT

In this chapter, we develop a more complete understanding of how the investor perceives risk and demands compensation for it. We eventually build toward a theory of portfolio management that incorporates many of these concepts. While some mathematics must be used to develop the concepts, we have attempted as much as possible to simplify the mathematical presentation, instead focusing on conceptual understanding rather than computational competency.

PORTFOLIO GOALS REVIEWED

Any portfolio manager must start with a set of goals and objectives and some planned strategy for meeting those goals. The investor's basic consideration is to decide between several conflicting goals. Should the investor pursue income or growth? Can growth be compatible with safety of principal? How much liquidity is needed in the portfolio? Is the investor in a high enough tax bracket to pursue tax advantaged investments? Should the investment orientation be long-term or short-term? (These issues were discussed more fully in Chapter 1.)

Of course, one goal common to all investors is an expected rate of return. The higher the desired rate of return, however, the greater the assumed risk. Investors have not always thought this way; they often neglected risk considerations and focused only on return.

THE RETURN TRAP

In the bull market days of the 1950s and part of the 1960s, many portfolio managers turned in performances that were vastly superior to the market averages. High returns were often achieved by taking larger than normal risks through investing in small growth companies or concentrating in a limited number of high-return industries. These portfolio managers or their representatives proclaimed their superior ability in managing money and often extrapolated past returns to tempt investors with their image of the future. There was very little attempt to relate rate of return directly to risk exposure or to provide caveats about the likelihood of replicating past performance. They projected an image that in terms of generating returns, people were either superior money managers or they were not.

Nevertheless, with the end of the bull market era of the 1960s, a new mentality developed. Many of the gunslinging super performers of the past were the worst performers in a bear market. Their high returns of the past were probably not so much a result of unusual insight but rather that they utilized unusually high risk. Actually some portfolio managers began to welcome the notion of risk-adjusted returns. A mutual fund manager or bank trust department head could rationally explain to a client, "although a competitor had a 2 percent higher return, it was actually inferior to our performance on a risk-adjusted basis." With the revival of a bull market mentality in

1983, investors must be careful not to fall into the return trap; they should continue looking at return on a risk-adjusted basis.

A BASIC LOOK AT RISK-RETURN TRADE-OFFS

As indicated in Chapter 1, risk is generally associated with uncertainty about future outcome. The greater the range of possible outcomes, the greater the risk. We also observed in Chapter 1 that most investors tend to be risk-averse; that is, all things being equal, investors prefer less risk to more risk and will only increase their risk-taking position if a premium for risk is involved. Each investor has a different attitude toward risk. The inducement one investor needs to withdraw his funds from a savings account to drill an oil well may be quite different from that required by another. For some, only a very small premium for risk is necessary, others won't participate unless there are exceptionally high rewards.

The first 18 chapters cover many types of investments. The individual features of stocks, bonds, convertible bonds, Treasury bills, real estate, options, and futures have been presented and discussed. Figure 19–1 lists these investments in a risk return tradeoff graph. While some may take exception to the placement of one or two investment types, the general concept of higher risk holds in moving from left to right along the horizontal axis. This

FIGURE 19–1   Risk-Return Trade-offs for Selected Investments

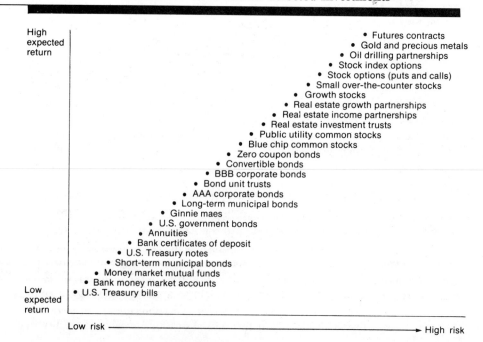

graph is relatively true for large portfolios of these asset types. But there are always exceptions. While an Eastern Airlines bond may be more risky than IBM stock, stocks in general are more risky than corporate bonds in general. As we move into the next section, we will present some basic quantitative methods of measuring risk so that Figure 19–1 can be quantified as well as conceptualized.

Expected Value

To determine the expected value, we multiply each possible outcome by its probability of occurrence. Assume we are considering two investment proposals where K represents a possible outcome and P represents the probability of that outcome based on the state of the economy. The total probability always equals 1.00 or 100 percent. If we were dealing with common stocks, K would represent the price appreciation potential plus the dividend yield (total return). Assume that we are examining two potential investments (investment i and j) and that the potential returns are based on the following data.

Economic possibilities	Probability P	Investment i potential returns K_i	Investment j potential returns K_j
Recession	.20	5%	20%
Slow growth	.30	7	8
Semistrong	.30	13	8
Strong economy	.20	15	6

Given the data for the economy and potential returns, an expected return value $\bar{K}$ can be calculated for each investment. The expected value $\bar{K}$ is equal to the sum (Σ) of K times P. In the case of both investments, the expected return is 10 percent. The calculation is as follows:

$$\bar{K} = \Sigma KP \qquad (19\text{--}1)$$

Economic possibilities	Probability P	K	Investment i potential returns KP	K	Investment j potential returns KP
Recession	.20	5%	1.0%	20%	4.0%
Slow growth	.30	7	2.1	8	2.4
Semistrong	.30	13	3.9	8	2.4
Strong economy	.20	15	3.0	6	1.2
			10.0% = $\bar{K}_i$		10.0% = $\bar{K}_j$

While both investments have the same expected rate of return, they may not necessarily have the same risk characteristics. We use the standard deviation as one measure of risk.

Standard Deviation

The commonly used measure of dispersion (variability) is the standard deviation denoted by the symbol (σ). The standard deviation measures the spread of the outcomes around the expected value and is represented by formula 19–2.

$$\sigma_i = \sqrt{\Sigma(K - \bar{K}_i)^2 P} \qquad (19\text{–}2)$$

Let's determine the standard deviation for investment i around the expected value ($\bar{K}_i$) of 10 percent.

K	$\bar{K}_i$	P	$(K - \bar{K}_i)$	$(K - \bar{K}_i)^2$	$(K - \bar{K}_i)^2 P$
5%	10%	.20	− 5%	25%	5.0%
7	10	.30	− 3	9	2.7
13	10	.30	+ 3	9	2.7
15	10	.20	+ 5	25	5.0
					15.4% $= \Sigma(K - \bar{K}_i)^2 P$

$$\sigma_i = \sqrt{\Sigma(K - \bar{K}_i)^2 P} = \sqrt{15.4\%} = 3.9\% \text{ (rounded)}$$

The standard deviation for investment j is:

$$\sigma_j = \sqrt{\Sigma(K - \bar{K}_i)^2 P}$$

K	$\bar{K}_j$	P	$(K - \bar{K}_j)$	$(K - \bar{K}_j)^2$	$(K_j)^2 P$
20%	10%	.20	+ 10%	100%	20.0%
8	10	.30	− 2	4	1.2
8	10	.30	− 2	4	1.2
6	10	.20	− 4	16	3.2%
					25.6% $= \Sigma(K - \bar{K}_i)^2 P$

$$\sigma_j = \sqrt{\Sigma(K - K_j)^2 P} = \sqrt{25.6\%} = 5.1\% \text{ (rounded)}$$

The standard deviation of investment i is 3.9 percent (rounded), while that of investment j is 5.1 percent (rounded). We assume that investment j is a countercyclical investment. It does well during a recession and poorly in a strong economy. Perhaps it represents a firm in the housing industry that is most profitable when the economy is sluggish and interest rates are low. Under these circumstances, people will avail themselves of low-cost financing to purchase a new home and the firm's stock will do well. In a booming economy, interest rates will advance rapidly, and the financing of housing will become quite expensive. Thus, we have a countercyclical investment.

Even though both investments have an expected value of 10 percent, investment i has less risk because its standard deviation of 3.9 percent is smaller than the standard deviation of 5.1 percent for investment j. The bigger the standard deviation, the greater the risk for two securities that have the same expected returns. The standard deviation measures dispersion of outcomes around the mean of a normal distribution and statistically tells us that 68.26 percent of the outcomes should be within one standard deviation from the expected value. Two standard deviations includes 95.45 percent of the expected outcomes. If we show investment i and j in a normal distribution with a range of expected returns based on the standard deviation, the potential riskiness of both investments can be compared. As shown in the Figure 19–2, approximately 68 percent of the time, investment i will have returns between 13.9 percent and 6.1 percent, while investment j will have returns between 15.1 percent and 4.9 percent. On the basis of two standard deviations (95.45 percent of the time), investment i will have returns between 17.8 percent and 2.2 percent, while investment j will be between 20.2 percent and −0.2 percent. The chance for bigger gains or losses is clearly higher (and therefore more risky) for investment j.

FIGURE 19–2   Investment i and j—Normally Distributed Returns

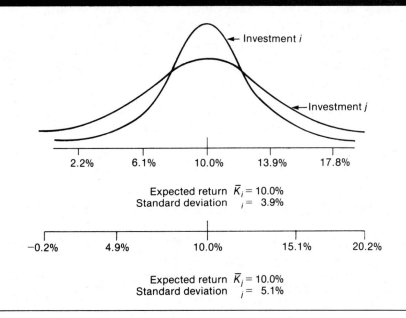

The above example demonstrates one measure of risk—the standard deviation of returns. The second basic measure of risk that we will discuss is called beta. The concept of beta is developed in the capital asset pricing model, which is presented in the next section.

THE CAPITAL ASSET PRICING MODEL

The capital asset pricing model (CAPM) relates the risk-return trade-offs of individual assets to market returns. Common stock returns over time have generally been used to test this model since stock prices are widely available and efficiently priced, as are market indexes of stock performance. In theory the CAPM encompasses all assets, but in practice it is difficult to measure returns on all types of assets or to find an all-encompassing market index. For our purposes, we will use common stock returns to explain the model and occasionally we will generalize to other assets.

The basic form of the CAPM is a linear relationship between returns on individual stocks and the market over time. By using least squares regression analysis, the return on an individual stock, K_j, is expressed in Formula 19–3

$$K_j = \alpha + \beta_j K_m + e \qquad (19\text{--}3)$$

where

K_j = Return on individual common stock of a company
α = Alpha, the intercept on the y-axis
B_j = Beta, the coefficient
K_m = Return on the market (usually an index of stock prices is used)
e = Error term of the regression equation

As indicated in Table 19–1 and Figure 19–3, this equation uses historical data to generate the beta coefficient (β_j), a measurement of the return performance of a given stock versus the return performance of the market. Assume that we want to calculate a beta for Parts Associates, Inc. (PAI), and that we have the performance data for that company and the market shown in Table 19–1. The relationship between PAI and the market appears graphically in Figure 19–3.

TABLE 19–1 Performance of PAI and the Market

	Rate of return on stock	
Year	PAI	Market
1	12.0%	10.0%
2	16.0	18.0
3	20.0	16.0
4	16.0	10.0
5	6.0	8.0
Mean return	14.0%	12.4%
Standard deviation	4.73%	3.87%

The alpha term in Figure 19–3 is 2.8 percent and the beta term is .9. The alpha term is the expected return on PAI stock if returns on the market are zero. However, if the returns on the market are expected to approximate the historical rate of 12.4 percent, the expected return on PAI would be K_j = 2.8 + 0.9(12.4) = 14.4 percent. This maintains the historical relationship. If the returns on the market are expected to rise to 18 percent next year, expected return on PAI would be K_j = 2.8 + 0.9(18.0) = 19 percent.

FIGURE 19–3   Linear Regression of Returns between PAI and the Market*

*Year	K_j	K_m	$\Sigma K_j K_m$	$\Sigma K_j \Sigma K_m$	ΣK_m^2	$(\Sigma K_m)^2$
			936	4,340	844	3,844
1	.12%	10%				
2	.16	18				
3	.20	16				
4	.16	10				
5	6	8				
	70%	62%				

$$\beta_j = \frac{n\Sigma K_j K_m - \Sigma K_j \Sigma K_m}{n\Sigma K_m^2 - (\Sigma K_m)^2} = \frac{5(936) - 4,340}{5(844) - 3,844} = 0.9$$

$$\alpha = \frac{\Sigma K_j - \beta \Sigma K_m}{n} = \frac{70 - 0.9(62)}{5} = 2.8$$

Notice that we are talking in terms of expectations. The CAPM is an expectational (ex ante) model, and there is no guarantee that historical data will reoccur. One area of empirical testing involves the stability and predictability of the beta coefficient based on historical data. Research has indicated that betas are more useful in a portfolio context (for groupings of stocks) because the betas of individual stocks are less stable from period to period than portfolio betas. In addition, there seems to be a tendency for individual betas to approach 1.0 over time.

Systematic and Unsystematic Risk

Previously, we mentioned that there are two major types of risk associated with a stock. One is the market movement or beta (β_j) risk. If the market moves up or down, a stock is assumed to change in value. This type of risk is referred to as *systematic* risk and was first introduced in Chapter 1. The second type of risk is represented by the error term (e_j) and indicates changes in value not associated with market movement. It may represent the temporary influence of a competitor's new product, changes in raw material prices, or unusual economic and government influences on a given firm. These changes are peculiar to an individual security or industry at a given point in time and are not directly correlated with the market. This second type of risk is referred to as *unsystematic* risk.

Recall that one type of risk is assumed to be compensated for under the capital asset pricing model, while another is not. The investor is presumed to receive a risk premium for the beta (or systematic) risk but not for unsystematic risk. Since the latter is associated with an individual company or industry, it may be diversified away in a large portfolio and is not a risk inherent in investing in common stocks. Thus, by picking stocks that are less than perfectly correlated, unsystematic risk may be eliminated. For example, the inherent risks of investing in semiconductor stocks may be diversified away by investing in the countercyclical housing stocks. Researchers have indicated that all but 15 percent of unsystematic risk may be eliminated with a carefully selected portfolio of 10 stocks and all but 11 percent with a portfolio of 20 stocks.[1] We thus can describe total risk as:

$$\text{Total risk} = \text{Systematic risk} + \text{Unsystematic risk}$$

But unsystematic risk can be diversified away, so that systematic risk (β_j) is the only relevant risk under the capital asset pricing model for which the investor can expect to receive compensation.

The Security Market Line

The capital asset pricing model evolved from Formula 19–3 into a risk premium model where the basic assumption is that in order for investors to take more risk they must be compensated by larger expected returns. Investors should also not accept returns that are less than they can get from a riskless asset. For CAPM purposes it is assumed that short-term U.S. Treasury bills may be considered a riskless asset.[2] When viewed in this context, an investor must achieve an extra return above that obtainable from a Treasury bill in order to induce the assumption of more risk. This brings us to the more common and theoretically useful model:

$$K_j = R_f + \beta_j(K_m - R_f) \tag{19–4}$$

where

$$R_f = \text{Risk-free rate of return}$$
$$\beta_j = \text{Beta coefficient from Formula 19–3}$$
$$K_m = \text{Return on the market index}$$

---

[1] Wagner and Lau, "The Effect of Diversification on Risk." *Financial Analysts Journal,* November–December 1971.

[2] A number of studies have also indicated that longer term government securities may appropriately represent R_f, or the risk-free rate.

$K_m - R_f =$ Premium or excess return of the market versus the risk-free rate (since the market is riskier than R_f, the assumption is that the expected K_m will be greater than R_f)

$\beta_j(K_m = R_f) =$ Expected return above the risk-free rate for the stock of company j, given the level of risk.

The model centers on "beta," the coefficient of the premium demanded by an investor to invest in an individual stock. For each individual security, beta measures the sensitivity (volatility) of the security's return to the market. By definition, the market has a beta of 1.0, so that if an individual company's beta is 1.0, it can expect to have returns as volatile as the market and total returns equal to the market. A company with a beta of 2.0 would be twice as volatile as the market and would be expected to generate more returns, whereas a company with a beta of 0.5 would be half as volatile as the market.

Since the beta factor is deemed to be important in analyzing potential risk and return, there is much emphasis placed on knowing the beta for a given security. Merrill Lynch, Value Line and various brokerage houses and investment services publish information on beta for a large number of securities. A representative list is presented in the table below.

Corporation	Beta (August 1984)
Georgia-Pacific	1.40
Digital Equipment	1.25
Ford Motor	1.05
Eli Lilly	.90
Colgate-Palmolive	.80
Cincinnati Gas and Electric	.60

In order to practically apply the model to determine expected returns, the investor must have some estimate of the market risk premium ($K_m - R_f$). While R_f, the one-year Treasury bill yield, is easily obtainable from *The Wall Street Journal* or other daily financial publications, estimating the expected market return, K_m, is not so easy. More often than not analysts will estimate the expected risk premium rather than K_m. A long-term study of security returns is updated each year by Ibbotson and Sinquefield and published by the Financial Analysts' Federation in Charlottesville, Virginia. This study provides useful insights into long-term risk premiums and the annual returns on stocks, bonds, and Treasury bills.

The Ibbotson-Sinquefield data ending the year 1985 shows that from 1926 through 1985 common stocks provided an annualized return of 9.84 percent while Treasury bills returned 3.41 percent annually over that same time period. If we substitute these values into the risk premium equation ($K_m - R_f$), we get a premium of 6.43 percent over the last 60 years. Using more current data from 1945–85, common stocks returned 11.46 percent while Treasury bills returned 4.6 percent for a 30-year risk premium of 6.87 percent. This data is shown in Table 19–2. The risk premium for the last 20 years is quite low because of low annual stock returns and high Treasury bill yields. Both were the victim of high rates of inflation. This is a good time to

TABLE 19–2   Annual Returns—Common Stock and Treasury Bills

Ibbotson-Sinquefield data	Common stock returns K_m	One-year T bills R_f	Risk premium $(K_m - R_f)$
1926–85	9.84%	3.41%	6.43%
1945–85	11.46	4.59	6.87
1965–85	8.23	6.95	1.28

remember that the capital asset pricing model is expectational and that we should not be blind slaves to past data. While history is important in setting expectations, we should not be so myopic that we use only the recent past to set our expectations. The risk premium calculated on an annual basis is extremely volatile having a standard deviation of almost 20 percent. The market does not always provide positive returns on an annual basis and as far as risk premiums are concerned, the long-term experience is a better measure of what our expectations should be. For example, the recent past performance of the stock market between 1982 and 1985 has increased the reported long-term risk premiums as stock returns rose and Treasury bill yields fell. The risk premium over longer periods is more stable; many analysts expect the average premium should be between 5.5 percent and 6.5 percent. For illustrative purposes, we will use an expected risk premium of 6.0 percent in the return equation.

For example, assuming that the risk-free rate is 7.0 percent and that the risk premium is 6 percent, the following returns would occur with stocks having betas of 0.5, 1.0, and 2.0.

$$K_j = R_f \quad + B_j (K_m - R_f)$$
$$K_5 = 7.0\% + \quad .5 (6.0\%) \quad = 10.0\%$$
$$K_{1.0} = 7.0\% + 1.0 (6.0\%) \quad = 13.0\%$$
$$K_{2.0} = 7.0\% + 2.0 (6.0\%) \quad = 19.0\%$$

Basically beta measures the riskiness of an investment relative to the market. In order to outperform the market, we would have to assume more risk by selecting assets with betas greater than 1.0. Another way of looking at the risk-return trade-off would be that if less risk than the market is desired, an investor should choose assets with a beta of less than 1.0. Beta is a good measure of a stock's risk when the stock is added to a diversified portfolio.

In Figure 19–3, individual stock returns were compared to market returns and the beta from Formula 19–3 was shown. From Formula 19–4, the risk premium model, a generalized risk-return graph called the security market line (SML) can be constructed that identifies the risk-return trade-off of any common stock (asset) relative to the company's beta. This is shown in Figure 19–4.

FIGURE 19–4   The Security Market Line (SML)

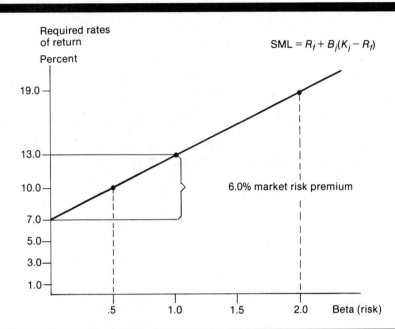

The required return for all securities can be expressed as the risk-free rate plus a premium for risk. Thus, we see that a stock with a beta of 1.0 would have a risk premium of 6.0 percent added to the risk-free rate of 7.0 percent to provide a required return of 13 percent. Since a beta of 1.0 implies risk equal to the market, the return is also at the overall market rate. If the beta is 2.0, twice the market risk premium of 6.0 percent must be earned, and we add 12 percent to the risk-free rate of 7.0 percent to determine the required return of 19 percent. For a beta of 0.5, the required return is 10.0 percent.

Assumptions of the Capital Asset Pricing Model

Having evaluated some of the implications of the CAPM, it is important to be aware of some of the assumptions that go into the model.

1. All investors can borrow or lend an unlimited amount of funds at a given risk-free rate.
2. All investors have the same one-period time horizon.
3. All investors wish to maximize their expected utility over this time horizon and evaluate investments on the basis of means and standard deviations of portfolio returns.
4. All investors have the same expectations—that is, all investors estimate identical probability distributions for rates of return.

5. All assets are perfectly divisible—it is possible to buy fractional shares of any asset or portfolio.

6. There are no taxes or transactions costs.

7. The market is efficient and in equilibrium or quickly adjusting to equilibrium.

The purpose of listing these assumptions is to indicate some of the necessary conditions to create the CAPM. While at first they may appear to be severely limiting, they are similar to those often used in the standard economic theory of the firm and in other basic financial models.

The primary usefulness in examining this model or similar risk-return trade-off models is to provide some reasonable basis for relating return opportunity with risk on the investment. Portfolio managers find risk-return models helpful in explaining their performance or the performance of their competitors to clients. A competitor's portfolio that has unusually high returns may have been developed primarily on the basis of high-risk assets. To the extent that this can be explained on the basis of capital market theory, the competitors' performance may look less like superior money management and more like a product of high risk taking. Many of the techniques for assessing portfolio performance on Wall Street are explicitly or implicitly related to the risk-return concepts discussed in this chapter.

Though empirical tests have somewhat supported the capital asset pricing model, a number of testing problems remain. In order to develop the SML in which stock returns (vertical axis) can be measured against beta (horizontal axis), an appropriate line must be drawn. Researchers have some disagreement about R_F. (Is it represented by short-term or long-term Treasury rates?) There is also debate about what is the appropriate K_M, or market rate of return. Some suggest the market proxy variable will greatly influence beta and that difficulties in dealing with this problem can bring the whole process under attack.[3]

When empirical data is compared to theoretical return expectations, there is some discrepancy in that the theoretical SML may have a slightly greater slope than the actual line fitted on the basis on real-world data as shown in Figure 19–5.[4]

There may also be a possible problem in that betas for individual securities are not necessarily stable over time (rather than remaining relatively constant at 1.3 or perhaps .7, they tend to approach 1 over time). Thus, a beta based on past risk may not always reflect current risk.[5] Because the beta

[3] Richard Roll. "A Critique of the Asset Pricing Theory's Test." *Journal of Financial Economics,* March 1977, pp. 129–76. Also, "Ambiguity When Performance is Measured by the Securities Market Line," *Journal of Finance,* September 1978, pp. 1051–69.

[4] Franco Modigliani and Gerald A. Pogue. "An Introduction to Risk and Returns." *Financial Analysts Journal,* March–April 1974, pp. 68–86, and May–June 1974, pp. 69–86.

[5] Robert A. Levy, "On the Short-Term Stationary of Beta Coefficients." *Financial Analysts Journal,* November–December 1971, pp. 55–62. Also Marshall E. Blume, "Beta and Their Regression Tendencies," *Journal of Finance,* June 1975, pp. 785–95.

FIGURE 19–5   Test of the Security Market Line

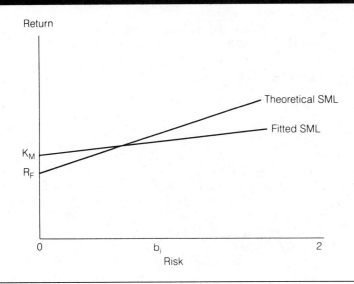

for a portfolio may be more stable than an individual stock's beta, portfolio betas are also used as a systematic risk variable.

By examining portfolio betas rather than individual stock betas, we overcome part of the criticism leveled at the instability of betas in the capital asset pricing model. Many of the other criticisms have also evoked new research that may provide different approaches or possible solutions to past deficiencies in the model. In any event, the capital asset pricing model is likely to remain relatively important in the future.

The major advantage of beta as a measure of risk is that the mathematical calculation to calculate the risk of a portfolio is much simpler than using the standard deviation as a portfolio risk measure. A portfolio beta is simply the weighted average of the betas of the individual stocks that make up the portfolio. The expected portfolio return is also a weighted average of the expected return for each stock. These relationships are expressed in formulas 19–5 and 19–6:

$$B_p \text{ (portfolio beta)} = XB_j \qquad (19\text{--}5)$$
$$K_p = R_f + B_p (K_m - R_f) \qquad (19\text{--}6)$$

where the subscript p represents the portfolio, X is the percentage of the portfolio invested in each stock, and j represents each individual stock in the portfolio. Perhaps a more practical way of presenting these concepts is to look at an actual portfolio of individual stocks. The first panel of Table 19–3 shows a five-stock portfolio where the expected return is 12.55 percent and the beta of the portfolio is 1.32. The second panel assumes that the same

TABLE 19–3   Portfolio Returns and Betas

				Beginning Portfolio				
Stock	Shares	Stock price	Amount	Percent of portfolio X	Expected return K	Weighted return XK_j	Beta B_j	XB_j
OWU	100	$20	$2,000	10%	10%	1.0%	1.00	.10
ISU	100	30	3,000	15	12	1.8	1.20	.15
UOI	100	40	4,000	20	14	2.8	1.50	.30
DPU	100	50	5,000	25	15	3.75	2.00	.50
TCU	100	60	6,000	30	9	2.7	.80	.24

Total portfolio value = $20,000 K_p = 12.05% B_p = 1.32

				Restructured Portfolio				
Stock	Shares	Stock price	Amount	Percent of portfolio X	Expected return K	Weighted return XK_j	Beta B_j	XB_j
OWU	250	$20	$5,000	25.0%	10%	2.5 %	1.00	.25
ISU	150	30	4,500	22.5	12	2.7	1.20	.27
UOI	50	40	2,000	10.0	14	1.4	1.50	.15
DPU	50	50	2,500	12.5	15	1.875	2.00	.25
TCU	100	60	6,000	30.0	9	2.7	.80	.24

Total portfolio value = $20,000 K_p = 11.175% B_p = 1.16

stocks are held in the portfolio but the percentage weights are changed to reduce the beta (risk) of the portfolio. As expected, the return also declines as risk decreases.

MEASUREMENT OF RETURN IN RELATION TO RISK

In examining the performance of fund managers, the return measure commonly used is "excess returns." Though the term excess returns has many definitions, the one most commonly used is: total return on a portfolio (capital appreciation plus dividends) minus the risk-free rate.

Excess returns = Total portfolio return − Risk-free rate

Thus excess returns represent returns over and above what could be earned on a riskless asset. The rate of U.S. government Treasury bills is often used to represent the risk-free rate of return in the economy (though other definitions are possible). Thus a fund that earns 12 percent when the Treasury bill rate is 6 percent has excess returns of 6 percent.

Once computed, excess returns are then compared to risk. We look at three different approaches to comparing excess returns to risk: the Sharpe approach, the Treynor approach, and the Jensen approach.

Sharpe Approach

In the Sharpe approach,[6] the excess returns on a portfolio are compared to the portfolio standard deviation.

$$\text{Sharpe measure} = \frac{\text{Total portfolio return} - \text{Risk-free rate}}{\text{Portfolio standard deviation}} \quad (19\text{--}7)$$

The portfolio manager is thus able to view his or her excess returns per unit of risk. If a portfolio has a total return of 10 percent, the risk-free rate is 6 percent, and the portfolio standard deviation is 18 percent, the Sharpe measure is .22.

$$\text{Sharpe measure} = \frac{10\% - 6\%}{18\%} = \frac{4\%}{18\%} = .22$$

This measure can be compared to other portfolios or to the market in general to assess performance. If the market return per unit of risk is greater than .22, then the portfolio manager has turned in an inferior performance. Assume there is a 9 percent total market return, a 6 percent risk-free rate, and a market standard deviation of 12 percent. Then the Sharpe measure for the overall market is:

$$\frac{9\% - 6\%}{12\%} = \frac{3\%}{12\%} = .25$$

The portfolio measure of .22 is less than the market measure of .25 and represents an inferior performance. Of course, a portfolio measure above .25 would have represented a superior performance.

Treynor Approach

The formula for the second approach for comparing excess returns to risk (developed by Treynor[7]) is:

$$\text{Treynor measure} = \frac{\text{Total portfolio return} - \text{Risk-free rate}}{\text{Portfolio beta}} \quad (19\text{--}8)$$

The only difference between the Sharpe and Treynor approach is in the denominator. While Sharpe uses the portfolio standard deviation—Formula (19–7), Treynor uses the portfolio beta—Formula (19–8). Thus, Sharpe uses total risk, while Treynor uses only the systematic, or beta, risk. Implicit in the Treynor approach is the assumption that portfolio managers have diversified away unsystematic risk and only systematic risk remains.

---

[6] William F. Sharpe, "Mutual Fund Performance," *Journal of Business,* January 1966, pp. 119–38.

[7] Jack L. Treynor, "How to Rate Management of Investment Funds," *Harvard Business Review,* January–February 1965, pp. 63–74.

If a portfolio has a total return of 10 percent, the risk-free rate is 6 percent, and the portfolio beta is .9, the Treynor measure would be:

$$\frac{10\% - 6\%}{.9} = \frac{4\%}{.9} = \frac{.04}{.9} = .044$$

This measure can be compared to other portfolios or to the market in general to determine whether there is a superior performance in terms of return per unit of risk. Assume that the total market return is 9 percent, the risk-free rate is 6 percent, and the market beta (by definition) is 1; then the Treynor measure as applied to the market is .03.

$$\frac{9\% - 6\%}{1.0} = \frac{3\%}{1.0} = \frac{.03}{1.0} = .03$$

This would imply that the portfolio has turned in a superior return to the market (.044 versus .03). Not only is the portfolio return higher than the market return (10 percent versus 9 percent), but the beta is less (.9 versus 1.0). Clearly, there is more return per unit of risk.

In the Sharpe and Treynor measures, we find that as long as the portfolios are well diversified, they usually provide the same rankings. The correlation coefficient R_{pm} is introduced in Table 19–4. It (R_{pm}) indicates how closely the market and the portfolio move together in generating returns. If a portfolio has a correlation coefficient of 1.00, the market and the portfolio have a perfect relationship with each other. In practice, as a portfolio becomes larger and more diversified, the correlation coefficient will usually be above .75 and move closer to 1.00. Table 19–4 demonstrates this point. Using both the Sharpe and Treynor measures, portfolios 4, 5, 6, 7, and 8 all outperform the market.

TABLE 19–4   Portfolio Risk-Return Comparisons Using Sharpe and Treynor Risk Measures (Risk-free rate R_f = 7.0%)

Portfolio Number	Returns K_p	Standard Deviation σ_p	Beta B_p	Sharpe $\frac{(K_p - R_f)}{\sigma_p}$	Treynor $\frac{(K_p - R_f)}{B_p}$	Correlation coefficient R_{pm}
1	10%	11.8%	.68	.2542 (7)	.0441 (7)	.7492
2	10%	12.1%	.78	.2479 (8)	.0385 (8)	.8380
Market	12%	13.0%	1.00	.3846 (6)	.0500 (6)	1.0000
4	13%	14.2%	1.00	.4225 (3)	.0600 (2)	.9155
5	13%	15.0%	1.15	.4000 (5)	.0522 (5)	.9967
6	14%	15.0%	1.10	.4667 (1)	.0636 (1)	.9533
7	14%	17.2%	1.30	.4070 (4)	.0538 (4)	.9826
8	15%	18.9%	1.40	.4233 (2)	.0571 (3)	.9630

Note: Numbers in parentheses indicate the ranking of the portfolio on a risk-return basis.
    Sharpe measures total risk versus excess returns, while Treynor assumes a diversified portfolio and measures systematic risk versus excess returns

Jensen Approach

In the third approach, Jensen also emphasizes using certain aspects of the capital asset pricing model to evaluate portfolio managers.[8] He compares their actual excess returns (total portfolio return—risk-free rate) to what should be required in the market, based on their portfolio beta.

The required rate of excess returns in the market for a given beta is shown in Figure 19–6 as the market line. If the beta is 0, the investor should

FIGURE 19–6   Risk-Adjusted Portfolio Returns

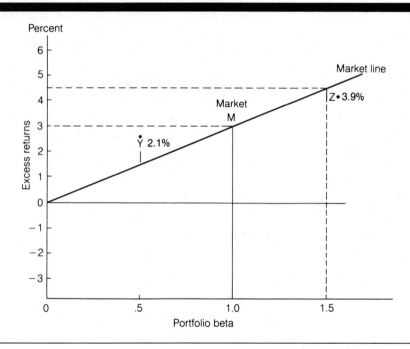

expect to earn no more than the risk-free rate of return since there is no systematic risk. If the portfolio manager earns only the risk-free rate of return, the excess returns will be 0. Thus with a beta of 0, the expected excess returns on the market line is 0. With a portfolio beta of 1, the portfolio has a systematic risk equal to the market, and the expected portfolio excess returns should be equal to market excess returns. If the market return (K_M) is 9 percent and the risk-free rate (R_F) is 6 percent, the market excess returns are 3 percent. A portfolio with a beta of 1 should expect to earn the market rate of excess returns ($K_M - R_F$), equal to 3 percent. Other excess returns

[8] Michael C. Jensen, "The Performance of Mutual funds in the Period 1945–1964," *Journal of Finance,* May 1968, pp. 389–416.

expectations are shown for beta ranging from 0 to 1.5. For example, a portfolio with a beta of 1.5 should provide excess returns of 4.5.

Adequacy of Performance

Using the Jensen approach, the adequacy of a portfolio manager's performance can be judged against the market line. Did he fall above or below the line? While it would appear that portfolio manager Y in Figure 19–6 had inferior excess returns in comparison to portfolio manager Z (2.1 percent versus 3.9 percent), this notion is quickly dispelled when one considers risk. Actually, portfolio manager Y performed above risk-return expectations as indicated by the market line, while portfolio manager Z was below his risk-adjusted expected level. The vertical difference from a fund's performance point to the market line can be viewed as a measure of performance. This value, termed *alpha* or *average differential return,* indicates the difference between the return on the fund and a point on the market line that corresponds to a beta equal to the fund. In the case of fund Z, the beta of 1.5 indicated an excess return of 4.5 percent along the market line, and the actual excess return was only 3.9 percent. We thus have a negative alpha of .6 percent (3.9% − 4.5%). Clearly, a positive alpha indicates a superior performance, while a negative alpha leads to the opposite conclusion.

FIGURE 19–7   Empirical Study of Risk-Adjusted Portfolio Returns—Systematic Risk and Return

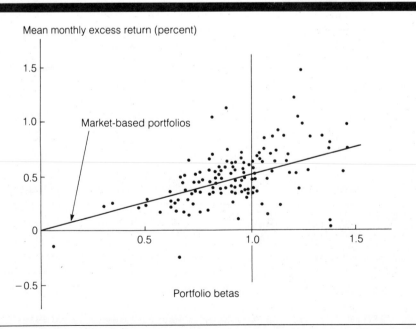

A key question for portfolio managers in general is, can they consistently perform at positive alpha levels? Can they generate returns better than those that are available along the market line, which are theoretically available to anyone? The results of a study conducted by John McDonald on 123 mutual funds are presented in Figure 19–7.

The upward-sloping line is the market line, or anticipated level of performance based on risk. The small dots represent performance of the funds. About as many funds underperformed (negative alpha below the line) as overperformed (positive alpha above the line). Although a few high-beta funds had an unusually strong performance on a risk-adjusted basis, there is no consistent pattern of superior performance.

DIVERSIFICATION

An important service that a money manager can provide is effective diversification of asset holdings. Once we accept the fact that superior performance on a risk-adjusted basis is a difficult achievement, we begin to look hard at other attributes that money managers may possess. We can ask, Are mutual fund managers effective diversifiers of their holdings?

As previously discussed, there are two measures of risk: systematic and unsystematic. Systematic risk is measured by the portfolio (or individual stock's) beta. Under the capital asset pricing model, higher betas are rewarded with relatively high returns, and vice versa. As the market goes up 10 percent, our portfolio might go up 12 percent (beta of 1.2), and a similar phenomenon may occur on the downside. Unsystematic risk is random or nonmarket related and may be generally diversified away by the astute portfolio manager. Under the capital asset pricing model, there is no market reward for unsystematic risk since it can be eliminated through diversification.

The question for a portfolio manager then becomes, How effective have you been at diversifying away the nonrewarded, unsystematic risk? Put another way, to what extent can a fund's movements be described as market-related rather than random in nature? If we plot a fund's excess returns over an extended period of time against market excess returns, we can determine the joint movement between the two as indicated in Figure 19–8. In Panel (a) we plot our basic points. In Panel (b) we draw a regression line through these points. Of importance to the present discussion is the extent to which our line fits the data. If the points of observation fall very close to the line, the independent variable, excess market returns, is largely responsible for describing the dependent variable, excess returns for fund X.

The degree of association between the independent and dependent variables is measured by R^2 (coefficient of determination).[9] R^2 may take on a

---

[9] R^2 also represents the correlation coefficient squared. Another statement is

$$R^2 = 1 - \frac{\Sigma(y - y_c)^2/n}{\Sigma(y - \bar{y})^2/n}$$

where y_c represents points along the regression line and y is the average value of the independent variable.

FIGURE 19–8   Relationship of Fund's Excess Returns to Market Excess Returns

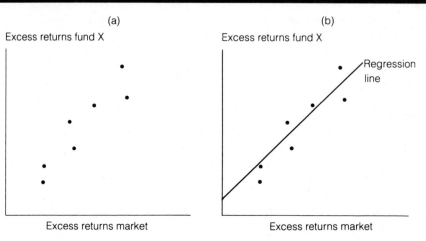

value anywhere between 0 and 1. A high degree of correlation between the independent and dependent variables will produce an R^2 of .7 or better. In Panel (b) it is assumed to be .90.

In Figure 19–9 the points do not fall consistently close to the regression line, and the R^2 value is assumed to be only .55. In this instance, we say that the independent variable (excess market returns) was not the only major variable in explaining changes in the dependent variable (excess returns for fund Y).

The points in Figure 19–9 imply that the portfolio manager for fund Y may have not been particularly effective in his diversification efforts. Many other factors besides market returns appear to be affecting the portfolio returns of fund Y, and these could have been diversified away rather than allowed to influence returns. In this instance, we say there is a high degree of unsystematic, or nonmarket-related, risk. Since unsystematic risk is presumed to go unrewarded in the marketplace under the capital asset pricing model, there is evidence of inefficient portfolio diversification.

What does empirical data tell us about the effectiveness of portfolio managers in achieving diversification. How have they stacked up in terms of R^2 values for their portfolios? As indicated in Figure 19–10, their record is generally quite good.

The Merrill Lynch study of 100 mutual funds between 1970 and 1974 shows an average R^2 value of approximately .90 with very few funds falling below .70. The actual range is between .66 and .98. Studies by McDonald, Jensen, Gentry, and Williamson have led to similar conclusions.

Although many mutual funds invest in 80 to 100 securities to achieve effective diversification, this is often more than is necessary. A high degree of

FIGURE 19–9   Example of Lower Correlation

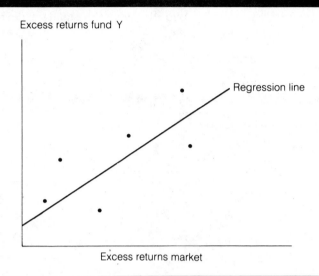

FIGURE 19–10   Quarterly Returns Attributable to Market Fluctuations: 100 Mutual Funds, 1970–1974

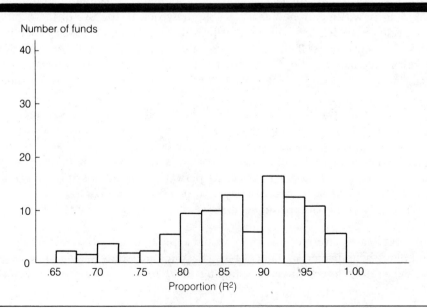

Source: Merrill Lynch, Pierce, Fenner & Smith, *Investment Performance Analysis, Comparative Survey, 1970–1974.*

diversification can be achieved with between 10 and 20 efficiently selected stocks, as is indicated in Table 19–5. The Wagner and Lau study shows the number of securities in the portfolio, the portfolio standard deviation, and correlation with return on the market index (R^2).

TABLE 19–5   Reduction in Portfolio Risk through Diversification

Number of securities in portfolio	Standard deviation of portfolio returns, σ_p (percent per month)	Correlation with return on market index*
1	7.0	0.54
2	5.0	0.63
3	4.8	0.75
4	4.6	0.77
5	4.6	0.79
10	4.2	0.85
15	4.0	0.88
20	3.9	0.89

* The market here refers to an unweighted index of all NYSE stocks.
Source: W. H. Wagner and C. S. Lau, "The Effect of Diversification on Risk," *Financial Analysts Journal,* November–December 1971, p. 53.

STABILITY OF BETAS

Earlier in the chapter, the lack of stability of the beta coefficient of an individual security was mentioned as a possible drawback to the use of the capital asset pricing model. Instability means prior beta values may not be reflective of future beta values. If this is the case, then, use of a beta based on prior performance may not be entirely accurate in reflecting future return potential. Since the beta coefficient is such an integral part of the analysis, we must address this issue.

We break down our discussion on beta stability as it relates to individual stocks, industry groupings, and portfolios. In regard to individual stocks, a study by Blume provided evidence that the betas of individual stocks tend to regress or approach 1 over time.[10] That is, a stock with a beta of 1.5 may tend to have a beta of 1.4 in the next period, 1.3 in a subsequent period, and so on. Stocks with betas below 1 also tend to approach 1 over time. While this is not an automatic occurrence, there is a tendency to follow this pattern.

The same pattern of instability would apply to betas for various industry groupings, as indicated in Table 19–6. The Valentine study shows the changing betas for different industry groupings over time. The pattern of typical

---

[10] Marshall E. Blume, "Betas and Their Regression Tendencies," *Journal of Finance,* June 1975, pp. 785–95.

TABLE 19–6   Industry Beta Values 1951–1970

	1951–55	1956–60	1961–65	1966–70
Aerospace	.96247	.66585	.72409	1.31815
Agricultural machinery	.78687	.90875	.81422	1.14613
Aluminum	1.18617	1.60756	1.13980	1.21376
Apparel manufacturing	.50733	.47428	1.23344	1.52437
Auto parts and accessories	.87577	1.03116	.84302	1.17786
Autos	1.21383	1.00899	.87593	1.00869
Auto tires and rubber goods	1.18350	1.20016	1.16497	.97226
Auto trucks and parts	.96299	1.24551	1.21358	1.24255
Biscuit bakers	.34377	.18935	.76037	.68711
Bituminous coal	1.02612	1.14341	1.11203	.80200
Bread and cake bakers	.35396	.35301	.93734	1.91074
Brewers	.18364	.56817	.74847	1.03782
Business and office equipment	1.12362	1.12134	1.44912	1.09700
—Canned foods	.65238	.55939	1.04155	1.01861
Cement	1.01518	.87642	.82306	1.53511
Chemicals	1.06482	1.04785	.94006	.85256
Cigarettes	.29077	.23970	1.29410	.55432
Confectionery	.35793	.35514	1.04756	.59934
Construction and material handling machinery	1.14771	1.18300	.91518	1.19976
Copper	1.17911	.97515	.94643	1.08206
Corn refiners	.32177	.44286	1.02606	.93099
Crude oil producers	.69844	1.03158	1.12971	.95093
Dairy products	.40212	.35200	.98700	1.04501
—Department stores	.60589	.53718	.66176	1.21765
Distillers	.74801	.79331	.86246	.90287
Drugs	.54110	1.05861	1.29238	.95521
Electrical equipment	.96542	1.25540	1.04542	1.19990
Electrical household appliances	.76593	1.01648	.91009	1.15041
Electronics	.90328	1.31251	1.55722	1.56784
Food Chain Stores	.38349	.51301	1.00418	.73317
Gold Mining	.54291	.63910	.06125	.07090
Heating and Plumbing	.64976	.86583	.95464	1.27624
Home Furnishings	.45473	.76023	1.18308	1.60301
Industrial Machinery	.81678	1.18670	1.03285	1.33398
Integrated domestic oil companies	.79546	1.09107	.82772	.96288
Integrated international oil comapnies	1.05360	.98599	.70443	.73875
Lead and zinc	.91563	.99167	1.07584	.72259

Source: Jerome L. Valentine, "Investment Analysis and Capital Market Theory," *Occasional Paper No. 1* (Charlottesville, Va.: The Financial Research Foundation, 1975), p. 34.

change can be found in such industries as canned goods and department stores.

While betas of individual stocks and industries may not be particularly stable over time, there is some evidence that portfolio betas are stable. This stability can be achieved with reasonably sized diversified portfolios of 10 to 20 stocks. We look to the research of Marshall Blume.

As indicated in Table 19–7, he measured the correlation between portfolio betas during different time periods. In each case, he compared one period to the next and determined the extent of correlation for different size portfolios. A high degree of correlation would indicate a stable beta because the past would be correlated with the future. For example, the last column shows the correlation of betas between the seven-year time periods of July 1954 to June 1961 and July 1961 to June 1968. With only one security, there was a correlation coefficient of .60; with 10 securities, .92; with 20 securities, .97; and finally with 50 securities, .98. The presumption is that reasonably large portfolios have stable betas over time, and this may be useful in assessing future risk considerations.

TABLE 19–7   Correlation Coefficients of Betas for Portfolios of *N* Securities

Number of securities per portfolio	7/26–6/33 and 7/33–6/40	7/33–6/40 and 7/40–6/47	7/40–6/47 and 7/47–6/54	7/47–6/54 and 7/54–6/61	7/54–6/61 and 7/61–6/68
1	0.63	0.62	0.59	0.65	0.60
2	0.71	0.76	0.72	0.76	0.73
4	0.80	0.85	0.81	0.84	0.84
7	0.86	0.91	0.88	0.87	0.88
10	0.89	0.94	0.90	0.92	0.92
20	0.93	0.97	0.95	0.95	0.97
35	0.96	0.98	0.95	0.97	0.97
50	0.98	0.99	0.98	0.98	0.98

Source: Abstracted from Marshall Blume, "On the Assessment of Risk," *Journal of Finance,* March 1971, p. 7.

THE MAKEUP OF INSTITUTIONAL INVESTORS

Having discussed measurement and portfolio management techniques for institutional investors, we will now take a more specific look at the participants. Institutional investors (as opposed to individual investors) represent organizations that are responsible for bringing together large pools of capital for purposes of reinvestment. Our coverage will center on investment companies (including mutual funds), pension funds, life insurance companies, bank trust departments, and endowments and foundations.

Investment Companies (Including Mutual Funds)

Investment companies take the proceeds of individual investors and reinvest them in other securities according to their specific objectives. Income and capital gains are generally distributed to stockholders and are subject to single taxation under Subchapter M of the Internal Revenue Code. Investments are discussed at some length in Chapter 20.

Other Institutional Investors

Other institutional investors (along with investment companies) and their extent of market participation are presented in Table 19–8. Total institutional holdings are approximately $2.5 trillion. We will briefly comment on pension funds, insurance companies, bank trust departments, and foundations and endowments.

TABLE 19–8   Percentage of Institutional Market Held by Institutional Investors

	Percent
1. Private noninsured pension funds	26.2
2. Open-end investment companies	15.5
3. Other investment companies	2.0
4. Life insurance companies	6.1
5. Property-liability insurance companies	4.9
6. Personal trust funds	27.8
7. Common trust funds	1.7
8. Mutual savings banks	1.1
9. State and local retirement funds	4.6
10. Foundations	7.4
11. Educational endowments	2.7
	100.0%

Source: Compiled from a review of annual reports from the Securities and Exchange Commission and the New York Stock Exchange.

Pension funds.   Pension funds represent an important and growing sector of the institutional market. Pension funds may be private or public in nature. Private funds represent well over 50 percent of the total. The benefits that accrue under private pension funds may be insured or uninsured, with the latter arrangement occurring most frequently. Public pension funds are run for the benefit of federal, state, or local employees.

Insurance companies.   Insurance companies may be categorized as either "life" or "property and casualty." Life insurance companies must earn a minimum rate of return assumed in calculating premiums, and public policy places great emphasis on safety of assets. Approximately 70 percent of life insurance company assets are in privately placed debt or mortgages, with the balance in bonds and stocks. Property and casualty insurance companies enjoy more lenient regulation of their activities and generally have a larger percentage of their assets in bonds and stocks.

Bank trust departments.   The emphasis in bank trust departments is on managing other people's funds for a fee. Banks may administer individual trusts or commingled (combined) funds in a common trust fund. Often a bank will establish more than one common trust fund to serve varying needs and objectives. The overall performance of bank trust departments has been mixed, with the usual number of leaders and laggards. Bank trust management is highly concentrated with a relatively small number of trust departments holding the majority of funds. Out of approximately 4,000 bank trust departments, the top 10 hold one third of all assets, and the largest 60 hold two thirds.

Foundations and endowments.   Foundations represent nonprofit organizations set up to accomplish social, educational, or charitable purposes. They are often established through the donation of a large block of stock in which the donor was one of the corporate founders. Examples include the Ford, Carnegie, and Rockefeller Foundations. Endowments, on the other hand, represent permanent capital funds that are donated to universities, churches, or civic organizations. The management of endowment funds is often quite difficult because of the pressure for current income to maintain operations (perhaps the university library) and simultaneous demands for capital appreciation. Measurement of performance for foundations and endowments has gone much more to a total-return basis (dividends plus capital appreciation) rather than the traditional interest-earned or dividend-received basis.

Chapter 20

Mutual Funds

INVESTMENT COMPANIES
Face-Amount Certificate Companies
Unit Investment Trusts (UITs)
Management Companies (Mutual Funds)

CLOSED- VERSUS OPEN-END FUNDS

INVESTING IN MUTUAL FUNDS
Load Funds
No-Load Funds
Buying and Selling

DIFFERING OBJECTIVES AND THE DIVERSITY OF MUTUAL FUNDS
Money Market Funds
Growth Funds
Growth with Income
Balanced Funds
Bond Funds
Sector Funds
Foreign Funds
Specialty Funds

SELECTION OF MUTUAL FUNDS
Measuring Risk Return Trade-offs
Matching Investment Objectives with Fund Types

THE PROSPECTUS
Investment Objectives and Policies
Portfolio
Management Fees and Expenses
Turnover Rate
Distributions and Taxation
Shareholder Services

INVESTMENT STRATEGIES USING MUTUAL FUNDS
Outguessing the Market
Building a Nest Egg
Retirement Plans
Living off Assets

Every investor is faced with two sets of problems:

> selecting investments that will meet specified objectives for income, appreciation, or tax benefits, and
> minimizing risks for a desired rate of return.

These problems were addressed in previous chapters. We learned that both equity and fixed-income securities can be valued by studying the overall economic environment and by conducting industry and company analysis. The preceding chapter illustrated how to eliminate a major source of risk through diversification. It also discussed how to combine investments in portfolios designed to meet investment objectives at acceptable levels of risk. All that is needed to effectively implement an investment program, then, is a thorough understanding of all previous chapters of this book and a pot of money large enough to achieve effective diversification. Thousands of professional money managers and wealthy investors are blessed with knowledge and capital—most individual investors lack one or both.

Both small investors and those who lack expertise encounter a number of practical problems. The investor with a small amount of capital ends up paying a larger proportion of his funds in commissions. As in other industries where the volume purchaser gets a better deal than the retail customer, the trader of small lots of stocks or bonds ends up paying more.

Diversification is also difficult to achieve. The normal trading unit for listed stocks—the "round lot"—is 100 shares. If proper diversification required a portfolio of at least 10 different stocks, the investor could purchase 100 shares of each of them. If each stock had a market value of $30, cost would be (excluding commission) $30,000 ($30 × $100 × 10). That's a big bite for most individuals just to get started.

Investors who have enough capital but are short on knowledge have their own handicaps. For example, physicians often set up pension plans for themselves and their employees. Although they have a large pool of investable funds, they may lack both knowledge of investment fundamentals and the time needed to manage such plans effectively.

Both of these types of investors—those who lack large amounts of capital and those who lack knowledge or time—have sought solutions to their problems in the "packaged" financial products offered by investment companies.

INVESTMENT COMPANIES

An investment company can be either a corporation or a trust through which investors pool their funds to achieve the benefits of diversification and professional management. Investment companies take the following forms.

Face-Amount Certificate Companies

These entities issue a certificate with a specific maturity date. Certificates may be purchased with a lump-sum payment or a series of payments. The face amount of the certificate is paid to the owner at a specific date, with interest paid periodically. The interest and face amount are guaranteed, and the guarantee is usually backed by a security interest in real property or other assets. Face-amount certificates are not common today.

Unit Investment Trusts (UITs)

UITs are investment companies organized for the purpose of purchasing a pool of securities—usually tax-exempt municipal bonds. UITs issue redeemable units to investors, representing a proportionate interest in the assets of the trust. Investors also receive a proportionate share in the interest or dividends received by the trust.

Unit trusts are passive investments. They normally purchase assets and hold them for the benefit of unit owners.

To understand unit trusts better, consider the following hypothetical example. Nuveen, Inc.—a prominent firm in this field—announces the formation of the next in their series of tax-exempt unit trusts: Nuveen Series 200. Through advertising and selling agents, Nuveen will raise $4 million dollars; investors will pay approximately $1,000 per unit. After deducting 3 to 4 percent for sales commissions, Nuveen will use the remaining cash to purchase large blocks of municipal securities from 10 to 20 different issuers. Once this diversified pool of bonds is acquired, Nuveen will play a passive role. It will collect and pass on to unit holders all interest payments received and all principal repayments resulting from maturing or recalled bonds. While UITs usually hold bonds until maturity, the trust custodian may sell off bonds whose future ability to pay interest and principal is altered by events.

The majority of unit trusts formed in the past decade have invested in tax-exempt securities. Often, trusts are formed to purchase tax-exempt securities from issuers in specific, high-tax states, such as New York, Massachusetts, and Minnesota. Unit holders residing in these states expect to receive a stream of income exempt from federal, state, and local taxation.

Even unit trusts dedicated to tax-exempt bonds have different investment objectives. Some deal strictly in long-term, high-rated issues. Others seek higher yields by purchasing issues with low ratings.

Units of a trust are redeemable under terms set forth in the prospectus. In most cases this means that a unit holder can sell units back to the trust at their net asset value, which is the current market value of each trust unit. If a trust is composed of fixed-income securities—like bonds—the market value of its assets will fluctuate inversely with the direction of market interest rates.

A secondary market for unit trusts is evolving among broker-dealers. Investors seeking to acquire or sell units can sometimes find a better deal in this market.

Investors in UITs benefit by professional selection of securities, by diversification, and by avoiding the housekeeping chores of collecting coupon payments. As a large buyer, a UIT can usually purchase securities at a better price than the individual who buys in small lots.

Management Companies (Mutual Funds)

Some investment companies hire the services of an investment advisory firm to actively manage their pools of capital—thus the name **management companies.** The most common forms of these entities are called **mutual funds,** and they have grown dramatically in popularity over the past decade. In 1985, investors plowed $110.5 billion into stock and bond mutual funds—double the 1984 volume.[1]

The concept of a mutual fund is best understood by an example. Suppose that you and your friends are too busy to develop the expertise needed to manage your own assets. One of your neighbors, however, has studied investments and securities markets extensively. He has also had years of hands-on experience as a trustee of his company's pension fund. You and your friends decide to pool your money and have this investment wizard act as your investment advisor. He will be compensated by receiving a small percentage of the average amount of assets under his management during the forthcoming year.

By common agreement, the pooled money is to be invested in the common stock of large, stable companies, with the objective of capital appreciation and moderate dividend income; funds not so invested are to be placed in short-term T bills to earn interest. Group members collectively contribute $100,000 and decide to issue shares in the fund at a rate of one share for each $10 contributed—a total of 10,000 shares. Since you put in $10,000, you receive 1,000 shares of the fund—or 10 percent of the funds shares. Over the next few weeks, your investment advisor uses $90,000 to purchase common stock in a number of companies representing several different industries and puts $10,000 in T bills. The portfolio looks like this:

Common stocks grouped by industry

Computers/semiconductors:
  Hewlett Packard
  National Semiconductor
  Digital Equipment
Financial services:
  Chemical Bank
  Merrill Lynch
  Northwestern National Life Insurance Co.
Consumer retail:
  K mart
  Toys R Us
  Dayton Hudson

Treasury bills
$10,000

Your group of investors has many characteristics of a management company: ownership interest represented by shares, professional management, stated investment objectives, and a diversified portfolio of assets.

---

[1] "Mutual Fund Sales Topple 1984's Record," *The Wall Street Journal,* January 2, 1986.

Since you own 10 percent of this portfolio, you are entitled to 10 percent of all income paid out to shareholders and 10 percent of all realized capital gains or losses.

The initial value of the portfolio is $100,000, or $10 per share. Your investment manager picked some winning stocks, and the portfolio rises to $115,000. Now each share is worth $11.50 per share.

CLOSED-VERSUS OPEN-END FUNDS

Management companies are of two kinds: closed-end and open-end funds. A closed-end fund is similar to the common stock of a corporation: the supply of shares is fixed, and the only way an investor can purchase fund shares is from another investor. Some closed-end funds trade on the stock exchanges and others over-the-counter. Purchase and sale of their shares is conducted through broker-dealers in the same way as corporate common stock. Because the assets of closed-end funds are generally marketable securities, the share prices of these funds fluctuate with the market values of the securities in their portfolios. REITs (real estate investment trusts) are an exception. Their portfolios are made up of properties or mortgages, whose values are difficult to establish

Closed-end funds represent a very minor percentage of the capital currently invested in management companies. Shares of closed-end funds usually sell at a discount from the market value of assets held (net asset value) because they are not as liquid as the shares of open-end funds. Occasionally, shares of a closed-end fund may sell at a premium over net asset value because one or more stocks in the portfolio is not publicly traded and is carried at a cost basis that the market believes to be artifically low.

The example above, where a group of like-minded individuals pool their money under the management of the local investment wizard, is a model for a closed-end fund. A fixed number of shares are available (10,000). Suppose the investors decide that they need a larger pool of capital to achieve adequate diversification, so they invite new investments on a continuous basis at the net asset value (NAV). NAV is the total market value of all the assets in the portfolio less any liabilities, divided by the number of shares outstanding.

$$\frac{Total\ market\ value\ of\ portfolio\ less\ liabilities}{Number\ of\ shares\ outstanding} = NAV$$

Issuing new shares at the NAV does not dilute the value of the original shares. For every share of new stock issued, the fund receives an infusion of cash equal to the NAV. This cash is invested in keeping with the fund's stated objectives. The closed-end fund has become an opened-end fund.

Open-end funds—or mutual funds—represent the vast majority of investment companies in terms of both numbers of funds and amount of capital invested. They allow investors to buy and redeem shares at the NAV (net of a possible purchase or redemption charge). Theoretically there is no limit to the number of new shares they may issue.

Table 20–1 sums up the essential difference between closed-end and mutual funds.

TABLE 20–1   Mutual Funds Compared with Closed-End Investment Companies

	Method of Purchase	Number of Shares Outstanding	Redeem Shares at Net Asset Value
Mutual fund	Salesman or direct from fund	Fluctuates	Yes
Closed-end fund	Stock exchange or over-the-counter	Fixed	No

Source: Donald Rugg, The Dow Jones-Irwin Guide to Mutual Funds, 3d ed. (Homewood, Ill.: Dow Jones-Irwin, 1986.)

INVESTING IN MUTUAL FUNDS (LOAD AND NO-LOAD)

The popularity of mutual funds, particularly among individual investors, is based on a combination of benefits and conveniences. In addition to the advantages of diversification and professional management, mutual funds usually offer a number of other conveniences.

While shares of closed-end funds trade on exchanges and over-the-counter, shares of open-end funds are purchased directly from the fund or through one of its selling agents. Investors wishing to sell their shares do so by direct redemption from the fund.

Load Funds

Some funds have established selling agreements with stockbrokers, financial planners, insurance agents, and others licensed to sell securities. Because fund managers' compensation is a percentage of all the money they manage, they are eager to enlarge their pool of money and are willing to pay a commission to selling agents. These funds are called *load funds*. The commission, or load, is paid to the selling agent directly from the investor's capital. The typical stock mutual fund has a load of 8.5 percent for investments under $10,000. Bond funds usually charge 3 to 4 percent. In both cases, the commission percentage normally decreases with larger purchases (see Table 20–2).

Several funds are referred to as *low-load* funds because their sales charges are 3 to 4 percent instead of the more normal 8 to 8.5 percent. In recent years several investment companies have introduced a number of *end-*

load funds. This type of fund has no sales charge on purchase but imposes a redemption charge of 5 percent that declines by 1 percent per year. After five years the fund can be sold without charge.

TABLE 20-2   Typical Sales Charges for Load Stock Fund

Purchase Amount	As Percent of Net Amount Invested	As Percent of Offering Price
Less than $15,000	9.29%	8.5%
$15,000–$24,999	8.11	7.5
$25,000–$49,000	6.67	6.25
$50,000–$99,000	4.99	4.75
$100,000–$250,000	3.63	3.50
$250,000–$499,000	2.83	2.75
⋮		
$5,000,000 and over	0.25	0.25

No-Load Funds

No-load funds do not charge commissions and are sold directly by the investment company through advertisements, prospectuses, and 800-number telephone orders. As of mid–1984, no-load funds made up about 25 percent of all stock fund assets and about half of the assets of recently started funds. For years there has been controversy over which type of fund performs better. Many feel that load funds, because of their larger size, have better management, while others feel that small funds have better potential to outperform the market. Studies indicate that there is no significant statistical difference in the performance of load and no-load funds. Consequently, most astute investors shop around for a no-load fund to fit their needs rather than pay a commission. But an inexperienced investor who seeks the advice of a competent stockbroker or financial planner should not expect that person to work for nothing. A sales commission may be worth the price if it saves a naive investor from a poor choioce of mutual funds. Investors interested in no-load funds can find information on mutual funds in Wiesenberger's "Investment Companies Service," *No-Load Mutual Funds* (Droms and Heerwagen, Dow Jones-Irwin), and *The Investor's Guide to No-Load Mutual Funds*, 5th edition (American Association of Individual Investors).

Buying and Selling

Opened-end funds are purchased on a *dollar-amount* basis, with a minimum initial investment usually in the $500 to $1,000 range. For example, an investor submits an order for $5,000 of the Fidelity Magellan Fund. The fund will purchase as many shares—and fractional shares—as $5,000 will buy at the

FIGURE 20–1

MUTUAL FUND QUOTATIONS

Thursday, March 6, 1986

Price ranges for investment companies, as quoted by the National Association of Securities Dealers. NAV stands for net asset value per share; the offering includes net asset value plus maximum sales charge, if any.

next determined NAV per share, plus any commission. The NAV is computed at closing time each day that the New York Stock Exchange is open.

Mutual fund prices are quoted in the financial presss (Figure 20–1 is taken from *The Wall Street Journal*). Because investment companies usually offer a family of funds, individual funds are listed under the name of the parent company. For example, the first mutual fund listed—Capital Growth Fund—is one of six funds offered by the AARP Investment Program.

The *Journal* listing gives a fund's NAV (net asset value) at the end of the business day prior to publication and the price at which shares can be redeemed to the fund. Offer price is the price at which shares are offered for purchase; NAV Chg. indicates the price change from the previous day's quotation.

Consider two mutual funds taken from Figure 20–1.

	NAV	Offer Price	NAV Chg.
AARP Invest Program:			
Cap Grw	21.38	N.L.	+.09
American Funds Group:			
Amcap F	10.30	11.26	+.05

"N.L." in the column for Offering Price indicates that the Capital Growth Fund is a no-load fund. New shares can be purchased at net asset value; old shares can be redeemed at the same price. The Amcap Fund is a load fund. The difference between the offer price and the net asset value is the sales charge ($11.26 − $10.30 = $0.96). The sales charge in this case is 8.5 percent of the offering price (.96/11.26).

Normally, outstanding shares can be redeemed without charge, although some funds do impose a small (usually 0.5 percent) redemption charge. The investor merely sends a written notice to the fund's transfer agent along with the share certificates he wants to redeem. The signature on such a redemption request must be "guaranteed" by an officer of a bank or brokerage firm.

DIFFERING OBJECTIVES AND THE DIVERSITY OF MUTUAL FUNDS

Recognizing that different investors have different objectives and sensitivities to risk, the mutual fund industry offers a potpourri of funds from which to choose. In 1985 there were over 1,300 mutual funds, each unique in terms of stated objectives, investment policies, and current portfolio. To make some sense out of this much variety, funds can be classified in terms of their stated objectives.

Money Market Funds

Money market funds have been the phenomenon of the late 1970s and the current decade (Forbes' Mutual Fund Survey lists over 250). Such funds had $210 billion in assets in early 1986. Money market mutual funds invest in short-term securities, such as U.S. Treasury bills and Euro-dollar deposits, commercial paper, jumbo bank certificates of deposit (CDs), and repurchase agreements.

Money market funds are no-load, and most require minimum deposits of $500 to $1,000. Most have check-writing privileges, but usually the checks must be written for at least $500.

Because the maturities of assets held in money market portfolios generally range from 20 to 50 days, the yields of these funds closely tracks short-term market interest rates. Money market funds give small investors an opportunity to invest in securities that were once out of reach.

Growth Funds

The pursuit of capital gains is what growth funds are all about. This class of funds includes those called *aggressive* growth funds and those concentrating on more stable and predictable growth. Both types invest primarily in common stock. Aggressive funds concentrate on speculative issues, emerging small companies, and "hot" sectors of the economy, and frequently use financial leverage to magnify returns. Regular growth funds generally invest in common stocks of more stable firms. They are less inclined to stay fully invested in stocks during periods of market decline, seldom use aggressive techniques like leverage, and tend to be long-term in orientation.

The best way to determine the type of growth fund is to carefully examine the fund's prospectus and current portfolio.

Growth with Income

A number of large, growing firms pay steady dividends. Their stocks are attractive to investors interested in capital growth potential with a base of dividend or interest income. Funds that invest in such stocks are less volatile and risky than growth funds investing in smaller companies paying low or no dividends.

Balanced Funds

These funds combine investments in common stock and bonds, and often preferred stock. They try to provide income plus some capital gains. Funds that invest in convertible securities are also considered balanced, since the convertible security is a hybrid fixed-income security with the opportunity for appreciation if the underlying common stock rises.

Bond Funds

Income-oriented investors have always been attracted to bonds. Because bonds represent a contractual obligation on the part of the issuer to the bondholder, they normally offer a certain return. But, as pointed out in Chapter 10, rising interest rates can undercut the market value of all classes of fixed-income securities. During the 1970s, a time of intense interest rate fluctuations, many bondholders watched the principal value of even their "safe" government bonds drop to 50 percent of face value. Bonds held in mutual funds were affected by the same market forces. Returns from bonds are historically lower than those from stocks, and bond funds are no exception.

Bond mutual funds can be roughly subdivided into corporate, government, and municipal funds. Tax-exempt bond funds have grown in popularity as inflation and income patterns push more people into high tax brackets. Because these funds buy only tax-exempt securities, interest income to shareholders is free of federal tax. As in the case of unit investment trusts, special tax-exempt funds have been established for the benefit of investors in states with high state and local income taxes. For example, fund managers of New York municipal bond funds establish portfolios of tax-exempt securities issued within the boundaries of that state. Under current tax law, interest income from these funds is exempt from federal, state, and local taxes for New York residents—a very appealing feature to high-bracket taxpayers.[2]

---

[2] How appealing? For a New Yorker in a combined marginal tax bracket of 40 percent, a 9 percent return from a tax-exempt fund is equivalent to earning 15 percent on a taxable investment of similar characteristics.

$$\frac{\text{Tax-exempt return}}{100\% - \text{Tax bracket}} = \frac{.09}{1.00 - .40} = 15\%$$

Sector Funds

Special funds have been created to invest in specific sectors of the economy. Sector funds exist for energy, medical technology, computer technology, leisure, and defense.

Because stock performance of companies within a particular industry, or sector, tend to be positively correlated, these funds offer investors less diversification and higher loss/reward potential.

Investors should be cautious of the initial offering of new sector funds. An initial offering usually occurs after the sector has already been the subject of intense interest based on recent spectacular performance. As a result, stocks in that sector are probably fully priced or overpriced.

Foreign Funds

As noted in Chapter 18, investors seeking participation in foreign markets and securities confront a number of obstacles, but the rewards can be remarkable. The mutual fund industry has made overseas investing convenient by establishing funds whose policies mandate investing on a global basis (Templeton World Fund), within the markets of a particular locale (Canadian Fund, Inc.), or within a region (Merrill Lynch Pacific). One fund even specializes in Third World countries.

Foreign funds as a group outperformed all other kinds of mutual funds in 1985.

Specialty Funds

Some mutual funds have specialized approaches that do not fit neatly into any of the preceding categories. Their names are often indicative of their investment objectives or policies: the Sunbelt Fund, the Phoenix Fund (rising from the ashes?), the Calvert Social Investment Fund, and United Services Gold Shares, to name just a few.

There is even a "fund of funds" (FundTrust) that manages a portfolio of different mutual fund shares.

Owing to fund managers' poor record in attempting to outperform the market, a number of funds have taken up the maxim that "if you can't beat 'em, join 'em!" Calling themselves index funds, these mutual funds establish portfolios that replicate some major market index, such as the S&P 500. Fund performance is exactly correlated with performance of "the market."

SELECTION OF MUTUAL FUNDS

Before putting cash to work in a fund, investors need to consider their investment objectives and willingness to accept risk. While a mutual fund provides diversification for a specific group of assets such as stocks or bonds, investors must consider their total portfolio, including company-sponsored pension funds (and where the pension assets are invested), real estate hold-

TABLE 20–3   Selected Risk/Return Characteristics for Mutual Funds Grouped by Investment Objective

Fund Class	Five-year Return 1980–1984	Current Yield	Standard Deviation	Beta
Aggressive growth	227%	1.4%	21.7%	1.24
Growth	163	2.4	15.8	0.96
Growth-income	148	4.0	11.7	0.83
Balanced	155	5.3	11.5	0.70
Bond funds	62	11.3	11.2	0.47
S&P index	122	4.3	14.6	1.00
Treasury bills	70	9.0	3.6	

Source: Gerald Perritt and L. Kay Shannon, *The Individual Investor's Guide to No-Load Mutual Funds,* 4th ed. (Chicago: Investment Information Services Press, 1985).

ings, and home equity. The selection of a mutual fund may actually boil down to several different types of funds such as a bond fund, growth stock fund, and money market fund. Table 20–3 lists mutual funds by broad categories that can then be matched with an investor's investment objectives and risk characteristics.

Measuring Risk Return Trade-offs

Many investors seem to go after the highest returns without considering the corresponding risk. Table 20–3 illustrates both return and risk characteristics of each broad group of funds. Remember that the higher the standard deviation of possible returns, the greater the risk. Additionally, stocks, portfolios and mutual funds with high standard deviations are also likely to have high betas, another measure of risk relative to the market. The higher the beta, the more volatile the returns of that investment relative to the volatility of market returns. The market in this case is measured by the Standard & Poor's 500 Index and has a beta of 1.00. Over the five-year period, aggressive growth funds have had higher returns but higher risk than the market. All other stock funds have had higher returns than the market and betas of less than 1.00—i.e., less risk than the market. This relationship probably won't hold over long periods of time. Notice that Treasury bills have the lowest standard deviation; since returns are never negative on 1-year T bills, these securities are considered risk free.

Matching Investment Objectives with Fund Types

Investors must consider how much volatility of return they can tolerate. Investors who require safety of principal with very little deviation of returns should choose Treasury bills (or money market funds) first and bond funds second. They should also expect to receive lower returns based on the above historical data. While aggressive growth funds provide the highest return, they also have the biggest risk.

Liquidity objectives are met by all mutual funds since redemption can take place any time. If investors need income, bond funds provide the highest annual current yield, while aggressive growth and growth funds provide the least. Growth-income and balanced funds are most appropriate for investors who want growth of principal with moderate current income. However, to protect investments from eroding purchasing power, investors may have to take some risk.

Many investors diversify by fund type. For example, at one stage in the business cycle an investor may want to have 50 percent of his assets in common stocks, 35 percent in bonds, 10 percent in money market funds, and 5 percent in an international stock fund. These percentages could change as market conditions change. If interest rates are expected to decline, it would be better to have a higher percentage of bonds and fewer money market securities. Investing with a "family of funds" allows the investor a choice of many different types of funds and the privilege of switching between funds at no or low cost. Some of the larger families of funds are managed by American Capital, Dryfus Group, Federated Funds, Fidelity Investments, Price Funds, and Vanguard Group. In addition, most major retail brokerage firms, such as Merrill Lynch, Dean Witter, Prudential Bache, and Shearson, have families of mutual funds.

Each mutual fund has a unique history and management team. There is no guarantee that past performance will be repeated in the future. Investors should check on a fund's longevity of management, historical returns, trading history, and management expenses. Since mutual funds are more widely followed today than at any time in history, countless publications provide analytical information—some of the most notable are Weisenberger Investment Service, *Forbes* September issue, *Money, Barron's, Business Week,* and more. However, for an in-depth study of a mutual fund and the details necessary for decision making, investors need a copy of the fund's prospectus.

THE PROSPECTUS

The Investment Companies Act of 1940, which established the standard of practice for all investment companies, requires that the purchaser of fund shares be provided with a current prospectus. This document is furnished to the SEC for its inspection prior to public distribution. It contains information deemed essential by the SEC in providing "full disclosure" to potential investors regarding the fund's investment objectives and policies, risks, management, expenses, and current portfolio. The prospectus also provides information on how shares can be purchased and redeemed, sales and redemption charges (if any), and shareholders services. Other fund documents are available to the public on request including the Statement of Additional Information and the fund's annual and quarterly reports.

While it is beyond the scope of this chapter to provide a complete discourse on interpreting a prospectus, investors need to understand the following essentials.

Investment Objectives and Policies

This section is always found in the beginning of the prospectus. It usually describes the fund's basic objectives:

> The Fund will invest only in securities backed by the full faith and credit of the U.S. Government. At least 70% of the Fund's assets will be invested in certificates issued by the Government National Mortgage Association (GNMA). It may also purchase other securities issued by the U.S. Government, its agencies, or instrumentalities as long as these securities are backed by the full faith and credit of the U.S. Government.

The prospectus goes on to detail investment management policies under which it intends to operate—typically with regard to the use of borrowed money, lending of securities, or something like the following:

> The Fund may, under certain circumstances, sell covered call options against securities it is holding for the purpose of generating additional income.

Portfolio (or "Investment Holdings")

This section lists the securities held by the fund as of the date indicated. Since investment companies are only required to publish their prospectuses every 16 months, the information is probably dated. Still, the portfolio should be compared to the stated objectives of the fund to see if they are consistent.

Management Fees and Expenses

Besides sales and redemption charges, the prospectus also provides information on figures on fund managers' reimbursement and the fund's housekeeping expenses. Annual fees for the investment advisor are expressed as a percentage of the average daily net assets during the year (usually 0.50 percent). Other expenses include legal and auditing fees, the cost of preparing and distributing annual reports and proxy statements, directors' fees, and transaction expenses. When lumped together with investment advisory fees, a fund's total yearly expenses typically range from 1 to 1.2 percent of fund assets. Experienced mutual fund investors cast a jaundiced eye on funds with expense ratios that exceed this figure.

A controversial new SEC ruling—Rule 12b-1—allows mutual funds to use fund assets for marketing expenses. Since marketing expenses have nothing to do with advancing shareholders' interests and everything to do with increasing the managers' fees, investors should be alert to this in the prospectus. Language such as the following indicates this practice:

The Fund may pay the Distributor a fee at the annual rate of up to 0.25% of the average daily net assets of the Fund. This distribution fee is intended to finance certain sales and promotional activities.

Turnover Rate

A portion of the expense ratio results from commissions paid when the fund manager trades securities. A number of mutual funds trade aggressively in pursuit of profits; others do just the opposite. In 1985 the Fidelity Contrafund had a 243 percent turnover rate; the rate for the Oppenheimer Special Fund was 9 percent.

As David Henry pointed out in a recent *Forbes* article:

> What does an investor get for a lot of furious trading? Sometimes, good performance. Sometimes, bad performance. Always trading costs.[3]

In reality, transaction costs amount to more than just commissions, and they are not always accounted for in the expense ratio. When fund assets are traded over-the-counter, the dealer's spread between the bid and asked price is not considered. Nor is the fact that large block trades—the kind mutual funds usually deal in—are made at less favorable prices than are smaller volume transactions.

The prospectus contains audited data on the turnover rate, the expense ratio, and other important data in the section on Per Share Income and Capital Changes (see Table 20–4 for an example).

Distributions and Taxation

The selling of securities in a mutual fund's portfolio results in capital losses or gains for the fund. These may be long or short term, depending on how long the securities were held. After netting losses against gains, most mutual funds distribute capital gains to shareholders annually.

Funds with securities that pay dividends or interest have a source of investment income. The fund, in turn, distributes such income to shareholders either quarterly or annually. This income is taxed as ordinary income.

A fund that distributes at least 90 percent of its net investment income and capital gains is not subject, as an entity, to federal income tax. It is simply acting as a "conduit" in channeling taxable sources of income from securities held in the portfolio to the fund's shareholders. Most funds operate this way. But while the mutual fund may not be subject to taxation, its shareholders are.

At the end of every calendar year, each fund shareholder receives a Form 1099-DIV. This document notifies the shareholder of the amount and tax status of his distributions. It tells which portion of capital gains qualifies for long-term tax treatment and which does not. The fund shareholder need

---

[3] David Henry, "High Churnover," *Forbes,* March 10, 1986.

TABLE 20–4   Per Share Income and Capital Changes (for a share outstanding throughout the year)

	Year Ending Dec. 31, 1985	Year Ending Dec. 31, 1984
Net asset value at beginning of year	$11.13	$12.00
Investment income	.18	.42
Expenses	.13	.13
Net investment income	.05	.29
Dividend from net investment income . . .	(.22)	—
Net realized gain and increase (decrease) in unrealized appreciation (depreciation) of investments	.296	(1.16)
Distribution from net realized gain on investments	(.026)	—
Increase (decrease) in net asset value . . .	.10	(.87)
Net asset value at end of year	$11.23	$11.13
Ratio of expenses to average net assets . .	1.20%	1.28%
Ratio of net investment income to average net assets	1.20%	1.28%
Ratio of net investment income to average net assets	.42%	2.74%
Portfolio turnover rate	92%	42%
Number of shares outstanding at end of period (thousands)	10,542	9,086

not have held his shares for more than six months to take advantage of long-term gain distributions. What matters is that *the fund* has held the assets that produced the gains. Form 1099-DIV also indicates the amount of dividends qualifying for the federal dividend exclusion.

Just as the share price of common and preferred stock tends to drop by the amount of the dividend on the *ex-dividend* date, so too does the net asset value of a mutual fund share drop on the *ex-distribution* date. Investors should avoid making a purchase until after the record date for a distribution. To understand why, consider a fund with an offering price of $8 per share that is about to make a $.50 distribution. The investor who purchases just before the ex-date will receive the $.50 distribution, but the share price will drop to $7.50. She is in the same net position but must now pay taxes on $.50. Mutual fund sales agents who recommend "buy today and you'll get a big dividend right away" are practicing an illegal ploy known as *selling dividends.*

The redemption or exchange of a mutual fund share also constitutes a taxable event. The normal tax rules governing gains or losses described in Chapter 3 apply.

Shareholders Services

Most mutual funds offer a number of services to their shareholders. Some can be used in the investor's strategy—a topic we will come to later. Common services include:

Automatic reinvestment.   The fund reinvests all distributions (usually without sales charge). Shares and fractional shares are purchased at the net asset value. Purchases are noted on annual and periodic account statements.

Safekeeping.   While shareholders are entitled to receive certificates for all whole shares, it is often convenient to let the fund's transfer agent hold the shares.

Exchange privilege.   Many large management companies sponsor a family of funds. They may have five or more funds, each dedicated to a different investment objective. Within certain limits, shareholders are free to move their money between the different funds in the family on a net asset value basis. Transfers can often be done by telephone; a minimal charge is common to cover paperwork.

Pre-authorized check plan.   Many people lack the discipline to save or invest regularly. Those who recognize this trait in themselves can authorize a management company to charge their bank account for predetermined amounts on a regular basis. The amounts withdrawn are used to purchase new shares.

Systematic withdrawal plan.   Every shareholder plans to convert his shares into cash at some time in the future. The investor who wants to receive a regular amount of cash each month or quarter can do so by arranging for such a plan. The fund sells enough shares on a periodic basis to meet the shareholder's cash requirement.

Checking privileges.   Most money market mutual funds furnish shareholders with checks that can be drawn against the account, provided that the account balance is above a minimum amount (usually $1,000). A per-check minimum of $500 is commonplace.

INVESTMENT STRATEGIES USING MUTUAL FUNDS

The characteristics of mutual funds suggest some unique investment strategies, but some strategies are *not* available to mutual fund shareholders.

Short selling—a technique used to capitalize on declining markets. Mutual fund shareholders must either sell out, change to other funds, or ride out the decline.

Buying or writing options cannot be done using the fund as the underlying security.

Buying on margin—a practice used to achieve leveraged results. Mutual fund shares are not marginable.

Outguessing the Market

A few individuals seem to have an uncanny ability to divine the future course of securities markets. A far greater number think they have it. These investors try to identify tops and bottoms in the market and position themselves accordingly. The same strategy can be employed using mutual funds.

Suppose you believe that the stock market is at a cyclical low point. The obvious thing to do is to purchase shares of a stock mutual fund. You might fine-tune your strategy by concentrating on sector funds that you think will be market leaders in the months ahead. In the last chapter we learned how stocks with high betas are more volatile than the general market. You might position yourself in funds with high betas in anticipation of a market upswing. Funds with high betas should outperform a rising market.

Assuming that your forecast is correct and timely, you will enjoy good results. But the market will eventually reach a high point that will make you fearful of a general market decline. You can sell out completely, or—using the exchange privilege common to most funds—change your high beta fund shares for those of a low beta, bond, or money market fund in the same family of funds. You will preserve your winnings, and be better positioned to ride out an impending market slump.

While this strategy is intuitively appealing, note the following two cautions. First, the ability to recognize peaks and troughs in the market is an illusive skill. Most academic research indicates that the whole notion of "market timing" is wishful thinking. Second, the manager of your fund may be pursuing a market timing or hedging strategy already. Information in the prospectus will reveal the investment strategies available to the fund manager.

Building a Nest Egg

Perhaps more than anything else, the liquidity and conveniences inherent in mutual funds lend themselves best to financial planning activities. The most important of these is the gradual accumulation of capital assets.

Using the pre-authorized check plan, investors can have fixed amounts regularly withdrawn from their checking accounts to purchase fund shares. Just as savers can have their banks channel a specific amount from their paychecks into savings accounts, so too can investors make regular, lump-sum fund share purchases on an "out of sight, out of mind" basis. Reinvestment of distributions enhances this strategy.

What distinguishes the mutual fund from the bank savings strategy is the fact that fund shares are purchased at different prices. The investor is using a passive strategy known as **dollar-cost averaging.** It applies to the acquisition of individual stocks, mutual fund shares, or other assets. Under dollar-cost averaging, the investor buys a fixed dollar's worth of a given security at regular intervals regardless of the security's price or the current market outlook. By using such a strategy, investors concede that they cannot outsmart the market. The intent of dollar-cost averaging is to avoid the com-

TABLE 20–5   Dollar-Cost Averaging

(1)	(2)	(3)	(4)
			Shares
Month	*Investment*	*Share Price*	*Purchased*
January	$200	$12	16.66
February	$200	$14	14.28
March	$200	$16	12.50
April	$200	$19	10.52
May	$200	$15	13.33
June	$200	$12	16.66
Totals	$1,200	$88	83.95 shares purchased

mon practice of buying high and selling low. In fact, investors are forced to do the opposite. Why? They commit a fixed-dollar amount each month (or year) and buy shares at the current market price. When the price is high, they are buying relatively fewer shares; when the price is low, they are accumulating more shares. An example is presented in Table 20–5. Suppose we use the pre-authorized check plan to channel $200 per month into a mutual fund. The price ranges from a low of $12 and a high of $19.

Note that when the share price is relatively low, such as in January, we purchased a larger number of shares than when the share prices were high, as in April. In this case, share price ended in June at the same price it was in January ($12).

What would happen if the price merely ended up at the average price over the six-month period? The values in column 3 total $88, so the average price over six months is $14.67 ($88/6). Actually, we would still make money under this assumption because the average *cost* is less than this amount. Consider that we invested $1,200 and purchased 83.95 shares. This translates to an average cost of only $14.29.

$$\frac{\text{Investment}}{\text{Shares purchased}} = \frac{\$1,200}{83.95} = \$14.29$$

The reason that the average cost ($14.29) is less than the average price ($14.67) is that we bought relatively more shares at the lower price levels and they weighed more heavily in our calculations. Thus, under dollar-cost averaging, investors can come out ahead over a period of investing fixed amounts, even if the share price ends up less than the average price paid on each transaction.[4]

The only time investors lose money is if the eventual price falls below the average cost ($14.29) and they sell at that point. While dollar-cost averaging has its advantages, it is not without criticism. Clearly, if the share price

---

[4] This does not consider any sales charges or commissions, which could be important.

continues to go down over a long period of time, it is hard to make a case for continued purchases. However, the long-term performance of most diversified mutual funds has been positive, and long-term investors may find this strategy useful in accumulating capital assets for retirement, childrens' education funds, or other purposes.

Retirement Plans

Millions of individuals are now contributing to individual retirement accounts (IRAs), and Keoghs. These retirement vehicles have favorable tax benefits to participants and are growing in popularity. IRS rules require that such retirement plans be administered by a qualified *custodian*. The custodian is responsible for the general administration of the plan, as well as reporting contributions and withdrawals to the IRS. Most large financial institutions— banks, insurance companies, investment companies, and brokerage firms— have been qualified as custodians.

Sponsors of corporate pension/profit-sharing plans, as well as those individuals (primarily employees of public schools and certain other nonprofit organizations) who qualify for Section 403b plans can and often do set up their plans with investment companies. Most mutual funds have prototype legal documents available to facilitate setting up individual plans.

Living off Assets

Many investors spend years methodically building up a pool of savings and capital assets to provide a supplementary source of retirement income or finance the education of children. Mutual funds are useful in this regard because most have a systematic withdrawal provision. Investors have the choice of either receiving the cash income from their shares and leaving the principal intact or selling off shares to provide regular cash (as would be done with growth stock funds, which traditionally invest in companies that pay few or no dividends).

Consider a hypothetical case. Mrs. Jones has accumulated shares in the XYZ Growth Fund with a market value of $50,000. She intends to begin drawing on her account this year to finance her son's education through four years of private college and two years of graduate school. She knows that she will need $12,000 for education expenses during each of the six years.

The XYZ Growth Fund has maintained a compound growth rate over the past decade of 12 percent. XYZ also has a bond fund that has had a compound growth rate of 9 percent over the same period; almost all of that growth resulted from interest income.

Mrs. Jones could exchange her shares of the Growth Fund for those of the Bond Fund, but the cash distributions alone would be insufficient to meet her expenses ($50,000 \times .09 = $4,500$). Clearly, she will have to withdraw some of the principal value.

FIGURE 20–2 $50,000 Account with Six Equal Withdrawals @ $12,162 at the End of Each Year (assumes annual growth rate of 12 percent)

```
50,000 starting balance
+ 12%
56,000 end of 1st year
− 12,162
43,838 + 12%  =    49,098 end of 2nd year
             − 12,162
            36,936 + 12%  =    41,368 end of 3rd year
                       − 12,162
                      29,206 + 12%  =    32,711 end of 4th year
                                 − 12,162
                                20,549 + 12%  =    23,015 end 5th year
                                          − 12,162
                                         10,853 + 12%  =    12,156
                                                    − 12,162
                                                      − 6 end of 6th year
```

Note: For greater convenience, systematic withdrawals can be made at more frequent intervals.
* Negative final balance due to rounding.

If she assumes the growth rate over the next six years will roughly approximate that of the previous decade, Mrs. Smith could structure her withdrawals like an *annuity*. She could arrange for a fixed-dollar payout at the end of each of the six years. The balance that remained in her account each year is assumed to grow at 12 percent. The sixth payment would reduce her principal balance to near $0.00. Figure 20–2 illustrates the concept. In this particular case, Mrs. Jones could arrange for a $12,162 fixed-dollar payment at the end of each year.[5]

This chapter began by describing the advantages of investing through investment companies. Of course, for every advantage, there must be some associated disadvantage. The following are some disadvantages normally associated with mutual funds:

> *They are passive investment.*   Except for purchasing and redemption, the investor has little control over the portfolio.
>
> *Broadly diversified portfolios generally lead to "average" results.*   In fact, the completely diversified fund becomes an index fund—a de-

---

[5] To find the payment amount of an annuity, use the table found in appendix D. Look up the present value of an annuity factor for six periods at 12% (4.111) and use it in the equation:

$$\text{Payment} = \text{Present amount/factor}$$
$$= \$50,000/4.111$$
$$= \$12,162$$

facto average. (Sector funds and foreign funds represent a departure from this sense of diversification.)

Tax-timing is controlled by the fund.

Each investor has to decide for himself whether these represent serious disadvantages. But the growing popularity of investing through investment companies indicates that they are serving a distinct need of the investing public.

GLOSSARY

Abnormal return Gains beyond what the market would normally provide after adjustment for risk.

Adjustable rate mortgage A mortgage in which the interest rate is adjusted regularly to current market conditions. It is sometimes referred to as a variable rate mortgage.

Advances Increases in the prices of various stocks as measured between two points in time. Significant advances in a large number of stocks indicate a particular degree of market strength. Also see **Declines.**

After-acquired property clause The stipulation in a mortgage bond indenture requiring all real property subsequently obtained by the issuing firm to serve as additional bond security.

After-market performance The price experience of new issues in the market.

Alpha The value representing the difference between the return on a portfolio and a return on the market line that corresponds to a beta equal to the portfolio. If a portfolio manager performs at positive alpha levels, he would generate returns better than those available along the market line.

American depository receipts (ADRs) These securities represent the ownership interest in a foreign company's common stock. The process is as follows: the shares of the foreign company are purchased and put in trust in a foreign branch of a New York bank. The bank, in turn, receives and can issue depository receipts to the American sharehold-

ers of the foreign firm. These ADRs (i.e., depository receipts) allow foreign shares to be traded in the United States much like any other security. Through ADRs, one can purchase the stock of Sony Corporation, Honda Motor Co., Ltd., and hundreds of other foreign corporations.

American Exchange Market Value Index An index comprising all stocks on the American Stock Exchange. It is value-weighted.

Anticipated realized yield The return received on a bond held for a period other than that ending on the call date or the maturity date. In computing the anticipated realized yield, the investor considers both coupon payments and expected capital gains.

Arbitrage pricing theory A theory for explaining stock prices and stock returns. While the capital asset pricing model bases return solely on one form of systematic risk (market risk), arbitrage pricing theory can utilize several sources of systematic risk (GNP, unemployment, etc.). Under this theory, it is assumed that the investor will not be allowed to earn a return greater than that dictated by the various sources of systematic risk. To the extent that he does, arbitrageurs will eliminate the extra returns by selling the security and buying other comparable securities—thus the term *artibrage pricing theory.* Unlike the capital asset pricing model, there is no necessity to define K_M (the market rate of return).

Asset utilization ratios Ratios that indicate the number of times per year that assets are

493

turned over. They show the activity in the various asset accounts.

Average differential return The alpha value which indicates the difference between the return on a portfolio or fund and a return on the market line that corresponds to a beta equal to the portfolio or fund.

Balance sheet A financial statement that indicates, at a given point in time, what the firm owns and how these assets are financed in the form of liabilities and ownership interest.

Balanced fund A type of mutual fund that invests in common stock, bonds, and often preferred stock to try to provide income plus some capital gains.

Bankers' acceptance A short-term debt instrument usually issued in conjunction with a foreign trade transaction. The acceptance is a draft that is drawn on a bank for approval for future payment and is subsequently presented to the payer.

Barron's Confidence Index An indicator utilized by technical analysts who follow smart money rules. Movements in the index measure the expectations of bond investors, whom some technical analysts see as astute enough to foresee economic trends before the stock market has time to react.

Barron's Group Stock Averages Barron's publishes stock averages covering 32 industry groups. These averages are especially useful to the analyst who is following the performance of a specific industry relative to the general market.

Basis The difference between the futures price and the value of the underlying item. Thus on a stock index futures contract, basis represents the difference between the stock index futures price and the value of the underlying index. The basis may be either positive or negative, with the former indicating optimism and the latter signifying pessimism.

Basis point The unit of measure of change on interest-bearing instruments. One basis point is equal to .01 percent.

Best efforts The issuing firm, rather than the investment banker, assumes the risk for a distribution. The investment banker merely agrees to provide his best effort to sell the securities.

Beta A measurement of movement of a security with the market in general. It measures volatility. A high beta coefficient indicates high amounts of systematic risk.

Beta-related hedge A stock index futures hedge in which the relative volatility of the portfolio to the market is considered in determining the number of contracts necessary to offset a given dollar level of exposure. If a portfolio has a beta greater than one, then extra contracts may be necessary to compensate for high volatility.

Beta stability The amount of consistency in beta values over time. Instability means prior beta values may not be reflective of future beta values.

Black-Scholes Option Pricing Model A formal model used to determine the theoretical value of an option. Such factors as the riskless interest rate, the length of the option, and the volatility of the underlying security are considered. For a more complete discussion, see Appendix 13B.

Blind pool A form of limited partnership for real estate investments in which funds are provided to the general partner to select properties for investment.

Bond price sensitivity The sensitivity of a change in bond prices to a change in interest rates. Bond price sensitivity is influenced by the duration of the bond, in that the longer the duration of a bond, the greater the price sensitivity. A less sophisticated, but acceptable approach, is to tie price sensitivity to the maturity of the bond rather than the duration.

Bond swaps The term refers to selling out of a given bond position and immediately buying into another one with similar attributes in an attempt to improve overall portfolio return or performance.

Breadth of market indicators Overall market rules used by technical analysts in comparing broad market activity with trading activity in a few stocks. By comparing all advances and declines in NYSE-listed stocks, for example, with the Dow Jones Industrial Average, analysts attempt to judge when the market has changed directions.

Bull spread An option strategy utilized when the expectation is that the stock price will rise. The opposite is a bear spread.

Business cycle Short-term swings in economic activity encompassing expansionary and recessionary periods and generally occurring over two- to four-year periods.

Buying the spread A term indicating the cost from writing the call is more than the revenue of the short position. The opposite results in "selling the spread."

Call An option to buy 100 shares of common stock at a specified price for a given period of time.

Call provision A mechanism for repaying funds advanced through a bond issue. A provision of the bond indenture allows the issuer to retire bonds prior to maturity by paying holders a premium above principal.

Capital appreciation A growth in the value of a stock or other investments as opposed to income from dividends or interest.

Capital asset pricing model A model by which assets are valued based on their risk characteristics. The required return for an asset is related to its beta.

Capital market line The graphic representation of the relationship of risks and returns with various portfolios of assets. The line is part of the capital asset pricing model.

Cash settlement Closing out a futures or options contract for cash rather than calling for actual delivery of the underlying item specified in the contract—i.e., pork bellies, T-bills. The stock index futures markets and stock index options markets are *purely* cash settlement markets. There is never even the implied

potential for future delivery of the S&P 500 Stock Index or other indexes.

CBOE Chicago Board Options Exchange, the first exchange for call options.

Certificates of deposit Savings certificates which entitle the holder to the receipt of interest. These instruments are issued by commercial banks and savings and loans (or other thrift institutions) and have traditionally been in small amounts such as $1,000 to $10,000 or large amounts such as $100,000 (jumbo CDs).

Chartered Financial Analyst (CFA) A security analyst or portfolio manager who has been appropriately certified through experience requirements and testing.

Charting The use by technical analysts of charts and graphs to plot past stock price movements, which are used to predict future prices.

Closed-end fund An investment fund with a limited number of shares. Shares are available in the market only if present owners wish to sell their holdings. See **Open-end fund.**

Closing purchase transaction A transaction in which an investor who is a writer of an option intends to terminate his obligation.

Closing sale transaction A transaction in which an investor who is the holder of an outstanding security intends to liquidate his position as a holder.

Combined earnings and dividend model A model combining earnings per share and an earnings multiplier with a finite dividend model. Value is derived from both the present value of dividends and the present value of the future price of the stock based on the earnings multiplier (P/E).

Commercial paper A short-term credit instrument which is issued by large business corporations to the public. Commercial paper usually comes in minimum denominations of $25,000 and represents an unsecured promissory note.

Commission broker An individual who represents a stock brokerage firm at an exchange and who executes sales and purchases stocks for the firm's clients across the nation.

Commodities Such tangible items as livestock, farm produce, and precious metals. Users and producers of comomodities hedge against future price fluctuations by transferring risks to speculators through futures contracts.

Constant dollar method Adjusting for inflation in the financial statements by using the consumer price index.

Constant growth model A dividend valuation model that assumes a constant growth rate for dividends.

Construction and development trust A type of REIT that makes short-term loans to developers during their construction period.

Consumer price index An index used to measure the changes in the general price level.

Contrary opinion rules Guidelines, based on such factors as the odd-lot or the short sales position, used by technical analysts who predict stock market activity on the assumption that such groups as small traders or short sellers are often wrong. Also see **Smart money rules.**

Contributory pension plan An arrangement in which both the employer and employee contribute to the pension plan.

Conversion premium The amount, expressed as a dollar value or as a percentage, by which the price of the convertible security exceeds the current market value of the common stock into which it may be converted.

Conversion price The face value of a convertible security divided by the conversion ratio, giving the price of the underlying common stock at which the security is convertible. An investor would usually not convert the security into common stock unless the market price was greater than the conversion price.

Conversion ratio The number of shares of common stock an investor receives in exchanging convertible bonds or shares of con-

vertible preferred stock for shares of common stock.

Conversion value The value of the underlying common stock represented by convertible bonds or convertible preferred stock. This dollar value is obtained by multiplying the conversion ratio by the per-share market price of the common stock.

Convertible security A corporate bond or a share of preferred stock which, at the option of the holder, can be converted into shares of common stock of the issuing corporation.

Correlation coefficient The measurement of joint movement between two variables.

Coupon rate The stated, fixed rate of interest paid on a bond.

Covered writer A writer of an option who owns the stock on which the option is written. If the stock is not owned, the writer is deemed naked.

Creditor claims Claims represented by debt instruments offered by financial institutions, industrial corporations, or the government.

Cross hedge A hedging position in which one form of security is used to hedge another form of security (often because differences in maturity dates or quality characteristics make a perfect hedge difficult to establish).

Currency fluctuations Changes in the relative value of one currency to another. For example, the French franc may advance or decline in relation to the dollar. To the extent a foreign currency appreciates relative to the dollar, returns on foreign investments will increase in terms of dollars. The opposite would be true for declining foreign currencies.

Currency futures Futures contracts for speculation or hedging in different nations' currencies.

Current cost method Adjusting for inflation in the financial statements by revaluing assets at their current cost.

Current ratio Current assets divided by current liabilities.

Current yield The annual dollar amount of interest paid on a bond divided by the price at which the bond is currently trading in the market.

Cyclical Indicators Factors that economists can observe to measure the progress of economic cycles. Leading indicators move in a particular direction in advance of the movement of general business conditions, while lagging indicators change direction after general conditions, and coincident indicators move in unison with the economy.

Cyclical Industry An industry, such as automobiles, whose financial health is closely tied to the condition of the general economy. Such industries tend to make the type of products whose purchase can be postponed until the economy improves.

Data base A form of organized, stored data. It is usually fed into the computer for additional analysis.

Debenture An unsecured corporate bond.

Debt utilization ratios Ratios that indicate how the firm is financed between debt (lenders) and equity (owners), and the firm's ability for meeting cash payments due on fixed obligations, such as interest, lease payments, licensing fees, or sinking fund charges.

Declines Decreases in the prices of various stocks as measured between two points in time. Significant declines in a large number of stocks indicate a particular degree of market weakness. Also see **Advances.**

Deep discount bond A bond that has a coupon rate far below rates currently available on investments and which consequently can be traded only at a significant discount from par value. It may offer an opportunity for capital appreciation.

Defined benefit plan Under a defined benefit plan, the employee can calculate his or her pension based on a formula using such factors as years of service and average earnings.

Defined contribution plan Under a defined contribution plan, retirement benefits are a function of total contributions over the life of the plan and are not based on such factors as years of service or average earnings.

Diagonal spread A combination of a vertical and horizontal spread.

Dilution The reduction in earnings per share that occurs when earnings remain unchanged yet the number of shares outstanding increases, as in the conversion of convertible bonds or preferred stock into common stock.

Direct equity claim Representation of ownership interests through common stock or other instruments to purchase common stock, such as warrants and options.

Discount rate The interest rate at which future cash flows are discounted to a present value.

Dispersion The distribution of values or outcomes around an expected value.

Diversification Lack of concentration in any one item. A portfolio composed of many different securities is diversified.

Diversification benefits Risk reduction through a diversification of investments. Investments that are negatively correlated or that have low positive correlation provide the best diversification benefits. Such benefits may be particularly evident in an internationally diversified portfolio.

Dividend valuation model Any one of a number of stock valuation models based on the premise that the value of stock lies in the present value of its future dividend stream.

Dividend yield Annual dividends per share divided by market price.

Dollar-cost averaging Under this system, a fixed-dollar investment is placed in a given security (or portfolio) each period regardless of its price or the current market outlook. This reflects an attempt to buy more shares at a lower average price.

Dow Jones Industrial Average An index of stock market activity based on the price movements of 30 large corporations. The average is price-weighted, which means that each stock is effectively weighted by the magnitude of its price.

Dow theory The theory, developed by Charles Dow in the late 1890s and still in use today, states that the analysis of long-term (primary) stock market trends can yield accurate predictions for future price movements.

Downside protection The protection that a convertible bond investor enjoys during a period of falling stock prices. While the underlying common stock and the convertible bond may both fall in value, the bond will fall only to a particular level because it has a fundamental, or pure, bond value based on its assured income stream.

Downside risk The possibility that an asset, such as a security, may fall in value as a result of fundamental factors or external market forces. The limit of the downside risk for a convertible bond can be computed as the difference between the bond's market price and its pure bond value divided by the market price.

Du Pont analysis A system of analyzing return on assets through examining the profit margin and asset turnover. Also, the value of return on equity is analyzed through evaluating return on assets and the debt/total assets ratio. Figure 7–2 summarizes the major components of the Du Pont system of analysis.

Duration The weighted average life of a bond. The weights are based on the present values of the individual cash flows relative to the present value of the total cash flows. Duration is a better measure than maturity when assessing the price sensitivity of bonds; that is, the impact of interest rate changes on bond prices can be more directly correlated to duration than to maturity.

Earnings per share The earnings available to holders of common stock divided by the number of common stock shares outstanding.

Earnings valuation model Any one of a number of stock valuation models based on the premise that a stock's value is some appropriate multiple of earnings per share.

Effective diversification The diversification of a portfolio to remove unsystematic risk.

Efficient frontier A set of portfolios of investments in which the investor receives maximum return for a given level of risk or a minimum risk for a given level of return.

Efficient hedge A hedge in which one side of the transaction effectively covers the exposed side in terms of movement.

Efficient market The capacity of the market to react to new information, to avoid rapid price fluctuations, and to engage in increased or reduced trading volume without realizing significant price changes. In an efficient market environment, securities are assumed to be correctly priced at any point in time.

Efficient market hypothesis The concept that there are many participants in the securities markets who are profit maximizing and alert to information so that there is almost instant adjustment to new information. The weak form of this hypothesis suggests that there is no relationship between past and future prices. The semi-strong form maintains that all forms of public information are already reflected in the price of a security so fundmental analysis cannot determine under- or overvaluation. The strong form suggests that all information, insider as well as public, is impounded in the value of a security.

Efficient portfolio A portfolio that combines assets so as to minimize the risk for a given level of return.

Equal-weighted index Each stock, regardless of total market value or price, is weighted equally. It is as if there were $100 invested in each and every stock in the index. The Value Line Index is a prime example of an equal-weighted index.

Equipment trust certificate A secured debt instrument used by firms in the transportation industry that provides for bond proceeds to purchase new equipment, which in turn is collateral for the bond issue.

Equity participation The lender also participates in an ownership interest in the property.

Equity trust A type of REIT that buys, operates, and sells real estate as an investment as opposed to construction and development trusts and mortgage trusts.

ERISA Employee Retirement Income Security Act of 1974 (commonly called the Pension Reform Act of 1974). The act requires that vesting after a certain period of time must take place. ERISA also prescribes minimum standards of eligibility for participation, disclosure to participant rules, and employer fiscal responsibility.

Estate and gift taxes Estate taxes are imposed on the estate of a deceased person, and gift taxes are imposed on lifetime gifts that exceed the $10,000-per-year gift allowance. For purposes of computation of taxes payable, the two types of tax obligations are combined (estate and gift), and a unified tax is applied to both.

Excess returns Returns in excess of the risk-free rate or in excess of a market measure such as the S&P 500 stock index.

Exchange listing A firm lists its shares on an exchange (such as the American or New York Stock Exchange).

Exercise price (warrant) The price at which the stock can be bought using the warrant.

Expectations hypothesis The hypothesis which explains the term structure of interest rates, stating that a long-term interest rate is the average of expected short-term interest rates over the applicable time period. If, for example, long-term rates are higher than short-term rates, then according to the expectations hypothesis, investors must expect that short-term rates will be increasing in coming periods.

Expected value The sum of possible outcomes times their probability of occurrence.

Extraordinary gains and losses Gains or losses from the sale of corporate fixed assets, lawsuits, or similar events that would not be expected to occur often, if ever again.

Fed The Federal Reserve serves as the central banking authority for the United States. The Fed enacts monetary policy, and it plays a major role in regulating commercial banking operations and controlling the money supply.

Federal deficit A situation in which the federal government spends more money than it receives through taxes and other revenue sources.

Federal surplus A situation in which taxes and other government revenues provide more money than is needed to cover government expenditures.

FIFO A method of inventory valuation in which it is assumed that inventory purchased first is sold first (first-in, first-out).

Financial asset A financial claim on an asset (rather than physical possession of a tangible asset) usually documented by a legal instrument, such as a stock certificate.

Financial service companies Firms that provide a broad range of financial services in order to diversify their consumer base. Services may include brokerage activities, insurance, banking, etc.

Fiscal policy Government spending and taxing practices designed to promote or inhibit various economic activities.

Floor broker An independent stockbroker who is a member of a stock exchange and who executes trades, for a fee, for commission brokers experiencing excessive volumes of trading.

Floor value A value which an income-producing security will not fall below because of the fundamental value attributable to its assured income stream.

Flow of funds analysis Analysis of the pattern of financial payments between business, government, and households.

Foreign currency effects To the extent a foreign currency appreciates relative to the dollar, returns on foreign investments will increase in terms of dollars. The opposite would be true for declining foreign currencies.

Foreign political risks The risks associated with investing in firms operating in foreign countries. There is the danger of nationalization of foreign firms or the blockage of capital flows to investors. There also may be the danger of violent overthrow of the political party in power, with all the associated implications. Punitive legislation against foreign firms or investors is another political risk.

Fourth market The direct trading between large institutional investors in blocks of listed stocks. The participants avoid paying brokerage commissions.

Fully diluted earnings per share The value of earnings per share that would be realized if all outstanding securities convertible into common stock were, in fact, converted.

Fundamental analysis The valuation of stocks based on fundamental factors, such as company earnings, growth prospects, etc.

Funded pension plan Current income is charged with pension liabilities in advance of the actual payment, and funds are set aside.

Futures contract An agreement that provides for sale or purchase of a specific amount of a commodity at a designated time in the future at a given price.

General obligation bonds A municipal bond backed by the full faith, credit, and "taxing power" of the issuing unit rather than the revenue from a given project.

Gift splitting Each spouse giving a child $10,000 per year for a total of $20,000, rather than the usual $10,000 available under the 1981 Economic Recovery Tax Act.

GNMA pass-through certificates These securities represent an undivided interest in a pool of federally insured mortgages. Actually, GNMA (the Government National Mortgage Association) buys a pool of mortgages from various lenders at a discount and then issues securities to the public against the mortgages. They are pass-through in that the holder of a GNMA certificate receives the interest and principal payment on the mortgages on a monthly basis.

Going public Selling formerly privately held shares to new investors on the over-the-counter market for the first time.

Government securities Bonds issued by federal, state, or local governmental units or government agencies. Whereas corporate securities' returns are paid through company earnings, government securities are repaid through taxes or the revenues from projects financed by the bonds.

Graduated payment mortgage A type of mortgage in which payments start out on a relatively low basis and increase over the life of the loan.

Greed index A contrary opinion index that measures how "greedy" investors are. Greed is thought to be synonymous with bullish sentiment, or optimism. Under the assumptions of the greed index, the more greedy or optimistic investors are, the more likely the market is to fall and vice versa.

Gross national product implicit price deflator A calculation made by the Department of Commerce which adjusts the prices of all goods and services in the GNP estimate for the effects of price change. It's a measure of inflation.

Growth company A company that exhibits rising returns on assets each year and sales that are growing at an increasing rate (growth phase of the life-cycle curve). Growth companies may not be as well known as growth stocks.

Growth stock The stock of a firm generally growing faster than the economy or market norm.

Hedging A process for lessening or eliminating risk by taking a position in the market opposite to your original position. For example, someone who owns wheat can sell a futures contract to protect against future price declines.

Horizontal spread Buying and writing two options with the same strike price but maturing in different months.

Ibbotson and Singuefield study A University of Chicago study examining comparative returns on stocks and fixed-income securities from the mid-1920s into the 1980s.

Immunization Immunizing or protecting a bond portfolio against the effects of changing interest rates on the ending value of the portfolio. The process is usually tied to a time horizon. In the process if interest rates go up, there will be a decline in the value of the portfolio, but a higher reinvestment rate opportunity for inflows. Conversely, if interest rates go down, there will be capital appreciation for the portfolio, but a lower reinvestment rate opportunity. By tying all the investment decisions to a specified duration period, the portfolio manager can take advantage of these counter forces to ensure a necessary outcome.

Income bond A corporate debt instrument on which interest is paid only if funds are available from current income.

Income statement A financial statement that shows the profitability of a firm over a given period of time.

Income statement method A method of forecasting earnings per share based on a projected income statement.

Indenture A lengthy, complicated legal document which spells out the borrowing firm's responsibilities to the individual lenders in a bond issue.

Index fund A fund investing in a portfolio of corporate stocks, the composition of which is determined by the Standard & Poor's 500 or some other index.

Indirect equity claim An indirect claim on common stock such as that achieved by placing funds in investment companies.

Individual retirement accounts (IRAs) Individual retirement plans. The maximum annual contribution is $2,000 for one person and $2,250 if there is a nonworking spouse. If there are two working spouses, the maximum contribution is $4,000. Contributions reduce taxable income and allow for the accumulation of funds that are not currently taxed.

Taxation only begins when withdrawals are made.

Individual retirement annuity A tax-deferred retirement annuity purchased from an insurance company. Benefits may be guaranteed in advance.

Industry factors The unique attributes that must be considered in analyzing a given industry or group of industries. Examples include industry structure, supply/demand of labor and materials, and government regulation.

Industry life cycle The movement of a firm or industry through stages of development, growth, expansion, and maturity.

Inflation A general increase in the prices of goods and services.

Inflation-adjusted accounting Restating financial statements to show the effect of inflation on the balance sheet and income statement. This is supplemental to the normal presentation based on historical data.

Inflationary expectations A value representing future expectations about the rate of inflation. This value, combined with the real rate of return, provides the risk-free required return for the investor.

Institutional investor A type of investor (as opposed to individual investors) representing organizations responsible for bringing together large pools of capital for investment. Institutional investors include investment companies, pension funds, life insurance companies, bank trust departments, and endowments and foundations.

In-the-money A term that indicates when the market price of a stock is above the striking price of the option. When the strike price is above the market price, the option is out-of-the-money.

Interest rate futures Futures contracts involving Treasury bills, Treasury bonds, Treasury notes, commercial paper, certificates of deposit, and GNMA certificates.

International tax problems Many foreign countries impose a 7.5 percent to 15 percent withholding tax against the dividends or interest paid to nonresident holders of equity or debt securities. However, it is often possible for tax-exempt U.S. investors to secure an exemption or rebate on part or all of the withholding tax. Also, taxable U.S. investors can normally claim a U.S. tax credit for taxes paid in foreign countries. The problem is more likely to be one of inconvenience and paper shuffling rather than loss of funds.

Internationally oriented funds Mutual funds and closed-end investment companies that invest in worldwide securities. Some funds specialize in Asian holdings, others in South African, and so on. A listing of internationally oriented funds is presented in Table 18–12.

Intrinsic value Value of an option equal to market price minus the strike price.

Inverse pyramiding A process of leveraging to control commodities contracts in which the profits from one contract are used to purchase another contract on margin, and profits on this contract are applied to a third, and so on.

Investment The commitment of current funds in anticipation of the receipt of an increased return of funds at some point in the future.

Investment banker One who is primarily involved in the distribution of securities from the issuing corporation to the public. An investment banker also advises corporate clients on their financial strategy and may help to arrange mergers and acquisitions.

Investment banking The underwriting and distribution of a new securities issue in the primary market. The investment banker advises the issuing concern on price and other terms and normally guarantees sale, while overseeing distribution of the securities through the selling brokerage houses.

Investment companies A type of financial institution that takes proceeds of individual investors and reinvests them in securities according to their specific objectives. A popular

type of investment company is the mutual fund.

Irrevocable trust The creator may not dissolve the trust and take back the property.

Jensen Measure of Portfolio Performance Jensen compares excess returns (total portfolio returns minus the risk-free rate) to what should be required in the market based on the portfolio beta. For example, if the portfolio beta is one, the portfolio has a systematic risk equal to the market, and the expected portfolio excess returns should be equal to market excess returns (the market rate of return minus the risk-free rate). The question then becomes, did the portfolio manager do better or worse than what is expected? The portfolio manager's excess returns can be compared to the market line of expected excess returns for any beta level.

Junk bonds High risk, low-grade bonds. They often perform like common stock and may provide interesting investment opportunities.

K_e The term representing anticipated rate of return equal to dividend yield plus expected growth in earnings and dividends. It is the discount rate applied to future dividends.

Keogh plan A retirement plan for self-employed individuals. The current rules permit 25 percent of annual earned income up to a maximum of $30,000 to be deducted from taxable income and to earn returns on a nontaxable basis until paid out at retirement. The funds may be invested in stocks, bonds, etc. Effectively, the maximum allowable deduction is closer to 20 percent because the contribution to the plan must be deducted from gross income to determine the base against which the 25 percent can be applied.

Key indicators Various market observations used by technical analysts to predict the directions of future market trends. Examples include the contrary opinion and smart money rules.

Least squares trendline A statistically developed linear trendline that minimizes the distance of the individual observations from the line.

Less developed countries Foreign countries that have not fully developed their economic system and productive capacity. Examples might include Chile, Jordan, Korea, Thailand, and Zimbabwe. A number of these less developed countries may represent good risk-reduction potential for U.S. investors because the factors that influence their economic welfare may be quite different from critical factors in the United States. Investments in these countries, at times, may also provide high returns.

LIFO A method of inventory valuation in which it is assumed that inventory purchased last is sold first (last-in, first-out).

Limit order A condition placed on a transaction executed through a stockbroker to assure that securities will be sold only if a specified minimum price is received, or purchased only if the price to be paid is no more than a given maximum.

Limited partnership A business arrangement in which there is the limited liability protection of a corporation with the tax provisions of a regular partnership. All profits or losses are directly assigned to the partners for tax purposes. The general partner has unlimited liability.

Lipper Mutual Fund Investment Performance Averages Lipper publishes indexes for growth funds, growth-with-income funds, and balanced funds. Lipper also shows year-to-date and weekly performance for many other categories of funds.

Liquidity The capacity of an investment to be retired for cash in a short period of time with a minimum capital loss.

Liquidity preference theory A theory related to the term structure of interest rates. The theory states that the term structure tends to be upward sloping more than any other pattern. This reflects a recognition of the fact that long maturity obligations are sub-

ject to greater price change movements than short maturity obligations when interest rates change. Because of increased risk of holding longer-term maturities, investors demand a higher return to hold such securities. Thus they have a preference for short-term liquid obligations.

Liquidity ratios Ratios that demonstrate the firm's ability to pay off short-term obligations as they come due.

Living trust (Inter vivos) A trust that is established during the lifetime of the creator.

Long position A market transaction in which an investor purchases securities with the expectation of holding the securities for cash income or for resale at a higher price in the future. See also **Short position.**

Long-term gain and losses Gains and losses on securities held over six months. The capital gains tax rate applied to long-term transactions is 40 percent of that for short-term transactions.

Lorie and Fisher study A University of Chicago study indicating comparative returns on financial assets over half a decade. It is similar to the Ibbotson and Sinquefield study in many respects.

Margin account A trading account maintained with a brokerage firm on which the investor may borrow a percentage of the funds for the purchase of securities. The broker loans the fund at interest slightly above the prime rate.

Margin maintenance requirement The amount of money that must be "deposited" to hold a margin position if losses reduce the initial margin that was put up.

Margin requirements The amount of money that must be "deposited" to purchase a commodity contract or shares of stock on margin.

Marital deduction The avoidance of any immediate tax consequence in passing an estate from one spouse to another.

Market A mechanism for facilitating the exchange of assets through buyer-seller communication. The communication, and not a central negotiating location, is the requisite condition for a market to exist, though some transactions (e.g., trades at the various stock exchanges) do involve a direct meeting of buyers and sellers or their agents.

Market capitalization The total market value of the firm. It is computed by multiplying shares outstanding times stock price.

Market line On a graph, excess returns are shown on the vertical axis and the portfolio beta is shown on the horizontal axis and the market line describes the relationship between the two.

Market rate of interest The coupon rate of interest paid on bonds currently issued. Of course, a previously issued bond which is currently traded may be sold at a discount or a premium so that the buyer in effect receives the market rate even if the coupon rate on this older bond is substantially higher or lower than market rates. The market rate is also known as the yield to maturity.

Market segmentation theory A theory related to the term structure of interest rates that focuses on the demand side of the market. There are several large institutional participants in the bond market, each with its own maturity preferences. Banks tend to prefer short-term liquid securities to match the nature of their deposits, whereas life insurance companies prefer long-term bonds to match their long-run obligations. The behavior of these two institutions and of savings and loans often creates pressure on short-term or long-term rates but very little on the intermediate market of five- to seven-year maturities. This theory helps to focus on the accumulation or liquidation of securities by institutions during the different phases of the business cycle and the resultant impact on the yield curve.

Maturity date The date at which outstanding principal must be repaid to bondholders.

Merger price premium The difference between the offering price per share and the market price per share of the merger candidate (before the impact of the offer).

Monetarist An economic analyst who feels that monetary policy tools, and not fiscal policy, can best provide a stable environment of sustained economic growth.

Monetary policy Direct control of interest rates or the money supply undertaken by the Federal Reserve to achieve economic objectives. Used in some cases to augment or offset the use of fiscal policy.

Money market account Accounts offered by financial institutions to compete with money market funds. The minimum deposit is $1,000, with a maximum of three checks drawn per month.

Money market fund A type of mutual fund which invests in short-term government securities, commercial paper, and repurchase agreements. Most offer check-writing privileges in minimums of $500.

Money supply The level of funds available at a given time for conducting transactions in our economy. The Federal Reserve can influence the money supply through its monetary policy tools. There are many different definitions of the money supply. For example, M1 is currency in circulation plus private checking deposits, including those in interest-bearing NOW accounts. M2 adds in savings accounts and money market mutual funds and so on.

Mortgage trust A form of REIT in which long-term loans are made to real estate investors.

Multinational corporations Firms that have operations in a number of foreign countries. Though precise definitions are difficult, a true multinational will probably operate in at least five different countries, with foreign sales equal to at least 40 to 50 percent of total sales. Multinationals are frequently found in such industries as oil, mainframe computers, and banking.

Municipal bonds Tax-exempt debt securities issued by state and local governments (including special political subdivisions).

Mutual fund A type of investment company that pools funds from investors and reinvests them. It is thought of as an open-end investment company because new shares can be sold to investors.

Mutual fund cash position An overall market rule which asserts that by examining the level of uncommitted funds held by large institutional investors, analysts can measure the potential demand for stocks and thereby anticipate market movements.

NASDAQ OTC Indexes Index measures for components of the over-the-counter market. The OTC Indexes are value-weighted.

National Association of Securities Dealers Automated Quotations System (NASDAQ) A computerized system that provides up-to-the-minute price quotations on over 4,000 of the more actively traded OTC stocks.

Net asset value A term often used in reference to the price of a share of a mutual fund. It is equal to the market value of the portfolio minus liabilities divided by the total number of shares outstanding in the fund.

Net debtor-creditor hypothesis Since inflation makes each dollar worth less, it is often argued that a person or firm that is a net debtor gains from inflation because payments of interest and return of principal are made with continually less valuable dollars. Conversely, a net creditor loses real capital because the loans are repaid in less valuable dollars.

Net working capital Current assets minus current liabilities.

New York Stock Exchange Index A market value-weighted measure of stock market changes for all stocks listed on the NYSE.

No-load mutual fund A mutual fund on which no sales commission must be paid. The funds' shares are sold, not through brokers but rather through the mail or other direct channels.

Nominal GNP Gross national product expressed in current, noninflation adjusted dollars.

Nominal return A return that has not been adjusted for inflation.

Nonconstant growth model A dividend valuation model that does not assume a constant growth rate for dividends.

Noncontributory pension plan An arrangement in which only the employer contributes to the pension plan. It is noncontributory for the employee.

Odd-lot dealer A member of a stock exchange who maintains an inventory of a particular firm's stock in order to sell odd lots (trades of less than 100 shares) to customers of the exchange.

Odd-lot theory The contrary opinion rule stating that small traders (who generally buy or sell odd lots) often misjudge market trends, selling just before upturns and buying before downturns. The theory has not been useful in predicting trends observed in recent years.

One hundred seventy-five percent declining-balance depreciation An accelerated depreciation method which represents the most rapid write-off of depreciation allowable on real estate (over 18 years) under the 1981 Economic Recovery Tax Act. In the IRS tables there is also an assumed shift to straight-line in the mid-life of the asset.

Open-end fund An investment company without a specified number of shares for trading; new shares can be created for new investors. It is called a mutual fund. See **Closed-end fund.**

Open-market operations The Federal Reserve's action of buying or selling government securities in order to expand or contract the amount of money in the economy.

Opening purchase transaction A transaction in which an investor intends to become the holder of an option.

Opening sale transaction A transaction in which an investor intends to be a writer of an option.

Operating margin Operating income divided by sales.

Option The right acquired for a consideration

to buy or sell something at a fixed price within a specified period of time.

Option premium The intrinsic value plus a speculative premium.

Option price The specified price at which the holder of a warrant may buy the shares to which the warrant entitles purchase.

Options Clearing Corporation Issues all options listed on the exchanges which trade in options.

Options on industry indexes An option index contract specifically tailored to a given industry. Thus, one who wishes to speculate on a given industry's performance or hedge against holdings in that industry can use industry index options (subindexes). Contracts apply to the S&P Computer and Business Equipment Index, the S&P Integrated International Oil Index, the S&P Transportation Index, and to many other industries.

Options on stock index futures An *option* to purchase a stock index *futures* contract at a specified price over a given time period. This security combines the options concept with the futures concept.

Organized exchanges Institutions, such as the New York Stock Exchange, the American Stock Exchange, or any of the smaller regional exchanges, that provide a central location for the buying and selling of securities.

OTC National Market System A segment of the OTC stock market made up of stocks that have a diversified geographical stockholder base and relatively large activity in their securities. Stocks in the National Market system receive enhanced market activity reporting through the NASDAQ system.

Overall market rules Guidelines, such as breadth of market indicators or mutual fund cash positions, used by technical analysts who predict stock market activity based on past activity.

Over-the-counter market Not a specific location but rather a communications network through which trades of bonds, nonlisted stocks, and other securities take place. Trad-

ing activity is overseen by the National Association of Securities Dealers (NASD).

Par bonds Bonds that are selling at their par or maturity values rather than at premium or discounted prices. Par value on a corporate bond is generally $1,000.

Par value (bond) The face value of a bond, generally $1,000 for corporate issues, higher denominations for government issues.

Partial hedge A hedge position in which only part of the risk is eliminated or lessened.

Payout ratio Annual dividends per share divided by annual earnings per share.

Peak The point in an economic cycle at which expansion ends and a recession begins.

Perpetual bond A bond with no maturity date.

Personal savings/personal disposable income The rate at which people are saving their disposable income. This has implications for the generation of funds to modernize plant and equipment and increase productivity.

Portfolio The term applied to a collection of securities or investments.

Portfolio effect The effect obtained when assets are combined into a portfolio. The interaction of the assets can provide risk reduction such that the portfolio standard deviation may be less than the standard deviation of any one asset in it.

Portfolio manager One who has responsibility for managing large pools of funds. Portfolio managers may be employed by insurance companies, mutual funds, bank trust departments, pension funds, and other institutional investors.

Preferred stock A hybrid security that generally provides fixed returns. Preferred stockholders are paid returns after bondholder claims are satisfied but before any returns are paid to common stockholders. Though preferred stock returns are fixed in amount, they are classified as dividends (not interest) and are not tax-deductible to the issuing firm.

Price/earnings ratio The multiplier applied to earnings per share to determine current value. The P/E ratio is influenced by the earnings and sales growth of the firm, the risk or volatility of its performance, the debt-equity structure, and other factors.

Price ratios Ratios that relate the internal performance of the firm to the external judgment of the marketplace in terms of value.

Price-weighted average Each stock in the average is weighted by its price. The higher the price, the greater the relative weighting. The Dow Jones Industrials Average represents a price-weighted average.

Primary earnings per share A firm's adjusted earnings after taxes divided by the number of shares of common stock outstanding plus common stock equivalents. Common stock equivalents include warrants and other options along with convertible securities that are paying low returns at time of issue compared to other comparable securities.

Primary market A market in which an investor purchases an asset (via an investment banker) from the issuer of that asset. The purchase of newly issued shares of corporate stock is an example of primary market activity. Subsequent transfers of the particular asset take place in the secondary market. Also see the definition for **Secondary market.**

Private pension plans Nongovernment-sponsored pension plans. About 60 percent of nongovernmental employees are covered by a private pension plan.

Private placement The company sells its securities to private investors such as insurance companies, pension funds, etc. rather than through the public markets. Investment bankers may also aid in a private placement on a fee basis. Most private placements involve debt rather than common stock.

Profitability ratios Ratios that allow the analyst to measure the ability of the firm to earn an adequate return on sales, total assets, and invested capital.

Prospectus A document that must accompany a new issue of securities. It contains the same information appearing in the registration statement, such as a list of directors and officers, financial reports certified by a CPA, the underwriters, the purpose and use for the funds, and other reasonable information that investors need to know.

Public placement Public distribution of securities through the financial markets.

Pure bond value The fundamental value of a bond that represents a floor price below which the bond's value should not fall. The pure bond value is computed as the present value of all future interest payments added to the present value of the bond principal.

Pure pickup yield swap A bond swap where a bond owner thinks that he or she can increase the yield to maturity by selling a bond and buying a different bond of equal risk. This implies market disequilibrium.

Put An option to sell 100 shares of common stock at a specified price for a given period of time.

Qualified pension plan Under the provisions of the Internal Revenue Service, a qualified pension plan allows the employer to deduct annual contributions to the pension plan as a tax-deductible item. From the employees' perspective, a qualified plan allows funds in the plan to earn income without immediate taxation, and no tax is paid on the employer's contribution until benefits are received. A qualified pension plan must meet the appropriate requirements established under ERISA.

Quick ratio Current assets minus inventory (i.e., cash, marketable securities, and accounts receivables) divided by current liabilities.

R^2 The coefficient of determination. It measures the degree of association between the independent variable(s) and the dependent variable. It may take on a value anywhere between 0 and 1.

Real asset A tangible piece of property that may be seen, felt, held, or collected, such as real estate, gold, diamonds, etc.

Real estate investment trust (REIT) An organization similar to a mutual fund where investors pool funds that are invested in real estate or used to make construction or mortgage loans.

Real GNP Gross national product expressed in dollars that have been adjusted for inflation.

Real rate of return The return that investors require for allowing others to use their money for a given time period. This is the value that investors demand for passing up immediate consumption and allowing others to use their savings until the funds are returned. Because the term *real* is employed, this means it is a value determined *before* inflation is added.

Recaptured depreciation When accelerated depreciation is taken and then the property is sold, part of the profit may be considered recaptured depreciation for tax purposes. It is taxed as ordinary income.

Registered trader A member of a stock exchange who trades for his or her own account rather than for the client of a brokerage firm.

Reinvestment assumption with bonds The assumed rate of reinvestment for inflows from a bond investment. It is normally assumed that inflows can be reinvested at the yield to maturity of the bond. This, however, may not be valid. Interest rates may go up or down as inflows from coupon payments come in and need to be reinvested. A more valid approach is to assign appropriate reinvestment rates to inflows and then determine how much the total investment will be worth at the end of a given time period. This process is known as terminal wealth analysis.

Reported income versus adjusted earnings Reported income is generally based on historical cost accounting, whereas adjusted earnings have been modified for the effect of inflation (on inventory and plant and equipment).

Reserve requirements Percentages of bank deposit balances stipulated by the Federal Reserve as unavailable for lending. By increasing or reducing reserve requirements, the Fed can contract or expand the money supply.

Resistance level The technical analyst's view that as long as a given long-term trend continues, prices of a particular stock or of the market as a whole will not rise above the upper end of the normal trading range (the resistance level) because at that point investors sell in an attempt to get even or take a profit.

Return on equity Net income divided by stockholders' equity.

Revenue bond A municipal bond supported by the revenue from a specific project, such as a toll road, bridge, or municipal colosseum.

Revocable trust The creator may eventually dissolve the trust and take back the property.

Risk Uncertainty concerning the outcome of an investment or other situation. It is often defined as variability of returns from an investment. The greater the range of possible outcomes, the greater the risk.

Risk-adjusted return The amount of return after adjustment for the level of risk incurred to achieve the return.

Risk-free rate The required rate of return before risk is explicitly considered. It is composed of the real rate of return plus a rate equivalent to inflationary expectations. It is referred to as R_F.

Risk premium A premium assumed to be paid to an investor for the risk inherent in an investment. It is added to the risk-free rate to get the overall required return on an investment.

Secondary market A market in which an investor purchases an asset from another investor rather than the issuing corporation. The activity of secondary markets sets prices and provides liquidity. Also see **Primary market.**

Secured bond A bond which is collateralized by the pledging of assets.

Securities Act of 1933 Enacted by Congress to curtail abuses by securities issuers, the law requires full disclosure of pertinent investment information and provides for penalties to officers of firms that do not comply.

Securities Acts Amendments of 1975 Enacted to increase competition in the securities markets, this legislation prohibits fixed commissions on public offerings of securities and directs the Securities and Exchange Commission to develop a single, nationwide securities market.

Securities and Exchange Commission (SEC) The federal government agency created in 1934 to enforce securities laws. Issuers of securities must register detailed reports with the SEC, and the SEC polices such activities as insider trading, investor conspiracies, and the functionings of the securities exchanges.

Securities Exchange Act of 1934 Created the Securities and Exchange Commission to regulate the securities markets. The act further empowers the Board of Governors of the Federal Reserve System to control margin requirements.

Securities Investor Protection Corporation Created under the Securities Investor Protection Act of 1970, this agency oversees the liquidation of insolvent brokerage firms and provides insurance on investors' trading accounts.

Security analyst One who studies various industries and companies and provides research reports and valuation studies.

Security market line The graphic representation of risk (as measured by beta) and return for an individual security.

Selling short against the box A short sale of securities with the objective of deferring the payment of taxes. This requires a short sale against shares already owned so that shares owned are delivered to cover the short position as the transaction is completed.

Semi-strong form of efficient market hypothesis The hypothesis states that all public information is already impounded into the value of a security.

Serial bond A mechanism for repaying funds advanced through a bond issue. Regular payments systematically retire individual bonds with increasing maturities until, after many years, the entire series has been repaid.

Settle price The term for the closing price on futures contracts.

Shared appreciation mortgage A type of mortgage in which the lender participates in any increase in value associated with the property being mortgaged.

Sharpe Measure of Portfolio Performance Total portfolio return minus the risk-free rate divided by the portfolio standard deviation. It allows the portfolio manager to view his or her excess returns in relation to total risk. Comparisons between various portfolios can be made based on this relative risk measure.

Short position (short sale) A market transaction in which an investor sells borrowed securities in anticipation of a price decline. The investor's expectation is that the securities can be repurchased (to replace the borrowed shares) at a lower price in the future. Also see the definition for **Long position.**

Short sales position theory The contrary opinion rule stating that large volumes of short sales can signal an impending market upturn because short sales must be covered and thereby create their own demand. Also, the average short seller is often thought to be wrong.

Short-term gains and losses Gains and losses on securities held for six months or less. The stockholders' ordinary marginal tax rate applies.

Sinking fund A mechanism for repaying funds advanced through a bond issue. The issuer makes periodic payments to the trustee, who retires part of the issue by purchasing the bonds in the open market.

Small-firm effect A market theory that suggests that small firms produce superior returns compared to larger firms on both an absolute and risk-adjusted basis.

Smart money rules Guidelines, such as *Barron's* Confidence Index, used by technical analysts who predict stock market activity based on the assumption that sophisticated investors will correctly predict market trends and that their lead should be followed. Also see **Contrary opinion rules.**

Sources-and-uses-of-funds statement A

presentation of how changes in the balance sheet were financed over a period of time. Sources of funds include increases in stockholders' equity, decreases in assets, and increases in liabilities. Uses are represented by decreases in stockholders' equity, increases in assets, and decreases in liabilities.

Specialist or dealer hedge A specialist on an exchange or dealer in the over-the-counter market buys and sells stocks for his own inventory for temporary holding (as part of his market making function). At times, he may assume a larger temporary holding than desired with all the risks associated with that exposure. Stock index futures or options can reduce the market, or systematic, risk, although they cannot reduce the specific risk associated with a security.

Speculative premium The difference between an option or warrant's price and its intrinsic value. That an investor would pay something in excess of the intrinsic value indicates a speculative desire to hold the security in anticipation of future increases in the price of the underlying stock.

Spot market The term applied to the cash price for immediate transfer of a commodity as opposed to the futures market where no physical transfer takes place immediately.

Spreads A combination of options which consists of buying one option (going long) and writing an option (going short) on the same stock.

Standard & Poor's 500 Stock Index An index of 500 major U.S. Corporations. There are 400 industrial firms, 20 transportation firms, 40 utilities, and 40 financial firms. This index is value-weighted.

Standard & Poor's 400 Industrial Index An index which measures price movements in the stocks of 400 large industrial corporations listed on the New York Stock Exchange.

Standard & Poor's International Oil Index A value-weighted index of six oil firms. Options on the index have been traded on the Chicago Board Options Exchange.

Standard deviation A measure of dispersion that considers the spread of outcomes around the expected value.

Stock dividend A dividend paid by issuing more stock which results in retained earnings being capitalized.

Stock index futures A futures contract on a specific stock index, such as the Standard & Poor's 500 Stock Index or the NYSE Composite Index.

Stock index options An option contract to purchase (call) or sell (put) a stock index. Popular contracts include the S&P 100 Index, the American Exchange Major Market Index, and others. The purchaser of a stock index option pays an initial premium and then closes out the option at a given price in the future.

Stock repurchase A purchase by a firm of its own shares in the marketplace.

Stock split The result of a firm dividing its shares into more shares with a corresponding decrease in par value.

Stop order A mechanism for locking in gains or limiting losses on securities transactions. The investor is not assured of paying or receiving a particular price but rather agrees to accept the price prevailing when the broker is able to execute the order after prices have reached some predetermined figure.

Straddle A combination of a put and call on the same stock with the same strike price and expiration date.

Straight-line depreciation A method of depreciation in which the project cost is divided by the project life to calculate each year's depreciation amount.

Strong form of the efficient market hypothesis A hypothesis that says that all information, insider as well as public, is reflected in the price of a security.

Support level The technical analyst's view that as long as a given long-term trend continues, prices of a particular stock or of the market as a whole will not fall below the lower end of normal trading range (the support level) because at that point low prices stimulate demand.

Swaps The procedure of selling out of a given bond position and immediately buying into another one with similar attributes in an attempt to improve overall portfolio return or performance.

Syndicate A group of investment bankers which jointly shares the underwriting and distribution responsibilities in a large offering of new securities. Each participant is responsible for a predetermined sales volume. One or a few firms serve as the managing underwriters.

Synergy A more than proportionate increase in performance from the combination of two or more parts.

Systematic risk Risk inherent in an investment related to movements in the market that cannot be diversified away.

Tax hedge An investor may have accumulated a large return on a diversified portfolio in a given year. In order to maintain the profitable position, but defer the taxable gains until the next year, stock index future or options contracts may be employed. Of course, for individual securities, individual stock options may be used when available.

Tax swaps Selling out of one bond position and buying into a similar one in order to take advantage of a tax situation. For example, one might sell a bond that has a short-term capital loss in order to take the deduction, and replace it with a similar bond.

Technical analysis An analysis of price and volume data as well as other related market indicators to determine past trends that are believed to be predictable into the future. Charts and graphs are often utilized.

Term structure of interest rates This depicts the relationship between maturity and interest rates for a 20- to 25-year time horizon.

Terminal wealth table A table that indicates the ending or terminal wealth from a bond investment based on the reinvestment of the inflows at a specified rate (which may be different from the coupon rate). The initial in-

vestment can then be compared to the terminal wealth (compound interest plus principal) and an overall rate of return computed.

Testamentary trust A trust created by a will.

Third market The trading between dealers and institutional investors, through the over-the-counter market, of NYSE-listed stocks. The third market accounts for an extremely small share of total trading activity.

Trading range The spread of prices that a stock normally sells within.

Treasury bill A short-term U.S. government obligation. A Treasury bill is purchased at a discount and is negotiable.

Treasury bond A long-term (7 to 25 years) U.S. government bond.

Treasury note An intermediate-term (one to seven years) U.S. government bond.

Treasury stock Stock issued but not outstanding by virtue of being held (after it is repurchased) by the firm.

Trend analysis Comparative analysis of performance over time.

Treynor Measure of Portfolio Performance Total portfolio return minus the risk-free rate divided by the portfolio beta. Unlike the Sharpe Measure, which uses the portfolio standard deviation in the denominator, the risk measure here is the beta, or systematic risk. It enables the portfolio manager to view his or her excess returns in relation to non-diversifiable risk. The assumption is that all other types of risk have been diversified away. Once computed, the Treynor Measure allows for comparisons between different portfolios.

Trough The point in an economic cycle at which recession ends and expansion begins.

Trust A legal entity in which transfer of ownership of property from an original owner (the creator of the trust) to another person (the trustee) takes place for the benefit of someone else (the beneficiary).

Underpricing In selling formerly privately held shares to new investors in the over-the-counter market, the price might not fully reflect the value of the issue. Underpricing is used to attempt to ensure the success of the initial distribution.

Underwriter hedge A hedge, based on stock index futures or options contracts, used to offset the risk exposure associated with the underwriting of new securities by an investment banker. If the market goes down, presumably the loss on the stock being underwritten will be compensated for by the gain on the stock index futures or option contract as a result of being able to repurchase it at a lower price. This, of course, is not a perfect hedge. It is possible that the stock could go down while the market is going up, and losses on both the stock and stock index contract would take place (writing options directly against the stock may be more efficient, but in many cases such options are not available).

Unfriendly takeover A merger or acquisition in which the firm acquired does not wish to be acquired.

Unfunded pension plan Payments to retirees are made out of current income and not out of prior funding.

Unified tax credit A credit against the estate and gift tax. Under the 1981 Economic Recovery Tax Act, the credit goes from $47,000 in 1981 to $192,800 in 1987. In 1987, this will provide an equivalent exemption of $600,000 for estate taxes.

Unified tax rate schedule The schedule applied to estate and gift taxes on a unified basis.

Unseasoned issue An issue that has not been formerly traded in the public markets.

Unsystematic risk Risk of an investment that is random in nature. It is not related to general market movements. It may represent the temporary influence of a competitor's new product, changes in raw material prices, or unusual economic or government influences on a firm. It may generally be diversified away.

Valuation The process of attributing a value to a security based on expectations of the future performance of the issuing concern, the relevant industry, and the economy as a whole.

Valuation model A representation of the components that provide the value of an investment, such as a dividend valuation model used to show the value of a common stock.

Value Line Index The index represents 1,700 companies from the New York and American Stock Exchanges and the over-the-counter market. Many individual investors use the Value Line Index because it more closely corresponds to the variety of stocks the average investor may have in his or her portfolio. It is an equal-weighted index, which means that each of the 1,700 stocks, regardless of market price, or total market value, is weighted equally.

Value-weighted index Each company in the index is weighted by its own total market value as a percentage of the total market value for all firms in the index. Most major indexes, such as the S&P 500, S&P 400, the NYSE Index, and the American Exchange Market Value Index, are value-weighted. With value-weighted indexes, large firms tend to be weighted more heavily than smaller firms.

Variability The possible different outcomes of an event. As an example, an investment with many possible different levels of return would have great variability.

Variable rate mortgage A mortgage in which the interest rate is adjusted regularly.

Vertical spread Buying and writing two contracts at different striking prices with the same month of expiration.

Vesting A legal term meaning that pension benefits or rights cannot be taken away.

Warrant A right or option to buy a stated number of shares of stock at a specified price over a given time period. It is usually of longer duration than a call option.

Warrant break-even The price movement in the underlying stock necessary for the warrant purchaser to break-even, that is, recover the initial purchase price of the warrant.

Weak form of efficient market hypothesis A hypothesis suggesting there is no relationship between past and future prices of securities.

White knight A firm that "rescues" another firm from an unfriendly takeover by a third firm.

Wiesenberger Financial Services An advisory service that provides important information on mutual funds.

Wilshire 5,000 Equity Index A stock market measure comprising 5,000 equity securities. It includes all New York Stock Exchange and American Stock Exchange issues and the most active over-the-counter issues. The index represents the *total dollar value* of all 5,000 stocks. By measuring total dollar value, it is, in effect, a value-weighted measure.

World Index A value-weighted index of the performance in 19 major countries as compiled by Capital International, S.A., of Geneva, Switzerland. The United States alone makes up approximately 50 percent of the index because it is value-weighted by market size.

Yield curve A curve that shows interest rates at a specific point in time for all securities having equal risk but different maturity dates. Usually, government securities are used to construct such curves. The yield curve is also referred to as the term structure of interest rates.

Yield spread The difference between the yields received on two different types of bonds, or bonds with different ratings. It is important to investment strategy because during periods of economic uncertainty, spreads increase because investors demand larger premiums on risky issues to compensate for the greater chance of default.

Yield to call The interest yield that will be realized on a callable bond if it is held from a given purchase date until the date when it can be called by the issuer. The yield to call reflects the fact that lower overall returns may be realized if the issuer avoids some later payments by retiring the bonds early.

Yield to maturity The annualized rate of return that an investor will receive if a bond is held until its maturity date. It is the market rate of return. The yield-to-maturity formula includes any capital gains or losses that arise because the par value is greater or less than the current market price.

Ying, Lewellen, Schlarbaum, and Lease study A research study that indicates there may be an opportunity for abnormal returns on a risk-adjusted basis in the many weeks between announcement of listing and actual listing of a security.

Zero-coupon bonds Bonds that are designed to pay no interest, in which the return to the investor is in the form of capital appreciation over the life of the issue.

APPENDIXES

APPENDIX A

Compound sum of $1

Period	1%	2%	3%	4%	5%	6%	7%	8%	9%	10%	11%
1	1.010	1.020	1.030	1.040	1.050	1.060	1.070	1.080	1.090	1.100	1.110
2	1.020	1.040	1.061	1.082	1.103	1.124	1.145	1.166	1.188	1.210	1.232
3	1.030	1.061	1.093	1.125	1.158	1.191	1.225	1.260	1.295	1.331	1.368
4	1.041	1.082	1.126	1.170	1.216	1.262	1.311	1.360	1.412	1.464	1.518
5	1.051	1.104	1.159	1.217	1.276	1.338	1.403	1.469	1.539	1.611	1.685
6	1.062	1.126	1.194	1.265	1.340	1.419	1.501	1.587	1.677	1.772	1.870
7	1.072	1.149	1.230	1.316	1.407	1.504	1.606	1.714	1.828	1.949	2.076
8	1.083	1.172	1.267	1.369	1.477	1.594	1.718	1.851	1.993	2.144	2.305
9	1.094	1.195	1.305	1.423	1.551	1.689	1.838	1.999	2.172	2.358	2.558
10	1.105	1.219	1.344	1.480	1.629	1.791	1.967	2.159	2.367	2.594	2.839
11	1.116	1.243	1.384	1.539	1.710	1.898	2.105	2.332	2.580	2.853	3.152
12	1.127	1.268	1.426	1.601	1.796	2.012	2.252	2.518	2.813	3.138	3.498
13	1.138	1.294	1.469	1.665	1.886	2.133	2.410	2.720	3.066	3.452	3.883
14	1.149	1.319	1.513	1.732	1.980	2.261	2.579	2.937	3.342	3.797	4.310
15	1.161	1.346	1.558	1.801	2.079	2.397	2.759	3.172	3.642	4.177	4.785
16	1.173	1.373	1.605	1.873	2.183	2.540	2.952	3.426	3.970	4.595	5.311
17	1.184	1.400	1.653	1.948	2.292	2.693	3.159	3.700	4.328	5.054	5.895
18	1.196	1.428	1.702	2.206	2.407	2.854	3.380	3.996	4.717	5.560	6.544
19	1.208	1.457	1.754	2.107	2.527	3.026	3.617	4.316	5.142	6.116	7.263
20	1.220	1.486	1.806	2.191	2.653	3.207	3.870	4.661	5.604	6.727	8.062
25	1.282	1.641	2.094	2.666	3.386	4.292	5.427	6.848	8.623	10.835	13.585
30	1.348	1.811	2.427	3.243	4.322	5.743	7.612	10.063	13.268	17.449	22.892
40	1.489	2.208	3.262	4.801	7.040	10.286	14.974	21.725	31.409	45.259	65.001
50	1.645	2.692	4.384	7.107	11.467	18.420	29.457	46.902	74.358	117.39	184.57

Percent

APPENDIX A (concluded)

Compound sum of $1

Percent

Period	12%	13%	14%	15%	16%	17%	18%	19%	20%	25%	30%
1	1.120	1.130	1.140	1.150	1.160	1.170	1.180	1.190	1.200	1.250	1.300
2	1.254	1.277	1.300	1.323	1.346	1.369	1.392	1.416	1.440	1.563	1.690
3	1.405	1.443	1.482	1.521	1.561	1.602	1.643	1.685	1.728	1.953	2.197
4	1.574	1.630	1.689	1.749	1.811	1.874	1.939	2.005	2.074	2.441	2.856
5	1.762	1.842	1.925	2.011	2.100	2.192	2.288	2.386	2.488	3.052	3.713
6	1.974	2.082	2.195	2.313	2.436	2.565	2.700	2.840	2.986	3.815	4.827
7	2.211	2.353	2.502	2.660	2.826	3.001	3.185	3.379	3.583	4.768	6.276
8	2.476	2.658	2.853	3.059	3.278	3.511	3.759	4.021	4.300	5.960	8.157
9	2.773	3.004	3.252	3.518	3.803	4.108	4.435	4.785	5.160	7.451	10.604
10	3.106	3.395	3.707	4.046	4.411	4.807	5.234	5.696	6.192	9.313	13.786
11	3.479	3.836	4.226	4.652	5.117	5.624	6.176	6.777	7.430	11.642	17.922
12	3.896	4.335	4.818	5.350	5.936	6.580	7.288	8.064	8.916	14.552	23.298
13	4.363	4.898	5.492	6.153	6.886	7.699	8.599	9.596	10.699	18.190	30.288
14	4.887	5.535	6.261	7.076	7.988	9.007	10.147	11.420	12.839	22.737	39.374
15	5.474	6.254	7.138	8.137	9.266	10.539	11.974	13.590	15.407	28.422	51.186
16	6.130	7.067	8.137	9.358	10.748	12.330	14.129	16.172	18.488	35.527	66.542
17	6.866	7.986	9.276	10.761	12.468	14.426	16.672	19.244	22.186	44.409	86.504
18	7.690	9.024	10.575	12.375	14.463	16.879	19.673	22.091	26.623	55.511	112.46
19	8.613	10.197	12.056	14.232	16.777	19.748	23.214	27.252	31.948	69.389	146.19
20	9.646	11.523	13.743	16.367	19.461	23.106	27.393	32.429	38.338	86.736	190.05
25	17.000	21.231	26.462	32.919	40.874	50.658	62.669	77.388	95.396	264.70	705.64
30	29.960	39.116	50.950	66.212	85.850	111.07	143.37	184.68	237.38	807.79	2,620.0
40	93.051	132.78	188.88	267.86	378.72	533.87	750.38	1,051.7	1,469.8	7,523.2	36,119.
50	289.00	450.74	700.23	1,083.7	1,670.7	2,566.2	3,927.4	5,988.9	9,100.4	70,065.	497,929.

Source: Maurice Joy, *Introduction to Financial Management* (Homewood, Ill.: Richard D. Irwin, Inc. 1977).

Present value of $1

Period	1%	2%	3%	4%	5%	6%	7%	8%	9%	10%	11%	12%
1	0.990	0.980	0.971	0.962	0.952	0.943	0.935	0.926	0.917	0.909	0.901	0.893
2	0.980	0.961	0.943	0.925	0.907	0.890	0.873	0.857	0.842	0.826	0.812	0.797
3	0.971	0.942	0.915	0.889	0.864	0.840	0.816	0.794	0.772	0.751	0.731	0.712
4	0.961	0.924	0.885	0.855	0.823	0.792	0.763	0.735	0.708	0.683	0.659	0.636
5	0.951	0.906	0.863	0.822	0.784	0.747	0.713	0.681	0.650	0.621	0.593	0.567
6	0.942	0.888	0.837	0.790	0.746	0.705	0.666	0.630	0.596	0.564	0.535	0.507
7	0.933	0.871	0.813	0.760	0.711	0.665	0.623	0.583	0.547	0.513	0.482	0.452
8	0.923	0.853	0.789	0.731	0.677	0.627	0.582	0.540	0.502	0.467	0.434	0.404
9	0.914	0.837	0.766	0.703	0.645	0.592	0.544	0.500	0.460	0.424	0.391	0.361
10	0.905	0.820	0.744	0.676	0.614	0.558	0.508	0.463	0.422	0.386	0.352	0.322
11	0.896	0.804	0.722	0.650	0.585	0.527	0.475	0.429	0.388	0.350	0.317	0.287
12	0.887	0.788	0.701	0.625	0.557	0.497	0.444	0.397	0.356	0.319	0.286	0.257
13	0.879	0.773	0.681	0.601	0.530	0.469	0.415	0.368	0.326	0.290	0.258	0.229
14	0.870	0.758	0.661	0.577	0.505	0.442	0.388	0.340	0.299	0.263	0.232	0.205
15	0.861	0.743	0.642	0.555	0.481	0.417	0.362	0.315	0.275	0.239	0.209	0.183
16	0.853	0.728	0.623	0.534	0.458	0.394	0.339	0.292	0.252	0.218	0.188	0.163
17	0.844	0.714	0.605	0.513	0.436	0.371	0.317	0.270	0.231	0.198	0.170	0.146
18	0.836	0.700	0.587	0.494	0.416	0.350	0.296	0.250	0.212	0.180	0.153	0.130
19	0.828	0.686	0.570	0.475	0.396	0.331	0.277	0.232	0.194	0.164	0.138	0.116
20	0.820	0.673	0.554	0.456	0.377	0.312	0.258	0.215	0.178	0.149	0.124	0.104
25	0.780	0.610	0.478	0.375	0.295	0.233	0.184	0.146	0.116	0.092	0.074	0.059
30	0.742	0.552	0.412	0.308	0.231	0.174	0.131	0.099	0.075	0.057	0.044	0.033
40	0.672	0.453	0.307	0.208	0.142	0.097	0.067	0.046	0.032	0.022	0.015	0.011
50	0.608	0.372	0.228	0.141	0.087	0.054	0.034	0.021	0.013	0.009	0.005	0.003

Percent

APPENDIX B (concluded)

Present value of $1

Period	13%	14%	15%	16%	17%	18%	19%	20%	25%	30%	35%	40%	50%
1	0.885	0.877	0.870	0.862	0.855	0.847	0.840	0.833	0.800	0.769	0.741	0.714	0.667
2	0.783	0.769	0.756	0.743	0.731	0.718	0.706	0.694	0.640	0.592	0.549	0.510	0.444
3	0.693	0.675	0.658	0.641	0.624	0.609	0.593	0.579	0.512	0.455	0.406	0.364	0.296
4	0.613	0.592	0.572	0.552	0.534	0.515	0.499	0.482	0.410	0.350	0.301	0.260	0.198
5	0.543	0.519	0.497	0.476	0.456	0.437	0.419	0.402	0.320	0.269	0.223	0.186	0.132
6	0.480	0.456	0.432	0.410	0.390	0.370	0.352	0.335	0.262	0.207	0.165	0.133	0.088
7	0.425	0.400	0.376	0.354	0.333	0.314	0.296	0.279	0.210	0.159	0.122	0.095	0.059
8	0.376	0.351	0.327	0.305	0.285	0.266	0.249	0.233	0.168	0.123	0.091	0.068	0.039
9	0.333	0.300	0.284	0.263	0.243	0.225	0.209	0.194	0.134	0.094	0.067	0.048	0.026
10	0.295	0.270	0.247	0.227	0.208	0.191	0.176	0.162	0.107	0.073	0.050	0.035	0.017
11	0.261	0.237	0.215	0.195	0.178	0.162	0.148	0.135	0.086	0.056	0.037	0.025	0.012
12	0.231	0.208	0.187	0.168	0.152	0.137	0.124	0.112	0.069	0.043	0.027	0.018	0.008
13	0.204	0.182	0.163	0.145	0.130	0.116	0.104	0.093	0.055	0.033	0.020	0.013	0.005
14	0.181	0.160	0.141	0.125	0.111	0.099	0.088	0.078	0.044	0.025	0.015	0.009	0.003
15	0.160	0.140	0.123	0.108	0.095	0.084	0.074	0.065	0.035	0.020	0.011	0.006	0.002
16	0.141	0.123	0.107	0.093	0.081	0.071	0.062	0.054	0.028	0.015	0.008	0.005	0.002
17	0.125	0.108	0.093	0.080	0.069	0.060	0.052	0.045	0.023	0.012	0.006	0.003	0.001
18	0.111	0.095	0.081	0.069	0.059	0.051	0.044	0.038	0.018	0.009	0.005	0.002	0.001
19	0.098	0.083	0.070	0.060	0.051	0.043	0.037	0.031	0.014	0.007	0.003	0.002	0
20	0.087	0.073	0.061	0.051	0.043	0.037	0.031	0.026	0.012	0.005	0.002	0.001	0
25	0.047	0.038	0.030	0.024	0.020	0.016	0.013	0.010	0.004	0.001	0.001	0	0
30	0.026	0.020	0.015	0.012	0.009	0.007	0.005	0.004	0.001	0	0	0	0
40	0.008	0.005	0.004	0.003	0.002	0.001	0.001	0.001	0	0	0	0	0
50	0.002	0.001	0.001	0.001	0	0	0	0	0	0	0	0	0

Percent

Source: Maurice Joy, *Introduction to Financial Management* (Homewood, Ill.: Richard D. Irwin, Inc. 1977).

APPENDIX C

Compound sum of an annuity of $1

Percent

Period	1%	2%	3%	4%	5%	6%	7%	8%	9%	10%	11%
1	1.000	1.000	1.000	1.000	1.000	1.000	1.000	1.000	1.000	1.000	1.000
2	2.010	2.020	2.030	2.040	2.050	2.060	2.070	2.080	2.090	2.100	2.110
3	3.030	3.060	3.091	3.122	3.153	3.184	3.215	3.246	3.278	3.310	3.342
4	4.060	4.122	4.184	4.246	4.310	4.375	4.440	4.506	4.573	4.641	4.710
5	5.101	5.204	5.309	5.416	5.526	5.637	5.751	5.867	5.985	6.105	6.228
6	6.152	6.308	6.468	6.633	6.802	6.975	7.153	7.336	7.523	7.716	7.913
7	7.214	7.434	7.662	7.898	8.142	8.394	8.654	8.923	9.200	9.487	9.783
8	8.286	8.583	8.892	9.214	9.549	9.897	10.260	10.637	11.028	11.436	11.859
9	9.369	9.755	10.159	10.583	11.027	11.491	11.978	12.488	13.021	13.579	14.164
10	10.462	10.950	11.464	12.006	12.578	13.181	13.816	14.487	15.193	15.937	16.722
11	11.567	12.169	12.808	13.486	14.207	14.972	15.784	16.645	17.560	18.531	19.561
12	12.683	13.412	14.192	15.026	15.917	16.870	17.888	18.977	20.141	21.384	22.713
13	13.809	14.680	15.618	16.627	17.713	18.882	20.141	21.495	22.953	24.523	26.212
14	14.947	15.974	17.086	18.292	19.599	21.015	22.550	24.215	26.019	27.975	30.095
15	16.097	17.293	18.599	20.024	21.579	23.276	25.129	27.152	29.361	31.772	34.405
16	17.258	18.639	20.157	21.825	23.657	25.673	27.888	30.324	33.003	35.950	39.190
17	18.430	20.012	21.762	23.698	25.840	20.213	30.840	33.750	36.974	40.545	44.501
18	19.615	21.412	23.414	25.645	28.132	30.906	33.999	37.450	41.301	45.599	50.396
19	20.811	22.841	25.117	27.671	30.539	33.760	37.379	41.446	46.018	51.159	56.939
20	22.019	24.297	26.870	29.778	33.066	36.786	40.995	45.762	51.160	57.275	64.203
25	28.243	32.030	36.459	41.646	47.727	54.865	63.249	73.106	84.701	98.347	114.41
30	34.785	40.588	47.575	56.085	66.439	79.058	94.461	113.28	136.31	164.49	199.02
40	48.886	60.402	75.401	95.026	120.80	154.76	199.64	259.06	337.89	442.59	581.83
50	64.463	84.579	112.80	152.67	209.35	290.34	406.53	573.77	815.08	1,163.9	1,668.8

APPENDIX C (concluded)

Compound sum of an annuity of $1

Period	12%	13%	14%	15%	16%	17%	18%	19%	20%	25%	30%
1	1.000	1.000	1.000	1.000	1.000	1.000	1.000	1.000	1.000	1.000	1.000
2	2.120	2.130	2.140	2.150	2.160	2.170	2.180	2.190	2.200	2.250	2.300
3	3.374	3.407	3.440	3.473	3.506	3.539	3.572	3.606	3.640	3.813	3.990
4	4.779	4.850	4.921	4.993	5.066	5.141	5.215	5.291	5.368	5.766	6.187
5	6.353	6.480	6.610	6.742	6.877	7.014	7.154	7.297	7.442	8.207	9.043
6	8.115	8.323	8.536	9.754	8.977	9.207	9.442	0.683	9.930	11.259	12.756
7	10.089	10.405	10.730	11.067	11.414	11.772	12.142	12.523	12.916	15.073	17.583
8	12.300	12.757	13.233	13.727	14.240	14.773	15.327	15.902	16.499	19.842	23.858
9	14.776	15.416	16.085	16.786	17.519	18.285	19.086	19.923	20.799	25.802	32.015
10	17.549	18.420	19.337	20.304	21.321	22.393	23.521	24.701	25.959	33.253	42.619
11	20.655	21.814	23.045	24.349	25.733	27.200	28.755	30.404	32.150	42.566	56.405
12	24.133	25.650	27.271	29.002	30.850	32.824	34.931	37.180	39.581	54.208	74.327
13	28.029	29.985	32.089	34.352	36.786	39.404	42.219	45.244	48.497	68.760	97.625
14	32.393	34.883	37.581	40.505	43.672	47.103	50.818	54.841	59.196	86.949	127.91
15	37.280	40.417	43.842	47.580	51.660	56.110	60.965	66.261	72.035	109.69	167.29
16	42.753	46.672	50.980	55.717	60.925	66.649	72.939	79.850	87.442	138.11	218.47
17	48.884	53.739	59.118	65.075	71.673	78.979	87.068	96.022	105.93	173.64	285.01
18	55.750	61.725	68.394	75.836	84.141	93.406	103.74	115.27	128.12	218.05	371.52
19	63.440	70.749	78.969	88.212	98.603	110.29	123.41	138.17	154.74	273.56	483.97
20	72.052	80.947	91.025	102.44	115.38	130.03	146.63	165.42	186.69	342.95	630.17
25	133.33	155.62	181.87	212.79	249.21	292.11	342.60	402.04	471.98	1,054.8	2,348.80
30	241.33	293.20	356.79	434.75	530.31	647.44	790.95	966.7	1,181.9	3,227.2	8,730.0
40	767.09	1,013.7	1,342.0	1,779.1	2,360.8	3,134.5	4,163.21	5,529.8	7,343.9	30,089.	120,393.
50	2,400.0	3,459.5	4,994.5	7,217.7	10,436.	15,090.	21,813.	31,515.	45,497.	280,256.	165,976.

Source: Maurice Joy, *Introduction to Financial Management* (Homewood, Ill.: Richard D. Irwin, Inc. 1977).

APPENDIX D

Present value of an annuity of $1

Percent

Period	1%	2%	3%	4%	5%	6%	7%	8%	9%	10%	11%	12%
1	0.990	0.980	0.971	0.962	0.952	0.943	0.935	0.926	0.917	0.909	0.901	0.893
2	1.970	1.942	1.913	1.886	1.859	1.833	1.808	1.783	1.759	1.736	1.713	1.690
3	2.941	2.884	2.829	2.775	2.723	2.673	2.624	2.577	2.531	2.487	2.444	2.402
4	3.902	3.808	3.717	3.630	3.546	3.465	3.387	3.312	3.240	3.170	3.102	3.037
5	4.853	4.713	4.580	4.452	4.329	4.212	4.100	3.993	3.890	3.791	3.696	3.605
6	5.795	5.601	5.417	5.242	5.076	4.917	4.767	4.623	4.486	4.355	4.231	4.111
7	6.728	6.472	6.230	6.002	5.786	5.582	5.389	5.206	5.033	4.868	4.712	4.564
8	7.652	7.325	7.020	6.733	6.463	6.210	5.971	5.747	5.535	5.335	5.146	4.968
9	8.566	8.162	7.786	7.435	7.108	6.802	6.515	6.247	5.995	5.759	5.537	5.328
10	9.471	8.983	8.530	8.111	7.722	7.360	7.024	6.710	6.418	6.145	5.889	5.650
11	10.368	9.787	9.253	8.760	8.306	7.887	7.499	7.139	6.805	6.495	6.207	5.938
12	11.255	10.575	9.954	9.385	8.863	8.384	7.943	7.536	7.161	6.814	6.492	6.194
13	12.134	11.348	10.635	9.986	9.394	8.853	8.358	7.904	7.487	7.103	6.750	6.424
14	13.004	12.106	11.296	10.563	9.899	9.295	8.745	8.244	7.786	7.367	6.982	6.628
15	13.865	12.849	11.939	11.118	10.380	9.712	9.108	8.559	8.061	7.606	7.191	6.811
16	14.718	13.578	12.561	11.652	10.838	10.106	9.447	8.851	8.313	7.824	7.379	6.974
17	15.562	14.292	13.166	12.166	11.274	10.477	9.763	9.122	8.544	8.022	7.549	7.102
18	16.398	14.992	13.754	12.659	11.690	10.828	10.059	9.372	8.756	8.201	7.702	7.250
19	17.226	15.678	14.324	13.134	12.085	11.158	10.336	9.604	8.950	8.365	7.839	7.366
20	18.046	16.351	14.877	13.590	12.462	11.470	10.594	9.818	9.129	8.514	7.963	7.469
25	22.023	19.523	17.413	15.622	14.094	12.783	11.654	10.675	9.823	9.077	8.422	7.843
30	25.808	22.396	19.600	17.292	15.372	13.765	12.409	11.258	10.274	9.427	8.694	8.055
40	32.835	27.355	23.115	19.793	17.159	15.046	13.332	11.925	10.757	9.779	8.951	8.244
50	39.196	31.424	25.730	21.482	18.256	15.762	13.801	12.233	10.962	9.915	9.042	8.304

APPENDIX D (concluded)

Present value of an annuity of $1

Percent

Period	13%	14%	15%	16%	17%	18%	19%	20%	25%	30%	35%	40%	50%
1	0.885	0.877	0.870	0.862	0.855	0.847	0.840	0.833	0.800	0.769	0.741	0.714	0.667
2	1.668	1.647	1.626	1.605	1.585	1.566	1.547	1.528	1.440	1.361	1.289	1.224	1.111
3	2.361	2.322	2.283	2.246	2.210	2.174	2.140	2.106	1.952	1.816	1.696	1.589	1.407
4	2.974	2.914	2.855	2.798	2.743	2.690	2.639	2.589	2.362	2.166	1.997	1.849	1.605
5	3.517	3.433	3.352	3.274	3.199	3.127	3.058	2.991	2.689	2.436	2.220	2.035	1.737
6	3.998	3.889	3.784	3.685	3.589	3.498	3.410	3.326	2.951	2.643	2.385	2.168	1.824
7	4.423	4.288	4.160	4.039	3.922	3.812	3.706	3.605	3.161	2.802	2.508	2.263	1.883
8	4.799	4.639	4.487	4.344	4.207	4.078	3.954	3.837	3.329	2.925	2.598	2.331	1.922
9	5.132	4.946	4.772	4.607	4.451	4.303	4.163	4.031	3.463	3.019	2.665	2.379	1.948
10	5.426	5.216	5.019	4.833	4.659	4.494	4.339	4.192	3.571	3.092	2.715	2.414	1.965
11	5.687	5.453	5.234	5.029	4.836	4.656	4.486	4.327	3.656	3.147	2.752	2.438	1.977
12	5.918	5.660	5.421	5.197	4.988	4.793	4.611	4.439	3.725	3.190	2.779	2.456	1.985
13	6.122	5.842	5.583	5.342	5.118	4.910	4.715	4.533	3.780	3.223	2.799	2.469	1.990
14	6.302	6.002	5.724	5.468	5.229	5.008	4.802	4.611	3.824	3.249	2.814	2.478	1.993
15	6.462	6.142	5.847	5.575	5.324	5.092	4.876	4.675	3.859	3.268	2.825	2.484	1.995
16	6.604	6.265	5.954	5.668	5.405	5.162	4.938	4.730	3.887	3.283	2.834	2.489	1.997
17	6.729	6.373	6.047	5.749	5.475	5.222	4.988	4.775	3.910	3.295	2.840	2.492	1.998
18	6.840	6.467	6.128	5.818	5.534	5.273	5.033	4.812	3.928	3.304	2.844	2.494	1.999
19	6.938	6.550	6.198	5.877	5.584	5.316	5.070	4.843	3.942	3.311	2.848	2.496	1.999
20	7.025	6.623	6.259	5.929	5.628	5.353	5.101	4.870	3.954	3.316	2.850	2.497	1.999
25	7.330	6.873	6.464	6.097	5.766	5.467	5.195	4.948	3.985	3.329	2.856	2.499	1.999
30	7.496	7.003	6.566	6.177	5.829	5.517	5.235	4.979	3.995	3.332	2.857	2.500	2.000
40	7.634	7.105	6.642	6.233	5.871	5.548	5.258	4.997	3.999	3.333	2.857	2.500	2.000
50	7.675	7.133	6.661	6.246	5.880	5.554	5.262	4.999	4.000	3.333	2.857	2.500	2.000

Source: Maurice Joy, *Introduction to Financial Management* (Homewood, Ill.: Richard D. Irwin, Inc. 1977).

Tables of squares and square roots

N	N²	√N	√10N	N	N²	√N	√10N
				50	2 500	7.071 068	22.36068
1	1	1.000 000	3.162 278	51	2 601	7.141 428	22.58318
2	4	1.414 214	4.472 136	52	2 704	7.211 103	22.80351
3	9	1.732 051	5.477 226	53	2 809	7.280 110	23.02173
4	16	2.000 000	6.324 555	54	2 916	7.348 469	23.23790
5	25	2.236 068	7.071 068	55	3 025	7.416 198	23.45208
6	36	2.449 490	7.745 967	56	3 136	7.483 315	23.66432
7	49	2.645 751	8.366 600	57	3 249	7.549 834	23.87467
8	64	2.828 427	8.944 272	58	3 364	7.615 773	24.08319
9	81	3.000 000	9.486 833	59	3 481	7.681 146	24.28992
10	100	3.162 278	10.00000	60	3 600	7.745 967	24.49490
11	121	3.316 625	10.48809	61	3 721	7.810 250	24.69818
12	144	3.464 102	10.95445	62	3 844	7.874 008	24.89980
13	169	3.605 551	11.40175	63	3 969	7.937 254	25.09980
14	196	3.741 657	11.83216	64	4 096	8.000 000	25.29822
15	225	3.872 983	12.24745	65	4 225	8.062 258	25.49510
16	256	4.000 000	12.64911	66	4 356	8.124 038	25.69047
17	289	4.123 106	13.03840	67	4 489	8.185 353	25.88436
18	324	4.242 641	13.41641	68	4 624	8.246 211	26.07681
19	361	4.358 899	13.78405	69	4 761	8.306 824	26.26785
20	400	4.472 136	14.14214	70	4 900	8.366 600	26.45751
21	441	4.582 576	14.49138	71	5 041	8.426 150	26.64583
22	484	4.690 416	14.83240	72	5 184	8.485 281	26.83282
23	529	4.795 832	15.16575	73	5 329	8.544 004	27.01851
24	576	4.898 979	15.49193	74	5 476	8.602 325	27.20294
25	625	5.000 000	15.81139	75	5 625	8.660 254	27.38613
26	676	5.099 020	16.12452	76	5 776	8.717 798	27.56810
27	729	5.196 152	16.43168	77	5 929	8.774 964	27.74887
28	784	5.291 503	16.73320	78	6 084	8.831 761	27.92848
29	841	5.385 165	17.02939	79	6 241	8.888 194	28.10694
30	900	5.477 226	17.32051	80	6 400	8.944 272	28.28427
31	961	5.567 764	17.60682	81	6 561	9.000 000	28.46050
32	1 024	5.656 854	17.88854	82	6 724	9.055 385	28.63564
33	1 089	5.744 563	18.16590	83	6 889	9.110 434	28.80972
34	1 156	5.830 952	18.43909	84	7 056	9.165 151	28.98275
35	1 225	5.916 080	18.70829	85	7 225	9.219 544	29.15476
36	1 296	6.000 000	18.97367	86	7 396	9.273 618	29.32576
37	1 369	6.082 763	19.23538	87	7 569	9.327 379	29.49576
38	1 444	6.164 414	19.49359	88	7 744	9.380 832	29.66479
39	1 521	6.244 998	19.74842	89	7 921	9.433 981	29.83287
40	1 600	6.324 555	20.00000	90	8 100	9.486 833	30.00000
41	1 681	6.403 124	20.24846	91	8 281	9.539 392	30.16621
42	1 764	6.480 741	20.49390	92	8 464	9.591 663	30.33150
43	1 849	6.557 439	20.73644	93	8 649	9.643 651	30.49590
44	1 936	6.633 250	20.97618	94	8 836	9.695 360	30.65942
45	2 025	6.708 204	21.21320	95	9 025	9.746 794	30.82207
46	2 116	6.782 330	21.44761	96	9 216	9.797 959	30.98387
47	2 209	6.855 655	21.67948	97	9 409	9.848 858	31.14482
48	2 304	6.928 203	21.90890	98	9 604	9.899 495	31.30495
49	2 401	7.000 000	22.13594	99	9 801	9.949 874	31.46427
50	2 500	7.071 068	22.36068	100	10 000	10.00000	31.62278

Tables of squares and square roots

N	N^2	$\sqrt{N}$	$\sqrt{10N}$	N	N^2	$\sqrt{N}$	$\sqrt{10N}$
100	10 000	10.00000	31.62278	150	22 500	12.24745	38.72983
101	10 201	10.04988	31.78050	151	22 801	12.28821	38.85872
102	10 404	10.09950	31.93744	152	23 104	12.32883	39.98718
103	10 609	10.14889	32.09361	153	23 409	12.36932	39.11521
104	10 816	10.19804	32.24903	154	23 716	12.40967	39.24283
105	11 025	10.24695	32.40370	155	24 025	12.44990	39.37004
106	11 236	10.29563	32.55764	156	24 336	12.45000	39.49684
107	11 449	10.34408	32.71085	157	24 649	12.52996	39.62323
108	11 664	10.39230	32.86335	158	24 964	12.56981	39.74921
109	11 881	10.44031	33.01515	159	25 281	12.60952	39.87480
110	12 100	10.48809	33.16625	160	25 600	12.64911	40.00000
111	12 321	10.53565	33.31666	161	25 921	12.68858	40.12481
112	12 544	10.58301	33.46640	162	26 244	12.72792	40.24922
113	12 769	10.63015	33.61547	163	26 569	12.76715	40.37326
114	12 996	10.67708	33.76389	164	26 896	12.80625	40.49691
115	13 225	10.72381	33.91165	165	27 225	12.84523	40.62019
116	13 456	10.77033	34.05877	166	27 556	12.88410	40.74310
117	13 689	10.81665	34.20526	167	27 889	12.92285	40.86563
118	13 924	10.86278	34.35113	168	28 224	12.96148	40.98780
119	14 161	10.90871	34.49638	169	28 561	13.00000	41.10961
120	14 400	10.95445	34.64102	170	28 900	13.03840	41.23106
121	14 641	11.00000	34.78505	171	29 241	13.07670	41.35215
122	14 884	11.04536	34.92850	172	29 584	13.11488	41.47288
123	15 129	11.09054	35.07136	173	29 929	13.15295	41.59327
124	15 376	11.13553	35.21363	174	30 276	13.19091	41.71331
125	15 625	11.18034	35.35534	175	30 625	13.22876	41.83300
126	15 876	11.22497	35.49648	176	30 976	13.26650	41.95235
127	16 129	11.26943	35.63706	177	31 329	13.30413	42.07137
128	16 384	11.31371	35.77709	178	31 684	13.34166	42.19005
129	16 641	11.35782	35.91657	179	32 041	13.37909	42.30839
130	16 900	11.40175	36.05551	180	32 400	13.41641	42.42641
131	17 161	11.44552	36.19392	181	32 761	13.45362	42.54409
132	17 424	11.48913	36.33180	182	33 124	13.49074	42.66146
133	17 689	11.53256	36.46917	183	33 489	13.52775	42.77850
134	17 956	11.57584	36.60601	184	33 856	13.56466	42.89522
135	18 225	11.61895	36.74235	185	34 225	13.60147	43.01163
136	18 496	11.66190	36.87818	186	34 596	13.63818	43.12772
137	18 769	11.70470	37.01351	187	34 969	13.67479	43.24350
138	19 044	11.74734	37.14835	188	35 344	13.71131	43.35897
139	19 321	11.78983	37.28270	189	35 721	13.74773	43.47413
140	19 600	11.83216	37.41657	190	36 100	13.78405	43.58899
141	19 881	11.87434	37.54997	191	36 481	13.82027	43.70355
142	20 164	11.91638	37.68289	192	36 864	13.85641	43.81780
143	20 449	11.95826	37.81534	193	37 249	13.89244	43.93177
144	20 736	12.00000	37.94733	194	37 636	13.92839	44.04543
145	21 025	12.04159	38.07887	195	38 025	13.96424	44.15880
146	21 316	12.08305	38.20995	196	38 416	14.00000	44.27189
147	21 609	12.12436	38.34058	197	38 809	14.03567	44.38468
148	21 904	12.16553	38.47077	198	39 204	14.07125	44.49719
149	22 201	12.20656	38.60052	199	39 601	14.10674	44.60942
150	22 500	12.24745	38.72983	200	40 000	14.14214	44.72136

Tables of squares and square roots

N	N²	√N	√10N	N	N²	√N	√10N
200	40 000	14.14214	44.72136	250	62 500	15.81139	50.00000
201	40 401	14.17745	44.83302	251	63 001	15.84298	50.09990
202	40 804	14.21267	44.94441	252	63 504	15.87451	50.19960
203	41 209	14.24781	45.05552	253	64 009	15.90597	50.29911
204	41 616	14.28296	45.16636	254	64 516	15.93738	50.39841
205	42 025	14.31782	45.27693	255	65 025	15.96872	50.49752
206	42 436	14.35270	45.38722	256	65 536	16.00000	50.59644
207	42 849	14.38749	45.49725	257	66 049	16.03122	50.69517
208	43 264	14.42221	45.60702	258	66 564	16.06238	50.79370
209	43 681	14.45683	45.71652	259	67 081	16.09348	50.89204
210	44 100	14.49138	45.82576	260	67 600	16.12452	50.99020
211	44 521	14.52584	45.93474	261	68 121	16.15549	51.08816
212	44 944	14.56022	46.04346	262	68 644	16.18641	51.18594
213	45 369	14.59452	46.15192	263	69 169	16.21727	51.28353
214	45 796	14.62874	46.26013	264	69 696	16.24808	51.38093
215	46 225	14.66288	46.36809	265	70 225	16.27882	51.47815
216	46 656	14.69694	46.47580	266	70 756	16.30951	51.57519
217	47 089	14.73092	46.58326	267	71 289	16.34013	51.67204
218	47 524	14.76482	46.69047	268	71 824	16.37071	51.76872
219	47 961	14.79865	46.79744	269	72 361	16.40122	51.86521
220	48 400	14.83240	46.90415	270	72 900	16.43168	51.96152
221	48 841	14.86607	47.01064	271	73 441	16.46208	52.05766
222	49 284	14.89966	47.11688	272	73 984	16.49242	52.15362
223	49 729	14.93318	47.22288	273	74 529	16.52271	52.24940
224	50 176	14.96663	47.32864	274	75 076	16.55295	52.34501
225	50 625	15.00000	47.43416	275	75 625	16.58312	52.44044
226	51 076	15.03330	47.53946	276	76 176	16.61325	52.53570
227	51 529	15.06652	47.64452	277	76 729	16.64332	52.63079
228	51 984	15.09967	47.74935	278	77 284	16.67333	52.72571
229	52 441	15.13275	47.85394	279	77 841	16.70329	52.82045
230	52 900	15.16575	47.95832	280	78 400	16.73320	52.91503
231	53 361	15.19868	48.06246	281	78 961	16.76305	53.00943
232	53 824	15.23155	48.16638	282	79 524	16.79286	53.10367
233	54 289	15.26434	48.27007	283	80 089	16.82260	53.19774
234	54 756	15.29706	48.37355	284	80 656	16.85230	53.29165
235	55 225	15.32971	48.47680	285	81 225	16.88194	53.38539
236	55 696	15.36229	48.57983	286	81 796	16.91153	53.47897
237	56 169	15.39480	48.68265	287	82 369	16.94107	53.57238
238	56 644	15.42725	48.78524	288	82 944	16.97056	53.66563
239	57 121	15.45962	48.88763	289	83 521	17.00000	53.75872
240	57 600	15.49193	48.98979	290	84 100	17.02939	53.85165
241	58 081	15.52417	49.09175	291	84 681	17.05872	53.94442
242	58 564	15.55635	49.19350	292	85 264	17.08801	54.03702
243	59 049	15.58846	49.29503	293	85 849	17.11724	54.12947
244	59 536	15.62050	49.39636	294	86 436	17.14643	54.22177
245	60 025	15.65248	49.49747	295	87 025	17.17556	54.31390
246	60 516	15.68439	49.59839	296	87 616	17.20465	54.40588
247	61 009	15.71623	49.69909	297	88 209	17.23369	54.49771
248	61 504	15.74802	49.79960	298	88 804	17.26268	54.58938
249	62 001	15.77973	49.89990	299	89 401	17.29162	54.68089
250	62 500	15.81139	50.00000	300	90 000	17.32051	54.77226

Tables of squares and square roots

N	N²	√N	√10N	N	N²	√N	√10N
300	90 000	17.32051	54.77226	350	122 500	18.70829	59.16080
301	90 601	17.34935	54.86347	351	123 201	18.73499	59.24525
302	91 204	17.37815	54.95453	352	123 904	18.76166	59.32959
303	91 809	17.40690	55.04544	353	124 609	18.78829	59.41380
304	92 416	17.43560	55.13620	354	125 316	18.81489	59.49790
305	93 025	17.46425	55.22681	355	126 025	18.84144	59.58188
306	93 636	17.49288	55.31727	356	126 736	18.86796	59.66574
307	94 249	17.52142	55.40758	357	127 449	18.89444	59.74948
308	94 864	17.54993	55.49775	358	128 164	18.92089	59.83310
309	95 481	17.57840	55.58777	359	128 881	18.94730	59.91661
310	96 100	17.60682	55.67764	360	129 600	18.97367	60.00000
311	96 721	17.63519	55.76737	361	130 321	19.00000	60.08328
312	97 344	17.66352	55.85696	362	131 044	19.02630	60.16644
313	97 969	17.69181	55.94640	363	131 769	19.05256	60.24948
314	98 596	17.72005	56.03670	364	132 496	19.07878	60.33241
315	99 225	17.74824	56.12486	365	133 225	19.10497	60.41523
316	99 856	17.77639	56.21388	366	133 956	19.13113	60.49793
317	100 489	17.80449	56.30275	367	134 689	19.15724	60.58052
318	101 124	17.83255	56.39149	368	135 424	19.18333	60.66300
319	101 761	17.86057	56.48008	369	136 161	19.20937	60.74537
320	102 400	17.88854	56.56854	370	136 900	19.23538	60.82763
321	103 041	17.91647	56.65686	371	137 641	19.26136	60.90977
322	103 684	17.94436	56.74504	372	138 384	19.28730	60.99180
323	104 329	17.97220	56.83309	373	139 129	19.31321	61.07373
324	104 976	18.00000	56.92100	374	139 876	19.33908	61.15554
325	105 625	18.02776	57.00877	375	140 625	19.36492	61.23724
326	106 276	18.05547	57.09641	376	141 376	19.39072	61.31884
327	106 929	18.08314	57.18391	377	142 129	19.41649	61.40033
328	107 584	18.11077	57.27128	378	142 884	19.44222	61.48170
329	108 241	18.13836	57.35852	379	143 641	19.46792	61.56298
330	108 900	18.16590	57.44563	380	144 000	19.49359	61.64414
331	109 561	18.19341	57.53260	381	145 161	19.51922	61.72520
332	110 224	18.22087	57.61944	382	145 924	19.54483	61.80615
333	110 889	18.24829	57.70615	383	146 689	19.57039	61.88699
334	111 556	18.27567	57.79273	384	147 456	19.59592	61.96773
335	112 225	18.30301	57. 87918	385	148 225	19.62142	62.04837
336	112 896	18.33030	57.96551	386	148 996	19.64688	62.12890
337	113 569	18.35756	58.05170	387	149 769	19.67232	62.20932
338	114 224	18.38478	57.13777	388	150 544	19.69772	62.28965
339	114 921	18.41195	58.22371	389	151 321	19.72308	62.36986
340	115 600	18.43909	58.30952	390	152 100	19.74842	62.44998
341	116 281	18.46619	58.39521	391	152 881	19.77372	62.52999
342	116 694	18.49324	58.48077	392	153 664	19.79899	62.60990
343	117 649	18.52026	58.56620	393	154 449	19.82423	62.68971
344	118 336	18.54724	58.65151	394	155 236	19.84943	62.76942
345	119 025	18.57418	58.73670	395	156 025	19.87461	62.84903
346	119 716	18.60108	58.82176	396	156 816	19.89975	62.92853
347	120 409	18.62794	58.90671	397	157 609	19.92486	63.00794
348	121 104	18.65476	58.99152	398	158 404	19.94994	63.08724
349	121 801	18.68154	59.07622	399	159 201	19.97498	63.16645
350	122 500	18.70829	59.16080	400	160 000	20.00000	63.24555

Tables of squares and square roots

N	N²	√N	√10N	N	N²	√N	√10N
400	160 000	20.00000	63.24555	450	202 500	21.21320	67.08204
401	160 801	20.02498	63.32456	451	203 401	21.23676	67.15653
402	161 604	20.04994	63.40347	452	204 304	21.26029	67.23095
403	162 409	20.07486	63.48228	453	205 209	21.28380	67.30527
404	163 216	20.09975	63.56099	454	206 116	21.30728	67.37952
405	164 025	20.12461	63.63961	455	207 025	21.33073	67.45369
406	164 836	20.14944	63.71813	456	207 936	21.35416	67.52777
407	165 649	20.17424	63.79655	457	208 849	21.37756	67.60178
408	166 464	20.19901	63.87488	458	209 764	21.40093	67.67570
409	167 281	20.22375	63.95311	459	210 681	21.42429	67.74954
410	168 100	20.24846	64.03124	460	211 600	21.44761	67.82330
411	168 921	20.27313	64.10928	461	212 521	21.47091	67.89698
412	169 744	20.29778	64.18723	462	213 444	21.49419	67.97058
413	170 569	20.32240	64.26508	463	214 369	21.51743	68.04410
414	171 396	20.34699	64.34283	464	215 296	21.54066	68.11755
415	172 225	20.37155	64.42049	465	216 225	21.56386	68.19091
416	173 056	20.39608	64.49806	466	217 156	21.58703	68.26419
417	173 889	20.42058	64.57554	467	218 089	21.61018	68.33740
418	174 724	20.44505	64.65292	468	219 024	21.63331	68.41053
419	175 561	20.46949	64.73021	469	219 961	21.65641	68.48357
420	176 400	20.49390	64.80741	470	220 900	21.67948	68.55655
421	177 241	20.51828	64.88451	471	221 841	21.70253	68.62944
422	178 084	20.54264	64.96153	472	222 784	21.72556	68.70226
423	178 929	20.56696	65.03845	473	223 729	21.74856	68.77500
424	179 776	20.59126	65.11528	474	224 676	21.77154	68.84706
425	180 625	20.61553	65.19202	475	225 625	21.79449	68.92024
426	181 476	20.63977	65.26808	476	226 576	21.81742	68.99275
427	182 329	20.66398	65.34524	477	227 529	21.84033	69.06519
428	183 184	20.68816	65.42171	478	228 484	21.86321	69.13754
429	184 041	20.71232	65.49809	479	229 441	21.88607	69.20983
430	184 900	20.73644	65.57439	480	230 400	21.90800	69.28203
431	185 761	20.76054	65.65059	481	231 361	21.93171	69.35416
432	186 624	20.78461	65.72671	482	232 324	21.95450	69.42622
433	187 489	20.80865	65.80274	483	233 280	21.97726	69.50820
434	188 356	20.83267	65.87868	484	234 256	22.00000	69.57011
435	189 225	20.85665	65.95453	485	235 225	22.02272	69.64194
436	190 096	20.88061	66.03030	486	236 196	22.04541	69.71370
437	190 969	20.90454	66.10598	487	237 169	22.06808	69.78530
438	191 844	20.92845	66.18157	488	238 144	22.09072	69.85700
439	192 721	20.95233	66.25708	489	239 121	22.11334	69.92853
440	193 600	20.97618	66.33250	490	240 100	22.13594	70.00000
441	194 481	21.00000	66.40783	491	241 081	22.15852	70.07139
442	195 364	21.02380	66.48308	492	242 064	22.18107	70.14271
443	196 249	21.04757	66.55825	493	243 049	22.20360	70.21396
444	197 136	21.07131	66.63332	494	244 036	22.22611	70.28513
445	198 025	21.09502	66.70832	495	245 025	22.24860	70.35624
446	198 916	21.11871	66.78323	496	246 016	22.27106	70.42727
447	199 809	21.14237	66.85806	497	247 009	22.29350	70.49823
448	200 704	21.16601	66.93280	498	248 004	22.31519	70.56912
449	201 601	21.18962	67.00746	499	249 001	22.33831	70.63993
450	202 500	21.21320	67.08204	500	250 000	22.36068	70.71068

Tables of squares and square roots

N	N²	√N	√10N	N	N²	√N	√10N
500	250 000	22.36068	70.71068	550	302 500	23.45208	74.16198
501	251 001	22.38303	70.78135	551	303 601	23.47339	74.22937
502	252 004	22.40536	70.85196	552	304 704	23.49468	74.29670
503	253 009	22.42766	70.92249	553	305 809	23.51595	74.36397
504	254 016	22.44994	70.99296	554	306 916	23.53720	74.43118
505	255 025	22.47221	71.06335	555	308 025	23.55844	74.49832
506	256 036	22.49444	71.13368	556	309 136	23.57965	74.56541
507	257 049	22.51666	71.20393	557	310 249	23.60085	74.63243
508	258 064	22.53886	71.27412	558	311 364	23.62202	74.69940
509	259 081	22.56103	71.34424	559	312 481	23.64318	74.76630
510	260 100	22.58318	71.41428	560	313 600	23.66432	74.83315
511	261 121	22.60531	71.48426	561	314 721	23.68544	74.89993
512	262 144	22.62742	71.55418	562	315 844	23.70654	74.96666
513	263 169	22.64950	71.62402	563	316 969	23.72762	75.03333
514	264 196	22.67157	71.69379	564	318 096	23.74686	75.09993
515	265 225	22.69361	71.76350	565	319 225	23.76973	75.16648
516	266 256	22.71563	71.83314	566	320 356	23.79075	75.23297
517	267 289	22.73763	71.90271	567	321 489	23.81176	75.29940
518	268 324	22.75961	71.97222	568	322 624	23.83275	75.36577
519	269 361	22.78157	72.04165	569	323 761	23.85372	75.43209
520	270 400	22.80351	72.11103	570	324 900	23.87467	75.49834
521	271 441	22.82542	72.18033	571	326 041	23.89561	75.56454
522	272 484	22.84732	72.24957	572	327 184	23.91652	75.63068
523	273 529	22.86919	72.31874	573	328 329	23.93742	75.69676
524	274 576	22.89105	72.38784	574	329 476	23.95830	75.76279
525	275 625	22.91288	72.45688	575	330 625	23.97916	75.82875
526	276 676	22.93469	72.52586	576	331 776	24.00000	75.89466
527	277 729	22.95648	72.59477	577	332 929	24.02082	75.96052
528	278 784	22.97825	72.66361	578	334 084	24.04163	76.02631
529	279 841	23.00000	72.73239	579	335 241	24.06242	76.09205
530	280 900	23.02173	72.80110	580	336 400	24.08319	76.15773
531	281 961	23.04344	72.86975	581	337 561	24.10394	76.22336
532	283 024	23.06513	72.93833	582	338 724	24.12468	76.28892
533	284 089	23.08679	73.00685	583	339 889	24.14539	76.35444
534	285 156	23.10844	73.07530	584	341 056	24.16609	76.41989
535	286 225	23.13007	73.14369	585	342 225	24.18677	76.48529
536	287 296	23.15167	73.21202	586	343 396	24.20744	76.55064
537	288 369	23.17326	73.28028	587	344 569	24.22808	76.61593
538	289 444	23.19483	73.34848	588	345 744	24.24871	76.68116
539	290 521	23.21637	73.41662	589	346 921	24.26932	76.74634
540	291 600	23.23790	73.48469	590	348 100	24.28992	76.81146
541	292 681	23.25941	73.55270	591	349 281	24.31049	76.87652
542	293 764	23.28089	73.62056	592	350 464	24.33105	76.94154
543	294 849	23.30236	73.68853	593	351 649	24.35159	77.00649
544	295 936	23.32381	73.75636	594	352 836	24.37212	77.07140
545	297 025	23.34524	73.82412	595	354 025	24.39262	77.13624
546	298 116	23.36664	73.89181	596	355 216	24.41311	77.20104
547	299 209	23.38803	73.95945	597	356 409	24.43358	77.26578
548	300 304	23.40940	74.02702	598	357 604	24.45404	77.33046
549	301 401	23.43075	74.09453	599	358 801	24.47448	77.39509
550	302 500	23.45208	74.16198	600	360 000	24.49490	77.45967

Tables of squares and square roots

N	N^2	$\sqrt{N}$	$\sqrt{10N}$	N	N^2	$\sqrt{N}$	$\sqrt{10N}$
600	360 000	24.49490	77.45967	650	422 500	25.49510	80.62258
601	361 201	24.51530	77.52419	651	423 801	25.51470	80.68457
602	362 404	24.53569	77.58868	652	425 409	25.53240	80.80130
603	363 609	24.55606	77.65307	653	426 409	25.55386	80.80842
604	364 816	24.57641	77.71744	654	427 716	25.57342	80.87027
605	366 025	24.59675	77.78175	655	429 025	25.59297	80.93207
606	367 736	24.61707	77.84600	656	430 336	25.61250	80.99383
607	368 449	24.63737	77.91020	657	431 649	25.63201	81.05554
608	369 664	24.65766	77.97435	658	432 964	25.65151	81.11720
609	370 881	24.67793	78.03845	659	434 281	25.67100	81.17881
610	372 100	24.69818	78.10250	660	435 600	25.69047	81.24038
611	373 321	24.71841	78.16649	661	436 921	25.70992	81.30191
612	374 544	24.73863	78.23043	662	438 244	25.72936	81.36338
613	375 769	24.75884	78.29432	663	439 569	25.74879	81.42481
614	376 996	24.77902	78.35815	664	440 896	25.76820	81.48620
615	378 225	24.79919	78.42194	665	442 225	25.78759	81.54753
616	379 456	24.81935	78.48567	666	443 556	25.80698	81.60882
617	380 689	24.83948	78.54935	667	444 889	25.82634	81.67007
618	381 924	24.85961	78.61298	668	446 224	25.84570	81.73127
619	383 161	24.87971	78.67655	669	447 561	25.86503	81.79242
620	384 400	24.89980	78.74008	670	448 900	25.88436	81.85353
621	385 641	24.91987	78.80355	671	450 241	25.90367	81.91459
622	386 884	24.93993	78.86698	672	451 584	25.92296	81.97561
623	388 129	24.95997	78.93035	673	452 929	25.94224	82.03658
624	389 376	24.97999	78.99367	674	454 276	25.96151	82.09750
625	390 625	25.00000	79.05694	675	455 625	25.98076	82.15838
626	391 876	25.01999	79.12016	676	456 976	26.00000	82.21922
627	393 129	25.03997	79.18333	677	458 329	26.01922	82.28001
628	394 384	25.05993	79.24645	678	459 684	26.03843	82.34076
629	395 641	25.07987	79.30952	679	461 041	26.05763	82.40146
630	396 900	25.09980	79.37254	680	462 400	26.07681	82.46211
631	398 161	25.11971	79.43551	681	463 761	26.09598	82.52272
632	399 424	25.13961	79.49843	682	465 124	26.11513	82.58329
633	400 689	25.15949	79.56130	683	466 489	26.13427	82.64381
634	401 956	25.17936	79.62412	684	467 856	26.15339	82.70429
635	403 225	25.19921	79.68689	685	469 225	26.17250	82.76473
636	404 496	25.21904	79.74961	686	470 596	26.19160	82.82512
637	405 769	25.23886	79.81228	687	471 969	26.21068	82.88546
638	407 044	25.25866	79.87490	688	473 344	26.22975	82.94577
639	408 321	25.27845	79.93748	689	474 721	26.24881	83.00602
640	409 600	25.29822	80.00000	690	476 100	26.26785	83.06624
641	410 881	25.31798	80.06248	691	477 481	26.28688	83.12641
642	412 164	25.33772	80.12490	692	478 864	26.30589	83.18654
643	413 449	25.35744	80.18728	693	480 249	26.32489	83.24662
644	414 736	25.37716	80.24961	694	481 636	26.34388	83.30666
645	416 025	25.39685	80.31189	695	483 025	26.36285	83.36666
646	417 316	25.41653	80.37413	696	484 416	26.38181	83.42661
647	418 609	25.43619	80.43631	697	485 809	26.40076	83.48653
648	419 904	25.45584	80.49845	698	487 204	26.41969	83.54639
649	421 201	25.47548	80.56054	699	488 601	26.43861	83.60622
650	422 500	25.49510	80.62258	700	490 000	26.45751	83.66600

Tables of squares and square roots

N	N²	√N	√10N	N	N²	√N	√10N
700	490 000	26.45751	83.66600	750	562 500	27.38613	86.60254
701	.491 401	26.47640	83.72574	751	564 001	27.40438	86.66026
702	492 804	26.49528	83.78544	752	565 504	27.42262	86.71793
703	494 209	26.51415	83.84510	753	567 009	27.44085	86.77557
704	495 616	26.53300	83.90471	754	568 516	27.45906	86.83317
705	497 025	26.55184	83.96428	755	570 025	27.47726	86.89074
706	498 436	26.57066	84.02381	756	571 536	27.49545	86.94826
707	499 849	26.58947	84.08329	757	573 049	27.51363	87.00575
708	501 264	26.60827	84.14274	758	574 564	27.53180	87.06320
709	502 681	26.62705	84.20214	759	576 081	27.54995	87.12061
710	504 100	26.64583	84.26150	760	577 600	27.56810	87.17798
711	505 521	26.66458	84.32082	761	579 121	27.58623	87.23531
712	506 944	26.68333	84.38009	762	580 644	27.60435	87.29261
713	508 369	26.70206	84.43933	763	582 169	27.62245	87.34987
714	509 796	26.72078	84.49852	764	583 696	27.64055	87.40709
715	511 225	26.73948	84.55767	765	585 225	27.65863	87.46428
716	512 656	26.75818	84.61578	766	586 756	27.67671	87.52143
717	514 089	26.77686	84.67585	767	588 289	27.69476	87.57854
718	515 524	26.79552	84.73488	768	589 824	27.71281	87.63561
719	516 961	26.81418	84.79387	769	591 361	27.73085	87.69265
720	518 400	26.83282	84.85281	770	592 900	27.74887	87.74964
721	519 841	26.85144	84.91172	771	594 441	27.76689	87.80661
722	521 284	26.87006	84.97058	772	595 984	27.78489	87.86353
723	522 729	26.88866	85.02941	773	597 529	27.80288	87.92042
724	524 176	26.90725	85.08819	774	599 076	27.82086	87.97727
725	525 625	26.92582	85.14693	775	600 625	27.83882	88.03408
726	527 076	26.94439	85.20563	776	602 176	27.85678	88.09086
727	528 529	26.96294	85.26429	777	603 729	27.87472	88.14760
728	529 984	26.98148	85.32294	778	605 284	27.89265	88.20431
729	531 411	27.00000	85.38150	779	606 841	27.91057	88.26098
730	532 900	27.01851	85.44004	780	608 400	27.92848	88.31761
731	534 361	27.03701	85.49854	781	609 961	27.94638	88.37420
732	535 824	27.05550	85.55700	782	611 524	27.96426	88.43076
733	537 289	27.07397	85.61542	783	613 089	27.98214	88.48729
734	538 756	27.09243	85.67380	784	614 656	28.00000	88.54377
735	540 225	27.11088	85.73214	785	616 225	28.01785	88.60023
736	541 696	27.12932	85.79044	786	617 796	28.03569	88.65664
737	543 169	27.14774	85.84870	787	619 369	28.05352	88.71302
738	544 644	27.16616	85.90693	788	620 944	28.07134	88.76936
739	546 121	27.18455	85.96511	789	622 521	28.08914	88.82567
740	547 600	27.20294	86.02325	790	624 100	28.10694	88.88194
741	549 081	27.22132	86.08136	791	625 681	28.12472	88.93818
742	550 564	27.23968	86.13942	792	627 264	28.14249	88.99438
743	552 049	27.25803	86.20745	793	628 849	28.16026	89.05055
744	553 536	27.27636	86.25543	794	630 436	28.17801	89.10668
745	555 025	27.29469	86.31338	795	632 025	28.19574	89.16277
746	556 516	27.31300	86.37129	796	633 616	28.21347	89.21883
747	558 009	27.33130	86.42916	797	635 209	28.23119	89.27486
748	559 504	27.34959	86.48609	798	636 804	28.24889	89.33085
749	561 001	27.36786	86.54479	799	638 401	28.26659	89.38680
750	562 500	27.38613	86.60254	800	640 000	28.28427	89.44272

Tables of squares and square roots

N	N^2	$\sqrt{N}$	$\sqrt{10N}$	N	N^2	$\sqrt{N}$	$\sqrt{10N}$
800	640 000	28.28427	89.44272	850	722 500	29.15476	92.19544
801	641 601	28.30194	89.49860	851	724 201	29.17190	92.24966
802	643 204	28.31960	89.55445	852	725 904	29.18904	92.30385
803	644 809	28.33725	89.61027	853	727 609	29.20616	92.35800
804	646 416	28.35489	89.66605	854	729 316	29.22328	92.41212
805	648 025	28.37252	89.72179	855	731 025	29.24038	92.46621
806	649 636	28.39014	89.77750	856	732 736	29.25748	92.52027
807	651 249	28.40775	89.83318	857	734 449	29.27456	92.57429
808	652 864	28.42534	89.88882	858	736 164	29.29164	92.62829
809	654 481	28.44293	89.94443	859	737 881	29.30870	92.68225
810	656 100	28.46050	90.00000	860	739 600	29.32576	92.73618
811	657 721	28.47806	90.05554	861	741 321	29.34280	92.79009
812	659 344	28.49561	90.11104	862	743 044	29.35984	92.84396
813	660 969	28.51315	90.16651	863	744 769	29.37686	92.89779
814	662 596	28.53069	90.22195	864	746 496	29.39388	92.95160
815	664 225	28.54820	90.27735	865	748 225	29.41088	93.00538
816	665 856	28.56571	90.33272	866	749 956	29.42788	93.05912
817	667 489	28.58321	90.38805	867	751 689	29.44486	93.11283
818	669 124	28.60070	90.44335	868	753 424	29.46184	93.16652
819	670 761	28.61818	90.49862	869	755 161	29.47881	93.22017
820	672 400	28.63564	90.55385	870	756 900	29.49576	93.27379
821	674 041	28.65310	90.60905	871	758 641	29.51271	93.32738
822	675 684	28.67054	90.66422	872	760 384	29.52965	93.38094
823	677 329	28.68798	90.71935	873	762 129	29.54657	93.43447
824	678 976	28.70540	90.77445	874	763 876	29.56349	93.48797
825	680 625	28.72281	90.82951	875	765 625	29.58040	93.54143
826	682 276	28.74022	90.88454	876	767 376	29.59730	93.59487
827	683 929	28.75761	90.93954	877	769 129	29.61419	93.64828
828	685 584	28.77499	90.99451	878	770 884	29.63106	93.70165
829	687 241	28.79236	91.04944	879	772 641	29.64793	93.75500
830	688 900	28.80972	91.10434	880	774 400	29.66479	93.80832
831	690 561	28.82707	91.15920	881	776 161	29.68164	93.86160
832	692 224	28.84441	91.21403	882	777 924	29.69848	93.91486
833	693 889	28.86174	91.26883	883	779 689	29.71532	93.96808
834	695 556	28.87906	91.32360	884	781 456	29.73214	94.02027
835	697 225	28.89637	91.37833	885	783 225	29.74895	94.07444
836	698 896	28.91366	91.43304	886	784 996	29.76575	94.12757
837	700 569	28.93095	91.48770	887	786 769	29.78255	94.10868
838	702 244	28.94823	91.54234	888	788 544	29.79933	94.23375
839	703 921	28.96550	91.59694	889	790 321	29.81610	94.28680
840	705 600	28.98275	91.65151	890	792 100	29.83287	94.33981
841	707 281	29.00000	91.70605	891	793 881	29.84962	94.39280
842	708 964	29.01724	91.76056	892	795 664	29.86637	94.44575
843	710 649	29.03446	91.81503	893	797 449	29.88311	94.49868
844	712 336	29.05168	91.86947	894	799 236	29.89983	94.55157
845	714 025	29.06888	91.92388	895	801 025	29.91655	94.60444
846	715 716	29.08608	91.97826	896	802 816	29.93326	94.65728
847	717 409	29.10326	92.03260	897	804 609	29.94996	94.71008
848	719 104	29.12044	92.08692	898	806 404	29.96665	94.76286
849	720 801	29.13760	92.14120	899	808 201	29.98333	94.81561
850	722 500	29.15476	92.19544	900	810 000	30.00000	94.86833

Tables of squares and square roots

N	N^2	$\sqrt{N}$	$\sqrt{10N}$	N	N^2	$\sqrt{N}$	$\sqrt{10N}$
900	810 000	30.00000	94.86833	950	902 500	30.82207	97.46794
901	811 801	30.01666	94.92102	951	904 401	30.83829	97.51923
902	813 604	30.03331	94.97368	952	906 304	30.85450	97.57049
903	815 409	30.04996	95.02631	953	908 209	30.87070	97.62172
904	817 216	30.06659	95.07891	954	910.116	30.88689	97.67292
905	819 025	30.08322	95.13149	955	912 025	30.90307	97.72410
906	820 836	30.09938	95.18403	956	913 936	30.91925	97.77525
907	822 649	30.11644	95.23655	957	915 849	30.93542	97.82638
908	824 464	30.13304	95.28903	958	917 764	30.95158	97.87747
909	826 281	30.14963	95.34149	959	919 681	30.96773	97.92855
910	828 100	30.16621	95.39392	960	921 600	30.98387	97.97959
911	829 921	30.18278	95.44632	961	923 521	31.00000	98.03061
912	831 744	30.19934	95.49869	962	925 444	31.01612	98.08160
913	833 569	30.21589	95.55103	963	927 369	31.03224	98.13256
914	835 396	30.23243	95.60335	964	929 296	31.04835	98.18350
915	837 225	30.24897	95.65563	965	931 225	31.06445	98.23441
916	839 056	30.26549	95.70789	966	933 156	31.08054	98.28530
917	840 889	30.28201	95.76012	967	935 089	31.09662	98.33616
918	842 724	30.29851	95.81232	968	937 024	31.11270	98.38699
919	844 561	30.31501	95.86449	969	938 961	31.12876	98.43780
920	846 400	30.33150	95.91663	970	940 900	31.14482	98.48858
921	848 241	30.34798	95.96874	971	942 841	31.16087	98.53933
922	850 084	30.36445	96.02083	972	944 784	31.17691	98.59006
923	851 929	30.38092	96.07289	973	946 729	31.19295	98.64076
924	853 776	30.39735	96.12492	974	948 676	31.20897	98.69144
925	855 625	30.41381	96.17692	975	950 625	31.22499	98.74209
926	857 476	30.43025	96.22889	976	952 576	31.24100	98.79271
927	859 329	30.44667	96.28084	977	954 529	31.25700	98.84331
928	861 184	30.46309	96.33276	978	956 484	31.27299	98.89388
929	863 041	30.47950	96.38465	979	958 441	31.28898	98.94443
930	864 900	30.49590	96.43651	980	960 400	31.30495	98.99495
931	866 761	30.51229	96.48834	981	962 361	31.32092	99.04544
932	868 624	30.52868	96.54015	982	964 324	31.33688	99.09591
933	870 489	30.54505	96.59193	983	966 144	31.34021	99.10321
934	872 356	30.56141	96.64368	984	968 256	31.36877	99.19677
935	874 225	30.57777	96.69540	985	970 225	31.38471	99.24717
936	876 096	30.59412	96.74709	986	972 196	31.40064	99.29753
937	877 969	30.61046	96.79876	987	974 169	31.41656	99.34787
938	879 844	30.62679	96.85040	988	976 144	31.43247	99.39819
939	881 721	30.64311	96.90201	989	978 121	31.44837	99.44848
940	883 600	30.65942	96.95360	990	980 100	31.46427	99.49874
941	885 481	30.67572	97.00515	991	982 081	31.48015	99.54898
942	887 364	30.69202	97.05668	992	984 064	31.49603	99.54920
943	889 249	30.70831	97.10819	993	986 049	31.51190	99.64939
944	891 136	30.72458	97.15966	994	988 036	31.52777	99.69955
945	893 025	30.74085	97.21111	995	990 025	31.54362	99.74969
946	894 916	30.75711	97.26253	996	992 016	31.55947	99.79980
947	896 809	30.77337	97.31393	997	994 009	31.57531	99.84989
948	898 704	30.78961	97.36529	998	996 004	31.59114	99.89995
949	900 601	30.80584	97.41663	999	998 001	31.60696	99.94999
950	902 500	30.82207	97.46794	1000	1 000 000	31.62278	100.00000

Source: Donald H. Sanders, A. Franklin Murph, Robert J. Eng, *Statistics, A Fresh Approach* (New York: McGraw-Hill, Inc. 1976).

APPENDIX F: *Financial and Economic Data Bases*

PART I
Stock Market Data, p. 667.

PART II
Interest Rate Data, p. 686.

PART III
Economic Data, p. 696.

PART I: STOCK MARKET DATA

DOW JONES INDUSTRIAL AVERAGES

1975–84 Quarterly Data
Closing averages, EPS, DPS, P/E ratios, dividend yields, and payout ratios, p. 667.

1946–83 Quarterly Data
Closing averages, EPS, DPS, preceding 12 months EPS, and P/E ratios, p. 668.

1908–83 Annual Data
Highs and lows for the industrial, transportation and utility averages, p. 673.

STANDARD AND POOR'S INDEXES

1957–83 Annual Data on S&P's 500 Composite Index
EPS, DPS, payout ratio, high-low price, high-low P/E ratios, high-low dividend yield, p. 675.

1953–83 Annual Data on S&P's 400 Industrial Index (per share data)
Sales, operating profit, profit margin, depreciation, income taxes, EPS, aftertax profit margin, DPS, payout ratio, high-low price, high-low P/E, high-low dividend yields, book value, return on book value (ROE), working capital, capital expenditures, p. 676.

1978–83 Annual Data on S&P's 400 Industrial Index (per share data)
Income statement, balance sheet, financial ratios, p. 677.

1926–83 Monthly Data on S&P's 500 Composite Index and S&P's 400 Industrials
Index average monthly prices and annual range, and close of daily indexes, p. 678.

Quarterly Dow Jones Industrial Stock Average

The table below lists the earnings (losses) of the Dow Jones Industrial Average based upon generally accepted accounting principles. The P/E ratio for the DJI correctly reflects deficit/negative earnings for the 1982 September and December quarters. The 1984 December 12-months dividend reflects $1.87½ GM dividend distribution value of one share of class E common for each 20 shares of common held. N.A.-Not available. d-Deficit.

Year	Quarter Ended		Clos. Avg.	Qtrly Chg.		% Chg.		Qtrly Earns	12-Mth Earns	P/E Ratio	12-Mth Divs	Divs Yield	Payout Ratio
1984	Dec.	31	1211.57	+	4.86	+	0.40	N.A.	N.A.	N.A.	60.63	5.00	N.A.
	Sept.	28	1206.71	+	74.31	+	6.56	29.08	108.11	11.2	58.41	4.84	.5402
	June	29	1132.40	−	32.49	−	2.79	35.02	102.07	11.1	57.67	5.09	.5650
	Mar.	30	1164.89	−	93.75	−	7.45	30.12	87.38	13.3	56.39	4.84	.6453
1983	Dec.	30	1258.64	+	25.51	+	2.07	13.89	72.45	17.4	56.33	4.47	.7775
	Sept.	30	1233.13	+	11.17	+	0.91	23.04	56.12	30.0	54.59	4.43	.9727
	June	30	1221.96	+	91.93	+	8.13	20.33	11.59	105.4	54.05	4.42	4.6635
	Mar.	31	1130.03	+	83.49	+	7.98	15.19	9.52	118.7	54.10	4.79	5.6828
1982	Dec.	31	1046.54	+	150.29	+	16.77	d2.44	9.15	114.4	54.14	5.17	5.9169
	Sept.	30	896.25	+	84.32	+	10.38	d21.49	35.15	25.5	55.55	6.20	1.5804
	June	30	811.93	−	10.84	−	1.32	18.26	79.90	10.2	55.84	6.88	.6989
	Mar.	31	822.77	−	52.23	−	5.97	14.82	97.13	8.5	56.28	6.84	.5794
1981	Dec.	31	875.00	+	25.02	+	2.94	23.56	113.71	7.7	56.22	6.42	.4944
	Sept.	30	849.98	−	126.90	−	12.99	23.26	123.32	6.9	56.18	6.61	.4539
	June	30	976.88	−	26.99	−	2.69	35.49	128.91	7.6	55.98	5.73	.4266
	Mar.	31	1003.87	+	39.88	+	4.14	31.40	123.60	8.1	54.99	5.48	.4449
1980	Dec.	31	963.99	+	31.57	+	3.39	33.17	121.86	7.9	54.36	5.64	.4461
	Sept.	30	932.42	+	64.50	+	7.43	28.85	111.58	8.4	53.83	5.77	.4824
	June	30	867.92	+	82.17	+	10.46	30.18	116.40	7.5	52.81	6.08	.4537
	Mar.	31	785.75	−	52.99	−	6.32	29.66	120.77	6.5	52.10	6.63	.4314
1979	Dec.	31	838.74	−	39.93	−	4.54	22.89	124.46	6.7	50.98	6.08	.4096
	Sept.	28	878.67	+	36.69	+	4.36	33.67	136.26	6.4	51.45	5.85	.3776
	June	29	841.98	−	20.20	−	2.34	34.55	128.99	6.5	50.35	5.98	.3903
	Mar.	30	862.18	+	57.17	+	7.10	33.35	124.10	6.9	49.48	5.74	.3987
1978	Dec.	29	805.01	−	60.81	−	7.02	34.69	112.79	7.1	48.52	6.03	.4302
	Sept.	29	865.82	+	46.87	+	5.72	26.40	101.59	8.5	47.42	5.48	.4668
	June	30	818.95	+	61.59	+	8.13	29.66	91.37	9.0	46.74	5.71	.5115
	Mar.	31	757.36	−	73.81	−	8.88	22.04	89.23	8.5	46.53	6.14	.5215
1977	Dec.	30	831.17	−	15.94	−	1.88	23.49	89.10	9.3	45.84	5.51	.5145
	Sept.	30	847.11	−	69.19	−	7.55	16.18	89.86	9.4	44.73	5.28	.4978
	June	30	916.30	−	2.83	−	0.31	27.52	97.18	9.4	43.85	4.79	.4512
	Mar.	31	919.13	−	85.52	−	8.51	21.91	95.51	9.6	42.63	4.64	.4463
1976	Dec.	31	1004.65	+	14.46	+	1.46	24.25	96.72	10.4	41.40	4.12	.4280
	Sept.	30	990.19	−	12.59	−	1.27	23.50	95.81	10.3	38.90	3.93	.4060
	June	30	1002.78	+	3.33	+	0.33	25.85	90.68	11.1	38.10	3.80	.4202
	Mar.	31	999.45	+	147.04	+	17.25	23.12	81.87	12.2	36.88	3.69	.4505
1975	Dec.	31	852.41	+	58.53	+	7.37	23.34	75.66	11.3	37.46	4.39	.4951
	Sept.	30	793.88	−	85.11	−	10.72	18.37	75.47	10.5	38.28	4.82	.5072
	June	30	878.99	+	110.84	+	12.61	17.04	83.83	10.5	38.66	4.40	.4612
	Mar.	31	768.15	+	151.91	+	24.65	16.91	93.47	8.2	38.56	5.02	.4125

Dow Jones Industrial Average
Earnings, Dividends and Price-Earnings Ratio

		Price	Earnings (by qtrs)	Preceding 12 mos. earnings	Price Earnings Ratio (col. 1 ÷ col. 3)	Dividends
1983	December 30	1258.94	. . . .	. . . .	. . . .	14.77
	September 30	1233.13	23.04	56.12	30.0	13.98
	June 30	1221.96	20.33	11.59	105.4	13.70
	March 31	1130.03	15.19	9.52	118.7	13.88
						56.33
1982	December 31	1046.54	d2.44	9.15	114.4	13.03
	September 30	896.25	d21.49	35.15	25.5	13.44
	June 30	811.93	18.26	79.90	10.2	13.75
	March 31	822.77	14.82	97.13	8.5	13.92
			9.15			54.14
1981	December 31	875.00	23.56	113.71	7.7	14.44
	September 30	849.98	23.26	123.32	6.9	13.73
	June 30	976.88	35.49	128.91	7.6	14.19
	March 31	1003.87	31.40	123.60	8.1	13.86
			113.71			56.22
1980	December 31	963.99	33.17	121.86	7.9	14.40
	September 30	932.42	28.85	111.58	8.4	13.53
	June 30	867.92	30.18	116.40	7.5	13.20
	March 31	785.75	29.66	120.77	6.5	13.23
			121.86			54.36
1979	December 31	838.74	22.89	124.46	6.7	13.87
	September 28	878.67	33.67	136.26	6.4	12.51
	June 29	841.98	34.55	128.99	6.5	12.49
	March 30	862.18	33.35	124.10	6.9	12.11
			124.46			50.98
1978	December 29	805.01	34.69	112.79	7.1	14.34
	September 29	865.82	26.40	101.59	8.5	11.41
	June 30	818.95	29.66	91.37	9.0	11.62
	March 31	757.36	22.04	89.23	8.5	11.15
			112.79			48.52

Earnings and Price-Earnings Ratio

Earnings on the Dow Jones industrial average are computed by adding the per share results of the latest quarter of each of the 30 components. This total is then divided by the then-current divisor. Having obtained the figure for the quarter, the four most recent quarterly figures are totaled to give the 12-month figure.

The industrial average stood at 1233.13 on September 30, 1983, for instance (see above). The 12-month earnings for that date were $56.12, being the sum of the four previous quarters ended September.

To obtain the price-earnings ratio on the industrials, the industrial average on a given date is divided by the 12-month earnings of the same date.

Source: *The Dow Jones Investor's Handbook* (Homewood, Ill.: Dow Jones-Irwin, 1984).

Dow Jones Industrial Average
Earnings, Dividends and Price-Earnings Ratio

		Price	Earnings (by qtrs)	Preceding 12 mos. earnings	Price Earnings Ratio (col. 1 ÷ col. 3)	Dividends
1977	December 30	831.17	23.49	89.10	9.3	13.24
	September 30	847.11	16.18	89.86	9.4	10.73
	June 30	916.30	27.52	97.18	9.4	11.41
	March 31	919.13	21.91	95.51	9.6	10.46
			89.10			45.84
1976	December 31	1004.65	24.25	96.72	10.4	12.13
	September 30	990.19	23.50	95.81	10.3	9.85
	June 30	1002.78	25.85	90.68	11.1	10.19
	March 31	999.45	23.12	81.87	12.2	9.23
			96.72			41.40
1975	December 31	852.41	23.34	75.66	11.3	9.63
	September 30	793.88	18.37	75.47	10.5	9.05
	June 30	878.99	17.04	83.83	10.5	8.97
	March 31	768.15	16.91	93.47	8.2	9.81
			75.66			37.46
1974	December 31	616.24	23.15	99.04	6.2	10.45
	September 30	607.87	26.73	99.73	6.1	9.43
	June 28	802.41	26.68	93.26	8.6	8.87
	March 29	846.68	22.48	89.46	9.5	8.97
			99.04			37.72
1973	December 31	850.86	23.84	86.17	9.9	10.62
	September 28	947.10	20.26	82.09	11.5	8.36
	June 29	891.71	22.88	77.56	11.5	8.27
	March 30	951.01	19.19	71.98	13.2	8.08
			86.17			35.33
1972	December 29	1020.02	19.76	67.11	15.2	8.99
	September 29	953.27	15.73	62.15	15.3	7.76
	June 30	929.03	17.30	58.87	15.8	7.87
	March 30	940.70	14.32	56.76	16.6	7.65
			67.11			32.27
1971	December 31	890.20	14.80	55.09	16.2	7.85
	September 30	887.19	12.45	53.43	16.6	7.51
	June 30	891.14	15.19	53.45	16.7	7.80
	March 31	904.37	12.65	52.36	17.3	7.70
			55.09			30.86
1970	December 31	838.92	13.14	51.02	16.4	8.25
	September 30	760.68	12.47	51.83	14.7	7.80
	June 30	683.53	14.10	53.18	12.8	7.80
	March 31	785.57	11.31	54.07	14.5	7.68
			51.02			31.53

Source: *The Dow Jones Investor's Handbook* (Homewood, Ill.: Dow Jones-Irwin, 1984).

Dow Jones Industrial Average
Earnings, Dividends and Price-Earnings Ratio

		Price	Earnings (by qtrs)	Preceding 12 mos. earnings	Price Earnings Ratio (col. 1 ÷ col. 3)	Dividends
1969	December 31	800.36	13.95	57.02	14.0	8.63
	September 30	813.09	13.82	59.60	13.6	7.82
	June 30	873.19	14.99	59.47	14.7	8.08
	March 28	935.48	14.26	59.34	15.8	9.37
			57.02			33.90
1968	December 31	943.75	16.53	57.89	16.3	8.59
	September 30	935.79	13.69	57.05	16.4	7.73
	June 28	897.80	14.86	55.71	16.1	7.73
	March 29	840.67	12.81	53.98	15.6	7.29
			57.89			31.34
1967	December 29	905.11	15.69	53.87	16.8	8.03
	September 29	926.66	12.35	52.73	17.6	7.25
	June 30	860.26	13.13	54.27	15.8	7.36
	March 31	865.98	12.70	56.67	15.3	7.55
			53.87			30.19
1966	December 30	785.69	14.55	57.68	13.6	10.01
	September 30	774.22	13.89	57.36	13.5	7.18
	June 30	870.10	15.53	56.23	15.5	7.26
	March 31	924.77	13.71	55.05	16.8	7.44
			57.68			31.89
1965	December 31	969.26	14.23	53.67	18.1	8.54
	September 30	930.58	12.76	52.74	17.6	6.58
	June 30	868.03	14.35	50.84	17.1	6.79
	March 31	889.05	12.33	48.55	18.3	6.70
			53.67			28.61
1964	December 31	874.13	13.30	46.43	18.8	10.46
	September 30	875.37	10.86	45.88	19.1	5.79
	June 30	831.50	12.06	44.46	18.7	7.16
	March 31	813.29	10.21	42.60	19.1	7.83
			46.43			31.24
1963	December 31	762.95	12.75	41.21	18.5	7.39
	September 30	732.79	9.44	40.18	18.2	5.35
	June 28	706.68	10.20	38.71	18.3	5.52
	March 29	682.52	8.82	37.35	18.3	5.15
			41.21			23.41
1962	December 31	652.10	11.72	36.43	17.9	7.66
	September 28	578.98	7.97	35.52	16.3	5.26
	June 29	561.28	8.84	34.74	16.2	5.23
	March 30	706.95	7.90	34.11	20.7	5.15
			36.43			23.30

Source: *The Dow Jones Investor's Handbook* (Homewood, Ill.: Dow Jones-Irwin, 1984).

Dow Jones Industrial Average
Earnings, Dividends and Price-Earnings Ratio

		Price	Earnings (by qtrs)	Preceding 12 mos. earnings	Price Earnings Ratio (col. 1 ÷ col. 3)	Dividends
1961	December 29	731.13	10.81	31.91	22.9	7.57
	September 29	701.21	7.19	29.03	24.2	5.09
	June 30	683.96	8.21	29.29	23.4	5.05
	March 30	676.63	5.70	29.53	22.9	5.00
			31.91			22.71
1960	December 31	615.89	7.93	32.21	19.1	6.55
	September 30	580.14	7.45	31.64	18.3	4.86
	June 30	640.62	8.45	31.26	20.5	4.83
	March 31	610.59	8.38	33.82	18.2	5.12
			32.21			21.36
1959	December 31	679.36	7.36	34.31	19.8	6.73
	September 30	631.68	7.07	35.70	17.7	4.53
	June 30	643.60	11.01	35.71	18.0	4.59
	March 31	601.71	8.87	31.04	19.4	4.89
			34.31			20.74
1958	December 31	583.65	8.75	27.95	20.9	5.83
	September 30	532.09	7.08	27.97	19.0	4.59
	June 30	478.18	6.34	29.41	16.3	4.62
	March 31	446.76	5.78	32.56	13.7	4.96
			27.95			20.00
1957	December 31	435.69	8.78	36.08	12.1	6.91
	September 30	456.30	8.51	36.70	12.4	4.91
	June 28	503.29	9.49	34.82	14.4	4.79
	March 29	474.81	9.30	34.30	13.8	5.00
			36.08			21.61
1956	December 31	499.47	9.40	33.34	15.0	8.17
	September 28	475.25	6.63	33.65	14.1	4.83
	June 29	492.78	8.97	35.51	13.9	4.98
	March 29	511.79	8.34	36.02	14.2	5.01
			33.34			22.99
1955	December 30	488.40	9.71	35.78	13.7	8.13
	September 30	466.62	8.49	34.41	13.6	4.25
	June 30	451.38	9.48	32.11	14.1	4.24
	March 31	409.70	8.10	29.65	13.8	4.96
			35.78			21.58
1954	December 31	404.39	8.34	28.18	14.4	5.76
	September 30	360.46	6.19	26.99	13.4	3.75
	June 30	333.53	7.02	27.52	12.1	3.92
	March 31	303.51	6.63	27.20	11.2	4.04
			28.18			17.47

Source: *The Dow Jones Investor's Handbook* (Homewood, Ill.: Dow Jones-Irwin, 1984).

Dow Jones Industrial Average
Earnings, Dividends and Price-Earnings Ratio

		Price	Earnings (by qtrs)	Preceding 12 mos. earnings	Price Earnings Ratio (col. 1 ÷ col. 3)	Dividends
1953	December 31	280.90	7.15	27.23	10.3	4.86
	September 30	264.04	6.72	27.63	9.6	3.53
	June 30	268.26	6.70	26.93	10.0	3.95
	March 31	279.87	6.66	25.78	10.9	3.77
			27.23			16.11
1952	December 31	291.90	7.55	24.78	11.8	4.62
	September 30	270.61	6.02	24.37	11.1	3.55
	June 30	274.35	5.55	24.06	11.4	3.55
	March 31	269.46	5.66	25.11	10.7	3.71
			24.78			15.43
1951	December 31	269.23	7.14	26.59	10.1	5.25
	September 28	271.16	5.71	29.02	9.3	3.72
	June 29	242.64	6.60	31.83	7.6	3.48
	March 31	247.94	7.14	32.40	7.7	3.89
			26.59			16.34
1950	December 30	235.41	9.57	30.70	7.7	6.26
	September 29	226.36	8.52	27.15	8.3	3.87
	June 30	209.11	7.17	24.99	8.4	2.98
	March 31	206.05	5.44	23.20	8.9	3.02
			30.70			16.13
1949	December 31	200.13	6.02	23.54	8.5	5.02
	September 30	182.51	6.36	24.66	7.4	2.32
	June 30	167.42	5.38	23.95	7.0	2.85
	March 31	177.10	5.78	23.79	7.4	2.60
			23.54			12.79
1948	December 31	177.30	7.14	23.07	7.7	4.32
	September 30	178.30	5.65	20.94	8.5	2.42
	June 30	189.46	5.22	19.60	9.7	2.59
	March 31	177.20	5.06	19.01	9.3	2.17
			23.07			11.50
1947	December 31	181.16	5.01	18.80	9.6	2.98
	September 30	177.49	4.31	18.66	9.5	2.09
	June 30	177.30	4.63	18.10	9.8	2.22
	March 31	177.20	4.85	16.62	10.7	1.92
			18.80			9.21
1946	December 31	177.20	4.87	13.63	13.0	2.45
	September 30	172.42	3.75	11.56	14.9	1.70
	June 28	205.62	3.15	10.24	20.1	1.78
	March 30	199.75	1.86	9.76	20.5	1.57
			13.63			7.50

Source: *The Dow Jones Investor's Handbook* (Homewood, Ill.: Dow Jones-Irwin, 1984).

YEARLY HIGHS AND LOWS OF DOW JONES AVERAGES

	—Industrials—		—Transportation—		—Utilities—	
	High	Low	High	Low	High	Low
1983	1287.20	1027.04	612.57	434.24	140.70	119.51
1982	1070.55	776.92	464.55	292.12	122.83	103.22
1981	1024.05	824.01	447.38	335.48	117.81	101.28
1980	1000.17	759.13	425.68	233.69	117.34	96.04
1979	897.61	796.67	271.77	205.78	109.74	98.24
1978	907.74	742.12	261.49	199.31	110.98	96.35
1977	999.75	800.85	246.64	199.60	118.67	104.97
1976	1014.79	858.71	237.03	175.69	108.38	84.52
1975	881.81	632.04	174.57	146.47	87.07	72.02
1974	891.66	577.60	202.45	125.93	95.09	57.93
1973	1051.70	788.31	228.10	151.97	120.72	84.42
1972	1036.27	889.15	275.71	212.24	124.14	105.06
1971	950.82	797.97	248.33	169.70	128.39	108.03
1970	842.00	631.16	183.31	116.69	121.84	95.86
1969	968.85	769.93	279.88	169.03	139.95	106.31
1968	985.21	825.13	279.48	214.58	141.30	119.79
1967	943.08	786.41	274.49	205.16	140.43	120.97
1966	995.15	744.32	271.72	184.34	152.39	118.96
1965	969.26	840.59	249.55	187.29	163.32	149.84
1964	891.71	766.08	224.91	178.81	155.71	137.30
1963	767.21	646.69	179.46	142.03	144.37	129.19
1962	726.01	535.76	149.83	114.86	130.85	103.11
1961	734.91	610.25	152.92	131.06	135.90	99.75
1960	685.47	566.05	160.43	123.37	100.07	85.02
1959	679.36	574.46	173.56	146.65	94.70	85.05
1958	583.65	436.89	157.91	99.89	91.00	68.94
1957	520.77	419.79	157.67	95.67	74.61	62.10
1956	521.05	462.35	181.23	150.44	71.77	63.03
1955	488.40	388.20	167.83	137.84	66.68	61.39
1954	404.39	279.87	146.23	94.84	62.47	52.22
1953	293.79	255.49	112.21	90.56	53.88	47.87
1952	292.00	256.35	112.53	82.03	52.64	47.53
1951	276.37	238.99	90.08	72.39	47.22	41.47
1950	235.47	196.81	77.89	51.24	44.26	37.40
1949	200.52	161.60	54.29	41.03	41.31	33.36
1948	193.16	165.39	64.95	48.13	36.04	31.65
1947	186.85	163.21	53.42	41.16	37.55	32.28
1946	212.50	163.12	63.31	44.69	43.74	33.20
1945	195.82	151.35	64.89	47.03	39.15	26.15
1944	152.53	134.22	48.40	33.45	26.37	21.74
1943	145.82	119.26	38.30	27.59	22.30	14.69
1942	119.71	92.92	29.28	23.31	14.94	10.58
1941	133.59	106.34	30.88	24.25	20.65	13.51

Source: *The Dow Jones Investor's Handbook* (Homewood, Ill.: Dow Jones-Irwin, 1984).

YEARLY HIGHS AND LOWS OF DOW JONES AVERAGES

	—Industrials—		—Transportation—		—Utilities—	
	High	Low	High	Low	High	Low
1940	152.80	111.84	32.67	22.14	26.45	18.03
1939	155.92	121.44	35.90	24.14	27.10	20.71
1938	158.41	98.95	33.98	19.00	c25.19	c15.14
1937	194.40	113.64	64.46	28.91	37.54	19.65
1936	184.90	143.11	59.89	40.66	36.08	28.63
1935	148.44	96.71	41.84	27.31	29.78	14.46
1934	110.74	85.51	52.97	33.19	31.03	16.83
1933	108.67	50.16	56.53	23.42	37.73	19.33
1932	88.78	41.22	41.20	13.23	36.11	16.53
1931	194.36	73.79	111.58	31.42	73.40	30.55
1930	294.07	157.51	157.94	91.65	108.62	55.14
1929	381.17	198.69	189.11	128.07	144.61	64.72
1928	300.00	191.33	b152.70	b132.60	....	....
1927	202.40	152.73	144.82	119.92	....	....
1926	166.64	135.20	123.23	102.41	....	....
1925	159.39	115.00	112.93	92.82	....	....
1924	120.51	88.33	99.50	80.23	....	....
1923	105.38	85.76	90.63	76.78	....	....
1922	103.43	78.59	93.99	74.43	....	....
1921	81.50	63.90	77.56	65.52	....	....
1920	109.88	66.75	85.37	67.83	....	....
1919	119.62	79.15	91.13	73.63	....	....
1918	89.07	73.38	92.91	77.21	....	....
1917	99.18	65.95	105.76	70.75	....	....
1916	110.15	84.96	112.28	99.11	....	....
1915	99.21	54.22	108.28	87.85	....	....
1914	a83.43	a71.42	a109.43	a89.41	....	....
1913	88.57	72.11	118.10	100.50	....	....
1912	94.15	80.15	124.35	114.92	....	....
1911	87.06	72.94	123.86	109.80	....	....
1910	98.34	73.62	129.90	105.59	....	....
1909	100.53	79.91	134.46	113.90	....	....
1908	87.67	58.62	120.05	86.04	....	....

a—The high and low figures for the industrials and transportation are for the period ended July 31, 1914. The industrial average was composed of 12 stocks when the New York Stock Exchange closed in July 1914 because of World War I. In September 1916, a new list of 20 stocks was adopted and computed back to the opening of the Exchange on December 12, 1914. On October 1, 1928, the stocks comprising the industrial average was increased to 30. The high and low for the industrial average for December 1914 was 56.76 and 53.17, respectively. The high and low for transportation for December 1914 was 92.29 and 86.40.

b—On March 7, 1928, transportation components were increased to 20 from 12.

c—Since June 2, 1938, the utility average has been based on 15 stocks instead of 20.

Source: *The Dow Jones Investor's Handbook* (Homewood, Ill.: Dow Jones-Irwin, 1984).

Standard and Poor's 500 Composite Index

COMPOSITE—500 STOCKS

Per Share Data—Adjusted to stock price index level. Average of stock price indexes, 1941-1943=10

	Earnings Per Share	Dividends Per Share	% of Earn.	Price 1941-1943=10 High	Low	Price/Earn. Ratio High	Low	Div. Yields % High	Low
1957	3.37	1.79	53.12	49.13	38.98	14.58	11.57	4.59	3.64
1958	2.89	1.75	60.55	55.21	40.33	19.10	13.96	4.33	3.17
1959	3.39	1.83	53.98	60.71	53.58	17.91	15.81	3.42	3.01
1960	3.27	1.95	59.63	60.39	52.30	18.47	15.99	3.73	3.23
1961	3.19	2.02	63.32	72.64	57.57	22.77	18.05	3.51	2.78
1962	3.67	2.13	58.04	71.13	52.53	19.38	14.26	4.07	2.99
1963	4.02	2.28	56.72	75.02	62.69	18.66	15.59	3.64	3.04
1964	4.55	2.50	54.95	86.28	75.43	18.96	16.58	3.31	2.90
1965	5.19	2.72	52.41	92.63	81.60	17.85	15.72	3.33	2.94
1966	5.55	2.87	51.71	94.06	73.20	16.95	13.19	3.92	3.05
1967	5.33	2.92	54.78	97.59	80.38	18.31	15.08	3.63	2.99
1968	5.76	3.07	53.30	108.37	87.72	18.81	15.23	3.50	2.83
1969	5.78	3.16	54.67	106.16	89.20	18.37	15.43	3.54	2.98
1970	5.13	3.14	61.21	93.46	69.29	18.22	13.51	4.53	3.36
1971	5.70	3.07	53.86	104.77	90.16	18.38	15.82	3.41	2.93
1972	6.42	3.15	49.07	119.12	101.67	18.55	15.84	3.10	2.64
1973	8.16	3.38	41.42	120.24	92.16	14.74	11.29	3.67	2.81
1974	8.89	3.60	40.49	99.80	62.28	11.23	7.01	5.78	3.61
1975	7.96	3.68	46.23	95.61	70.04	12.01	8.80	5.25	3.85
1976	9.91	4.05	40.87	107.83	90.90	10.88	9.17	4.46	3.76
1977	10.89	4.67	42.88	107.00	90.71	9.83	8.33	5.15	4.36
1978	12.33	5.07	41.12	106.99	86.90	8.68	7.05	5.83	4.74
1979	14.86	5.65	38.02	111.27	96.13	7.49	6.47	5.88	5.08
1980	14.82	6.16	41.57	140.52	98.22	9.48	6.63	6.27	4.38
1981	15.36	6.63	43.16	138.12	112.77	8.99	7.34	5.88	4.80
1982	12.64	6.87	54.35	143.02	102.42	11.31	8.10	6.71	4.80
1983	14.03	7.09	50.54	172.65	138.34	12.31	9.86	5.13	4.11

Source: *Standard & Poor's Analyst's Handbook* (New York: Standard & Poor's Corporation, 1984).

400 INDUSTRIALS*

Per Share Data—Adjusted to stock price index level. Average of stock price indexes, 1941-1943=10

	Sales	Oper. Profit	Profit Margin %	Depr.	Income Taxes	Earnings Per Share	Earnings % of Sales	Dividends Per Share	Dividends % of Earn.	Price 1941-1943=10 High	Price Low	Price/Earn. Ratio High	Price/Earn. Ratio Low	Div. Yields % High	Div. Yields % Low	Book Value Per Share	% Return	Working Capital	Capital Expenditures
1953	49.50	6.99	14.12	1.53	2.95	2.57	5.19	1.34	52.14	26.99	22.70	10.50	8.83	5.90	4.96	20.76	12.38	11.70	2.77
1954	46.19	6.50	14.07	1.66	2.29	2.69	5.82	1.45	53.90	37.24	24.84	13.84	9.23	5.84	3.89	22.09	12.18	12.19	2.77
1955	54.14	8.58	15.85	1.92	3.23	3.58	6.61	1.74	48.60	49.54	35.66	13.84	9.96	4.88	3.51	25.09	14.27	14.03	3.03
1956	54.73	8.36	15.27	2.04	2.96	3.50	6.40	1.84	52.57	53.28	45.71	15.22	13.06	4.03	3.45	26.35	13.28	13.91	4.14
1957	55.81	8.79	15.75	2.41	2.87	3.53	6.33	1.94	54.96	53.25	41.98	15.08	11.89	4.62	3.64	29.44	11.99	13.50	4.84
1958	53.48	7.70	14.40	2.38	2.40	2.95	5.52	1.86	63.05	58.97	43.20	19.99	14.64	4.31	3.15	30.66	9.62	14.27	3.58
1959	57.83	8.84	15.29	2.47	2.99	3.47	6.00	1.95	56.20	65.32	57.02	18.82	16.43	3.42	2.99	32.26	10.76	14.93	3.65
1960	59.47	8.73	14.68	2.56	2.87	3.40	5.72	2.00	58.82	65.02	55.34	19.12	16.28	3.61	3.08	33.74	10.08	15.29	4.23
1961	59.51	8.75	14.70	2.66	2.80	3.37	5.66	2.07	61.42	76.69	60.87	22.76	18.06	3.40	2.70	34.85	9.67	15.84	3.97
1962	64.63	9.81	15.18	2.89	3.16	3.83	5.93	2.20	57.44	75.22	54.80	19.64	14.31	4.01	2.92	36.37	10.53	16.85	4.41
1963	68.50	10.73	15.66	3.04	3.51	4.24	6.19	2.36	55.66	79.25	65.48	18.69	15.44	3.60	2.98	38.17	11.11	17.64	4.41
1964	73.19	11.67	15.94	3.24	3.70	4.85	6.63	2.58	53.20	91.29	79.74	18.82	16.44	3.24	2.83	40.23	12.06	18.07	5.71
1965	80.69	13.11	16.25	3.52	4.14	5.50	6.82	2.82	51.27	98.55	86.43	17.92	15.71	3.26	2.86	43.50	12.64	18.80	6.87
1966	88.46	14.48	16.37	3.87	4.35	5.87	6.64	2.95	50.26	100.60	77.89	17.14	13.27	3.79	2.93	45.59	12.88	19.48	8.26
1967	91.86	14.28	15.55	4.25	4.11	5.62	6.12	2.97	52.85	106.15	85.31	18.89	15.18	3.48	2.80	47.78	11.76	20.74	8.35
1968	101.49	16.08	15.84	4.56	5.14	6.16	6.07	3.16	51.30	118.03	95.05	19.16	15.43	3.32	2.68	50.21	12.27	21.08	8.65
1969	108.53	16.63	15.32	4.87	5.14	6.13	5.65	3.25	53.02	116.24	97.75	18.96	15.95	3.32	2.80	51.70	11.86	21.05	9.70
1970	109.85	15.54	14.15	5.17	4.23	5.41	4.92	3.20	59.15	102.87	75.58	19.01	13.97	4.23	3.11	52.65	10.28	20.70	10.25
1971	118.23	17.22	14.56	5.45	4.98	5.97	5.04	3.16	52.93	115.84	99.36	19.40	16.64	3.18	2.73	55.28	10.80	22.61	9.96
1972	128.79	19.39	15.06	5.76	5.90	6.83	5.30	3.22	47.14	132.95	112.19	19.47	16.43	2.87	2.42	58.34	11.71	24.41	10.08
1973	149.22	23.64	15.84	6.25	7.59	8.89	5.96	3.46	38.92	134.54	103.37	15.13	11.63	3.35	2.57	62.84	14.15	26.49	11.65
1974	182.10	27.97	15.36	6.86	10.22	9.61	5.28	3.71	38.61	111.65	69.53	11.62	7.24	5.34	3.32	67.81	14.17	28.47	14.65
1975	185.16	26.63	14.38	7.36	9.40	8.58	4.63	3.72	43.36	107.40	77.71	12.52	9.06	4.79	3.46	70.84	12.11	30.47	14.43
1976	202.66	29.23	14.42	7.58	10.21	10.69	5.27	4.22	39.48	120.89	101.64	11.31	9.51	4.15	3.49	76.26	14.02	31.89	14.92
1977	224.24	32.20	14.36	8.53	11.14	11.45	5.11	4.95	43.23	118.92	99.88	10.39	8.72	4.96	4.16	82.21	13.93	33.28	17.02
1978	251.32	36.19	14.40	9.64	12.14	13.04	5.19	5.37	41.18	118.71	95.52	9.10	7.33	5.63	4.53	89.34	14.60	34.88	19.70
1979	292.38	42.01	14.37	10.82	14.02	16.29	5.57	5.92	36.34	124.49	107.08	7.64	6.57	5.53	4.76	98.71	16.50	36.32	26.44
1980	327.36	43.08	13.16	12.37	13.67	16.12	4.92	6.49	40.26	160.96	111.09	9.99	6.89	5.84	4.03	108.33	14.88	36.52	29.86
1981	344.31	44.50	12.92	13.82	12.95	16.74	4.86	7.01	41.88	157.02	125.93	9.38	7.52	5.57	4.46	116.06	14.42	35.98	33.03
R1982	333.86	42.67	12.78	15.30	10.95	13.20	3.95	7.13	54.02	159.66	114.08	12.10	8.64	6.25	4.47	118.60	11.13	34.41	31.30
1983	334.58	45.81	13.69	16.16	12.13	14.78	4.42	7.32	49.53	194.84	154.95	13.18	10.48	4.72	3.76	121.66	12.15	36.74	24.86

NOTE: 1983 data incls. results of 'old' A.T.'; excls. $5.5 bil. charge
*Based on 68 individual groups.
Stock Price Indexes for this group extend back to 1918.

Source: *Standard & Poor's Analyst's Handbook* (New York: Standard & Poor's Corporation, 1984).

Standard and Poor's 400 Industrial Index
(Income Statement, Balance Sheet, Financial Ratios)

S & P 400
Per Share Data - Adjusted to Stock Price Index Level
Average of Stock Price Indexes, 1941 - 1943 = 10

Income Account —

	1983	1982	1981	1980	1979	1978
Sales	329.32	333.86	344.31	327.36	292.38	251.32
Costs & expenses	283.72	291.19	299.81	284.28	250.37	215.13
Operating income	45.61	42.67	44.50	43.08	42.01	36.19
Other income	5.10	5.42	6.93	5.55	4.14	2.84
Total income	50.70	48.09	51.42	48.63	46.15	39.02
Depreciation	16.09	15.30	13.82	12.37	10.82	9.64
Interest	7.56	8.23	7.49	5.95	4.58	3.84
Minority interest	0.21	0.19	0.22	0.33	0.29	0.23
Income taxes	11.98	10.95	12.95	13.67	14.02	12.14
Net income	14.87	13.41	16.94	16.31	16.45	13.17
Preferred dividends	0.34	0.26	0.24	0.22	0.19	0.16
Savings fr. com. stk. equiv.	0.03	0.04	0.04	0.04	0.03	0.03
Common earnings	14.56	13.20	16.74	16.12	16.29	13.04
Common dividends	7.25	7.13	7.01	6.49	5.92	5.37
Balance after dividends	7.31	6.06	9.73	9.63	10.38	7.67

Financial Ratios—

	1983	1982	1981	1980	1979	1978
Current ratio	1.5	1.5	1.5	1.6	1.6	1.7
Quick ratio	0.9	0.9	0.9	0.9	0.9	1.0
Debt to total assets (%)	23	24	23	22	22	22
Times interest earned	4.6	4.0	5.0	6.0	7.7	7.6
Inventory turnover	8.0	7.4	7.8	7.6	7.2	7.2
Total assets turnover	1.1	1.2	1.3	1.3	1.3	1.3
Profit margin (%)	13.85	12.78	12.92	13.16	14.37	14.40
Return on total assets (%)	5.08	4.64	6.22	6.47	7.24	6.58

Balance Sheet

Assets —

	1983	1982	1981	1980	1979	1978
Cash & equivalent	20.32	15.67	14.69	15.17	15.27	15.34
Receivables	44.90	41.90	40.68	39.93	38.80	33.39
Income tax refund	0.28	0.34	0.23	0.24	0.07	0.04
Inventories	41.30	44.99	44.02	42.83	40.42	35.09
Other current assets	4.88	5.21	4.71	4.12	3.19	2.68
Total current assets	107.04	104.68	103.29	101.51	97.65	86.44
Net property, plant, & equipment	141.15	144.06	134.37	120.03	106.89	94.15
Inv. & adv. to uncons. subs.	13.12	12.58	11.87	10.87	10.03	8.89
Intangibles	3.88	3.76	3.19	2.66	2.69	2.22
Other assets	16.79	15.72	15.58	13.23	7.65	6.43
Total assets	286.62	284.22	269.32	249.08	225.00	198.24

Liabilities —

	1983	1982	1981	1980	1979	1978
Notes payable	13.30	13.94	10.05	8.96	8.01	5.89
Current portion of long term debt	2.40	2.44	2.17	1.94	1.79	1.85
Accounts payable	27.03	25.16	26.07	25.71	23.75	19.88
Income tax payable	6.78	6.70	7.07	7.94	7.26	5.87
Accrued expenses	15.54	15.12	14.85	13.61	12.61	11.11
Other current liabilities	8.95	9.12	9.01	8.53	7.91	6.96
Total current liabilities	70.69	70.26	67.31	64.99	61.33	51.56
Long term debt	49.70	52.72	49.06	43.27	39.22	36.23
Deferred income tax	18.38	17.74	15.97	13.43	10.83	8.93
Minority interest	1.82	1.95	2.02	2.14	2.06	1.83
Other liabilities	17.20	15.04	12.31	10.97	6.90	5.45
Preferred stock	3.21	3.48	2.82	2.57	2.19	1.82
Common stock	9.40	11.33	11.17	10.64	10.37	10.34
Capital surplus	20.53	16.20	14.64	12.72	11.90	11.29
Retained earnings	95.71	95.50	94.03	88.35	80.20	70.78
Total liabilities	286.62	284.22	269.32	249.08	225.00	198.24

NA - Not Available
NM - Not Meaningful

Note: Data presented in the above format reflects results for only those companies which have reported; no estimates are used. This holds true for all industry groups. The tables in the front of the book do reflect estimated results for those companies which have not reported for fiscal 1983.

Source: *Standard & Poor's Analyst's Handbook* (New York: Standard & Poor's Corporation, 1984).

STOCK PRICE INDEXES—COMPOSITE†

(500 Stocks)

1941-1943 = 10 — Monthly Averages of Daily Indexes

Year	Jan.	Feb.	Mar.	Apr.	May	June	July	Aug.	Sept.	Oct.	Nov.	Dec.	Avg.
1926	12.65	12.67	11.81	11.48	11.56	12.11	12.62	13.12	13.32	13.02	13.19	13.49	12.59
1927	13.40	13.66	13.87	14.21	14.70	14.89	15.22	16.03	16.94	16.68	17.06	17.46	15.34
1928	17.53	17.32	18.25	19.40	20.00	19.02	19.16	19.78	21.17	21.60	23.06	23.15	19.95
1929	24.86	24.99	25.43	25.28	25.66	26.15	28.48	30.10	31.30	27.99	20.58	21.40	26.02
1930	21.71	23.07	23.94	25.46	23.94	21.52	21.06	20.79	20.78	17.92	16.62	15.51	21.03
1931	15.98	17.20	17.53	15.86	14.33	13.87	14.33	13.90	11.83	10.25	10.39	8.44	13.66
1932	8.30	8.23	8.26	6.28	5.51	4.77	5.01	7.53	8.26	7.12	7.05	6.82	6.93
1933	7.09	6.25	6.23	6.89	8.87	10.39	11.23	10.67	10.58	9.55	9.78	9.97	8.96
1934	10.54	11.32	10.74	10.92	9.81	9.94	9.47	9.10	8.88	8.95	9.20	9.26	9.84
1935	9.26	8.98	8.41	9.04	9.75	10.12	10.65	11.37	11.61	11.92	13.04	13.04	10.60
1936	13.76	14.55	14.86	14.88	14.09	14.69	15.56	15.87	16.05	16.89	17.36	17.06	15.47
1937	17.59	18.11	18.09	17.01	16.25	15.64	16.57	16.74	14.37	12.28	11.20	11.02	15.41
1938	11.31	11.04	10.31	9.89	9.98	10.21	12.24	12.31	11.75	13.06	13.07	12.69	11.49
1939	12.50	12.40	12.39	10.83	11.23	11.43	11.71	11.54	12.77	12.90	12.67	12.37	12.06
1940	12.30	12.22	12.15	12.27	10.58	9.67	9.99	10.20	10.63	10.73	10.98	10.53	11.02
1941	10.55	9.89	9.95	9.64	9.43	9.76	10.26	10.21	10.24	9.83	9.37	8.76	9.82
1942	8.93	8.65	8.18	7.84	7.93	8.33	8.64	8.59	8.68	9.32	9.47	9.52	8.67
1943	10.09	10.69	11.07	11.44	11.89	12.10	12.35	11.74	11.99	11.88	11.33	11.48	11.50
1944	11.85	11.77	12.10	11.89	12.67	13.00	12.61	12.60	12.91	12.82	13.10	12.47	12.47
1945	13.49	13.94	13.93	14.28	14.82	15.09	14.78	14.83	15.84	16.50	17.04	17.33	15.16
1946	18.02	18.07	17.53	18.66	18.70	18.58	18.05	17.70	15.09	14.75	14.69	15.13	17.08
1947	15.21	15.80	15.16	14.60	14.34	14.84	15.77	15.46	15.06	15.45	15.27	15.03	15.17
1948	14.83	14.10	14.30	15.40	16.15	16.82	16.42	15.94	15.76	16.19	15.29	15.19	15.53
1949	15.36	14.77	14.91	14.89	14.78	13.97	14.76	15.29	15.49	15.89	16.11	16.54	15.23
1950	16.88	17.21	17.35	17.84	18.44	18.74	17.38	18.43	19.08	19.87	19.83	19.75	18.40
1951	21.21	22.00	21.63	21.92	21.93	21.55	21.93	22.89	23.48	23.36	22.71	23.41	22.34
1952	24.19	23.75	23.81	23.74	23.73	24.38	25.08	25.14	24.78	24.26	25.03	26.04	24.50
1953	26.18	25.86	25.99	24.71	24.84	23.95	24.29	24.39	23.27	23.97	24.50	24.83	24.73
1954	25.46	26.02	26.57	27.63	28.73	28.96	30.13	30.73	31.45	32.18	33.44	34.97	29.69
1955	35.60	36.79	36.50	37.76	37.60	39.78	42.69	42.43	44.34	44.95	45.37	45.37	40.49
1956	44.15	44.43	47.49	48.05	45.54	46.27	48.78	48.49	46.84	46.24	45.76	46.44	46.62
1957	45.43	43.47	44.03	45.05	46.78	47.55	48.51	45.84	43.98	41.24	40.35	40.33	44.38
1958	41.12	41.26	42.11	42.34	43.70	44.75	45.98	47.70	48.96	50.95	52.50	53.49	46.24
1959	55.62	54.77	56.15	57.10	57.96	57.46	59.74	59.40	57.05	57.00	57.23	59.06	57.38
1960	58.03	55.78	55.02	55.73	55.22	57.26	55.84	56.51	53.73	55.47	55.47	56.80	55.85
1961	59.72	62.17	64.12	65.83	66.50	65.62	65.44	67.79	67.26	68.00	71.08	71.74	68.27
1962	69.07	70.22	70.29	68.05	62.99	55.63	56.97	58.52	58.00	56.17	60.04	62.64	62.38
1963	65.06	65.92	65.67	68.76	70.14	70.11	69.07	70.98	72.85	73.03	72.62	74.17	69.87
1964	76.45	77.39	78.80	79.94	80.72	80.24	83.22	82.00	83.41	84.85	85.44	83.96	81.37
1965	86.12	86.75	86.83	87.97	89.28	85.04	84.91	86.49	89.38	91.39	92.15	92.43	88.17
1966	93.32	92.69	88.88	91.60	86.78	86.06	85.84	80.65	77.81	77.13	80.99	81.33	85.26
1967	84.45	87.36	89.42	90.96	92.59	91.43	93.01	94.49	95.81	95.66	92.66	95.30	91.93
1968	95.04	90.75	89.09	95.67	97.87	100.5	100.3	98.11	101.3	103.8	105.4	106.5	98.69
1969	102.0	101.5	99.30	101.3	104.6	99.14	94.71	94.18	94.51	95.52	96.21	91.11	97.84
1970	90.31	87.16	88.65	85.95	76.06	75.59	75.72	77.92	82.58	84.37	84.28	90.05	83.22
1971	93.49	97.11	99.60	103.0	101.6	99.72	99.00	97.24	99.40	97.29	92.78	99.17	98.29
1972	103.3	105.2	107.7	108.8	107.7	108.0	107.2	111.0	109.4	109.6	115.1	117.5	109.2
1973	118.4	114.2	112.4	110.3	107.2	104.8	105.8	103.8	105.6	109.3	102.2	94.78	107.4
1974	96.11	93.45	97.44	92.46	89.67	89.79	82.82	76.03	68.12	69.44	71.74	67.07	82.85
1975	72.56	80.10	83.78	84.72	90.10	92.40	92.49	85.71	84.67	88.57	90.07	88.70	86.16
1976	96.86	100.6	101.1	101.9	101.2	101.8	104.2	103.3	105.5	101.9	101.2	104.7	102.0
1977	103.8	101.0	100.6	99.05	98.76	99.29	100.2	97.75	96.23	93.74	94.28	93.82	98.20
1978	90.25	88.98	88.82	92.71	97.41	97.66	97.19	103.9	103.9	100.6	94.71	96.11	96.02
1979	99.71	98.23	100.1	102.1	99.73	101.7	102.7	107.4	108.6	104.5	103.7	107.8	103.0
1980	110.9	115.3	104.7	103.0	107.7	114.6	119.8	123.5	126.5	130.2	135.7	133.5	118.8
1981	133.0	128.4	133.2	134.4	131.7	132.3	129.1	129.6	118.3	119.8	122.9	123.8	128.1
1982	117.3	114.5	110.8	116.3	116.4	109.7	109.4	109.7	122.4	132.7	138.1	139.4	119.7
1983	144.3	146.8	151.9	157.7	164.1	166.4	167.0	162.4	167.2	167.7	165.2	164.4	160.4

Annual Range, and Close, of Daily Indexes

Year	High	Low	Close	Year	High	Low	Close	Year	High	Low	Close
1926	13.66	10.93	13.49	1946	19.25	14.12	15.30	1966	94.06	73.20	80.33
1927	17.71	13.18	17.66	1947	16.20	13.71	15.30	1967	97.59	80.38	96.47
1928	24.35	16.95	24.35	1948	17.06	13.84	15.20	1968	108.4	87.72	103.9
1929	31.92	17.66	21.45	1949	16.79	13.55	16.76	1969	106.2	89.20	92.06
1930	25.92	14.44	15.34	1950	20.43	16.65	20.41	1970	93.46	69.29	92.15
1931	18.17	7.72	8.12	1951	23.85	20.69	23.77	1971	104.8	90.16	102.1
1932	9.31	4.40	6.89	1952	26.59	23.09	26.57	1972	119.1	101.7	118.1
1933	12.20	5.53	10.10	1953	26.66	22.71	24.81	1973	120.2	92.16	97.55
1934	11.82	8.36	9.50	1954	35.98	24.80	35.98	1974	99.80	62.28	68.56
1935	13.46	8.06	13.43	1955	46.41	34.58	45.48	1975	95.61	70.04	90.19
1936	17.69	13.40	17.18	1956	49.74	43.11	46.67	1976	107.8	90.90	107.5
1937	18.68	10.17	10.55	1957	49.13	38.98	39.99	1977	107.0	90.71	95.10
1938	13.79	8.50	13.21	1958	55.21	40.33	55.21	1978	107.0	86.90	96.11
1939	13.23	10.18	12.49	1959	60.71	53.58	59.89	1979	111.3	96.13	107.9
1940	12.77	8.99	10.58	1960	60.39	52.30	58.11	1980	140.5	98.22	135.8
1941	10.86	8.37	8.69	1961	72.64	57.57	71.55	1981	138.1	112.8	122.6
1942	9.77	7.47	9.77	1962	71.13	52.32	63.10	1982	143.0	102.4	140.6
1943	12.64	9.84	11.67	1963	75.02	62.69	75.02	1983	172.7	138.3	164.9
1944	13.29	11.56	13.28	1964	86.28	75.43	84.75				
1945	17.68	13.21	17.36	1965	92.63	81.60	92.43				

INDUSTRIAL STOCKS†

(400 Stocks)

Monthly Averages of Daily Indexes — 1941-1943-10

Year	Jan.	Feb.	Mar.	Apr.	May	June	July	Aug.	Sept.	Oct.	Nov.	Dec.	Avg.
1926	10.04	10.10	9.38	9.06	9.12	9.59	10.06	10.52	10.67	10.46	10.58	10.84	10.04
1927	10.74	10.96	11.16	11.42	11.85	12.01	12.38	13.18	14.08	13.80	14.20	14.61	12.53
1928	14.68	14.43	15.34	16.35	16.74	15.96	16.18	16.80	18.11	18.70	19.94	19.75	16.92
1929	21.22	21.12	21.68	21.62	21.70	21.55	22.95	23.89	24.68	22.26	16.44	17.03	21.35
1930	17.13	18.06	18.73	19.93	18.60	16.68	16.41	16.33	16.21	13.84	12.97	12.17	16.42
1931	12.34	13.27	13.45	12.18	10.97	10.56	10.95	10.72	9.15	7.91	8.09	6.54	10.51
1932	6.39	6.33	6.35	4.83	4.27	3.80	4.00	5.94	6.39	5.49	5.45	5.18	5.37
1933	5.35	4.74	4.93	5.75	7.41	8.61	9.40	9.15	9.37	8.48	8.92	9.16	7.61
1934	9.56	10.11	9.63	9.86	8.88	8.96	8.60	8.41	8.22	8.31	8.70	8.81	9.00
1935	8.88	8.72	8.19	8.67	9.40	9.64	10.14	10.71	11.01	11.39	12.43	12.38	10.13
1936	12.96	13.71	14.12	14.20	13.44	13.93	14.66	14.96	15.17	16.04	16.69	16.41	14.69
1937	16.87	17.51	17.52	16.45	15.74	15.24	16.30	16.17	14.03	12.04	10.82	10.68	14.97
1938	11.10	10.89	10.22	9.57	9.78	10.07	12.11	11.37	11.15	12.56	12.60	12.35	11.19
1939	12.30	12.12	12.09	10.56	10.91	11.11	11.37	11.15	12.56	12.60	12.35	12.09	11.77
1940	11.95	11.87	11.84	11.94	10.28	9.34	9.55	9.79	10.26	10.39	10.73	10.34	10.69
1941	10.30	9.64	9.73	9.43	9.27	9.66	10.19	10.14	10.21	9.81	9.41	8.86	9.72
1942	8.95	8.67	8.24	7.93	8.01	8.47	8.82	8.76	8.84	9.45	9.56	9.68	8.78
1943	10.22	10.81	11.13	11.44	11.87	12.14	12.29	11.66	11.91	11.77	11.25	11.42	11.49
1944	11.78	11.63	11.95	11.75	11.98	12.58	12.90	12.67	12.47	12.76	12.87	12.90	12.34
1945	13.23	13.63	13.63	13.94	14.44	14.58	14.23	14.39	15.43	16.03	16.41	16.73	14.72
1946	17.34	17.38	16.85	18.02	18.04	17.85	17.42	17.12	14.65	14.35	14.20	14.58	16.48
1947	14.69	15.31	14.73	14.23	14.02	14.58	15.48	15.15	14.76	15.19	15.15	14.93	14.85
1948	14.60	13.88	14.07	15.19	15.92	16.55	16.21	15.74	15.53	16.02	15.16	15.11	15.34
1949	15.23	14.57	14.72	14.66	14.51	13.69	14.55	15.04	15.20	15.83	16.15	16.29	15.00
1950	16.56	16.90	17.03	17.58	18.27	18.68	17.31	18.47	19.18	20.06	20.05	19.92	18.33
1951	21.38	22.22	21.84	22.24	22.29	21.88	22.31	23.35	23.98	23.80	23.09	23.83	22.68
1952	24.61	24.05	24.04	23.98	23.94	24.66	25.49	25.53	25.06	24.48	25.24	26.29	24.78
1953	26.45	26.07	26.18	24.84	25.01	24.12	24.41	24.44	23.26	23.94	24.85	24.84	24.84
1954	25.55	26.12	26.72	27.97	29.21	29.43	30.64	31.26	32.20	33.17	34.56	36.14	30.25
1955	36.79	38.06	37.65	39.04	38.88	41.45	44.94	44.56	46.88	44.52	47.78	48.25	42.40
1956	46.88	47.13	50.59	51.38	49.64	49.38	52.27	51.89	50.15	49.52	48.92	49.79	49.80
1957	48.43	46.10	46.86	48.06	50.14	50.30	51.30	52.54	49.51	47.52	44.43	43.41	43.29	47.63
1958	43.98	44.01	44.97	45.09	46.51	47.62	48.96	51.00	52.40	54.55	56.11	57.09	49.36
1959	59.30	58.33	59.79	60.92	62.09	61.57	64.23	63.74	61.21	61.04	61.46	63.56	61.45
1960	62.27	59.60	58.71	59.46	58.84	61.06	59.25	59.96	57.96	56.90	58.89	60.22	59.43
1961	63.20	65.71	67.83	69.64	70.34	69.48	69.15	71.69	70.80	71.42	74.72	75.81	69.99
1962	72.99	74.22	74.22	71.64	66.32	58.32	59.61	62.39	60.67	58.66	62.60	65.59	65.54
1963	68.00	68.41	68.71	72.17	73.60	73.61	72.45	74.43	76.63	77.09	76.69	78.38	73.39
1964	80.85	81.96	83.64	84.92	85.79	85.13	88.19	86.70	88.27	89.75	90.38	88.71	86.19
1965	91.04	91.64	91.75	93.08	94.69	90.19	89.92	91.68	94.93	97.20	98.02	97.66	93.48
1966	99.56	99.11	95.04	98.17	92.85	92.14	91.95	86.40	83.11	82.01	86.10	86.50	91.08
1967	89.88	93.35	95.86	97.54	99.59	98.61	100.4	102.1	103.8	104.2	100.9	103.9	99.18
1968	103.1	98.33	96.77	104.4	107.0	109.7	109.2	106.8	110.5	113.3	114.8	116.0	107.5
1969	111.0	110.2	108.2	110.7	114.5	108.6	103.7	103.4	104.0	105.1	105.9	100.5	107.2
1970	99.40	95.73	96.95	94.01	83.16	82.96	83.00	85.40	90.66	92.85	92.58	98.72	91.29
1971	102.2	106.6	109.6	113.7	112.0	110.3	109.3	109.0	107.3	109.0	103.7	108.4	
1972	114.1	116.9	119.7	121.3	122.0	120.6	120.0	124.4	122.3	122.4	128.3	131.1	121.8
1973	132.6	127.9	126.1	123.6	120.0	117.2	118.7	116.8	118.5	123.4	114.6	106.2	120.5
1974	107.2	104.1	109.0	103.7	101.2	101.6	93.54	85.51	76.54	77.57	80.17	74.80	92.91
1975	80.50	89.29	93.90	95.27	101.5	103.7	103.8	96.21	94.96	99.29	100.9	99.31	96.56
1976	108.5	113.0	113.7	114.7	113.8	114.5	117.0	115.6	118.2	114.0	113.0	116.3	114.3
1977	115.2	112.1	111.9	109.9	109.1	109.5	110.1	107.5	105.9	103.2	103.7	103.1	108.4
1978	99.34	96.95	97.65	102.1	107.7	108.0	107.4	115.0	115.1	111.6	105.2	106.9	106.2
1979	111.2	109.5	111.7	114.0	111.2	113.0	113.6	118.9	121.1	117.0	116.1	120.8	114.8
1980	124.7	130.9	118.7	115.6	120.8	128.8	135.2	142.0	143.7	148.4	155.1	152.2	134.5
1981	151.1	145.7	151.0	152.3	149.1	148.7	145.4	146.0	132.7	134.0	136.8	138.4	144.3
1982	131.1	127.6	122.9	129.2	129.7	122.6	122.5	123.2	137.1	148.1	153.9	156.0	133.6
1983	162.0	165.2	170.3	176.8	184.1	187.4	188.3	183.2	188.6	189.0	185.9	185.2	180.5

Annual Range, and Close, of Daily Indexes

Year	High	Low	Close	Year	High	Low	Close	Year	High	Low	Close
1926	11.01	8.63	10.83	1946	18.53	13.64	14.75	1966	100.6	77.89	85.24
1927	14.88	10.56	14.82	1947	15.83	13.40	15.18	1967	106.2	85.31	105.11
1928	20.85	14.05	20.85	1948	16.93	13.58	15.12	1968	118.0	95.05	113.0
1929	25.38	14.18	16.99	1949	16.79	13.23	16.49	1969	116.2	97.75	101.5
1930	20.32	11.33	11.90	1950	20.60	16.34	20.57	1970	102.9	75.58	100.9
1931	14.07	6.02	6.32	1951	24.33	20.85	24.24	1971	115.8	99.36	112.7
1932	7.26	3.52	5.18	1952	26.92	23.30	26.89	1972	130.0	112.2	131.9
1933	10.25	4.24	9.26	1953	26.99	22.70	24.87	1973	134.5	103.4	109.1
1934	10.54	7.63	9.12	1954	37.24	24.84	37.24	1974	111.7	69.53	76.47
1935	12.84	7.90	12.77	1955	49.54	35.66	48.44	1975	107.4	77.71	100.9
1936	17.02	12.67	16.50	1956	53.28	45.71	50.08	1976	120.9	101.6	119.5
1937	18.10	9.73	10.26	1957	53.25	41.98	42.86	1977	118.9	99.88	104.7
1938	13.66	8.39	13.07	1958	58.97	43.20	58.97	1978	118.7	95.52	107.2
1939	13.08	9.92	12.17	1959	65.32	57.02	64.50	1979	124.5	107.1	121.0
1940	12.47	8.70	10.37	1960	65.02	55.34	61.49	1980	161.0	111.1	154.5
1941	10.62	8.47	8.78	1961	76.69	60.87	75.72	1981	157.0	125.9	137.1
1942	9.94	7.54	9.93	1962	75.22	54.80	66.00	1982	159.7	114.1	157.6
1943	12.58	10.00	11.61	1963	79.25	65.48	79.25	1983	194.8	155.0	186.2
1944	13.18	11.43	13.05	1964	91.29	79.74	89.62				
1945	17.06	12.97	16.79	1965	98.55	86.43	98.47				

Source: *Standard & Poor's Statistics* (New York: Standard & Poor's Corporation, 1984).

PREFERRED STOCK PRICE INDEXES

Dollars per $100 par value

The indexes are based upon one price weekly (as of Wednesday's close), the monthly index being an average of the four or five weekly indexes of the month. These indexes have been based upon ten high grade non-callable issues, the yield for each being determined and the average of the four median yields representing the group yield. The average yield has, in turn, been converted into an equivalent price basis (7%) for the composite price index.

Monthly Averages of Weekly Indexes

Year	Jan.	Feb.	Mar.	Apr.	May	June	July	Aug.	Sept.	Oct.	Nov.	Dec.	Avg.
1933	121.8	120.6	115.3	114.5	117.8	123.3	126.6	127.3	128.1	126.3	121.9	121.1	122.1
1934	123.6	128.2	129.7	131.4	132.6	133.6	135.6	135.2	132.7	131.6	135.7	140.5	132.5
1935	142.8	144.5	145.6	149.2	153.5	153.8	153.9	154.4	153.5	152.6	154.6	157.9	151.4
1936	159.2	160.8	162.6	162.7	161.4	161.7	162.4	163.1	162.1	161.4	160.9	164.5	161.9
1937	167.6	166.5	159.0	154.8	153.1	155.3	155.2	157.1	156.6	155.2	153.8	156.5	157.6
1938	157.2	158.2	156.0	154.3	157.2	158.8	160.9	163.6	165.5	166.9	169.7	168.9	161.4
1939	170.1	170.6	169.4	168.3	169.1	170.7	172.8	172.0	156.1	156.9	165.3	169.0	167.5
1940	172.2	171.0	169.6	170.5	166.5	159.9	166.1	167.0	168.6	170.8	171.6	176.2	169.2
1941	177.9	172.9	171.5	170.8	168.9	168.9	173.1	174.3	173.4	172.1	170.5	168.7	171.9
1942	166.3	165.1	159.8	154.8	156.3	159.2	162.0	164.0	164.0	165.5	165.4	166.9	162.4
1943	168.0	170.8	171.5	171.5	172.1	173.8	175.9	176.4	175.9	175.1	172.6	169.1	172.7
1944	171.2	172.7	173.4	174.1	173.2	175.8	177.6	176.9	177.4	177.4	178.5	180.9	175.8
1945	183.3	185.5	187.7	190.9	191.2	190.9	189.6	188.1	186.7	188.0	192.2	195.3	189.1
1946	197.9	200.5	203.1	204.9	201.9	202.4	204.1	203.4	196.2	191.6	189.3	186.2	198.5
1947	187.3	189.0	188.1	186.5	186.2	186.2	188.4	188.7	188.3	181.2	174.5	172.1	184.7
1948	169.5	167.5	170.1	169.8	171.6	172.8	169.5	166.9	166.5	163.8	166.2	168.7	168.6
1949	171.4	173.2	172.2	172.2	173.2	176.1	176.6	179.5	182.1	180.3	179.8	180.6	176.4
1950	182.8	182.4	183.8	183.5	183.1	182.0	178.5	181.9	181.7	180.5	180.7	179.9	181.7
1951	180.9	180.9	174.9	170.4	168.9	167.9	166.7	169.4	168.5	167.0	165.4	163.7	170.4
1952	164.2	165.9	168.2	172.2	173.4	173.3	171.1	170.2	168.3	169.8	170.3	169.7	169.7
1953	168.4	166.3	165.7	161.7	160.0	156.8	160.1	163.1	162.8	167.3	168.8	166.5	164.0
1954	168.7	171.8	173.3	174.3	173.8	172.9	173.3	174.7	175.8	178.1	178.3	178.5	174.5
1955	175.8	175.0	174.6	176.0	175.6	175.7	176.7	174.4	172.7	173.5	174.7	172.9	174.8
1956	173.9	175.7	174.5	168.7	166.0	167.8	168.2	165.1	159.6	158.5	153.7	151.4	165.3
1957	155.1	156.7	157.2	156.8	154.6	149.5	147.3	145.1	146.2	145.9	146.5	156.0	151.4
1958	160.7	159.9	158.3	160.4	162.4	163.5	160.5	157.5	153.0	150.8	150.7	151.1	157.4
1959	154.4	155.1	156.3	155.0	149.7	146.0	147.2	149.0	146.0	145.6	145.4	144.3	149.5
1960	143.8	145.3	147.1	148.6	147.3	147.7	148.9	151.9	149.2	147.5	146.3	144.8	147.4
1961	148.0	149.8	150.2	150.1	151.0	150.2	149.4	149.2	149.3	151.8	152.7	150.9	150.2
1962	152.6	153.0	156.2	157.2	157.3	155.0	152.7	154.0	157.5	155.4	157.4	158.3	155.6
1963	161.3	164.1	164.9	162.4	163.4	163.2	161.4	162.7	162.9	164.5	163.6	161.9	163.0
1964	162.4	162.6	161.2	160.1	158.8	158.9	160.3	163.5	164.8	164.8	164.7	165.6	162.3
1965	167.5	166.1	164.2	163.7	162.8	159.7	159.8	161.3	162.2	159.8	158.9	156.6	161.9
1966	155.2	151.1	144.8	146.5	145.0	142.1	139.9	135.3	133.8	132.7	134.5	133.5	141.2
1967	138.3	140.7	138.9	139.2	135.5	132.0	131.1	131.0	129.4	125.3	120.8	117.8	131.7
1968	122.9	123.9	130.8	119.5	118.0	118.7	121.9	125.2	124.4	121.6	120.3	118.1	121.3
1969	118.2	117.9	115.0	114.0	113.0	110.6	109.1	108.6	106.1	103.1	102.3	97.4	109.6
1970	99.8	99.3	100.6	100.3	96.5	92.4	92.0	94.6	95.8	95.6	95.9	101.7	97.0
1971	107.3	110.7	108.1	106.4	102.7	100.1	99.6	99.5	101.5	103.7	103.4	102.9	103.8
1972	106.7	105.0	103.6	101.3	101.4	101.0	100.1	101.5	100.0	99.5	101.2	101.2	101.9
1973	102.1	101.4	99.5	98.6	98.1	96.7	95.3	94.2	94.9	97.6	94.6	90.2	96.9
1974	92.2	93.7	92.7	89.5	86.3	84.9	83.3	81.4	78.4	79.8	81.4	79.7	85.3
1975	84.1	86.8	87.1	84.7	82.2	83.9	85.0	83.2	81.8	81.6	82.4	82.8	83.8
1976	85.8	87.5	86.8	87.1	86.9	86.4	86.7	87.7	88.6	89.9	89.8	90.9	87.8
1977	92.9	92.7	92.6	92.1	91.8	91.9	90.3	92.7	92.4	91.9	91.2	89.2	92.1
1978	88.35	87.66	86.80	86.88	86.37	84.23	83.26	84.76	85.02	84.50	83.02	79.27	85.01
1979	79.61	79.87	79.80	80.01	79.33	78.94	78.40	77.62	76.67	74.01	70.42	69.60	77.02
1980	68.84	66.40	61.57	62.83	68.63	71.59	71.40	69.76	69.02	65.84	61.72	58.63	66.35
1981	60.62	59.19	59.27	59.26	56.94	57.23	56.30	55.45	53.82	53.50	54.88	54.58	56.75
1982	53.06	53.02	53.98	54.30	55.67	54.03	52.86	54.80	56.41	59.83	62.60	62.55	56.09
1983	62.37	62.92	64.45	64.84	65.72	64.75	63.32	63.27	63.32	63.82	62.94	60.96	63.56

Annual Range, and Close, of Weekly Indexes

Year	High	Low	Close	Year	High	Low	Close	Year	High	Low	Close
1931	145.2	117.1	117.1	1949	183.3	169.1	181.4	1967	141.5	116.7	118.4
1932	121.5	99.3	119.9	1950	184.2	178.1	179.8	1968	125.8	116.3	116.5
1933	128.7	113.5	120.7	1951	181.7	161.9	161.9	1969	118.9	95.6	97.7
1934	141.4	121.3	140.9	1952	173.8	161.6	169.6	1970	103.0	89.3	101.2
1935	159.1	141.4	159.1	1953	169.6	156.2	166.7	1971	112.2	98.5	103.6
1936	165.5	158.7	165.5	1954	179.1	167.0	177.5	1972	107.9	99.2	101.0
1937	168.3	152.5	156.6	1955	177.4	172.0	172.6	1973	102.7	88.6	88.6
1938	170.7	153.5	167.5	1956	178.4	150.7	151.9	1974	94.7	77.6	78.7
1939	173.7	152.5	168.7	1957	158.2	144.2	157.7	1975	88.4	80.4	82.5
1940	178.1	159.1	178.1	1958	164.4	150.0	151.7	1976	91.5	83.1	91.5
1941	179.5	166.7	166.7	1959	157.3	142.7	142.8	1977	94.5	89.0	89.3
1942	167.1	152.5	166.7	1960	153.1	143.5	146.4	1978	89.42	78.32	78.52
1943	176.4	167.1	169.9	1961	153.0	146.4	150.7	1979	80.90	68.93	69.03
1944	181.9	170.7	181.9	1962	159.1	151.0	159.1	1980	73.16	57.96	57.88
1945	196.7	182.3	196.7	1963	165.2	159.1	161.2	1981	61.04	52.62	52.62
1946	205.3	185.7	185.7	1964	166.2	158.0	166.0	1982	65.35	52.43	61.47
1947	189.2	167.9	167.9	1965	165.7	155.2	155.2	1983	66.10	60.02	60.02
1948	173.7	163.6	169.5	1966	155.6	131.2	135.3				

PREFERRED STOCK YIELD INDEXES

Yield in percent.

The indexes are based upon one price weekly (as of Wednesday's close), the monthly index being an average of the four or five weekly indexes of the month. These indexes have been based upon ten high-grade non-callable issues, the yield for each being determined and the average of the four median yields representing the group yield. The average yield has, in turn, been converted into an equivalent price basis (7%) for the composite price index.

Monthly Averages of Weekly Indexes

Year	Jan.	Feb.	Mar.	Apr.	May	June	July	Aug.	Sept.	Oct.	Nov.	Dec.	Avg
1933	5.75	5.81	6.07	6.12	5.95	5.68	5.53	5.50	5.47	5.55	5.74	5.78	5.75
1934	5.66	5.46	5.40	5.33	5.28	5.24	5.16	5.18	5.28	5.32	5.16	4.99	5.29
1935	4.90	4.85	4.81	4.69	4.56	4.55	4.55	4.54	4.56	4.59	4.53	4.43	4.63
1936	4.40	4.36	4.31	4.30	4.34	4.33	4.31	4.29	4.32	4.34	4.35	4.26	4.33
1937	4.18	4.21	4.40	4.52	4.57	4.51	4.51	4.46	4.47	4.51	4.55	4.47	4.45
1938	4.45	4.43	4.49	4.54	4.46	4.43	4.35	4.28	4.23	4.20	4.12	4.15	4.34
1939	4.12	4.11	4.13	4.16	4.14	4.10	4.05	4.07	4.09	4.47	4.24	4.14	4.19
1940	4.07	4.10	4.13	4.11	4.21	4.38	4.22	4.19	4.15	4.10	4.08	3.97	4.14
1941	3.94	4.05	4.08	4.10	4.15	4.15	4.05	4.02	4.04	4.07	4.01	4.15	4.08
1942	4.21	4.24	4.38	4.52	4.48	4.40	4.32	4.27	4.27	4.23	4.23	4.19	4.31
1943	4.17	4.10	4.08	4.08	4.07	4.03	3.98	3.97	3.98	4.00	4.06	4.14	4.06
1944	4.09	4.06	4.04	4.02	4.04	3.98	3.94	3.96	3.95	3.95	3.92	3.87	3.99
1945	3.82	3.78	3.73	3.67	3.66	3.67	3.69	3.72	3.75	3.72	3.64	3.59	3.70
1946	3.54	3.49	3.45	3.42	3.47	3.46	3.43	3.44	3.57	3.65	3.70	3.76	3.53
1947	3.74	3.71	3.72	3.75	3.76	3.76	3.72	3.71	3.72	3.86	4.01	4.07	3.79
1948	4.13	4.18	4.12	4.12	4.08	4.05	4.13	4.20	4.20	4.28	4.21	4.15	4.15
1949	4.09	4.04	4.07	4.07	4.04	3.98	3.97	3.90	3.85	3.88	3.89	3.89	3.85
1950	3.84	3.84	3.81	3.82	3.82	3.85	3.92	3.85	3.85	3.88	3.88	3.89	3.85
1951	3.87	3.87	4.00	4.11	4.15	4.17	4.20	4.13	4.18	4.19	4.23	4.28	4.11
1952	4.26	4.22	4.16	4.07	4.04	4.04	4.09	4.12	4.12	4.16	4.12	4.11	4.13
1953	4.16	4.21	4.23	4.33	4.38	4.47	4.37	4.30	4.30	4.19	4.15	4.20	4.27
1954	4.15	4.08	4.04	4.02	4.03	4.05	4.04	4.01	3.98	3.93	3.92	3.93	4.02
1955	3.98	4.00	4.01	3.98	3.99	3.98	3.96	4.01	4.06	4.04	4.01	4.05	4.01
1956	4.03	3.99	4.01	4.15	4.22	4.17	4.16	4.24	4.39	4.42	4.56	4.63	4.25
1957	4.51	4.47	4.46	4.47	4.53	4.69	4.75	4.83	4.79	4.80	4.78	4.49	4.63
1958	4.36	4.38	4.42	4.37	4.31	4.28	4.36	4.45	4.58	4.64	4.65	4.63	4.45
1959	4.54	4.52	4.48	4.51	4.68	4.79	4.75	4.70	4.80	4.81	4.81	4.85	4.69
1960	4.87	4.82	4.76	4.71	4.75	4.74	4.70	4.61	4.69	4.75	4.78	4.84	4.75
1961	4.73	4.68	4.66	4.67	4.63	4.66	4.69	4.69	4.62	4.59	4.64	4.66	4.66
1962	4.59	4.52	4.48	4.45	4.45	4.52	4.59	4.55	4.50	4.49	4.45	4.42	4.50
1963	4.34	4.27	4.24	4.31	4.29	4.29	4.34	4.30	4.30	4.28	4.28	4.32	4.30
1964	4.31	4.31	4.34	4.37	4.41	4.41	4.37	4.29	4.25	4.25	4.25	4.23	4.32
1965	4.18	4.22	4.26	4.28	4.30	4.38	4.38	4.34	4.32	4.39	4.44	4.49	4.32
1966	4.51	4.63	4.83	4.78	4.83	4.93	5.00	5.18	5.23	5.28	5.21	5.24	4.97
1967	5.07	4.98	5.04	5.03	5.17	5.30	5.34	5.35	5.41	5.59	5.79	5.95	5.34
1968	5.70	5.65	5.80	5.86	5.92	5.90	5.76	5.59	5.63	5.76	5.82	5.93	5.78
1969	5.93	5.94	6.09	6.14	6.20	6.33	6.42	6.45	6.61	6.79	6.84	7.19	6.41
1970	7.02	7.04	6.97	6.98	7.26	7.57	7.62	7.41	7.31	7.33	7.30	6.88	7.22
1971	6.53	6.32	6.48	6.59	6.82	6.99	7.03	7.04	6.90	6.75	6.78	6.81	6.75
1972	6.57	6.67	6.76	6.91	6.90	6.93	6.99	6.94	7.00	7.03	6.93	6.92	6.88
1973	6.85	6.91	7.03	7.11	7.13	7.25	7.35	7.43	7.38	7.18	7.40	7.76	7.23
1974	7.60	7.47	7.56	7.83	8.11	8.25	8.40	8.61	8.93	8.78	8.60	8.78	8.24
1975	8.33	8.07	8.04	8.27	8.51	8.34	8.24	8.41	8.56	8.58	8.50	8.46	8.36
1976	8.26	8.00	8.07	8.04	8.06	8.10	8.08	7.99	7.90	7.80	7.80	7.70	7.98
1977	7.54	7.55	7.56	7.60	7.63	7.62	7.51	7.55	7.58	7.62	7.67	7.85	7.61
1978	7.92	7.99	8.07	8.06	8.11	8.31	8.42	8.26	8.24	8.29	8.43	8.84	8.25
1979	8.79	8.77	8.77	8.75	8.82	8.87	8.93	9.02	9.13	9.46	9.95	10.06	9.11
1980	10.17	10.55	11.37	11.16	10.20	9.78	9.81	10.04	10.14	10.64	11.35	11.94	10.60
1981	11.55	11.83	11.81	11.81	12.30	12.23	12.43	12.63	13.01	13.09	12.76	12.83	12.36
1982	13.79	13.20	12.97	12.90	12.58	12.96	13.24	12.78	12.41	11.71	11.18	11.20	12.53
1983	11.23	11.13	10.86	10.80	10.65	10.81	11.06	11.07	11.06	10.97	11.12	11.49	11.02

Annual Range, and Close, of Weekly Indexes

Year	High	Low	Close	Year	High	Low	Close	Year	High	Low	Close
1933	6.17	5.44	5.82	1950	3.93	3.80	3.89	1967	6.00	4.95	5.91
1934	5.77	4.95	4.97	1951	4.32	3.85	4.32	1968	6.02	5.57	6.01
1935	4.95	4.40	4.40	1952	4.33	4.03	4.13	1969	7.33	5.88	7.16
1936	4.41	4.23	4.23	1953	4.48	4.13	4.20	1970	7.84	6.79	6.89
1937	4.59	4.16	4.47	1954	4.19	3.91	3.95	1971	7.10	6.24	6.76
1938	4.56	4.10	4.18	1955	4.09	3.94	4.06	1972	7.06	6.49	6.93
1939	4.59	4.03	4.15	1956	4.65	3.97	4.61	1973	7.90	6.82	7.90
1940	4.40	3.93	3.93	1957	4.86	4.42	4.44	1974	9.02	7.39	8.89
1941	4.20	3.90	4.20	1958	4.67	4.26	4.62	1975	8.70	7.92	8.48
1942	4.59	4.19	4.27	1959	4.90	4.45	4.90	1976	8.42	7.65	7.65
1943	4.19	3.97	4.12	1960	4.88	4.57	4.81	1977	7.87	7.41	7.84
1944	4.11	3.85	3.85	1961	4.78	4.58	4.65	1978	8.94	7.83	8.92
1945	3.84	3.56	3.56	1962	4.64	4.40	4.40	1979	10.16	8.71	10.14
1946	3.77	3.41	3.77	1963	4.40	4.24	4.34	1980	12.09	9.57	12.09
1947	4.17	3.70	4.17	1964	4.41	4.21	4.22	1981	13.30	11.47	13.30
1948	4.28	4.03	4.13	1965	4.51	4.15	4.51	1982	13.35	10.71	11.39
1949	4.14	3.82	3.86	1966	5.34	4.50	5.17	1983	11.66	10.59	11.66

Source: *Standard & Poor's Statistics* (New York: Standard & Poor's Corporation, 1984).

New York Stock Exchange

Composite Stock Index

Year	Open	High	Low	Close	Chg.
1983	79.79	*99.63	79.79	95.18	+14.15
1982	81.33	82.35	58.80	81.03	+ 9.92
1981	78.26	79.14	64.96	71.11	— 6.75
1980	60.69	81.02	55.30	77.86	+15.91
1979	53.93	63.39	53.88	61.95	+ 8.33
1978	51.82	60.38	48.37	53.62	+ 1.12
1977	57.69	57.69	49.78	52.50	— 5.38
1976	48.04	57.88	48.04	57.88	+10.24
1975	37.06	51.24	37.06	47.64	+11.51
1974	51.98	53.37	32.89	36.13	—15.69
1973	65.06	65.48	49.05	51.82	—12.66
1972	56.23	65.14	56.23	64.48	+ 8.05
1971	49.73	57.76	49.60	56.43	+ 6.20
1970	52.10	52.36	37.69	50.23	— 1.30
1969	58.94	59.32	49.31	51.53	— 7.37
1968	53.68	61.27	48.70	58.90	+ 5.07
1967	43.74	54.16	43.74	53.83	+10.11
1966	49.86	51.06	39.37	43.72	— 6.28
1965	45.37	50.00	43.64	50.00	+ 4.35
1964	40.47	46.49	40.47	45.65	+ 5.73
1963	34.41	39.92	34.41	39.92	+ 6.11
1962	37.34	38.02	28.20	33.81	— 4.58
1961	31.17	38.60	31.17	38.39	+ 7.45
1960	31.99	31.99	28.38	30.94	— 1.21
1959	29.54	32.39	28.94	32.15	+ 3.30
1958	21.71	28.85	21.45	28.85	+ 7.74
1957	24.43	26.30	20.92	21.11	— 3.24
1956	23.56	25.90	22.55	24.35	+ 0.64
1955	19.05	23.71	19.05	23.71	+ 4.31
1954	13.70	19.40	13.70	19.40	+ 5.80
1953	14.65	14.65	12.62	13.60	— 0.89
1952	13.70	14.49	13.31	14.49	+ 0.89
1951	12.28	13.89	12.28	13.60	+ 1.59
1950	10.06	12.01	9.85	12.01	+ 2.10

*Record high.

The New York Stock Exchange composite stock index has been computed on a daily basis since June 1, 1964. Prior to that date it was on a weekly basis. December 31, 1965, equals 50.

Source: *The Dow Jones Investor's Handbook* (Homewood, Ill.: Dow Jones-Irwin, 1984).

New York Stock Exchange

Cash Dividends and Yields on Common Stocks

Calendar Year	Number of Issues Listed at Year End	Number Paying Cash Dividends During Year	Estimated Aggregate Cash Payments (Millions)	a-Median Yield (%)	Calendar Year	Number of Issues Listed at Year End	Number Paying Cash Dividends During Year	Estimated Aggregate Cash Payments (Millions)	a-Median Yield (%)
1982	1,499	1,287	$62,224	4.1	1960	1,126	981	$9,872	4.2
1981	1,534	1,337	60,628	5.0	1959	1,092	953	9,337	3.8
1980	1,540	1,361	53,072	4.6	1958	1,086	961	8,711	4.1
1979	1,536	1,359	46,937	5.0	1957	1,098	991	8,807	6.1
1978	1,552	1,373	41,151	4.8	1956	1,077	975	8,341	5.2
1977	1,549	1,360	36,270	4.5	1955	1,076	982	7,488	4.6
1976	1,550	1,340	30,608	4.0	1954	1,076	968	6,439	4.7
1975	1,531	1,273	26,901	5.0	1953	1,069	964	5,874	6.3
1974	1,543	1,308	25,662	7.4	1952	1,067	975	5,595	6.0
1973	1,536	1,276	23,627	5.0	1951	1,054	961	5,467	6.5
1972	1,478	1,195	21,490	3.0	1950	1,039	930	5,404	6.7
1971	1,399	1,132	20,256	3.2	1949	1,017	887	4,235	7.0
1970	1,330	1,120	19,781	3.7	1948	986	883	3,806	7.8
1969	1,290	1,121	19,404	3.6	1947	964	851	3,255	6.3
1968	1,253	1,104	18,124	2.6	1946	933	798	2,669	4.8
1967	1,255	1,116	16,866	3.2	1945	881	746	2,275	3.6
1966	1,267	1,127	16,151	4.1	1944	864	717	2,223	5.0
1965	1,254	1,111	15,300	3.2	1943	845	687	2,063	6.1
1964	1,227	1,066	13,555	3.3	1942	834	648	1,997	7.8
1963	1,194	1,032	12,096	3.6	1941	834	627	2,281	9.3
1962	1,168	994	11,203	3.8	1940	829	577	2,099	6.1
1961	1,145	981	10,430	3.3	1939	825	504	1,833	..

a-Based on cash payments during the year and price at end of year for dividend-paying stocks only.

Source: *The Dow Jones Investor's Handbook* (Homewood, Ill.: Dow Jones-Irwin, 1984).

INTRODUCTION: THE VALUE LINE AVERAGES

Value Line computes four stock market averages; the Value Line Composite (based on the 1,700 stocks reviewed in the Value Line Investment Survey); the 1,500-stock Value Line Industrial Average (which eliminates railroad and utility stocks); the Value Line Railroad Average (14 stocks) and the Value Line Utility Average (177 stocks).

Value Line Averages are computed as follows: Every market day, the closing price of each stock is divided by the preceding day's close. Thus, for example, if a stock rises from 50 to 51½ (a 3 percent increase) the change would be expressed as 1.03; 51½ ÷ 50 = 1.03. Conversely, if a stock fell 3 percent from 50 to 48½, the change would be .97; 48½ ÷ 50 = .97. The changes for all stocks in the group would be geometrically averaged.[1] This final average change for the day is then multiplied by the prior day's closing Value Line Average. For example, if Monday's closing Value Line Composite is 140.10 and Tuesday's average change is 1.025, Tuesday's Value Line Composite is 143.60; 140.10 × 1.025 = 143.60. (The Value Line Averages use June 30, 1961, as a starting point; the averages for that day are set at 100.00.)

When stock dividends or splits occur, the preceding day's price is adjusted accordingly, and the index of change is computed using the above method. As stocks are added to the Value Line Investment Survey, the average is enlarged. Additions and deletions of stocks present no problem to the average because of its large base.

Like the Value Line Averages, the New York Stock Exchange Indices and the Standard & Poor's Averages use many stocks. But the NYSE and S&P measures focus on changes in *market value* rather than changes in stock price. (The market value of a company is its stock price multiplied by the number of shares outstanding.) Thus, a $50 stock with 10 million shares outstanding that moves by 3 percent has a greater impact on the "weighted" averages than another $50 stock that also moves by 3 percent but has only 2 million shares outstanding. Also, even if both companies have the same number of shares, a 3 percent price change in the stock that sells for $50 a share will have a greater impact on the average than a 3 percent change in the price of a stock that sells for $20. Although the Dow Jones Industrial Average is neither weighted by number of shares, nor broad—including as it does, only 30 stocks—the fluctu-

---

[1] A geometric average of n items is:

$$\sqrt[n]{\text{the product of all } n \text{ items.}}$$

Thus, the geometric average of 3, 4 and 5 (3 items) is:

$$\sqrt[3]{3 \times 4 \times 5} = \sqrt[3]{60} = 3.91$$

This is in contrast to an arithmetic average, which is:

$$\text{the sum of all } n \text{ items} \div n.$$

For 3, 4 and 5, the arithmetic average would be:

$$(3 + 4 + 5) \div 3 = 12 \div 3 = 4$$

ations of the Dow are similar to those of the S&P and NYSE averages. That's because the 30 Dow stocks are the shares of the largest companies in the country, and they account for about 25 percent of the total market value of all outstanding shares.

The NYSE and the S&P averages, because they are value weighted, are better measures of the *value of all shares outstanding* in the marketplace than of stock prices. Nor is the Dow an effective barometer of stock prices. Smaller companies are ignored. And those companies that are included don't have equal impacts on the index: The Dow is more responsive to trends in the price of a $20 stock than those of a $5 security.

Value Line's Averages give as much weight to a 3 percent fluctuation in the price of a stock with 2 million shares outstanding as to a 3 percent move in the price of a stock with 100 million shares. Also, the Value Line Averages give equal consideration to stocks that sell for $20 or $5 per share. Thus the Value Line Averages reflect changes in the *price of the typical stock.* The investor who wants to measure the performance of his individual stocks (as opposed to the performance of a diversified portfolio) or monitor trends in stock prices can better do so by referring to Value Line's broadly based, *equally weighted average* of stock prices than to weighted averages which are heavily dependent on large "blue chip" stocks.

Annual High-Low Ranges, 1961–1981

Value Line Composite Averages

Year	High	Date	Low	Date	Last
1961	106.78	12-1	99.62	7-21	105.33
1962	106.03	2-16	76.58	10-26	88.20
1963	102.64	9-13	91.23	1-4	100.21
1964	116.36	11-20	102.03	1-3	113.55
1965	135.47	12-21	111.09	6-28	135.11
1966	141.14	4-21	105.98	10-7	118.45
1967	156.27	10-9	119.25	1-3	152.89
1968	188.64	12-13	138.92	3-25	183.18
1969	183.63	1-2	127.40	12-17	130.56
1970	135.46	1-5	84.23	7-7	103.60
1971	125.76	4-28	97.36	11-23	112.94
1972	125.98	4-12	107.11	10-16	114.05
1973	116.20	1-3	70.50	12-13	73.61
1974	83.41	3-14	47.03	12-23	48.97
1975	80.88	7-15	51.12	1-2	70.69
1976	93.47	12-31	71.62	1-2	93.47
1977	96.34	7-22	86.53	10-25	93.92
1978	119.77	9-12	88.67	1-16	97.97
1979	125.25	10-5	98.88	1-2	121.91
1980	149.76	11-20	100.60	3-27	144.20
1981	159.03	6-15	125.66	9-25	137.81

Value Line Industrial Averages

Year	High	Date	Low	Date	Last
1961	105.72	12-8	99.61	7-21	104.71
1962	105.41	2-16	74.30	10-26	85.68
1963	99.77	10-25	88.65	1-4	97.52
1964	113.06	11-20	99.42	1-3	110.22
1965	135.10	12-17	108.22	6-28	134.34
1966	142.53	4-21	105.21	10-7	118.17
1967	163.09	10-9	119.03	1-3	160.00
1968	199.99	12-13	144.03	3-5	193.80
1969	194.38	1-3	133.80	12-17	137.00
1970	142.27	1-5	85.40	7-7	104.67
1971	129.92	4-28	98.89	11-23	115.84
1972	131.65	4-12	110.09	10-16	116.97
1973	119.33	1-3	70.45	12-13	73.53
1974	84.30	3-14	46.50	12-23	48.52
1975	82.22	7-15	50.61	1-2	70.93
1976	94.33	12-31	71.87	1-2	94.33
1977	96.67	7-22	86.48	10-25	94.52
1978	124.35	9-12	89.02	1-11	100.38
1979	130.33	10-5	101.33	1-2	127.01
1980	158.61	11-20	104.39	3-27	152.14
1981	169.62	6-15	132.01	9-25	145.06

Value Line Rail Averages

Year	High	Date	Low	Date	Last
1961	110.52	11-17	95.85	7-21	104.05
1962	110.65	2-9	79.93	6-22	96.68
1963	131.61	8-30	104.25	1-18	127.30
1964	177.80	10-21	129.90	1-8	160.87
1965	199.09	12-17	149.37	6-28	198.65
1966	224.12	2-15	144.06	10-7	157.18
1967	202.69	7-21	159.76	1-3	175.56
1968	213.69	12-13	160.74	3-25	210.01
1969	218.52	2-12	129.29	12-23	132.76
1970	140.71	3-3	81.66	7-7	112.64
1971	145.21	9-7	104.10	11-24	122.57
1972	127.86	1-28	101.98	10-31	104.05
1973	107.17	1-3	70.60	8-22	86.93
1974	94.22	1-3	56.98	9-16	60.66
1975	75.07	7-16	63.12	1-3	68.12
1976	100.25	12-29	69.27	1-2	99.94
1977	115.50	5-20	95.57	10-25	102.69
1978	122.26	9-8	97.32	10-31	103.02
1979	144.44	8-15	105.07	1-2	134.17
1980	207.16	11-28	122.27	3-27	198.12
1981	213.42	4-20	163.06	9-25	181.40

Value Line Utility Averages

Year	High	Date	Low	Date	Last
1961	116.94	11-24	100.00	6-30	111.70
1962	113.03	3-23	89.55	6-22	105.49
1963	118.45	9-6	107.66	1-4	114.09
1964	128.73	11-28	114.99	1-3	127.95
1965	134.10	3-4	123.50	6-29	127.90
1966	128.79	1-10	101.40	8-30	112.38
1967	118.79	4-20	105.89	11-20	109.59
1968	126.34	11-29	105.33	3-25	121.84
1969	123.14	2-7	91.88	12-17	94.65
1970	99.95	12-31	80.68	7-23	99.95
1971	105.40	1-19	89.69	11-24	96.93
1972	101.40	11-24	88.15	7-31	99.48
1973	100.21	1-8	75.11	12-5	79.13
1974	84.05	1-7	52.19	9-13	55.91
1975	76.98	6-25	58.79	1-2	75.63
1976	95.11	12-31	76.50	1-2	95.11
1977	101.63	7-22	92.45	3-28	96.57
1978	96.17	1-3	85.89	11-14	86.94
1979	98.63	8-31	87.53	1-2	93.86
1980	100.81	7-17	79.34	3-27	98.43
1981	101.71	1-6	89.72	9-25	96.26

Source: *Value Line Investment Survey,* Arnold Bernhardt & Company, Inc.

1973–83 Yearly Highs, Lows, Closes & Percent Changes for the Year

Index		1973	1974	1975	1976	1977
Composite	High	136.84 1/11	96.53 3/15	88.00 7/15	97.88 12/31	105.05 12/30
	Low	88.67 12/24	54.87 10/03	60.70 1/02	78.06 1/02	93.66 4/05
	Close	92.19	59.82	77.62	97.88	105.05
	% Change	−31.1	−35.1	+29.8	+26.1	+ 7.3
Industrial	High	136.97 1/11	89.78 3/15	93.79 7/15	100.12 12/31	109.43 12/30
	Low	80.15 12/24	54.21 10/03	57.22 1/02	81.44 1/02	96.29 4/26
	Close	83.57	56.46	80.95	100.12	109.43
	% Change	−36.9	−32.4	+43.4	+23.7	+ 9.3
Other Finance	High	151.93 1/11	111.60 1/23	88.47 6/24	101.57 12/31	105.65 7/25
	Low	102.93 12/24	57.16 10/03	64.70 1/02	79.36 1/02	97.04 4/06
	Close	107.50	63.43	79.02	101.57	105.53
	% Change	−27.8	−41.0	+24.6	+28.5	+ 3.9
Insurance	High	149.69 1/03	113.46 1/17	91.19 7/15	105.21 12/31	115.01 11/25
	Low	103.22 5/21	57.57 10/03	73.47 9/17	81.60 1/02	96.14 4/04
	Close	110.15	74.69	80.90	105.21	114.51
	% Change	−26.1	−32.2	+ 8.3	+30.0	+ 8.8
Bank	High	123.57 1/22	105.11 1/17	82.76 7/15	92.72 12/31	96.02 12/05
	Low	96.50 12/05	59.43 10/04	62.22 1/02	72.73 1/02	89.64 5/31,6/06
	Close	100.42	61.49	72.37	92.72	95.28
	% Change	−15.7	−38.8	+17.7	+28.1	+ 2.8
Utility	High	101.30 2/20	76.55 3/06	69.52 6/30	86.91 12/31	101.68 12/23
	Low	69.85 12/05	48.22 12/24	50.44 1/02	66.15 1/02	87.04 1/03
	Close	72.07	49.60	65.95	86.91	101.03
	% Change	−26.9	−31.2	+33.0	+31.8	+16.2
Transportation	High	124.95 1/12	96.66 3/15	90.92 7/14	105.78 4/20	104.40 7/22
	Low	77.65 12/21	61.24 12/23	66.67 1/06	85.97 1/02	91.60 4/25
	Close	81.04	65.79	85.52	101.28	97.68
	% Change	−31.0	−18.8	+30.0	+18.4	− 3.6

Index		1978	1979	1980	1981	1982	1983
Composite	High	139.25 9/13	152.29 10/05	208.15 11/28	223.47 5/29	240.70 12/08	328.91 06/24
	Low	99.09 1/11	117.84 1/02	124.09 3/27	175.03 9/28	159.14 8/13	230.59 01/03
	Close	117.98	151.14	202.34	195.84	232.41	278.60
	% Change	+12.3	+28.1	+33.9	− 3.2	+18.7	+19.9
Industrial	High	155.79 9/12	175.18 12/31	274.70 11/28	283.03 5/29	281.64 12/08	408.42 06/24
	Low	101.91 1/11	126.88 1/02	145.03 3/27	204.62 9/25	177.70 8/13	270.55 01/03
	Close	126.85	175.18	261.36	229.29	273.58	323.68
	% Change	+15.9	+38.1	+49.2	−12.3	+19.3	+18.3
Other Finance	High	129.85 9/13	139.50 8/24	154.07 12/31	182.10 6/25	216.40 12/08	284.39 09/26
	Low	101.11 1/16	114.18 1/02	106.35 3/27	154.61 1/02	152.45 8/13	206.86 01/04
	Close	114.43	130.92	154.07	176.20	207.50	227.53
	% Change	+ 8.4	+14.4	+17.7	+14.4	+17.8	+33.7
Insurance	High	144.14 9/11	166.31 10/05	184.71 9/23	204.77 6/15	236.76 12/06	287.34 05/10
	Low	106.71 1/16	126.58 1/02	128.74 3/27	166.10 2/13	163.78 8/13	217.33 01/24
	Close	127.24	162.03	166.81	194.31	226.40	257.63
	% Change	+11.1	+27.3	+ 3.0	+16.5	+16.5	+13.8

NASDAQ Index Comparisons, 1973–1983 (*continued*)

Index		1978	1979	1980	1981	1982	1983
Bank	High	111.56 10/13	115.81 8/31	118.58 12/24	144.06 12/01	160.73 11/12	203.75 12/30
	Low	93.96 1/11	102.09 1/03	91.99 3/27	118.59 1/02	127.84 8/13	155.68 01/12
	Close	102.33	108.24	118.39	143.13	156.37	203.75
	% Change	+ 7.4	+ 5.8	+ 9.4	+20.9	+ 9.3	+30.3
Utility	High	116.73 9/13	130.41 12/31	165.92 11/28	191.18 11/30	316.17 12/08	293.76 11/30
	Low	93.23 1/20	106.27 1/02	106.01 3/27	148.69 2/04	168.02 3/12	194.27 01/04
	Close	106.04	130.41	165.70	181.67	286.23	280.80
	% Change	+ 5.0	+23.0	+27.1	+ 9.6	+57.6	+43.6
Transportation	High	128.71 9/13	133.42 10/04	179.20 10/10	201.71 6/15	205.81 11/05	391.37 06/16
	Low	92.92 1/23	100.76 1/02	100.55 3/27	155.99 1/08	145.26 3/16	257.12 10/12
	Close	100.53	118.47	164.19	167.77	195.48	269.39
	% Change	+ 2.9	+17.8	+39.0	+ 2.2	+16.5	− 5.9

Source: *NASDAQ 1928 & 83 Fact Book*, National Association of Security Dealers, Inc.

PART II: INTEREST RATE DATA

MOODY'S U.S. GOVERNMENT BOND YIELD AVERAGES (Monthly Data)

1941–83 3–5 Year Maturities, p. 687.

1941–83 Long-Term Bonds, p. 687.

1943–83 3–Year Treasury, p. 688.

1943–83 5–Year Treasury, p. 688.

1941–83 91–day T-Bill Rate—Average for Last Offering of Month, p. 689.

1943–83 10–Year Treasury, p. 689.

MOODY'S CORPORATE and INDUSTRIAL BOND YIELDS (Monthly Data)

1919–84 Average of Yields on *Aaa* Corporate Bonds, p. 690.

1919–84 Average of Yields on *Aa* Corporate Bonds, p. 691.

1919–84 Average of Yields on *A* Corporate Bonds, p. 692.

1919–84 Average of Yields on *Baa* Corporate Bonds, p. 693.

1919–84 Average of Yields on *Aaa* Industrial Bonds, p. 694.

1919–84 Average of Yields on *Baa* Industrial Bonds, p. 695.

MOODY'S GOVERNMENT BOND YIELD AVERAGES

3-5 YEAR MATURITY, SELECTED ISSUES [1]

	Annual	Jan.	Feb.	Mar.	Apr.	May	June	July	Aug.	Sept.	Oct.	Nov.	Dec.
1941	.73	.76	.81	.84	.81	.72	1.41	.67	.62	.72	.98		1.10
1942	1.46	1.05	1.02	1.02	1.06	1.11	1.32	1.45	1.47	1.47	1.48	1.49	1.48
1943	1.34	1.43	1.41	1.40	1.39	1.36	.68	1.30	1.29	1.31	1.31	1.29	1.30
1944	1.33	1.30	1.32	1.36	1.36	1.35	1.34	1.31	1.30	1.31	1.35	1.34	1.35
1945	1.18	1.31	1.22	1.18	1.14	1.16	1.16	1.16	1.17	1.19	1.17	1.14	1.13
1946	1.16	1.06	.99	.96	1.10	1.16	1.15	1.15	1.19	1.27	1.29	1.28	1.30
1947	1.32	1.26	1.26	1.24	1.24	1.27	1.29	1.33	1.31	1.28	1.35	1.47	1.54
1948	1.62	1.63	1.63	1.60	1.58	1.51	1.49	1.56	1.65	1.69	1.71	1.69	1.64
1949	1.43	1.59	1.57	1.54	1.53	1.49	1.42	1.26	1.26	1.34	1.38	1.37	1.37
1950	1.50	1.39	1.44	1.45	1.45	1.45	1.47	1.45	1.45	1.55	1.65	1.62	1.64
1951	1.93	1.66	1.67	1.86	2.03	2.04	2.00	1.94	1.89	1.93	2.00	2.01	2.09
1952	2.13	2.08	2.07	2.02	1.93	1.95	2.04	2.14	2.29	2.28	2.26	2.25	2.30
1953	2.56	2.39	2.42	2.46	2.61	2.86	2.92	2.72	2.77	2.69	2.38	2.32	2.22
1954	1.82	2.04	1.84	1.80	1.71	1.78	1.79	1.69	1.74	1.80	1.85	1.90	1.94
1955	2.50	2.11	2.18	2.30	2.39	2.40	2.42	2.54	2.73	2.77	2.72	2.70	2.98
1956	3.12	2.74	2.65	2.83	3.11	3.04	2.87	2.97	3.36	3.43	3.29	3.49	3.65
1957	3.62	3.40	3.33	3.38	3.48	3.60	3.77	3.89	3.91	3.93	3.99	3.63	3.04
1958	2.90	2.77	2.67	2.50	2.33	2.25	2.25	2.54	3.11	3.57	3.63	3.60	3.65
1959	4.33	3.86	3.85	3.88	4.03	4.16	4.33	4.40	4.45	4.78	4.69	4.74	4.95
1960	3.99	4.87	4.66	4.24	4.23	4.42	4.06	3.71	3.50	3.61	3.64	3.68	3.51
1961	3.60	3.53	3.54	3.43	3.39	3.28	3.70	3.69	3.80	3.77	3.64	3.68	3.82
1962	3.57	3.84	3.77	3.55	3.48	3.53	3.51	3.71	3.57	3.56	3.46	3.46	3.44
1963	3.72	3.47	3.48	3.50	3.56	3.57	3.67	3.78	3.81	3.88	3.91	3.97	4.04
1964	4.06	4.06	4.02	4.15	4.18	4.07	4.03	3.99	3.99	4.03	4.04	4.04	4.07
1965	4.22	4.06	4.08	4.12	4.12	4.11	4.09	4.10	4.19	4.24	4.33	4.46	4.77
1966	5.16	4.89	5.02	4.94	4.86	4.94	5.01	5.22	5.58	5.62	5.38	5.43	5.43
1967	5.05	4.71	4.73	4.52	4.46	4.69	4.96	5.17	5.28	5.40	5.52	5.73	5.07
1968	5.60	5.52	5.58	5.77	5.69	5.95	5.71	5.44	5.32	5.31	5.42	5.47	5.99
1969	6.86	6.04	6.16	6.33	6.16	6.32	6.64	7.02	7.07	7.58	7.47	7.58	7.98
1970	7.34	8.14	7.80	7.20	7.49	7.97	7.86	7.58	7.56	7.24	7.06	6.36	5.87
1971	5.74	5.73	5.32	4.74	5.42	6.02	6.30	6.69	6.33	5.89	5.63	5.43	5.32
1972	5.77	5.28	5.43	5.64	5.92	5.58	5.65	5.74	5.84	6.09	6.07	6.88	6.72
1973	6.84	6.21	6.54	6.78	6.67	6.72	6.69	7.41	8.32	8.31	7.91	7.58	7.15
1974	7.73	6.87	6.70	7.26	7.92	8.16	8.06	8.32	8.57	8.14	7.73	7.42	7.41
1975	7.46	7.22	6.78	6.91	7.66	7.39	7.16	7.62	8.03	7.90	7.80	7.62	7.50
1976	6.83	7.08	7.09	7.14	6.87	6.52	6.70	6.53	6.60	6.83	6.87	6.40	5.85
1977	6.79	6.44	6.62	6.67	6.52	6.70	6.70	6.83	7.18	7.21	7.33	7.58?	—
1978	8.23	7.64	7.69	7.71	7.84	8.02	8.24	8.46	8.24	8.32	8.53	8.91	9.13
1979	9.52	9.30	9.10	9.20	9.27	9.24	8.85	8.82	9.03	9.48	10.67	10.90	10.35
1980	11.29	10.67	12.48	13.31	11.50	9.44	8.97	9.34	10.63	11.44	11.77	12.83	13.12
1981	14.06	12.59	13.25	13.23	13.80	14.57	13.75	14.63	15.41	15.81	15.24	13.03	13.45
1982	12.83	14.39	14.38	13.77	13.77	13.45	14.12	13.81	12.64	12.17	10.81	10.32	10.27
1983	10.52	9.98	10.19	10.03	9.92	9.85	10.45	10.99	11.33	11.15	10.96	10.07	11.33

LONG-TERM BONDS [2]

	Annual	Jan.	Feb.	Mar.	Apr.	May	June	July	Aug.	Sept.	Oct.	Nov.	Dec.
1941	2.05	2.12	2.22	2.12	2.07	2.04	2.01	1.98	2.01	2.02	1.98	2.34	2.47
1942	2.46	2.48	2.48	2.46	2.44	2.45	2.43	2.46	2.47	2.46	2.45	2.47	2.49
1943	2.47	2.46	2.46	2.48	2.48	2.46	2.45	2.45	2.46	2.48	2.48	2.48	2.49
1944	2.48	2.49	2.49	2.48	2.48	2.49	2.49	2.49	2.48	2.47	2.48	2.48	2.48
1945	2.37	2.44	2.38	2.40	2.39	2.39	2.35	2.34	2.36	2.37	2.35	2.33	2.33
1946	2.19	2.21	2.12	2.09	2.08	2.19	2.16	2.18	2.23	2.24	2.26	2.25	2.24
1947	2.25	2.21	2.21	2.19	2.19	2.19	2.22	2.25	2.24	2.24	2.27	2.36	2.39
1948	2.44	2.45	2.45	2.44	2.44	2.42	2.41	2.41	2.45	2.45	2.44	2.44	2.44
1949	2.31	2.42	2.39	2.38	2.38	2.38	2.38	2.27	2.24	2.22	2.22	2.20	2.19
1950	2.32	2.20	2.24	2.27	2.30	2.31	2.33	2.34	2.33	2.36	2.38	2.38	2.39
1951	2.57	2.39	2.40	2.47	2.56	2.63	2.65	2.61	2.57	2.71	2.74	2.66	2.70
1952	2.68	2.74	2.71	2.70	2.64	2.57	2.61	2.61	2.70	2.71	2.74	2.71	2.75
1953	2.94	2.80	2.83	2.89	2.97	3.12	3.13	3.04	3.05	3.01	2.87	2.86	2.79
1954	2.55	2.69	2.62	2.53	2.48	2.54	2.55	2.47	2.48	2.52	2.54	2.57	2.59
1955	2.84	2.68	2.77	2.78	2.82	2.81	2.82	2.91	2.95	2.92	2.87	2.89	2.91
1956	3.08	2.88	2.85	2.93	3.07	2.97	2.93	3.00	3.17	3.21	3.20	3.30	3.40
1957	3.47	3.34	3.22	3.26	3.32	3.40	3.58	3.60	3.63	3.66	3.73	3.57	3.30
1958	3.43	3.24	3.26	3.25	3.12	3.14	3.19	3.36	3.60	3.75	3.76	3.70	3.80
1959	4.07	3.90	3.92	3.92	4.01	4.08	4.09	4.11	4.10	4.26	4.11	4.12	4.27
1960	4.01	4.37	4.22	4.08	4.17	4.16	3.99	3.86	3.79	3.82	3.91	3.93	3.88
1961	3.90	3.89	3.81	3.78	3.80	3.73	3.88	3.90	4.00	4.02	3.98	3.98	4.06
1962	3.95	4.08	4.09	4.01	3.89	3.88	3.90	4.02	3.97	3.94	3.89	3.87	3.87
1963	4.00	3.88	3.92	3.93	3.97	3.97	4.00	4.01	3.99	4.04	4.07	4.10	4.14
1964	4.15	4.15	4.14	4.18	4.20	4.16	4.13	4.13	4.14	4.16	4.16	4.12	4.14
1965	4.21	4.14	4.16	4.15	4.15	4.14	4.14	4.15	4.19	4.25	4.28	4.34	4.43
1966	4.65	4.43	4.61	4.63	4.55	4.57	4.63	4.75	4.80	4.79	4.70	4.74	4.65
1967	4.85	4.40	4.47	4.45	4.51	4.76	4.86	4.86	4.95	4.98	5.18	5.24	5.36
1968	5.26	5.17	5.15	5.38	5.28	5.39	5.23	5.09	5.04	5.10	5.24	5.36	5.66
1969	6.12	5.74	5.86	6.05	5.86	5.85	6.06	6.07	6.02	6.32	6.27	6.51	6.81
1970	6.58	6.86	6.44	6.39	6.53	6.94	6.99	6.57	6.75	6.63	6.59	6.25	5.98
1971	5.70	5.93	5.85	5.73	5.77	6.00	5.88	5.80	5.68	5.47	5.36	5.40	5.53
1972	5.54	5.53	5.58	5.57	5.65	5.54	5.50	5.49	5.51	5.61	5.60	5.42	5.25
1973	6.21	5.80	5.99	6.11	6.02	6.18	6.24	6.92	7.07	7.21	7.19	7.11	6.82
1974	6.88	6.45	6.46	6.70	6.92	6.98	6.92	7.07	7.21	7.29	7.28	7.20	7.16
1975	6.96	6.58	6.51	6.65	6.99	6.94	6.85	6.93	6.88	6.86	6.72	6.66	6.37
1976	6.79	6.92	6.92	6.86	6.72	6.98	6.93	6.88	6.86	6.72	6.66	6.62	6.37
1977	7.53	7.35	7.53	7.57	7.50	7.57	7.43	7.45	7.50	7.45	7.60	7.67	7.77
1978	8.40	8.02	8.10	8.10	8.22	8.37	8.45	8.61	8.38	8.37	8.60	8.68	8.84
1979	9.26	8.93	8.94	8.99	9.03	9.11	8.84	8.85	8.89	9.14	9.93	10.38	10.08
1980	11.23	10.54	12.01	12.26	11.22	10.15	9.74	10.20	10.94	11.36	11.63	12.30	12.35
1981	13.31	12.05	12.68	12.59	13.08	13.44	12.82	13.49	14.05	14.59	14.59	13.08	13.28
1982	12.61	14.16	14.07	13.37	13.24	13.05	13.75	13.40	12.54	11.86	10.84	10.46	10.60
1983	11.17	10.64	10.89	10.65	10.49	10.52	10.95	11.44	11.78	11.62	11.55	11.68	11.81

[1] Selected notes and bonds maturing within 3 to 5 years. [2] Long-term: due or callable after 15 years, Jan. 1941-March 1952; after 12 years, Apr. 1952-Mar. 1953; 10 years or more, beginning Apr. 1953.

Source: *Moody's Municipal & Government Manual,* vol. 2 (New York: Moody's Investor's Service Inc., 1984).

3-YEAR TREASURY*

Year	Jan.	Feb.	Mar.	Apr.	May	June	July	Aug.	Sept.	Oct.	Nov.	Dec.
1943	1.22	1.22	1.23	1.27	1.19	1.16	1.15	1.18	1.20	1.20	1.20	1.19
1944	1.22	1.24	1.27	1.23	1.21	1.24	1.20	1.19	1.17	1.23	1.25	1.30
1945	1.23	1.17	1.19	1.16	1.18	1.14	1.19	1.22	1.20	1.15	1.10	1.07
1946	0.96	0.92	1.00	1.10	1.12	1.09	1.11	1.13	1.23	1.22	1.23	1.20
1947	1.15	1.18	1.13	1.19	1.23	1.23	1.26	1.22	1.24	1.37	1.44	1.49
1948	1.48	1.49	1.47	1.47	1.39	1.46	1.49	1.56	1.61	1.63	1.60	1.54
1949	1.49	1.51	1.47	1.48	1.43	1.37	1.25	1.22	1.25	1.25	1.28	1.26
1950	1.33	1.33	1.36	1.41	1.39	1.43	1.39	1.45	1.59	1.64	1.62	1.68
1951	1.70	1.71	1.97	2.00	2.05	2.08	1.93	1.87	1.95	2.07	2.04	2.11
1952	2.06	2.10	2.04	1.94	1.96	2.07	2.20	2.34	2.30	2.24	2.25	2.34
1953	2.30	2.31	2.37	2.59	2.68	2.62	2.52	2.60	2.39	2.20	2.24	1.96
1954	1.88	1.57	1.52	1.43	1.60	1.44	1.49	1.49	1.66	1.75	1.73	1.79
1955	1.95	2.19	2.24	2.40	2.29	2.42	2.56	2.73	2.54	2.56	2.76	2.90
1956	2.62	2.68	2.88	3.14	2.93	2.94	3.20	3.42	3.43	3.39	3.66	3.66
1957	3.33	3.42	3.44	3.54	3.67	3.82	3.93	3.95	4.04	4.00	3.43	2.78
1958	2.65	2.41	2.32	2.12	1.97	2.15	2.43	3.33	3.65	3.57	3.56	3.70
1959	3.93	3.85	4.02	4.10	4.24	4.54	4.59	4.77	4.93	4.68	4.86	5.17
1960	4.86	4.83	4.14	4.32	4.37	3.98	3.47	3.42	3.41	3.52	3.71	3.34
1961	3.46	3.42	3.38	3.29	3.36	3.56	3.51	3.62	3.63	3.55	3.60	3.64
1962	3.75	3.57	3.40	3.35	3.34	3.48	3.66	3.41	3.34	3.26	3.35	3.38
1963	3.39	3.38	3.44	3.51	3.57	3.56	3.76	3.77	3.81	3.88	3.88	4.00
1964	3.99	4.00	4.16	4.10	4.02	3.96	3.93	3.95	3.99	4.01	4.07	4.09
1965	4.15	4.20	4.18	4.17	4.14	4.08	4.12	4.19	4.33	4.36	4.48	4.88
1966	4.89	5.04	4.92	4.91	5.05	5.04	5.21	6.11	5.72	5.38	5.42	4.93
1967	4.62	4.76	4.29	4.41	4.55	5.10	5.24	5.29	5.45	5.64	5.64	5.71
1968	5.53	5.69	5.81	5.95	6.05	5.87	5.52	5.53	5.46	5.61	5.73	6.51
1969	6.17	6.38	6.34	6.31	6.61	6.88	7.32	7.34	8.06	7.41	7.79	8.41
1970	8.20	7.62	7.20	7.73	8.14	7.72	7.57	7.43	7.01	6.90	5.71	5.75
1971	5.60	5.08	4.48	5.13	5.89	6.20	6.59	6.18	5.74	5.46	5.21	5.14
1972	5.00	5.19	5.45	5.78	5.38	5.54	5.65	5.69	5.95	5.89	5.82	5.89
1973	6.15	6.46	6.86	6.76	6.83	6.73	7.43	7.85	7.27	6.74	6.96	6.75
1974	6.87	6.66	7.20	7.97	8.16	8.09	8.33	8.64	8.40	7.91	7.62	7.20
1975	7.03	6.51	6.87	7.65	7.13	7.28	7.78	8.02	8.24	7.41	7.51	7.01
1976	6.91	6.93	6.95	6.84	7.37	7.10	7.05	6.74	6.62	6.36	5.80	5.61
1977	6.49	6.52	6.49	6.28	6.46	6.22	6.49	6.68	6.91	7.27	7.10	7.36
1978	7.52	7.66	7.67	7.82	8.12	8.37	8.39	8.34	8.50	8.76	9.04	9.55
1979	9.18	9.45	9.33	9.48	9.34	8.95	9.03	9.50	9.60	11.60	10.58	10.72
1980	11.06	13.79	13.76	10.32	8.92	9.27	9.44	11.64	12.44	12.49	13.19	12.43
1981	13.01	13.29	13.36	14.24	14.66	14.12	15.03	16.21	16.03	15.40	12.67	13.97
1982	14.74	13.87	14.39	13.67	14.90	13.82	12.45	12.04	12.04	10.81	10.31	10.03
1983	10.12	9.68	9.82	10.25	10.58	11.04	11.23	10.73	10.92	10.81	10.89	10.93

5-YEAR TREASURY*

Year	Jan.	Feb.	Mar.	Apr.	May	June	July	Aug.	Sept.	Oct.	Nov.	Dec.
1943	1.63	1.66	1.68	1.69	1.63	1.55	1.56	1.60	1.61	1.61	1.63	1.61
1944	1.62	1.61	1.62	1.62	1.62	1.64	1.64	1.62	1.62	1.64	1.64	1.66
1945	1.54	1.48	1.47	1.36	1.40	1.37	1.39	1.40	1.40	1.36	1.26	1.24
1946	1.14	1.11	1.15	1.29	1.31	1.27	1.29	1.33	1.43	1.43	1.46	1.44
1947	1.36	1.40	1.35	1.38	1.39	1.41	1.42	1.37	1.40	1.51	1.61	1.76
1948	1.76	1.77	1.74	1.73	1.62	1.68	1.73	1.83	1.84	1.86	1.81	1.74
1949	1.69	1.69	1.63	1.63	1.58	1.51	1.41	1.36	1.40	1.40	1.41	1.39
1950	1.45	1.45	1.48	1.54	1.50	1.57	1.49	1.55	1.68	1.72	1.71	1.76
1951	1.78	1.79	2.03	2.09	2.14	2.15	2.15	2.00	1.96	2.04	2.14	2.20
1952	2.14	2.19	2.12	2.04	2.13	2.13	2.22	2.33	2.42	2.44	2.34	2.39
1953	2.42	2.45	2.49	2.70	2.80	2.74	2.74	2.65	2.49	2.36	2.43	2.16
1954	2.09	1.98	1.85	1.75	1.95	1.80	1.85	1.87	1.95	2.05	2.07	2.13
1955	2.32	2.39	2.50	2.57	2.51	2.63	2.79	2.88	2.76	2.71	2.89	2.95
1956	2.74	2.75	3.00	3.17	2.95	3.03	3.24	3.48	3.40	3.46	3.65	3.58
1957	3.33	3.37	3.39	3.57	3.71	3.85	3.98	3.88	4.03	4.00	3.42	2.84
1958	2.76	2.66	2.54	2.38	2.38	2.54	2.88	3.48	3.77	3.78	3.60	3.87
1959	4.04	3.87	4.02	4.19	4.32	4.50	4.55	4.72	4.87	4.70	4.72	5.10
1960	4.85	4.78	4.24	4.38	4.43	4.07	3.65	3.64	3.64	3.72	3.96	3.60
1961	3.73	3.63	3.60	3.57	3.55	3.80	3.80	3.91	3.79	3.78	3.84	3.89
1962	4.00	3.83	3.64	3.62	3.61	3.72	3.87	3.65	3.64	3.55	3.62	3.56
1963	3.61	3.65	3.71	3.73	3.75	3.79	3.88	3.88	3.92	3.98	3.96	4.08
1964	4.07	4.08	4.21	4.16	4.11	4.04	4.06	4.06	4.06	4.09	4.12	4.14
1965	4.17	4.21	4.19	4.19	4.17	4.14	4.16	4.24	4.33	4.38	4.49	4.83
1966	4.87	5.04	4.90	4.91	5.03	5.04	5.21	5.98	5.38	5.21	5.37	4.88
1967	4.64	4.77	4.45	4.57	4.72	5.22	5.29	5.34	5.46	5.69	5.67	5.69
1968	5.55	5.70	5.83	5.92	6.04	5.86	5.55	5.58	5.52	5.57	5.77	6.45
1969	6.19	6.38	6.38	6.34	6.62	6.80	7.02	7.04	7.97	7.31	7.58	8.33
1970	8.14	7.56	7.24	7.82	8.10	7.79	7.61	7.50	7.18	7.15	6.18	6.05
1971	6.03	5.73	5.13	5.69	6.32	6.61	6.88	6.48	6.04	5.86	5.73	5.64
1972	5.48	5.63	5.88	6.14	5.80	5.88	5.94	6.00	6.25	6.15	6.06	6.12
1973	6.30	6.59	6.89	6.71	6.88	6.60	7.25	7.59	7.01	6.70	6.87	6.75
1974	6.83	6.75	7.22	7.87	7.99	7.88	8.15	8.50	8.25	7.88	7.63	7.32
1975	7.33	6.95	7.28	7.82	7.48	7.55	7.84	8.01	8.35	7.67	7.80	7.38
1976	7.35	7.32	7.27	7.24	7.60	7.46	7.46	7.19	7.08	6.82	6.25	6.19
1977	6.91	6.96	6.94	6.80	6.86	6.62	6.81	6.93	7.09	7.41	7.28	7.56
1978	7.70	7.83	7.85	8.00	8.23	8.43	8.47	8.26	8.42	8.65	8.81	9.24
1979	8.96	9.17	9.15	9.20	9.20	8.75	8.86	9.19	9.25	11.07	10.43	10.40
1980	10.85	13.43	12.90	10.22	9.28	9.58	9.79	11.84	12.28	12.21	12.71	12.09
1981	12.66	13.20	13.24	14.08	14.17	13.78	14.62	16.05	16.06	15.63	12.99	13.96
1982	14.50	13.54	14.17	13.34	13.32	14.55	13.50	12.20	12.22	11.31	10.99	10.51
1983	10.69	10.19	10.56	10.30	10.70	11.00	11.43	11.70	11.28	11.41	11.36	11.36

Source: *Moody's Municipal & Government Manual,* vol. 2 (New York: Moody's Investor's Service Inc., 1984).

91-DAY BILL RATE-AVG. FOR LAST OFFERING OF MONTH

	Jan.	Feb.	Mar.	Apr.	May	June	July	Aug.	Sept.	Oct.	Nov.	Dec.
1941	neg.	.086	.055	.097	.107	.087	.094	.090	.062	.151	.242	.310
1942	.220	222	.221	.335	.365	.360	.372	.367	.373	.373	.368	.357
1943	.369	.369	.374	.373	.374	.375	.374	.375	.375	.375	.375	.373
1944	.374	.375	.375	.374	.375	.375	.375	.375	.375	.375	.375	.373
1945	.375	.375	.376	.375	.375	.375	.375	.375	.375	.375	.376	.374
1946	.375	.375	.375	.375	.376	.376	.740	.766	.817	.895	.944	.952
1947	.376	.376	.376	.376	.376	.376	.998	.997	.996	.997	.997	.998
1948	.990	.997	.996	.997	.997	.998	.997	1.072	1.109	1.120	1.147	1.157
1949	1.160	1.164	1.162	1.156	1.159	1.158	1.017	1.031	1.076	1.036	1.052	1.087
1950	1.103	1.132	1.145	1.166	1.167	1.172	1.174	1.285	1.324	1.316	1.383	1.382
1951	1.389	1.390	1.507	1.506	1.600	1.527	1.591	1.645	1.647	1.593	1.609	1.865
1952	1.589	1.563	1.592	1.616	1.728	1.682	1.877	1.899	1.635	1.757	1.931	2.228
1953	1.961	2.070	2.036	2.243	2.084	1.954	2.157	2.001	1.634	1.220	1.488	1.574
1954	0.998	0.986	1.030	0.886	0.718	0.635	0.800	0.983	0.984	1.007	0.897	1.175
1955	1.349	1.355	1.374	1.697	1.471	1.401	1.720	1.875	2.122	2.231	2.440	2.688
1956	2.245	2.429	2.422	2.788	2.573	2.535	2.303	2.832	2.986	2.907	3.174	3.217
1957	3.283	3.288	3.034	3.054	3.245	3.232	3.158	3.497	3.534	3.622	3.158	3.174
1958	2.202	1.202	1.189	1.055	0.635	1.006	0.984	2.162	2.511	2.647	2.723	2.739
1959	2.975	2.589	2.766	2.831	2.878	3.281	3.047	3.824	3.958	4.022	4.279	4.516
1960	4.116	4.168	2.792	3.317	3.497	2.399	2.404	2.518	2.286	2.129	2.396	2.120
1961	2.230	2.496	2.392	2.186	2.354	2.219	2.244	2.321	2.233	2.325	2.606	2.594
1962	2.688	2.664	2.719	2.740	2.656	2.792	2.892	2.806	2.749	2.742	2.853	2.894
1963	2.917	2.870	2.919	2.884	2.974	2.979	3.206	3.396	3.379	3.452	3.480	3.522
1964	3.501	3.547	3.550	3.446	3.475	3.478	3.475	3.513	3.542	3.567	3.758	3.867
1965	3.848	3.989	3.922	3.916	3.889	3.789	3.803	3.855	3.983	4.040	4.104	4.457
1966	4.596	4.696	4.555	4.630	4.641	4.477	4.423	4.818	5.087	5.503	5.246	5.202
1967	4.486	4.538	4.150	3.715	3.477	3.462	4.747	4.490	4.629	4.542	4.957	4.989
1968	4.646	5.063	5.186	5.499	5.696	5.238	5.190	5.194	5.182	5.471	5.488	6.199
1969	6.167	6.080	6.065	6.053	6.124	6.456	7.172	7.098	7.106	7.030	7.476	8.096
1970	7.888	6.812	6.330	6.876	7.133	6.421	6.345	6.342	5.807	5.831	5.084	4.803
1971	4.201	3.497	3.521	3.865	4.344	5.080	5.554	4.549	4.676	4.443	4.324	3.731
1972	3.367	3.446	3.849	3.513	3.762	4.023	3.794	4.332	4.644	4.767	4.886	5.111
1973	5.689	5.811	6.251	6.278	6.694	7.228	8.320	8.778	7.331	7.163	7.695	7.406
1974	7.778	7.188	8.300	8.909	7.983	7.841	7.698	9.908	7.002	7.892	7.328	7.113
1975	5.606	5.455	5.562	5.716	5.206	5.665	6.318	6.593	6.547	5.685	5.520	5.208
1976	4.763	4.870	4.929	4.909	5.495	5.368	5.194	5.091	5.072	4.929	4.466	4.296
1977	4.720	4.708	4.609	4.518	4.993	4.965	5.163	5.574	5.982	6.278	6.057	6.144
1978	6.440	6.429	6.310	6.294	6.658	6.967	6.895	7.323	8.106	8.454	9.166	9.388
1979	9.324	9.451	9.498	9.498	9.526	8.802	9.154	9.855	9.989	12.256	11.018	12.105
1980	12.038	13.700	15.037	10.788	7.675	8.149	8.221	10.124	11.524	11.331	14.384	13.908
1981	15.199	14.103	12.501	14.190	16.750	13.909	15.065	15.583	14.669	13.352	10.400	11.690
1982	13.364	12.430	13.399	12.469	11.520	13.269	10.550	8.604	7.801	8.031	8.280	7.975
1983	8.122	7.944	8.680	8.150	8.650	9.090	9.130	9.280	8.730	8.410	8.900	8.940

10-YEAR TREASURY*

	Jan.	Feb.	Mar.	Apr.	May	June	July	Aug.	Sept.	Oct.	Nov.	Dec.
1943	2.08	2.06	2.09	2.08	2.02	2.02	2.00	2.03	2.03	2.05	2.08	2.09
1944	2.09	2.06	2.05	2.06	2.06	2.07	2.07	2.05	2.05	2.07	2.06	2.06
1945	1.96	1.87	1.85	1.75	1.75	1.71	1.70	1.72	1.71	1.64	1.58	1.49
1946	1.38	1.43	1.45	1.58	1.61	1.59	1.64	1.71	1.74	1.75	1.79	1.70
1947	1.68	1.70	1.67	1.70	1.69	1.72	1.70	1.65	1.66	1.78	1.87	2.17
1948	2.17	2.17	2.12	2.08	1.96	2.08	2.07	2.16	2.15	2.19	2.11	2.05
1949	2.00	1.98	1.91	1.89	1.86	1.79	1.73	1.66	1.70	1.70	1.70	1.66
1950	1.74	1.73	1.74	1.79	1.76	1.82	1.75	1.80	1.91	1.95	1.93	1.96
1951	1.96	2.01	2.20	2.27	2.26	2.29	2.15	2.19	2.25	2.27	2.28	2.35
1952	2.31	2.35	2.29	2.20	2.35	2.37	2.42	2.51	2.64	2.52	2.50	2.52
1953	2.61	2.66	2.74	2.87	3.02	2.92	2.85	2.87	2.62	2.56	2.63	2.41
1954	2.37	2.37	2.41	2.33	2.37	2.39	2.36	2.43	2.45	2.44	2.49	2.51
1955	2.59	2.64	2.65	2.73	2.65	2.76	2.94	2.94	2.83	2.83	2.89	2.92
1956	2.80	2.83	2.99	3.13	2.90	2.99	3.14	3.37	3.26	3.39	3.53	3.51
1957	3.29	3.30	3.30	3.50	3.60	3.84	3.87	3.75	3.88	3.88	3.35	2.96
1958	2.92	2.88	2.79	2.67	2.69	2.92	3.23	3.52	3.79	3.78	3.62	4.01
1959	4.06	3.88	4.00	4.22	4.32	4.38	4.41	4.54	4.68	4.46	4.47	4.87
1960	4.78	4.57	4.31	4.37	4.29	4.09	3.80	3.79	3.76	3.92	4.10	3.81
1961	3.86	3.72	3.76	3.75	3.76	3.91	3.91	3.96	3.88	3.93	4.05	4.15
1962	4.19	4.09	3.91	3.86	3.91	3.97	4.03	3.92	3.94	3.89	3.95	3.85
1963	3.85	3.94	3.96	3.98	3.95	3.99	3.99	3.99	4.05	4.13	4.09	4.14
1964	4.16	4.14	4.22	4.22	4.20	4.15	4.21	4.21	4.18	4.19	4.18	4.18
1965	4.18	4.22	4.21	4.21	4.21	4.21	4.22	4.26	4.33	4.37	4.50	4.64
1966	4.70	4.96	4.84	4.85	4.89	4.89	5.05	5.53	5.12	4.94	5.13	4.72
1967	4.51	4.73	4.50	4.65	4.80	5.16	5.21	5.26	5.33	5.59	5.64	5.65
1968	5.51	5.63	5.78	5.70	5.93	5.70	5.37	5.45	5.40	5.56	5.72	6.18
1969	6.00	6.24	6.33	6.05	6.34	6.50	6.54	6.60	7.35	6.97	7.34	7.99
1970	7.64	7.10	7.00	7.77	8.20	7.66	7.28	7.35	7.16	7.30	6.29	6.46
1971	6.02	6.03	5.42	5.81	6.26	6.78	6.66	6.26	5.96	5.82	3.74	5.70
1972	5.88	5.66	6.01	6.11	5.96	5.96	5.82	6.21	6.37	6.31	6.29	6.40
1973	6.51	6.74	6.73	6.59	6.78	6.78	7.31	7.00	6.52	6.58	6.71	6.67
1974	6.91	6.85	7.16	7.61	7.72	7.53	7.75	8.19	7.89	7.35	7.12	7.12
1975	6.96	6.93	7.05	7.55	7.14	7.28	7.31	7.41	7.92	7.66	7.81	7.36
1976	7.24	7.26	7.12	7.18	7.34	7.34	7.26	7.23	7.05	6.98	6.77	6.22
1977	7.33	7.44	7.44	7.34	7.34	7.31	7.09	7.11	7.21	7.30	7.58	7.77
1978	7.93	8.00	8.04	8.15	8.33	8.49	8.52	8.29	8.45	8.67	8.72	9.02
1979	8.86	9.11	9.08	9.12	9.12	8.92	8.90	9.00	9.22	10.74	10.24	10.33
1980	11.00	13.07	12.50	10.53	9.88	9.97	10.31	11.48	11.97	12.06	12.34	11.82
1981	12.48	13.11	13.02	13.75	13.70	13.34	14.13	15.37	15.51	15.19	12.96	14.00
1982	14.57	13.83	14.11	13.25	13.21	14.30	13.54	12.45	11.80	10.78	10.53	10.32
1983	10.64	10.10	10.35	10.08	10.53	10.84	11.28	11.52	11.27	11.44	11.37	11.43

*Taken from a line, commonly called a yield curve, on last Tuesday of month.

Source: *Moody's Municipal & Government Manual*, vol. 2 (New York: Moody's Investor's Service Inc., 1984).

MOODY'S AVERAGE OF YIELDS ON Aaa CORPORATE BONDS (IN PERCENT)

Year	Aver.	Jan.	Feb.	Mar.	Apr.	May	June	July	Aug.	Sept.	Oct.	Nov.	Dec.
1984..	...	12.20	12.08	12.57	12.81	13.28	...	...	...	...	...	...	...
1983..	12.04	11.79	12.01	11.73	11.51	11.46	11.74	12.15	12.51	12.37	12.25	12.41	12.57
1982..	13.79	15.18	15.27	14.58	14.46	14.26	14.81	14.61	13.71	12.94	12.12	11.68	11.83
1981..	14.17	12.81	13.35	13.33	13.88	14.32	13.75	14.38	14.89	15.49	15.40	14.22	14.23
1980..	11.94	11.09	12.38	12.96	12.04	10.99	10.58	11.07	11.64	12.02	12.31	12.97	13.21
1979..	9.63	9.25	9.26	9.37	9.38	9.50	9.29	9.20	9.23	9.44	10.13	10.76	10.74
1978..	8.73	8.41	8.47	8.47	8.56	8.69	8.76	8.88	8.69	8.69	8.89	9.03	9.16
1977..	8.02	7.96	8.04	8.10	8.04	8.05	7.95	7.94	7.98	7.92	8.04	8.08	8.19
1976..	8.43	8.60	8.55	8.52	8.40	8.58	8.62	8.56	8.45	8.38	8.32	8.25	7.98
1975..	8.83	8.83	8.62	8.67	8.95	8.90	8.77	8.84	8.95	8.95	8.86	8.78	8.79
1974..	8.57	7.83	7.85	8.01	8.25	8.37	8.47	8.72	9.00	9.24	9.27	8.89	8.89
1973..	7.44	7.15	7.22	7.29	7.26	7.29	7.37	7.45	7.68	7.63	7.60	7.67	7.68
1972..	7.21	7.19	7.27	7.24	7.30	7.30	7.23	7.21	7.19	7.22	7.21	7.12	7.08
1971..	7.39	7.36	7.08	7.21	7.25	7.53	7.64	7.64	7.59	7.44	7.39	7.26	7.25
1970..	8.04	7.91	7.93	7.84	7.83	8.11	8.48	8.44	8.13	8.09	8.03	8.05	7.64
1969..	7.03	6.59	6.66	6.85	6.89	6.79	6.98	7.08	6.97	7.14	7.33	7.35	7.72
1968..	6.18	6.17	6.10	6.11	6.21	6.27	6.28	6.24	6.02	5.97	6.09	6.19	6.45
1967..	5.51	5.20	5.03	5.13	5.11	5.24	5.44	5.58	5.62	5.65	5.82	6.07	6.19
1966..	5.13	4.74	4.78	4.92	4.96	4.98	5.07	5.16	5.31	5.49	5.41	5.35	5.39
1965..	4.49	4.43	4.41	4.42	4.43	4.44	4.46	4.48	4.49	4.52	4.56	4.60	4.68
1964..	4.40	4.37	4.36	4.38	4.40	4.41	4.41	4.40	4.41	4.42	4.42	4.43	4.44
1963..	4.26	4.21	4.19	4.19	4.21	4.22	4.23	4.26	4.29	4.31	4.32	4.33	4.35
1962..	4.33	4.42	4.42	4.39	4.33	4.28	4.28	4.34	4.35	4.32	4.28	4.25	4.24
1961..	4.35	4.32	4.27	4.22	4.25	4.27	4.33	4.41	4.45	4.45	4.42	4.39	4.42
1960..	4.41	4.61	4.56	4.49	4.45	4.46	4.45	4.41	4.28	4.25	4.30	4.31	4.35
1959..	4.38	4.12	4.14	4.13	4.23	4.37	4.46	4.47	4.43	4.52	4.57	4.56	4.58
1958..	3.79	3.60	3.59	3.63	3.60	3.57	3.57	3.67	3.85	4.09	4.11	4.09	4.08
1957..	3.89	3.77	3.67	3.66	3.67	3.74	3.91	3.99	4.10	4.12	4.10	4.08	3.81
1956..	3.36	3.11	3.08	3.10	3.24	3.28	3.26	3.28	3.43	3.56	3.59	3.69	3.75
1955..	3.06	2.93	2.93	3.02	3.01	3.04	3.05	3.06	3.11	3.13	3.10	3.10	3.15
1954..	2.90	3.06	2.95	2.86	2.85	2.88	2.90	2.89	2.87	2.89	2.87	2.89	2.90
1953..	3.20	3.02	3.07	3.12	3.23	3.34	3.40	3.28	3.24	3.29	3.16	3.11	3.13
1952..	2.96	2.98	2.93	2.96	2.93	2.93	2.94	2.95	2.94	2.95	3.01	2.98	2.97
1951..	2.86	2.66	2.66	2.78	2.87	2.89	2.94	2.94	2.94	2.95	2.89	2.96	3.01
1950..	2.62	2.57	2.58	2.58	2.60	2.61	2.62	2.65	2.61	2.64	2.67	2.67	2.67
1949..	2.66	2.71	2.71	2.70	2.70	2.71	2.71	2.67	2.62	2.60	2.61	2.60	2.58
1948..	2.82	2.86	2.85	2.83	2.78	2.76	2.76	2.81	2.84	2.84	2.84	2.84	2.79
1947..	2.61	2.57	2.55	2.55	2.53	2.53	2.55	2.55	2.56	2.61	2.70	2.77	2.86
1946..	2.53	2.54	2.48	2.47	2.46	2.51	2.49	2.48	2.51	2.58	2.60	2.59	2.61
1945..	2.62	2.69	2.65	2.62	2.61	2.62	2.61	2.60	2.61	2.62	2.62	2.62	2.61
1944..	2.72	2.72	2.74	2.74	2.74	2.73	2.73	2.72	2.71	2.72	2.72	2.72	2.70
1943..	2.73	2.79	2.77	2.76	2.76	2.74	2.72	2.69	2.69	2.69	2.70	2.71	2.74
1942..	2.83	2.83	2.85	2.86	2.83	2.85	2.85	2.83	2.81	2.80	2.80	2.79	2.81
1941..	2.77	2.75	2.78	2.80	2.82	2.81	2.77	2.74	2.74	2.75	2.73	2.72	2.80
1940..	2.84	2.88	2.86	2.84	2.82	2.93	2.96	2.88	2.85	2.82	2.79	2.75	2.71
1939..	3.01	3.01	3.00	2.99	3.02	2.97	2.92	2.89	2.93	3.25	3.15	3.00	2.94
1938..	3.19	3.17	3.20	3.22	3.30	3.22	3.26	3.22	3.18	3.21	3.15	3.10	3.08
1937..	3.26	3.10	3.22	3.32	3.42	3.33	3.28	3.25	3.24	3.28	3.27	3.24	3.21
1936..	3.24	3.37	3.32	3.29	3.29	3.27	3.24	3.23	3.21	3.18	3.18	3.15	3.10
1935..	3.60	3.77	3.69	3.67	3.66	3.65	3.61	3.56	3.60	3.59	3.52	3.47	3.44
1934..	4.00	4.35	4.20	4.13	4.07	4.01	3.93	3.89	3.93	3.96	3.90	3.86	3.81
1933..	4.49	4.44	4.48	4.68	4.78	4.63	4.46	4.36	4.30	4.36	4.34	4.54	4.50
1932..	5.01	5.20	5.23	4.98	5.17	5.36	5.41	5.26	4.91	4.70	4.64	4.63	4.59
1931..	4.58	4.42	4.43	4.39	4.40	4.37	4.36	4.36	4.40	4.55	4.99	4.94	5.32
1930..	4.55	4.66	4.69	4.62	4.69	4.60	4.57	4.52	4.47	4.42	4.42	4.47	4.52
1929..	4.83	4.62	4.66	4.70	4.69	4.70	4.70	4.77	4.77	4.79	4.77	4.76	4.67
1928..	4.55	4.46	4.46	4.46	4.46	4.49	4.57	4.61	4.64	4.61	4.61	4.58	4.61
1927..	4.57	4.66	4.67	4.62	4.58	4.57	4.58	4.60	4.56	4.54	4.51	4.49	4.46
1926..	4.73	4.82	4.77	4.79	4.74	4.71	4.72	4.71	4.72	4.72	4.71	4.68	4.68
1925..	4.88	4.95	4.95	4.91	4.87	4.83	4.83	4.87	4.90	4.87	4.85	4.84	4.85
1924..	5.00	5.09	5.09	5.10	5.08	5.04	4.99	4.95	4.95	4.95	4.92	4.94	4.95
1923..	5.12	5.07	5.07	5.18	5.22	5.16	5.15	5.14	5.08	5.12	5.11	5.09	5.09
1922..	5.10	5.34	5.29	5.23	5.15	5.13	5.08	5.00	4.96	4.93	4.97	5.09	5.08
1921..	5.97	6.14	6.08	6.08	6.06	6.11	6.18	6.12	5.99	5.93	5.84	5.60	5.50
1920..	6.12	5.75	5.86	5.92	6.04	6.25	6.38	6.34	6.30	6.22	6.05	6.08	6.26
1919..	5.49	5.35	5.35	5.39	5.44	5.39	5.40	5.44	5.56	5.60	5.54	5.66	5.73

Source: *Moody's Industrial Manual* (New York: Moody's Investor's Service, 1984).

MOODY'S AVERAGE OF YIELDS ON Aa CORPORATE BONDS (IN PERCENT)

Year	Aver.	Jan.	Feb.	Mar.	Apr.	May	June	July	Aug.	Sept.	Oct.	Nov.	Dec.
1984..	...	12.71	12.70	13.22	13.48	14.10	...	...	...	...	...	...	...
1983..	12.42	12.35	12.58	12.32	12.06	11.95	12.15	12.39	12.72	12.62	12.49	12.61	12.76
1982..	14.41	15.75	15.72	15.21	14.90	14.77	15.26	15.21	14.48	13.72	12.97	12.51	12.44
1981..	14.75	13.52	13.89	13.90	14.39	14.88	14.41	14.79	15.42	15.95	15.82	14.97	15.00
1980..	12.50	11.56	12.73	13.51	13.06	11.91	11.39	11.43	12.09	12.52	12.68	13.34	13.78
1979..	9.94	9.48	9.50	9.61	9.65	9.86	9.66	9.49	9.53	9.70	10.46	11.22	11.15
1978..	8.92	8.59	8.65	8.66	8.73	8.84	8.95	9.07	8.96	8.92	9.07	9.24	9.33
1977..	8.24	8.16	8.26	8.28	8.28	8.28	8.19	8.12	8.17	8.15	8.26	8.34	8.40
[†]1976..	8.75	9.13	9.02	9.01	8.89	8.92	8.89	8.81	8.66	8.54	8.48	8.46	8.24
[†]1975..	9.17	9.13	8.91	8.92	9.19	9.24	9.13	9.13	9.23	9.35	9.32	9.23	9.25
[†]1974..	8.84	8.00	8.05	8.18	8.43	8.58	8.75	9.01	9.28	9.66	9.64	9.34	9.20
1973..	7.66	7.37	7.47	7.49	7.49	7.49	7.55	7.64	7.84	7.86	7.84	7.90	7.92
1972..	7.48	7.52	7.52	7.53	7.57	7.56	7.51	7.50	7.43	7.41	7.45	7.39	7.36
1971..	7.78	7.90	7.67	7.73	7.74	7.84	7.96	7.96	7.93	7.81	7.69	7.56	7.57
1970..	8.32	8.15	8.13	8.06	8.03	8.24	8.58	8.64	8.49	8.47	8.44	8.42	8.13
1969..	7.20	6.73	6.77	6.95	7.02	6.96	7.12	7.24	7.23	7.36	7.53	7.58	7.93
1968..	6.38	6.29	6.27	6.28	6.38	6.48	6.50	6.45	6.25	6.23	6.32	6.45	6.66
1967..	5.66	5.30	5.18	5.23	5.26	5.42	5.63	5.72	5.76	5.87	6.01	6.23	6.35
1966..	5.23	4.83	4.90	5.05	5.10	5.10	5.16	5.25	5.38	5.58	5.50	5.46	5.48
1965..	4.57	4.48	4.46	4.48	4.48	4.49	4.52	4.56	4.59	4.63	4.66	4.69	4.80
1964..	4.49	4.49	4.46	4.47	4.49	4.50	4.51	4.50	4.49	4.48	4.49	4.49	4.50
1963..	4.39	4.37	4.36	4.34	4.35	4.36	4.36	4.39	4.40	4.41	4.43	4.44	4.46
1962..	4.47	4.55	4.56	4.53	4.49	4.43	4.44	4.44	4.49	4.46	4.41	4.40	4.38
1961..	4.48	4.48	4.40	4.33	4.37	4.41	4.45	4.53	4.57	4.59	4.56	4.54	4.56
1960..	4.56	4.77	4.71	4.62	4.58	4.61	4.60	4.56	4.44	4.41	4.44	4.47	4.50
1959..	4.51	4.22	4.24	4.23	4.32	4.46	4.56	4.58	4.58	4.69	4.76	4.70	4.74
1958..	3.94	3.81	3.77	3.78	3.78	3.78	3.78	3.83	3.98	4.20	4.21	4.21	4.18
1957..	4.03	3.89	3.83	3.80	3.79	3.83	3.98	4.10	4.21	4.26	4.28	4.29	4.08
1956..	3.45	3.19	3.16	3.18	3.30	3.34	3.35	3.39	3.50	3.63	3.69	3.76	3.85
1955..	3.16	3.06	3.10	3.13	3.13	3.15	3.14	3.14	3.20	3.22	3.19	3.18	3.22
1954..	3.06	3.22	3.12	3.03	3.00	3.03	3.06	3.04	3.03	3.04	3.04	3.04	3.04
1953..	3.31	3.09	3.14	3.18	3.29	3.41	3.50	3.42	3.39	3.43	3.33	3.27	3.28
1952..	3.04	3.05	3.01	3.03	3.01	3.00	3.03	3.04	3.06	3.07	3.08	3.06	3.05
1951..	2.91	2.71	2.71	2.82	2.93	2.93	2.99	2.99	2.92	2.88	2.93	3.02	3.06
1950..	2.69	2.65	2.65	2.66	2.66	2.69	2.69	2.72	2.67	2.71	2.72	2.72	2.72
1949..	2.75	2.81	2.80	2.79	2.79	2.78	2.78	2.75	2.71	2.69	2.70	2.68	2.67
1948..	2.90	2.94	2.93	2.90	2.87	2.86	2.85	2.89	2.94	2.93	2.94	2.92	2.88
1947..	2.70	2.65	2.64	2.64	2.63	2.63	2.64	2.64	2.64	2.69	2.79	2.85	2.94
1946..	2.62	2.62	2.56	2.54	2.56	2.58	2.59	2.59	2.62	2.68	2.70	2.69	2.69
1945..	2.71	2.76	2.73	2.72	2.73	2.72	2.69	2.68	2.70	2.70	2.70	2.68	2.68
1944..	2.81	2.83	2.83	2.82	2.82	2.81	2.81	2.80	2.79	2.79	2.81	2.80	2.76
1943..	2.86	2.93	2.89	2.88	2.88	2.87	2.85	2.82	2.81	2.82	2.83	2.84	2.87
1942..	2.98	2.96	2.98	3.00	2.98	3.00	3.01	2.99	2.99	2.98	2.95	2.94	2.96
1941..	2.94	2.95	3.00	3.01	3.04	2.99	2.95	2.90	2.90	2.91	2.87	2.86	2.95
1940..	3.02	3.08	3.05	3.04	2.99	3.08	3.10	3.01	3.03	3.01	3.01	2.96	2.92
1939..	3.22	3.32	3.26	3.22	3.22	3.16	3.13	3.08	3.11	3.49	3.35	3.16	3.14
1938..	3.56	3.50	3.51	3.56	3.73	3.56	3.68	3.62	3.57	3.60	3.53	3.46	3.42
1937..	3.46	3.30	3.40	3.50	3.57	3.48	3.43	3.41	3.41	3.46	3.53	3.54	3.50
1936..	3.46	3.57	3.55	3.55	3.57	3.53	3.51	3.48	3.44	3.41	3.37	3.31	3.28
1935..	3.95	4.21	4.13	4.11	4.08	4.03	3.99	3.89	3.87	3.85	3.82	3.73	3.65
1934..	4.44	5.00	4.70	4.55	4.43	4.37	4.30	4.28	4.34	4.42	4.36	4.28	4.27
1933..	5.23	5.30	5.35	5.61	5.81	5.40	5.09	4.83	4.77	4.96	4.97	5.35	5.27
1932..	5.98	6.08	6.13	5.85	6.11	6.38	6.60	6.51	5.83	5.54	5.51	5.57	5.60
1931..	5.05	4.70	4.70	4.67	4.76	4.76	4.81	4.81	4.85	5.08	5.57	5.61	6.26
1930..	4.77	4.86	4.89	4.80	4.78	4.77	4.76	4.74	4.68	4.65	4.67	4.75	4.85
1929..	4.93	4.79	4.86	4.92	4.91	4.91	4.98	4.97	4.99	5.01	5.01	4.94	4.84
1928..	4.71	4.61	4.61	4.59	4.60	4.64	4.75	4.79	4.82	4.79	4.78	4.75	4.77
1927..	4.77	4.87	4.87	4.83	4.80	4.79	4.80	4.80	4.73	4.73	4.69	4.65	4.62
1926..	4.97	5.07	5.04	5.05	4.99	4.94	4.92	4.95	4.95	4.97	4.95	4.93	4.89
1925..	5.20	5.30	5.25	5.24	5.24	5.19	5.15	5.17	5.21	5.18	4.17	5.14	5.14
1924..	5.44	5.55	5.52	5.57	5.56	5.49	5.43	5.38	5.38	5.38	5.35	5.32	5.31
1923..	5.62	5.42	5.49	5.62	5.73	5.66	5.66	5.69	5.63	5.65	5.65	5.63	5.63
1922..	5.59	5.94	5.80	5.79	5.71	5.62	5.64	5.57	5.44	5.35	5.36	5.45	5.41
1921..	6.55	6.64	6.60	6.59	6.68	6.69	6.76	6.78	6.64	6.56	6.47	6.18	5.95
1920..	6.59	6.19	6.28	6.42	6.54	6.78	6.79	6.69	6.76	6.65	6.56	6.63	6.84
1919..	5.86	5.75	5.79	5.76	5.80	5.75	5.71	5.76	5.85	5.96	5.96	6.02	6.21

Source: *Moody's Industrial Manual* (New York: Moody's Investor's Service, 1984).

MOODY'S AVERAGE OF YIELDS ON A CORPORATE BONDS (IN PERCENT)

Year	Aver.	Jan.	Feb.	Mar.	Apr.	May	June	July	Aug.	Sept.	Oct.	Nov.	Dec.
1984..	...	13.13	13.11	13.54	13.77	14.37	...	...	...	...	...	...	...
1983..	13.10	13.53	13.52	13.15	12.86	12.68	12.88	12.99	13.17	13.11	12.97	13.09	13.21
1982..	15.43	16.19	16.35	16.12	15.95	15.70	16.07	16.20	15.70	15.07	14.34	13.81	13.66
1981..	15.29	13.83	14.27	14.47	14.82	15.43	15.08	15.36	15.76	16.36	16.47	15.82	15.75
1980..	12.89	11.88	12.99	13.97	13.55	12.35	11.89	11.95	12.44	12.97	13.05	13.59	14.03
1979..	10.20	9.72	9.68	9.81	9.88	10.00	9.89	9.75	9.85	10.03	10.83	11.50	11.46
1978..	9.12	8.76	8.79	8.83	8.93	9.05	9.18	9.33	9.18	9.11	9.26	9.48	9.53
1977..	8.49	8.45	8.49	8.55	8.55	8.55	8.46	8.40	8.40	8.37	8.48	8.56	8.57
⊡1976.	9.09	9.54	9.43	9.40	9.26	9.28	9.24	9.14	8.98	8.81	8.73	8.69	8.53
⊡1975.	9.65	9.81	9.51	9.37	9.62	9.79	9.67	9.61	9.68	9.74	9.72	9.64	9.67
⊡1974.	9.20	8.17	8.25	8.32	8.61	8.83	9.07	9.40	9.67	10.04	10.29	9.96	9.80
1973..	7.84	7.53	7.60	7.66	7.64	7.64	7.71	7.86	8.11	8.11	7.98	8.07	8.11
1972..	7.66	7.70	7.70	7.66	7.74	7.75	7.69	7.71	7.64	7.64	7.64	7.58	7.50
1971..	8.03	8.15	7.85	7.96	7.99	8.14	8.20	8.21	8.20	8.04	7.97	7.88	7.81
1970..	8.57	8.35	8.31	8.17	8.22	8.49	8.76	8.92	8.85	8.78	8.71	8.74	8.48
1969..	7.40	6.93	6.97	7.13	7.21	7.12	7.28	7.40	7.41	7.56	7.79	7.84	8.21
1968..	6.54	6.48	6.41	6.43	6.57	6.62	6.65	6.60	6.38	6.39	6.47	6.59	6.85
1967..	5.86	5.53	5.38	5.49	5.46	5.60	5.77	5.88	5.94	6.06	6.19	6.43	6.58
1966..	5.35	4.91	4.96	5.12	5.18	5.17	5.29	5.36	5.48	5.69	5.67	5.65	5.69
1965..	4.63	4.57	4.54	4.54	4.54	4.55	4.58	4.62	4.65	4.69	4.71	4.75	4.85
1964..	4.57	4.57	4.56	4.56	4.59	4.60	4.60	4.58	4.57	4.55	4.55	4.57	4.58
1963..	4.48	4.48	4.46	4.45	4.46	4.46	4.45	4.47	4.48	4.50	4.51	4.54	4.54
1962..	4.65	4.74	4.74	4.71	4.66	4.62	4.62	4.65	4.66	4.62	4.61	4.59	4.54
1961..	4.70	4.69	4.63	4.57	4.59	4.63	4.69	4.75	4.80	4.81	4.79	4.75	4.74
1960..	4.77	4.93	4.92	4.86	4.79	4.84	4.81	4.77	4.65	4.63	4.67	4.69	4.71
1959..	4.67	4.43	4.43	4.40	4.45	4.61	4.71	4.75	4.74	4.87	4.87	4.86	4.89
1958..	4.17	4.01	4.00	4.06	4.01	4.02	4.00	4.04	4.19	4.40	4.45	4.43	4.42
1957..	4.19	4.01	3.99	3.97	3.95	3.99	4.09	4.20	4.35	4.43	4.46	4.50	4.31
1956..	3.57	3.30	3.28	3.30	3.41	3.47	3.48	3.52	3.63	3.73	3.81	3.90	3.98
1955..	3.24	3.15	3.17	3.18	3.19	3.21	3.22	3.24	3.28	3.31	3.30	3.29	3.33
1954..	3.18	3.35	3.25	3.16	3.15	3.15	3.18	3.17	3.15	3.13	3.14	3.13	3.14
1953..	3.47	3.25	3.30	3.36	3.44	3.58	3.67	3.62	3.56	3.56	3.47	3.40	3.40
1952..	3.23	3.32	3.25	3.24	3.20	3.20	3.20	3.19	3.21	3.22	3.24	3.24	3.22
1951..	3.13	2.89	2.88	3.00	3.11	3.15	3.21	3.23	3.17	3.15	3.18	3.26	3.31
1950..	2.89	2.85	2.86	2.86	2.86	2.88	2.90	2.92	2.87	2.88	2.91	2.92	2.91
1949..	3.00	3.08	3.05	3.05	3.05	3.04	3.04	3.04	2.96	2.95	2.94	2.93	2.89
1948..	3.12	3.17	3.17	3.13	3.08	3.06	3.03	3.03	3.07	3.13	3.15	3.18	3.16
1947..	2.87	2.79	2.79	2.80	2.81	2.82	2.83	2.82	2.81	2.86	2.95	3.01	3.16
1946..	2.75	2.73	2.70	2.69	2.69	2.73	2.73	2.72	2.74	2.80	2.84	2.84	2.83
1945..	2.87	2.98	2.94	2.92	2.90	2.88	2.86	2.85	2.85	2.85	2.84	2.81	2.79
1944..	3.06	3.11	3.10	3.10	3.09	3.07	3.07	3.05	3.04	3.05	3.01	3.01	2.98
1943..	3.13	3.20	3.17	3.14	3.14	3.13	3.11	3.09	3.08	3.10	3.10	3.11	3.13
1942..	3.28	3.30	3.29	3.32	3.30	3.31	3.31	3.28	3.27	3.26	3.24	3.24	3.23
1941..	3.30	3.36	3.38	3.37	3.38	3.34	3.31	3.26	3.24	3.24	3.21	3.19	3.27
1940:..	3.57	3.69	3.68	3.65	3.59	3.65	3.70	3.57	3.55	3.52	3.48	3.40	3.36
1939..	3.89	3.97	3.94	3.87	3.97	3.92	3.86	3.83	3.80	4.05	3.94	3.78	3.74
1938..	4.22	4.20	4.24	4.34	4.49	4.28	4.41	4.21	4.13	4.20	4.08	4.02	4.02
1937..	4.01	3.77	3.85	3.97	4.04	3.98	3.96	3.94	3.94	4.02	4.16	4.24	4.20
1936..	4.02	4.21	4.12	4.10	4.12	4.11	4.09	4.05	3.99	3.94	3.90	3.85	3.78
1935..	4.55	4.74	4.63	4.67	4.69	4.59	4.52	4.46	4.49	4.48	4.49	4.45	4.35
1934..	5.08	5.72	5.24	5.12	4.97	4.96	4.96	4.93	5.09	5.17	5.00	4.93	4.86
1933..	6.09	6.16	6.30	6.64	6.85	6.29	5.88	5.58	5.51	5.70	5.76	6.22	6.21
1932..	7.20	7.06	7.06	6.80	7.48	8.40	8.50	8.19	6.84	6.45	6.44	6.53	6.61
1931..	6.01	5.26	5.29	5.30	5.52	5.65	5.75	5.64	5.88	6.29	6.88	6.90	7.70
1930..	5.13	5.23	5.25	5.15	5.12	5.07	5.08	5.06	5.00	4.94	5.06	5.21	5.43
1929..	5.28	5.10	5.14	5.24	5.23	5.24	5.31	5.32	5.39	5.43	5.38	5.33	5.21
1928..	5.01	4.91	4.92	4.92	4.91	4.96	5.07	5.09	5.10	5.07	5.04	4.99	5.08
1927..	5.04	5.11	5.13	5.12	5.06	5.05	5.06	5.04	5.01	5.01	4.97	4.94	4.92
1926..	5.24	5.38	5.33	5.34	5.27	5.18	5.18	5.21	5.23	5.23	5.23	5.17	5.16
1925..	5.55	5.70	5.61	5.66	5.63	5.46	5.44	5.51	5.56	5.53	5.54	5.51	5.46
1924..	5.93	6.16	6.18	6.10	6.09	6.00	5.90	5.79	5.84	5.83	5.78	5.72	5.72
1923..	6.17	6.04	6.07	6.24	6.25	6.17	6.19	6.21	6.06	6.15	6.23	6.22	6.20
1922..	6.03	6.41	6.33	6.22	6.05	5.93	5.97	5.88	5.85	5.79	5.91	5.99	6.04
1921..	7.28	7.52	7.50	7.53	7.53	7.50	7.58	7.53	7.43	7.23	7.03	6.62	6.39
1920..	7.41	6.88	7.15	7.11	7.34	7.60	7.58	7.62	7.69	7.48	7.34	7.45	7.71
1919..	6.48	6.42	6.45	6.48	6.40	6.35	6.26	6.26	6.44	6.56	6.52	6.70	6.91

Source: *Moody's Industrial Manual* (New York: Moody's Investor's Service, 1984).

MOODY'S AVERAGE OF YIELDS ON Baa CORPORATE BONDS (IN PERCENT)

Year	Aver.	Jan.	Feb.	Mar.	Apr.	May	June	July	Aug.	Sept.	Oct.	Nov.	Dec.
1984..	...	13.65	13.59	13.99	14.31	14.74	...	...	...	...	...	...	...
1983..	13.55	13.94	13.95	13.61	13.29	13.09	13.37	13.39	13.64	13.55	13.46	13.61	13.75
1982..	16.11	17.10	17.18	16.82	16.78	16.64	16.92	16.80	16.32	15.63	14.73	14.30	14.14
1981..	16.04	15.03	15.37	15.34	15.56	15.95	15.80	16.17	16.34	16.92	17.11	16.39	16.55
1980..	13.67	12.42	13.57	14.45	14.19	13.17	12.71	12.65	13.15	13.70	14.23	14.64	15.14
1979..	10.69	10.13	10.08	10.26	10.33	10.47	10.38	10.29	10.35	10.54	11.40	11.99	12.06
1978..	9.49	9.17	9.20	9.22	9.32	9.49	9.60	9.60	9.48	9.42	9.59	9.83	9.94
1977..	8.97	9.08	9.12	9.12	9.07	9.01	8.91	8.87	8.82	8.80	8.89	8.95	8.99
[1]1976..	9.75	10.41	10.24	10.12	9.94	9.86	9.89	9.82	9.64	9.40	9.29	9.23	9.12
[1]1975..	10.61	10.81	10.65	10.48	10.58	10.69	10.62	10.55	10.59	10.61	10.62	10.56	10.56
[1]1974..	9.50	8.48	8.53	8.62	8.87	9.05	9.27	9.48	9.77	10.18	10.48	10.60	10.63
1973..	8.24	7.90	7.97	8.03	8.09	8.06	8.13	8.24	8.53	8.63	8.41	8.42	8.48
1972..	8.16	8.23	8.23	8.24	8.24	8.23	8.20	8.23	8.19	8.09	8.06	7.99	7.93
1971..	8.56	8.74	8.39	8.46	8.45	8.62	8.75	8.76	8.76	8.59	8.48	8.38	8.38
1970..	9.11	8.86	8.78	8.63	8.70	8.98	9.25	9.40	9.44	9.39	9.33	9.38	9.12
1969..	7.81	7.32	7.30	7.51	7.54	7.52	7.70	7.84	7.86	8.05	8.22	8.25	8.65
1968..	6.94	6.84	6.80	6.85	6.97	7.03	7.07	6.98	6.82	6.79	6.84	7.01	7.23
1967..	6.23	5.97	5.82	5.85	5.83	5.96	6.15	6.26	6.33	6.40	6.52	6.72	6.93
1966..	5.67	5.06	5.12	5.32	5.41	5.48	5.58	5.68	5.83	6.09	6.10	6.13	6.18
1965..	4.87	4.80	4.78	4.78	4.80	4.81	4.85	4.88	4.88	4.91	4.93	4.95	5.02
1964..	4.83	4.83	4.83	4.83	4.85	4.85	4.85	4.83	4.82	4.82	4.81	4.81	4.81
1963..	4.86	4.91	4.89	4.88	4.87	4.85	4.84	4.84	4.83	4.84	4.83	4.84	4.85
1962..	5.02	5.08	5.07	5.04	5.02	5.00	5.02	5.05	5.06	5.03	4.99	4.96	4.92
1961..	5.08	5.10	5.07	5.02	5.01	5.01	5.03	5.09	5.11	5.12	5.13	5.11	5.10
1960..	5.19	5.34	5.34	5.25	5.20	5.28	5.26	5.22	5.08	5.01	5.11	5.08	5.10
1959..	5.05	4.87	4.89	4.85	4.86	4.96	5.04	5.08	5.09	5.18	5.28	5.26	5.28
1958..	4.73	4.83	4.66	4.68	4.67	4.62	4.55	4.53	4.67	4.87	4.92	4.87	4.85
1957..	4.71	4.49	4.47	4.43	4.44	4.52	4.63	4.73	4.82	4.93	4.99	5.09	5.03
1956..	3.88	3.60	3.58	3.60	3.68	3.73	3.76	3.80	3.93	4.07	4.17	4.24	4.37
1955..	3.53	3.45	3.47	3.48	3.49	3.50	3.51	3.52	3.56	3.59	3.59	3.58	3.62
1954..	3.51	3.71	3.61	3.51	3.47	3.47	3.49	3.50	3.49	3.47	3.46	3.45	3.45
1953..	3.74	3.51	3.53	3.57	3.65	3.78	3.86	3.86	3.85	3.88	3.82	3.75	3.74
1952..	3.52	3.59	3.53	3.51	3.50	3.49	3.50	3.50	3.51	3.52	3.54	3.53	3.51
1951..	3.41	3.17	3.16	3.23	3.35	3.40	3.49	3.53	3.50	3.46	3.50	3.56	3.61
1950..	3.24	3.24	3.24	3.24	3.23	3.25	3.28	3.32	3.23	3.21	3.22	3.22	3.20
1949..	3.42	3.46	3.45	3.47	3.45	3.45	3.47	3.46	3.40	3.37	3.36	3.35	3.31
1948..	3.47	3.52	3.53	3.53	3.47	3.38	3.34	3.37	3.44	3.45	3.50	3.53	3.53
1947..	3.24	3.13	3.12	3.15	3.16	3.17	3.21	3.18	3.17	3.23	3.35	3.44	3.52
1946..	3.05	3.01	2.95	2.94	2.96	3.02	3.03	3.03	3.03	3.10	3.15	3.17	3.17
1945..	3.29	3.46	3.41	3.38	3.36	3.32	3.29	3.26	3.26	3.24	3.20	3.15	3.10
1944..	3.61	3.76	3.72	3.70	3.68	3.63	3.59	3.57	3.55	3.56	3.55	3.53	3.49
1943..	3.91	4.16	4.08	4.01	3.96	3.91	3.88	3.81	3.81	3.83	3.82	3.83	3.82
1942..	4.28	4.29	4.29	4.30	4.26	4.27	4.33	4.30	4.28	4.26	4.24	4.25	4.28
1941..	4.33	4.38	4.42	4.38	4.33	4.32	4.31	4.28	4.27	4.30	4.28	4.28	4.38
1940..	4.75	4.86	4.83	4.80	4.74	4.94	5.11	4.80	4.76	5.00	4.56	4.48	4.45
1939..	4.96	5.12	5.05	4.89	5.15	5.07	4.91	4.84	4.85	5.00	4.88	4.85	4.92
1938..	5.80	5.89	5.97	6.30	6.47	6.06	6.25	5.63	5.49	5.65	5.36	5.23	5.27
1937..	5.03	4.49	4.53	4.68	4.84	4.84	4.93	4.91	4.92	5.16	5.52	5.82	5.73
1936..	4.77	5.00	4.80	4.86	4.91	4.94	4.90	4.84	4.74	4.62	4.54	4.52	4.53
1935..	5.75	5.98	5.95	6.20	6.13	5.94	5.77	5.67	5.58	5.53	5.54	5.43	5.30
1934..	6.32	7.01	6.27	6.26	6.01	6.05	6.06	6.13	6.49	6.57	6.40	6.37	6.23
1933..	7.76	8.01	8.37	8.91	9.12	7.74	7.07	6.62	6.77	7.27	7.49	7.98	7.75
1932..	9.30	9.13	8.87	8.83	10.46	11.63	11.52	10.79	8.22	7.61	7.87	8.24	8.42
1931..	7.62	6.41	6.38	6.44	6.72	7.15	7.36	7.08	7.47	8.07	9.04	8.93	10.42
1930..	5.90	5.92	5.89	5.73	5.70	5.72	5.78	5.77	5.73	5.65	5.94	6.25	6.71
1929..	5.90	5.63	5.66	5.79	5.80	5.80	5.94	5.95	6.04	6.12	6.11	6.03	5.95
1928..	5.48	5.35	5.33	5.32	5.33	5.42	5.55	5.58	5.61	5.59	5.58	5.55	5.60
1927..	5.48	5.61	5.59	5.54	5.48	5.50	5.55	5.55	5.48	5.42	5.38	5.35	5.32
1926..	5.87	6.09	6.02	6.05	5.98	5.86	5.80	5.79	5.81	5.79	5.81	5.77	5.68
1925..	6.27	6.44	6.36	6.36	6.41	6.30	6.18	6.20	6.24	6.20	6.17	6.17	6.15
1924..	6.83	7.24	7.14	7.08	7.03	6.97	6.82	6.67	6.69	6.73	6.62	6.54	6.46
1923..	7.24	6.98	6.97	7.09	7.17	7.17	7.21	7.34	7.38	7.38	7.46	7.40	7.38
1922..	7.08	7.70	7.55	7.45	7.14	6.89	6.97	6.89	6.85	6.75	6.78	6.98	7.02
1921..	8.35	8.50	8.42	8.55	8.53	8.52	8.56	8.48	8.51	8.34	8.34	7.88	7.61
1920..	8.20	7.78	7.94	7.97	8.17	8.39	8.39	8.52	8.39	8.14	7.99	8.21	8.56
1919..	7.25	7.12	7.20	7.15	7.23	7.09	7.04	7.06	7.13	7.27	7.34	7.54	7.77

[1]As of December 20, 1976, railroad bonds were removed from the combined Corporate Averages, retroactive to January 1974. This adjustment was necessary because of a lack of comparability to the Industrial and Public Utility averages, reflecting the limited availability of reasonably-current-coupon railroad bonds.

Source: *Moody's Industrial Manual* (New York: Moody's Investor's Service, 1984).

MOODY'S AVERAGE OF YIELDS ON Aaa INDUSTRIAL BONDS (IN PERCENT)

Year	Aver.	Jan.	Feb.	Mar.	Apr.	May	June	July	Aug.	Sept.	Oct.	Nov.	Dec.
1984..	...	12.01	12.08	12.57	12.81	13.28	...	...	...	...	...	...	...
1983..	11.56	11.28	11.54	11.27	11.03	10.91	11.25	11.61	11.99	11.87	11.83	12.00	12.14
1982..	13.35	14.57	14.66	14.09	14.07	13.83	14.30	14.24	13.43	12.64	11.81	11.24	11.34
1981..	13.70	12.31	12.75	12.81	13.33	13.81	13.35	13.87	14.36	14.92	14.97	13.99	13.93
1980..	11.57	10.85	12.01	12.59	11.81	10.74	10.27	10.65	11.17	11.58	11.83	12.53	12.79
1979..	9.39	9.01	9.01	9.11	9.15	9.30	9.08	8.98	8.99	9.18	9.87	10.52	10.51
1978..	8.58	8.31	8.37	8.36	8.43	8.54	8.60	8.73	8.52	8.54	8.72	8.87	8.98
1977..	7.86	7.77	7.86	7.92	7.86	7.87	7.77	7.78	7.82	7.76	7.88	7.93	8.04
1976..	8.23	8.33	8.29	8.30	8.20	8.43	8.40	8.33	8.26	8.18	8.14	8.12	7.81
1975..	8.61	8.65	8.44	8.52	8.78	8.75	8.61	8.62	8.69	8.68	8.57	8.52	8.51
1974..	8.42	7.65	7.70	7.87	8.13	8.26	8.34	8.60	8.89	9.12	9.03	8.69	8.74
1973..	7.28	6.96	7.04	7.12	7.08	7.13	7.23	7.28	7.56	7.48	7.43	7.50	7.50
1972..	6.97	6.90	7.00	6.93	7.01	7.00	6.93	6.98	6.96	7.03	7.01	6.94	6.90
1971..	7.05	7.01	6.68	6.80	6.91	7.21	7.28	7.32	7.28	7.14	7.08	6.97	6.95
1970..	7.77	7.76	7.73	7.61	7.58	7.76	8.16	8.19	7.83	7.79	7.75	7.75	7.31
1969..	6.93	6.47	6.53	6.73	6.81	6.69	6.88	7.03	6.95	7.04	7.08	7.21	7.58
1968..	6.12	6.09	6.05	6.08	6.16	6.22	6.24	6.20	5.97	5.91	6.04	6.12	6.18
1967..	5.49	5.13	5.04	5.14	5.13	5.21	5.41	5.58	5.62	5.66	5.77	6.06	6.14
1966..	5.12	4.72	4.81	4.95	4.97	4.98	5.05	5.11	5.29	5.49	5.37	5.32	5.36
1965..	4.45	4.36	4.35	4.35	4.36	4.39	4.44	4.46	4.47	4.50	4.52	4.58	4.67
1964..	4.32	4.28	4.24	4.27	4.31	4.32	4.31	4.32	4.35	4.36	4.38	4.37	4.37
1963..	4.14	4.06	4.04	4.04	4.07	4.08	4.09	4.15	4.19	4.21	4.22	4.23	4.26
1962..	4.18	4.30	4.31	4.28	4.19	4.11	4.14	4.22	4.22	4.16	4.09	4.07	4.08
1961..	4.21	4.16	4.09	4.04	4.09	4.11	4.20	4.28	4.29	4.32	4.29	4.27	4.33
1960..	4.28	4.49	4.44	4.37	4.33	4.34	4.34	4.29	4.13	4.12	4.15	4.16	4.21
1959..	4.27	4.00	4.03	4.01	4.15	4.28	4.38	4.35	4.30	4.43	4.44	4.43	4.45
1958..	3.61	3.42	3.43	3.46	3.39	3.33	3.32	3.46	3.68	4.03	3.98	3.93	3.93
1957..	3.76	3.68	3.53	3.54	3.52	3.63	3.89	3.91	4.01	3.97	3.93	3.94	3.58
1956..	3.30	3.05	3.01	3.08	3.22	3.22	3.17	3.21	3.36	3.50	3.51	3.59	3.70
1955..	3.00	2.86	2.93	2.97	2.95	2.99	3.00	2.98	3.06	3.07	3.05	3.03	3.10
1954..	2.82	3.00	2.85	2.78	2.78	2.81	2.84	2.81	2.79	2.80	2.77	2.80	2.84
1953..	3.12	2.97	3.01	3.05	3.16	3.29	3.37	3.19	3.12	3.17	3.06	3.03	3.05
1952..	2.88	2.87	2.82	2.87	2.85	2.86	2.87	2.87	2.86	2.87	2.95	2.91	2.91
1951..	2.78	2.59	2.60	2.74	2.82	2.81	2.87	2.87	2.80	2.74	2.81	2.86	2.88
1950..	2.55	2.50	2.51	2.52	2.53	2.53	2.54	2.58	2.54	2.57	2.60	2.60	2.60
1949..	2.58	2.60	2.61	2.61	2.61	2.63	2.64	2.59	2.53	2.52	2.53	2.53	2.51
1948..	2.71	2.76	2.74	2.71	2.67	2.65	2.65	2.70	2.74	2.73	2.73	2.73	2.67
1947..	2.53	2.49	2.47	2.46	2.45	2.46	2.47	2.46	2.47	2.53	2.60	2.68	2.76
1946..	2.44	2.42	2.38	2.39	2.43	2.47	2.42	2.40	2.42	2.51	2.50	2.48	2.51
1945..	2.49	2.54	2.50	2.47	2.50	2.52	2.51	2.49	2.47	2.48	2.46	2.48	2.48
1944..	2.57	2.49	2.53	2.57	2.59	2.58	2.59	2.59	2.58	2.58	2.58	2.59	2.56
1943..	2.49	2.54	2.52	2.51	2.51	2.49	2.48	2.46	2.46	2.47	2.48	2.50	2.50
1942..	2.57	2.59	2.59	2.61	2.56	2.60	2.60	2.57	2.56	2.56	2.54	2.54	2.56
1941..	2.50	2.36	2.44	2.51	2.57	2.57	2.52	2.52	2.49	2.51	2.48	2.48	2.56
1940..	2.44	2.47	2.44	2.41	2.38	2.60	2.57	2.57	2.46	2.45	2.40	2.34	2.28
1939..	2.67	2.62	2.61	2.63	2.69	2.65	2.57	2.57	2.51	3.03	2.90	2.68	2.59
1938..	2.85	2.87	2.93	2.92	2.96	2.85	2.86	2.86	2.82	2.87	2.82	2.74	2.72
1937..	3.06	2.90	3.05	3.10	3.27	3.12	3.04	3.04	3.02	3.12	3.06	2.99	2.97
1936..	3.03	3.13	3.08	3.05	3.07	3.08	3.07	3.06	3.01	2.95	2.99	2.94	2.91
1935..	3.53	3.82	3.72	3.69	3.65	3.62	3.57	3.50	3.53	3.48	3.31	3.24	3.25
1934..	4.02	4.37	4.23	4.19	4.13	4.04	3.93	3.87	3.91	3.93	3.89	3.85	3.84
1933..	4.53	4.50	4.56	4.74	4.88	4.74	4.50	4.42	4.35	4.39	4.36	4.46	4.46
1932..	5.09	5.45	5.37	5.18	5.26	5.35	5.47	5.30	4.96	4.75	4.67	4.68	4.64
1931..	4.71	4.59	4.57	4.51	4.54	4.54	4.49	4.47	4.47	4.65	5.12	5.07	5.50
1930..	4.69	4.80	4.84	4.76	4.71	4.72	4.69	4.64	4.60	4.57	4.57	4.64	4.68
1929..	4.86	4.77	4.81	4.83	4.82	4.85	4.90	4.91	4.90	4.92	4.91	4.91	4.80
1928..	4.73	4.66	4.66	4.68	4.66	4.69	4.73	4.79	4.82	4.79	4.77	4.76	4.77
1927..	4.76	4.85	4.84	4.81	4.80	4.77	4.76	4.78	4.77	4.75	4.68	4.68	4.64
1926..	4.93	5.03	5.01	5.04	5.00	4.95	4.93	4.89	4.88	4.88	4.83	4.85	4.86
1925..	5.11	5.19	5.19	5.18	5.10	5.10	5.11	5.09	5.12	5.10	5.03	5.04	5.05
1924..	5.28	5.33	5.34	5.35	5.34	5.33	5.29	5.26	5.24	5.25	5.23	5.21	5.21
1923..	5.37	5.33	5.33	5.38	5.42	5.42	5.41	5.40	5.38	5.36	5.33	5.31	5.31
1922..	5.35	5.60	5.52	5.45	5.38	5.38	5.37	5.27	5.23	5.19	5.21	5.26	5.37
1921..	6.15	6.34	6.25	6.23	6.21	6.22	6.28	6.26	6.16	6.16	6.15	5.87	5.65
1920..	6.19	5.74	5.83	5.91	6.01	6.21	6.47	6.44	6.41	6.42	6.26	6.26	6.35
1919..	5.55	5.53	5.51	5.53	5.58	5.53	5.44	5.45	5.50	5.57	5.60	5.65	5.69

Source: *Moody's Industrial Manual* (New York: Moody's Investor's Service, 1984).

MOODY'S AVERAGE OF YIELDS ON Baa INDUSTRIAL BONDS (IN PERCENT)

Year	Aver.	Jan.	Feb.	Mar.	Apr.	May	June	July	Aug.	Sept.	Oct.	Nov.	Dec.
1984..	...	13.24	13.13	13.42	13.78	14.21	...	...	...	...	...	...	...
1983..	12.90	13.33	13.27	12.89	12.52	12.12	12.57	12.76	13.07	12.99	12.95	13.10	13.27
1982..	15.77	16.36	16.51	16.47	16.55	16.60	16.63	16.50	16.28	15.57	14.35	13.79	13.58
1981..	15.48	14.76	14.87	14.84	14.98	15.24	15.29	15.35	15.48	16.08	16.50	16.28	16.07
1980..	13.39	11.92	12.73	13.64	14.03	13.41	12.78	12.54	12.79	13.33	14.03	14.48	14.98
1979..	10.42	9.96	9.89	9.98	9.98	10.11	10.24	10.19	10.11	10.20	10.29	10.91	11.50	11.61
1978..	9.35	9.07	9.11	9.07	9.10	9.27	9.40	9.45	9.43	9.36	9.49	9.66	9.79
1977..	8.87	8.99	9.04	9.04	8.97	8.88	8.80	8.75	8.72	8.74	8.77	8.84	8.90
1976..	9.67	10.26	10.17	10.07	9.92	9.81	9.76	9.75	9.61	9.33	9.17	9.12	9.03
1975..	10.26	10.02	9.98	10.01	10.30	10.42	10.39	10.30	10.31	10.35	10.34	10.33	10.33
1974..	9.14	8.38	8.37	8.42	8.69	8.85	9.03	9.23	9.39	9.78	9.92	9.81	9.85
1973..	8.07	7.80	7.85	7.94	8.00	7.89	7.99	8.10	8.34	8.35	8.12	8.17	8.29
1972..	7.99	8.01	8.02	8.07	8.07	8.10	8.01	8.01	8.00	7.95	7.96	7.86	7.80
1971..	8.37	8.46	8.04	8.18	8.19	8.51	8.71	8.74	8.60	8.43	8.34	8.16	8.13
1970..	9.00	8.84	8.76	8.57	8.65	8.82	9.05	9.22	9.32	9.29	9.22	9.28	8.92
1969..	7.76	7.29	7.26	7.44	7.41	7.47	7.65	7.76	7.87	8.02	8.17	8.15	8.58
1968..	6.90	6.79	6.79	6.81	6.86	6.95	7.05	6.98	6.75	6.76	6.82	7.01	7.25
1967..	6.21	6.02	5.90	5.90	5.81	5.87	6.06	6.24	6.31	6.43	6.53	6.67	6.82
1966..	5.68	5.09	5.14	5.29	5.32	5.44	5.61	5.74	5.92	6.18	6.14	6.13	6.18
1965..	4.92	4.85	4.84	4.83	4.88	4.88	4.91	4.93	4.95	4.96	4.98	5.00	5.05
1964..	4.87	4.90	4.88	4.88	4.89	4.91	4.91	4.88	4.85	4.84	4.84	4.84	4.85
1963..	4.90	4.90	4.89	4.90	4.91	4.91	4.89	4.90	4.90	4.89	4.89	4.89	4.90
1962..	4.98	5.07	5.05	4.96	4.93	4.93	5.00	5.06	5.04	4.96	4.91	4.91	4.90
1961..	5.10	5.13	5.08	5.02	5.05	5.05	5.06	5.12	5.13	5.14	5.16	5.13	5.10
1960..	5.11	5.17	5.17	5.08	5.06	5.20	5.20	5.17	5.05	4.99	5.05	5.05	5.11
1959..	4.91	4.77	4.80	4.76	4.77	4.80	4.87	4.92	4.96	5.02	5.07	5.09	5.12
1958..	4.59	4.75	4.63	4.60	4.56	4.50	4.44	4.39	4.44	4.64	4.71	4.72	4.74
1957..	4.79	4.62	4.64	4.57	4.55	4.60	4.73	4.81	4.90	5.00	5.03	5.04	4.97
1956..	3.84	3.55	3.52	3.55	3.65	3.69	3.71	3.75	3.89	4.02	4.13	4.22	4.42
1955..	3.47	3.38	3.40	3.41	3.42	3.44	3.45	3.47	3.53	3.54	3.53	3.53	3.56
1954..	3.40	3.59	3.46	3.35	3.31	3.34	3.39	3.43	3.40	3.38	3.37	3.36	3.36
1953..	3.55	3.27	3.29	3.34	3.44	3.54	3.65	3.69	3.70	3.72	3.68	3.63	3.64
1952..	3.20	3.18	3.15	3.16	3.17	3.16	3.16	3.17	3.18	3.21	3.25	3.29	3.28
1951..	3.04	2.84	2.84	2.91	2.98	3.02	3.10	3.13	3.11	3.09	3.12	3.15	3.18
1950..	2.86	2.86	2.85	2.83	2.85	2.85	2.86	2.88	2.86	2.85	2.86	2.86	2.85
1949..	3.02	3.10	3.09	3.07	3.06	3.05	3.06	3.03	2.99	2.96	2.96	2.93	2.90
1948..	3.13	3.18	3.18	3.19	3.16	3.10	3.04	3.04	3.11	3.12	3.16	3.16	3.15
1947..	2.92	2.87	2.85	2.86	2.85	2.83	2.86	2.88	2.90	2.92	3.01	3.08	3.16
1946..	2.84	2.83	2.80	2.80	2.81	2.84	2.83	2.83	2.80	2.83	2.86	2.88	2.91
1945..	2.96	3.02	2.99	2.99	2.98	2.96	2.97	2.97	2.98	2.95	2.93	2.89	2.88
1944..	3.15	3.30	3.25	3.24	3.24	3.17	3.09	3.10	3.11	3.10	3.10	3.08	3.05
1943..	3.38	3.49	3.47	3.48	3.44	3.42	3.38	3.30	3.29	3.31	3.31	3.33	3.33
1942..	3.55	3.62	3.63	3.62	3.54	3.50	3.49	3.47	3.49	3.54	3.56	3.54	3.56
1941..	3.65	3.78	3.78	3.76	3.74	3.70	3.67	3.61	3.58	3.54	3.48	3.50	3.60
1940..	4.08	4.13	4.11	4.07	4.02	4.22	4.38	4.20	4.15	4.06	3.96	3.88	3.82
1939..	4.25	4.27	4.27	4.25	4.39	4.33	4.22	4.20	4.19	4.37	4.27	4.14	4.15
1938..	4.49	4.48	4.53	4.67	4.73	4.54	4.60	4.44	4.39	4.49	4.37	4.32	4.36
1937..	4.25	3.94	3.99	4.13	4.21	4.16	4.16	4.16	4.12	4.22	4.49	4.69	4.70
1936..	4.07	4.16	4.13	4.13	4.15	4.13	4.12	4.11	4.06	4.02	3.99	3.93	3.96
1935..	4.51	4.74	4.70	4.67	4.67	4.68	4.57	4.54	4.43	4.45	4.36	4.30	4.28
1934..	5.15	5.54	5.31	5.28	5.09	5.06	5.03	4.98	5.13	5.22	5.17	5.05	4.88
1933..	6.36	7.04	7.54	7.99	7.71	6.64	6.03	5.59	5.44	5.49	5.52	5.68	5.70
1932..	8.76	9.78	9.16	8.53	9.35	10.30	10.64	10.29	7.93	7.21	7.25	7.39	7.32
1931..	8.03	6.59	6.55	6.72	7.17	7.93	8.08	7.65	7.88	8.61	9.46	9.22	10.50
1930..	6.09	6.21	6.11	5.91	5.82	5.84	5.99	5.95	5.88	5.81	6.21	6.43	6.90
1929..	6.02	5.82	5.79	5.88	5.84	5.89	6.05	5.98	6.01	6.13	6.19	6.35	6.25
1928..	5.71	5.54	5.49	5.51	5.55	5.68	5.80	5.86	5.84	5.80	5.79	5.84	5.85
1927..	5.61	5.80	5.75	5.63	5.54	5.60	5.63	5.63	5.64	5.56	5.49	5.50	5.52
1926..	6.11	6.29	6.23	6.22	6.21	6.12	6.06	6.09	6.04	6.05	6.06	6.06	5.89
1925..	6.37	6.54	6.46	6.45	6.47	6.48	6.34	6.35	6.32	6.29	6.21	6.25	6.23
1924..	6.87	7.16	7.11	7.08	7.02	6.96	6.87	6.80	6.84	6.75	6.71	6.60	6.55
1923..	7.06	7.02	6.99	6.97	6.93	6.84	6.90	7.10	7.17	7.15	7.21	7.24	7.21
1922..	7.12	7.50	7.51	7.45	7.15	6.92	6.97	6.92	6.91	6.81	6.86	7.16	7.22
1921..	8.10	8.50	8.23	8.42	8.33	8.16	8.14	8.07	8.11	8.14	8.07	7.68	7.36
1920..	7.94	7.48	7.63	7.82	7.81	8.04	8.12	8.23	8.12	7.83	7.64	8.06	8.54
1919..	6.99	6.96	7.04	7.00	7.07	6.97	6.78	6.78	6.83	6.90	6.97	7.22	7.35

The tables above give the monthly average yields of 40 long-term industrial bonds (10 Aaa, 10 Aa, 10 A and 10 Baa). Prior to 1928, 20 bonds were used. All yields are calculated to maturity dates and the list of bonds used is adjusted when required to reflect rating changes or other reasons so that each of the series is comparable throughout the entire period. Average yields for the periods presented are not intended to be indicative of yields which may prevail in the future.

Source: *Moody's Industrial Manual* (New York: Moody's Investor's Service, 1984).

PART III: ECONOMIC DATA

SUMMARY NATIONAL INCOME AND PRODUCT SERIES, ANNUALLY AND QUARTERLY: 1950—82

Table A.—Gross National Product

[Billions of dollars; quarterly data are seasonally adjusted at annual rates]

Year and quarter	GNP	Personal consumption expenditures				Gross private domestic investment				Net exports			Government purchases of goods and services			Final sales	Percent change from preceding period	
		Total	Durable goods	Nondurable goods	Services	Total	Nonresidential	Residential	CBI	Net	Exports	Imports	Total	Federal	State and local		GNP	Final sales
1950	286.5	192.0	30.8	98.2	63.0	53.8	27.3	19.8	6.8	2.2	14.4	12.2	38.5	18.7	19.8	279.7	10.9	7.0
1951	330.8	207.1	29.8	108.8	68.5	59.2	31.3	17.6	10.3	4.4	19.7	15.3	60.1	38.3	21.8	320.5	15.5	14.6
1952	348.0	217.1	29.1	113.9	74.0	52.1	31.3	17.7	3.1	3.2	19.1	15.9	75.6	52.4	23.2	344.8	5.2	7.6
1953	366.8	229.7	32.5	116.5	80.6	53.3	34.5	18.4	.4	1.3	18.0	16.7	82.5	57.5	25.0	366.3	5.4	6.2
1954	366.8	235.8	31.8	118.0	86.1	52.7	34.2	20.1	-1.5	2.5	18.7	16.2	75.8	47.9	27.8	368.4	0	.6
1955	400.0	253.7	38.6	122.9	92.1	68.4	38.5	23.9	6.0	3.0	21.0	18.0	75.0	44.5	30.6	394.1	9.0	7.0
1956	421.7	266.0	37.9	128.9	99.2	71.0	44.0	22.3	4.7	5.3	25.0	19.8	79.4	45.9	33.5	417.0	5.4	5.8
1957	444.0	280.4	39.3	135.2	105.9	69.2	47.0	20.9	1.3	7.3	28.1	20.8	87.1	50.0	37.1	442.6	5.3	6.1
1958	449.7	289.5	36.8	139.8	112.8	61.9	42.0	21.4	-1.5	3.3	24.2	21.0	95.0	53.9	41.1	451.2	1.3	1.9
1959	487.9	310.8	42.4	146.4	121.9	78.1	45.9	26.6	5.7	1.4	24.8	23.4	97.6	53.9	43.7	482.2	8.5	6.9
1960	506.5	324.9	43.1	151.1	130.7	75.9	48.5	24.5	3.0	5.5	28.9	23.4	100.3	53.7	46.5	503.6	3.8	4.4
1961	524.6	335.0	41.6	155.3	138.1	74.8	48.0	24.5	2.3	6.6	29.9	23.3	108.2	57.4	50.8	522.2	3.6	3.7
1962	565.0	355.2	46.7	161.6	147.0	85.4	52.2	27.0	6.3	6.4	31.8	25.4	118.0	63.7	54.3	558.8	7.7	7.0
1963	596.7	374.6	51.4	167.1	156.1	90.9	54.8	30.1	6.0	7.6	34.2	26.6	123.7	64.6	59.0	590.7	5.6	5.7
1964	637.7	400.5	56.4	176.9	167.1	97.4	61.0	30.7	5.6	10.1	38.8	28.8	129.8	65.2	64.6	632.1	6.9	7.0
1965	691.1	430.4	63.0	188.6	178.7	113.5	72.7	30.9	9.9	8.8	41.1	32.3	138.4	67.3	71.1	681.2	8.4	7.8
1966	756.0	465.1	68.0	204.7	192.4	125.7	83.1	28.5	14.1	6.5	44.6	38.1	157.7	78.8	79.8	741.9	9.4	8.9
1967	799.6	490.3	70.1	212.6	207.6	122.8	83.9	28.6	10.3	6.3	47.3	41.0	180.2	90.9	89.3	789.3	5.8	6.4
1968	873.4	536.9	80.5	230.6	225.8	133.3	90.7	34.8	7.9	4.3	52.4	48.1	199.0	98.0	101.0	865.5	9.2	9.7
1969	944.0	581.8	85.7	247.8	248.2	149.3	101.3	38.2	9.8	4.2	57.5	53.3	208.8	97.6	111.2	934.2	8.1	7.9
1970	992.7	621.7	85.2	265.7	270.8	144.2	103.9	37.1	3.2	6.7	65.7	59.0	220.1	95.7	124.4	989.5	5.2	5.9
1971	1,077.6	672.2	97.2	278.8	296.2	166.4	107.9	50.9	7.7	4.1	68.8	64.7	234.9	96.2	138.7	1,070.0	8.6	8.1
1972	1,185.9	737.1	111.1	300.6	325.3	195.0	121.0	63.8	10.2	.7	77.5	76.7	253.1	101.7	151.4	1,175.7	10.1	9.9
1973	1,326.4	812.0	123.3	333.4	355.2	229.8	143.3	68.0	18.5	14.2	109.6	95.4	270.4	102.0	168.5	1,307.9	11.8	11.2
1974	1,434.2	888.1	121.5	373.4	393.2	228.7	156.6	57.9	14.1	13.4	146.2	132.8	304.1	111.0	193.1	1,420.1	8.1	8.6
1975	1,549.2	976.4	132.2	407.3	437.0	206.1	157.7	55.3	-6.9	26.8	154.9	128.1	339.9	122.7	217.2	1,556.1	8.0	9.6
1976	1,718.0	1,084.3	156.8	441.7	485.7	257.9	174.1	72.0	11.8	13.8	170.9	157.1	362.1	129.2	232.9	1,706.2	10.9	9.6
1977	1,918.3	1,204.4	178.2	478.8	547.4	324.1	205.2	95.8	23.0	-4.0	182.7	186.7	393.8	143.4	250.4	1,895.3	11.7	11.1
1978	2,163.9	1,346.5	200.2	528.2	618.0	386.6	248.9	111.2	26.5	-1.1	218.7	219.8	431.9	153.6	278.3	2,137.4	12.8	12.8
1979	2,417.8	1,507.2	213.4	600.0	683.7	423.0	290.2	118.6	14.3	13.2	281.4	268.1	474.4	168.3	306.0	2,403.5	11.7	12.4
1980	2,631.7	1,668.1	214.7	668.8	784.5	401.9	308.8	102.9	-9.8	23.9	338.8	314.8	537.8	197.0	340.8	2,641.5	8.8	9.9
1981	2,954.1	1,857.2	236.1	733.9	887.1	474.9	352.2	104.3	18.5	26.3	368.8	342.5	595.7	229.2	366.5	2,935.6	12.2	11.1
1982	3,073.0	1,991.9	244.5	761.0	986.4	414.5	348.3	90.8	-24.5	17.4	347.6	330.2	649.2	258.7	390.5	3,097.5	4.0	5.5
1950: I	267.6	182.9	27.7	94.8	60.3	43.6	23.8	17.5	2.4	3.4	13.5	10.1	37.7	18.6	19.1	265.2	17.9	4.9
II	277.1	186.8	28.1	96.3	62.3	50.5	26.1	19.6	4.8	3.0	13.8	10.8	36.9	17.4	19.4	272.3	15.0	11.2
III	294.8	200.4	35.6	100.9	63.9	55.4	29.1	21.5	4.9	.9	14.5	13.6	38.0	18.0	20.0	289.9	28.0	28.4
IV	306.3	197.8	31.5	100.9	65.4	65.6	30.1	20.5	15.1	1.5	15.8	14.3	41.4	20.9	20.5	291.2	16.6	1.8
1951: I	320.4	208.3	33.8	107.6	66.9	60.7	30.3	19.9	10.5	1.7	17.3	15.6	49.6	28.7	20.9	309.9	19.7	28.2
II	328.3	203.8	28.9	107.1	67.9	63.9	31.3	17.4	15.2	3.8	19.7	15.9	56.7	35.1	21.6	313.1	10.2	4.1
III	335.0	206.2	28.3	109.0	69.0	58.7	31.9	16.4	10.4	5.8	20.7	15.0	64.4	42.3	22.1	324.7	8.5	15.7
IV	339.2	209.9	28.3	111.4	70.1	53.4	31.6	16.7	5.1	6.4	21.0	14.7	69.6	47.2	22.4	334.1	5.1	12.1
1952: I	341.9	211.1	28.9	110.8	71.5	54.1	31.8	17.1	5.2	5.7	21.3	15.6	70.9	48.3	22.6	336.7	3.2	3.2
II	342.1	215.1	29.0	113.0	73.1	47.5	32.3	17.6	-2.3	4.0	19.3	15.3	75.5	52.2	23.3	344.4	.3	9.5
III	347.8	217.2	27.3	115.0	74.9	51.1	29.2	17.6	4.3	2.0	17.9	15.9	77.5	54.3	23.1	343.5	6.8	-1.1
IV	360.0	225.0	31.4	116.9	76.7	55.7	31.9	18.4	5.4	1.0	18.0	17.0	78.3	54.6	23.8	354.6	14.8	13.5
1953: I	366.1	228.3	32.9	117.0	78.4	54.8	33.7	18.7	2.4	1.3	17.8	16.5	81.7	57.2	24.5	363.7	7.0	10.6
II	369.4	229.9	32.8	116.9	80.2	56.1	34.2	18.8	3.2	.8	18.0	17.1	82.6	58.1	24.4	366.3	3.7	2.9
III	368.4	230.5	32.5	116.2	81.8	54.2	35.2	18.2	.7	1.3	18.3	17.0	82.4	57.2	25.1	367.7	-1.1	1.6
IV	363.1	230.0	31.9	116.0	82.1	48.2	34.8	18.0	-4.5	1.6	17.8	16.3	83.4	57.6	25.8	367.6	-5.6	-.1
1954: I	362.5	231.9	31.2	117.1	83.6	49.5	33.9	18.1	-2.5	1.7	17.2	15.5	79.5	52.8	26.7	365.1	-.7	-2.8
II	362.3	234.3	31.8	117.1	85.3	50.4	33.8	19.4	-2.7	2.3	19.2	16.9	75.4	48.0	27.4	365.1	-.2	0
III	366.7	236.4	31.3	118.1	87.0	53.1	34.5	20.8	-2.2	2.6	18.7	16.0	74.6	46.2	28.4	368.9	5.0	4.3
IV	375.6	240.8	33.0	119.5	88.3	57.8	34.5	22.1	1.3	3.5	19.7	16.2	73.4	44.8	28.7	374.3	10.0	6.0
1955: I	388.2	246.8	36.2	120.5	90.1	63.5	35.0	23.9	4.6	3.6	20.5	16.9	74.3	44.5	29.8	383.5	14.1	10.2
II	396.2	251.9	38.6	122.2	91.1	67.9	37.4	24.5	6.1	2.3	20.2	17.9	74.1	43.7	30.3	390.1	8.5	7.0
III	404.8	256.0	40.3	123.3	92.4	70.1	39.9	24.1	6.0	3.3	21.5	18.3	75.4	44.7	30.7	398.7	9.0	9.2
IV	411.0	260.0	39.4	125.7	94.9	72.0	41.8	23.1	7.1	2.9	21.8	18.9	76.2	44.9	31.3	404.0	6.3	5.3
1956: I	412.8	261.4	37.6	127.2	96.5	70.8	42.3	22.5	6.0	3.4	23.2	19.8	77.2	44.9	32.3	406.8	1.7	2.8
II	418.4	263.9	37.6	128.1	98.1	70.4	43.4	22.7	4.3	4.9	24.6	19.8	79.3	46.2	33.1	414.1	5.5	7.4
III	423.5	266.8	37.3	129.4	100.1	71.3	44.9	22.3	4.1	5.6	25.7	20.1	79.7	45.8	33.9	419.4	4.9	5.2
IV	432.1	271.9	38.9	130.8	102.1	71.6	45.5	21.8	4.3	7.2	26.6	19.4	81.3	46.7	34.6	427.7	8.4	8.2
1957: I	440.2	276.1	40.0	132.5	103.6	69.8	46.5	21.3	2.1	8.0	29.0	21.0	86.2	50.3	35.9	438.1	7.7	10.1
II	442.3	278.3	39.5	133.9	104.9	69.8	46.6	20.8	2.3	7.6	28.7	21.1	86.6	49.9	36.7	440.0	1.9	1.7
III	449.4	282.8	39.1	137.2	106.5	71.8	47.9	20.7	3.2	7.4	28.0	20.6	87.5	50.1	37.5	446.3	6.6	5.8
IV	444.0	284.4	38.8	136.9	108.7	65.4	47.0	20.6	-2.2	6.1	26.6	20.5	88.1	49.6	38.5	446.2	-4.8	-.1
1958: I	436.8	284.0	36.8	137.6	109.6	57.8	43.2	20.0	-5.4	3.8	24.2	20.4	91.2	51.6	39.5	442.2	-6.3	-3.5
II	440.7	286.8	36.0	138.9	111.9	56.5	41.5	20.1	-5.1	3.2	24.2	21.0	94.2	53.6	40.6	445.8	3.7	3.3
III	453.9	291.7	36.7	140.8	114.2	62.5	40.9	21.6	.1	3.5	24.2	20.7	96.1	54.4	41.7	453.8	12.5	7.3
IV	467.0	295.4	38.0	141.9	115.5	70.4	42.4	23.9	4.1	2.4	24.2	21.8	98.7	55.9	42.7	462.8	12.1	8.3
1959: I	477.0	303.5	41.2	144.3	117.9	74.5	43.9	26.4	4.2	1.1	23.5	22.4	97.8	54.3	43.6	472.8	8.9	8.9
II	490.6	309.1	43.0	145.6	120.5	83.0	45.6	27.3	10.2	.4	24.0	23.6	98.0	54.3	43.7	480.4	11.9	6.6
III	489.0	314.2	43.9	147.1	123.2	75.2	47.1	26.7	1.4	2.1	26.0	24.0	97.5	53.7	43.8	487.6	-1.3	6.1
IV	495.0	316.2	41.6	148.7	125.9	79.7	47.1	25.9	6.8	2.1	25.7	23.6	97.0	53.3	43.7	488.2	5.0	.5
1960: I	506.9	319.8	43.0	148.8	128.0	86.0	49.0	26.6	10.5	3.8	27.7	23.9	97.3	52.3	44.9	496.4	10.0	6.9
II	506.3	325.9	43.9	151.8	130.2	76.4	49.2	24.3	2.8	4.7	28.7	24.0	99.3	53.1	46.2	503.4	-.5	5.8
III	508.0	326.0	43.4	151.4	131.2	74.2	48.0	23.5	2.6	6.1	29.5	23.4	101.8	54.6	47.2	505.4	1.4	1.5
IV	504.8	328.0	42.2	152.5	133.3	66.9	47.7	23.4	-4.2	7.3	29.5	22.3	102.7	54.8	47.9	509.0	-2.5	2.9
1961: I	508.2	328.5	39.7	153.9	135.0	66.9	46.7	23.4	-3.2	7.8	30.0	22.3	105.0	55.3	49.7	511.4	2.7	1.9
II	519.2	333.1	40.7	154.7	137.6	72.9	47.8	23.6	1.5	6.4	28.9	22.5	106.8	56.9	49.9	517.7	9.0	5.0
III	528.2	335.7	41.9	155.2	138.6	78.0	48.0	24.9	5.2	6.1	30.0	24.0	108.4	57.7	50.8	523.1	7.1	4.2
IV	542.6	342.7	44.0	157.4	141.4	81.3	49.6	25.9	5.8	6.3	30.8	24.5	112.3	59.6	52.7	536.7	11.3	10.9
1962: I	554.2	347.5	45.0	159.3	143.2	84.9	50.6	26.0	8.3	5.7	30.5	24.8	116.1	63.0	53.1	546.0	8.9	7.1
II	562.7	353.0	46.3	160.6	146.1	85.9	52.3	27.2	6.4	7.0	32.4	25.4	116.8	63.0	53.8	556.4	6.3	7.8
III	568.9	357.0	46.8	162.2	148.0	86.4	53.1	27.4	5.9	6.7	32.3	25.6	118.8	64.1	54.7	562.9	4.4	4.8
IV	574.3	363.4	48.8	164.1	150.5	84.5	52.7	27.3	4.5	6.0	32.0	26.0	120.4	64.8	55.6	569.8	3.9	5.0

Source: *Survey of Current Business* (Washington, D.C.: Department of Commerce, October 1983).

Table A.—Gross National Product—Continued

[Billions of dollars; quarterly data are seasonally adjusted at annual rates]

Year and quarter	GNP	Personal consumption expenditures				Gross private domestic investment				Net exports			Government purchases of goods and services			Final sales	Percent change from preceding period	
		Total	Durable goods	Nondurable goods	Services	Total	Nonresidential	Residential	CBI	Net	Exports	Imports	Total	Federal	State and local		GNP	Final sales
1963: I	582.0	367.2	49.8	165.2	152.1	86.4	52.5	28.3	5.7	6.3	31.9	25.6	122.1	64.9	57.2	576.3	5.4	4.6
II	590.7	371.2	51.1	165.9	154.1	90.4	54.0	30.3	6.1	7.9	34.3	26.4	121.3	63.3	58.0	584.6	6.1	5.9
III	601.8	377.8	51.9	168.3	157.7	92.3	55.6	30.3	6.5	7.3	34.6	27.2	124.3	64.5	59.8	595.3	7.7	7.5
IV	612.4	382.1	52.9	168.8	160.4	94.5	57.3	31.6	5.6	8.8	36.1	27.3	127.0	65.9	61.2	606.8	7.3	8.0
1964: I	625.3	390.6	55.0	172.7	162.9	95.6	58.3	31.9	5.4	10.7	38.3	27.6	128.3	65.9	62.4	619.9	8.7	8.9
II	634.0	397.9	56.4	175.7	165.7	96.7	60.2	30.7	5.9	9.4	37.8	28.4	130.0	65.8	64.2	628.2	5.7	5.5
III	642.8	405.9	58.2	179.1	168.5	96.8	62.1	30.3	4.5	10.1	39.2	29.1	130.0	64.7	65.3	638.3	5.7	6.6
IV	648.8	407.6	56.1	180.1	171.4	100.2	63.6	29.9	6.7	10.0	40.0	30.0	130.9	64.5	66.4	642.1	3.8	2.4
1965: I	668.8	417.9	61.6	182.6	173.7	111.5	68.2	31.0	12.3	7.9	36.9	29.1	131.6	63.9	67.7	656.5	13.0	9.3
II	681.7	424.3	61.5	186.0	176.9	111.8	71.1	31.2	9.5	10.0	42.6	32.7	135.6	65.8	69.8	672.2	7.9	9.9
III	696.4	432.9	63.3	189.5	180.1	114.2	74.0	31.0	9.2	9.2	42.3	33.0	140.1	67.6	72.6	687.2	8.9	9.3
IV	717.2	446.3	65.6	195.6	184.3	116.7	77.6	30.6	8.5	8.1	42.5	34.4	145.1	71.8	74.3	708.7	12.5	13.1
1966: I	738.5	456.2	68.7	200.5	187.0	124.8	80.8	30.9	13.1	7.5	43.4	36.0	150.0	73.6	76.4	725.4	12.4	9.8
II	750.0	460.6	66.0	203.9	190.6	127.4	82.9	29.9	14.5	6.7	43.8	37.0	155.3	76.8	78.5	735.4	6.4	5.6
III	760.6	469.4	68.5	206.8	194.1	123.5	84.0	28.1	11.3	5.7	45.0	39.4	162.0	81.5	80.5	749.3	5.8	7.8
IV	774.9	474.2	68.8	207.4	198.0	127.1	84.5	25.1	17.6	6.2	46.0	39.8	167.3	83.5	83.9	757.3	7.7	4.3
1967: I	780.7	478.7	67.3	209.6	201.9	120.2	83.0	24.8	12.4	7.0	47.5	40.6	174.9	88.6	86.3	768.4	3.1	6.0
II	788.6	487.5	70.6	211.2	205.7	117.1	83.5	27.6	6.0	6.7	46.8	40.1	177.3	89.4	88.0	782.7	4.1	7.6
III	805.7	494.0	70.8	213.4	209.8	123.5	83.6	29.7	10.2	6.3	46.9	40.6	182.0	92.1	89.9	795.6	9.0	6.8
IV	823.3	500.8	71.6	216.2	213.0	130.6	85.6	32.1	12.8	5.3	48.1	42.8	186.5	93.7	92.9	810.4	9.0	7.7
1968: I	841.2	517.6	76.8	223.1	217.8	127.1	89.5	33.0	4.6	4.1	49.8	45.7	192.4	96.0	96.4	836.6	9.0	13.6
II	867.2	530.2	78.7	228.2	223.2	133.6	88.5	34.5	10.7	4.9	51.8	46.9	198.6	98.8	99.7	856.5	13.0	9.9
III	884.9	545.7	83.0	234.2	228.4	133.8	90.3	35.0	8.5	4.4	54.3	49.9	201.0	98.6	102.3	876.3	8.4	9.6
IV	900.3	554.0	83.3	236.9	233.8	138.6	94.3	36.6	7.7	3.7	53.5	49.8	204.0	98.6	105.4	892.6	7.2	7.6
1969: I	921.2	565.8	85.3	241.3	239.2	147.1	97.8	38.9	10.4	3.9	49.7	45.9	204.5	97.0	107.5	910.8	9.6	8.4
II	937.4	576.9	85.7	245.9	245.3	149.4	100.0	39.1	10.4	3.7	59.0	55.3	207.4	97.2	110.3	927.1	7.2	7.3
III	955.3	586.7	85.9	249.9	250.9	154.1	103.4	38.4	12.3	3.9	59.5	55.6	210.7	98.3	112.4	943.1	7.9	7.1
IV	962.0	597.8	86.0	254.3	257.4	146.5	103.8	36.4	6.3	5.2	61.9	56.6	212.4	97.8	114.6	955.7	2.8	5.5
1970: I	972.0	607.8	84.9	260.2	262.8	141.3	103.3	36.4	1.6	6.5	63.6	57.1	216.4	98.0	118.4	970.5	4.2	6.3
II	986.3	616.9	86.3	263.5	267.1	143.6	104.3	34.9	4.4	8.1	66.7	58.6	217.7	95.8	122.0	981.9	6.0	4.8
III	1,003.6	628.1	87.3	267.3	273.6	147.8	105.2	36.5	6.0	6.6	66.1	59.6	221.1	94.2	126.9	997.6	7.2	6.5
IV	1,009.0	634.1	82.4	271.9	279.7	144.1	102.7	40.5	.9	5.5	66.2	60.7	225.3	95.0	130.3	1,008.1	2.2	4.3
1971: I	1,049.3	652.8	93.0	273.8	286.0	159.4	104.8	44.1	10.5	7.3	68.4	61.0	229.7	95.8	133.9	1,038.7	16.9	12.7
II	1,068.9	666.0	95.9	277.4	292.7	166.9	107.4	49.6	9.9	3.5	69.1	65.6	232.4	95.0	137.4	1,059.0	7.7	8.0
III	1,086.6	677.5	98.2	279.9	299.5	168.7	108.5	53.4	6.8	3.9	71.8	67.9	236.4	96.6	139.9	1,079.7	6.8	8.1
IV	1,105.8	692.6	102.0	284.0	306.6	170.6	110.9	56.4	3.3	1.7	66.0	64.3	240.9	97.4	143.4	1,102.4	7.3	8.7
1972: I	1,142.4	709.6	105.6	288.8	315.2	183.3	116.0	61.0	6.3	-.2	74.0	74.3	249.7	102.7	147.0	1,136.1	13.9	12.8
II	1,171.7	727.3	109.0	297.2	321.2	193.2	118.7	62.5	12.0	-.3	73.8	74.0	251.5	102.8	148.7	1,159.7	10.7	8.5
III	1,196.1	744.2	112.2	304.0	328.0	197.5	120.9	63.8	12.8	1.4	78.0	76.5	252.9	100.4	152.5	1,183.2	8.6	8.4
IV	1,233.5	767.0	117.6	312.6	336.8	206.1	128.4	68.0	9.8	2.1	84.1	82.1	258.3	100.8	157.5	1,223.7	13.1	14.4
1973: I	1,283.5	790.0	125.5	321.6	343.0	221.6	134.8	70.5	16.3	7.0	95.8	88.8	264.9	103.0	161.9	1,267.2	17.2	15.0
II	1,307.6	802.9	124.3	327.7	350.9	227.0	142.5	69.1	15.4	11.4	105.0	93.5	266.3	100.4	165.9	1,292.2	7.7	8.1
III	1,337.7	820.6	123.4	337.5	359.8	229.6	146.9	67.6	15.1	18.5	114.1	95.6	268.9	98.8	170.2	1,322.6	9.6	9.7
IV	1,376.7	834.3	120.2	346.8	367.3	240.9	149.0	64.8	27.1	19.8	123.5	103.6	281.6	105.8	175.9	1,349.6	12.2	8.4
1974: I	1,387.7	853.0	118.5	358.4	376.1	225.8	152.0	61.2	12.7	22.0	136.8	114.7	286.8	103.9	182.8	1,375.0	3.2	7.7
II	1,423.8	878.6	121.7	369.4	387.5	232.9	155.6	59.6	17.7	11.7	146.3	134.6	300.6	109.6	191.0	1,406.1	10.8	9.4
III	1,451.6	906.7	127.4	380.4	398.9	227.9	159.2	58.0	10.7	7.8	147.5	139.8	309.2	112.7	196.6	1,440.8	8.0	10.3
IV	1,473.8	914.1	118.5	385.1	410.4	228.0	159.5	53.1	15.4	12.1	154.2	142.1	319.7	117.8	201.9	1,458.4	6.3	5.0
1975: I	1,479.8	935.1	122.4	392.2	420.6	191.4	155.1	50.6	-14.3	25.6	156.0	130.3	327.7	119.2	208.5	1,494.1	1.6	10.2
II	1,516.7	961.6	127.1	402.5	432.0	193.0	155.2	52.5	-14.6	28.5	149.2	120.7	333.6	120.1	213.5	1,531.3	10.4	10.3
III	1,578.5	992.1	136.7	414.1	441.3	217.5	158.9	56.6	2.1	24.9	152.7	127.8	344.0	123.7	220.3	1,576.5	17.3	12.3
IV	1,621.8	1,016.9	142.6	420.4	453.9	222.4	161.8	61.4	-.8	28.1	161.9	133.8	354.3	127.9	226.4	1,622.5	11.4	12.2
1976: I	1,672.0	1,047.8	152.0	429.6	466.2	248.8	166.6	66.9	15.3	18.4	164.0	145.6	357.0	126.7	230.4	1,656.7	13.0	8.7
II	1,698.6	1,067.2	154.6	436.2	476.4	258.3	170.9	70.1	17.3	15.0	168.4	153.4	358.1	126.3	231.8	1,681.3	6.5	6.1
III	1,729.0	1,094.2	158.1	445.6	490.5	259.6	177.5	70.7	11.4	12.2	173.6	161.4	362.8	129.5	233.4	1,717.5	7.3	8.9
IV	1,772.5	1,127.9	162.6	455.5	509.8	264.7	181.3	80.2	3.3	9.4	177.5	168.1	370.4	134.3	236.2	1,769.2	10.5	12.6
1977: I	1,834.8	1,162.7	171.2	466.0	525.5	296.4	191.5	85.3	19.6	-2.1	177.9	180.0	377.9	135.8	242.1	1,815.2	14.8	10.8
II	1,895.1	1,186.8	175.5	474.5	536.8	319.4	200.8	95.4	23.3	-1.8	185.1	186.8	390.7	142.2	248.4	1,871.9	13.8	13.1
III	1,954.4	1,216.5	180.1	480.5	555.9	339.6	208.2	99.3	32.1	-.4	186.8	187.2	398.7	146.2	252.5	1,922.3	13.1	11.2
IV	1,988.9	1,251.8	186.0	494.3	571.5	340.7	220.5	103.2	17.1	-1.7	181.2	192.9	408.0	149.5	258.4	1,971.8	7.2	10.7
1978: I	2,031.7	1,276.4	184.9	502.7	588.8	354.2	226.8	102.1	25.3	-11.7	195.6	207.2	412.8	147.3	265.5	2,006.4	8.9	7.2
II	2,139.5	1,330.7	202.6	519.2	608.8	388.5	245.8	111.9	30.8	-4.1	213.1	217.2	424.4	149.2	275.3	2,108.7	23.0	22.0
III	2,202.5	1,367.5	203.7	534.9	628.8	394.6	256.4	114.8	23.5	1.2	224.0	222.9	439.3	156.1	283.2	2,179.1	12.3	14.0
IV	2,281.6	1,411.3	209.9	556.1	645.6	409.1	266.6	116.2	26.2	10.1	242.1	232.0	451.1	161.8	289.3	2,254.4	15.2	14.8
1979: I	2,335.5	1,446.3	211.1	569.3	666.0	415.1	277.1	116.4	21.5	17.2	256.1	238.9	456.9	164.4	292.5	2,314.0	9.8	10.8
II	2,377.9	1,476.0	208.7	586.0	681.3	428.3	283.7	118.2	26.4	9.1	268.2	259.1	464.5	163.2	301.2	2,351.5	7.5	6.6
III	2,454.8	1,528.3	217.3	609.3	701.7	431.9	294.4	121.8	11.8	16.1	290.6	274.5	478.5	168.0	310.5	2,443.1	13.6	16.5
IV	2,502.9	1,578.0	216.6	635.5	725.9	416.8	301.6	117.8	-2.6	10.5	310.5	300.0	497.6	177.8	319.8	2,505.5	8.1	10.6
1980: I	2,572.9	1,620.5	220.7	651.4	748.3	422.0	311.1	112.5	-1.6	12.8	335.3	322.5	517.6	188.1	329.6	2,574.5	11.7	11.5
II	2,578.8	1,626.4	200.8	658.2	767.5	394.3	299.3	92.0	3.0	22.5	336.8	314.2	535.5	199.0	336.5	2,575.7	.9	.2
III	2,639.1	1,683.4	213.8	671.9	797.6	379.5	307.5	97.5	-25.4	37.1	337.6	300.5	539.1	194.5	344.6	2,664.5	9.7	14.5
IV	2,736.0	1,741.9	223.6	693.7	824.6	411.7	317.3	109.5	-15.1	23.3	345.4	322.0	559.0	206.6	352.4	2,751.1	15.5	13.6
1981: I	2,866.6	1,802.8	236.9	716.3	849.6	455.5	333.1	111.6	10.9	31.9	367.3	335.4	576.3	215.7	360.5	2,855.7	20.5	16.1
II	2,912.5	1,835.8	233.4	730.6	871.8	472.1	347.6	109.5	15.0	21.1	369.2	348.1	583.5	220.4	363.2	2,897.5	6.6	6.0
III	3,004.9	1,886.1	243.5	741.1	901.5	495.8	360.6	101.7	33.6	22.8	367.5	344.7	600.3	232.4	367.9	2,971.4	13.3	10.6
IV	3,032.2	1,904.1	230.8	747.7	925.6	476.2	367.6	94.3	14.3	29.2	371.0	341.7	622.8	248.5	374.3	3,017.9	3.7	6.4
1982: I	3,021.4	1,938.9	239.4	749.7	949.7	422.9	361.3	87.3	-25.7	29.9	358.4	328.5	629.8	249.7	380.0	3,047.1	-1.4	3.9
II	3,070.2	1,972.8	242.9	754.7	975.2	432.5	352.7	91.0	-11.2	33.3	364.5	331.2	631.6	244.1	387.5	3,081.4	6.6	4.6
III	3,090.7	2,008.8	243.4	766.6	998.9	425.3	342.3	87.9	-4.9	.9	346.0	345.0	655.7	261.7	394.0	3,095.6	2.7	1.9
IV	3,109.6	2,046.9	252.1	773.0	1,021.8	377.4	337.0	96.8	-56.4	5.6	321.6	316.1	679.7	279.2	400.5	3,165.9	2.5	9.4

GNP Gross national product; CBI Change in business inventories.

Source: *Survey of Current Business* (Washington, D.C.: Department of Commerce, October 1983).

Table B.—Gross National Product in Constant Dollars

[Billions of 1972 dollars; quarterly data are seasonally adjusted at annual rates]

Year and quarter	GNP	Personal consumption expenditures				Gross private domestic investment				Net exports			Government purchases of goods and services			Final sales	Command GNP	Percent change from preceding period		
		Total	Durable goods	Non-durable goods	Services	Total	Nonresidential	Residential	CBI	Net	Exports	Imports	Total	Federal	State and local			GNP	Final sales	Command GNP
1950	534.8	337.3	42.6	161.8	132.9	93.5	50.0	33.0	10.6	5.9	23.6	17.7	98.1	47.3	50.8	524.2	532.1	8.7	5.6	8.2
1951	579.4	341.6	39.1	165.3	137.2	93.9	52.9	27.3	13.7	10.1	28.6	18.5	133.7	82.2	51.5	565.6	574.6	8.3	7.9	8.0
1952	600.8	350.1	38.0	171.2	140.9	83.0	52.1	26.6	4.3	7.9	27.9	20.0	159.8	107.2	52.7	596.5	596.8	3.7	5.5	3.9
1953	623.6	363.4	42.1	175.7	145.6	85.3	56.3	27.5	1.5	4.8	26.6	21.8	170.1	114.7	55.3	622.1	620.4	3.8	4.3	3.9
1954	616.1	370.0	42.5	177.0	150.5	83.1	55.4	29.9	-2.2	6.9	27.8	20.9	156.0	96.1	59.9	618.2	612.4	-1.2	-.6	-1.3
1955	657.5	394.1	51.1	185.4	157.6	103.8	61.3	34.8	7.7	7.3	30.7	23.4	152.3	88.2	64.1	649.8	654.1	6.7	5.1	6.8
1956	671.6	405.4	48.8	191.6	165.0	102.6	65.4	31.5	5.8	10.1	35.3	25.2	153.5	86.8	66.7	665.8	668.2	2.1	2.5	2.2
1957	683.8	413.8	48.6	194.9	170.3	97.0	66.2	29.2	1.5	11.8	38.0	26.1	161.2	90.6	70.6	682.2	681.1	1.8	2.5	1.9
1958	680.9	418.0	45.3	196.6	175.9	87.5	59.3	30.0	-1.8	5.6	33.2	27.6	169.8	93.4	76.4	682.7	679.6	-.4	.1	-.2
1959	721.7	440.4	50.7	205.0	184.8	108.0	63.6	37.4	7.0	2.7	33.8	31.1	170.6	91.4	79.2	714.7	720.9	6.0	4.7	6.1
1960	737.2	452.0	51.4	208.2	192.4	104.7	66.9	34.2	3.5	7.7	38.4	30.7	172.8	90.4	82.4	733.7	736.8	2.2	2.7	2.2
1961	756.6	461.4	49.3	211.9	200.2	103.9	66.7	34.3	3.0	8.5	39.3	30.9	182.9	95.3	87.5	753.7	757.0	2.6	2.7	2.7
1962	800.3	482.0	54.7	218.5	208.8	117.6	72.0	37.7	7.8	7.5	41.8	34.3	193.2	102.8	90.4	792.4	801.3	5.8	5.1	5.9
1963	832.5	500.5	59.7	223.0	217.8	125.1	75.1	42.5	7.5	9.4	44.8	35.4	197.6	101.8	95.8	825.0	833.2	4.0	4.1	4.0
1964	876.4	528.0	64.8	233.3	229.8	133.0	82.7	43.1	7.1	12.8	50.3	37.5	202.6	100.2	102.4	869.3	876.7	5.3	5.4	5.2
1965	929.3	557.5	72.6	244.0	240.9	151.9	97.4	42.7	11.8	10.1	51.7	41.6	209.8	100.3	109.5	917.5	930.5	6.0	5.5	6.1
1966	984.8	585.7	78.4	255.5	251.8	163.0	108.0	38.2	16.8	6.5	54.4	47.9	229.7	112.6	117.1	968.0	986.6	6.0	5.5	6.0
1967	1,011.4	602.7	79.5	259.5	263.7	154.9	105.6	37.1	12.2	5.4	56.7	51.3	248.5	125.1	123.4	999.2	1,013.9	2.7	3.2	2.8
1968	1,058.1	634.4	88.3	270.5	275.6	161.6	109.5	43.1	9.0	1.9	61.2	59.3	260.2	128.1	132.1	1,049.1	1,061.5	4.6	5.0	4.7
1969	1,087.6	657.9	91.8	277.3	288.8	171.4	116.8	43.6	11.1	.9	65.0	64.1	257.4	121.8	135.6	1,076.6	1,091.7	2.8	2.6	2.9
1970	1,085.6	672.1	89.1	283.7	299.3	158.5	113.8	41.0	3.8	3.9	70.5	66.6	251.1	110.6	140.5	1,081.8	1,089.2	-.2	.5	-.2
1971	1,122.4	696.8	98.2	288.7	309.9	173.9	112.2	53.7	8.1	1.6	71.0	69.3	250.1	103.7	146.4	1,114.3	1,125.2	3.4	3.0	3.3
1972	1,185.9	737.1	111.1	300.6	325.3	195.0	121.0	63.8	10.2	.7	77.5	76.7	253.1	101.7	151.4	1,175.7	1,185.9	5.7	5.5	5.4
1973	1,254.3	767.9	121.3	307.4	339.2	217.5	138.1	62.3	17.2	15.5	97.3	81.8	253.3	95.9	157.4	1,237.1	1,250.9	5.8	5.2	5.5
1974	1,246.3	762.8	112.3	302.5	348.0	195.5	135.7	48.2	11.6	22.7	108.5	80.7	260.3	96.6	163.6	1,234.7	1,226.7	-.6	-.2	-1.9
1975	1,231.6	779.4	112.7	307.5	359.3	154.8	119.3	42.2	-6.7	32.2	103.5	71.4	265.2	97.4	167.8	1,238.4	1,214.4	-1.2	.3	-1.0
1976	1,298.2	823.1	126.6	321.9	374.7	184.5	125.6	51.2	7.8	25.4	110.1	84.7	265.2	96.8	168.4	1,290.4	1,280.2	5.4	4.2	5.4
1977	1,369.7	864.3	138.0	333.4	393.0	214.2	140.3	60.7	13.3	22.0	112.9	90.9	269.2	100.4	168.8	1,356.4	1,345.8	5.5	5.1	5.1
1978	1,438.6	903.2	146.8	344.4	412.0	236.7	158.3	62.4	16.0	24.0	126.7	102.7	274.6	100.3	174.3	1,422.6	1,414.0	5.0	4.9	5.1
1979	1,479.4	927.6	147.2	353.1	427.3	236.3	169.9	59.1	7.3	37.2	146.2	109.0	278.3	102.1	176.2	1,472.2	1,447.6	2.8	3.5	2.4
1980	1,475.0	931.8	137.5	355.6	438.8	208.5	165.8	47.1	-4.4	50.3	159.1	108.8	284.3	106.4	177.9	1,479.4	1,433.0	-.3	.5	-1.0
1981	1,513.8	956.8	141.2	362.5	453.1	227.6	174.4	44.7	8.5	43.0	159.7	116.7	286.5	110.4	176.1	1,505.3	1,479.8	2.6	1.8	3.3
1982	1,485.4	970.2	139.8	364.2	466.2	194.5	166.1	37.8	-9.4	28.9	147.3	118.4	291.8	116.6	175.2	1,494.8	1,462.7	-1.9	-.7	-1.2
1950: I	512.6	327.7	38.9	160.1	128.6	79.6	44.8	30.3	4.4	6.8	22.6	15.9	98.6	48.1	50.4	508.2	511.3	19.1	8.1	18.6
II	526.4	333.6	39.2	161.7	132.7	89.8	48.9	33.2	7.7	6.8	23.3	16.5	96.2	45.4	50.8	518.7	524.1	11.2	8.5	10.5
III	543.8	348.0	49.0	164.4	134.6	96.0	53.0	35.0	8.0	4.3	23.8	19.5	95.5	44.5	50.9	535.8	540.7	13.9	13.8	13.3
IV	556.3	339.9	43.2	161.0	135.7	108.7	53.3	33.3	22.1	5.6	24.6	19.0	102.0	51.0	51.0	534.2	552.6	9.5	-1.2	9.1
1951: I	564.4	345.7	44.3	164.7	136.7	96.6	51.8	31.4	13.4	6.4	25.8	19.4	115.7	65.0	50.7	550.9	560.1	6.0	13.1	5.6
II	575.9	337.8	38.1	162.7	137.1	100.1	53.0	27.1	19.9	9.5	28.2	18.7	128.5	77.0	51.5	556.0	570.9	8.4	-3.7	7.9
III	587.9	340.7	37.1	166.0	137.6	93.8	53.9	25.3	14.6	12.2	30.0	17.8	141.2	89.5	51.8	573.3	582.5	8.6	13.1	8.4
IV	589.1	342.1	36.9	167.7	137.5	85.3	52.8	25.5	7.0	12.5	30.5	18.0	149.2	97.4	51.8	582.1	584.4	.8	6.3	1.3
1952: I	593.7	342.7	37.5	166.5	138.7	86.4	53.1	26.0	7.3	11.7	30.8	19.1	152.9	100.7	52.2	586.4	589.1	3.2	3.0	3.2
II	594.3	348.6	38.3	170.3	140.0	77.4	53.6	26.5	-2.7	9.0	28.0	19.0	159.4	106.3	53.1	597.0	590.3	.4	7.4	.8
III	600.5	350.2	35.9	172.8	141.5	80.5	48.9	26.2	5.4	6.1	26.2	20.1	163.7	111.6	52.1	595.1	596.9	4.2	-1.3	4.6
IV	614.6	358.8	45.0	174.9	143.4	87.6	52.8	27.6	7.2	4.9	26.6	21.7	163.3	110.0	53.2	607.4	610.9	9.7	8.5	9.7
1953: I	623.2	362.8	42.3	176.1	144.4	87.6	55.6	28.0	3.9	5.0	26.3	21.3	167.7	113.5	54.3	619.2	619.8	5.7	8.0	6.0
II	628.3	364.6	41.9	176.6	146.0	89.1	55.9	28.2	5.1	4.4	26.8	22.4	170.2	115.9	54.3	623.2	625.0	3.3	2.6	3.4
III	624.4	363.6	41.8	175.2	146.6	86.0	57.0	27.1	1.9	4.8	27.0	22.2	170.0	114.4	55.6	622.5	621.3	-2.4	-.4	-2.3
IV	618.2	362.6	42.5	174.9	145.3	78.6	56.7	26.9	-5.0	5.0	26.3	21.3	172.0	115.1	56.9	623.2	615.2	-3.9	.4	-3.9
1954: I	610.5	363.5	40.9	175.8	146.8	79.1	55.3	27.3	-3.4	5.2	25.7	20.5	162.6	103.9	58.7	613.9	607.5	-4.9	-5.8	-4.9
II	608.1	366.2	41.4	175.0	149.7	79.7	54.8	29.0	-4.1	6.7	28.4	21.8	155.6	96.5	59.0	612.2	604.4	-1.6	-1.1	-2.1
III	616.9	371.8	42.4	177.2	152.1	84.0	56.0	30.8	-2.7	7.3	27.9	20.6	153.8	93.3	60.6	619.6	613.0	5.9	4.9	5.8
IV	628.4	378.6	45.1	180.0	153.4	89.7	55.6	32.7	1.5	8.4	29.3	20.9	151.7	90.8	60.9	627.0	624.6	7.7	4.8	7.8
1955: I	644.1	385.2	48.1	181.4	155.7	97.7	55.6	35.2	5.9	8.4	30.3	21.9	152.7	89.5	63.3	638.2	640.3	10.3	7.4	10.4
II	653.2	392.2	51.3	184.4	156.5	103.9	60.2	35.7	8.0	6.3	29.7	23.4	150.9	86.8	64.1	645.2	649.9	5.8	4.5	6.2
III	663.2	396.4	52.7	185.9	157.7	105.8	63.2	34.9	7.8	7.5	31.2	23.8	150.5	89.2	64.3	655.4	660.0	6.3	6.5	6.3
IV	669.5	402.6	52.2	189.8	160.6	107.8	65.2	33.3	9.2	7.1	31.4	24.4	150.0	87.2	64.8	660.2	666.1	3.8	3.0	3.7
1956: I	666.8	403.2	49.4	191.6	162.2	103.9	64.3	32.1	7.5	7.7	33.0	25.3	152.1	86.6	65.5	659.3	663.5	-.6	-.6	-1.6
II	670.2	403.9	48.9	191.1	163.9	102.7	65.3	31.9	5.5	9.6	34.8	25.2	154.0	87.6	66.5	664.7	666.8	2.0	3.3	2.0
III	670.7	405.1	48.1	191.2	165.8	102.2	66.2	31.2	4.9	10.5	36.2	25.7	152.9	85.9	66.9	665.9	667.4	.3	.7	.4
IV	678.4	409.3	48.8	192.5	168.0	101.7	65.7	30.7	5.4	12.5	37.1	24.6	154.8	87.2	67.6	673.0	675.0	4.7	4.4	4.7
1957: I	683.5	411.7	49.9	193.1	168.7	98.4	66.1	29.9	2.5	13.2	39.4	26.2	160.1	91.0	69.2	681.0	680.3	3.0	4.8	3.2
II	684.1	412.4	48.8	193.9	169.7	98.0	65.3	29.2	2.9	12.6	39.1	26.4	161.1	91.3	69.8	681.2	681.0	.4	.1	.4
III	688.5	415.2	48.0	196.7	170.5	99.8	67.3	28.9	3.7	11.9	37.7	25.8	161.6	90.7	70.8	684.8	685.8	2.6	2.1	2.8
IV	679.1	416.0	47.9	195.7	172.3	91.7	65.7	29.0	-3.0	9.5	35.6	26.1	162.0	89.5	72.5	682.1	-677.3	-5.3	-1.6	-4.9
1958: I	665.5	411.0	45.1	193.4	172.5	82.9	61.5	28.2	-6.8	6.5	33.0	26.5	165.0	90.9	74.2	672.3	664.0	-7.8	-5.7	-7.7
II	669.9	414.7	44.5	194.9	175.3	80.8	58.8	28.2	-6.2	5.6	33.2	27.6	166.7	93.2	75.6	676.1	668.5	2.7	2.3	2.8
III	685.9	420.9	45.1	197.8	177.5	88.1	57.6	30.2	.3	5.9	33.2	27.3	171.0	93.9	77.2	685.6	684.7	9.9	5.8	10.0
IV	702.5	425.4	46.6	200.6	178.2	98.0	59.3	33.5	5.3	4.3	33.2	28.9	174.7	96.0	78.7	697.2	701.4	10.0	7.0	10.2
1959: I	711.5	434.1	49.5	203.2	181.5	103.7	61.1	37.1	5.5	2.1	32.1	30.0	171.6	92.3	79.3	706.0	710.9	5.2	5.1	5.5
II	726.2	439.7	51.3	204.6	183.8	114.1	63.1	38.4	12.6	1.2	32.7	31.5	171.3	92.0	79.3	713.6	725.5	8.5	4.4	8.5
III	721.2	443.3	52.1	205.5	185.7	104.0	65.0	37.6	1.4	3.6	35.4	31.8	170.2	90.8	79.4	719.8	720.3	-2.8	3.5	-2.8
IV	727.9	444.6	49.7	206.8	188.1	110.2	65.1	36.4	8.7	3.8	34.9	31.1	169.3	90.3	79.0	719.2	726.9	3.8	-.3	3.7
1960: I	740.7	448.1	51.0	207.2	189.9	117.4	67.4	37.3	12.7	6.0	37.3	31.3	169.2	88.9	80.3	728.0	739.7	7.2	5.0	7.3
II	738.4	454.1	52.3	209.5	192.3	105.1	67.8	34.1	3.3	6.8	38.2	31.5	172.4	90.4	82.0	735.1	737.8	-1.2	4.0	-1.0
III	737.7	452.7	51.8	208.1	192.7	102.5	66.2	32.9	3.4	8.1	38.9	30.7	174.4	91.1	83.3	734.3	737.5	-.4	-.4	-.1
IV	732.1	453.2	50.5	208.1	194.6	93.8	66.3	32.7	-5.3	9.8	39.2	29.4	175.4	91.3	84.1	737.4	731.9	-3.0	1.7	-3.0
1961: I	737.7	454.0	47.7	209.6	196.7	94.0	65.2	32.9	-4.1	10.4	39.9	29.5	179.4	92.6	86.8	741.8	737.6	3.1	2.4	3.1
II	750.1	459.9	48.4	211.7	199.9	101.1	66.3	33.1	1.8	8.0	37.8	29.8	181.0	94.6	86.4	748.3	750.6	6.9	3.5	7.2
III	759.6	461.4	49.4	211.7	200.2	107.9	66.5	34.9	6.5	7.7	39.4	31.7	182.7	95.4	87.3	753.2	760.0	5.2	2.6	5.1
IV	779.0	470.3	51.8	214.8	203.7	112.6	68.6	36.3	7.7	7.8	40.3	32.5	188.4	98.7	89.7	771.3	779.6	10.6	10.0	10.7
1962: I	789.2	474.5	52.9	216.5	205.1	116.8	70.0	36.4	10.4	6.6	40.0	33.3	191.3	102.2	89.1	778.8	790.2	5.3	3.9	5.6
II	798.4	479.8	54.2	217.4	208.3	118.3	72.2	38.0	8.1	8.5	42.6	34.1	191.8	102.1	89.7	790.4	799.4	4.8	6.1	4.7
III	805.5	483.7	54.7	219.3	209.7	119.1	73.3	38.3	7.5	8.0	42.6	34.6	194.6	103.7	90.9	797.9	806.6	3.7	3.9	3.7
IV	808.0	490.0	57.0	220.8	212.1	116.0	72.5	38.2	5.3	7.0	42.2	35.2	195.0	103.2	91.8	802.6	809.1	1.2	2.4	1.3

Source: *Survey of Current Business* (Washington, D.C.: Department of Commerce, October 1983).

Table B.—Gross National Product in Constant Dollars—Continued

[Billions of 1972 dollars; quarterly data are seasonally adjusted at annual rates]

Year and quarter	GNP	Personal consumption expenditures				Gross private domestic investment				Net exports			Government purchases of goods and services			Final sales	Com-mand GNP	Percent change from preceding period		
		Total	Durable goods	Non-durable goods	Serv-ices	Total	Nonresi-dential	Resi-dential	CBI	Net	Exports	Imports	Total	Federal	State and local			GNP	Final sales	Com-mand GNP
1963: I	815.0	493.1	58.2	221.5	213.4	118.7	71.8	39.5	7.4	7.4	41.9	34.5	195.8	102.2	93.6	807.6	816.0	3.5	2.5	3.5
II	826.7	497.4	59.4	222.4	215.7	124.6	74.1	42.6	7.9	9.6	44.8	35.2	195.1	100.6	94.4	818.8	827.6	5.8	5.7	5.8
III	839.8	503.9	60.1	224.1	219.7	127.3	76.1	43.1	8.0	9.2	45.2	36.0	199.3	102.3	96.9	831.7	840.2	6.5	6.5	6.2
IV	848.6	507.5	61.0	224.2	222.4	129.6	78.2	44.7	6.7	11.3	47.3	36.0	200.2	102.0	98.2	841.9	848.9	4.3	5.0	4.2
1964: I	864.2	516.6	63.2	228.2	225.2	131.8	79.3	45.6	6.9	14.0	50.0	36.0	201.7	101.8	99.9	857.3	864.1	7.5	7.5	7.4
II	873.7	525.6	64.8	232.2	228.7	132.4	81.6	43.4	7.4	12.3	49.2	36.9	203.4	101.3	102.1	866.3	873.7	4.5	4.3	4.5
III	880.9	534.3	66.8	236.1	231.4	131.5	83.9	42.1	5.5	12.8	50.6	37.9	202.3	99.1	103.3	875.4	881.3	3.3	4.3	3.5
IV	886.8	535.3	64.6	236.7	234.1	136.1	86.0	41.4	8.6	12.4	51.4	39.0	203.1	98.6	104.6	878.2	887.5	2.7	1.3	2.9
1965: I	906.7	546.0	70.5	239.2	236.2	149.4	91.7	42.9	14.8	9.0	46.7	37.7	202.3	96.8	105.5	891.9	907.9	9.3	6.4	9.5
II	919.7	550.7	70.6	240.9	239.2	150.5	95.6	43.6	11.3	11.2	53.6	42.4	207.2	99.0	108.2	908.3	921.4	5.8	7.6	6.1
III	934.1	559.2	73.1	244.1	242.1	152.4	98.9	42.5	11.0	10.6	53.1	42.5	211.8	100.5	111.3	923.1	935.3	6.4	6.6	6.2
IV	956.8	573.9	76.1	251.8	246.0	155.4	103.4	41.9	10.0	9.8	53.6	43.9	217.7	104.7	113.0	946.7	957.3	10.1	10.7	9.7
1966: I	975.4	581.2	79.7	253.5	248.0	164.8	106.7	42.4	15.6	8.2	54.1	45.8	221.2	106.5	114.7	959.8	976.7	8.0	5.6	8.4
II	979.3	582.3	76.3	255.4	250.6	165.0	108.1	39.8	17.1	7.1	53.8	46.7	224.8	108.8	116.0	962.2	980.7	1.6	1.0	1.6
III	987.9	588.6	78.8	257.2	252.6	160.3	109.0	37.7	13.6	5.1	54.6	49.5	234.0	116.8	117.2	974.3	989.9	3.6	5.1	3.8
IV	996.6	590.5	78.7	255.9	255.9	162.0	108.2	33.0	20.8	5.4	55.1	49.7	238.7	118.3	120.4	975.8	998.9	3.6	.6	3.7
1967: I	997.8	594.8	77.2	258.3	259.2	152.6	105.8	32.3	14.5	6.2	56.9	50.7	244.2	122.5	121.7	983.3	1,000.3	.5	3.1	.6
II	1,004.2	602.4	80.7	259.4	262.3	148.9	105.5	36.1	7.3	6.0	56.1	50.2	247.0	124.6	122.4	996.9	1,006.6	2.6	5.6	2.6
III	1,016.2	605.2	79.9	259.5	265.7	155.1	104.8	38.4	11.8	5.4	56.3	50.9	250.6	127.1	123.5	1,004.4	1,018.7	4.9	3.0	4.9
IV	1,027.3	608.2	80.1	260.8	267.4	163.0	106.3	41.5	15.2	3.9	57.4	53.5	252.2	126.3	125.9	1,012.2	1,030.1	4.4	3.1	4.5
1968: I	1,036.6	620.7	85.2	266.1	269.5	157.2	109.9	41.9	5.4	2.2	59.0	56.8	256.5	127.8	128.7	1,031.2	1,039.4	3.7	7.7	3.7
II	1,055.7	629.9	86.9	269.0	274.0	162.7	107.4	43.0	12.2	2.2	60.1	57.9	260.9	129.5	131.4	1,043.5	1,059.5	7.6	4.9	8.0
III	1,068.2	642.3	90.9	273.6	277.8	161.6	108.6	43.3	9.8	2.0	63.6	61.5	262.2	128.8	133.4	1,058.4	1,071.5	4.8	5.8	4.6
IV	1,071.8	644.7	90.4	273.3	281.0	164.9	112.3	44.0	8.6	1.2	62.3	61.1	261.1	126.5	134.6	1,063.2	1,075.2	1.4	1.9	1.4
1969: I	1,084.2	651.9	92.3	275.7	283.9	172.5	115.1	45.6	11.7	1.2	57.1	55.8	258.6	123.6	135.0	1,072.5	1,087.6	4.7	3.5	4.7
II	1,088.8	656.2	92.1	277.0	287.1	173.1	116.2	45.0	11.8	.4	67.4	67.0	259.2	123.5	135.7	1,077.0	1,092.9	1.7	1.7	2.0
III	1,092.0	659.6	91.7	277.7	290.2	175.4	118.5	43.2	13.7	.2	67.2	67.0	256.8	120.8	136.0	1,078.3	1,096.4	1.2	.5	1.3
IV	1,085.6	663.9	91.3	278.7	293.9	164.8	117.4	40.5	7.0	1.8	68.3	66.5	255.0	119.1	135.9	1,078.6	1,089.9	-2.3	.1	-2.4
1970: I	1,081.4	667.4	89.7	281.3	296.4	158.1	115.4	40.6	2.1	3.2	69.4	66.2	252.7	115.1	137.6	1,079.2	1,085.7	-1.5	.2	-1.5
II	1,083.0	670.5	90.7	282.4	297.4	158.3	115.0	38.4	5.0	4.5	71.5	67.0	249.6	110.9	138.7	1,077.9	1,087.7	.6	-.5	.7
III	1,093.3	676.5	91.1	284.5	300.8	161.6	114.7	40.4	6.5	4.3	70.6	66.3	250.9	108.8	142.1	1,086.8	1,096.3	3.9	3.3	3.2
IV	1,084.7	673.9	84.8	286.7	302.5	156.2	110.8	40.4	4.5	3.6	70.4	66.8	251.0	107.5	143.4	1,083.3	1,087.2	-3.1	-1.3	-3.3
1971: I	1,111.5	687.0	94.0	287.6	305.4	169.8	110.8	47.8	11.2	4.7	70.7	66.0	250.0	105.6	144.4	1,100.3	1,114.8	10.3	6.4	10.5
II	1,116.9	693.3	96.3	288.5	308.5	175.1	112.1	52.6	10.4	.3	71.2	70.9	248.3	102.6	145.7	1,106.5	1,120.5	2.0	2.3	2.1
III	1,125.7	698.2	99.0	288.4	310.8	175.3	112.2	56.0	7.0	1.7	74.2	72.5	250.6	104.1	146.5	1,118.7	1,128.2	3.2	4.5	2.8
IV	1,135.4	708.6	103.5	290.2	314.9	175.4	113.6	58.2	3.6	-.2	67.7	67.9	251.5	102.7	148.8	1,131.7	1,137.3	3.5	4.7	3.3
1972: I	1,157.2	718.6	106.2	292.4	320.0	186.0	117.3	62.4	6.3	-1.9	74.9	76.8	254.5	104.3	150.2	1,150.9	1,158.9	7.9	6.9	7.8
II	1,178.5	731.1	108.9	299.3	322.9	194.5	119.1	63.4	12.1	-.4	74.2	74.6	253.2	103.3	150.0	1,166.5	1,178.6	7.6	5.5	7.0
III	1,193.1	741.3	111.7	303.3	326.4	196.8	120.4	63.7	12.8	2.4	78.2	75.8	252.6	101.0	151.6	1,180.3	1,192.1	5.0	4.8	4.7
IV	1,214.8	757.1	117.6	307.6	331.9	202.7	127.2	65.7	9.7	2.9	82.5	79.6	252.1	98.1	154.0	1,205.1	1,213.9	7.5	8.7	7.5
1973: I	1,246.8	768.8	124.8	309.9	334.1	215.7	132.8	66.9	16.0	7.7	91.0	83.3	254.6	98.9	155.7	1,230.7	1,245.7	10.9	8.8	10.9
II	1,248.3	766.3	122.5	306.3	337.5	217.2	138.3	63.7	15.2	13.7	95.8	82.1	251.1	94.9	156.2	1,233.1	1,244.6	.5	.8	-.3
III	1,255.8	769.7	120.8	307.4	341.5	215.4	140.5	61.1	13.8	19.4	99.8	80.4	251.3	93.5	157.8	1,242.0	1,252.0	2.4	2.9	2.4
IV	1,266.1	766.7	117.2	306.0	343.5	221.8	140.7	57.4	23.7	21.2	102.4	81.2	256.4	96.3	160.1	1,242.4	1,260.4	3.3	.1	2.7
1974: I	1,253.3	761.2	114.4	302.6	344.2	206.3	140.3	52.8	13.2	28.2	108.0	79.8	257.5	95.3	162.2	1,240.1	1,240.4	-4.0	-.8	-6.2
II	1,254.7	764.1	114.7	302.6	346.8	200.9	138.2	50.1	12.6	28.9	111.4	82.5	260.8	96.9	163.9	1,242.1	1,232.9	.4	.7	-2.4
III	1,246.8	769.4	115.8	304.4	349.2	190.3	135.2	47.4	7.7	26.2	107.5	81.3	260.9	96.8	164.1	1,239.1	1,225.2	-2.5	-1.0	-2.5
IV	1,230.3	756.5	104.5	300.4	351.6	184.3	129.1	42.4	12.9	27.8	106.9	79.1	261.8	97.5	164.3	1,217.5	1,209.3	-5.2	-6.8	-5.1
1975: I	1,204.3	763.3	106.5	302.8	354.0	145.8	120.7	39.4	-14.3	32.1	104.0	71.9	263.0	96.8	166.2	1,218.6	1,186.3	-8.2	.4	-7.4
II	1,218.9	775.6	109.0	307.8	358.8	146.8	117.8	40.3	-11.3	33.5	100.3	66.8	263.0	96.5	166.5	1,230.2	1,201.1	4.9	3.9	5.1
III	1,246.1	785.4	115.9	309.0	360.5	163.3	119.2	43.1	1.0	30.8	102.5	71.7	266.6	98.1	168.4	1,245.1	1,229.3	9.2	4.9	9.7
IV	1,257.3	793.3	119.2	310.2	363.9	163.3	119.6	45.9	-2.3	32.3	107.4	75.1	268.3	98.2	170.2	1,259.5	1,240.7	3.6	4.7	3.8
1976: I	1,285.0	809.9	125.1	316.3	368.4	181.4	122.0	49.4	10.0	26.7	107.6	80.9	267.0	96.5	170.5	1,274.9	1,268.5	9.1	5.0	9.3
II	1,293.7	817.1	125.6	320.2	371.3	185.7	124.1	50.3	11.3	25.9	109.3	83.3	264.9	96.3	168.6	1,282.4	1,275.9	2.7	2.4	2.4
III	1,301.1	826.5	126.9	323.5	376.1	184.6	127.4	49.9	7.3	25.6	111.5	85.9	264.3	96.8	167.6	1,293.8	1,282.0	2.3	3.6	1.9
IV	1,313.1	838.9	128.5	327.5	382.8	186.3	128.9	56.5	2.4	23.4	111.9	88.5	264.5	97.4	167.1	1,310.6	1,294.6	3.7	5.3	4.0
1977: I	1,341.3	851.7	133.9	330.6	387.1	201.7	134.5	56.7	10.5	22.3	111.0	88.7	265.6	97.6	168.0	1,330.8	1,317.9	8.9	6.3	7.4
II	1,363.3	858.0	136.9	331.9	389.2	213.7	138.8	61.2	13.8	22.6	113.9	91.3	269.0	100.2	168.8	1,349.5	1,339.8	6.7	5.8	6.8
III	1,385.8	867.3	139.2	332.4	395.7	222.8	141.2	62.8	18.7	24.9	115.2	90.3	270.8	102.2	168.6	1,367.0	1,360.7	6.8	5.3	6.4
IV	1,388.4	880.4	142.0	338.7	399.7	218.5	146.5	61.9	10.1	18.1	111.4	93.2	271.4	101.8	169.6	1,378.3	1,364.7	.8	3.4	1.2
1978: I	1,400.0	883.8	139.4	339.1	405.3	226.7	148.5	60.9	17.3	19.1	118.1	99.0	270.4	98.8	171.6	1,382.8	1,375.4	3.4	1.3	3.2
II	1,437.0	901.1	149.8	341.0	410.3	239.9	157.9	63.7	18.4	22.4	124.3	101.9	273.6	99.0	174.7	1,418.6	1,412.7	11.0	10.8	11.3
III	1,448.8	908.6	147.9	345.3	415.4	238.0	161.6	63.1	13.3	25.3	128.8	103.5	276.8	101.1	175.7	1,435.5	1,424.0	3.3	4.9	3.2
IV	1,468.4	919.2	150.1	352.2	416.9	242.2	165.2	61.8	15.2	29.3	135.6	106.2	277.7	102.4	175.3	1,453.2	1,443.7	5.5	5.0	5.7
1979: I	1,472.6	921.2	148.6	349.9	422.8	241.5	168.0	60.7	12.9	33.4	138.8	105.4	276.4	102.2	174.2	1,459.7	1,446.8	1.1	1.8	.9
II	1,469.2	919.5	144.9	349.2	425.4	241.3	168.0	59.6	13.7	31.5	140.4	109.0	276.8	101.0	175.9	1,455.4	1,441.5	-.9	-1.2	-1.4
III	1,486.6	930.9	149.1	353.4	428.5	237.2	172.9	59.5	4.8	39.8	149.2	109.4	278.8	101.9	176.8	1,481.9	1,453.3	4.8	7.5	3.3
IV	1,489.3	938.6	146.3	359.8	432.6	225.3	170.9	56.7	-2.3	44.2	156.4	112.2	282.1	103.4	177.8	1,491.6	1,449.1	.7	2.7	-1.1
1980: I	1,496.4	938.3	145.2	358.5	434.5	224.3	171.8	53.0	-.5	49.8	164.4	114.5	284.0	105.8	178.1	1,496.9	1,451.1	1.9	1.4	.6
II	1,461.4	919.6	130.0	354.2	435.4	202.4	162.2	42.4	-2.1	52.6	161.0	108.4	286.8	109.3	177.5	1,463.6	1,416.6	-9.0	-8.6	-9.2
III	1,464.2	929.4	135.6	353.5	440.3	197.4	163.6	44.0	-10.1	53.4	156.4	102.9	284.0	106.2	177.8	1,474.4	1,423.5	.8	3.0	2.0
IV	1,477.9	940.0	139.0	356.2	444.7	210.0	165.7	49.0	-4.7	45.4	154.7	109.3	282.5	104.2	178.3	1,482.5	1,440.3	3.8	2.2	4.8
1981: I	1,510.1	953.6	145.4	359.8	448.3	222.7	170.9	48.8	3.0	48.3	160.6	112.4	285.6	107.3	178.3	1,507.0	1,472.5	9.0	6.8	9.2
II	1,512.5	954.7	140.5	362.7	451.5	229.5	173.4	47.3	8.9	44.1	160.7	116.6	284.1	107.9	176.2	1,503.6	1,475.5	.7	-.9	.8
III	1,525.8	962.9	143.9	363.8	455.5	236.3	177.0	43.1	16.1	39.8	159.0	119.1	286.8	111.8	175.0	1,509.7	1,493.9	3.6	1.6	5.1
IV	1,506.9	955.7	134.8	363.8	457.1	221.7	176.3	39.4	6.0	39.9	158.7	118.8	289.6	114.5	175.1	1,500.9	1,477.2	-4.9	-2.3	-4.4
1982: I	1,485.8	961.4	138.5	362.8	460.4	199.7	173.9	36.5	-10.2	35.2	151.8	116.6	289.4	114.5	174.9	1,495.9	1,461.2	-5.5	-1.3	-4.3
II	1,489.3	968.8	139.5	363.5	465.7	201.4	167.1	37.8	-3.4	33.4	154.5	121.1	285.8	110.3	175.4	1,492.7	1,468.1	1.0	-.8	1.9
III	1,485.7	971.0	138.2	364.7	468.2	198.4	163.3	36.5	-1.3	24.0	146.4	122.4	292.2	116.9	175.3	1,487.0	1,462.0	-1.0	-1.5	-1.6
IV	1,480.7	979.6	143.2	366.0	470.4	178.4	160.5	40.6	-22.7	23.0	136.5	113.5	299.7	124.4	175.2	1,503.4	1,459.7	-1.3	4.5	-.6

GNP   Gross national product; CBI   Change in business inventories.

Source: *Survey of Current Business* (Washington, D.C.: Department of Commerce, October 1983).

COMMODITY PRICES—CONSUMER PRICES

YEAR AND MONTH	All items, wage earners and clerical workers, revised (CPI-W) ★	All items, all urban consumers (CPI-U)	CONSUMER PRICE INDEX¹										Food	
			All items less shelter	All items less food	All items less medical care	Special group indexes					Services		Total⁴ ★	Food at home
						Commodities				Commod- ities less food²				
						Total² ★	Nondurables		Durables²		Total² ★	Services less rent²		
							Total	Nondura- bles less food						
						1967 = 100								
1961	89.6		89.9	89.7	90.3	92.0	90.2	91.2	96.6	93.4	85.2	83.9	89.1	90.4
1962	90.6		90.9	90.8	91.2	92.8	90.9	91.8	97.6	94.1	86.8	85.5	89.9	91.0
1963	91.7		92.1	92.0	92.3	93.6	92.0	92.7	97.9	94.8	88.5	87.3	91.2	92.2
1964	92.9		93.2	93.2	93.5	94.6	93.0	93.5	98.8	95.6	90.2	89.2	92.4	93.2
1965	94.5		94.6	94.5	94.9	95.7	94.6	94.8	98.4	96.2	92.2	91.5	94.4	95.5
1966	97.2		97.4	96.7	97.7	98.2	98.1	97.0	98.5	97.5	95.8	95.3	99.1	100.3
1967	100.0		100.0	100.0	100.0	100.0	100.0	100.0	100.0	100.0	100.0	100.0	100.0	100.0
1968	104.2		104.1	104.4	104.1	103.7	103.9	104.1	103.1	103.7	105.2	105.7	103.6	103.2
1969	109.8		109.0	110.1	109.7	108.4	108.9	108.8	107.0	108.1	112.5	113.8	108.9	108.2
1970	116.3		114.4	116.7	116.1	113.5	114.0	113.1	111.8	112.5	121.6	123.7	114.9	113.7
1971	121.3		119.3	122.1	120.9	117.4	117.7	117.0	116.5	116.8	128.4	130.8	118.4	116.4
1972	125.3		122.9	125.8	124.9	120.9	121.7	119.8	118.9	119.4	133.3	135.9	123.5	121.6
1973	133.1		131.1	130.7	132.9	129.9	132.8	124.8	121.9	123.5	139.1	141.8	141.4	141.4
1974	147.7		146.1	143.7	147.7	145.5	151.0	140.9	130.6	136.6	152.1	156.0	161.7	162.4
1975	161.2		159.1	157.1	160.9	158.4	163.2	151.7	145.5	149.1	166.6	171.9	175.4	175.8
1976	170.5		168.3	167.5	169.7	165.2	169.2	158.3	154.3	156.6	180.4	186.8	180.8	179.5
1977	181.5	181.5	179.1	178.4	180.3	174.7	178.9	166.5	163.2	165.1	194.3	201.6	192.2	190.2
1978	195.3	195.4	191.3	191.2	194.0	187.1	192.0	174.3	173.9	174.7	210.9	219.4	211.4	210.2
1979	217.7	217.4	210.8	213.0	216.1	208.4	215.9	198.7	191.1	195.1	234.2	244.9	234.5	232.9
1980	247.0	246.8	235.5	244.0	245.5	233.9	245.0	235.2	210.4	222.0	270.3	285.1	254.6	251.5
1981	272.3	272.4	258.5	270.6	270.9	253.6	266.3	257.5	227.1	241.2	305.7	324.3	274.6	269.9
1982	288.6	289.1	273.3	288.4	286.8	263.8	273.6	261.6	241.1	250.9	333.3	354.2	285.7	279.2
1979:														
January	204.7	204.7	199.5	199.8	203.2	195.8	201.0	180.3	182.0	181.9	221.1	230.4	223.9	223.1
February	207.1	207.1	201.6	201.8	205.5	198.3	204.0	182.2	183.6	183.7	223.3	232.9	228.2	228.0
March	209.3	209.1	203.7	203.8	207.6	200.5	206.9	185.7	184.9	185.9	225.1	235.0	230.4	229.9
April	211.8	211.5	206.0	206.3	210.1	203.3	209.9	189.6	187.2	188.9	227.0	237.1	232.3	231.7
May	214.3	214.1	208.4	208.9	212.7	205.8	212.8	193.2	189.2	191.6	229.5	239.8	234.3	233.4
June	216.9	216.6	210.7	211.8	215.2	208.4	215.7	197.6	191.1	194.7	232.1	242.6	235.4	234.2
July	219.4	218.9	212.7	214.2	217.6	210.5	218.3	201.1	192.6	197.0	234.7	245.6	236.9	235.5
August	221.5	221.1	214.2	216.9	219.7	212.2	220.4	205.4	193.6	199.5	237.6	248.8	236.3	233.9
September	223.7	223.4	216.1	219.6	222.1	214.1	223.1	209.6	194.5	201.8	240.7	252.1	237.1	234.7
October	225.6	225.4	217.4	221.8	224.1	215.6	224.5	211.3	196.0	203.4	243.6	255.1	238.2	235.4
November	227.6	227.5	218.6	224.1	226.2	217.4	225.8	212.9	198.4	205.4	246.2	258.2	239.1	236.0
December	230.0	229.9	220.6	226.4	228.6	219.4	228.2	215.2	199.8	207.2	249.3	261.6	241.7	238.7
1980:														
January	233.3	233.2	223.4	229.9	231.9	222.4	232.0	220.5	201.3	210.4	253.1	266.1	243.8	240.6
February	236.5	236.4	226.6	233.5	235.0	225.2	236.3	227.3	202.1	213.8	256.8	270.2	244.9	241.3
March	239.9	239.8	229.6	237.1	238.4	228.0	240.3	232.6	203.0	216.7	261.3	275.4	247.3	243.6
April	242.6	242.5	231.7	239.9	241.1	229.9	242.2	234.6	204.9	218.6	265.3	280.0	249.1	245.3
May	245.1	244.9	233.4	242.6	243.6	231.4	243.2	235.5	207.1	220.2	269.2	284.4	250.4	246.5
June	247.8	247.6	234.9	245.5	246.4	232.8	244.5	236.3	208.6	221.4	274.2	290.0	252.0	248.0
July	248.0	247.8	236.4	245.1	246.5	234.1	245.9	236.6	209.8	222.2	272.4	287.6	254.8	251.5
August	249.6	249.4	238.5	246.3	248.1	236.7	248.3	237.8	212.4	224.2	272.5	287.4	256.7	256.3
September	251.9	251.7	241.0	248.6	250.4	239.0	250.2	239.3	215.3	226.6	274.8	289.8	261.1	258.9
October	254.1	253.9	242.1	250.9	252.6	240.7	251.0	239.6	218.1	228.3	277.9	293.2	262.4	260.0
November	256.4	256.2	243.6	253.2	254.9	242.5	252.4	240.5	220.6	230.0	280.9	296.4	264.5	262.1
December	258.7	258.4	245.2	255.5	257.1	243.8	254.1	242.0	221.1	231.0	284.7	300.7	266.4	263.9
1981:														
January	260.7	260.5	247.6	257.6	259.2	245.4	256.9	245.3	221.0	232.4	287.7	304.2	268.6	265.6
February	263.5	263.2	251.2	260.4	261.9	248.3	262.3	253.2	220.3	235.4	290.1	306.9	270.8	267.3
March	265.2	265.1	253.3	262.3	263.7	249.8	265.2	257.5	219.8	237.0	292.5	309.5	272.2	268.6
April	266.8	266.8	254.9	264.2	265.4	250.8	265.9	258.1	221.1	238.0	295.4	312.8	272.9	268.7
May	269.1	269.0	256.2	267.0	267.6	251.9	265.8	258.2	223.9	239.6	299.6	317.4	272.5	267.7
June	271.4	271.3	257.8	269.5	269.9	253.2	266.2	258.0	226.6	241.1	303.5	321.9	273.6	268.7
July	274.6	274.4	259.9	272.7	273.0	255.0	267.1	257.5	229.6	242.6	308.8	328.1	276.2	271.6
August	276.5	276.5	261.4	274.9	274.9	256.2	268.1	258.4	230.9	243.8	312.2	331.7	277.4	272.8
September	279.1	279.3	263.5	278.2	277.8	257.7	269.5	260.3	232.6	244.5	317.3	337.5	278.0	273.2
October	279.7	279.9	264.5	279.0	278.3	257.9	269.5	260.7	232.2	245.9	318.6	338.7	277.6	272.1
November	280.4	280.7	265.4	280.1	279.0	258.0	269.8	261.1	233.2	246.2	320.6	340.8	277.1	271.0
December	281.1	281.5	266.0	280.8	279.6	258.4	269.8	261.1	233.7	246.5	321.8	342.0	277.8	271.7
1982:														
January	282.1	282.5	267.4	281.4	280.6	258.8	270.8	260.2	233.4	245.9	323.9	344.2	281.0	275.3
February	282.9	283.4	268.3	282.1	281.5	259.5	271.7	260.1	233.7	246.0	325.3	345.7	283.3	278.0
March	282.5	283.1	268.5	281.7	280.9	258.8	270.7	258.4	233.5	245.2	325.5	345.7	283.0	277.1
April	283.7	284.3	268.7	282.9	282.1	259.8	269.3	255.0	235.8	245.0	328.4	349.1	283.9	277.9
May	286.5	287.1	270.6	286.0	284.9	261.5	270.7	256.2	239.8	247.8	331.8	352.8	285.5	279.8
June	290.1	290.6	273.8	289.7	288.4	265.1	274.4	261.2	243.2	251.9	334.9	356.5	287.8	282.6
July	291.8	292.2	275.3	291.5	289.9	266.5	275.7	263.0	244.7	253.5	337.0	358.5	288.5	282.8
August	292.4	292.8	275.7	292.5	290.5	266.4	275.5	263.6	244.6	253.8	338.9	360.5	287.4	280.8
September	292.8	293.3	276.9	292.9	290.8	266.6	276.2	264.6	244.1	253.9	339.7	361.3	287.6	280.6
October	293.6	294.1	277.9	294.0	291.5	267.5	276.5	265.7	246.0	255.4	340.3	361.6	287.0	279.4
November	293.2	293.6	278.1	293.6	290.8	267.8	276.4	266.1	246.6	256.0	338.6	359.3	286.4	278.3
December	292.0	292.4	278.2	292.1	289.5	267.7	275.8	264.7	247.3	255.8	335.6	355.5	286.5	277.8

Footnotes giving source of data and description of series appear in the section immediately following these tables.

★Monthly data prior to 1979 are shown on pp. 156 and 157.

Source: *Business Statistics, a Supplement to the Survey of Current Business* (Washington, D.C.: U.S. Department of Commerce, Bureau of Economic Analysis, 1982).

FINANCE—PROFITS AND DIVIDENDS

YEAR AND QUARTER	MANUFACTURING CORPORATIONS (FEDERAL TRADE COMMISSION) [1]																Dividends paid (cash), quarterly, all industries
	Net profits after taxes																
	All industries	Food and kindred products	Textile mill products	Paper and allied products	Chemicals and allied products	Petroleum and coal products	Stone, clay, and glass products	Primary nonferrous metal	Primary iron and steel	Fabricated metal products	Machinery (except electrical)	Electrical and electronic equipment)	Transportation equipment (except motor vehicles and equipment)	Motor vehicles and equipment	All other manufacturing industries	
	Millions of dollars																
1961	15,311	1,325	280	583	2,045	3,090	543	488	803	445	1,061	1,024	298	1,488	1,722	8,551
1962	17,719	1,369	354	628	2,239	3,236	581	533	720	608	1,308	1,219	442	2,289	2,033	9,281
1963 [2]	19,483	1,449	354	634	2,427	3,831	593	563	938	668	1,432	1,299	444	2,562	2,041	9,868
1964	23,211	1,692	507	754	2,857	4,094	681	758	1,225	842	2,001	1,512	546	2,808	2,617	10,810
1965	27,521	1,896	694	[3] 753	3,188	4,442	761	970	1,401	1,151	2,499	1,926	721	3,496	[3] 3,285	11,979
1966	30,937	[4] 2,102	702	911	3,474	5,055	799	1,298	1,487	1,395	3,058	2,379	821	3,053	[4] 4,058	12,958
1967	29,008	2,130	540	[5] 796	3,261	5,497	672	1,061	1,165	1,316	2,893	2,297	809	2,356	3,884	13,262
1968	32,069	2,209	654	889	3,525	5,794	769	1,149	1,186	1,320	2,947	2,518	1,025	3,222	4,229	14,189
1969	33,248	2,382	621	987	3,591	5,884	822	1,414	1,221	1,326	3,138	2,594	945	2,845	4,835	15,058
1970	28,572	2,549	413	719	3,434	5,893	627	1,297	692	1,066	2,689	2,349	593	1,424	4,522	15,070
1971	31,038	2,754	558	501	3,780	5,829	853	621	748	1,070	2,489	2,563	585	3,097	4,990	15,252
1972	36,467	3,021	659	941	4,499	5,151	1,060	687	1,022	[6] 1,569	3,481	[6] 2,999	[6] 780	3,639	5,944	16,110
1973 [7]	48,259	3,723	831	1,427	5,670	[8] 7,759	1,266	1,343	1,695	2,207	4,936	3,883	933	4,122	7,079	17,734
1974	58,747	4,601	780	2,287	7,175	14,483	1,204	2,035	3,149	2,837	5,648	2,940	1,127	1,957	8,524	19,467
1975	49,135	5,154	409	1,801	6,703	9,307	968	663	2,280	2,523	6,311	2,564	1,039	1,737	7,481	19,968
1976	64,519	5,826	809	2,270	7,610	11,725	1,447	913	2,085	3,196	7,889	4,073	1,687	5,099	9,890	22,763
1977	70,366	5,575	828	2,367	8,060	12,179	1,686	873	864	3,458	9,131	5,383	1,989	6,133	11,840	26,585
1978	81,148	6,213	1,170	2,598	9,117	12,805	2,353	1,362	2,124	3,815	10,746	6,500	2,374	6,211	13,760	28,932
1979	98,698	7,340	1,340	3,723	10,896	21,936	2,373	2,691	2,185	4,431	11,530	7,386	3,189	4,382	15,314	32,491
1980	92,579	8,222	977	2,789	11,578	25,133	1,833	2,768	2,334	3,967	11,459	7,114	3,084	−3,424	14,745	36,495
1981	101,302	9,109	1,157	3,110	12,973	23,733	1,627	2,124	3,507	4,235	12,580	7,872	3,722	−209	15,762	40,317
1982	71,028	8,383	851	1,460	10,324	19,666	408	−333	−3,705	2,320	8,038	6,449	2,566	734	13,867	41,259
1979:																
January																
February																
March	22,666	1,456	246	867	2,746	3,976	287	607	617	1,017	2,682	1,808	666	2,164	3,527	7,126
April																
May																
June	26,795	1,919	355	917	2,938	5,256	749	749	966	1,272	3,006	1,926	884	1,917	3,941	8,170
July																
August																
September	24,746	2,171	381	1,162	2,632	5,732	770	609	743	1,091	2,763	1,735	815	−51	4,193	8,099
October																
November																
December	24,491	1,794	358	777	2,580	6,972	567	726	−141	1,051	3,079	1,917	824	352	3,635	9,096
1980:																
January																
February																
March	24,776	1,720	313	731	3,157	7,258	237	961	814	1,161	2,591	1,799	777	−210	3,467	8,788
April																
May																
June	22,423	1,844	230	740	2,774	6,675	480	769	529	928	2,890	1,694	804	−1,333	3,399	8,919
July																
August																
September	20,982	2,120	196	621	2,937	5,644	602	402	218	870	2,637	1,681	742	−1,626	3,938	8,920
October																
November																
December	24,398	2,538	238	697	2,710	5,556	514	636	773	1,008	3,341	1,940	761	−255	3,941	9,868
1981:																
January																
February																
March	24,372	2,106	243	769	3,525	5,395	238	835	921	1,022	2,745	2,164	1,111	−384	3,682	9,771
April																
May																
June	28,873	2,264	408	879	3,365	6,771	567	630	1,160	1,320	3,259	2,166	1,001	936	4,147	10,080
July																
August																
September	25,201	2,293	308	633	3,098	6,103	555	290	1,421	1,133	3,084	1,797	903	−622	4,205	9,703
October																
November																
December	22,856	2,446	198	829	2,985	5,464	267	369	5	760	3,492	1,745	707	−139	3,728	10,763
1982:																
January																
February																
March	19,042	1,895	110	418	2,963	5,164	−198	111	27	762	2,723	1,702	609	1	2,755	10,176
April																
May																
June	20,044	2,181	144	436	2,821	4,040	165	59	−276	833	2,377	1,717	653	1,072	3,822	10,437
July																
August																
September	17,828	1,845	258	408	2,478	5,225	280	−36	−906	433	1,786	1,602	706	−18	3,767	10,085
October																
November																
December	14,114	2,462	339	198	2,062	5,237	161	−467	−2,550	292	1,152	1,428	598	−321	3,523	10,561

Footnotes giving source of data and description of series appear in the section immediately following these tables.

Source: *Business Statistics, a Supplement to the Survey of Current Business* (Washington, D.C.: U.S. Department of Commerce, Bureau of Economic Analysis, 1982).

INDEX

169